THE ESSENTIAL VEGETARIAN COOKBOOK

Also by Diana Shaw

Almost Vegetarian
Grilling from the Garden
Sweet Basil, Garlic, Tomatoes, and Chives
Vegetarian Entertaining

DIANA SHAW

THE ESSENTIAL VEGETARIAN COOKBOOK

Your Guide to the Best Foods on Earth

• WHAT TO EAT • WHERE TO GET IT •
• HOW TO PREPARE IT •

Illustrations by Kathy Warinner

Clarkson Potter/Publishers
New York

Copyright © 1997 by Diana Shaw

Published by Clarkson Potter/Publishers, 201 East 50th Street, New
York, New York 10022. Member of the Crown Publishing Group.

Random House, Inc. New York, Toronto, London, Sydney, Auckland

http://www.randomhouse.com/

CLARKSON N. POTTER, POTTER, and colophon are trademarks of
Clarkson N. Potter, Inc.

Printed in the United States of America

Design and illustration by Kathy Warinner, Aufuldish & Warinner,
San Anselmo, California.

Library of Congress Cataloging-in-Publication Data
Shaw, Diana.
   The essential vegetarian cookbook/ Diana Shaw.
      p.   cm.
   Includes index.
   1. Vegetarian cookery.   I. Title.
   TX837.S46273   1997
   641.5'636—dc20   96-22290
      CIP

ISBN 0-517-59989-2 (hardcover)
ISBN 0-517-88268-X (paper)

10 9 8 7 6 5 4 3 2 1

First Edition

For James

ONE-DISH DINNERS 328

BREADS AND BREAD DISHES 390

GRILLING 444

DESSERTS 466

Acknowledgments

Despite various crises and other occurrences that delayed the delivery of this book, it's here thanks entirely to the emphatic encouragement and exuberant enthusiasm of my editor, Katie Workman. Katie's confidence in the concept of this book and in my ability to realize it kept me working through calamities, including a house burning down, and seeming miracles, such as the birth of my son. I am grateful also to her sister, Elizabeth Workman, who took on the tedious task of transferring the great bulk of the recipes to the nutrition analysis program. And, too, to Erica Youngren, who is meant to be Katie's assistant, but has given more than ample help to me as well.

Chavanne Hanson, MPH, RD, LD, director of nutrition services for University Synergy, the preventive cardiology program of University Hospitals of Cleveland, helped keep my nutrition claims honest and compiled the menus for special diets. The great fun of working with Chavanne is that, while driven to teach us how to eat for optimum health, she truly loves food; rather than go on about what we're doing wrong, she makes us *want* to eat "right."

There is more kindness, civility, and good taste (and superb cheese!) at Darien Cheese & Fine Foods than in most food retailers you're likely to find, all thanks to Ken and Tori Skovron, the proprietors, and their wonderful staff. Their store has come to feel like an extension of my home . . . the warmest room in the house.

As always, thanks to Ellen Rose, whose bookstore Cook's Library is in Los Angeles, three thousand miles away, but who's always there for me. And to my long-time agents, Gail Hochman and Marianne Merola, thanks again, and *still!*

My husband, Simon, doesn't want my thanks. "Thanks" don't go for long bike rides or walks at sunset or quiet dinners in the yard out back. Thanks don't help give the baby a bath, look for a new house, pore over the Sunday paper, or share a large order of sushi. I'll be right there, Simon. Meanwhile, thank you.

Finally, it's too soon to thank my son, Michael Anthony, for anything besides simply appearing on this earth to demonstrate that something can be more thrilling, exhilarating, and scrumptious in life than a bowl of Bell Pepper Risotto.

Foreword

As director of nutrition services for University Hospitals of Cleveland Synergy, a state-of-the-art preventative health program that empowers people to develop and maintain a healthy lifestyle through proper nutrition, culinary arts, exercise, and behavioral medicine, my primary focus is to teach people about food for the health of it! By definition, Synergy is "the cooperative action of two or more separate forces, in which the total effect is greater than the sum of their effects when acting independently." When nutrition and food are delicately and thoughtfully blended, the end result is a tremendous synergy of nourishing and delicious cuisine that supports outstanding health and well-being.

The key to helping individuals maintain a healthy diet is not to start from scratch, but to transform their current diet into a healthier one. Nutrition counseling and food preparation that suggests optimal nourishment, outstanding flavor, and ease of preparation are critical for installing a comprehensive and lasting change.

Diana Shaw's recipes do just this! Individuals will gain a realistic approach to proper nutrition coupled with enjoyable and exciting culinary techniques. They will learn the value of cooking to enhance the natural flavors of food which provide endless flavor. Diana's synergistic approach of shaping high-nutrient foods into delectable dishes is exceptional. Menus provide a complete foundation of nutritional knowledge on which people can begin to make the most of their diet and better understand how healthy food can work into their lifestyle. Readers will find that the ultimate goal of establishing an eating pattern which emphasizes balance, moderation, and appropriate food choices is soon within their reach.

These nutritious and satisfying recipes will provide you with an exhilarating new tool for preparing a lifetime of flavorful meals.

Chavanne B. Hanson, MPH, RD, LD
Director of Nutrition Services,
University Hospitals Synergy,
University Hospitals of Cleveland

THE ESSENTIAL VEGETARIAN COOKBOOK

INTRODUCTION

Eating Well to Live Well

Given so much that's so good, *why*, you have to wonder, have we been eating so badly?

"American food" has long been short for "cheeseburgers, French fries, and a Coke." But as we discover that a steady diet of this stuff can also mean obesity, heart disease, and diminished life expectancy, many of us are looking to make far better use of the foods that we have. We're tapping the best of everything at hand, from our abundant crops to the traditions of people who've moved here from other places, still hungry for what they had at home. While we are able to buy sacks of "all-purpose" potatoes, we can also get Katahdins, Red Dales, Purple Peruvians, and Yukon Golds. Iceberg lettuce is still on the shelf, but we can also choose among radicchio, mâche, and all manner of mesclun. We can buy plain, old baked beans in a can, but we can also get plump, glossy, fresh dried beans at the market or through the mail.

In fact, when you look at what's happening in supermarkets, restaurants, and homes around the country, you'll see a new cuisine evolving before your eyes: a *vegetarian* cuisine uniquely our own and as expansive as our appetite and imagination. We're making moo-shu mushrooms and serving them in flour tortillas; we're filling a calzone with chilies and black beans; making soup out of strawberries; and savory pancakes from leeks. Cooking with fresh produce, varied spices, new strains of grains, and heirloom legumes, we're integrating thoroughly our love of good food with our concern for good health.

Once vegetarian meals were called "meatless." But as you'll find in all that follows, vegetarian meals have become too inclusive to be named for what's not on the plate. Consequently, this book is for everyone who loves food of all kinds. And with comprehensive nutritional information accompanying each recipe, it proves, page after page, there need be no distinction between eating well and eating *well*.

Throughout the book, you'll find two standard features meant to help you make the most of the recipes. In the lists headed "Basics," you'll find general preparation advice for everything from muffins to couscous and crepes.

Lists headed "Make It Your Own" offer specific tips for adapting basic recipes, with advice about what to add to the basic recipe and when to add it during preparation.

You'll also find nutritional information with each recipe, as well as menus and guidance in meal planning that give equal consideration to your dietary needs and your desire for something good to eat.

A BALANCED, NOURISHING VEGETARIAN DIET

This type of diet depends on which type of vegetarian meals you may choose: almost-vegetarian, lacto-ovo, lacto, or vegan.

Almost Vegetarian: You eat vegetables, grains, dairy products, and eggs, and—occasionally—fish and/or chicken.

Anything Missing? If the chicken or fish is lean, your portions are moderate, and everything you eat is prepared without much fat or salt, an almost-vegetarian diet should provide everything you need.

Lacto-Ovo Vegetarian: You eat vegetables, grains, dairy products, and eggs.

Anything Missing? Provided you eat a variety of foods within those categories, you should get everything you need. If you have high cholesterol or a personal or family history of heart disease, limit yourself to two or three whole eggs each week (you can cook with as many whites as you'd like). For more on eggs, see page 56.

A Balanced, Nourishing Lacto-Ovo Menu

Breakfast
Fortified cereal (such as Complete Bran Flakes, Total, Multi Bran Chex) with nonfat milk
My Best Bran Muffins (page 72)
Orange juice or sliced fresh orange or berries

Lunch
Curried Egg Salad (page 145)
Whole wheat bread
Fresh fruit

Dinner
Butternut Squash Soup (page 181)
Pasta with Lovely Lentil Sauce (page 283)
Mesclun with Orange-Vinaigrette-Style Dressing (page 119)
Fig Glacé (page 488) with vanilla nonfat frozen yogurt

Lacto Vegetarian: You eat vegetables, grains, and dairy products.

Anything Missing? You may not be getting enough iron and zinc. Be sure to compensate by making meals of whole wheat bread and iron-fortified whole-grain breakfast cereal, chickpeas, kale, and collard greens. Take supplements only if your doctor recommends them; large doses of some minerals can be toxic and can prevent the absorption of others.

EVERYONE WANTS TO KNOW

Q. Will going vegetarian make me popular and good-looking, and allow me to live forever?
A. Probably not . . . but a *balanced,* nourishing vegetarian diet may help you enjoy better health overall, and all of the many benefits that go with it.

A Balanced, Nourishing Lacto Menu

Breakfast

Oatmeal cooked in nonfat milk (page 52)

Orange juice or sliced fresh orange or berries

Lunch

Pasta e Fagioli (page 194)

Whole wheat roll

Fruit-flavored nonfat yogurt

Dinner

Potato Curry (page 356)

Beet Raita (page 154)

Naan (page 415)

Mango Cream (page 496)

Vegan: You eat only vegetables and grains. *Anything Missing?* Without fortified foods, it's a pretty sure bet you're getting no vitamin B_{12}, and you may not be getting enough iron, calcium, zinc, and vitamin D. Check with a Registered Dietician to make sure you're meeting your needs.

A Balanced, Nourishing Vegan Menu

Breakfast

Granola (page 50), with fortified low-fat or nonfat soy milk

Grape-Nuts Bran Bread (page 406), toasted, with fruit preserves or whipped honey

Fresh orange juice

Lunch

Basic Hummus (page 254) in whole wheat pita with tomatoes and alfalfa sprouts

Tabbouleh (page 139)

Fresh fruit

Dinner

Mesclun with Orange-Sesame Dressing (page 121)

Apple-Turnip Soup (page 486)

Sweet Black Beans on Whole Wheat Penne (page 289)

Wheat Berry Bread (page 400) or any whole wheat bread

THE BENEFITS OF A BALANCED VEGETARIAN DIET

A balanced vegetarian diet may help you:

Lose weight. Many cuts of meats are full of fat. So if you're not eating meat, you've already cut a huge source of fat or calories from your diet. If you don't replace this fat with fat or calories from other sources, you should lose weight without having to cut back drastically on other foods. Choose lean proteins, such as legumes, grains, nonfat dairy products, reduced-fat tofu, and nonfat soy milk. Also, when you eat fiber-rich foods such as beans and grains, you'll feel full on fewer calories and won't be tempted to overeat.

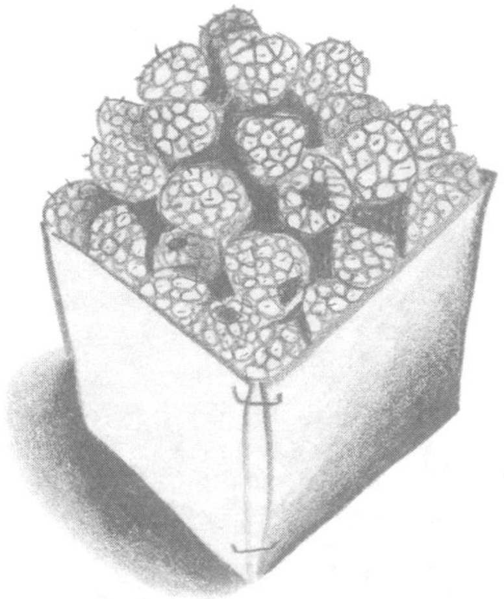

WHY WORRY ABOUT WHAT MAY BE MISSING FROM YOUR DIET?

Trying to go without key minerals and vitamins is like expecting a building to stand without critical girders. You may hold up for a while, but at some point you're bound to give way. Nutritional deficiencies can be hard to diagnose once they occur; it's much easier to avoid them altogether by considering what may be missing from your diet, then eating to compensate. For example, if you know you're at risk for iron deficiency, you'll know to eat lots of iron-rich legumes, greens, and fortified cereals. If you know your diet doesn't include vitamin B12 (which comes only from animal products), you'll also know to eat foods that are fortified with it. Ditto for calcium and vitamin D.

SHORTAGES AND CONSEQUENCES

When you go without *iron,* you may feel tired and have trouble concentrating and staying alert. To compensate eat iron-fortified breakfast cereal topped with strawberries and iron-fortified low-fat or nonfat soy milk, as well as chickpeas, kale, and collard greens. (The vitamin C in the berries and other fruits and vegetables boosts iron absorption.)

The long-term consequences of going without *vitamin B12* include a number of psychiatric disorders. To compensate, eat B12-fortified cereal and/or drink fortified soy milk.

You need *calcium* and *vitamin D* to build and preserve your bones and teeth. Drink fortified soy milk and orange juice and eat tofu and high-calcium legumes such as Great Northern beans and chickpeas. If practical, get twenty minutes of sun daily.

Long-term effects of inadequate *zinc* can include slow healing of wounds (which can lead to infection), arrested growth and sexual development, as well as impaired vision and immunity and a distorted sense of taste and smell. To compensate, eat whole wheat bread, wheat germ, and brewer's yeast, as well as zinc-fortified cereals.

If you suspect you're not getting enough of certain vitamins and/or minerals, consult with a Registered Dietician. You'll probably be asked to keep track of what you eat over a period of time, and the R.D. will then assess your overall intake, and suggest how to adjust your diet. Supplements can be toxic, so don't use them until you've tried improving your diet, then received your doctor's approval.

✐ *Lower your blood pressure.* As you lose excess weight, your blood pressure may drop, so everything mentioned before is relevant here, too. If you're overweight, eating the kind of vegetarian diet I've described above—moderate portions of fiber-rich, low-fat, and nonfat foods—and exercising regularly, you may lose enough weight to bring your blood pressure down. If your weight and blood pressure are normal, a vegetarian diet of this kind, along with regular exercise, should help you maintain your health, keeping your weight and blood pressure from rising over time.

Sodium contributes to high blood pressure in some people, so try to limit the amount in your diet. Although no official daily value has been established, most health advocacy groups suggest you eat no more than 2,400 milligrams each day. This can be difficult, since most prepared foods —including breakfast cereals, soups, and mixes of all kinds—contain salt. You can't

always tell how much sodium a food contains by how salty it tastes; many high-sodium foods don't taste of salt at all. Check the label.

✐ *Lower your cholesterol.* If you replace foods that are high in saturated fat, like meats, with vegetables and whole grains, you're losing foods that make your body produce LDL (harmful) cholesterol, and replacing it with fiber, which seems actually to lower cholesterol. No one knows why, but it seems that it's not just the laying off of fatty foods, but actually eating soy foods and vegetables that lowers the risk of heart disease among vegetarians. In fact several reputable studies have shown that vegetarians have lower cholesterol and lower rates of heart disease than people who eat meat.

✐ *Strengthen your bones.* If you're a lacto-ovo vegetarian or a lacto vegetarian, you're boosting the amount of bone-enforcing calcium in your diet by eating lean dairy products, such as nonfat yogurt and skim milk, in place of meat. If you're a vegan, you can get ample calcium by eating tofu, kale, and calcium-fortified low-fat or nonfat soy milk.

✐ *Defy certain cancers.* All of us harbor substances that may at any time become cell-mangling, tissue-mauling cancers. They're called free radicals, and a number of things, including smoking, breathing bad air, and eating too much fat, may set them off. Studies suggest eating vegetables and fruits that contain antioxidant vitamins (beta-carotene, vitamin A, vitamin C, and vitamin E) may cut your risk for certain

THREE KEY WORDS FOR VEGETARIANS OF ALL KINDS

Variety, fresh, simple: eat a variety of fresh foods, simply prepared.

Variety: The easiest, most sensible and effective way to get the nourishment you need is to eat the widest variety of foods within the vegetarian diet of your choice, supplementing with fortified products when necessary. The more types of foods you eat, the more likely it is you'll get enough nutrients, vitamins, and minerals.

Don't bother trying to work out to the gram how much of what you're getting each day, especially since you'd have to factor in which minerals and vitamins help, and which hinder, the absorption of the others. For instance, vitamin C helps the body absorb iron, while certain chemicals (phytates) in some iron-rich plants, such as spinach, prevent it. Excessive zinc also blocks iron. And while vitamin D facilitates the absorption of calcium, both excessive protein and zinc can hinder absorption. If you had to sort through all of that every time you planned a meal, you'd be too exasperated to eat anything at all.

Besides, your needs vary from day to day, depending on your general health, how much sleep you've been getting, and how much you've been exerting yourself. Your diet should vary, too—extra fiber when you're constipated, hot liquids when you have a cold, more complex carbohydrates when you've been running like crazy.

Finally, monotony is unnatural. If we were meant to eat the same thing every day, why are there apples *and* oranges, broccoli *and* cauliflower, cabbage *and* spinach?

Fresh: Foods contain more vitamins when they're fresh. Vitamins deteriorate with age and with exposure to light, heat, and moisture.

Simple: The less you do to a food, the more nutrients you preserve and the fewer calories you add. (See "The Basic Methods," page 500.)

types of cancer, including breast cancer, lung cancer, and colon cancer. So far, it seems that you get this protection only when the vitamins come from food; vitamin pills don't seem to do it. Studies suggest that soy products such as tofu and tempeh provide protection, too.

🖉 *Avoid constipation.* Meat has virtually no fiber, so when you eat vegetarian meals, you have lots of room for fiber-filled foods.

When you choose legumes, whole grains, and raw or lightly cooked fresh vegetables and fruits, you're adding the kind of roughage you need to prevent constipation.

❧ *Boost energy and stamina.* It's not easy to convert the main components of meat, namely protein and fat, into energy. Carbohydrates are the best source of fuel. When you replace meat with complex carbohydrates, such as legumes and grains, you get energy that's accessible immediately and that will burn steadily for the next few hours. With the extra energy, you may want to get more exercise, which will in turn build your stamina and give you more energy still.

❧ *Live longer.* When you add up all of the benefits—effective weight control, lower blood pressure and cholesterol, lower rates of cancer, and more energy and vitality—

A PLAUSIBLE PARADOX?

Q. Can I eat more and weigh less?
A. Within limits, for example, if you eat more complex carbohydrates and much less fat. Here's why.

First, fat has nine calories per gram, and carbohydrate has only four. So gram for gram, a fatty food has more than twice as many calories as a food that is mostly carbohydrate. Consider French fries. Three ounces of French fries have more than three times as many calories as three ounces of boiled or baked potato. So when you eat high-carbohydrate foods, instead of an equal measure of fatty foods, you're consuming far fewer calories, just like that.

Second, many studies indicate that it's not just the number of calories you eat, but the proportion of fat in your diet that determines whether you'll be overweight. Your body tends to turn fat into fat, and carbohydrate into fuel, storing the fat, and burning the fuel.

Q. For practical purposes, what does this mean?
A. Adapt recipes and meals to increase the proportion of carbohydrate to fat. For example, serve more pasta with less sauce (if it's a fatty sauce) and less cheese. Instead of spreading a pat of butter on a wedge of toast, cut a thicker slice of toast and top it with a fat-free spread (see page 103).

Q. What if I want to lose weight?
A. Don't cut back on calories drastically. Your body knows how much energy it needs to survive and will compensate for inadequate calories by burning whatever calories it gets more slowly. Instead, cut way back on the calories you get from fat, and combine a high-carbohydrate diet with regular exercise.

you get a longer life span. And with the increased energy and vitality, you'll get more living from that life.

Note: Some people become vegetarians to mask eating disorders. A balanced vegetarian diet should include more types of foods than it leaves out. In fact, healthy vegetarians tend to eat a wider variety of foods than meat eaters, who may eat burgers or bologna day after day. If you find that you're more concerned with excluding foods than broadening your diet, discuss this with your doctor or with a registered dietitian who specializes in eating disorders.

Getting the Most from the Nutritional Information in This Book

✐ Know *roughly* what you need, especially the amount of protein, fat, and carbohydrate appropriate for your age, height, and activity level. (See "How Many Calories Do I Need?" for basic guidelines.)

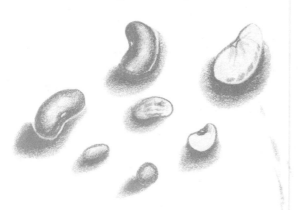

HOW MANY CALORIES DO I NEED?

Multiply your *ideal weight* by 10.

Then multiply your *activity level* by 100: Multiply 100 by 7 if you're *active* (work out rigorously—run, cycle, rollerblade, swim—for at least sixty minutes straight at least four times a week). Multiply by 5 if you're *moderately active* (work out at something fairly rigorous for at least thirty minutes straight at least three times a week). Multiply by 3 if you're *inactive* (rarely exercise and have no regularly scheduled physical activity).

Add up the numbers, and the total is roughly how many calories you need. Now you can use the information following each recipe to determine how many of your needed calories are in a serving.

This is not a case for a calculator. Unless you have a condition that requires strict calorie control—clinical obesity or diabetes, for example—a rough idea is all you need. Your general health is the best indication; if you have enough energy to get through the day and enjoy what you do, and if you're close to your ideal weight, chances are you're getting the right number of calories.

✐ While you should know roughly what you need and have some sense of what you're getting, you don't have to be obsessive about it. Eating a bit more or less on any given day isn't going to have crippling consequences. Chances are you're in good shape if you come close to your targets over the course of a week.

✐ Variations in ingredients may affect the total calories and fat content of a recipe.

When an alternative is given in a recipe's list of ingredients—for example, "nonfat or reduced-fat sour cream"—the nutrition information (calories, protein, carbohydrates, and so on) following the recipe pertains to the *first* ingredient, not the alternative, that is, the nonfat sour cream, not the reduced fat. Similarly, the nutrition information following each recipe doesn't include the values for optional ingredients.

AVOID SATURATION

All shortenings—butter, olive oil, Crisco, coconut oil—have the same number of calories: 120 per tablespoon. The difference among them is the type of fat they contain: unsaturated fat or saturated fat.

Saturated fat raises the levels of LDL cholesterol in the blood. LDL cholesterol is a sticky, fatlike substance that, in moderate amounts, regulates hormone production and helps build cells. But in excess it clogs arteries, causing high blood pressure and contributing to the risk of heart disease and stroke. Saturated fat comes primarily from animal foods, although the fat in coconut, palm kernel, and palm oil is saturated, too. *Less than 10 percent of the fat you eat should be saturated.*

To complicate things, there's HDL cholesterol, a "good" cholesterol that carries LDL cholesterol to the liver, which gets rid of it. You can increase the proportion of HDL to LDL cholesterol by substituting unsaturated fat, such as olive oil, for saturated fat, such as butter.

Then there's trans fat. Trans fat is what you get when you take an unsaturated fat, such as vegetable oil, and make it solid through a process called hydrogenation. It's then virtually the same as saturated fat, raising cholesterol and blood pressure and triggering all that ensues. When a food label lists hydrogenated vegetable oil as an ingredient, the product contains saturated fat.

Although unsaturated fats like olive and canola oils aren't as bad for you as saturated fats, all fats are high in calories and potentially fattening. Don't *add* unsaturated fats to your diet; substitute them for saturated fats, keeping total fat below 30 percent of your total number of calories.

KEY TO THE NUTRITION INFORMATION GRID

PER SERVING: CALORIES XX • PROTEIN XX G • CARBOHY-DRATE XX G • FAT XX G • CHOLESTEROL XX MG • SODIUM XX MG • XX% CALORIES FROM FAT • OUTSTANDING SOURCE OF XXXXX • VERY GOOD SOURCE OF XXXXX • GOOD SOURCE OF XXXXX

CALORIES

Calories are energy. Your body uses some energy just for the ordinary business of living: it takes energy to breathe, among other things, to think, replace cells, and make your hair and nails grow.

TO GET THE MOST OUT OF THE NUTRITIONAL INFORMATION ON PACKAGED FOOD LABELS

Q. Why should I read labels?

A. To keep track of what you're eating, to be sure the calories in each serving come with enough essential vitamins, minerals, and fiber for good health and the proper amount and proportion of protein, carbohydrate, and fat.

Food labels also allow you to compare products. If you're worried about sodium and fat, you can tell at a glance which cereals, for instance, contain the least of each.

Q. All food labels carry this line: "Percent Daily Value are based on a 2,000 calorie diet." What's that all about?

A. If you eat two thousand calories each day, the percentages let you know how much fat, saturated fat, total carbohydrate, and fiber a serving gives you in relation to how much you need that day.

Q. Why two thousand calories? Is that how many I should be eating?

A. Two thousand calories are appropriate for many Americans, but this is not a universal recommendation. If you're a woman who's five feet, seven inches, and you work out four or five times each week, two thousand should be about right for you. But if you're a small, sedentary women, you should probably eat fewer calories. If you're a large, active man, you'll certainly need more. See "How Many Calories Do I Need?" (page 9) to calculate the number of calories you require.

Q. What if I eat fewer than two thousand calories each day?

A. You can adjust the daily values proportionately. If you eat 1,500 calories a day, or a quarter fewer than 2,000, knock one-fourth off the percentage daily value. In other words, you'd want no more than 75 percent of the daily value for the nutrients given. If you eat 1,800 calories, you'd want no more than 80 percent. And so on.

INTERPRETING HEALTH CLAIMS

If the product's label says

Fat Free: The product contains no more than 0.5 grams of fat per serving.

Low Fat: It contains no more than 3 grams of fat per serving—unless it's an entrée (such as a frozen dinner), in which case it can contain 3 grams of fat for every 3½ ounces of weight. So a 9-ounce entrée, for example, may have up to 8 grams of fat.

Light: It contains less than half as much fat and sodium and fewer than a third as many calories as the full-fat version of the same food. "Light" cream cheese, for example, contains 50 percent less fat and 30 percent fewer calories per serving than regular cream cheese:

seventy calories per serving versus one hundred calories.

Low Fat Foods May Reduce Risk of Heart Disease: It is low in fat, saturated fat, and cholesterol.

Low Sodium Foods May Reduce High Blood Pressure: It is low in sodium.

Fruits, Vegetables, and Grains May Reduce the Risk of Cancer and/or Heart Disease: It is low in fat, saturated fat, and cholesterol and contains at least one gram of fiber per serving.

Dairy Products Can Prevent Osteoporosis: It is low in fat and high in calcium.

Since calories themselves provide only energy, it's possible to eat as many calories as you need in a day without getting any nourishment. If you ate a pound of brownies (even fat-free brownies), for instance, you'd have more than enough calories, and not anywhere near as many vitamins, minerals, and nutrients as you need. The information following each recipe—like the labels on packaged food—is meant to let you know how much nourishment comes with the calories in each serving.

How many calories you need depends on a number of things, including your age,

height, ideal weight, actual weight, activity level, and metabolism (the speed your body burns calories, determined partly by genetics—sorry—and partly by how active you are; regular exercise boosts your metabolism). (See "How Many Calories Do I Need?" page 9.)

PROTEIN

A little goes far enough.

It's impossible to overstate the importance of protein, which controls or affects everything your body does to sustain itself. Yet it's easy to overestimate how much you need. Because meat is a rich source of complete protein, many vegetarians (or their mothers) worry whether they're getting enough. Chances are, they're getting enough and then some.

Protein isn't a single substance, but a complicated chemical compound, which is complete—and able to be used by your body—only when eight of the *essential* amino acids that build usable protein are present. Animal foods contain all eight, but grains, legumes, and fresh produce don't; your body can't use protein from those sources until you match them in a way that fills out the set.

Unless your regimen is uncommonly eccentric, you won't have to think much about this. Just eat legumes of some kind with any type of grain, and you've got it. It's as simple as spreading peanut butter on bread—or tossing it with pasta (see cold sesame noodles, page 298), cooking beans with rice (see page 352), or making soup with pasta and beans (page 194).

When you combine vegetables and grains, you get plenty of protein plus more

fiber, more complex carbohydrates, and more of certain critical vitamins than you'd get from meat. And, provided you spare the butter and go easy on the oil, you get less fat and no cholesterol at all.

CARBOHYDRATE

We run on carbohydrates. While both protein and fat can provide energy, carbohydrates do it more efficiently. Carbohydrates aren't just a superior source of energy, but foods that are high in complex carbohydrates tend also to contain lots of vitamins, minerals, and fiber.

"Simple carbohydrates" is another name for sugar, which you can get in food, such as fruit (fructose) or milk (lactose), or straight, as sugar, honey, or molasses. When you eat fruit or milk products, you not only get sugar, you get vitamins and minerals, too. But when you eat sugars straight, you get calories—pure, quick-burning energy—and nothing else. If you use the energy, that's fine. But if you don't, the calories are stored as fat.

You get long-lasting energy, and a lot more nourishment, from complex carbohydrates, also known as starches. Most complex-carbohydrate foods are very low in fat, if not entirely fat free. And because a gram of carbohydrate has fewer than half as many calories as a gram of fat, when you replace a fatty food with an equal portion of complex carbohydrates, you cut calories drastically. Also, foods with abundant complex carbohydrates tend to contain a lot of fiber, too, so they're more filling than fatty foods.

FAT

Given all the advice to avoid it you may find it hard to believe that we all need some fat. It cushions your organs, regulates your body temperature, makes your hair glossy and your skin smooth, activates your hormones, and provides energy when other sources have been drained by illness or overexertion.

Although you need it, you don't need much of it. It's a well-established fact that excessive fat can lead to heart disease. And it's widely supposed that fat promotes cancer, too.

Set fat priorities. For everyday meals, use nonfat dairy and/or soy products, such as milk, yogurt, frozen yogurt, sour cream, cream cheese, and tofu. Also, use lean cooking methods, baking your potatoes and steaming your vegetables, saving your fat allowance for special foods, such as full-fat cheese or a splendid extra virgin olive oil.

The nutrition information following each recipe includes the grams of fat in each serving so you'll know how much of your daily allowance the dish provides. Again, keep in mind that some variations will change the fat content. Using part-skim ricotta cheese in place of nonfat ricotta, for example, will add several grams of fat, and additional calories, to a dish.

The nutrition information also includes the percentage of calories that come from fat in each serving. This is the easiest way to keep track of how much fat you're eating. Most of your meals should be made up of foods that get fewer than 30 percent of their calories from fat.

CHOLESTEROL

Here you'll find how much dietary cholesterol there is in each serving. Dietary cholesterol can raise your blood cholesterol

---

MORE NUTRITIONAL JARGON

Q. What do you mean by "daily value" on the food label?

A. The daily value is the amount of a nutrient, vitamin, or mineral you need for good health, as determined by government studies. The *percentage* of the daily value refers to *how much* of that critical nutrient, vitamin, or mineral a serving of the food contains.

Q. What does it mean to me?

A. It means you can tell by a glance at the nutrition information following each recipe whether a serving of that dish helps you meet your needs for the day. For example, if a recipe's nutritional information indicates that one serving of the dish is an outstanding source of iron, you know that a serving gives you nearly half (more than 40 percent) of the iron you need daily. If it's a good source of calcium, you know you'll have to get up to about 80 percent more calcium from other foods.

---

level, although saturated fat seems to do the real damage where that's concerned. Nevertheless, dietary cholesterol, which comes from animal products only, shouldn't exceed 300 milligrams each day. For more about cholesterol, see page 57.

For more about cholesterol, see page 57.

SODIUM

The amount you'll find here indicates how much sodium is in the dish *before* you add salt to taste. If you're adding salt, keep in mind that 1 teaspoon contains 2 thousand milligrams of sodium. If the dish serves 4, that's an extra 500 milligrams per portion. Your total for the day shouldn't exceed 2,400 milligrams. For more about sodium, see page 563.

FIBER

Fiber is the indigestible part of plant foods. Because bran is coarse and unappetizing, people have been refining wheat and other grains since ancient times. As a consequence, we suffer constipation and ever-increasing rates of colon cancer and high cholesterol.

There are two types of fiber: soluble, found in legumes, oat bran, brown rice, and some fruits and vegetables, and insoluble, which comes in wheat bran and legumes.

Soluble fiber helps lower blood cholesterol. It also helps regulate blood sugar, keeping it from entering your system too quickly, preventing that sugar surge that then leaves you lagging.

Insoluble fiber is the fiber that relieves constipation and may protect against colon cancer.

Fiber of both kinds fills you up without adding calories. As a bonus, most foods that are naturally fiber rich are low in fat.

If you haven't been eating much fiber, a sudden switch to a fiber-rich diet could be an uncomfortable (and, in some respects, antisocial) shock to the system. Gradually increase the amount of fiber you eat until you meet the daily value, drinking more water—at least eight glasses a day—as well.

VITAMINS A AND C

These vitamins are discussed on page 6 (antioxidants).

B VITAMINS

B vitamins enable your body to metabolize the other components of foods. B_1, B_2, and B_3 (thiamine, riboflavin, and niacin) help release the energy from carbohydrates. B_6 makes it possible for your body to use protein, and B_{12} (which comes only from animal products and fortified foods) helps form red blood cells and maintain the central nervous system.

Folacin is essential to the synthesis of DNA, and it's so critical to the healthy development of embryos that all women of child-bearing age are advised to eat lots of it—double the 200 micrograms recommended for most adults—before they get pregnant, and during the early weeks of pregnancy.

READING THE NUTRITIONAL ANALYSIS

When one serving of a recipe provides 10 percent or more of the daily value for a particular vitamin or mineral or for fiber, it will be listed in the nutrition information. The vitamins and minerals included are iron, calcium, zinc, vitamin A (beta-carotene), B vitamins, vitamin C, and folacin. The three categories, "outstanding," "very good," and "good," are defined as follows:

Outstanding Source: One serving provides over 40 percent of the daily value for the vitamins and minerals that are listed here. For example, the Early Spring Minestrone (page 196) is an outstanding source of vitamins A and C and folacin and iron.

Very Good Source: One serving of the recipe provides more than 20 percent of the daily value for the vitamins and minerals that are listed here. For example, Kidney Bean Hummus (page 254) is a very good source of folacin and iron.

Good Source: One serving of the recipe provides more than 10 percent of the daily value for the vitamins and minerals that are listed here. For example, Lentils with Spinach Ragout (page 282) is a good source of vitamin B₃ and zinc.

Food Labeling: The Highs and the Lows

You want a low percentage of the daily value for total fat, saturated fat, cholesterol, and sodium. In fact, you should try to keep the total of your daily percentages for these four well below 100.

You want a high percentage of the daily value for fiber, vitamins A and C, calcium, and iron in the foods you eat.

It's not as easy to determine whether you want a high percentage of the daily value for carbohydrate. While you *do* want lots of complex carbohydrates, you *don't* want much simple carbohydrate (sugar). Food labels distinguish between the two in a very subtle way. Here's how to tell the difference. If the number of grams listed next to "Sugars" is low compared with the number of grams for "Total Carbohydrate," then most of the carbohydrate in that food is complex. In this case, a high percentage of the daily value is a *good* thing.

But if the number of grams of sugar is close to the total number of grams of carbohydrate, the product may contain too much refined sugar. Check the ingredients list; if "sugar," "corn syrup," or any word ending in "ose" is at the lead, that confirms it. In this case, a high percentage daily value is not so great.

However, it may be that the number of sugar grams is high because the product is naturally sweet: pure orange, grape, or apple juice, for example. Again, check the ingredients list to see whether sugar is a natural part of the product. If so, it won't be listed.

GOOD CHOICE
(BREAKFAST CEREAL)

Nutrition Facts

Serving Size 1 cup (47g)
Servings Per Container 1

Amount Per Serving

Calories 160   Calories from Fat 5

	% Daily Value*
Total Fat 1g	1%
Saturated Fat 0g	0%
Cholesterol 0mg	0%
Sodium 0mg	0%
Total Carbohydrate 38g	13%
Dietary Fiber 6g	26%
Sugars 1g	
Protein 6g	

Vitamin A 0%		Vitamin C 0%
Calcium 2%		Iron 12%

*Percent Daily Values are based on a 2,000 calorie diet. Your daily values may be higher or lower depending on your calorie needs:

	Calories:	2,000	2,500
Total Fat	Less than	65g	80g
Saturated Fat	Less than	20g	25g
Cholesterol	Less than	300mg	300mg
Sodium	Less than	2,400mg	2,400mg
Total Carbohydrate		300g	375g
Dietary Fiber		25g	30g

Calories per gram:
Fat 9 • Carbohydrate 4 • Protein 4

NOT-SO-GOOD CHOICE
(BREAKFAST CEREAL)

Nutrition Facts

Serving Size 1/2 cup (56g)
Servings Per Container 1

Amount Per Serving

Calories 250   Calories from Fat 90

	% Daily Value*
Total Fat 10g	15%
Saturated Fat 6g	32%
Cholesterol 0mg	0%
Sodium 115mg	5%
Total Carbohydrate 38g	13%
Dietary Fiber 3g	12%
Sugars 12g	
Protein 6g	

Vitamin A 0%		Vitamin C 0%
Calcium 4%		Iron 11%

*Percent Daily Values are based on a 2,000 calorie diet. Your daily values may be higher or lower depending on your calorie needs:

	Calories:	2,000	2,500
Total Fat	Less than	65g	80g
Saturated Fat	Less than	20g	25g
Cholesterol	Less than	300mg	300mg
Sodium	Less than	2,400mg	2,400mg
Total Carbohydrate		300g	375g
Dietary Fiber		25g	30g

Calories per gram:
Fat 9 • Carbohydrate 4 • Protein 4

Menus for Special Diets

The menus with nutritional analysis were compiled by Chavanne Hanson, MPH, RD, LD, director of nutrition services for University Synergy, the preventive cardiology program of University Hospitals of Cleveland, Primary Affiliate of Case Western Reserve University.

While eating well involves some general principles—lots of complex carbohydrates, not much fat, plenty of fresh produce and whole grains—your needs may be more specific. This is true if you have a condition such as heart disease or diabetes that can be controlled, treated, or otherwise affected by diet. The menus that follow have been compiled to meet particular needs when diet may make a difference.

While the conditions and concerns these menus address are different, all of the meals are low in fat and high in complex carbohydrates. And, with the exception of fresh fruit and fortified breakfast cereals, every dish included can be found in this book.

More likely than not, you don't have the time to make each dish on every menu. But you can use the menus to discover how inclusive even a restricted diet can be. In other words, they're meant for inspiration and encouragement as much as for meal planning.

Each menu item is one serving size as indicated in the recipe or, if a prepared food such as cereal, on the package.

Also, the numbers given for calories and grams have been rounded off, so they are approximate. Moreover, the amounts of calories and nutrients in prepared food products such as broths, cheeses, and bread crumbs may vary from brand to brand, affecting the total calorie content of dishes that call for them.

PREGNANCY

I've never met someone who's followed a prescribed pregnancy diet. Nausea and/or cravings can confound any expectant mother (see "On That Which May Work in Theory"). In fact, the menus that follow may appeal to you only once you're into your second trimester, when your stomach is likely to be settled. Don't force yourself to eat foods that repulse you. First of all, you probably won't be able to keep them down. Second, according to one theory, certain foods may be less appetizing—particularly fruits and vegetables—because they contain small amounts of natural toxins. Food plants produce toxins to keep insects from eating them and your body may be hypersensitive to them while your

embryo is in its most vulnerable stage. Nevertheless, there are some fundamental guidelines you should try to follow when you're up to it.

First, to nourish the embryo and maintain your own strength, you probably need about three hundred calories more than before you were pregnant. You can get the additional calories by eating larger portions of foods you're eating already, provided they're high in complex carbohydrates, calcium, and iron and low in fat. Or you can supplement your calories by tacking a snack onto your regular meals. If you're too nauseous to eat much of anything, try to compensate for foods that repulse you with whatever you can stand to eat, most likely bland cereals, including plain rice.

Additional daily dietary requirements include 60 grams of protein; 300 milligrams of iron (preferably from foods, which include fortified cereals, not supplements, which can cause constipation); 1,200 milligrams of calcium (preferably from nonfat

ON THAT WHICH MAY WORK IN THEORY:
MY PREGNANCY DIET

While I was planning my pregnancy, I was happy to discover that most advice books decreed that the optimal diet was very similar to the one I've always eaten—lots of fresh produce, whole grains, and skim dairy products, few fats and simple sugars. But roughly three weeks into maternity, I lost my appetite—and everything I tried to eat. I couldn't face food in any form—raw, cooked, or depicted in photographs. For a food writer, pregnancy was proving an occupational hazard, something like being a gymnast in a full-body cast.

My eating habits turned from exemplary to exactly the opposite, as I went through mammoth roast beef sandwiches (rare) and grilled hamburgers (also rare). I spent one day in a frenzy, going from one butcher shop to another for the perfect veal shank for osso buco. I found it, braised it, and ate it—without pausing to wipe my mouth. Meanwhile I couldn't look at my former favorite foods: broccoli, strawberries, pineapple, oranges, mangoes, yogurt, and cottage cheese. But I *could* handle hummus—only, however, on toasted rye. And I could deal with waffles, too. I managed to gain the requisite weight by eating three of everything that would stay in my stomach.

I didn't eat "right" until my son was born, so I can't attribute the fact that he's healthy and strong to a diet anything like the one presented here. Yet I'm not suggesting you try to subsist on waffles and hummus. It's just that you can't predict how you'll feel when you're pregnant; food aversions may scuttle the best laid meal plans.

For insight into the source and significance of "pregnancy sickness," including nausea, cravings, and aversions, read *Protecting Your Baby-to-Be* by Margie Profet (Addison Wesley, 1995).

dairy products, not supplements, which, like iron, can cause constipation); 15 milligrams of zinc; 70 milligrams of vitamin C; 800 RE vitamin A; 400 international units of vitamin D; 10 milligrams of vitamin E; and 400 micrograms of folacin.

As for alcohol, artificial sweeteners, and caffeine, it's prudent to avoid them altogether throughout your pregnancy.

Note: *If you were overweight or underweight at the time you became pregnant, consult your doctor about your diet. In the following menus, all portions are one serving as indicated in the recipe or on the label if the food is a packaged product.*

Dinner

Angel-Hair Pasta with Asparagus and Cherry
Tomatoes *(page 294)*
Steamed broccoli
Carrot Cake *(page 474)*
Nonfat milk

Menu 2

CALORIES: ABOUT 2,360 • PROTEIN: 92 G • 15% CALORIES
FROM PROTEIN • CARBOHYDRATE: 380 G • 63% CALORIES
FROM CARBOHYDRATE • FAT: 57 G • 22% CALORIES FROM
FAT • FIBER: 40 G

Breakfast

Cornmeal Waffles *(page 92)*
Maple syrup
Nonfat milk
Mixed fresh berries or fresh orange and pink
grapefruit slices
Prune juice

Lunch

Your Basic Heartwarming Black Bean Soup
(page 188)
Grilled Vegetable Pockets *(page 462)*, made
with whole wheat pita
Fruit-flavored nonfat yogurt (without artificial
sweeteners)

Dinner

Spinach Risotto *(page 309)*
Chopped Caponata *(page 134)*
Mesclun with Orange-Sesame Dressing
(page 119)
Ricotta Cheesecake *(page 482)*

Menu 1

CALORIES: ABOUT 2,400 • PROTEIN: 86 G • 14% CALORIES
FROM PROTEIN • CARBOHYDRATE: 450 G • 72% CALORIES
FROM CARBOHYDRATE • FAT: 39 G • 14% CALORIES FROM
FAT • FIBER: 52 G

Breakfast

Fortified whole-grain cereal, such as Total
Fresh strawberries
Blueberry Buttermilk Pancakes *(page 86)*
Maple syrup
Nonfat milk
Orange juice

Lunch

Grilled Black Bean Patty *(page 461)*
Whole wheat pita bread
Grilled Corn and Pepper Salad with Tomatoes
(page 464)
Mango

Menu 3

CALORIES: ABOUT 2,270 • PROTEIN: 117 G • 20% CALORIES FROM PROTEIN • CARBOHYDRATE: 370 G • 63% CALORIES FROM CARBOHYDRATE • FAT: 45.5 G • 17% CALORIES FROM FAT • FIBER: 43 G

BREAKFAST
Baked Eggs on Polenta with Spinach (*page 327*)
Cantaloupe
Grape-Nuts Bran Bread (*page 406*), toasted
Nonfat milk

LUNCH
Lentil Salad with Minced Vegetables (*page 142*)
Whole wheat pita bread
Steamed broccoli
Fruit-flavored nonfat yogurt (without artificial sweeteners)

DINNER
Grain-Filled Onions (*page 365*)
Tofu and Mushrooms with Peanut Sauce
(*page 456*)
Angel Food Cake (*page 472*)
Nonfat milk

Menu 4

CALORIES: ABOUT 2,450 • PROTEIN: 120 G • 19% CALORIES FROM PROTEIN • CARBOHYDRATE: 380 G • 60% CALORIES FROM CARBOHYDRATE • FAT: 60 G • 21% CALORIES FROM FAT • FIBER: 47 G

BREAKFAST
Oat-Flour Scones (*page 82*)
Nonfat milk
Banana, strawberries, and kiwi or banana and orange

LUNCH
Spinach-Ricotta Calzone (*page 419*)
Salad of Baby Artichokes and Shiitake
Mushrooms (*page 126*)
Vanilla or cappuccino nonfat yogurt

DINNER
Grilled Ratatouille (*page 464*)
Cucumber Raita (*page 156*)
Lavosh (*page 412*)
Lemon-Berry Pudding (*page 495*)

300-CALORIE SNACKS
Granola (*page 50*) with 1 cup nonfat milk
Farina Prune Whip (*page 100*) and 1 apple
Sweet Potato Biscuit Strawberry Shortcake
(*page 481*) and 1 cup nonfat milk
1 cup fruit-flavored nonfat yogurt (without artificial sweeteners)
1 large bunch of grapes

NURSING MOTHER

I know, all you can think about (when you have a moment to think at all!) is losing the weight you gained when you were pregnant. So you may want to cut calories right away. Not so fast—now that you're nursing, you need even more calories than you did when you were pregnant, about two hundred more for a total of five hundred more than you need ordinarily. The fat you stored during pregnancy becomes milk, which your baby will drain in no time. Once that fat layer is gone, you'll have to eat enough food to make more milk. To keep your energy and milk supply up, get those additional calories from calcium-rich foods, such as nonfat yogurt, skim milk, or calcium-fortified, low-fat soy products. In addition to more calories each day you'll need: 65 grams of protein; 15 milligrams of iron; 1,200 milligrams of calcium; 19 mil-

ligrams of zinc; 1,300 RE vitamin A; 2.6 milligrams of vitamin B_{12}; 95 milligrams of vitamin C; and 400 international units of vitamin D.

In addition, be sure to drink eight to ten cups of water each day. You can substitute unsweetened fruit juice for some of the water, but not caffeinated drinks or sugary sodas.

Note: *In the following menus, all portions are one serving as indicated in the recipe or on the label if the food is a packaged product.*

Menu 1

CALORIES: ABOUT 2,370 • PROTEIN: 130 G • 22% CALORIES FROM PROTEIN • CARBOHYDRATE: 380 G • 62% CALORIES FROM CARBOHYDRATE • FAT: 43 G • 16% CALORIES FROM FAT • FIBER: 38 G

BREAKFAST
Angel-Hair Pasta with Eggs, Tomatoes, and
Avocado (*page 101*)
Whole wheat toast
Nonfat milk or nonfat yogurt
Orange or fresh orange juice

LUNCH
Raspberry-Cannellini Succotash (*page 137*)
Your Own Sourdough Bread (*page 410*)
Fresh grapes and pineapple

DINNER
Hummus (*page 254*)
Whole wheat pita bread
Eggplant Baked with Lentils (*page 346*)
Spicy Spinach Nuggets with Cooling Chive
Sauce (*page 216*)
Chocolate Soufflé Cake (*page 476*)

Menu 3

CALORIES: ABOUT 2,200 • PROTEIN: 105 G • 18% CALORIES FROM PROTEIN • CARBOHYDRATE: 382 G • 66% CALORIES FROM CARBOHYDRATE • FAT: 40 G • 16% CALORIES FROM FAT • FIBER: 39 G

BREAKFAST
Granola *(page 50)*
Nonfat milk
Apple-Buttermilk Bundt Muffins *(page 74)*
Orange juice

LUNCH
Red or Yellow Bell Pepper Soup *(page 171)*
Curried Egg Salad *(page 145)*
Carrot sticks
Whole wheat bread
Vanilla or fruit-flavored nonfat yogurt

DINNER
Salad of Baby Artichokes and Shiitake
Mushrooms *(page 126)*
Orange-Sesame-Tempeh Soba *(page 296)*
Cucumber Raita *(page 156)*
Mango Cream *(page 496)*

Menu 2

CALORIES: ABOUT 2,350 • PROTEIN: 86 G • 14% CALORIES FROM PROTEIN • CARBOHYDRATE: 427 G • 70% CALORIES FROM CARBOHYDRATE • FAT: 43 G • 16% CALORIES FROM FAT • FIBER: 38 G

BREAKFAST
Papaya or mango
Whole Wheat Pancakes *(page 88)*
Maple syrup
Nonfat milk or nonfat yogurt

LUNCH
Sweet and Creamy Carrot Calzone *(page 422)*
Asparagus Salad with Bell Peppers and Eggs
(page 146)
Kiwi and strawberries

DINNER
Grilled Fresh Corn and Chickpea Patty
(page 460)
Whole wheat pita bread
Radicchio with Potatoes and Celery *(page 125)*
Fruity Rice Pudding with Meringue *(page 494)*
Nonfat milk or nonfat yogurt

Menu 4

CALORIES: ABOUT 2,200 • PROTEIN: 90 G • 16% CALORIES FROM PROTEIN • CARBOHYDRATE: 384 G • 67% CALORIES FROM CARBOHYDRATE • FAT: 44 G • 17% CALORIES FROM FAT • FIBER: 48 G

BREAKFAST
French Toast *(page 93)*
Maple syrup
Mixed fresh berries: strawberries, blueberries,
raspberries
Fresh orange juice
Nonfat milk or nonfat yogurt

LUNCH
Baked Beans (page 214)
Savory Baked Corn Cakes (page 257)
Apple juice (pressed, not from concentrate)
Fruit-flavored nonfat yogurt (without artificial
sweeteners)

DINNER
Sun-Dried Tomato and Black Olive Frittata
(page 187)
Couscous (page 338) or bulgur
Baked Alaska (page 473)

WEIGHT LOSS

It may seem ironic that as the number of low-fat foods and calorie-free sweeteners proliferate in this country, so has the number of obese Americans. In fact, it makes perfect sense. Those products create the illusion that you can eat as much as you want without consequences, encouraging the very habit you must break if you're going to lose weight once and for all. Any sensible and successful weight-loss program involves eating fewer calories, and spending more of the calories you eat. You can start by substituting complex carbohydrates and nonfat dairy products for fatty foods, getting fewer than 25 percent of your calories from fat. And exercise for at least thirty minutes five or six days a week. If your appetite goes haywire between meals, eat four to six small meals throughout the day to control your hunger. Also, fill up with high-fiber foods, and water. Avoid sugary foods because, although sugar doesn't have many calories, many

sweets also contain lots of fat. Moreover, sugar stokes your appetite, which is one reason nonfat cookies, cakes, and such don't necessarily help you lose weight.

Finally, beer bellies usually don't come from beer, but from what you're likely to eat along with it. Recent studies indicate that alcohol tends to make people overeat, maybe because it lowers inhibitions or because it triggers the appetite, or both. Consequently, stick with the soft stuff when you're trying to lose weight.

Note: *In the following menus, all portions are one serving as indicated in the recipe or on the label if the food is a packaged product.*

Menu 1

CALORIES: ABOUT 1,500 • PROTEIN: 74.5 G • 19% CALORIES FROM PROTEIN • CARBOHYDRATE: 250 G • 64% CALORIES FROM CARBOHYDRATE • FAT: 29 G • 17% CALORIES FROM FAT • FIBER: 38 G

BREAKFAST
My Best Bran Muffins (page 72)
Nonfat yogurt or nonfat milk
Fresh strawberries

LUNCH
Grilled Pepper and Provolone Sandwich
(page 463)
Pretzel sticks

SNACK 1
Apple and lemon or vanilla nonfat yogurt

SNACK 2
Nonfat cocoa mix made with nonfat milk

DINNER
Cabbage-Filled Cabbage Stir-Fry *(page 376)*
Savory Fresh Peach Salad *(page 376)*

Menu 2

CALORIES: ABOUT 1,600 • PROTEIN: 78 G • 18% CALORIES
FROM PROTEIN • CARBOHYDRATE: 290 G • 67% CALORIES
FROM CARBOHYDRATE • FAT: 29 G • 15% CALORIES FROM
FAT • FIBER: 55 G

BREAKFAST
Scrambled Eggs *(page 61)*
Whole wheat toast
Papaya or mango

LUNCH
Barley Soup with Zucchini *(page 175)*
Fat-free wheat crackers or fat-free saltines
Fresh orange or tangerine

SNACK 1
Whole wheat pita bread
Red Lentil Spread *(page 256)*

SNACK 2
Granola *(page 50)*
Nonfat milk or nonfat yogurt
Fresh berries

DINNER
Bell Peppers with Double-Corn Filling
(page 361)
Chili Rice *(page 260)*

Menu 3

CALORIES: ABOUT 1,700 • PROTEIN: 90 G • 20% CALORIES
FROM PROTEIN • CARBOHYDRATE: 260 G • 58% CALORIES
FROM CARBOHYDRATE • FAT: 43 G • 22% CALORIES FROM
FAT • FIBER: 32 G

BREAKFAST
Cottage Cheese Pancakes *(page 86)*
Maple syrup
Cantaloupe

LUNCH
Chilled Filled Spinach Rolls *(page 369)*
Tomato Raita *(page 155)*

SNACK 1
Plain bagel
Strained Yogurt spread (*page 102*)

SNACK 2
Nonfat milk
Fat-free graham crackers

DINNER
Chunky Bean Burritos with Spicy Tomato
Sauce (*page 354*)
Fresh Corn Custard with Polenta Crust (*page 248*)
Sliced fresh tomato and cucumber

Menu 4

CALORIES: ABOUT 1,800 • PROTEIN: 77 G • 16% CALORIES
FROM PROTEIN • CARBOHYDRATE: 315 G • 67% CALORIES
FROM CARBOHYDRATE • FAT: 34 G • 16% CALORIES FROM
FAT • FIBER: 36 G

BREAKFAST
Waffles (*page 89*)
Maple syrup
Red grapefruit
Nonfat milk or nonfat yogurt

LUNCH
Incredible Corn Soup (*page 179*)
Pita Bread (*page 414*)
Peach, plum, or apple

SNACK 1
Swift, Delicious Bean Salad (*page 148*)

SNACK 2
Fresh Apple-Spice Cake (*page 477*)
Nonfat milk

DINNER
Speedy Summer Casserole (*page 333*)
Cucumber and Bulgur Wheat with
Fresh Herbs (*page 138*)
Fresh pear

ATHLETES
The three C's critical for athletes are: calories, carbohydrates, and calcium. You'll need enough calories to stay strong, perform well, and maintain your optimal body weight. Although you can consult "How Many Calories Do I Need?" page 9, the best guide to calorie consumption is your performance and your weight. If your energy drops during an event, or if you find you're losing weight and strength as you train, you may not be eating enough. But if you find that you're gaining weight despite rigorous workouts, you may be eating too much.

Roughly 70 percent of your calories should come from carbohydrate, ideally complex carbohydrates such as baked potatoes, pasta, and legumes. Carbohydrates provide a combination of fast- and slow-burning energy; you get a boost right off the bat, then energy that lasts for several hours afterward.

Rigorous exercise takes a double toll on bones. First, it strains them. Second, it can deplete calcium. Protect your bones by eating at least 1,000 milligrams of calcium each day, preferably in the form of nonfat dairy products.

You shouldn't get more than 20 percent of your calories from fat. Fat releases energy grudgingly and may slow you down. Besides, it's not good for your heart.

Drink lots of water *before* you get thirsty. By the time you feel thirsty, you're already dehydrated to a point that it affects your performance.

Finally, eat breakfast. A morning meal made up of complex carbohydrates and nonfat dairy products will get you off and running.

Note: *In the following menus, all portions are one serving as indicated in the recipe or on the label if the food is a packaged product.*

Menu 1

CALORIES: ABOUT 2,400 • PROTEIN: 83 G • 13% CALORIES FROM PROTEIN • CARBOHYDRATE: 470 G • 76% CALORIES FROM CARBOHYDRATE • FAT: 30.5 G • 11% CALORIES FROM FAT • FIBER: 42 G

BREAKFAST
Breakfast Kugel (*page 97*)
Grape-Nuts Bran Bread (*page 406*)
Red grapefruit
Nonfat milk or nonfat yogurt

LUNCH
Tamale-Style Fresh Corn Nuggets (*page 246*)
Steamed broccoli
Watermelon

DINNER
Strawberry Soup (*page 206*)
Cayote Calzone (*page 421*)
Mesclun with Avocado-Buttermilk Dressing
(*page 120*)
Jelly Roll (*page 480*)

Menu 2

CALORIES: ABOUT 2,280 • PROTEIN: 91 G • 15% CALORIES FROM PROTEIN • CARBOHYDRATE: 430 G • 72% CALORIES FROM CARBOHYDRATE • FAT: 34 G • 13% CALORIES FROM FAT • FIBER: 40 G

BREAKFAST
Cottage Cheese Pancakes (*page 86*)
Maple syrup
Fresh orange juice
Fresh banana
Nonfat milk or nonfat yogurt

LUNCH
Eggplant Salad with Red Bell Pepper *(page 133)*
Sun-Dried Tomato Flan *(page 243)*
Naan *(page 415)*
Grapes

DINNER
Butternut Squash Soup *(page 180)*
Nori Rolls *(page 370)*
Steamed broccoli
Fig Glace *(page 488)*

LUNCH
Early Spring Minestrone *(page 196)*
Swift Chapati-Style Flat Bread *(page 412)*
Nectarine

DINNER
Asparagus Risotto with Lemon and Mint
(page 314)
Artichoke and Mushroom Savory Pie
(page 434)
Vanilla nonfat yogurt with fresh fruit

Menu 3

CALORIES: ABOUT 2,230 • PROTEIN: 96.3 G • 17% CALORIES
FROM PROTEIN • CARBOHYDRATE: 360 G • 64% CALORIES
FROM CARBOHYDRATE • FAT: 49 G • 19% CALORIES FROM
FAT • FIBER: 39.5 G

BREAKFAST
Fruity Cream of Rice *(page 55)*
Nonfat milk or nonfat yogurt
Fresh orange juice or prune juice

Menu 4

CALORIES: ABOUT 2,220 • PROTEIN: 77 G • 13% CALORIES
FROM PROTEIN • CARBOHYDRATE: 430 G • 74% CALORIES
FROM CARBOHYDRATE • FAT: 34 G • 13% CALORIES FROM
FAT • FIBER: 42 G

BREAKFAST
Granola Bars *(page 51)*
Fruit Smoothie *(page 48)*

LUNCH
Spinach with Potatoes, Fennel,
and Pine Nuts *(page 219)*
Whole Wheat Chickpea Bread
(page 403)
Corn on the cob (steamed or boiled,
no butter)
Fresh fruit

DINNER
Gnocchi *(page 316)*
Simplest Fresh Tomato Sauce
(page 278)
Panzanella *(page 150)*
Citrus Pudding Cake *(page 478)*

DIABETES

As a diabetic, you're acutely sensitive to what you eat; meal planning is a balancing act you have to perform to avoid flooding your system with sugars it can't handle. Consequently, it's critical to get the right amount of calories. Don't determine your calorie level without discussing it with your doctor or a registered dietitian who specializes in diabetes. The following menus provide between 1,700 and 1,800 calories each, but you may need more or fewer depending on the many factors involved in managing diabetes. You can increase or decrease the number of calories in the menus by adding or eliminating snacks.

Although you've been told a million times, once again: avoid refined sugars, choosing complex carbohydrates instead. A majority of your calories should come from complex carbohydrates, high fiber foods such as whole grains and legumes.

Meanwhile, fewer than 30 percent of your calories should come from fat, fewer than 20 percent if your cholesterol is high and/or you're overweight.

Since you have to compensate for the fact that your body can't regulate the flow of energy from food, *when* you eat matters as much as what you eat. Establish a meal and snack schedule that allows you to keep your blood sugar level stable.

Note: *In the following menus, all portions are one serving as indicated in the recipe or on the label if the food is a packaged product.*

Menu 1

CALORIES: ABOUT 1,800 • PROTEIN: 80 G • 17% CALORIES FROM PROTEIN • CARBOHYDRATE: 330 G • 71% CALORIES FROM CARBOHYDRATE • FAT: 25 G • 12% CALORIES FROM FAT • FIBER: 40 G

BREAKFAST
Oatmeal made with nonfat milk (*page 52*)
Raisins
Fresh orange or orange juice

LUNCH
Strata (*page 440*)
Sorbet (*page 489*)

SNACK
Kidney Bean Hummus (*page 254*)
Whole wheat pita bread

DINNER
Short Pasta with Olive Pesto (*page 296*)
Soft and Chewy Dinner Rolls (*page 408*)
Assorted grapes

Menu 2

CALORIES: ABOUT 1,790 • PROTEIN: 94.5 G • 20% CALORIES FROM PROTEIN • CARBOHYDRATE: 300 G • 66% CALORIES FROM CARBOHYDRATE • FAT: 28 G • 14% CALORIES FROM FAT • FIBER: 39 G

BREAKFAST
Polenta Porridge (*page 54*)
Cantaloupe and honeydew
Nonfat milk or nonfat yogurt

LUNCH
Sweet Black Beans on Whole Wheat Penne
(*page 289*)
Mesclun with Orange-Sesame Dressing
(*page 121*) or bottled fat-free dressing
Whole wheat bread

SNACK
Sweet Potato Biscuit Strawberry
Shortcake (*page 481*)
Nonfat milk

DINNER
Lentil Terrines with Mixed-Vegetable Sauce
(*page 334*)
Brown rice
Your Own Sourdough Bread (*page 410*)
Apple Butter with yogurt (*page 103*)

Menu 3

CALORIES: ABOUT 1,700 • PROTEIN: 83 G • 18% CALORIES FROM PROTEIN • CARBOHYDRATE: 320 G • 70% CALORIES FROM CARBOHYDRATE • FAT: 25 G • 12% CALORIES FROM FAT • FIBER: 47 G

BREAKFAST
Oat Bran cereal made with nonfat milk
(*page 54*)
Fresh orange or red grapefruit

LUNCH
Parsnip and Apple Terrine (*page 236*)
Soft and Chewy Dinner Rolls
(*page 408*)

SNACK
Fruit-flavored nonfat yogurt (with artificial
sweeteners)

DINNER
Creamy Spinach Soup (*page 183*)
Sweet Potato Drop Gnocchi
(*page 320*)
Mixed Greens with Raspberry Dressing
(I or II) (*page 122*)

Menu 4

CALORIES: ABOUT 1,700 • PROTEIN: 82.5 G • 19% CALORIES FROM PROTEIN • CARBOHYDRATE: 270 G • 62% CALORIES FROM CARBOHYDRATE • FAT: 37 G • 19% CALORIES FROM FAT • FIBER: 42.5 G

BREAKFAST
Baked Eggs (*page 63*) on plain bagel
Cottage cheese
Fresh orange or grapefruit

LUNCH
Broccoli Rabe with Linguine *(page 292)*
Corn on the cob

SNACK
Carrot Bar Cookies *(page 483)*

DINNER
Grilled Mushrooms and Sour Cream *(page 226)*
Stewed Beans with Potatoes and
Olives *(page 332)*
Steamed asparagus
Fresh fruit

MENOPAUSE

You may be lucky and feel no effects when you "go through the change." If you're not so fortunate, you may be able to control many of the symptoms such as fatigue and mild depression, with a combination of hormone therapy and diet, or with diet alone. Complex carbohydrates can make you more energetic and stimulate the production of a natural antidepressant (seratonin) in your brain. Consequently, try to get 60 to 70 percent of your calories from complex carbohydrates.

You may burn calories from all foods more slowly as you age, and fat calories are always the last to go, so eat low-fat foods to control your weight, getting fewer than 30 percent of your calories from fat.

You'll need between 1,000 and 1,500 milligrams of calcium daily to avoid or arrest osteoporosis (degenerative bone disease). If you're on estrogen therapy, the lower amount may be fine. If not, shoot for more. And try to get it from nonfat dairy products rather than supplements, which may cause constipation.

Eating at least 30 grams of fiber each day should help keep you regular and may help you feel full enough to cut excess calories.

Finally, alcohol can contribute to bone loss, so don't overdo it. Consider the results of a study reported in the *Journal of the National Cancer Institute:* The risk of breast cancer is 39 percent higher among women who have one drink each day, and 69 percent higher among women who have two. So you may be better off saving the sauce for special occasions.

Note: *In the following menus, all portions are one serving as indicated in the recipe or on the label if the food is a packaged product.*

Menu 1

CALORIES: ABOUT 1,750 • PROTEIN: 97 G • 21% CALORIES FROM PROTEIN • CARBOHYDRATE: 270 G • 60% CALORIES FROM CARBOHYDRATE • FAT: 38 G • 19% CALORIES FROM FAT • FIBER: 33 G

BREAKFAST
Fruit Smoothie (*page 48*)

LUNCH
Lentil and Mushroom Stew (*page 340*)
Fat-free wheat crackers or saltines
Fresh pear or apple

DINNER
Spinach Strudel (*page 437*)
Pasta with Roasted Fresh Tomato (*page 290*)
Your Own Sourdough Bread (*page 410*)
Sorbet (*page 489*)

Menu 2

CALORIES: ABOUT 1,800 • PROTEIN: 82 G • 17% CALORIES FROM PROTEIN • CARBOHYDRATE: 290 G • 61% CALORIES FROM CARBOHYDRATE • FAT: 47.5 G • 22% CALORIES FROM FAT • FIBER: 32.5 G

BREAKFAST
French Toast (*page 93*)
Maple syrup
Nonfat milk or nonfat yogurt

LUNCH
Cold Cherry Soup (*page 204*)
Panzanella (*page 150*)

DINNER
Cheese Crepe Bundles in Minced Ratatouille
(*page 348*)
Rice
Whole wheat bread
Melon and fresh berries or Sorbet (*page 489*)

Menu 3

CALORIES: ABOUT 1,740 • PROTEIN: 70 G • 15% CALORIES FROM PROTEIN • CARBOHYDRATE: 330 G • 73% CALORIES FROM CARBOHYDRATE • FAT: 23.5 G • 12% CALORIES FROM FAT • FIBER: 40 G

BREAKFAST
Farina Prune Whip (*page 100*)
Nonfat milk or nonfat yogurt

LUNCH
Gazpacho *(page 202)*
Tamale-Style Fresh Corn Nuggets *(page 246)*

DINNER
Mango Salsa *(page 160)*
My Favorite Chickpeas *(page 360)*
Swift Chapati-Style Flat Bread *(page 412)* or
Naan *(page 415)*
Steamed spinach

Menu 4

CALORIES: ABOUT 1,730 • PROTEIN: 67 G • 15% CALORIES
FROM PROTEIN • CARBOHYDRATE: 290 G • 64% CALORIES
FROM CARBOHYDRATE • FAT: 41 G • 21% CALORIES FROM
FAT • FIBER: 33 G

BREAKFAST
Granola *(page 50)*
Nonfat milk

LUNCH
Fresh Corn Risotto *(page 312)*
Beet and Vidalia Onion Salad *(page 136)*
Fresh fruit

DINNER
Baked Ratatouille Terrine *(page 238)*
Creamy Rice with Potatoes and Leeks
(page 259)
Mesclun with Creamy Chive Dressing
(page 120)
Your Own Sourdough Bread *(page 410)*
Sorbet *(page 489)*

CANCER PREVENTION
The American Institute for Cancer Research has named the following dietary "cancer protectors," with demonstrated links to lower rates of cancer: vitamin A and beta-carotene, vitamin C, vitamin E, and fiber. It seems the prime dietary cancer promoter may be fat. It's easy to infer the advice from that information: eat at least nine servings of vitamin rich fruits and vegetables every day, at least 30 grams of fiber and very little fat. For cancer prevention, ideally fewer than 20 percent of your calories should come from fat, with only 10 percent coming from saturated fats. This is not only because fat itself may contribute to cancer, but because being overweight is a risk factor, too.

Note: *In the following menus, all portions are one serving as indicated in the recipe or on the label if the food is a packaged product.*

Menu 1

CALORIES: ABOUT 1,780 • PROTEIN: 110 G • 24% CALORIES FROM PROTEIN • CARBOHYDRATE: 270 G • 58% CALORIES FROM CARBOHYDRATE • FAT: 37 G • 18% CALORIES FROM FAT • FIBER: 47 G

BREAKFAST
Baked Blintz Casserole (*page 96*)
Fresh orange or berries

LUNCH
Tabbouleh (*page 138*)
Black Beans with Orange and Saffron
(*page 340*)
Spinach with bottled fat-free dressing

DINNER
Sweet Carrot Soup (*page 187*)
Sesame Grilled Tofu and Mushrooms
(*page 458*)
Cucumber Raita (*page 156*)
Naan (*page 415*)

DINNER
Carrot-Spinach Terrine (*page 237*)
Potato Gratin (*page 228*)
Steamed broccoli
Apple Butter (*page 103*) with vanilla nonfat
yogurt

Menu 2

CALORIES: ABOUT 1,680 • PROTEIN: 62 G • 14% CALORIES FROM PROTEIN • CARBOHYDRATE: 325 G • 75% CALORIES FROM CARBOHYDRATE • FAT: 22 G • 11% CALORIES FROM FAT • FIBER: 29 G

BREAKFAST
Waffles (*page 88*)
Maple syrup
Nonfat milk or nonfat yogurt
Fresh orange juice

LUNCH
Cold Teriyaki-Style Noodle Salad (*page 148*)
Pineapple and kiwi

Menu 3

CALORIES: ABOUT 1,740 • PROTEIN: 83 G • 18% CALORIES FROM PROTEIN • CARBOHYDRATE: 230 G • 61% CALORIES FROM CARBOHYDRATE • FAT: 41 G • 20% CALORIES FROM FAT • FIBER: 39 G

BREAKFAST
Fruity Cream of Rice (*page 55*)
Nonfat milk or nonfat yogurt

LUNCH
Lentil Salad with Minced Vegetables (*page 142*)
Whole wheat pita
Fruit-flavored nonfat yogurt (without artificial
sweeteners)

DINNER
Peanut Curry with Sweet Potato and Collard
Greens (*page 359*)
Bulgur Wheat with Spinach, Raisins,
and Pine Nuts (*page 262*)
Naan (*page 415*)

Menu 4

CALORIES: ABOUT 1,750 • PROTEIN: 72.5 G • 16% CALORIES
FROM PROTEIN • CARBOHYDRATE: 335 G • 73% CALORIES
FROM CARBOHYDRATE • FAT: 23 G • 11% CALORIES FROM
FAT • FIBER: 47 G

BREAKFAST
My Best Bran Muffins (*page 72*)
Nonfat milk
Fresh orange or grapefruit juice

LUNCH
Carrot Gnocchi (*page 318*)
Cannellini Bean and Spinach Salad (*page 138*)

DINNER
Mushroom Pâté (*page 240*)
Summer Market Salad (*page 141*)
Lavosh (*page 412*)
Pumpkin Soufflé (*page 499*)

HYPERTENSION
(HIGH BLOOD PRESSURE)
One of the principal risk factors in heart
disease, high blood pressure, may be the
most manageable. If you're overweight,
shedding the extra pounds may bring down
your blood pressure. Also, if you cut salt
and other sources of sodium, so that you're
eating fewer than 2,400 milligrams of
sodium each day, you can keep your blood
pressure down or keep it from rising in the
first place. To control your weight, get less
than 25 percent of your calories from fat
and at least 50 percent of your calories
from complex carbohydrates, such as
whole-grain products and legumes. If you
eat at least 35 grams of fiber daily, you'll
feel full while you're eating less. Also,
foods that are rich in fiber naturally tend to
be low in fat, too.

Finally, limit caffeine, having fewer
than 3 cups of coffee or cola each day.

Note: *In the following menus, all portions are
one serving as indicated in the recipe or on the label if
the food is a packaged product.*

Menu 1

CALORIES: ABOUT 1,745 • PROTEIN: 67.4 G • 15% CALORIES
FROM PROTEIN • CARBOHYDRATE: 285 G • 64% CALORIES
FROM CARBOHYDRATE • FAT: 41 G • 21% CALORIES FROM
FAT • FIBER: 31 G

BREAKFAST
Blueberry Spoonbread (*page 98*)
Fresh grapefruit half or grapefruit juice
Nonfat milk or nonfat yogurt

LUNCH
Cream of Fresh Tomato Soup (*page 182*)
Oven-Baked Leek and Fennel Pancakes
(*page 258*)
Whole wheat bread
Fresh fruit or Sorbet (*page 489*)

DINNER
Citrus-Marinated Asparagus with Sesame
Seeds and Pine Nuts (*page 131*)
Fresh Artichokes on Pasta (*page 293*)
Fresh tomato filled with Baba Ghanouj
(*page 220*)
Glace (*page 486*) or frozen yogurt

Menu 2

CALORIES: ABOUT 1,770 • PROTEIN: 77 G • 16% CALORIES
FROM PROTEIN • CARBOHYDRATE: 230 G • 63% CALORIES
FROM CARBOHYDRATE • FAT: 43 G • 21% CALORIES FROM
FAT • FIBER: 43 G

BREAKFAST
Oatmeal Bread (*page 405*)
Fruit preserves
Frittata (*page 68*)

LUNCH
Raspberry-Cannellini Succotash (*page 137*)
Asparagus-Potato Puffs (*page 222*)
Fruit-flavored nonfat yogurt

DINNER
Grilled Fajitas (*page 459*)
Rice
Corn and Red Pepper Salad with Caramelized
Sweet Onions (*page 129*)
Fresh fruit or Sorbet (*page 489*)

Menu 3

CALORIES: ABOUT 1,890 • PROTEIN: 73 G • 15% CALORIES
FROM PROTEIN • CARBOHYDRATE: 350 G • 71% CALORIES
FROM CARBOHYDRATE • FAT: 30 G • 14% CALORIES FROM
FAT • FIBER: 46 G

BREAKFAST
Pumpkin Waffles (*page 91*)
Maple syrup
Nonfat milk or nonfat yogurt
Fresh berries or fresh orange juice

LUNCH
Spicy Corn Salad with Jalapeño Peppers
(*page 130*)
Spicy Spinach Nuggets with Cooling
Chive Sauce (*page 216*)
Whole wheat bread
Fresh mango

DINNER
Baked Bean Soup (*page 191*)
Sour Cream and Onion Savory Pie
(*page 435*)
Frozen yogurt

Menu 4

CALORIES: ABOUT 1,710 • PROTEIN: 87.5 G • 19% CALORIES FROM PROTEIN • CARBOHYDRATE: 285 G • 63% CALORIES FROM CARBOHYDRATE • FAT: 34 G • 17% CALORIES FROM FAT • FIBER: 40 G

BREAKFAST
Oatmeal made with nonfat milk *(page 52)*
Fresh orange or grapefruit or fresh orange or grapefruit juice

LUNCH
Black Beans in Bell Peppers *(page 368)*
Roasted Fresh Tomatoes *(page 218)*
Naan *(page 415)*
Melon

DINNER
Spicy Tofu with Eggplant and Peppers
(page 342)
Bulgur Wheat Pilaf with Cool Mint Sauce
(page 261)
Lemon Tea Cakes *(page 478)*

HIGH CHOLESTEROL
The National Institutes of Health, citing high cholesterol as a prime risk factor for heart disease, recommends a two-step diet to lower LDL (aka "bad") cholesterol. Step one involves getting no more than 20 percent of your calories from fat, with saturated fats contributing no more than half of the total number of fat calories. The amount of cholesterol you consume daily should be less than 300 milligrams. Incidentally, most authorities agree that all of us should eat within these guidelines.

If your cholesterol level doesn't fall,

move on to step two, cutting saturated fat from no more than 10 percent to no more than 7 percent of your calories, and consume fewer than 200 milligrams of cholesterol each day.

Don't *add* unsaturated fats to your diet; substitute them for saturated and hydrogenated fats while cutting back on *all* fats altogether.

Cutting back on fat makes room for complex carbohydrates; at least 50 to 60 percent of your calories should come from foods such as legumes and whole grains. Fortuitously, many complex carbohydrate foods also contain lots of soluble fiber, which has been found to be as effective at lowering cholesterol as prescription medication, for some people. Try to eat at least 35 grams of fiber every day, with one-third of it soluble, the type of fiber you get from beans, oat bran, and fresh fruits and vegetables.

Note: *In the following menus, all portions are one serving as indicated in the recipe or on the label if the food is a packaged product.*

Menu 1

CALORIES: ABOUT 1,980 • PROTEIN: 115 G • 22% CALORIES FROM PROTEIN • CARBOHYDRATE: 345 G • 67% CALORIES FROM CARBOHYDRATE • FAT: 24 G • 10% CALORIES FROM FAT (2% SATURATED) • FIBER: 40 G

BREAKFAST
Breakfast Kugel (*page 96*)
Nonfat milk or soy milk or nonfat yogurt
Cantaloupe or fresh orange or grapefruit

LUNCH
Bulgur and Red Lentil Soup (*page 198*)
Whole wheat pita bread
Apple or pear

SNACK
(omit if you have to cut total calories to
reach your ideal weight)
Fruit Smoothie made with nonfat milk or
nonfat soy milk (*page 48*)

DINNER
Potato-Fennel Stew with Mixed Beans and
Tofu (*page 336*)
Rice
Lavosh (*page 412*)

Menu 2

CALORIES: ABOUT 1,750 • PROTEIN: 72 G • 16% CALORIES FROM PROTEIN • CARBOHYDRATE: 330 G • 71% CALORIES FROM CARBOHYDRATE • FAT: 27 G • 13% CALORIES FROM FAT (2.4% SATURATED) • FIBER: 45 G

BREAKFAST
Oat Bran cereal made with nonfat milk
(*page 54*)
Banana
Fresh orange or grapefruit juice

LUNCH
Artichoke and Mushroom Savory Pie (*page 434*)
Fresh spinach with Orange-Sesame Dressing
(*page 121*) or bottled nonfat dressing

SNACK
Kidney Bean Hummus (*page 254*)
Swift Chapati-Style Flat Bread (*page 412*)

DINNER
Supper Fruit Salad (*page 144*)
Whole Wheat Chickpea Bread (*page 403*)
Lemon Filling (*page 496*)

Menu 3

CALORIES: ABOUT 1,980 • PROTEIN: 71.5 G • 14% CALORIES FROM PROTEIN • CARBOHYDRATE: 400 G • 77% CALORIES FROM CARBOHYDRATE • FAT: 22 G • 10% CALORIES FROM FAT (2% SATURATED) • FIBER: 49 G

BREAKFAST
Whole Wheat Pancakes (*page 88*)
Maple syrup
Nonfat milk or nonfat yogurt
Fresh berries or orange juice

LUNCH
Lemon-Spiked Lentil Salad *(page 143)*
Whole Wheat Chickpea Bread *(page 403)*
Fresh fruit

SNACK
Granola Bar *(page 51)*

DINNER
Sweet Onion Focaccia *(page 427)*
Pasta e Fagioli *(page 194)*

Menu 4

CALORIES: ABOUT 1,780 • PROTEIN: 88 G • 18% CALORIES FROM PROTEIN • CARBOHYDRATE: 345 G • 71% CALORIES FROM CARBOHYDRATE • FAT: 24.5 G • 11% CALORIES FROM FAT (3% SATURATED) • FIBER: 64 G

BREAKFAST
Oat Bran Muffins *(page 75)*
Nonfat milk
Fresh orange or red grapefruit or fresh orange
or red grapefruit juice

LUNCH
Black Beans with Orange and Saffron *(page 341)*
Savory Carrot Flan *(page 245)*
Sliced tomatoes with Creamy Chive Dressing
(page 120)
Naan *(page 415)*

DINNER
Classic Leek and Potato Soup with Watercress
(page 182)
Caesar-Style Summertime Panzanella *(page 152)*
Sweet-Potato-Biscuit Strawberry Shortcake
(page 481)

HIGH TRIGLYCERIDES
It's a bit trickier to manage high triglycerides than high cholesterol because a very low-fat diet can actually make the condition worse. Nevertheless, if you have high triglycerides you should modify your diet, eating fewer calories overall to reach your ideal body weight. Be sure you're getting some fat, but that it is mostly unsaturated, and that it contributes no more than 25 percent of your total calories each day. You should steer clear of simple sugars, including dried fruit, fruit juice, soda, and alcohol of all kinds, choosing whole fruits and whole grains instead.

Note: *In the following menus, all portions are one serving as indicated in the recipe or on the label if the food is a packaged product.*

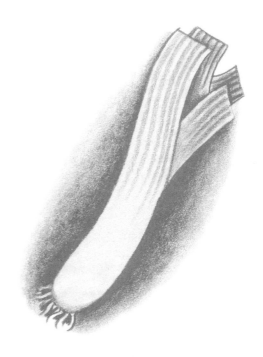

Menu 1

CALORIES: ABOUT 1,627 • PROTEIN: 72 G • 17% CALORIES FROM PROTEIN • CARBOHYDRATE: 290 G • 68% CALORIES FROM CARBOHYDRATE • FAT: 28 G • 15% CALORIES FROM FAT • FIBER: 35 G

BREAKFAST
Polenta Porridge (*page 54*)
Fresh orange slices

LUNCH
Cream of Fresh Tomato Soup (*page 182*)
Rice with corn and beans
Your Own Sourdough Bread (*page 410*)

DINNER
Gnocchi (*page 316*)
Grilled Mushrooms and Sour Cream (*page 226*)
Whole wheat bread

Menu 2

CALORIES: ABOUT 1,650 • PROTEIN: 67.5 G • 16% CALORIES FROM PROTEIN • CARBOHYDRATE: 285 G • 66% CALORIES FROM CARBOHYDRATE • FAT: 35 G • 18% CALORIES FROM FAT • FIBER: 50 G

BREAKFAST
Oatmeal cooked in nonfat milk (*page 52*)
Fresh red grapefruit

LUNCH
Tabbouleh (*page 139*)
Eggplant, Potato and Spinach with
Aromatic Herbs (*page 344*)
Apple

DINNER
Chili (*page 352*)
Spring Garden Tortillas (*page 355*)
Glace (*page 486*) or frozen yogurt

Menu 3

CALORIES: ABOUT 1,595 • PROTEIN: 87 G • 21% CALORIES FROM PROTEIN • CARBOHYDRATE: 250 G • 61% CALORIES FROM CARBOHYDRATE • FAT: 31 G • 17% CALORIES FROM FAT • FIBER: 33 G

BREAKFAST
Grape-Nuts cereal
Nonfat milk
Oatmeal Bread (*page 405*)
Fruit preserves

LUNCH
Cold Cream of Broccoli Soup (*page 200*)
Leek and Onion Potato Pie (*page 350*)
Fruit-flavored nonfat yogurt

DINNER
Rolled Roasted Red Peppers (*page 249*)
Artichokes, Mushrooms and Potatoes with
Whole Wheat Pasta (*page 288*)
Your Own Sourdough Bread (*page 410*)

Menu 4

CALORIES: ABOUT 1,600 • PROTEIN: 77 G • 18% CALORIES FROM PROTEIN • CARBOHYDRATE: 285 G • 67% CALORIES FROM CARBOHYDRATE • FAT: 26 G • 14% CALORIES FROM FAT • FIBER: 37 G

BREAKFAST
Oat-Flour Scones (*page 82*)
Nonfat milk
Fresh berries or melon

LUNCH
Mushroom Crepes (*page 430*)
Papaya or mango

DINNER
Tamale-Style Fresh Corn Nuggets with Bean
Filling (*page 246*)
Romaine lettuce, grated carrot, sliced tomatoes
with Avocado-Buttermilk Dressing (*page 120*)

ADDITIONAL MENUS
The following are menus organized by
occasion. Use them as they are, or to guide
you as you create your own.

PICNICS
Carrot-Spinach Terrine (*page 237*)
Tahini Tabbouleh (*page 149*)

Leek and Onion Potato Pie (*page 350*)
Cucumber and Bulgur Wheat with
Fresh Herbs (*page 138*)

Cantaloupe Soup (*page 207*)
Sweet Onion Focaccia (*page 427*)

Summer Market Salad (*page 141*)
Chilled Cream of Carrot Soup with
Ginger and Lime (*page 200*)

Rice Salad with Snow Peas, Red Beans,
and Sweet Corn (*page 146*)
Strawberry Soup (*page 206*)

Chilled Filled Spinach Rolls (*page 369*)
Panzanella (*page 150*)

ELABORATE DINNER PARTIES
Sweet and Simple Borscht (*page 184*)
Lentil Terrines with Mixed-Vegetable Sauce
(*page 334*)
Baby spinach with Orange-Sesame Dressing
(*page 121*)
Torta di Budino di Riso Integrale (*page 482*)

Butternut Squash Soup (*page 181*)
Grain-Filled Onions (*page 365*)
Potato-Fennel Stew with Mixed Beans and
Tofu (*page 336*)
Maple-Apple-Cranberry Crumble (*page 479*)

Creamy Herb Soup (*page 180*)
Cheese Crepe Bundles in Minced Ratatouille
(*page 348*)
Rice
Endive, Radicchio, and Mushroom Salad
(*page 124*)
Jelly Roll (*page 480*)

BREAKFAST

Nutritionists can rattle off a number of reasons to eat a good breakfast: it keeps you alert and energetic, stops you from craving high-calorie midmorning snacks, and provides a number of essential nutrients, vitamins, minerals, and fiber.

But I prefer my reason, which is that breakfast is a hedge against a lousy day. If you eat something delicious first thing in the morning, no matter what happens to you later on, you'll have had *something* to enjoy.

I'm disposed—by metabolism and habit—toward big breakfasts; I've always woken up hungry, preferring to eat blueberry pancakes than to sleep through the twenty minutes it takes to make them. And I've come to believe that no one—even those who rarely eat breakfast—would refuse it if *time* weren't an issue.

Throughout this section you'll find tips for preparing your favorite breakfast foods the night before while you're still alert, leaving only a simple step or two for the morning. Once breakfast becomes a habit, you'll wonder how you ever got along without it.

Breakfast in Meal Planning •

Breakfast Pantry • Breakfast Menus

• Weekday Breakfast Strategies •

 Brunch Strategies • Smoothies

• Granola • Hot Cereals • Eggs •

Muffins, Quick Breads, and Rolls •

Pancakes • Waffles • Puddings,

Casseroles, and Breakfast Pastas •

Toppings and Spreads for Pancakes,

Waffles, and Breakfast Breads

Breakfast in Meal Planning

Breakfast can include a substantial share of critical minerals and vitamins, especially calcium, iron, and vitamin C, D, and B12. And it can be a major source of complex carbohydrates, which give you energy that lasts at least until lunch.

Here are just a few of the supremely nourishing breakfast foods you'll find in this section.

BLUEBERRY BUTTERMILK PANCAKES (PAGE 87)
39% daily value for protein
30% daily value for calcium
25% daily value for vitamins B1, 2, 3
21% daily value for zinc
18% daily value for iron
12% daily value for folacin

STRAWBERRY SMOOTHIE (PAGE 48)
25% daily value for protein
50% daily value for vitamin C
38% daily value for calcium
27% daily value for vitamin B2
13% daily value for zinc

OATMEAL MADE WITH NONFAT MILK (PAGE 52)
29% daily value for protein
33% daily value for calcium
15% daily value for vitamin A
11% daily value for zinc

MY BEST BRAN MUFFINS (PAGE 72)
24% daily value for iron
20% daily value for calcium
15% daily value for zinc

FARINA PRUNE WHIP (PAGE 100)
24% daily value for protein
28% daily value for calcium
22% daily value for iron
21% daily value for vitamin C
12% daily value for zinc

Breakfast Pantry

You'll find my brand-name recommendations for many of these items on page 595. If you can't find what you want where you shop, see the mail-order information on page 596.

Flours
All-purpose flour
Whole wheat flour
Oatmeal flour
Whole wheat pastry flour* or kamut flour*

Other Grains
Rolled oats
Cornmeal (polenta), preferably stone-ground
Wheat bran
Oat bran
Farina/Cream of Wheat*
Cream of Rice*

Sweeteners
Sugar, preferably raw (turbinado) sugar
Light brown sugar
Dark brown sugar
Honey
Molasses
Maple syrup
Fruit juice concentrate
Barley-malt syrup*
Fruit preserves, preferably all-fruit

Miscellaneous Baking Staples
Baking soda
Baking powder
Cornstarch or arrowroot
Cocoa
Vanilla extract
Nonfat dry milk* (refrigerate after opening)

In the Refrigerator
Large eggs
Nonfat milk or soy milk

Plain nonfat yogurt
Low-fat cottage cheese
Nonfat or reduced-fat sour cream
Nonfat or part-skim ricotta cheese
Nonfat or reduced-fat cream cheese
Nonfat or low-fat buttermilk
Fresh orange juice or grapefruit juice
Fresh fruit

*Optional, not called for often.

NONFAT BUTTERMILK? AN OXYMORON?

No. Originally buttermilk was the tangy liquid left over from churning milk into butter. Today, it's made by adding bacterial culture to nonfat or low-fat milk. Except in the rare instances when dairies garnish the product with small slivers of butter (in which case it's *not* labeled "Fat free"), buttermilk has nothing to do with butter, and fat-free buttermilk is—as billed—fat free. It can be harder to come by than low-fat buttermilk, which has only slightly more fat and calories than nonfat. If you can't find either, you can substitute plain nonfat yogurt in most recipes.

Breakfast Menus

Muesli (*page 56*)
Breakfast Bread Pudding (*page 94*)
Fresh fruit or juice

Soft-Boiled Egg (*page 65*)
Toasted Grape-Nut Bran Bread (*page 406*)
Strained Yogurt spread (*page 102*) and Fruit Jam
(*page 105*)
Fresh fruit or juice

Oatmeal Pudding (*page 98*)
Fresh fruit or juice

Scrambled Eggs (*page 61*)
Popovers (*page 83*)
Fresh fruit or juice

Granola (*page 50*)
Smoothie (*page 48*)

DO-AHEAD BRUNCH MENUS
Baked Blintz Casserole (*page 96*)
Cinnamon-Raisin Rolls (*page 80*)
Fresh fruit and/or juice

Breakfast Kugel (*page 97*)
Toasted Wheat Berry Bread (*page 400*)
Fresh fruit and/or juice

Prune and Barley or Wheat Berry Pudding
(*page 99*)
Apple-Buttermilk Bundt Muffins (*page 74*)
Fresh fruit and/or juice

Frittatas (*page 68*)
Toasted Oatmeal Bread (*page 405*)
Apple Butter (*page 103*)
Fresh fruit and/or juice

LAST-MINUTE BRUNCH DISHES
Souffléed Frittata (*page 69*)
Blueberry Spoonbread (*page 98*)
Angel-Hair Pasta with Eggs, Tomatoes, and
Avocado (*page 101*)
(Serve with fruit and/or juice, and store-
bought breads and spread)

BRUNCH ENTRÉES FROM OTHER
SECTIONS
Savory Cheesecakes (*page 377*)
Tortilla-Style Frittata (*page 389*)
Torta di Budino di Riso Integrale (*page 482*)
Maple-Apple-Cranberry Crumble (*page 479*)
Spinach and Eggs in Cheese Soufflé (*page 382*)
Crepes (*page 428*)
Baked Eggs on Polenta with Spinach (*page 327*)

Weekday Breakfast Strategies

You love eating breakfast, but you hate making it.

Maybe you only hate making it in the morning . . . maybe if you set it up the night before, you'll enjoy sitting down to the meal you prepared.

ON THE WEEKEND

• Shop. Check the breakfast pantry list, look over the recipes, and take it from there.

• Make granola and/or a batch or two of muffins, scones, or date nut or zucchini bread. Store the granola in a jar in the refrigerator and put the muffins in the freezer. Slice the date nut or zucchini bread before you freeze it.

AT NIGHT

• Pour a serving of cereal or granola in a bowl and put it in the refrigerator.

• Take a muffin, scone, or slice of bread out of the freezer, put it on a plate, cover it with plastic wrap, and leave it out.

• If you're going to have hot cereal, combine the cereal and water or milk in a saucepan, cover it with plastic wrap or the saucepan lid, and refrigerate it.

• If you're going to have a smoothie, make sure your blender's clean and plugged in. Put all of the ingredients at the front of the refrigerator or freezer so you won't have to root around for fifteen minutes just to assemble them.

• If you're going to be having pancakes or waffles, measure and mix the dry ingredients, and cover them with plastic wrap. Measure and mix the wet ingredients, cover, and refrigerate them. Take out the griddle or waffle iron so it's ready to go.

• If you're going to have coffee, prepare the pot, measuring out the coffee. (Wait until the morning to add the water.)

• Set your place.

I use the time between dinner and dessert to prepare breakfast things. While I'm getting out dessert, which on weeknights is always something simple and ready-made, such as frozen yogurt and fruit, I also pour the cereal, measure the coffee, and put out bread, bagels, or muffins that I will toast or warm in the morning.

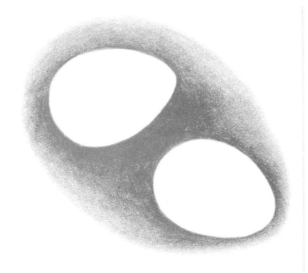

Brunch Strategies

Having people to brunch always seems like a great idea. Heck, it will be Sunday, and you'll have nothing else to do. But inevitably, when Sunday comes, sleeping in seems more urgent—or desirable—than getting up to cook. So the first step is to decide whether you *really* want to be responsible for preparing a meal on Sunday morning.

Once committed, here's how to cope:

• Plan the menu the week before. And keep it simple. Plan to supplement a dish you'll make with store-bought salads, baked goods, and fruit juices.

• Shop during the week. If there's a chance someone might get to the food before it's meant to be eaten, label it "Off-limits" (and post an appropriate penalty—such as having to pick up a replacement, prepare the brunch, or clean up after it).

• Freeze store-bought baked goods, if you

know you won't have time to buy them fresh on Sunday.

• Choose a main dish that tastes best the day after it's been made. On Saturday, make Baked Blintz Casserole (see page 96), Breakfast Kugel (see page 97), Savory Cheesecake (see page 377), Ratatouille (see page 343), or Frittatas (see pages 68 to 70).

• For muffins, pancakes, or waffles, prepare the dry and wet ingredients separately the night before. Refrigerate the wet ingredients, and cover the dry. Combine them just before baking or cooking on Sunday.

• For French toast, prepare the egg-milk mixture, and put the bread in to soak the night before. Cover and refrigerate. (Make sure you use thick bread slices, or the French toast will be soggy.)

• For omelettes, prepare the fillings up to two days ahead.

• Set the table on Saturday.

• If your guests ask what they can bring, tell them flowers. Or have them stop and pick up the bagels, so you can use that time to make something to spread on them.

Smoothies

FRUIT SMOOTHIE

Serves 1

TOTAL TIME: ABOUT 3 TO 10 MINUTES, DEPENDING ON THE INGREDIENTS
TIME TO PREPARE: 3 TO 10 MINUTES, DEPENDING ON THE INGREDIENTS
COOKING TIME: NONE
DO AHEAD: YOU CAN MAKE THIS DRINK UP TO 1 DAY IN ADVANCE.
REFRIGERATION: KEEPS 1 DAY IN THE REFRIGERATOR

My husband's favorite "my crazy wife" story concerns the morning our son was born. I woke up at 4:30 A.M. in advanced labor. "Shouldn't we call the doctor?" he asked. My due date was 2 weeks away, and I was reluctant to acknowledge that my time had come. As far as I knew, wishful thinking had never caused contractions to cease, but I was willing to give it a try. "Maybe after breakfast," I said.

I went to the kitchen and set out cereal and a bagel for Simon. Ordinarily I would have had the same. But things were becoming less ordinary by the moment. As he ate, I blended yogurt and frozen strawberries and drank it down, pausing periodically to writhe on the floor. When at last we left for the hospital, we got stuck in morning traffic. Minutes after we arrived, so did our son.

I offer this anecdote to show that no matter what your rush, you can make a simple, sustaining morning meal. These instant breakfasts taste infinitely better than the commercial products that go by that name, not only because they're fresh and all natural, but because you choose the ingredients to suit yourself.

½ cup nonfat vanilla frozen yogurt

½ cup lemon nonfat yogurt

1 medium banana or ½ cup sliced frozen strawberries

1 teaspoon sugar (optional)

Place the frozen yogurt, lemon yogurt, banana or strawberries, and sugar, if using, in a blender, and process until smooth.

PER SERVING (WITH BANANA): CALORIES 300 • PROTEIN 11 G • CARBOHYDRATE 65 G • FAT 0 G • CHOLESTEROL 3.30 MG • SODIUM 143 MG • 3% CALORIES FROM FAT • OUTSTANDING SOURCE OF VITAMIN B₆; CALCIUM • VERY GOOD SOURCE OF VITAMINS B₂, B₁₂, C • GOOD SOURCE OF ZINC
PER SERVING (WITH STRAWBERRIES): CALORIES 220 • PROTEIN 10 G • CARBOHYDRATE 45 G • FAT 0 G • CHOLESTEROL 3.34 MG • SODIUM 143 MG • 2% CALORIES FROM FAT • OUTSTANDING SOURCE OF VITAMIN C; CALCIUM • VERY GOOD SOURCE OF VITAMINS B₂, B₁₂ • GOOD SOURCE OF ZINC

Make It Your Own

There's only one rule when it comes to smoothies: don't add anything that will bend the blade of your blender. Try for a combination of ingredients that will give you a good dose of vitamins, minerals, and fiber and a thick, satisfying drink. Some suggestions:

Frozen vanilla or strawberry nonfat yogurt combined with fresh peeled and seeded fruit.

Plain or vanilla nonfat yogurt with a frozen banana or frozen strawberries or blueberries. (When the fruit is frozen, it thickens the mixture.)

Fruit-flavored nonfat kefir (a cultured-milk drink, like fluid yogurt) with a frozen banana, along with a third complementary fruit. Try blending strawberry kefir with the frozen banana and kiwifruit; peach kefir with the frozen banana and a mango; raspberry kefir with the frozen banana and strawberries.

Make a date shake by combining vanilla nonfat yogurt, honey, and chopped dates.

✐ Plump up dried fruit by pouring boiling water over it and letting it soak for up to thirty minutes. Drain the fruit and puree it with non-fat yogurt, milk, or a complementary fruit juice.

Granola

BEST GRANOLA FORMULA

Serves 10 to 12

TOTAL TIME: ABOUT 30 MINUTES
TIME TO PREPARE: 15 MINUTES
COOKING TIME: 15 MINUTES
REFRIGERATION/FREEZING: KEEPS UP TO 6 MONTHS IN A
   COOL, DRY PLACE

*I*n the 1970s and '80s, granola meant health food. Now we know better. In addition to whole grains and dried fruit, most brands contain enough oil and nuts to provide a whole day's share of fat in one bowlful.

The choice was clear: switch to shredded wheat,

or go on eating granola and admit you don't care if it kills you.

But here's another option: oil-free granola. It tastes as good as the original, but it's genuinely wholesome. Try it once, and you'll be glad to know that you can double this recipe.

¼ cup honey
¼ cup barley-malt syrup (see mail-order
   information, page 596) or honey
¼ cup mixed fruit juice concentrate (see Note;
   see mail-order information, page 596)
5 cups rolled oats, preferably organic
1 cup raisins

Heat the oven to 350° F.

In a large saucepan, combine the honey, barley-malt syrup, and fruit juice concentrate. Heat over medium heat until you can stir the mixture easily, but before it starts to boil, about 5 minutes.

Place the oats in a large mixing bowl. Add the honey mixture and stir rapidly and thoroughly to coat the oats.

Spread the oats in a thin, even layer on a large nonstick baking sheet (you may need two). Place it in the oven and bake until the granola is crisp, no more than 15 minutes. Watch carefully, or the granola may burn.

Remove the baking sheet to a cooling rack. Let the granola cool thoroughly on the baking sheet. Place the granola in a large bowl, break up any large chunks, stir in the raisins, and transfer to a tightly covered container. Store in a cool place.

Note: This is a syrup made from fruit juice—not a frozen concentrate—which you may be able to find at a health-food market, on the sweetener shelf, next to molasses and maple syrup.

PER SERVING: CALORIES 220 • PROTEIN 6 G • CARBOHYDRATE 46 G • FAT 2.2 G • CHOLESTEROL 0 MG • SODIUM 3.54 MG • 9% CALORIES FROM FAT • VERY GOOD SOURCE OF VITAMIN B₁ • GOOD SOURCE OF VITAMIN C; IRON

Make It Your Own

Although it's hardy stuff, granola is sensitive to subtle changes in ingredients. Switch the sweetener or the fruit juice, and you have a whole new flavor. Consider other add-ins too, such as coconut, chopped dried fruits, and nuts.

WHAT TO ADD AND WHEN TO ADD IT

✑ Use maple syrup instead of barley-malt syrup.

✑ Use the same amount of undiluted, thawed frozen apple juice concentrate in place of mixed fruit juice concentrate. Add diced dried apples along with the raisins.

✑ Use the same amount of undiluted thawed orange juice concentrate in place of mixed fruit juice concentrate. Add dried cranberries and/or diced dried mango instead of, or along with, the raisins.

✑ For other fruit flavors, use the undiluted frozen or bottled juice concentrate of any fruit you want, such as blueberry, cherry, or apple.

✑ Before baking, add slivered almonds or chopped peanuts to the oats. Stir thoroughly. Remember nuts are fatty, so go easy with this option, adding about ⅓ cup per recipe.

✑ Before baking, add ¼ cup shredded unsweetened coconut to the mixture. Stir well.

✑ Before baking, stir in ½ cup wheat bran or oat bran. Substitute barley flakes or wheat flakes for half of the oats. (If you can't find

them where you shop, see mail-order information, page 596.)

•

GRANOLA BARS

Serves 8

TOTAL TIME: 1 HOUR, 10 TO 15 MINUTES, INCLUDING TIME TO SOAK THE FIGS
TIME TO PREPARE: 10 MINUTES
COOKING TIME: 30 TO 35 MINUTES
DO AHEAD: YOU CAN MAKE THE GRANOLA UP TO 1 WEEK IN ADVANCE.
REFRIGERATION/FREEZING: REFRIGERATE UP TO 5 DAYS. FREEZE UP TO 6 MONTHS.

Everyone's heard that, like vegetables, breakfast is Good for You. Yet some of the very same people who never have to be told to eat their greens skip the morning meal without a second thought—or with an inappropriate one, like "Hey, I'll grab a granola bar." Most granola bars are no more nourishing than the oil and sweeteners that contribute most of their calories. You can buy low-fat granola bars, but none, I'm sure, as good as these.

½ cup loosely packed dried figs
½ cup brown sugar
2 large egg whites
1 teaspoon vanilla extract
¼ cup whole wheat or oat flour
2 cups nonfat or low-fat granola, store-bought or homemade (see page 50)
½ cup raisins (if the granola doesn't contain raisins)

Place the figs in a bowl and pour 1 cup boiling water over them. Let them soak for 30 minutes.

Heat the oven to 350°F. Drain the water

and puree the figs in a food processor or blender. Transfer the figs to a mixing bowl. Add the brown sugar, egg whites, vanilla, and flour. Beat with an electric hand mixer until smooth. Stir in the granola and the raisins, if using.

Use your hands to press the mixture evenly into a nonstick 8-inch square pan. Bake until firm and lightly browned, about 30 minutes.

Let the pan cool on a wire rack for 10 minutes, then cut the baked granola into 8 squares or rectangles while it is still slightly warm. Remove the bars from the pan, and place them directly on the rack to cool completely.

For crispier bars, place the cut granola bars on a baking sheet and continue to bake at 350° F. for an additional 5 minutes. Remove from the baking sheet and let them cool completely on a rack.

PER SERVING (1 BAR): CALORIES 250 • PROTEIN 5.3 G • CARBOHYDRATE 57.2 G • FAT 1.5 G • CHOLESTEROL 0 MG • SODIUM 21.5 MG • 5% CALORIES FROM FAT • GOOD SOURCE OF VITAMIN B₁; IRON

Hot Cereals

Like local produce, certain dishes have seasons. Pumpkin pie in August could be seriously disorienting; strawberry shortcake in November could spark an existential crisis.

Hot cereals have a season, too. A bowl of oatmeal, for instance, is best in winter because for all its sweet, nutty flavor much of the pleasure is in the comfort of having something warm inside you when it's cold outdoors.

While comfort is a critical component, a bowl of oatmeal—or farina, Cream of Rice, or polenta—provides more than that.

TIMESAVING TIP

Hot cereal will cook more rapidly in the morning if you put it in the saucepan with the water, milk, or juice, cover the pan, and let it sit and soak—refrigerated—overnight.

You get fiber and complex carbohydrates to start. If you cook it in nonfat milk instead of water, you're adding calcium and protein. Cook the cereal in fruit juice, and you're fortifying it with vitamins. Toss in some chopped dried fruit, and you're adding fiber and iron.

But as any four-year-old will tell you, knowing something's good for you doesn't make it taste any better, and all this business about fiber and fortification would be pointless if, in your experience, hot cereal is a bland bowlful of mush. The following recipes may change your perspective on porridges.

OATMEAL

Serves 1

TOTAL TIME: 15 MINUTES
TIME TO PREPARE: 15 MINUTES
COOKING TIME: INCLUDED IN TIME TO PREPARE
DO AHEAD: THE OATMEAL WILL SOFTEN AND COOK FASTER IF YOU PLACE IT IN THE SAUCEPAN WITH THE MILK THE NIGHT BEFORE. COVER AND REFRIGERATE UNTIL THE MORNING. STIR WELL BEFORE COOKING.

When you cook the oats in milk instead of water, you make them better altogether, cooking up a sweeter, creamier bowl of cereal, richer in calcium and protein.

⅓ cup rolled oats, preferably organic

1 cup nonfat milk, plus additional for serving

2 teaspoons maple syrup or light or dark brown sugar

1 tablespoon raisins

Place the oats, milk, and maple syrup or brown sugar in a heavy saucepan. Bring to a simmer over medium heat, stirring often to prevent burning. Reduce the heat to medium-low, and continue cooking until the porridge is thick and creamy, about 10 minutes. Stir in the raisins. Serve, topped with additional milk if you'd like.

PER SERVING: CALORIES 254 • PROTEIN 13 G • CARBOHYDRATE 47 G • FAT 2.2 G • CHOLESTEROL 4.41 MG • SODIUM 130 MG • 8% CALORIES FROM FAT • VERY GOOD SOURCE OF VITAMINS B₁, B₂; CALCIUM • GOOD SOURCE OF VITAMINS A, B₁₂; ZINC

MICROWAVE OATMEAL: Combine the oats, milk, and maple syrup or brown sugar in a large (4-cup-capacity) Pyrex bowl. Cook on the highest power for 3 minutes. Stir well, and return the oatmeal to the microwave, cooking and stirring at 3- to 4-minute intervals until it's done, about 10 minutes total. Stir in the raisins and serve with additional milk, if you'd like.

Make It Your Own

Each type of cereal grain has a distinct flavor— once you've tasted each of them, you'll never mistake cornmeal for Cream of Wheat, which, in turn, you'll never confuse with oatmeal, and

so on. Experiment to see which liquids and sweeteners go best with each grain.

WHAT TO ADD AND WHEN TO ADD IT

Apple Juice or Nonfat Milk. Cook the cereal in these rather than water. Place the cereal and juice or milk in the saucepan and heat them together. Just remember when you use a liquid other than water, increase the amount of liquid by ½ cup. Stir often, especially if you're using milk, which may burn.

Sweetener. Stir in brown sugar, honey, maple syrup, fruit syrup, fruit preserves, or ginger marmalade (1 to 2 teaspoons per serving) while the cereal is cooking. For a lighter touch, spoon the sweetener on top of your serving, to taste.

Chopped Dried Fruits. Try raisins, prunes, figs, dates, cherries, or apricots, about 2 tablespoons per serving. Cook them with the cereal and they'll be plump and juicy. If you prefer them chewy, stir them in just before serving.

Toasted Almonds or Chopped Fresh Apples. For a crunchy contrast to the creamy cereal, sprinkle the top of each serving with 2 tablespoons of one or both of these. Season with a tiny pinch of ground cinnamon, nutmeg, or ginger.

Nonfat milk or vanilla or blended-fruit-flavored nonfat yogurt. Even if you've cooked your cereal in milk, it doesn't hurt to add about ½ cup more when you serve it. Or swirl in your favorite flavored nonfat yogurt.

•

POLENTA PORRIDGE

Serves 1

TOTAL TIME: ABOUT 20 MINUTES
TIME TO PREPARE: ABOUT 20 MINUTES
COOKING TIME: INCLUDED IN TIME TO PREPARE
DO AHEAD: THE PORRIDGE WILL SOFTEN AND COOK FASTER
    IF YOU PLACE IT IN THE SAUCEPAN WITH THE MILK THE
    NIGHT BEFORE. COVER AND REFRIGERATE UNTIL THE
    MORNING. STIR WELL BEFORE COOKING.

Once called "hasty pudding," cornmeal cooked with milk and molasses isn't all that hasty, compared with pouring dry cereal out of a box. But it's worth the time up front because it sticks with you well into the day. Moreover, it's yummy.

¼ cup stone-ground cornmeal

1 cup nonfat milk, plus additional for serving

½ teaspoon molasses

1 teaspoon dark brown sugar

In a heavy saucepan, combine the cornmeal and milk. Bring to a simmer over medium heat, stirring often with a wire whisk. Turn down the heat to medium-low, and continue cooking and whisking until the porridge is thick, about 20 minutes. Whisk in the molasses and brown sugar. Serve hot, with additional milk, if you'd like.

PER SERVING: CALORIES 215 • PROTEIN 11 G • CARBOHYDRATE 40 G • FAT 1.5 G • CHOLESTEROL 4.4 MG • SODIUM 140 MG • 6% CALORIES FROM FAT • VERY GOOD SOURCE OF VITAMINS B₁, B₂; CALCIUM • GOOD SOURCE OF VITAMINS A, B₁₂; ZINC

MICROWAVE POLENTA PORRIDGE: Place the cornmeal and milk in a large (4-cup-capacity) Pyrex bowl. Cook on the highest power for 4 minutes. Stir well, and return the porridge to the microwave, cooking and stirring at 4 minute intervals until its done, about 20 minutes total. Serve hot, with additional milk, if you'd like.

•

OAT BRAN

Serves 1

TOTAL TIME: ABOUT 6 MINUTES
TIME TO PREPARE: ABOUT 6 MINUTES
COOKING TIME: INCLUDED IN TIME TO PREPARE

No one had heard of oat bran until a controversial study released a few years ago made extravagant claims for its ability to lower cholesterol. While many of those health claims seem to be justified, the authors of the study would have been on safe ground altogether, if they'd simply stated this significant fact: It's delicious.

⅓ cup oat bran

1 cup nonfat milk, plus additional for serving

2 teaspoons maple syrup or light or dark brown sugar

2 tablespoons raisins

Place the oat bran, milk, and maple syrup or brown sugar in a heavy saucepan. Bring to a simmer over medium heat, stirring often with a wire whisk to keep lumps from forming and to prevent burning. Reduce the heat to medium-low, and continue cooking until the porridge is thick and creamy, about 5 minutes. Stir in the raisins. Serve, topped with additional milk, if you'd like.

PER SERVING: CALORIES 197 • PROTEIN 14 G • CARBOHYDRATE 41 G • FAT 2.65 G • CHOLESTEROL 4.41 MG • SODIUM 128 MG • 10% CALORIES FROM FAT • VERY GOOD SOURCE OF VITAMINS B₁, B₂; CALCIUM • GOOD SOURCE OF VITAMINS A, B₁₂; IRON, ZINC

MICROWAVE OAT BRAN: Combine the oats, milk, and maple syrup or brown sugar in a large (4-cup-capacity) Pyrex bowl. Cook on the highest power for 2 minutes. Stir well with a wire whisk, and return to the microwave, cooking and stirring at 2-minute intervals until its done, about 6 minutes total. Serve with additional milk if you'd like.

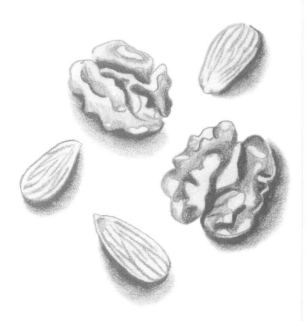

FRUITY CREAM OF RICE

Serves 1

TOTAL TIME: ABOUT 15 MINUTES
TIME TO PREPARE: ABOUT 15 MINUTES
COOKING TIME: INCLUDED IN TIME TO PREPARE
DO AHEAD: THE CEREAL WILL SOFTEN AND COOK FASTER IF YOU PLACE IT IN THE SAUCEPAN WITH THE JUICE THE NIGHT BEFORE. COVER AND REFRIGERATE UNTIL THE MORNING. STIR WELL BEFORE COOKING.

A luscious option if you're allergic to wheat, tired of oats, or just very fond of rice. You can use nonfat milk or soy milk in place of the apple juice, if you'd like.

¼ cup Cream of Rice
1 cup apple juice
2 teaspoons light brown sugar
1 tablespoon diced dried apples
1 tablespoon chopped almonds, toasted
   (optional; see page 56)

In a heavy saucepan, combine the Cream of Rice, apple juice, and brown sugar. Bring to a boil over medium-high heat. Reduce the heat to medium-low and simmer, stirring occasionally, until you have a thick porridge, about 10 minutes. Stir in the dried apples. Serve hot, sprinkled with toasted almonds, if you'd like.

PER SERVING: CALORIES 251 • PROTEIN 2 G • CARBOHYDRATE 60 G • FAT .50 G • CHOLESTEROL 0 MG • SODIUM 17 MG • 20% CALORIES FROM FAT • NOT A CONCENTRATED SOURCE OF ANY PARTICULAR VITAMIN OR NUTRIENT, BUT CONTAINS A VARIETY, INCLUDING VITAMINS B₁, B₆, AND IRON

MICROWAVE FRUITY CREAM OF RICE: Combine the Cream of Rice and apple juice in a large (4-cup-capacity) Pyrex bowl. Cook on the highest power until the mixture boils, about 4 minutes, stir, and return the cereal to the microwave, stirring and cooking at 3-minute intervals until cooked, about 12 minutes. Stir in the dried apples and serve with the toasted almonds on top, if you'd like.

LEFTOVER HOT CEREAL? Make a breakfast pudding to serve the next day. Follow the directions for Oatmeal Pudding (see page 98).

•

MUESLI

Serves 4

TOTAL TIME: 5 TO 7 MINUTES, NOT INCLUDING TIME TO
    SOAK THE CEREAL
TIME TO PREPARE: 5 TO 7 MINUTES
COOKING TIME: NONE
REFRIGERATION: REFRIGERATE UP TO 24 HOURS.

If you were only to read the ingredients and preparation directions, you wouldn't imagine that this dish would be any good at all. I mean, what could you expect of a mix of rolled oats, dried fruits, and nuts soaked in water? Quite a lot, as it happens; it is delicious. If you're still skeptical, make this Muesli just once, and you'll find—I promise— how deceptive a mere recipe can be.

Serve the Muesli topped with plain or vanilla nonfat yogurt or milk.

1⅓ cups rolled oats, preferably organic
1⅓ cups water
1 tablespoon fresh lemon or orange juice
3 tablespoons maple syrup
½ cup chopped prunes
½ cup chopped dried apples
¼ cup currants or chopped raisins
2 tablespoons slivered or chopped almonds,
    toasted (see Note)

In a large ceramic or glass bowl, combine the oats, water, lemon or orange juice, maple syrup, prunes, apples, currants or raisins, and almonds. Stir well, cover with plastic wrap, and refrigerate overnight. Stir well before serving.

Note: To toast almonds, heat the oven or toaster oven to 350° F. Place the almonds in a single layer on a sheet of foil. Bake until they're golden brown, about 5 minutes for slivered almonds and 8 minutes for whole. Watch closely to prevent burning.

PER SERVING: CALORIES 245 • PROTEIN 5 G • CARBOHYDRATE 52 G • FAT 3.6 G • CHOLESTEROL 0 MG • SODIUM 16.9 MG • 13% CALORIES FROM FAT • GOOD SOURCE OF VITAMINS B₁, E; IRON, ZINC

NOW TRY THIS: Add 2 tablespoons unsweetened coconut to the basic mixture, or add ¼ cup chopped dried cherries, or add a pinch of cinnamon.

Eggs

Generally, I'm willing to comply with current nutritional recommendations; I'm happy to eat complex carbohydrates, get plenty of calcium, and avoid copious portions of fats in most forms.

But while I have some degree of faith in research that points to the dangers of bologna, bacon, and Big Macs, I suspect that studies indicating a problem with eggs were conducted by people who spent their youth at boarding schools or summer camps where powdered egg products were served. No one who's enjoyed fresh eggs properly cooked could possibly think there's anything wrong with them . . . at least in moderation.

THE UNJUST FALL AND GLORIOUS REDEMPTION OF THE EGG

First they said to avoid eggs altogether because they're too high in cholesterol. Then they said that dietary cholesterol (the cholesterol in the foods we eat, as opposed to the cholesterol that builds up in our bloodstream) isn't so bad after all. Saturated fat is the real enemy, because it, rather than dietary cholesterol, has a larger role in raising the level of cholesterol in the blood. Eggs contain only two grams of saturated fat, less than half the amount in an ounce of cheddar cheese. Moreover, all of the fat is in the yolk, which means that egg whites are fat free.

Unfortunately, the campaign against the egg was so successful, many people don't know that a truce has been declared, and that most of us can enjoy up to four whole eggs each week (and cook with an unlimited number of egg whites) without worrying about gumming up our arteries. If you have low cholesterol and no heart disease in the family, you may be able to eat more than that. But if your cholesterol is high and your family is prone to heart trouble, consult with a specialist before eating any at all.

KEEPING THE FAT OUT

With fewer than ninety calories each, eggs aren't fattening unless you cook them with lots of butter or oil. You may not realize how little shortening you need to make them the way you like them. The following basic recipes call for the minimum fat necessary, which for some is none at all.

EGG LABEL

Nutrition Facts

Serving Size 1 (50g)
Servings Per Container 1

Amount Per Serving

Calories 70	Calories from Fat 45
	% Daily Value*
Total Fat 5g	**8%**
Saturated Fat 1.5g	**8%**
Cholesterol 215mg	**70%**
Sodium 65mg	**3%**
Total Carbohydrate 1g	**0%**
Dietary Fiber 0g	**0%**
Sugars 1g	
Protein 6g	

Vitamin A 6%	Vitamin C 0%
Calcium 2%	Iron 4%

*Percent Daily Values are based on a 2,000 calorie diet. Your daily values may be higher or lower depending on your calorie needs:

	Calories:	2,000	2,500
Total Fat	Less than	65g	80g
Saturated Fat	Less than	20g	25g
Cholesterol	Less than	300mg	300mg
Sodium	Less than	2,400mg	2,400mg
Total Carbohydrate		300g	375g
Dietary Fiber		25g	30g

Calories per gram:
Fat 9 • Carbohydrate 4 • Protein 4

Q. What is salmonella and what does it have to do with eggs?

A. Salmonella is bacteria that is able to penetrate eggshells. It causes a particularly unpleasant form of food poisoning.

Q. Is it common?

A. Fewer than 1 percent of eggs are contaminated with the bacteria. And even fewer eggs contain enough bacteria to make you sick.

Q. So what are my chances of getting sick from salmonella?

A. According to the USDA, about 1 in 238,500.

Q. If the chances of getting sick are so remote, why worry about it?

A. You might decide not to worry about it. But if you're pregnant or have low immunity, or if you're cooking for someone very young or very old, you should be concerned about all potential sources of infections, including eggs.

Q. How will I know if I have salmonella poisoning?

A. You'll feel as if you've been struck—suddenly—with a killer flu. You'll be leveled by stomach cramps, nausea, fever, headache, and diarrhea.

Q. How can I make sure I won't get sick?

A. Try the following:

• Refrigerate eggs at a temperature below 40°F.

• Discard cracked eggs.

• Check the last date of sale on the egg carton and don't buy the eggs if that day has come and gone. If you've got a dated carton at home, don't use the eggs more than one week past the date, or if the egg smells foul or looks milky.

• Don't leave eggs or mixtures containing raw eggs at room temperature for more than an hour.

• Cook eggs thoroughly so that the whites are set and not runny, and the yolk has an opaque veil.

• Cook eggs at 140°F. for at least five minutes.

• Because the bacteria lodges just inside the shell, don't use the eggshell to separate the white from the yolk. Instead, wash your hands thoroughly and spread the fingers of your left hand (your right hand if you're left-handed). Break the egg and drop the egg into your open hand. Let the white run through your fingers into one bowl and place the yolk in another.

• Don't take raw-egg products on picnics, such as mayonnaise.

• You control how your eggs are handled at home, but you can't be sure that restaurants are as conscientious as you'd like. When you're eating out, don't order anything that calls for raw or lightly cooked eggs, such as classic Caesar salad, eggnog, or poached or soft-boiled eggs.

SHOP TALK/DECODING EGG CARTONS

Grade AA or A: Eggs are graded according to regulations concerning their appearance and condition. Grades don't have anything to do with size, which is rated separately, or with nutritional content. To rate tops (AA), an egg must be oval, with one end longer and more tapered than the other. The shell must be perfectly smooth and clean, the white clear and thick, and the yolk firm. Grade-A eggs don't have to be quite as perfect, but they can't be misshapen, spotted, or runny. There are grade-B eggs, but although they're safe and good, you won't find them at the supermarket. They're just not pretty enough. And so they go into packaged foods such as cookies, cakes, and so on.

Expiration Date: To ensure that eggs are fresh and safe, packers must stamp the carton with an expiration date that's not more than thirty days after the date that the eggs are gathered and boxed. Although it isn't meant to be a "use by" date, you may find that it indicates with some accuracy when the eggs will lose their flavor. Don't use the eggs more than two weeks after the "expiration" date, or if the egg smells foul or looks milky, or the shell is cracked.

Size: The quality and amount of feed, the size of the hens, and weather conditions down on the farm help determine whether eggs will be jumbo or small or something in between. Recipes for cakes, quiches, custards, or whatever calling for eggs usually mean large eggs. But there are also jumbo (the biggest), extra large (one size down from jumbo), medium, and small. The nutrition content varies with the size; the larger eggs have more of everything, and the smaller, naturally enough, have less. You can cut the amount of saturated fat and calories in any basic egg dish by using medium or small eggs rather than large. For scrambled eggs, omelettes, or frittatas, try following the steps in the basic recipes (pages 61, 66, and 68 respectively), using one whole medium egg and the white of a large, extra large, or jumbo egg. You'll get more volume with less fat.

Free Range: Most commercial eggs aren't produced in what you'd call humane conditions. The hens are confined in small cages and fed by machines. While cruel to the chickens, these operations are cost-efficient, making it possible for most Americans to afford a very nourishing food.

If your conscience balks at conventional egg farming and you don't mind paying extra (sometimes almost triple), you can buy free-range eggs, which are gathered from hens raised outdoors or uncaged on open floors. Free-range eggs have no nutritional advantages over conventional eggs, they may just make you feel better about eating them. The eggs are expensive because free-range farms have to pay lots of hands to gather the eggs, while conventional farmers switch on a conveyor belt to collect theirs. Also, free-range farms accommodate fewer hens, so they produce fewer eggs. There's a big demand for these eggs now, and that, combined with the low yield, means higher prices.

Organic: Organic eggs come from hens raised on feed that's been grown without chemical pesticides or fertilizer on land that's been pesticide free for at least seven years. They often taste better than conventional eggs, simply because farms produce fewer of them and get them to the market faster—and fresher. Like free-range eggs, organic eggs cost much more than conventional eggs. And like free-range eggs, they may offer peace of mind, but they provide nothing more than normal eggs in the way of nutrition.

Feed: Some farmers feed their hens special diets to fortify their eggs with certain vitamins or to reduce the amount of saturated fat or cholesterol in the yolks. Compare the labels on egg cartons to find which offers the most of what you want and least of what you don't.

A FRIED EGG

Serves 1

TOTAL TIME: ABOUT 10 MINUTES
TIME TO PREPARE: 5 MINUTES
COOKING TIME: 3 MINUTES

Many films from the 1940s or '50s feature a scene in a diner where the star or her nemesis is having breakfast. And for a time what I enjoyed most about fried eggs was ordering them "sunny-side up," or "over easy," the way I'd heard Veronica Lake or Joan Crawford do it. The eggs themselves were always disappointing—greasy and bland, with rubbery whites, and yolks like glue. After a while the kick I got from my routine wasn't worth what I'd have to eat as a result of doing it.

Maybe those movie stars got sick of greasy eggs, too, and would have liked to know how to "fry" them as follows. Served sunny-side up or over easy, these eggs are uncommonly light, with a fresh, clean taste.

1 large egg
2 teaspoons water

Squirt a small nonstick pan with nonstick spray, or rub it lightly with canola oil.

Heat the pan over medium-high heat. When it is hot, crack the eggshell on the side of the pan and drop the egg in the center.

Reduce the heat to medium-low. When the white starts to set, add 2 teaspoons of water. Cover the pan and continue to cook until the white is completely set and the yolk is firm enough to stay in place, but still glossy and soft, about 3 minutes. Check after 2 minutes to prevent overcooking. Serve right away.

PER SERVING: CALORIES 75 • PROTEIN 6.25 G • CARBOHYDRATE 0 G • FAT 5 G • CHOLESTEROL 213 MG • SODIUM 63 MG • 62% CALORIES FROM FAT • GOOD SOURCE OF VITAMINS A, B₂

S C R A M B L E D   E G G S

Serves 1

TOTAL TIME: ABOUT 10 MINUTES
TIME TO PREPARE: 10 MINUTES
COOKING TIME: INCLUDED IN TIME TO PREPARE

For those who romanticize the French way of life, there's no better way to contrast American "crassness" with Gallic civility than to compare scrambled eggs with omelettes, or vice versa. Making an omelette involves skill and concentration (see page 66); you have to slow down and pay attention. Also, you have to eat it with some degree of ceremony. You don't just hack it off, mash it on toast with jam, and shove it in your mouth.

Scramble means haste, and that's about all you need to make the eggs in question. Pour the eggs in a pan, scrape and stir, wait a few seconds, scrape and stir again, toss them onto a plate, and mash them on

your toast (with jam!). For champions of the American Way, this is what the pursuit of happiness is all about.

1 large egg
1 large egg white
3 tablespoons low-fat cottage cheese (see Note)
Salt and freshly ground black pepper to taste

In a small bowl, beat together the egg and egg white. Beat in the cottage cheese.

Heat a small nonstick pan over medium heat. When it is hot, add the eggs. Reduce the heat to medium-low and wait until the eggs start to set, about 40 seconds.

Using a nonmetallic spatula, turn the eggs gently by folding them over, making large creamy curds. Don't stir vigorously, or you'll

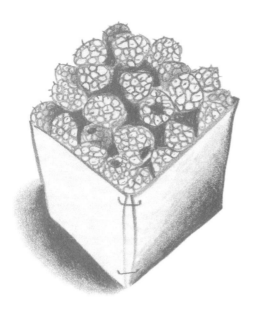

get a crumbly consistency. When the eggs are nearly as firm as you'd like, take them from the stove and turn them out onto a plate. They'll cook a bit more once they're away from the heat. Season with salt and pepper.

Note: Cottage cheese keeps the eggs light and fluffy in the absence of butter.

PER SERVING: CALORIES 122 · PROTEIN 15 G · CARBOHYDRATE 2.12 G · FAT 5.4 G · CHOLESTEROL 215 MG · SODIUM 290 MG · 42% CALORIES FROM FAT · VERY GOOD SOURCE OF VITAMIN B₂ · GOOD SOURCE OF VITAMINS A, B₁₂

Make It Your Own

The basic recipe is easy, and the flavor is just as uncomplicated. Whatever you add will give them a whole new taste.

WHAT TO ADD AND WHEN TO ADD IT

Grated Cheese. Stir 1 tablespoon in with the egg mixture after you've beaten together the eggs and cottage cheese.

Fresh Minced Herbs or Crumbled Dried Herbs. Sprinkle 2 teaspoons minced fresh herbs on top just before serving, along with the salt and pepper, or beat ½ teaspoon crumbled dried herbs in with the cottage cheese before scrambling. For the fresh herbs, try chives, parsley, cilantro, sage, or marjoram, or use dried oregano, thyme, or tarragon.

Fruit Preserves. As the eggs start to set, add 1 to 2 teaspoons of preserves to the pan and continue cooking as directed in the basic recipe.

•

A POACHED EGG

Serves 1

TOTAL TIME: 5 MINUTES
TIME TO PREPARE: NONE
COOKING TIME: 5 MINUTES

Ask people to name their favorite foods, and each is likely to list a number of things that need no explanation: chocolate cake, strawberry ice cream, pizza. . . . They may also include something that can't be understood in any objective way, but can only be explained in terms of some soothing subconscious association.

For me it's poached eggs on toast. The toast must be spread thick with cottage cheese, and the yolk must be firm but still runny. It makes a mess on my plate and my chin, and calls for at least two napkins. It is not something I eat in public, but gives me great pleasure on those melancholy occasions when I've no one to cook for and must eat alone.

1 large egg

Bring 3 inches of water to a simmer in a medium skillet.

Crack the eggshell on the side of the skillet and drop the egg in from above.

Cover the skillet and turn off the heat. (If you're using an electric stove, transfer the skillet to another burner.) Let the egg sit, covered, for 5 minutes, or until the white is set and a thin film covers the yolk. Lift it out with a slotted spatula and let it drain before placing it on toast, if you'd like.

PER SERVING: CALORIES 75 • PROTEIN 6.25 G • CARBOHYDRATE 0 G • FAT 5 G • CHOLESTEROL 213 MG • SODIUM 63 MG • 62% CALORIES FROM FAT • GOOD SOURCE OF VITAMINS A, B₂

•

A BAKED EGG

Serves 1

TOTAL TIME: ABOUT 15 MINUTES
TIME TO PREPARE: 5 MINUTES
COOKING TIME: 8 MINUTES

Baked eggs are more popular in some other countries than they are here. In France, for instance, every café menu offers oefs sur le plat. We like our eggs fast and foolproof: scrambled, boiled, or fried, and using the oven adds a level of complexity that defeats the purpose. So why bother with baking? For one thing, this method captures more true egg flavor than the others. For another thing: brunch.

When you're cooking for a crowd, this method beats frying, poaching, or scrambling. The eggs cook evenly, since you have them at the same steady temperature for the same amount of time, and you can use them to compile a one-dish meal by baking them on toast (below) or on a casserole made with spinach and polenta (see page 327).

1 large egg
1 tablespoon nonfat or low-fat buttermilk, half-and-half, or cream
Salt and freshly ground black pepper to taste

Heat the oven to 325°F. Squirt a 6-ounce ramekin or custard cup with nonstick spray, or grease lightly with butter or canola oil.

Break the egg into the center of the ramekin or custard cup. Spoon the buttermilk, half-and-half, or cream over the egg.

Bake until the white is set and the yolk is firm but not solid, about 8 minutes. Season with salt and pepper. Serve right away.

PER SERVING: CALORIES 80 • PROTEIN 6.7 G • CARBOHYDRATE 1.3 G • FAT 5 G • CHOLESTEROL 214 MG • SODIUM 79 MG • 59% CALORIES FROM FAT • GOOD SOURCE OF VITAMINS A, B₂

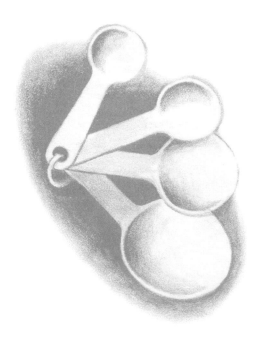

Make It Your Own

Because the basic Baked Egg recipe calls for so little seasoning, it's asking to be adapted. Just mind the timing. Make sure whatever you bake with the egg won't burn before the egg is cooked and, similarly, that the egg won't be done ahead of the rest of the dish.

WHAT TO ADD AND WHEN TO ADD IT

✐ *Grains and Potatoes.* Try polenta (see page 324), grits (see page 577), or seasoned mashed potatoes (see page 226), preparing ⅓ to ½ cup per egg and place in a lightly greased baking dish. Using the back of a spoon, make an indentation that will be a well for each egg. Drop an egg into each well. If you'd like, sprinkle with the grated cheese of your choice before baking. Be sure to grate the cheese finely, or it may not melt before the eggs are cooked. Bake at 325°F. for 8 minutes.

✐ *Ratatouille and Fillings.* Use leftover ratatouille (see page 343) or any of the fillings for pastas (see page 301) or savory pies (see page 433). Place the ratatouille or filling—about ½ cup per egg—in the baking dish. Make an indentation as described for the grains and potatoes, above, and bake at 325°F. for 8 minutes.

Baked Egg on Toast

Serve a baked egg on bread as a base or to sop up the yolk. Before baking, slice the bread at least ⅓ inch thick and no more than ⅔ inch thick, then toast it lightly. (Thinner slices will burn, thicker slices won't be crisp enough.) Experiment with different types of toast, such as challah, raisin, rye, and sourdough. Don't use pita, though, which is too thin. A thin slice of bagel is great because you can drop the egg into it so that the yolk plops into the hole.

1 slice whole wheat toast or thin slice
    toasted bagel
½ teaspoon unsalted butter, or 1 tablespoon
    low-fat cottage cheese
1 large egg
1 tablespoon nonfat or low-fat buttermilk,
    half-and-half, or cream
Salt and freshly ground black pepper to
    taste

Heat the oven to 325°F. If using toast, cut a whole in the center about the size of an egg yolk.

Butter the toast or bagel slice or spread it with cottage cheese. Place it in a small baking dish. Break the egg over the hole in the toast or bagel. Spoon the buttermilk, half-and-half, or cream over the egg. Bake until the white is set and the yolk is firm but not solid, about 8 minutes. Season with salt and pepper.

PER SERVING: CALORIES 180 • PROTEIN 9.9 G • CARBOHYDRATE 16 G • FAT 8.4 G • CHOLESTEROL 219 MG • SODIUM 251 MG • 42% CALORIES FROM FAT • VERY GOOD SOURCE OF VITAMIN B₂ • GOOD SOURCE OF VITAMIN A; IRON

A HARD-BOILED EGG

Serves 1

TOTAL TIME: 20 MINUTES
TIME TO PREPARE: 5 MINUTES
COOKING TIME: 15 MINUTES
REFRIGERATION: REFRIGERATE HARD-BOILED EGGS IN THEIR
 SHELLS UP TO 3 DAYS.

Food writers have to be careful not to alienate readers by slighting a dish that might be a favorite of any number of them. But I think I'm safe in saying that plain old hard-boiled eggs aren't very exciting, and that anyone presented with one for the first time could be forgiven for wondering why, given the splendid versatility of the egg, someone would come up with such a thing.

Let's be charitable and assume it was not their creator's intention to serve hard-boiled eggs straight from the shell, but to slice and chop them for salads or soup garnishes, stuff them with herbs and spices, or stir them into a sweet and crunchy curry sauce (see page 145). In this context, a food you might tend to dismiss as insipid seems inspired.

1 large egg

Place the egg at the bottom of a deep saucepan. Add water to cover.

Bring the water to a boil over medium-high heat. Cover the pan and remove from the heat.

Let the egg sit for 15 minutes. Drain and let cool water run over it to stop the cooking process. Peel just before serving.

PER SERVING: CALORIES 75 • PROTEIN 6.25 G • CARBOHYDRATE 0 G • FAT 5 G • CHOLESTEROL 213 MG • SODIUM 63 MG • 62% CALORIES FROM FAT • GOOD SOURCE OF VITAMINS A, B₂

A SOFT-BOILED EGG

Serves 1

TOTAL TIME: ABOUT 10 MINUTES
TIME TO PREPARE: 5 MINUTES
COOKING TIME: 5 MINUTES

Doomsayers will tell you that eating soft boiled eggs is like playing Russian roulette. Eggs that aren't cooked long enough to pass for Indian rubber, they say, carry the risk of deadly salmonella bacteria.

Call me reckless if you will, but every once in a while, I like to play the odds, which in the case of getting sick from salmonella amount to one chance in eighty lifetimes. I'm willing to bet this is one of the seventy-nine lifetimes in which I can enjoy soft-boiled eggs with impunity.

The odds improve when you hold the eggs at a temperature of 140° F. for at least five minutes. Since you have to keep eggs at a high temperature for a full five minutes to soft boil them, you're bound to kill any active bacteria that might be present.

For more on minimizing the risk of salmonella poisoning, see page 58.

1 large egg

Place the egg at the bottom of a deep saucepan. Add water to cover.

Bring the water to a boil over medium-high heat. Cover the pan and remove from the heat.

Let the egg sit for 5 minutes. Drain and let cold water run over it to stop the cooking process. Place the egg in an eggcup, or peel and place on toast, and serve right away.

PER SERVING: CALORIES 75 • PROTEIN 6.25 G • CARBOHYDRATE 0 G • FAT 5 G • CHOLESTEROL 213 MG • SODIUM 63 MG • 62% CALORIES FROM FAT • GOOD SOURCE OF VITAMINS A, B₂

THE OMELETTE

Serves 1

TOTAL TIME: ABOUT 8 TO 13 MINUTES, DEPENDING ON THE FILLING

TIME TO PREPARE: 5 TO 10 MINUTES, DEPENDING ON THE FILLING

COOKING TIME: ABOUT 3 MINUTES

DO AHEAD: YOU CAN MAKE AND REFRIGERATE A FILLING UP TO 3 DAYS IN ADVANCE.

They say practice makes perfect. But they also say there are exceptions to every rule. Here's what I mean.

When I was nine, I saw Julia Child make an omelette on television. She intended to demonstrate how simple it was, but succeeded only in impressing me with her superhuman dexterity.

I'm still impressed. I've cracked a lot of eggs in the decades since that broadcast, but I'm still no match for the Master where omelettes are concerned. Practice has made me competent, though, and gives me the know-how to offer these tips for preparation and improvisation.

2 large eggs

1 tablespoon nonfat or low-fat buttermilk, or nonfat milk

1 recipe filling (see "Make It Your Own")

Salt and freshly ground black pepper to taste

Beat together the eggs and milk. Squirt an 8- or 9-inch nonstick skillet with nonstick spray, or rub lightly with vegetable oil. Heat over medium-high heat.

When the skillet is hot, pour in the eggs. As the bottom sets, gently lift up the edge with a nonmetallic spatula and let the egg run underneath. Place the filling in the center, and using the spatula, fold the top portion over to cover the filling.

Hold the serving plate over the pan and flip the omelette onto it. Season with salt and pepper, and serve right away.

PER SERVING (OMELETTE WITHOUT FILLING): CALORIES 156 • PROTEIN 13 G • CARBOHYDRATE 2 G • FAT 10 G • CHOLESTEROL 427 MG • SODIUM 142 MG • 60% CALORIES FROM FAT • GOOD SOURCE OF VITAMINS A, B₂, B₁₂; FOLACIN

Make It Your Own

Omelettes were made to be made to order. You can fill them with anything you like provided you watch the proportions—too much can overwhelm the eggs and make them cook unevenly. Also, because the eggs cook so quickly, make sure that a filling that's meant to be cooked is completely done before you add it.

WHAT TO ADD AND WHEN TO ADD IT

☙ *Shredded or Grated Cheese.* Sprinkle 2 to 3

OMELETTE OR FRITTATA?

It's an *omelette* if it's folded in a dainty fashion over a filling.

It's a *frittata* if it's flat and puffy and studded with filling.

It's an *omelette* if you're trying to figure out how on earth to get the eggs to fold in a dainty fashion over the filling. (Tip: Use a very good nonstick pan and a wide plastic spatula. When the egg has set on the bottom but is still runny on the surface, sprinkle the filling down the center. Quickly slide the spatula under the egg and flip it over to enclose the filling.)

It's a *frittata* if you just pour the eggs over the filling, wait for them to set on the bottom, then stick them in the oven until firm.

It's an *omelette* if you can't make out how you'll get it from the pan to the plate without having it collapse or tear. (Tip: Wait a few seconds after you've folded the egg over the filling, then slide the spatula under the omelette to loosen it. Tilt the omelette pan over the serving plate and flip the omelette onto it.)

It's a *frittata* if you just run a spatula underneath to loosen it, then flip it onto a plate.

---

teaspoons cheese (cheddar, Swiss, jalapeño-studded Jack . . .) inside the omelette just before you fold it over. The heat from the eggs will melt the cheese.

✎ *Minced Fresh or Crumbled Dried Herbs.* Beat ¼ to ½ teaspoon dried herbs into the eggs before cooking. Sprinkle ½ to 1 teaspoon fresh herbs on top (see page 557 for herb suggestions).

✎ *Steamed or Sautéed Vegetables.* Follow the steps in the basic recipe, and use about ½ cup vegetables. For additional flavor, sprinkle with cheese before folding the omelette over.

✎ *Peeled, Seeded Fresh Fruit.* Beat 1 tablespoon sugar into the eggs before cooking. Make sure the fruit is ripe but not too juicy, and use no more than ⅓ cup for each single-serving omelette. Follow the steps for filling in the basic recipe.

✎ *Fruit Preserves.* Using about ¼ cup for each omelette, spoon the preserves in a line along the center just before you fold the omelette over.

✎ *Ricotta Cheese.* Sweeten about ¼ cup ricotta per omelette with 2 to 3 teaspoons confectioners' sugar or make it savory with 1 tablespoon grated Parmesan and a pinch of crumbled dried herbs, such as oregano or basil. Spoon the ricotta mixture along the center of the omelette just before you fold it over.

●

THE FRITTATA

Serves 1

TOTAL TIME: ABOUT 10 TO 20 MINUTES, DEPENDING ON
   THE FILLING
TIME TO PREPARE: 5 TO 15 MINUTES, DEPENDING ON THE
   FILLING
COOKING TIME: 4 MINUTES
REFRIGERATION/FREEZING: REFRIGERATE UP TO 1 DAY. DO
   NOT FREEZE.

Frittatas are much like omelettes, but easier to prepare. Like omelettes, they call for beaten eggs and a filling. But they don't require the precise timing and deft handling perfect omelettes demand. And they don't involve more than one pan; you can make the filling and the frittata in the same skillet (see Note). Moreover, they're wonderful hot, cold, or at room temperature, so you don't have to rush them—or your guests—to the table, as you do omelettes, which must be served hot or warm.

2 large eggs, or 1 large egg plus 2 large egg
   whites
1 recipe filling (see "Make It Your Own")
Salt and freshly ground black pepper to taste

Place a rack in the upper third of the oven. Heat the oven to 350°F. Break the eggs into a bowl, and beat lightly with a fork or whisk.

Squirt an 8- or 9-inch ovenproof nonstick skillet with nonstick spray or rub lightly with canola oil. Heat over medium-high heat.

Put the filling in the pan. Give the eggs another stir, then pour them into the pan, covering the filling, and stir lightly with a fork until the eggs start to set, about 30 seconds. Reduce the heat to medium-low. Once the bottom is firm and about ½ inch thick, about 2 minutes, use a nonmetallic spatula to lift the edge of the frittata. Tilt the pan toward that edge so that the uncooked egg runs underneath. Lower the edge and swirl the pan gently to distribute the egg evenly. Continue cooking until the egg on top—while still not set—is no longer runny, about 4 minutes.

Place the skillet in the oven until the top is set and just dry to the touch, 2 to 4 minutes. Check each minute after two, because the frittata will turn tough if cooked too long. Run a spatula around the edges and underneath to loosen the frittata, and invert or slide it onto a serving plate. Season to taste with salt and pepper. Serve at once, let cool to room temperature, or refrigerate and serve chilled.

Note: To double the servings, use 4 large eggs or 2 whole eggs and the volume of 3 additional eggs and cook in a 12-inch nonstick skillet.

PER SERVING (WITH HERBS): CALORIES 95 • PROTEIN 9.9 G • CARBOHYDRATE 1.8 G • FAT 5 G • CHOLESTEROL 213 MG • SODIUM 118 MG • 49% CALORIES FROM FAT • GOOD SOURCE OF VITAMINS A, B₂

Make It Your Own

When you're making a frittata, you're meant to improvise. The basic idea is to enjoy the fact that you're not making an omelette.

WHAT TO ADD AND WHEN TO ADD IT

Grated or Crumbled Cheese. Beat it in with the eggs before you put the eggs in the pan. Use no more than 2 tablespoons for each single-serving frittata.

Vegetables. Slice or chop vegetables such as mushrooms, spinach, asparagus, and so on fine, using no more than ⅔ cup for each single-serving frittata, and sauté them in the skillet using a drop of oil until they're nearly cooked. (They'll finish cooking after you've added the eggs.) You'll get a more satisfying flavor if you include at least 1 tablespoon chopped onions or shallots along with the vegetable of your choice. When the vegetables are cooked, pour the eggs on top and cook as directed in the basic recipe. For more detailed instructions, see page 68.

✐ *Fresh or Dried Herbs.* For each single-serving frittata, beat about 2 tablespoons minced fresh herbs into the eggs before pouring them into the heated skillet. Or use ½ teaspoon crumbled dry herbs. Try parsley, basil, chives, marjoram, tarragon, or oregano.

✐ *Pasta.* Put about ½ cup of a leftover pasta dish, sauce and all, at the bottom of the heated nonstick skillet. Pour the eggs on top and cook as directed. You can do the same with leftover risotto.

THE SOUFFLÉED FRITTATA

Serves 1

TOTAL TIME: ABOUT 20 TO 25 MINUTES, DEPENDING ON THE FILLING
TIME TO PREPARE: 8 TO 15 MINUTES, DEPENDING ON THE FILLING
COOKING TIME: ABOUT 10 MINUTES

This puffy (and pretty!) variation involves only one step more than The Frittata (see preceding recipe). You separate the eggs, whip the whites until stiff, fold them back into the yolks, cook on the stovetop, then finish in the oven. (For more servings, see Note, page 68.) Use any of the fillings suggested in "Make It Your Own" (see page 68), or serve it plain or dusted with confectioners' sugar.

2 large eggs, separated
1 teaspoon unsalted butter or canola oil
1 recipe filling (see "Make It Your Own")
Salt and freshly ground black pepper to taste

Place a rack in the upper third of the oven and heat the oven to 400°F.

Lightly beat the egg yolks to blend them together. Beat the egg whites until stiff but not dry. Gently fold the whites into the yolks.

Melt the butter or heat the oil in a 7-inch ovenproof nonstick skillet over medium heat. When it's hot, swirl the pan to distribute it evenly. Gently pour the egg mixture into the skillet and let it cook over medium heat until the bottom and sides are set, about 5 minutes.

Transfer the eggs to the oven and bake until slightly puffy and the top is set and golden brown, 3 to 4 minutes. Season with salt and pepper.

To loosen the frittata from the skillet, run a plastic spatula around the rim. Gently slide the frittata onto a serving plate. Do not invert it as you would an ordinary frittata, or it will collapse.

PER SERVING: CALORIES 183 • PROTEIN 12.5 G • CARBOHYDRATE 1.2 G • FAT 13.8 G • CHOLESTEROL 436 MG • SODIUM 127 MG • 69% CALORIES FROM FAT • VERY GOOD SOURCE OF VITAMIN B2 • GOOD SOURCE OF VITAMINS A, B12; FOLACIN

NOW TRY THIS: Omit the salt and pepper, and sprinkle with confectioners' sugar instead.

Muffins, Quick Breads, and Rolls

THE MUFFIN

Makes 6

TOTAL TIME: ABOUT 45 MINUTES
TIME TO PREPARE: 15 MINUTES
COOKING TIME: ABOUT 30 MINUTES
DO AHEAD: YOU CAN MIX THE BATTER THE NIGHT BEFORE, THEN REFRIGERATE.
REFRIGERATION/FREEZING: REFRIGERATE UP TO 4 DAYS. FREEZE UP TO 6 MONTHS.

As a child I had the world mapped out according to the foods I could get in various places. New York City was bagels, soft pretzels, and Carnegie Deli cheesecake. The Shenandoah Valley was crisp fresh apples and pulpy cider, and Boston—my favorite—was muffins: big giant corn, blueberry, and, best of all, bran muffins. If I were to be honest I'd have to say that my decision to go to Radcliffe College had more to do with being able to get a good muffin every morning than with anything you'd normally consider in choosing a place of higher learning.

It's been years since I've lived in the Boston area, but only hours since I've had a good muffin. Made as follows, they contain no added fat. And while that's true of a number of commercial muffins, most of those are oversweetened, thanks to misguided efforts to compensate for the lack of shortening.

1 cup unbleached all-purpose flour
1 cup whole wheat flour
1/3 cup granulated sugar or brown sugar
1 teaspoon baking powder
1/2 teaspoon baking soda
1 cup nonfat buttermilk
3 large egg whites, lightly beaten

Heat the oven to 500° F.

Using a whisk or a long-tined fork, combine the flours, sugar, baking powder, and baking soda in a mixing bowl. In a separate bowl, combine the buttermilk and egg whites.

Using the whisk or fork, stir the wet ingredients into the flour mixture, just until everything is moistened, about 30 seconds. It's likely the batter will be lumpy. Leave it that way, and you'll be rewarded for your restraint with light, tender muffins.

Fill the cups of a 6-cup nonstick muffin tin three-fourths full. Place the tin in the oven, close the door, and lower the heat to 400° F. Bake until a paring knife or toothpick inserted in the center of a muffin comes out clean, about 30 minutes. Let the tin cool on a cooling rack for 10 minutes before removing the muffins. To store, let the muffins cool completely. Seal them inside a plastic bag, and refrigerate or freeze.

PER SERVING (1 MUFFIN): CALORIES 210 • PROTEIN 7.4 G • CARBOHYDRATE 44 G • FAT 0 G • CHOLESTEROL 1.43 MG • SODIUM 187 MG • 4% CALORIES FROM FAT • GOOD SOURCE OF VITAMINS B₁, B₂, B₃; CALCIUM, IRON

MUFFIN BASICS

• Make sure your baking powder and soda are no more than six months old. They lose their leavening powers over time, and old leavening makes heavy muffins. Store both in a cool place, away from direct sunlight.

• Don't overbeat the batter! Beating toughens it up, making the muffins chewy and heavy. Stir it just enough to moisten all of the ingredients. Ordinarily, a thirty-second stir will do it (don't use an electric beater).

• For lovely peaks, heat the oven to 500° F. before baking, then lower it to 400° F. after you put in the muffins.

• Although you'll want to eat them right away, let the muffins cool in the tin, on a wire cooling rack, for about ten minutes first. If you'll be storing them, remove the muffins and let them cool completely. Seal them in a plastic bag and refrigerate or freeze.

Make It Your Own

As you might infer from the variety of muffins on the market, it's easy to customize the basic item. Pancakes, too. Any alteration gives them a whole new taste.

WHAT TO ADD AND WHEN TO ADD IT
🌿 *Fresh Fruits.* When you're adding fresh fruit, make sure it's not too juicy, or the muffins or pancakes will be soggy. Select firm, *just*-ripe peaches (peeled), apricots (peeled), strawberries (hulled), raspberries, and, of course, blueberries. Finely chop the fruit (except blueberries) before using. You can use fresh or canned pineapple as long as you chop it finely and drain it well.

Taste the fruit before you begin making the batter. If it's not sweet enough for you, place it —already chopped—in a bowl, sprinkle it with 1 tablespoon sugar or drizzle it with 2 teaspoons of honey. Toss gently and let it sit for 20 minutes. Use no more than ⅔ cup finely chopped fresh fruit for the basic recipe. Add the fruit to the wet ingredients before combining the wet and dry. The basic rule for beating the final batter applies: Easy does it!

🍃 *Citrus Fruit.* Don't use the fruit of oranges or lemons. For citrus flavor, add 1 tablespoon finely grated orange or lemon zest plus 1 tablespoon fresh orange or lemon juice to the wet ingredients before adding them to the dry.

🍃 *Dried Fruit.* Use any kind you want—currants, raisins, dates, prunes, apricots, cherries, cranberries, mangoes, and so on— chopping them very fine (except currants, which are small enough). Don't add more than ½ cup, chopped, to the batter, or the muffins or pancakes will be heavy. Add dried fruit to the dry ingredients before combining the wet and dry.

🍃 *Fruit Preserves or Purees.* For jam-filled muffins, use any flavor you'd like. First spoon a tablespoon of batter into each muffin cup. Place 2 teaspoons of preserves (or a tablespoon if you want a bigger burst of jam in the center) on top. Fill the cups three-fourths full with the remaining batter, and bake as directed.

🍃 *Nuts.* Walnuts, almonds, pecans, macadamia nuts, hazelnuts, and Brazil nuts. Chop them very fine. Add no more than ⅓ cup chopped nuts to the basic recipe or the muffins or pancakes will be heavy. To enhance the flavor of almonds, toast them lightly before using them (see page 56). Add chopped nuts to the dry ingredients before combining the wet and the dry.

🍃 *Seeds.* Poppy seeds, sesame seeds, sunflower seeds. Pour the batter into the tins, then sprinkle 1 to 2 teaspoons seeds over each muffin before baking, or blend ¼ cup seeds into the batter.

🍃 *Combinations.* Once you know how to customize muffins and pancakes, it's easy to get carried away and risk weighing down the batter and muddying up the flavor. You'll do best if you keep the combinations simple, and add no more to the basic batter than 1 cup total additional ingredients (e.g., ⅔ cup chopped apples plus ⅓ cup chopped walnuts). Add even less—no more than ¾ cup— when you're combining dried fruits and nuts, both of which are heavy (e.g., ⅓ cup chopped raisins and ⅓ cup chopped pecans).

•

MY BEST BRAN MUFFINS

Makes 6

TOTAL TIME: 45 MINUTES
TIME TO PREPARE: 10 MINUTES
COOKING TIME: 35 MINUTES
DO AHEAD: YOU CAN MIX THE BATTER THE NIGHT BEFORE, THEN REFRIGERATE. STIR LIGHTLY BEFORE POURING INTO THE TIN.
REFRIGERATION/FREEZING: REFRIGERATE UP TO 1 WEEK. FREEZE UP TO 6 MONTHS.

Moist, molasses-y, and deceptively rich, these muffins are "best" because they're also fat free, but amply full of flavor, nourishment, and fiber.

1 cup whole wheat flour

1 teaspoon baking soda

1 teaspoon baking powder

½ teaspoon salt

1½ cups wheat bran

⅓ cup brown sugar

¼ cup molasses

2 large egg whites

1 cup nonfat buttermilk or plain nonfat yogurt

Heat the oven to 500° F.

In a large mixing bowl, sift together the flour, baking soda, baking powder, and salt. Stir in the bran with a whisk or a long-tined fork.

In another large mixing bowl, beat together the brown sugar, molasses, egg whites, and buttermilk or yogurt.

Add the dry ingredients to liquid ingredients, and stir just to moisten, about 30 seconds. Fill each cup in a 6-cup nonstick muffin tin three-fourths full and place the tin in the oven. Reduce the heat to 400° F. and bake until a toothpick inserted in the center of a muffin comes out clean, about 35 minutes. Let the tin cool on a cooling rack for 10 minutes before removing the muffins. To store, let the muffins cool completely on the rack. Seal them inside a plastic bag, and refrigerate or freeze.

PER SERVING (1 MUFFIN): CALORIES 164 • PROTEIN 8.59 G • CARBOHYDRATE 36.6 G • FAT 1.09 G • CHOLESTEROL 0.735 MG • SODIUM 267 MG • 5% CALORIES FROM FAT • VERY GOOD SOURCE OF CALCIUM, IRON • GOOD SOURCE OF VITAMINS B₁, B₂, B₃, B₆

PUMPKIN BRAN MUFFINS

Makes 6

TOTAL TIME: 40 MINUTES
TIME TO PREPARE: 10 MINUTES
COOKING TIME: 30 MINUTES
DO AHEAD: YOU CAN MIX THE BATTER THE NIGHT BEFORE, THEN REFRIGERATE. STIR LIGHTLY BEFORE POURING INTO THE TIN.
REFRIGERATION/FREEZING: REFRIGERATE UP TO 1 WEEK. FREEZE UP TO 6 MONTHS.

Pumpkin enriches these muffins in two ways, with its familiar sweet flavor and a bit of beta-carotene. You can replicate the taste and multiply the vitamins by using sweet potato instead.

1 cup pumpkin or sweet potato puree
1 cup wheat bran
3 large egg whites
¾ cup nonfat buttermilk or plain nonfat yogurt
⅓ cup molasses
⅓ cup granulated sugar or brown sugar
1¼ cups whole wheat flour
2 teaspoons baking powder
½ teaspoon baking soda
1 teaspoon ground cinnamon
1 teaspoon ground ginger
1 cup raisins

Heat the oven to 500° F.

In a large mixing bowl, combine the pumpkin or sweet potato puree, wheat bran, egg whites, buttermilk or yogurt, molasses, and sugar. Stir with a whisk until smooth.

In a separate bowl, whisk together the flour, baking powder, baking soda, cinnamon, and ginger.

Stir the wet ingredients into the dry, mixing just enough to moisten, about 30 seconds. Fold in the raisins.

Fill the cups of a 6-cup nonstick muffin tin two-thirds full. Place the tin in the oven. Lower the temperature to 400°F. Bake until the tops are golden brown and springy to the touch and a knife or toothpick inserted in the center of a muffin tests clean, about 30 minutes. Let the tin cool on a cooling rack for 10 minutes before removing the muffins. To store, let the muffins cool completely on the rack. Seal them inside a plastic bag, and refrigerate or freeze.

PER SERVING (1 MUFFIN): CALORIES 229 • PROTEIN 6.4 G • CARBOHYDRATE 56 G • FAT 0 G • CHOLESTEROL 0.551 MG • SODIUM 292 MG • 3% CALORIES FROM FAT • OUTSTANDING SOURCE OF VITAMIN A • VERY GOOD SOURCE OF CALCIUM, IRON • GOOD SOURCE OF VITAMINS B₂, B₃

APPLE-BUTTERMILK BUNDT MUFFINS

Makes 4 Bundts or 6 muffins

TOTAL TIME: ABOUT 35 TO 45 MINUTES
TIME TO PREPARE: 15 MINUTES
COOKING TIME: 20 TO 30 MINUTES
REFRIGERATION/FREEZING: REFRIGERATE UP TO 4 DAYS.
 FREEZE UP TO 6 MONTHS.

Oat flour and buttermilk make these apple-flavored muffins/cakes sweet and light. Bundt pans are fun, but optional. They taste just as good baked in conventional muffin tins.

1 cup whole wheat flour
1 cup oat flour
1 1/2 teaspoons baking powder
1 1/2 teaspoons baking soda
Pinch ground cinnamon
2 large egg whites
2/3 cup plus 2 tablespoons nonfat buttermilk
1/2 cup unsweetened unseasoned apple butter
1/2 cup packed dark brown sugar
1/3 cup maple syrup

Heat the oven to 400°F.

In a mixing bowl, whisk together the whole wheat flour, oat flour, baking powder, baking soda, and cinnamon.

In a separate bowl, combine the egg whites, buttermilk, apple butter, brown sugar, and maple syrup. Beat until smooth.

Add the dry ingredients to the buttermilk mixture. Stir just until moistened, about 30 seconds. Distribute the batter evenly among the cups in a nonstick Bundt pan or nonstick muffin tin.

Bake for 20 to 30 minutes, or until a knife inserted in the center of a muffin or Bundt comes out clean. Let the Bundt pan or muffin tin cool on a cooling rack for about 10 minutes before removing the muffins. To store, let the muffins cool completely on the rack. Seal them inside a plastic bag, and refrigerate or freeze.

PER SERVING (1 MUFFIN): CALORIES 298 • PROTEIN 8 G • CARBOHYDRATE 64 G • FAT 2 G • CHOLESTEROL 0.972 MG • SODIUM 461 MG • 6% CALORIES FROM FAT • GOOD SOURCE OF VITAMIN B₁; CALCIUM, IRON

•

O A T   B R A N   M U F F I N S

Makes 6

TOTAL TIME: 30 MINUTES
TIME TO PREPARE: 5 MINUTES
COOKING TIME: 25 MINUTES
REFRIGERATION/FREEZING: REFRIGERATE UP TO 3 DAYS.
    FREEZE UP TO 6 MONTHS.

Oat bran muffins were the rage for a spell following the release of a study revealing that oat bran can lower blood cholesterol as effectively as a number of prescription drugs. The trend died, not because researchers retracted their results, but because most of the muffins were so bad that medicine was a more appetizing option. If more had tasted like these, they'd still be in high demand, and no one would miss out on the benefits of oat bran.

1 cup oat bran
1 cup whole wheat flour
½ cup dark brown sugar
1 teaspoon baking powder
½ teaspoon baking soda
1 cup nonfat buttermilk or plain nonfat yogurt
3 large egg whites

Heat the oven to 500° F.

In a mixing bowl, combine the oat bran, flour, brown sugar, baking powder, and baking soda using a long-tined fork or a wire whisk. In a separate bowl, beat together the buttermilk or yogurt and egg whites until well combined.

Pour the wet mixture into the flour mixture, and stir until the flour mixture is thoroughly moistened, but still lumpy, about 30 seconds. Fill the cups of a 6-cup nonstick muffin tin three-fourths full.

Place the tin in the oven; as you shut the door, lower the temperature to 400° F. Bake until golden brown, about 25 minutes, or until a toothpick inserted in the center of a muffin comes out clean. Let the tin cool on a cooling rack for 10 minutes before removing the muffins. To store, let the muffins cool completely on the rack. Seal them inside a plastic bag, and refrigerate or freeze.

PER SERVING (1 MUFFIN): CALORIES 183 • PROTEIN 9.5 G • CARBOHYDRATE 40 G • FAT 1.5 G • CHOLESTEROL 0.735 MG • SODIUM 251 MG • 7% CALORIES FROM FAT • VERY GOOD SOURCE OF VITAMIN B • GOOD SOURCE OF VITAMIN B₁; CALCIUM, ZINC

CORN MUFFINS

Makes 6

TOTAL TIME: 45 MINUTES
TIME TO PREPARE: 15 MINUTES
COOKING TIME: 30 MINUTES
REFRIGERATION/FREEZING: REFRIGERATE UP TO 4 DAYS.
    FREEZE UP TO 6 MONTHS.

When I first set out to make fat-free corn muffins, I hoped they'd taste the same as the conventional kind, which call for lots of vegetable oil. But they actually taste better. It seems that what you lose in fat, you gain in true corn flavor. Try them toasted.

1 cup whole wheat flour
1 cup stone-ground cornmeal
½ cup sugar
2 teaspoons baking powder
1 teaspoon baking soda
1 cup fresh or frozen blueberries or cranberries,
    or ⅓ cup dried blueberries or cranberries
    (optional)
1 cup nonfat buttermilk or plain nonfat yogurt
3 large egg whites

Heat the oven to 500°F.

In a mixing bowl, whisk together the flour, cornmeal, sugar, baking powder, baking soda, and blueberries or cranberries, if using.

In a separate bowl, beat together the buttermilk or yogurt and egg whites. Add them to the flour mixture and stir just until everything is moistened, about 30 seconds.

Fill the cups of a 6-cup nonstick muffin tin three-fourths full. Place the tin in the oven, close the door, and lower the heat to 400°F. Bake until a paring knife or toothpick inserted in the center of a muffin comes out clean, about 30 minutes. Let the tin cool on a cooling rack for 10 minutes before removing the muffins. To store, let the muffins cool completely on the rack. Seal them inside a plastic bag, and refrigerate or freeze.

PER SERVING (1 MUFFIN): CALORIES 232 • PROTEIN 7.5 G • CARBOHYDRATE 49 G • FAT 1.47 G • CHOLESTEROL 1.43 MG • SODIUM 409 MG • 5% CALORIES FROM FAT • GOOD SOURCE OF VITAMINS B₁, B₂, B₃; CALCIUM

•

DATE-NUT BREAD

Serves 8

TOTAL TIME: ABOUT 1 HOUR
TIME TO PREPARE: 15 MINUTES
COOKING TIME: 40 MINUTES
REFRIGERATION/FREEZING: REFRIGERATE UP TO 4 DAYS.
    FREEZE UP TO 6 MONTHS.

Prune puree replaces shortening to update this classic quick bread. Serve it spread with cream cheese (reduced-fat if there's a brand you like), and enjoy it not just for breakfast, but late in the day with coffee or tea.

1 cup nonfat buttermilk or plain nonfat yogurt
2 large eggs, lightly beaten
2 tablespoons prune puree (page 468) or
    unsweetened prune baby food
½ cup packed dark brown sugar
2 cups whole wheat flour
1 teaspoon baking soda
1 cup dates, chopped
1 cup walnuts, chopped
2 teaspoons grated orange zest

Heat the oven to 350°F. Lightly grease a 9 ×
5-inch loaf pan or squirt with nonstick spray.

In a mixing bowl, stir the buttermilk or
yogurt, eggs, prune, and brown sugar until
smooth. In a separate bowl, combine the flour
and baking soda with a whisk.

Pour the wet ingredients into the flour
mixture, and stir just until everything's moist,
about 30 seconds. Fold the dates, walnuts, and
orange zest into the batter.

Pour the batter into the prepared loaf pan.
Bake until a toothpick inserted in the center of
the loaf tests clean, about 40 minutes. Let the
pan cool on a cooling rack for 10 to 15 minutes
before removing the bread. To store, let the
loaf cool completely on the rack. Seal it inside
a plastic bag, and refrigerate or freeze.

PER SERVING (1 SLICE): CALORIES 260 • PROTEIN 9.4 G • CARBOHYDRATE 37 G •
FAT 9.9 G • CHOLESTEROL 0.551 MG • SODIUM 50 MG • 32% CALORIES FROM FAT •
GOOD SOURCE OF VITAMINS B₁, B₂, B₃, B₆; CALCIUM, IRON, ZINC

•

ZUCCHINI BREAD

Serves 8

TOTAL TIME: 50 MINUTES
TIME TO PREPARE: 10 MINUTES
COOKING TIME: 40 MINUTES
REFRIGERATION/FREEZING: REFRIGERATE UP TO 1 WEEK.
    FREEZE UP TO 6 MONTHS.

Check out the label on most zucchini breads,
and you'll find oil of some kind pretty far
up on the list of ingredients. There's not
much point to it, though, because zucchini adds so
much moisture of its own, you can make a perfectly
scrumptious bread from the squash with no oil at all.

1⅓ cups whole wheat flour
⅔ cup oat bran
½ cup sugar
1 tablespoon nonfat dry milk
2 teaspoons baking powder
½ teaspoon ground cinnamon
1 teaspoon baking soda
1 cup nonfat buttermilk
3 large egg whites
1 medium zucchini, peeled and shredded (about
    1½ cups)

Heat the oven to 425°F. Lightly grease a 9 ×
5-inch loaf pan or 2 miniature loaf pans, or
squirt with nonstick spray.

In a mixing bowl, whisk together the flour,
oat bran, sugar, dry milk, baking powder, cinnamon, and baking soda.

In a separate bowl, blend together the buttermilk, egg whites, and zucchini.

Stir the wet ingredients into the dry only
until moistened, taking care not to overbeat,
about 30 seconds.

Pour into the loaf pan or miniature loaf
pans. Bake until a toothpick inserted in the
center of the loaf comes out clean, about 40
minutes. Let the pan cool on a cooling rack for
10 to 15 minutes before removing the bread.
To store, let the loaf cool completely on the
rack. Seal it inside a plastic bag, and refrigerate
or freeze.

PER SERVING (1 SLICE): CALORIES 159 • PROTEIN 6.6 G • CARBOHYDRATE 34.7 G
• FAT 1.23 G • CHOLESTEROL 1.07 MG • SODIUM 303 MG • 6% CALORIES FROM FAT •
GOOD SOURCE OF VITAMINS B₁, B₂; CALCIUM

•

BREAKFAST
GINGERBREAD

Serves 8

TOTAL TIME: ABOUT 1 HOUR
TIME TO PREPARE: ABOUT 20 MINUTES
COOKING TIME: 35 MINUTES
REFRIGERATION/FREEZING: REFRIGERATE UP TO 4 DAYS.
    FREEZE UP TO 6 MONTHS.

Gingerbread's one of those toss-up things: fine for dessert and after-school snacks, but even better—I think—for breakfast. Try it lightly toasted, with yogurt spread (see page 102) and marmalade.

2½ cups whole wheat pastry flour (see mail-
    order information, page 596)
1 teaspoon baking soda
1 teaspoon ground ginger
½ teaspoon ground nutmeg
½ teaspoon ground cinnamon
1¼ cups nonfat buttermilk or plain nonfat yogurt
2 large egg whites

1 cup loosely packed dark brown sugar
½ cup molasses

Heat the oven to 350°F.

In a mixing bowl, combine the flour, baking soda, ginger, nutmeg, and cinnamon. Mix with a whisk to blend. In a separate bowl, beat together the buttermilk or yogurt, egg whites, brown sugar, and molasses until the texture is light and fluffy, about 5 minutes using an electric hand mixer.

Gradually (in about 5 additions) beat the buttermilk mixture into the flour mixture. Pour into a nonstick 8-inch square pan. Bake until golden and springy to the touch and a toothpick inserted in the center of the gingerbread comes out clean, about 35 minutes. Let the pan cool on a cooling rack for 10 to 15 minutes before removing and slicing the gingerbread. To store, let the gingerbread cool completely on the rack. Seal it inside a plastic bag, and refrigerate or freeze.

PER SERVING (1 SLICE): CALORIES 277 • PROTEIN 8.14 G • CARBOHYDRATE 62.3 G • FAT 0 G • CHOLESTEROL 0.689 MG • SODIUM 211 MG • 3% CALORIES FROM FAT • GOOD SOURCE OF VITAMINS B₁, B₂, B₃, B₆; CALCIUM, ZINC

•

ENGLISH MUFFINS

Serves 8

TOTAL TIME: ABOUT 2 HOURS, 20 MINUTES, INCLUDING
    TIME TO RISE AND BAKE
TIME TO PREPARE: ABOUT 20 MINUTES, FEWER IF YOU USE A
    FOOD PROCESSOR OR MIXMASTER
COOKING TIME: 20 MINUTES
EQUIPMENT: MUFFIN RINGS, A BISCUIT CUTTER, OR AN ALU-
    MINUM CAN (3 TO 4 INCHES IN DIAMETER), WITH BOTH
    ENDS REMOVED
FREEZING: FREEZE UP TO 9 MONTHS.

*S*ince several brands of English muffins taste just fine, you may well wonder whether it's worth the time to make them yourself. Try these once, and I'll bet you'll be glad you did. Made with buttermilk or yogurt, they're chewier than any packaged kind I know, with a slight tang that you can play up with marmalade or subdue with strawberry jam.

1 ½ teaspoons dry active yeast

2 tablespoons warm water

¾ cup nonfat or low-fat buttermilk, or ½ cup milk mixed with ¼ cup plain yogurt, at room temperature

1 tablespoon sugar

1 teaspoon salt

3 cups unbleached all-purpose flour or up to half whole wheat (1 ½ cups unbleached all-purpose flour plus 1 ½ cups whole wheat flour)

In a small mixing bowl, dissolve the yeast in the water. When it's bubbly, about 3 minutes, transfer to a large mixing bowl or to the work bowl of a food processor or Mixmaster.

Stir in the buttermilk, sugar, salt, and enough flour to make a dough that is soft and pliable.

Turn out onto a lightly floured surface and knead until smooth and springy, about 10 minutes. Or knead the dough in the work bowl of the processor or with the dough hook of the Mixmaster.

Shape the dough into a ball and place in a deep ceramic or glass bowl. Cover with plastic wrap and set aside until doubled in bulk, about 1 hour.

Punch the dough down and turn it out onto a lightly floured surface. With a rolling pin, roll it to about ½ inch thick. Using your muffin rings, biscuit cutter, or tin can, cut out eight rounds. (You may have to gather the scraps after you've cut a few, then roll them out to cut some more.)

Sprinkle a baking tray with stone-ground cornmeal or lightly grease it with vegetable oil. Place the rounds on the tray, and cover loosely with a towel. Let them rest for 40 minutes, until puffy.

About 20 minutes before baking, preheat the oven to 400°F.

Remove the towel, and place the tray in the oven. After 10 minutes, turn the muffins over and bake for another 10 minutes.

Let the muffins cool on a rack. To serve, split them by prying open with the tines of a fork (this makes the insides fluff up, which makes crunchy toast). Toast, and serve with your favorite spread.

PER SERVING (1 MUFFIN): CALORIES 187 • PROTEIN 5.7 G • CARBOHYDRATE 38.6 G • FAT 0 G • CHOLESTEROL 0 MG • SODIUM 292 MG • 3% CALORIES FROM FAT • GOOD SOURCE OF VITAMINS B₁, B₂, B₃; IRON

CINNAMON-RAISIN ROLLS

Makes 8

TOTAL TIME: 1 HOUR
TIME TO PREPARE: 35 MINUTES
COOKING TIME: 25 MINUTES
DO AHEAD: YOU CAN MAKE THE DOUGH UP TO 3 DAYS IN
   ADVANCE. KEEP WRAPPED AND REFRIGERATED UNTIL
   READY TO USE.
REFRIGERATION/FREEZING: DOUGH KEEPS, UNBAKED, UP TO
   3 DAYS IN THE REFRIGERATOR OR UP TO 6 MONTHS IN
   THE FREEZER. ROLLS KEEP 2 DAYS REFRIGERATED, UP TO 6
   MONTHS FROZEN.

A cross between biscuits and buns . . . delicious however you describe them. Be sure to bake plenty if there are other people in the house; the aroma of cinnamon is so appetizing, you'll be handing these out fresh from the oven.

¼ cup raisins

1 cup whole wheat flour

1 cup unbleached all-purpose flour

1 tablespoon baking powder

1 cup low-fat cottage cheese

⅓ cup granulated sugar

⅓ cup nonfat buttermilk

1 teaspoon vanilla extract

⅓ cup loosely packed brown sugar

2 teaspoons ground cinnamon

Heat the oven to 400°F.

    Place the raisins in a small bowl. Bring ¼ cup water to a boil and pour it over the raisins. Set aside.

    In a mixing bowl, whisk together the flours and baking powder.

    In a food processor puree the cottage cheese until smooth. Add the granulated sugar, buttermilk, and vanilla. Process again until smooth. Add the flour mixture and process in short pulses just until a dough forms, about 4 to 5 pulses.

    Dust a flat work surface with flour. Pat the dough into a ball. Place it in the center of the work surface and roll it out into a rectangle, about 10 by 12 inches.

    Combine the brown sugar and cinnamon, and sprinkle evenly over the dough. Drain the raisins and distribute them over the dough. Roll the dough up from the long side as if it were a jelly roll. Slice it into 8 pieces.

    Place the pieces flat on a nonstick baking sheet. Bake for 25 minutes, or until golden brown. Leave the rolls on the baking sheet and cool on a rack for 5 minutes. Serve warm. To store, let the rolls cool completely. Seal them inside a plastic bag and refrigerate or freeze.

PER SERVING (1 ROLL): CALORIES 185 • PROTEIN 8 G • CARBOHYDRATE 36.6 G • FAT 1 G • CHOLESTEROL 2.73 MG • SODIUM 263 MG • 5% CALORIES FROM FAT • GOOD SOURCE OF VITAMINS B₁, B₂, B₃; CALCIUM

CRUMPETS

Makes 12

TOTAL TIME: ABOUT 2 HOURS, 25 MINUTES, INCLUDING
   TIME TO RISE
TIME TO PREPARE: ABOUT 15 MINUTES
COOKING TIME: ABOUT 10 MINUTES
EQUIPMENT: ENGLISH-MUFFIN RINGS
DO AHEAD: YOU CAN MIX THE FIRST BATTER (BEFORE
   ADDING THE BAKING SODA) THE NIGHT BEFORE. COVER
   AND REFRIGERATE. RESUME THE RECIPE THE NEXT
   MORNING.
REFRIGERATION/FREEZING: DO NOT REFRIGERATE. FREEZE
   THE CRUMPETS UP TO 6 MONTHS. WRAP EACH INDIVIDU-
   ALLY IN PLASTIC.

If you've never had a crumpet, imagine a thick, yeasty pancake the size of an English muffin, pocked with craters. Now imagine spreading the surface lightly with butter and jam, which seep in through the craters, making the crumpet so sweet and delicious, you'll wish you could live your life over again to eat the crumpets you've missed until now. And even if you have had crumpets—the cello-wrapped kind you can buy at the supermarket—you don't know how good the dimpled cakes can be until you griddle some up from scratch.

1 cup warm nonfat milk

1 cup warm water (about 95 to 103°F.)

1 tablespoon (1 packet) dry active yeast

1 teaspoon sugar

1 cup unbleached all-purpose flour

¾ cup whole wheat pastry or kamut flour (see
   mail-order information, page 596)

½ teaspoon salt

¼ teaspoon baking soda

1 tablespoon hot water

In a large mixing bowl, combine the milk, warm water, yeast, and sugar. Stir lightly, then let the mixture stand until creamy, about 5 minutes.

In a separate mixing bowl, whisk together the flours and salt. Using a wooden spoon, beat the flour mixture into the yeast mixture. Keep stirring until the batter is very elastic, about 5 minutes.

Cover the bowl with plastic wrap and let the batter rise until doubled and bubbly, about 1 hour, 30 minutes.

Place the baking soda in a small bowl and add the hot water to dissolve it. Beat the baking soda into the batter, cover again, and let rise until bubbly, about 30 minutes.

Generously grease the inside of 6 English-muffin rings. Heat a nonstick griddle over medium heat, and place the rings (or as many as will fit) on the griddle. Stir down the batter, and ladle it into the rings, only ½ inch full. Be careful not to add too much batter, or the crumpet will be too thick and won't cook all the way through. Cook until the bottom is firmly set, the top starts to dry, and small holes begin to form on the surface, about 7 minutes. Slip off the muffin rings (they may be hot, so use pot holders), flip the crumpets with a spatula, and cook the other side until firm, about 3 minutes. Transfer to a cooling rack and cool completely before toasting. Repeat with the remaining batter.

PER SERVING (1 CRUMPET): CALORIES 73 • PROTEIN 3 G • CARBOHYDRATE 15 G • FAT 0 G • CHOLESTEROL 0.367 MG • SODIUM 126 MG • 4% CALORIES FROM FAT

OAT-FLOUR SCONES

Makes 6

TOTAL TIME: 25 MINUTES
TIME TO PREPARE: 10 MINUTES
COOKING TIME: 15 MINUTES
REFRIGERATION/FREEZING: REFRIGERATE UP TO 3 DAYS.
  FREEZE UP TO 3 MONTHS.

I f you are not baking with oat flour yet, you're in for a treat. Inside each speck is a substance that mimics, of all things, butter. Since scones should taste buttery, but we shouldn't eat all that much butter, the oat flour offers a means to have the flavor without the fat.

If you can't find oat flour where you shop, order it by mail (see page 596), or put an equal amount of old-fashioned rolled oats (not instant) in your food processor and pulverize.

1½ cups oat flour

1 tablespoon baking powder

½ teaspoon baking soda

¼ cup plus 1 tablespoon nonfat or reduced-fat
    sour cream (see Note)

2 large eggs, lightly beaten

1 tablespoon barley-malt syrup (see mail-order
    information, page 596) or honey

Heat the oven to 350°F.

In a medium mixing bowl, combine the oat flour, baking powder, and baking soda. Stir with a fine whisk or long-tined fork to blend thoroughly.

In a separate bowl, beat together the sour cream, eggs, and barley-malt syrup or honey. Add the sour cream mixture to the flour mixture, and stir to make a stiff batter.

Drop by spoonfuls 2 inches apart onto a nonstick baking sheet. Bake until lightly browned, about 15 minutes.

Let the baking sheet cool on a cooling rack for 10 minutes before removing the scones. To store, let the scones cool completely on the rack, then seal them in a plastic bag and refrigerate or freeze.

Note: Don't substitute plain yogurt for the sour cream as you might elsewhere; it's too thin.

PER SERVING (1 SCONE): CALORIES 122 • PROTEIN 6.18 G • CARBOHYDRATE 18.5 G • FAT 2.94 G • CHOLESTEROL 71 MG • SODIUM 212 MG • 21% CALORIES FROM FAT • VERY GOOD SOURCE OF CALCIUM • GOOD SOURCE OF VITAMIN B₁

NOW TRY THIS: Add 2 tablespoons currants to the flour mixture; just before baking, top each mound of batter with a teaspoon of fruit preserves; or just before baking, sprinkle each mound of batter with cinnamon sugar or maple sugar.

THE POPOVER

Makes 6 small or 4 large

TOTAL TIME: ABOUT 45 TO 50 MINUTES
TIME TO PREPARE: ABOUT 10 MINUTES
COOKING TIME: 20 TO 25 MINUTES
EQUIPMENT: NONSTICK POPOVER CUPS
DO AHEAD: YOU CAN MIX THE BATTER THE NIGHT BEFORE, COVER, AND REFRIGERATE. BEAT WITH AN ELECTRIC MIXER BEFORE BAKING.

To write about a subject—any subject— you have to think long and hard about it. And the longer and harder I think about popovers—how you break through the light, crisp crust to find filaments of custard that open onto an ideal receptacle for jam or honey, scrambled eggs, fruit salad, and more—the more I want to quit writing and start baking. Let's say (strictly hypothetically) I were to give in to this impulse; here's how I'd proceed.

2 large eggs, lightly beaten
1 cup nonfat milk
1 cup whole wheat pastry or unbleached all-purpose flour

Heat the oven to 400°F. With an electric hand mixer, beat together the eggs and the milk in a mixing bowl until frothy. Add the flour and beat until large bubbles form, at least 1 minute.

Lightly grease the inside of 4 or 6 popover cups. Pour the batter either two-thirds of the way (for 4 higher, airier popovers) or halfway (for 6 smaller, denser popovers) to the top.

Bake, without opening the oven door, until they've risen above the top of the pan and turned golden, about 20 minutes. Immediately prick the top with the point of a sharp knife to let the steam escape. If you like your popovers

custardy, serve them right away. If you like a drier interior, return them to the oven for 5 minutes after you've pricked them, and serve right away.

PER SERVING (1 SMALL POPOVER): CALORIES 94 • PROTEIN 5 G • CARBOHYDRATE 16 G • FAT 1.2 G • CHOLESTEROL 36 MG • SODIUM 32 MG • 12% CALORIES FROM FAT

POPOVER BASICS

• If you have time, start with the eggs and milk at room temperature, putting them out about forty minutes ahead of time.
• Even if they're nonstick, grease the cups well with unsalted butter, canola oil, or non-stick spray. The sides have to be very slick for the popovers to rise without tearing.
• Don't open the oven door during the first twenty minutes of baking at least, or the popovers will collapse.
• Beat the batter rigorously so it takes in as much air as possible. Since popovers contain no leavening, they depend on air to rise.

Make It Your Own

Unlike muffin or pancake batter, good popover batter is too light to handle much in the way of additional ingredients. You can still make your popovers distinct by filling them imaginatively.

WHAT TO ADD AND WHEN TO ADD IT
🖉 *Cheese.* Beat in ¼ cup grated or finely shredded cheese along with the milk. Try, for example, Parmesan, Gruyère, or sharp cheddar. Seasoned with cheese, popovers go well with soup or salad.
🖉 *Herbs.* Beat in about 2 tablespoons finely

minced fresh herbs or ½ teaspoon crumbled dried herbs along with the milk. You can add small amounts of herbs and cheese without worrying about weighing down the batter. Try fresh or dried basil or oregano with Parmesan, or fresh parsley or chives with cheddar.

 Fillings. Slice the top off a popover and place about 2 heaping tablespoons of filling such as egg salad, ricotta cheese, sautéed vegetables, or jam into the hollow center. Replace the top, and serve right away. Filled large popovers make a great brunch offering.

Pancakes

THE PANCAKE

Serves 4

TOTAL TIME: ABOUT 20 MINUTES
TIME TO PREPARE: 20 MINUTES
COOKING TIME: INCLUDED IN TIME TO PREPARE
DO AHEAD: YOU CAN MAKE THE BATTER THE NIGHT BEFORE. COVER AND REFRIGERATE. WHISK BEFORE USING.

In one of my favorite movies, Barbara Stanwyck plays a food writer for a popular women's magazine. Without consulting her, the publisher sponsors a contest, awarding as first prize Christmas dinner cooked by Stanwyck's character and served at the idyllic Connecticut farmhouse she has vividly and repeatedly described for her readers as her home.

Problem is, Stanwyck lives in a Midtown walk-up and has never made a meal in her life. In the nick of time, she manages to borrow a house, a baby, a husband, and a chef. The scam is going off nicely, until her guest asks her to flip a pancake—a "week-end ritual" she's bragged about in print. Tension is high when Stanwyck grabs the griddle with both hands, closes her eyes, and tosses a flapjack toward the ceiling. It comes down as it should, and her secret is safe.

I don't even pretend to be able to flip pancakes. The purpose of flipping is to keep them light, which I manage with buttermilk rather than acrobatics. I make them lighter still by omitting shortening from the batter, counting again on nonfat buttermilk for the tender consistency that ordinarily comes from butter or oil.

1 ½ cups unbleached all-purpose flour
2 tablespoons granulated sugar or brown sugar
2 teaspoons baking powder
½ teaspoon baking soda
1 large egg, lightly beaten, or 2 large egg whites
1 ⅓ cups nonfat buttermilk or plain nonfat yogurt

Using a wire whisk, combine the flour, sugar, baking powder, and baking soda in a mixing bowl. In a separate bowl, blend together the egg or egg whites and buttermilk or yogurt.

Add the liquid ingredients to the flour mixture. Stir just to moisten. If the batter's still lumpy, don't be tempted to make it smooth, or the pancakes may be tough.

Unless you know from experience that the pancakes won't stick to the surface, squirt a nonstick griddle with nonstick spray, or rub it lightly with vegetable oil. Heat the griddle on medium-high. The griddle's ready to go when a teaspoon of water dropped on the surface spits back at you.

Lower the heat to medium. For each pancake, use a ladle or a ¼-cup measure to pour the batter onto the griddle. Bake until the sur-

PANCAKE BASICS

• Make sure your baking powder and baking soda are no more than six months old, or your pancakes may be heavy. Store them in a cool place away from direct sunlight.

• When you add the wet ingredients to the dry ingredients, stir just enough to moisten the flour. Fight the urge to beat them into a smooth, thin batter, and you'll be rewarded with tender pancakes. Overbeaten batter makes them tough and chewy.

• Make sure your griddle's nonstick surface is up to the job. If you have any doubts, squirt with nonstick spray or grease lightly with canola oil before heating.

• Test the temperature of the surface of your griddle by dropping a teaspoon of water onto it. If the water breaks up into little bubbles that shimmy and hop on the surface, the griddle's ready for the batter.

• For light, fluffy pancakes, separate the eggs. Add the yolks to the wet ingredients. After you've combined the wet and dry ingredients, beat the egg whites until they're stiff. Fold them into the batter, then proceed as normal.

• Wait until the pancake surface is pitted with holes before flipping it over to cook the other side. Turning pancakes more than once makes them tough. If your pancakes are burning on the bottom before the pits appear on the surface, turn down the heat, and let the griddle cool for four or five minutes before you add fresh batter.

• Give your pancakes plenty of space. If you crowd them, the batter may run together.

face is pitted with tiny holes, about 2 minutes. Flip with a spatula and bake the other side until golden brown, about 1 minute. Serve right away, or place, covered loosely with foil, in a 200° F. oven for up to 10 minutes, while you cook the rest.

PER SERVING (1 PANCAKE): CALORIES 250 • PROTEIN 11 G • CARBOHYDRATE 49 G • FAT 0 G • CHOLESTEROL 1.47 MG • SODIUM 429 MG • 2% CALORIES FROM FAT • VERY GOOD SOURCE OF VITAMINS B₁, B₂; CALCIUM • GOOD SOURCE OF VITAMIN B₃; IRON

•

COTTAGE CHEESE PANCAKES

Serves 4

TOTAL TIME: 20 MINUTES
TIME TO PREPARE: 20 MINUTES
COOKING TIME: INCLUDED IN TIME TO PREPARE

Pancakes may be misleading. These are lighter and fluffier than anything else by that name. (Tip: Because they're so light, they tend to stick to the griddle, so lightly grease the griddle with oil or unsalted butter before you drop the batter onto it.)

2 large eggs, separated
Pinch cream of tartar
¼ cup sugar
⅔ cup low-fat cottage cheese
¼ cup nonfat buttermilk
⅔ cup whole wheat pastry flour
1 teaspoon grated lemon zest

In a large mixing bowl, beat the egg whites to soft peaks. Add the cream of tartar and sugar, and continue beating until the whites are stiff but not dry.

In a separate bowl, blend together the egg yolks, cottage cheese, buttermilk, pastry flour, and lemon zest until smooth. Fold in the egg whites.

Heat a nonstick griddle over medium heat.

Drop the batter onto the griddle 2 tablespoons at a time, and cook over medium-low heat until bubbles form on the surface and the pancake is golden underneath, about 3 minutes. Turn and cook the other side until golden, about 1½ minutes.

PER SERVING: CALORIES 190 • PROTEIN 11.3 G • CARBOHYDRATE 29.6 G • FAT 3.69 G • CHOLESTEROL 108 MG • SODIUM 196 MG • 5% CALORIES FROM FAT • GOOD SOURCE OF VITAMINS B₂, B₁₂

•

POPOVER PANCAKES

Serves 4

TOTAL TIME: 30 TO 35 MINUTES
TIME TO PREPARE: 5 MINUTES
COOKING TIME: 25 TO 30 MINUTES

More popover than pancake. Outside it's billowy and golden brown; inside, it's like custard. Make sure to have everyone seated at the table before you serve them—these tend to collapse quickly.

⅔ cup unbleached all-purpose flour
Pinch salt
3 large eggs
⅔ cup low-fat or nonfat milk
1 tablespoon confectioners' sugar
Fruit or preserves

Place a rack on the lowest rung of the oven. Heat the oven to 425°F.

In a mixing bowl, sift together the flour and salt. In another bowl, beat the eggs lightly with a whisk and add the milk. Add the flour mixture and beat with an electric mixer just until bubbly.

Pour the batter into an 8- or 9-inch ovenproof nonstick skillet, and place the skillet on the lowest rack of the oven. Bake for 15 minutes, without opening the oven. Pierce the pancake to let steam escape.

Lower the heat to 375°F. and bake 10 to 15 minutes longer, until puffy and golden brown.

Serve immediately topped with confectioners'
sugar and fruit or preserves.

PER SERVING: CALORIES 155 • PROTEIN 7.44 G • CARBOHYDRATE 22.3 G • FAT 4 G
• CHOLESTEROL 22.3 MG • SODIUM 201 MG • 23% CALORIES FROM FAT • GOOD
SOURCE OF VITAMINS B₁, B₂

●

BLUEBERRY
BUTTERMILK
PANCAKES

Serves 4

TOTAL TIME: 15 MINUTES
TIME TO PREPARE: 15 MINUTES
COOKING TIME: INCLUDED IN TIME TO PREPARE
DO AHEAD: YOU CAN MIX THE BATTER THE NIGHT BEFORE,
  COVER, AND REFRIGERATE. WHISK BEFORE COOKING.

*As you enjoy these pancakes, spare a moment
to pity the Italians who have nothing in the
morning but tooth-cracking biscotti and a
slug of strong espresso.*

1 cup unbleached all-purpose flour or whole
  wheat pastry flour
½ cup oat flour, or ½ cup unbleached all-
  purpose or whole wheat pastry flour
1 tablespoon sugar
1½ teaspoons baking powder
¾ teaspoon baking soda
2 large egg whites
1½ cups nonfat buttermilk or plain nonfat
  yogurt
1 teaspoon vanilla extract
1 cup fresh blueberries, rinsed and picked over

In a large bowl, whisk together the flours, sugar,
baking powder, and baking soda. In a separate
bowl, whisk together the egg whites, buttermilk
or yogurt, and vanilla. Whisk the wet ingredients into the dry until just smooth. Stir in the
blueberries.

Lightly grease a nonstick griddle, or coat it
with nonstick spray. Heat the griddle over
medium-high heat until droplets of water splat-
ter when you sprinkle them on the surface.
Cooking 2 or 3 pancakes at once, drop batter
¼ cup at a time onto the griddle. Let cook until
bubbles form on the surface, about 1½ minutes. Flip each pancake to cook the other side
until golden, about 1 minute. Transfer to a
warm plate.

PER SERVING: CALORIES 350 • PROTEIN 17.5 G • CARBOHYDRATE 70 G • FAT
1.78 G • CHOLESTEROL 1.65 MG • SODIUM 522 MG • 4% CALORIES FROM FAT • VERY
GOOD SOURCE OF VITAMINS B₁, B₂, B₃; CALCIUM, ZINC • GOOD SOURCE OF VITA-
MINS B₆, B₁₂; FOLACIN, IRON

●

WHOLE WHEAT PANCAKES

Serves 4

TOTAL TIME: 20 MINUTES
TIME TO PREPARE: 10 MINUTES
COOKING TIME: 10 MINUTES
DO AHEAD: YOU CAN MIX THE BATTER, EXCEPT THE EGG
   WHITE, THE NIGHT BEFORE, THEN REFRIGERATE, COVERED,
   OVERNIGHT. BEAT THE EGG WHITE AND FOLD IT IN THE
   NEXT DAY.

These pancakes call for just enough whole wheat flour for flavor and fiber, but not for producing hockey pucks, a common liability in whole wheat baking.

⅔ cup whole wheat flour

⅓ cup unbleached all-purpose flour

2 tablespoons wheat bran

½ teaspoon salt

1 teaspoon baking soda

3 tablespoons currants

1 large egg, separated

1 cup nonfat buttermilk or plain nonfat yogurt

1 tablespoon brown sugar

Heat a griddle with a nonstick surface over medium heat. Whisk together the flours, bran, salt, and baking soda in a mixing bowl until well blended. Add the currants and stir to distribute throughout.

   In another bowl, use a fork to beat the egg yolk into the buttermilk or yogurt. Add the brown sugar and beat again to blend. Stir into the flour mixture.

   Beat the egg white until soft peaks form. Gently but thoroughly fold the white into the batter.

Using a ladle or a ¼-cup measure, pour some batter onto the griddle. Cook over medium heat until the bottom sets and bubbles start to form on the surface, about 1½ minutes. Use a heavy plastic spatula to turn the pancake over. Brown the other side, about 1 minute. Serve right away, or place, covered loosely with foil, in a 200°F. oven for up to 10 minutes, while you cook the rest.

PER SERVING: CALORIES 194 • PROTEIN 9.5 G • CARBOHYDRATE 36 G • FAT 1.9 G • CHOLESTEROL 54.4 MG • SODIUM 513 MG • 9% CALORIES FROM FAT • GOOD SOURCE OF VITAMINS B₁, B₂, B₃: CALCIUM, IRON, ZINC

Waffles

THE WAFFLE

Serves 4

TOTAL TIME: ABOUT 20 MINUTES
TIME TO PREPARE: 10 MINUTES
COOKING TIME: UP TO 8 MINUTES
DO AHEAD: YOU CAN MIX THE BATTER THE NIGHT BEFORE,
   EXCEPT FOR THE EGG WHITE, THEN REFRIGERATE,
   COVERED, OVERNIGHT.
REFRIGERATION/FREEZING: COOL THE WAFFLES COM-
   PLETELY, WRAP INDIVIDUALLY IN PLASTIC, AND FREEZE UP
   TO 3 MONTHS.

Go figure. You call someone "muffin," "honey pie," and "cookie," and you're expressing affection. But call a person a "waffler," and you're looking for a fight. What gives?

As it happens, this isn't a slur on waffles. An unfortunate phonetic coincidence links the delicious breakfast dish with an unattractive characteristic. You see, the root word for "waffles"—the food—is wabo, German for "honeycomb," which is precisely what a waffle looks like.

But "to waffle," as in "to equivocate," comes from waff, Old English for "yelp."

I don't think waffles are in danger of suffering on account of the inapt association with waffling. If anything has harmed the reputation of waffles, it's the frozen kind. Sure they're convenient, but they don't taste as good.

Instead of settling for second-rate waffles, plan ahead. Make fresh batter the night before and refrigerate it. Set out the waffle iron so it's ready to go the next day. Before you get into the shower in the morning, squirt the iron with nonstick spray and turn it on. After your bath, pour the batter into the iron and make the coffee. Presto; instant waffles. Or close enough.

1 cup unbleached all-purpose flour, or ½ cup
   unbleached all-purpose plus ½ cup whole
   wheat flour
1 tablespoon stone-ground cornmeal
¼ teaspoon salt
1 teaspoon baking soda
1 large egg, separated
1 cup plus 2 tablespoons nonfat buttermilk

Coat the waffle iron with nonstick spray, and plug it in to heat.

Sift the flour, cornmeal, salt, and baking soda together in a large mixing bowl.

In a separate bowl, lightly beat together the egg yolk and the buttermilk. Stir the mixture into the dry ingredients.

Whip the egg white until soft peaks form. Gently but thoroughly fold the white into the batter.

For a round waffle iron that makes one 8-inch waffle, pour ¼ cup of batter into the center of the waffle iron. For a square waffle iron that makes 4 waffles, pour half the batter into the center of the waffle iron.

Cook until the indicator light goes out, or until the waffle is deep golden brown. Timing varies considerably depending on the waffle iron. This could take anywhere from 2½ minutes to 8 minutes. Repeat with the remaining batter. Serve immediately, or place each waffle directly on the rack in the center of a warm (no more than 150° F.) oven. Serve within 10 minutes, or the waffles will cook through, becoming hard.

PER SERVING (I WAFFLE): CALORIES 174 • PROTEIN 8.47 G • CARBOHYDRATE 30 G • FAT 1.7 G • CHOLESTEROL 54 MG • SODIUM 512 MG • 9% CALORIES FROM FAT • VERY GOOD SOURCE OF VITAMINS B₁, B₂ • GOOD SOURCE OF VITAMIN B₃; CALCIUM, IRON

WAFFLE BASICS

• Whipping the egg white makes the waffles light and crispy.

• Buttermilk makes waffles tender, so you don't have to add shortening of any kind.

• A tablespoon of cornmeal added to the batter makes the waffles crisp.

• Mix the waffle batter before you start making the topping. A short resting period softens the gluten in the flour and makes a lighter, more tender interior.

• Bake the waffles *just* before serving or as you serve them. Don't stack them as they're done; the steam from each waffle will make the others soggy.

Make It Your Own

While you *can* throw all sorts of things into the batter, I don't recommend it. First, waffles should be light, and additional ingredients will weigh them down. Second, whatever you add may bake onto your waffle iron, leaving a mess. I've seen recipes that call for putting cheese into the batter. Please! You might as well apply it to the iron with a glue gun. Instead of tinkering with the batter, use different toppings to make your waffles distinct. You'll find some suggestions on page 102.

PUMPKIN WAFFLES

Serves 4

TOTAL TIME: ABOUT 30 MINUTES
TIME TO PREPARE: ABOUT 20 MINUTES
COOKING TIME: UP TO 8 MINUTES
DO AHEAD: YOU CAN MIX THE BATTER THE NIGHT BEFORE,
    EXCEPT FOR THE EGG WHITES, THEN REFRIGERATE, COV-
    ERED, OVERNIGHT. BEAT THE EGG WHITES AND FOLD
    THEM INTO THE BATTER THE NEXT DAY.
REFRIGERATION/FREEZING: COOL THE WAFFLES COM-
    PLETELY, WRAP INDIVIDUALLY IN PLASTIC, AND FREEZE UP
    TO 6 MONTHS.

Y ou'd order these out, wouldn't you? Then
why not make them at home? (And why
not add a scoop of frozen vanilla yogurt?
And some chopped pecans? And maple syrup?)

1 cup unbleached all-purpose flour, or ½ cup
    unbleached all-purpose plus ½ cup whole
    wheat flour
1 tablespoon stone-ground cornmeal
¼ teaspoon salt
1 teaspoon baking soda
½ teaspoon ground cinnamon (see Note)
½ teaspoon ground ginger (see Note)
2 large egg whites
⅔ cup nonfat buttermilk or plain nonfat yogurt
⅓ cup canned or fresh pumpkin puree
2 tablespoons sugar
1 tablespoon molasses

Coat the waffle iron with nonstick spray, and
plug it in to heat. Sift the flour, cornmeal, salt,
baking soda, cinnamon, and ginger together
into a large mixing bowl. In a separate bowl,
lightly beat together the egg yolks, buttermilk
or yogurt, pumpkin, sugar, and molasses. Stir
the mixture into the dry ingredients.

In another bowl, whip the egg whites until
soft peaks form. Gently but thoroughly fold
the whites into the batter.

For a round waffle iron that makes one 8-
inch waffle, pour ¼ cup of batter into the center of the waffle iron. For a square waffle iron
that makes 4 waffles, pour half the batter into
the center of the waffle iron.

Cook until the indicator light goes out, or
until the waffle is deep golden brown. Timing
varies considerably depending on the waffle
iron. This could take anywhere from 2½ minutes to 8 minutes. Serve immediately, or place
each waffle directly on the rack in the center of
a warm (no more than 150° F.) oven. Serve
within 10 minutes, or the waffles will cook
through, becoming hard.

*Note: You can substitute 1 teaspoon pumpkin pie spice for
the cinnamon and ginger.*

PER SERVING: CALORIES 177 • PROTEIN 5.3 G • CARBOHYDRATE 36.5 G • FAT 0 G •
CHOLESTEROL 0 MG • SODIUM 236 MG • 2% CALORIES FROM FAT • OUTSTANDING
SOURCE OF VITAMIN A • GOOD SOURCE OF VITAMINS B₁, B₂, B₃; IRON

CORNMEAL WAFFLES

Serves 4

TOTAL TIME: ABOUT 20 MINUTES

TIME TO PREPARE: 10 MINUTES

COOKING TIME: UP TO 8 MINUTES

DO AHEAD: YOU CAN MIX THE BATTER THE NIGHT BEFORE, EXCEPT FOR THE EGG WHITE, THEN REFRIGERATE, COVERED, OVERNIGHT. BEAT THE EGG WHITE AND FOLD IT INTO THE BATTER THE NEXT DAY.

REFRIGERATION/FREEZING: COOL THE WAFFLES COMPLETELY, WRAP INDIVIDUALLY IN PLASTIC, AND FREEZE UP TO 3 MONTHS.

I*n addition to the conventional syrup or preserves, savory brunch toppings such as egg salad or sautéed mushrooms taste terrific on these hearty waffles. For a true corn taste, use stone-ground cornmeal.*

⅓ cup stone-ground yellow cornmeal

⅔ cup unbleached all-purpose flour

¼ teaspoon salt

1 teaspoon baking soda

1 large egg, separated

1 cup plus 2 tablespoons nonfat buttermilk

Coat the waffle iron with nonstick spray, and plug it in to heat.

Sift the cornmeal, flour, salt, and baking soda into a large mixing bowl. In a separate bowl, lightly beat together the egg yolk and the buttermilk. Stir the mixture into the dry ingredients.

In another bowl, whip the egg white until soft peaks form. Gently but thoroughly fold the white into the batter.

For a round waffle iron that makes one 8-inch waffle, pour ¼ cup of batter into the center of the waffle iron. For a square waffle iron that makes 4 waffles, pour half the batter into the center of the waffle iron.

Cook until the indicator light goes out, or until the waffle is deep golden brown. Timing varies considerably depending on the waffle iron. This could take anywhere from 2½ minutes to 8 minutes. Serve immediately, or place each waffle directly on the rack in the center of a warm (no more than 150° F.) oven. Serve within 10 minutes, or the waffles will cook through, becoming hard.

PER SERVING: CALORIES 158 • PROTEIN 7.85 G • CARBOHYDRATE 27 G • FAT 1.9 G • CHOLESTEROL 54.4 MG • SODIUM 514 MG • 11% CALORIES FROM FAT • GOOD SOURCE OF VITAMINS B₁, B₂; CALCIUM

FRENCH TOAST

Serves 4

TOTAL TIME: ABOUT 15 MINUTES
TIME TO PREPARE: 5 MINUTES
COOKING TIME: 8 MINUTES
DO AHEAD: YOU CAN MIX THE MILK AND EGG THE NIGHT
BEFORE, COVER, AND REFRIGERATE. STIR WELL THE NEXT
DAY BEFORE DIPPING THE BREAD.

*W*hat, you may wonder, does French toast have to do with France? Did it originate there? Is such a thing even served in France, or is the name simply meant to give some class to what's basically a slice of bread soaked in milk and eggs?

Larousse Gastronomique, the definitive source on French food, isn't much help. On the one hand, it affirms that what we call French toast is in fact served in France, as a dessert called pain perdu. Pain perdu *means "lost bread" and refers to the main ingredient, bread that's gone stale and is therefore lost for any other purpose.*

But the answer's not complete. Larousse goes on to say that the French used to refer to pain perdu *as* pain à la romaine, *or "Roman bread." And*

sure enough, the Romans had made something called pandorado, *or "golden bread," a dish that we would recognize as French toast.*

No matter what it's called or why, French toast is versatile, lending itself to infinite adaptation. You can make it as light or rich as you please, use any type of bread you'd like, prepare it overnight or on the spot, bake it or grill it, stuff it with fruit or top it with syrup, yogurt, honey, or cheese.

2 large eggs
2 large egg whites
$^1/_2$ cup nonfat milk
1 tablespoon granulated sugar, brown sugar,
    maple syrup, or honey
1 teaspoon vanilla extract
Pinch ground cinnamon (optional)
Eight $^1/_2$-inch-thick slices whole wheat bread
Topping (see page 102)

In a wide, shallow bowl or pie plate, combine the eggs, egg whites, milk, sugar, syrup, or honey, vanilla, and cinnamon, if using. Stir well to blend.

Squirt a nonstick griddle or wide skillet with nonstick spray. Heat the griddle or skillet over medium-high heat. Dip the bread slices into the milk mixture, moistening each side. Be careful not to soak the slices or they will fall apart. Place the slices on the griddle or in the skillet and cook until the underside is nicely browned and crisp, about 4 minutes. Turn and cook the other side, about 4 minutes.

Serve right away with the topping of your choice, or keep warm by placing slices in a single layer in a 150° F. oven. Don't stack the slices or the toast will get soggy.

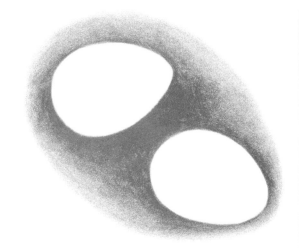

one slice and top it with another. Bake at 425°F. until the top slice has browned. Turn the sandwich to bake the other side. Or cook on the griddle as directed for French Toast.

✐ *Toppings.* Add confectioners' sugar, fruit preserves, ginger marmalade, maple syrup, or fruit-flavored nonfat yogurt just before serving.

Note: Nutritional values will vary depending upon the type of bread you use. To keep fat and calories down choose a bread with no added fat, or make your own (see page 393)!

PER SERVING (SEE NOTE): CALORIES 239 • PROTEIN 13.3 G • CARBOHYDRATE 38.7 G • FAT 4.66 G • CHOLESTEROL 109 MG • SODIUM 444 MG • 17% CALORIES FROM FAT • GOOD SOURCE OF VITAMINS B₁, B₂, B₃; FOLACIN, CALCIUM, IRON, ZINC

Make It Your Own

French toast is a concept, not a recipe. Make it your way any way you'd like.

WHAT TO ADD AND WHEN TO ADD IT

✐ *Different Breads.* Try challah, raisin bread, and Grape-Nuts Bran Bread (see page 406).

✐ *Fruit Juice.* Substitute it for the milk.

✐ *Fresh Grated Ginger.* Add it to the milk-and-egg soak.

✐ *Fruit Preserves.* Add them to the milk-and-egg soak.

✐ *Fillings.* Try Vanilla Ricotta Icing (see page 475), reduced-fat cream cheese and jam, thinly sliced broiled bananas or apples. After the bread has soaked, spread a layer of filling on

Puddings, Casseroles, and Breakfast Pastas

BREAKFAST BREAD PUDDING

Serves 4

TOTAL TIME: ABOUT 1 HOUR, NOT INCLUDING TIME TO SOAK THE BREAD
TIME TO PREPARE: 10 MINUTES
COOKING TIME: 50 MINUTES
DO AHEAD: PREPARE THE NIGHT BEFORE SERVING. KEEP REFRIGERATED UNTIL READY TO BAKE.
REFRIGERATION/FREEZING: REFRIGERATE LEFTOVERS UP TO 2 DAYS. DO NOT FREEZE.

A casserole with the luscious flavor of French toast and the texture of smooth, dense pudding, this is as easy as they come. Just chuck some bread into the dish, pour in the eggs and milk, top with sugar, and let it bake.

4 cups loosely packed 1-inch day-old whole wheat or white bread cubes
2 large eggs
2 large egg whites
1 cup nonfat milk
¼ cup maple syrup or honey
2 tablespoons brown sugar
1 teaspoon vanilla extract
1 teaspoon ground cinnamon

Place the bread in the bottom of a 9-inch baking dish.

In a mixing bowl, beat together the eggs, egg whites, milk, syrup or honey, brown sugar, vanilla, and cinnamon until thoroughly blended. Pour the mixture evenly over the bread. Cover tightly with plastic wrap and refrigerate overnight.

Place a rack in the center of the oven and preheat the oven to 350° F. Bake until golden brown and firm to the touch, about 50 minutes. Serve warm.

Note: Nutritional values will vary depending upon the type of bread you use. To keep fat and calories down choose a bread with no added fat, or make your own (see page 393)!

PER SERVING: CALORIES 260 • PROTEIN 10 G • CARBOHYDRATE 45 G • FAT 4.87 G • CHOLESTEROL 108 MG • SODIUM 343 MG • 16% CALORIES FROM FAT • GOOD SOURCE OF VITAMINS B₁, B₂, B₃; FOLACIN, CALCIUM, IRON, ZINC

Make It Your Own

Although it's excellent as it is, you may want to put your mark on this pudding by adding fruit purees, dried or fresh fruit, and various sweeteners and syrups. For more on bread puddings (and stratas) see page 440.

WHAT TO ADD AND WHEN TO ADD IT

✏ *Fruit Purees.* In place of half of the milk, add ½ cup pureed bananas, prunes, or dried apricots. (Plump the dried fruit first by soaking it in hot water to cover until soft.) Blend the fruit puree with the remaining ½ cup milk, and proceed as directed in the bread pudding recipe.

✏ *Pumpkin or Sweet Potato Puree.* In place of half of the milk, substitute pumpkin or sweet potato puree. Blend the puree with the remaining ½ cup milk and proceed as directed. For an additional twist, stir 2 teaspoons of ginger preserves into the milk mixture.

✏ *Dried or Fresh Fruit.* Stir about ½ cup dried or fresh fruit such as pitted and halved cherries, blueberries, cranberries, diced apples, and/or chopped prunes, into the bread-milk-egg mixture. Bake as directed.

✏ *Jams or Marmalade.* Spread the bread lightly with fruit jam or marmalade before cutting it into cubes for the pudding.

BAKED BLINTZ CASSEROLE

Serves 8

TOTAL TIME: ABOUT 2 HOURS TO 2 HOURS, 15 MINUTES, INCLUDING TIME TO REST THE BASE

TIME TO PREPARE: 15 MINUTES

COOKING TIME: 1 HOUR, 30 MINUTES

DO AHEAD: YOU CAN MAKE THIS DISH UP TO 2 DAYS BEFORE, IF YOU SERVE IT COLD. DO NOT REHEAT.

REFRIGERATION/FREEZING: REFRIGERATE UP TO 3 DAYS. DO NOT FREEZE OR REHEAT.

My grandmother was not a cook, so her blintzes were perplexing because they were very, very good. While not haute cuisine, blintzes (crepes filled with cottage cheese or jam and lightly fried in butter) are hard to get just right. How did she make them so light? And how was it that her fillings were consistently the right consistency?

When I graduated college and moved to New York City, my grandmother gave me a care package and came clean in the bargain. Along with a pint of sour cream, there were four cartons of Tabachnik's frozen blintzes.

This simple casserole—the same components as blintzes, but served in a different configuration—is almost as convenient and easily as good. (Moreover, you get bragging rights.)

Blintz Base

3 large eggs

1 cup water

¼ teaspoon salt

1 cup sifted unbleached all-purpose flour

Filling

2 cups nonfat ricotta cheese

½ cup nonfat or reduced-fat cream cheese

½ cup nonfat or reduced-fat sour cream

2 large eggs

3 large egg whites

2 tablespoons fresh lemon juice

1 teaspoon grated lemon zest

Fresh fruit, such as strawberries, blueberries, or sliced peaches (optional)

Heat the oven to 350°F. Lightly grease a 9-inch baking dish or squirt with nonstick spray.

To make the Blintz Base

Beat together the eggs, water, salt, and flour in a mixing bowl. Let the mixture rest at room temperature for 15 to 30 minutes. Beat again. Pour into the baking dish and bake until set, about 30 minutes. It may puff up, in which case use a sharp knife to poke several airholes in the surface. The base will settle.

To make the Filling

In a blender or food processor, combine the ricotta, cream cheese, sour cream, eggs, egg whites, lemon juice, and lemon zest. Process until smooth.

Pour the filling over the base. Place the casserole in the oven and bake until set and golden brown, about 1 hour. Cool slightly before serving topped with fruit, if you'd like. Or chill and serve cold.

PER SERVING: CALORIES 195 • PROTEIN 20 G • CARBOHYDRATE 18 G • FAT 3.2 G • CHOLESTEROL 137 MG • SODIUM 308 MG • 16% CALORIES FROM FAT • VERY GOOD SOURCE OF VITAMIN B₂ • GOOD SOURCE OF VITAMINS A, B₁

BREAKFAST KUGEL
A Noodle Pudding
Serves 6

TOTAL TIME: ABOUT 1 HOUR, 10 MINUTES
TIME TO PREPARE: ABOUT 20 MINUTES
COOKING TIME: 50 MINUTES
DO AHEAD: YOU CAN MAKE THE KUGEL, UNCOOKED, UP TO
  2 DAYS IN ADVANCE. KEEP REFRIGERATED UNTIL READY
  TO BAKE.
REFRIGERATION/FREEZING: REFRIGERATE LEFTOVERS UP TO 3
  DAYS. DO NOT FREEZE.

The problem with most kugels is that the noodles sink into the general muck, making a gummy mess. It doesn't look very nice, and it tastes . . . well . . .

This one is different. The noodles hold their own, staying springy and chewy in a firm, sweet pudding. It's also easy and nourishing, and something you can make two days ahead of Sunday and serve for brunch.

8 ounces dried whole wheat penne or elbow
  noodles
1 large egg
2 large egg whites
2 cups low-fat cottage cheese or low-fat farmer
  cheese
²⁄₃ cup nonfat or reduced-fat sour cream
¹⁄₂ cup sugar
1 tablespoon grated lemon or orange zest
1 teaspoon vanilla extract
¹⁄₂ cup soft bread crumbs, from whole wheat or
  French bread
¹⁄₃ cup raisins or dried cherries

Heat the oven to 350°F. Lightly grease an 8-inch baking pan or squirt with nonstick spray.

Bring a large pot of water to a boil. Stir in the pasta, and cook until not quite done (test it with your teeth, it should still be a bit hard in the center when you bite into one), about 6 minutes.

In a food processor or blender, combine the egg and egg whites. Add the cottage or farmer cheese, sour cream, sugar, lemon or orange zest, and vanilla extract. Process until smooth.

Transfer the mixture to a mixing bowl and stir in the bread crumbs and raisins or cherries. Spoon into the baking pan and bake until golden brown, about 50 minutes.

Let sit at room temperature for 15 minutes before cutting and serving. Serve warm right away or refrigerate, covered, and serve cold.

PER SERVING: CALORIES 239 • PROTEIN 15.9 G • CARBOHYDRATE 40.7 G • FAT 1.9 G • CHOLESTEROL 38.9 MG • SODIUM 374 MG • 7% CALORIES FROM FAT • GOOD SOURCE OF VITAMINS B₂, B₁₂

OATMEAL PUDDING

Serves 6

TOTAL TIME: ABOUT 50 MINUTES, NOT INCLUDING TIME TO
    COOK THE OATMEAL
TIME TO PREPARE: 5 MINUTES
COOKING TIME: 40 MINUTES
DO AHEAD: MAKE THE OATMEAL UP TO 2 DAYS AHEAD. THE
    PUDDING CAN BE MADE 3 DAYS IN ADVANCE.
REFRIGERATION/FREEZING: REFRIGERATE UP TO 3 DAYS. DO
    NOT FREEZE.

O ccasionally in life we get the opportunity to prove a truism false. I got my chance one winter day when I had to abandon a pot of oatmeal to make a train. Later, it was hard to determine which'd be worse, throwing out the oatmeal or reheating it the next day. Then I remembered a third option.

In her definitive Breakfast Book, Marion Cunningham offers a recipe calling for cooked oatmeal and cottage cheese. Here's my version of that dish. (This pudding makes it possible to serve oatmeal to guests; it doesn't have to be piping hot or topped with milk in the usual way.)

1 cup low-fat cottage cheese

4 cups cooked oatmeal (1 cup oats cooked in 2
    cups nonfat milk; see page 52)

1 large egg, lightly beaten

1 large egg white

1 cup nonfat milk

3 tablespoons brown sugar

3 tablespoons maple syrup

Pinch ground nutmeg or mace

⅓ cup raisins

Heat the oven to 350° F.

In a food processor, combine the cottage cheese, oatmeal, egg, egg white, milk, brown sugar, maple syrup, and nutmeg or mace. Process until smooth. Stir in the raisins.

Pour into a 1½-quart baking dish or 6 individual ovenproof dishes, and bake until golden and set, about 40 minutes.

PER SERVING: CALORIES 247 • PROTEIN 14 G • CARBOHYDRATE 41 G • FAT 3 G •
CHOLESTEROL 39 MG • SODIUM 232 MG • 11% CALORIES FROM FAT • VERY GOOD
SOURCE OF CALCIUM • GOOD SOURCE OF VITAMINS A, B₁, B₂, B₁₂; ZINC

•

BLUEBERRY
SPOONBREAD

Serves 4

TOTAL TIME: 50 MINUTES
TIME TO PREPARE: 5 MINUTES
COOKING TIME: 45 MINUTES
REFRIGERATION/FREEZING: REFRIGERATE OVERNIGHT. DO
    NOT FREEZE.

A blueberry muffin soufflé you can whip up in no time—and will—time and time again. When local blues aren't in season (i.e., most of the year), use frozen berries. Frozen local fruit has much more flavor than fresh blueberries from somewhere far off.

2 large eggs

1/2 cup stone-ground yellow cornmeal

2 cups nonfat buttermilk

1/3 cup sugar

1 cup fresh blueberries, rinsed and picked over

Place a rack in the center of the oven and pre-heat the oven to 350°F. Lightly grease a 1½-quart baking dish or soufflé dish.

Beat together the eggs, cornmeal, butter-milk, and sugar until frothy. Stir in the blueber-ries and pour into the prepared dish.

Bake until puffy and lightly browned, about 45 minutes.

Let cool on a rack for 5 minutes before serving.

PER SERVING: CALORIES 250 • PROTEIN 12 G • CARBOHYDRATE 43 G • FAT 3.8 G • CHOLESTEROL 126 MG • SODIUM 138 MG • 13% CALORIES FROM FAT • VERY GOOD SOURCE OF VITAMINS B₂, B₁₂; CALCIUM • GOOD SOURCE OF VITAMINS B₁, C; ZINC

PRUNE AND BARLEY OR WHEAT BERRY PUDDING

Serves 2

TOTAL TIME: 2 HOURS, 45 MINUTES
TIME TO PREPARE: 10 MINUTES
COOKING TIME: 2 HOURS
DO AHEAD: YOU CAN COOK THE BARLEY OR WHEAT BERRIES IN MILK UP TO 2 DAYS AHEAD, KEEPING THE GRAIN COV-ERED AND REFRIGERATED.
REFRIGERATION/FREEZING: REFRIGERATE UP TO 3 DAYS. DO NOT FREEZE.

A great way to get to know these grains. Make the pudding the night before because it needs time to set. You can reheat it before serving, or serve it cold.

2 cups nonfat milk

1/4 cup barley or wheat berries

1 egg, lightly beaten

2 tablespoons sugar

1 teaspoon vanilla extract

1/2 cup chopped prunes

1 teaspoon grated lemon zest

Heat the oven to 300°F.

Place the milk and barley or wheat berries in a medium, heavy ovenproof saucepan. Bring the mixture to a simmer over medium-high heat, stirring often to prevent burning. As soon as it reaches a simmer, remove it from the heat, cover, and transfer to the oven.

Bake until most of the milk has been absorbed and the grain is tender, about 1 hour. Remove from the oven and transfer the grain to a mixing bowl.

Turn up the oven to 350°F.

Let the grain cool for 15 minutes, stirring

often to help it along. In a separate bowl, beat together the egg, sugar, vanilla, prunes, and lemon zest. Stirring constantly, add the mixture to the grain.

Spoon it into 2 6-ounce custard cups. Place the cups inside a deep baking dish. Pour water into the outer dish until it comes halfway up the pan. Cover loosely with foil. Bake until firm, about 1 hour, checking the water level occasionally, and adding more as necessary to maintain it.

Place the custard cups on a cooling rack and let them sit for 30 minutes. Serve the pudding warm, or transfer it to the refrigerator and serve chilled, or reheat it when ready to serve.

PER SERVING: CALORIES 324 • PROTEIN 14 G • CARBOHYDRATE 60 G • FAT 3.36 G • CHOLESTEROL 111 MG • SODIUM 161 MG • 9% CALORIES FROM FAT • OUTSTANDING SOURCE OF CALCIUM • VERY GOOD SOURCE OF VITAMINS A, B₂, B₁₂ • GOOD SOURCE OF VITAMINS B₁, B₆; IRON, ZINC

FARINA PRUNE WHIP

Serves 1

TOTAL TIME: 3 HOURS, 10 MINUTES, INCLUDING TIME TO CHILL
TIME TO PREPARE: 10 MINUTES
COOKING TIME: INCLUDED IN TIME TO PREPARE
DO AHEAD: MAKE THIS DISH THE NIGHT BEFORE OR UP TO 3 DAYS AHEAD. WRAP AND REFRIGERATE.
REFRIGERATION: REFRIGERATE UP TO 3 DAYS.

I love prunes, something I owe to the time I've spent in France, where they appear in desserts of all kinds. In this country we tend to think of prunes as a prescription rather than a treat. But try this for breakfast, and I'll bet you'll come to share my enthusiasm for them.

1 cup prune juice
1 teaspoon sugar
2½ tablespoons farina or Cream of Wheat (not instant)
½ cup plain nonfat yogurt
½ teaspoon grated lemon or orange zest

In a medium saucepan, bring the prune juice to a simmer over medium-high heat. Stir in the sugar and the farina. Bring to a simmer again, and stir constantly until the cereal has thickened, about 10 minutes. Remove it from the heat and let it cool.

When the mixture's no longer steaming, use an electric hand beater to whip the yogurt and zest into it. Refrigerate until it's thick and creamy, about 3 hours. Serve in individual bowls or parfait glasses.

PER SERVING: CALORIES 344 • PROTEIN 10.8 G • CARBOHYDRATE 74.8 G • FAT 0 G • CHOLESTEROL 2.2 MG • SODIUM 104 MG • 1% CALORIES FROM FAT • OUTSTANDING SOURCE OF VITAMINS B₂, B₆ • VERY GOOD SOURCE OF VITAMIN C; CALCIUM, IRON • GOOD SOURCE OF VITAMINS B₃, B₁₂; ZINC

ANGEL-HAIR PASTA WITH EGGS, TOMATOES, AND AVOCADO

Serves 2

TOTAL TIME: ABOUT 16 MINUTES
TIME TO PREPARE: ABOUT 10 MINUTES
COOKING TIME: ABOUT 6 MINUTES

Pasta for breakfast? Why not? It's made of grain, like cereal or toast. And it's as hearty and comforting as a bowl of oats, especially when you make it as follows.

Although it's a spur-of-the-moment dish, the trick to turning out perfect pasta and eggs is taking your time at the mixing stage. Beating swiftly with the heat up high coats the pasta with clots. But stirring slowly with the heat set low makes a silky, cream-style sauce that clings to the strands.

6 ounces dried angel-hair pasta (capellini)
2 large eggs, lightly beaten, or 1 large egg plus 2 large egg whites, lightly beaten
2 tablespoons nonfat or reduced-fat sour cream
1 medium tomato, chopped
¼ teaspoon minced garlic
1 tablespoon minced fresh cilantro
2 tablespoons shredded sharp cheddar cheese
¼ cup chopped avocado
Salt and freshly ground black pepper to taste

Bring a large pot of water to a boil and prepare the pasta according to the package directions. Meanwhile, in a mixing bowl, combine the eggs, sour cream, tomato, garlic, cilantro, cheese, avocado, and salt and pepper.

When the pasta has cooked, drain it quickly in a colander. Set the colander over the cooking pot for 15 to 20 seconds so some of the cooking water drips into the pot. Toss the pasta back into the pot and, using a wooden spoon, swiftly stir the egg mixture into the pasta. Turn the heat to the lowest setting and stir constantly, until the pasta is coated with a creamy sauce (see Note), about 2 minutes. Remove from the heat and serve at once.

Note: Be careful not to overcook at this stage, or the eggs will scramble instead of binding into a sauce.

PER SERVING: CALORIES 286 • PROTEIN 14.1 G • CARBOHYDRATE 31.3 G • FAT 12 G • CHOLESTEROL 219 MG • SODIUM 210 MG • 37% CALORIES FROM FAT • VERY GOOD SOURCE OF VITAMINS A, B₁, B₂, C • GOOD SOURCE OF VITAMINS B₃, B₆, B₁₂, FOLACIN, IRON

L.A. STORY

When I lived in Los Angeles, a film magazine occasionally called me last minute to write profiles to replace columns they'd killed for one reason or another. To meet my deadlines, I'd have to interview my subject in the morning—some trick, since actors, by definition, do not get up before noon. I could coerce them if I said we'd meet at Hugos, where "*tout* L.A." started the day. *Everyone* ate there, and not just because everyone ate there. The food was excellent, especially this breakfast pasta, L.A.'s answer to eggs with bacon, sausage, and grits.

Toppings and Spreads for Pancakes, Waffles, and Breakfast Breads

STRAINED YOGURT

Makes 1 cup; serves 6

TOTAL TIME: ABOUT 8 HOURS
TIME TO PREPARE: 3 MINUTES
COOKING TIME: NONE
REFRIGERATION/FREEZING: REFRIGERATE UP TO 5 DAYS. DO NOT FREEZE.

When you strain yogurt, the bite drains away along with much of the liquid, rendering a thick spread that's much like cream cheese. (If you use nonfat yogurt, it's fat free.) Make it with plain yogurt for a neutral spread you can use as is or season to taste. Or make it with flavored yogurt for a sweet or fruity spread.

4 cups plain, vanilla, or smooth fruit-flavored (blended, not fruit-on-bottom) nonfat yogurt

Fit a sieve or a coffee filter holder inside the mouth of a 2-cup-capacity measuring cup, canister, or bowl, making sure the sieve or filter holder is sufficiently suspended to allow liquid to drain freely into the receptacle.

Line the sieve or filter holder with a clean paper coffee filter or a piece of 2-ply-thick cheesecloth. Stir the yogurt well and pour it into the coffee filter or cheesecloth. Place the works in the refrigerator to drain overnight, or until the yogurt has drained enough to make a thick spread similar to cream cheese.

PER SERVING (2 TABLESPOONS): CALORIES 69 • PROTEIN 7 G • CARBOHYDRATE 9.4 G • FAT 0 G • CHOLESTEROL 2.2 MG • SODIUM 93.5 MG • 3% CALORIES FROM FAT

Make It Your Own

Once plain yogurt is strained, it tastes very mild and takes well to flavoring.

WHAT TO ADD AND WHEN TO ADD IT

Pureed Dried Fruit. For each cup of strained plain yogurt, soften 1 cup of prunes, dried apricots, or dried Bing cherries in warm water to cover for about 30 minutes. When the fruit is tender, drain the water and puree the fruit. In a mixing bowl, combine the puree and strained yogurt, and stir until well blended.

Fruit Preserves. In a mixing bowl, combine the strained yogurt with ¼ cup fruit preserves of your choice. Add 1 tablespoon honey, and stir until well blended.

Honey or Maple or Fruit Syrup. Stirring by hand, blend with the strained yogurt. Start with 1 tablespoon, adding more to taste.

✏ *Minced Fresh Chives or Dill.* For spreading on plain, rye, or pumpernickel bread or bagels stir about ¼ cup into the strained yogurt

✏ *Cottage Cheese.* For a thicker spread, puree ½ to 1 cup low-fat cottage cheese with the strained yogurt.

✏ *Ricotta Cheese, Confectioners' Sugar, and Lemon Zest.* For each cup of strained yogurt blend in a food processor or blender with 1 cup nonfat or reduced-fat ricotta, ½ cup confectioners' sugar, and 2 teaspoons lemon zest. This makes a great topping for French toast and pancakes.

•

A P P L E   B U T T E R

Makes 2 cups

TOTAL TIME: 30 TO 40 MINUTES
TIME TO PREPARE: 15 MINUTES
COOKING TIME: 15 TO 25 MINUTES
REFRIGERATION/FREEZING: REFRIGERATE UP TO 2 WEEKS.
  DO NOT FREEZE.

Serve this hearty spread with muffins, French toast, pancakes, or waffles. Or use it to replace fat in baked goods (see page 468).

4 pounds Granny Smith apples, or another
    sweet-tart variety (see listing on page 548),
    peeled, seeded, and sliced
⅓ cup fresh-pressed apple juice (not from
    concentrate)
⅔ cup maple syrup or dark brown sugar
2 teaspoons vanilla extract
1 tablespoon fresh lemon juice
Ground cinnamon, nutmeg, ginger, and/or cloves
    to taste

To make this on the stovetop, place the apples, apple juice, maple syrup or brown sugar, vanilla, lemon juice, cinnamon, nutmeg, ginger, and/or cloves in a large stockpot with a tight-fitting lid. (Alternatively, place the ingredients in a pressure cooker, and consult your owner's manual for the correct pressure and time. If you have a pressure cooker, by all means use it. It seals in flavor more effectively than either the stovetop or microwave method.)

Bring the mixture to a boil over medium-high heat. Reduce the heat to medium-low, and simmer until the apples are soft enough to mash with the back of a wooden spoon, between 15 and 25 minutes, depending on the size and type of apples.

Remove the apple mixture from the heat and puree with an immersion blender. Or transfer to a food processor and process in short spurts until smooth. Don't overdo it, or the results will be watery.

PER SERVING (2 TABLESPOONS): CALORIES 42 • PROTEIN 0 G • CARBOHYDRATE 10 G • FAT 0 G • CHOLESTEROL 0 MG • SODIUM 0 MG • 4% CALORIES FROM FAT

MICROWAVE APPLE BUTTER: To make this in a microwave (which retains flavor nearly as well as a pressure-cooker), reduce the amount of apple juice to 2 tablespoons. Place the apples, apple juice, maple syrup or sugar, vanilla, lemon juice, and cinnamon, nutmeg, ginger, and/or cloves in a microwavable bowl. Cover with plastic wrap or a microwave-resistant plate. Cook on full power for 8 minutes, turning the bowl 180 degrees once halfway through. Check, and if the apples aren't soft enough to mash with the back of a wooden spoon, repeat for 4 minutes. Test again, repeating if necessary. Puree as directed above.

FRUIT SAUCE

Makes 3 cups; serves 6

TOTAL TIME: 3 HOURS, 15 MINUTES, INCLUDING TIME TO CHILL
TIME TO PREPARE: ABOUT 15 MINUTES
COOKING TIME: INCLUDED IN TIME TO PREPARE
REFRIGERATION/FREEZING: REFRIGERATE UP TO 1 WEEK. FREEZE UP TO 6 MONTHS.

*S*erve this over pancakes, waffles, and French toast. You can also stir it into yogurt, or add it to a Fruit Smoothie (page 48).

½ cup apple juice
¼ cup sugar
2 tablespoons fresh lemon juice
2 teaspoons cornstarch
4 cups chopped fresh or frozen fruit of any kind, such as hulled strawberries; whole fresh blueberries; peeled peaches, apricots, or mangoes; pitted cherries; raspberries; rhubarb (see Note)

To make the sauce on the stovetop, in a heavy saucepan, whisk together the apple juice, sugar, lemon juice, and cornstarch. Heat gently over medium heat, stirring often until slightly thickened, about 4 minutes. Add the fruit, cover, and simmer gently, stirring often, until the fruit cooks down into a thick sauce, about 10 minutes.

Remove the sauce from the heat and let cool, stirring often to prevent lumps from forming. Chill thoroughly before serving, at least 3 hours.

Note: To peel peaches or apricots, bring water to a boil in a large pot. Drop in the fruit and allow the water to return to a boil. Let the fruit boil 40 seconds. Remove the fruit with a slotted spoon. When the fruit is cool enough to handle, slip off the skin.

To peel the mango, make 4 equally spaced slits in the skin, lengthwise from the stem. Pull back the skin as if peeling a banana. Slice the fruit off the pit.

For rhubarb, use an additional ½ cup sugar, or ¾ cup sugar total.

PER SERVING (2 TABLESPOONS): CALORIES 92 • PROTEIN 0 G • CARBOHY-DRATE 20.4 G • FAT 0 G • CHOLESTEROL 0 MG • SODIUM 1.95 MG • 4% CALORIES FROM FAT • OUTSTANDING SOURCE OF VITAMIN C

MICROWAVE FRUIT SAUCE: To make this sauce in the microwave, place the apple juice, sugar, lemon juice, and cornstarch in a large glass bowl. Whisk well. Microwave at full power for 1 minute. Whisk again. Add the fruit. Microwave at full power for 3 to 4 minutes, until the fruit has cooked down into a thick sauce. Whisk well and let cool. Cover and chill the fruit thoroughly before serving.

•

F R U I T   J A M

Makes 2 pints

TOTAL TIME: ABOUT 3 HOURS, 30 MINUTES, INCLUDING TIME TO STERILIZE THE JARS AND REST THE FRUIT
TIME TO PREPARE: 2 HOURS
COOKING TIME: 30 MINUTES
EQUIPMENT: 4 HALF-PINT JARS WITH VACUUM SEALS, TONGS, WIDEMOUTHED FUNNEL.
REFRIGERATION/FREEZING: YOU CAN REFRIGERATE THE JAM IN UNSTERILIZED JARS UP TO 2 WEEKS. YOU CAN REFRIG-ERATE JAM IN STERILIZED JARS THAT HAVE BEEN OPENED UP TO 2 WEEKS.

O rdinarily, being "in a jam" is a bad thing —unless the jam you're in happens to be one that you're making. And the way this splatters, you'll be in it for sure.

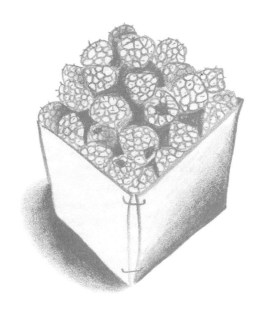

The basic jam recipe below makes a loose jam, jelled by the fruit's natural thickener, pectin. For a firmer consistency, buy a packet of commercial pectin and follow the instructions on the package.

Jam making is a process that calls for more organization than creativity. Take it step by step.

2 cups prepared fruit (see "Preparing the Fruit," page 107)
⅔ cup sugar

Assemble the equipment
Buy at least 4 half-pint glass jars with double-rubber-vacuum-seal lids. You'll also need a rack that fits inside a large saucepan, a good set of tongs, and a widemouthed funnel that tapers down to fit into the jars.

Sterilize the jars
Rinse the jars well, lids and all.

Place them in a large saucepan and add water to cover. Bring to a boil over medium-high heat. Boil for 3 minutes. Remove the pan from the heat and set it aside.

Prepare the fruit

Seed, hull, and/or peel the fruit, depending on type (see below). In a heavy, nonreactive saucepan, combine the prepared fruit with the sugar. Mash with a wide-tined fork or potato masher. Let the fruit rest for 1 to 2 hours, stirring occasionally, until the juices are fully released.

CONSCIENTIOUS COOKS WANT TO KNOW

Q. Do I have to use sugar? Can I substitute fruit concentrate or honey?

A. You *can*, but sugar brings out the fruit flavor more effectively than other sweeteners, including fruit concentrates. It also facilitates jelling, making a firmer jam than you'd get otherwise. Moreover, sugar and other sweeteners have roughly the same number of calories, all of which come from carbohydrates. The amount of vitamins and minerals in honey is so small, it's insignificant. So choose the sweetener that tastes best to you.

Cook the fruit

Bring the mixture to a boil in the heavy saucepan over medium-high heat. Reduce the heat to medium and simmer until the jam is very thick, about 20 to 30 minutes, stirring often and skimming off the white foam that may come to the surface. Pay close attention toward the end, stirring constantly as the jam thickens, or it may stick and burn.

Jar the jam

Spread a double layer of paper towels on a counter. Using tongs, remove the jars from the saucepan and turn them upside down on the paper towels to drain briefly. Place a rack at the bottom of a large saucepan. Fill the pan halfway with water and bring it to a simmer. Fill a tea kettle with water and bring it to a simmer, too. Using a ladle, pour the jam through a funnel into the jars to reach ½ inch from the top. Clamp each jar shut.

Sterilize the jam

(If you're going to eat the jam within 2 weeks, you can skip this step. Simply let it cool and put it in the refrigerator.) Using tongs, place the jars in the saucepan of simmering water. Pour simmering water from the kettle over the jars, covering them by at least 2 inches. Cover the saucepan and simmer over medium-low heat for 10 minutes. Use the tongs to remove the jars. Let them drain on the paper towels.

PER SERVING (2 TABLESPOONS): CALORIES 30.5 • PROTEIN 0 G • CARBOHY-DRATE 7.8 G • FAT 0 G • CHOLESTEROL 0 MG • SODIUM 0.232 MG • 2% CALORIES FROM FAT

PREPARING THE FRUIT

• Peel apricots, peaches, and plums by plunging them into boiling water and waiting for the water to return to a boil. Let the fruit boil for 40 seconds, then remove it with a slotted spoon. When the fruit is cool enough to handle, slip off the skin.
• Pit cherries.
• Hull strawberries and cut them in half.
• Pick over blueberries, removing the stems.
• Trim the stems from figs and cut the fruit in half.
• Use raspberries and blackberries as they are

SALADS

Here's a stumper for you.

What makes something a salad? Greens? Then what about potato salad, pasta salad, three-bean, or lentil salad?

That it's "light"? "Light" would hardly describe the grain salads of the Middle East, the bread salads of Italy, or your average dressing-drenched Caesar.

That it's served cold or at room temperature? Then what about warm grilled vegetable salads?

Is something a salad because it's made of a bunch of different ingredients thrown together? If so, why isn't a stew a salad?

Actually, the very word "salad" is a clue to the definition of the dish. "Salad" comes from the Roman word for "salt." Salt, pure and simple, was a popular dressing in ancient times, the oil and vinegar of its day. This suggests that a salad was anything dressed with salt. In other words, a salad is defined by its dressing; *dressing* makes a salad a salad. A salad, then, is any number of ingredients united by a common dressing.

A salad is supper when those ingredients are varied, wholesome, and substantial enough to make a main course. A salad is a supplement when its flavors, colors, and textures enhance and complement other dishes, rounding out a meal.

Salads in Meal Planning

A well-composed salad can provide a substantial share of your daily values for critical vitamins and minerals. Serve these salads often for a big boost toward the nourishment you need.

TAHINI TABBOULEH (PAGE 149)
150% daily value for vitamin C
53% daily value for folacin
26% daily value for iron
50% daily value for fiber

RICE SALAD WITH SNOW PEAS, RED BEANS, AND SWEET CORN (PAGE 146)
252% daily value for vitamin C
57% daily value for for folacin
31% daily value for iron
41% daily value for thiamin (vitamin B_1)
25% daily value for niacin (vitamin B_3)
60% daily value for fiber

LEMON-SPIKED LENTIL SALAD (PAGE 143)
70% daily value for folacin
33% daily value for iron
28% daily value for fiber

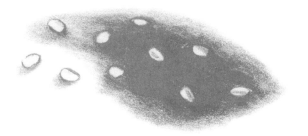

CANNELLINI BEAN AND SPINACH SALAD (PAGE 138)
85% daily value for vitamin C
44% daily value for folacin
35% daily value for vitamin A
28% daily value for vitamin E
28% daily value for fiber

ASPARAGUS SALAD WITH BELL PEPPERS AND EGGS (PAGE 146)
472% daily value for vitamin C
87% daily value for folacin
66% daily value for vitamin E
43% daily value for vitamin A
30% daily value for vitamin B_6
35% daily value for fiber
27% daily value for thiamin (vitamin B_1) and riboflavin (vitamin B_2)

Salad Pantry

You'll find my brand-name recommendations for most of these items on page 595. If you can't find what you want where you shop, see the mail-order information on page 596.

Extra virgin olive oil
Other oils, such as walnut oil, sesame oil, peanut oil
Balsamic vinegar
Wine vinegars (red, white, champagne)
Raspberry vinegar
Rice vinegar
Dijon mustard
Tahini (refrigerate after opening)
Dry-packed sun-dried tomatoes
Bread, for bread salads and croutons

In the Refrigerator
Plain nonfat yogurt
Nonfat or reduced-fat ricotta cheese
Olives (oil cured and salt cured)
Capers
Fresh herbs such as chives, basil, cilantro,
    parsley
Salad greens (see page 112)
Nonfat or reduced-fat sour cream

Simple Salad Menus

Here are some suggestions for serving salads for lunch or supper, paired with a soup, bread, or entrée from other sections of this book.

30-MINUTE MEALS
Quick Fresh Corn Salad (*page 128*)
Creamy Spinach Soup (*page 183*)

Cannellini Bean and Spinach Salad (*page 138*)
Supper Frittata (*page 383*) with herbs and/or
cheese

Tahini Tabbouleh (*page 149*)
Pita Bread (*page 414*)

Summer Market Salad (*page 141*)
Soft and Chewy Dinner Rolls (*page 408*)

Panzanella (*page 150*)
Chickpea and Rosemary Passata (*page 192*)

Peanut Curry with Sweet Potato and Collard
Greens (*page 359*)
Rice
Beet Raita (*page 154*)
Mango Cream (*page 496*)

My Favorite Chickpeas (*page 360*)
Rice
Spinach Raita (*page 156*)

Lemon-Spiked Lentil Salad (*page 143*)
Spinach Risotto (*page 309*)

Cool and Spicy Eggplant Salad with Roasted
Garlic, Ginger, and Mint (*page 135*)
Bulgur and Red Lentil Soup (*page 199*)

Grilled Fresh Corn and Chickpea Patties
(*page 460*)
Mango Salsa (*page 160*)

Curried Egg Salad (*page 145*)
Chilled Cream of Carrot Soup with Ginger
and Lime (*page 201*)

Salad Greens

When you sample the greens below, you'll find that lettuce isn't just lettuce—it's peppery arugula and sharp radicchio, sweet tender Bibb, and crisp, bittersweet romaine, among others.

When you're in the market for greens, look for the following:

Living Color: Fresh greens look alive—vibrant and clear, not dull and cloudy. Make sure the leaves aren't brown around the edges or bruised along the ribs or stems.

Perfect Posture: The leaves should stand up, not droop or curl up at the edges. (Kale, curly endive, and escarole are special cases because they're curly all over. Kale curls should be tight and firm, not limp.)

Clean, Fresh Scent: If you can smell the greens without burrowing your nose into them, back off and buy them elsewhere. Fresh greens should smell only faintly, and that smell should be like fresh air, clean and slightly sweet.

Packaged Greens: When you buy washed, packaged greens, check the sell-by date and inspect the contents, checking for dark rims and bruises on the leaves and other signs of soggy, wilted lettuce, such as faded colors and flattened ribs. Choose packs containing leaves with vibrant colors, and use them as soon as you get them home. Or punch small airholes in the pack and store it in a crisper for one day.

WHAT'S THAT SMELL?, OR THE DISPIRITING TRUTH ABOUT STORING SALAD GREENS

When you get greens home, blot moisture from the leaves with a paper towel. Place them in a large paper bag or a plastic bag with holes in it, and toss them in the crisper compartment of your refrigerator. Do all of this, do what you will, but your greens will be good for only two days. After that they get slimy, and before you know it, those tender little leaves stink like skunk cabbage. So, eat your greens swiftly.

Type of Green: Arugula
How It Looks: Small, flat, oval leaves on stems, sold loose with roots attached
How It Tastes: Strong peppery flavor when raw; much milder pepper flavor when cooked
How Much Makes One Serving: 1 cup, chopped
Try It With: A mixture of other salad

greens, including romaine, baby spinach, radicchio, and mâche and a light oil and vinegar dressing

Type of Green: Baby spinach
How It Looks: Small, oval, light-jade-colored leaves on slender stems, often with roots attached. Unlike mature spinach, the ribs aren't prominent
How It Tastes: Mild, grassy when raw; sweeter, more spinachy, when cooked
How Much Makes One Serving: 1 cup
Try It With: That Japanese Dressing (see page 122)

Type of Green: Belgian endive
How It Looks: Yellow-green leaves in compact, torpedo-shaped heads approximately five inches long
How It Tastes: Sharp, bittersweet when raw; mildly sweet when sautéed
How Much Makes One Serving: 1 small endive
Try It With: Radicchio, walnuts, and mushrooms in a mild lemon dressing (see page 124)

Type of Green: Butterhead (Boston and Bibb) lettuce
How It Looks: Round head; light green, short, rounded leaves clustered in a bouquet-shaped head
How It Tastes: Mild, sweet
How Much Makes One Serving: 1 cup
Try It With: A mixture of other salad greens, including romaine, baby spinach,

radicchio, and mâche and any salad dressing you'd like (see pages 117 to 123)

Type of Green: Collards
How It Looks: Long, wide (approximately eight by five inches at the widest point), firm muted-green leaves with prominent rib in center; sold on sturdy stems. For use raw in salads, buy tender, light-green collards.
How It Tastes: Strong, bitter. Use sparingly, finely shredded, to season other greens.
How Much Makes One Serving: 1 cup, chopped
Try It In: Peanut Curry with Sweet Potato and Collard Greens (see page 359)

Type of Green: Dandelion greens
How It Looks: Long, narrow, saw-toothed leaves
How It Tastes: Strong, bitter
How Much Makes One Serving: 1/2 cup, chopped
Try It With: Baby spinach, tossed with Orange-Sesame Dressing (see page 121)

Type of Green: Escarole
How It Looks: Round head; broad, curly light green floppy leaves; white core; and smooth underside
How It Tastes: Mild, bitter
How Much Makes One Serving: 1 cup, chopped
Try It With: A mixture of other salad greens, including romaine, baby spinach, radicchio, and mâche and the Multipurpose Creamy Dressing (see page 119)

Type of Green: Kale
How It Looks: Large round heads, curly dark green leaves, sometimes purple in the center
How It Tastes: Very pungent when raw; still has substantial kick when cooked
How Much Makes One Serving: 1 cup, chopped
Try It In: Any dish calling for spinach or collards

Type of Green: Mâche (lamb's lettuce)
How It Looks: Tiny, light-jade-colored oval leaves on slender stems
How It Tastes: Delicate, sweet
How Much Makes One Serving: ½ cup, chopped
Try It With: A mixture of other salad greens, including romaine, baby spinach, radicchio, and Raspberry Dressing I (see page 122)

Type of Green: Mustard greens
How It Looks: Wide, saw-toothed, pea-green leaves with a tender rib running into a short stem
How It Tastes: Strong peppery flavor; pungent, milder pepper flavor when stir-fried or sautéed
How Much Makes One Serving: 1 cup, chopped
Try It In: Moo-Shu Mushrooms (see page 374)

Type of Green: Radicchio
How It Looks: Round head, maroon and white leaves packed into tight heads

How It Tastes: Strong, bittersweet flavor when raw; winy, faintly sweet when sautéed
How Much Makes One Serving: 1 cup, chopped
Try It With: Arborio rice and grated Parmesan for Radicchio Risotto (see page 310); endive, walnuts, and mushrooms in a mild lemon dressing (see page 124)

Type of Green: Romaine lettuce
How It Looks: Narrow head, long light green leaves with firm ribs joined at a solid core at the base. The outer leaves may be dark green and floppy, while the inner leaves (the heart) are stiff, ice green, and crisp.
How It Tastes: Strong, bittersweet
How Much Makes One Serving: 1 cup, chopped
Try It With: A creamy Caesar-style Parmesan dressing and fresh croutons in Caesar-Style Summertime Panzanella (see page 152)

Type of Green: Sorrel
How It Looks: Small, light-jade-green leaves shaped like baby spinach, sold in bunches with tender stems attached
How It Tastes: Delicate, lemony
How Much Makes One Serving: ½ cup, chopped
Try It With: A mixture of other salad greens, including romaine, baby spinach, radicchio, and mâche and Raspberry Dressing I (see page 122).

Type of Green: Swiss chard, or chard
How It Looks: Long, wide leaves from thick stems that may be either red or white
How It Tastes: Pungent when raw, slightly milder—but still sharp—when steamed or sautéed
How Much Makes One Serving: 1 cup, chopped
Try It In: Any dish calling for spinach or collards

Type of Green: Watercress
How It Looks: Small, round, dark green leaves on thin stems, sold in clusters
How It Tastes: Strong peppery flavor
How Much Makes One Serving: 1 cup, chopped
Try It In: Mixed fresh herbs in refreshing Creamy Herb Soup (see page 180)

Vinegars

You can infuse vinegar with any flavor you want, then use it to season salads and sauces and to "sweat" instead of sauté (see page 512). The vinegar you infuse should be light and clean tasting, so nothing blocks the flavor of the herbs or fruit you steep in it.

HERB VINEGAR
Makes about 2½ cups

TOTAL TIME: ABOUT 2 WEEKS
TIME TO PREPARE: ABOUT 10 MINUTES
COOKING TIME: ABOUT 2 WEEKS, INCLUDING TIME TO STEEP.
REFRIGERATION: REFRIGERATE UP TO 1 YEAR, IF DESIRED.

1 cup loosely packed fresh herbs (see Note)
2 cups white wine vinegar, champagne vinegar, or rice vinegar

Place the herbs in a sterile jar with an airtight, rubber-rimmed, clamp-top lid.

Bring the vinegar to a boil in a small saucepan. Pour over the herbs.

Seal the jar and let the mixture steep at room temperature for 2 weeks.

Using a fine-mesh sieve and a funnel, if necessary, strain the vinegar into a sterile bottle. Seal with a cork. (For sources of corked bottles, see mail-order information on page 596.)

Store in a cool dark place for up to 1 year.

Note: The herbs to use, alone or in combination, include rosemary, tarragon, thyme, bay leaf, oregano, and basil.

FRUIT VINEGAR

Makes about 1½ cups

TOTAL TIME: ABOUT 2 WEEKS
TIME TO PREPARE: ABOUT 10 MINUTES
COOKING TIME: ABOUT 2 WEEKS, INCLUDING TIME TO
    STEEP
REFRIGERATION: REFRIGERATE UP TO 6 MONTHS,
    IF DESIRED.

½ pound chopped fresh fruit, peeled and seeded
    if necessary (see "Preparing the Fruit")
2½ cups rice vinegar or white wine vinegar
1 tablespoon sugar or honey

Place the fruit in a sterile jar with an airtight, rubber-rimmed, clamp-top lid. Add the vinegar.

Seal the jar and place it in the refrigerator to steep for 2 weeks.

Place a sieve over a nonreactive small saucepan, and strain the vinegar, pressing the fruit against the mesh to express as much juice as possible into the pan. Add the sugar or honey.

Bring the vinegar to a simmer over medium heat. Let it simmer for about 10 minutes, stirring to dissolve the sugar or honey.

Transfer the vinegar to a sterilized bottle and seal with a cork. (For sources of corked bottles, see mail-order information on page 596.)

Store in a cool dark place or in the refrigerator for up to 6 months.

•

PREPARING THE FRUIT

• Peel ripe apricots and peaches by plunging them into boiling water and waiting for the water to return to a boil. Let the fruit boil for 40 seconds, then remove with a slotted spoon. When the fruit is cool enough to handle, slip off the skin and remove the pits. Crush the fruit with a potato masher or the back of a wooden spoon.
• Pick over blueberries, removing the stems. Crush them with a potato masher or the back of a wooden spoon.
• Pit cherries and crush them with a potato masher or the back of a wooden spoon.
• Peel ripe mangoes by making four evenly spaced slices lengthwise from the stem end to the bottom. Pull off the skin as if you were peeling a banana. Cut the fruit away from the pit and chop it into pulp.
• Crush raspberries and blackberries with a potato masher or the back of a wooden spoon.
• Hull strawberries and cut them in half. Crush them with a potato masher or the back of a wooden spoon.

Salad Dressings

A good dressing is a well-balanced blend of sharp and mellow flavors that complements a salad's ingredients and doesn't dominate them.

WHICH TYPE OF DRESSING?

- For tender greens such as Bibb and butter lettuce, and delicate vegetables such as snow peas and asparagus, use light oil and vinegar or low-fat vinaigrette-style dressings.
- For sturdy greens such as romaine and radicchio, hearty vegetables such as cauliflower and potatoes, and substantial main-dish salads, you can use a light oil-and-vinegar-based dressing or a richer cream-style dressing.
- For more flavor with less dressing, chop fresh herbs and toss them with the salad greens.
- If you use a mixture of flavorful greens (see listings on pages 112 to 115), you can skip the oil entirely and dress your salad lightly with a good fruit or balsamic vinegar or with fresh lemon, lime, or orange juice.

VINAIGRETTE-STYLE DRESSING
Greatly Reduced Fat
Makes 1 cup

TOTAL TIME: 15 MINUTES
TIME TO PREPARE: 5 MINUTES
COOKING TIME: ABOUT 10 MINUTES
REFRIGERATION/FREEZING: REFRIGERATE UP TO 1 WEEK.
    DO NOT FREEZE.

Here's how to use vegetable broth to make a reduced-fat version of classic vinaigrette. Thickened with arrowroot or cornstarch, the broth provides a creamy, flavorful base that incorporates the oil into a full-bodied dressing. Dressing made this way has fewer than half the calories in conventional vinaigrette.

½ cup vegetable broth
1½ teaspoons arrowroot or cornstarch
¼ cup extra virgin olive oil
¼ cup balsamic or red wine vinegar
Salt
Seasonings to taste (see "Now Try This," page
    118)

Place all but 2 tablespoons of the broth in a small saucepan and bring to a boil over medium-high heat. Reduce the heat to medium, keeping the broth at a simmer. Put the remaining broth in a small mixing bowl and stir in the arrowroot or cornstarch.

Stirring constantly, whisk the arrowroot or cornstarch mixture into the simmering broth. Continue whisking until the mixture is just thick enough to coat the whisk with a fine film, about 5 minutes.

Remove from the heat and let cool completely. Season with salt.

Using an electric hand mixer or a Mixmaster fitted with a whisk, whip the oil and vinegar into the thickened broth. The mixture should incorporate the oil and vinegar in a smooth dressing.

PER SERVING (2 TABLESPOONS): CALORIES 32.5 • PROTEIN 0.1 G • CARBOHYDRATE 0.4 G • FAT 3.4 G • CHOLESTEROL 0 MG • SODIUM 24.3 MG • 92% CALORIES FROM FAT

NOW TRY THIS: Add 1 teaspoon Dijon mustard when you add the oil and vinegar.

Stir in 1 teaspoon minced, drained, and rinsed capers at the end.

Stir in ½ teaspoon grated garlic plus 1 teaspoon grated lemon zest at the end; or stir in 2 tablespoons minced fresh herbs, such as chives, basil, or cilantro.

DRESSING BASICS

• The classic proportion for oil and vinegar dressing is 3 parts oil to 1 part vinegar, for example:

3 tablespoons extra virgin olive oil
1 tablespoon balsamic vinegar

• If you use an oil with intense flavor, such as walnut oil or premium extra virgin olive oil, you can lower the ratio to 2 to 1 or even 1½ to 1:

1½ tablespoons walnut oil
1 tablespoon balsamic vinegar

• You can reduce the proportion of oil to 1 to 1 by using a mild vinegar, such as rice vinegar, or fruit vinegar:

1 tablespoon walnut oil
1 tablespoon raspberry vinegar

• You can extend the flavor of any oil and vinegar dressing without additional fat by adding an amount of rich vegetable broth equal to the amount of oil:

1 tablespoon extra virgin olive oil
1 tablespoon vegetable broth
1 tablespoon balsamic vinegar

• Now that many good fat-free dairy products are available—such as yogurt, ricotta cheese, and sour cream—you can make low-fat cream-style dressings. However, the quality of these products varies widely from one company to another. Some are delicious; some are dreadful. Read the labels and choose products made without artificial ingredients. Then sample several of those to find which taste best to you. (You'll find my brand-name recommendations on page 595.)

SERVING BASICS

• Wait until you're about to serve the salad before you dress it, or it will get soggy. Pour or spoon the dressing evenly over the leaves and fold it—rather than toss it—gently but thoroughly into the greens so it's evenly distributed. Use just enough to make the leaves glisten. They shouldn't look slick or soaked.

• To save time, mix the dressing in the salad bowl and fold the greens into the dressing.

• You can squirt the dressing on your salad using a plant mister. Adjust the nozzle to fine mist, squirt the greens lightly, and gently fold them until dressed.

•

ORANGE-VINAIGRETTE-STYLE DRESSING
Oil Free

Makes about 1 cup

TOTAL TIME: 5 MINUTES
TIME TO PREPARE: 5 MINUTES
COOKING TIME: INCLUDED IN TIME TO PREPARE
REFRIGERATION/FREEZING: REFRIGERATE UP TO 5 DAYS. DO NOT FREEZE.

1 cup fresh orange or pineapple juice
2 tablespoons rice vinegar
1 tablespoon low-sodium soy sauce
1 teaspoon Dijon mustard
2 teaspoons light honey
2 teaspoons cornstarch

Combine the juice, vinegar, soy sauce, mustard, honey, and cornstarch in a small saucepan. Bring to a gentle simmer over medium-high heat, whisking constantly. Reduce the heat to medium-low and continue whisking until the dressing is thickened, about 5 minutes.

Remove from the heat and let the dressing cool. Stir well before serving. If the dressing is too thick, dilute it with additional fruit juice.

PER SERVING (2 TABLESPOONS): CALORIES 34.2 • PROTEIN 0.4 G • CARBOHYDRATE 8.3 G • FAT 0 G • CHOLESTEROL 0 MG • SODIUM 110 MG • 2% CALORIES FROM FAT • GOOD SOURCE OF VITAMIN C

•

MULTIPURPOSE CREAMY DRESSING

Makes 2 1/2 cups

TOTAL TIME: FEWER THAN 5 MINUTES
TIME TO PREPARE: FEWER THAN 5 MINUTES
COOKING TIME: NONE

1 cup nonfat or part-skim ricotta cheese
1 1/2 cups plain nonfat yogurt or nonfat sour cream
1/2 teaspoon Dijon mustard
1 tablespoon fresh lemon juice
2 teaspoons balsamic or fruit vinegar, such as raspberry, blueberry, or strawberry
1 scallion, including greens, minced (optional)
2 tablespoons minced fresh herbs, such as chives, parsley, basil

Combine the ricotta, yogurt or sour cream, mustard, lemon juice, vinegar, scallion if using, and herbs in a food processor or blender. Process until smooth.

PER SERVING (2 TABLESPOONS): CALORIES 25 • PROTEIN 3.59 G • CARBOHYDRATE 2.61 G • FAT 0 G • CHOLESTEROL 0 MG • SODIUM 17.6 MG • 2% CALORIES FROM FAT

•

CREAMY CHIVE DRESSING

Makes about 3 cups

TOTAL TIME: 5 MINUTES
TIME TO PREPARE: 5 MINUTES
COOKING TIME: NONE
REFRIGERATION/FREEZING: REFRIGERATE UP TO 5 DAYS. DO
   NOT FREEZE.

Great on potato salads, fresh chopped tomatoes, and lettuces of all kinds, it's equally good as a dip for steamed vegetables. Flecked with green, it's also very pretty.

1/2 teaspoon grated garlic

2 cups nonfat yogurt

1 cup low-fat cottage cheese or nonfat ricotta cheese

1/2 cup minced fresh chives

4 scallions, white part and 1 inch of greens, chopped

1 teaspoon Dijon mustard

2 tablespoons fresh lemon juice

1 tablespoon honey

1 teaspoon low-sodium soy sauce

Combine the garlic, yogurt, and cottage cheese or ricotta in a food processor or blender, and process until smooth.

Transfer the mixture to a mixing bowl and stir in the chives, scallions, mustard, lemon juice, honey, and soy sauce.

PER SERVING (2 TABLESPOONS): CALORIES 45 • PROTEIN 4.2 G • CARBOHYDRATE 6 G • FAT 0 G • CHOLESTEROL 1.5 MG • SODIUM 130 MG • 6% CALORIES FROM FAT • GOOD SOURCE OF CALCIUM

•

AVOCADO-BUTTERMILK DRESSING

Makes about 1 1/4 cups

TOTAL TIME: 10 MINUTES
TIME TO PREPARE: 10 MINUTES
COOKING TIME: NONE
REFRIGERATION/FREEZING: REFRIGERATE UP TO 4 DAYS. DO
   NOT FREEZE.

Avocado gives body and a buttery finish to this multipurpose cream-style dressing. Enjoy it over mixed greens or as a dressing for chilled, steamed vegetables such as broccoli, potatoes, sugar snap peas, or fresh corn. Taste the basic mixture before you decide which of the optional ingredients to add. Also consider what you're serving, adding cilantro and cumin to complement a Southwest entrée, for example, or ginger and garlic to go with a Far Eastern dish.

1/2 ripe avocado, cut into chunks

1/2 cup nonfat buttermilk

1/4 cup nonfat or reduced-fat sour cream

1 teaspoon Dijon mustard

2 tablespoons fresh lemon juice

1 scallion, including greens, chopped

Additional Seasonings to Mix and Match (optional)

1 tablespoon minced fresh chives

¼ teaspoon grated garlic

1 tablespoon minced fresh cilantro

1 teaspoon grated peeled fresh ginger

½ teaspoon ground cumin

2 teaspoons minced reconstituted dried ancho chili

Combine the avocado, buttermilk, sour cream, mustard, lemon juice, and scallion in a food processor or blender. Process until smooth. Add any of the seasonings you'd like and process again.

PER SERVING (2 TABLESPOONS): CALORIES 35 • PROTEIN 1.7 G • CARBOHY-DRATE 3.3 G • FAT 1.9 G • CHOLESTEROL 0 MG • SODIUM 26.8 MG • 46% CALORIES FROM FAT

ORANGE-SESAME DRESSING

Makes about 1½ cups

TOTAL TIME: ABOUT 1 HOUR, 35 MINUTES, INCLUDING TIME TO COOL
TIME TO PREPARE: 20 MINUTES
COOKING TIME: 10 MINUTES
REFRIGERATION/FREEZING: REFRIGERATE UP TO 5 DAYS. DO NOT FREEZE.

Serve this sweet, creamy, Asian-influenced low-fat dressing on chilled steamed asparagus or broccoli, or drizzle it over mixed leafy greens.

½ cup fresh orange juice

½ teaspoon grated garlic

1 teaspoon grated peeled fresh ginger

½ teaspoon Dijon mustard

1 teaspoon low-sodium soy sauce

1 tablespoon rice vinegar

1 teaspoon cornstarch

1 cup plain nonfat yogurt or soft tofu

1 tablespoon sesame seeds, toasted (see Note)

In a small saucepan, combine the orange juice, garlic, ginger, mustard, soy sauce, vinegar, and cornstarch. Bring the mixture to a simmer over medium-high heat, stirring often until it thickens, about 10 minutes. Remove from the heat and let it cool to room temperature, stirring often to keep it from getting gelatinous, about 1 hour. Meanwhile, in a small bowl, whisk or beat the yogurt or tofu until it's smooth and creamy. When the orange mixture is thoroughly cool, beat in the yogurt or tofu with a hand mixer. Stir in the sesame seeds.

Note: To toast sesame seeds, spread the seeds in a single layer on a sheet of aluminum foil. Bake in a toaster oven or conventional oven at 350° F. until the seeds turn golden brown, about 3 minutes. Watch closely to prevent burning.

PER SERVING (2 TABLESPOONS): CALORIES 44 • PROTEIN 2.6 G • CARBOHYDRATE 7 G • FAT 0 G • CHOLESTEROL 0 MG • SODIUM 92.5 MG • 13% CALORIES FROM FAT • GOOD SOURCE OF VITAMIN C

•

THAT JAPANESE DRESSING

Makes about ¼ cup

TOTAL TIME: 3 MINUTES
TIME TO PREPARE: 3 MINUTES
REFRIGERATION/FREEZING: REFRIGERATE UP TO 1 MONTH.
  DO NOT FREEZE.

You know, the sweet and tangy one you get with your meal at Japanese restaurants. Serve this over crisp mixed greens, or over fresh cleaned spinach.

2 tablespoons low-sodium soy sauce
1 tablespoon rice vinegar
1 tablespoon light sesame oil (see Note)
1 teaspoon sugar
1 teaspoon grated fresh ginger

In a small bowl, combine the soy sauce, rice vinegar, sesame oil, sugar, and ginger. Mix until well blended.

Note: Don't use dark sesame oil; the flavor will dominate.

PER SERVING (1 TABLESPOON): CALORIES 38.5 • PROTEIN 0 G • CARBOHYDRATE 1.44 G • FAT 3.4 G • CHOLESTEROL 0 MG • SODIUM 405 MG • 78% CALORIES FROM FAT

•

RASPBERRY DRESSING I

Makes about 1 cup

TOTAL TIME: FEWER THAN 5 MINUTES
TIME TO PREPARE: FEWER THAN 5 MINUTES
COOKING TIME: NONE
REFRIGERATION/FREEZING: REFRIGERATE UP TO 5 DAYS. DO
  NOT FREEZE.

Smooth, tangy, and just sweet enough, this dressing goes well with mixed greens or steamed vegetables.

¼ teaspoon minced garlic
½ teaspoon Dijon mustard
½ cup nonfat or part-skim ricotta cheese
½ cup plain nonfat yogurt
1 tablespoon fresh lemon juice
1 tablespoon raspberry vinegar
2 tablespoons minced fresh chives

Combine the garlic, mustard, ricotta, yogurt, lemon juice, raspberry vinegar, and chives in a food processor or blender. Process until smooth.

PER SERVING (2 TABLESPOONS): CALORIES 29 • PROTEIN 4.25 G • CARBOHYDRATE 2.9 G • FAT 0 G • CHOLESTEROL 0 MG • SODIUM 21 MG • 2% CALORIES FROM FAT

•

RASPBERRY DRESSING II

Makes about ½ cup

TOTAL TIME: FEWER THAN 5 MINUTES
TIME TO PREPARE: FEWER THAN 5 MINUTES
COOKING TIME: NONE
REFRIGERATION/FREEZING: REFRIGERATE UP TO 5 DAYS. DO
  NOT FREEZE.

I *personally would never suggest such a thing, but* *if you were the type to go in for corny food* *analogies you might compare raspberry vinegar* *to a soprano and walnut oil to a bass, then go on to* *say that together they make fresh salad greens sing.*

2 tablespoons raspberry vinegar

3 tablespoons nonfat or reduced-fat sour cream

3 tablespoons vegetable broth

2 teaspoons walnut oil

1 teaspoon Dijon mustard

Whisk together the vinegar, sour cream, vegetable broth, walnut oil, and mustard.

PER SERVING (2 TABLESPOONS): CALORIES 27 • PROTEIN 0 G • CARBOHYDRATE 1.2 G • FAT 2.3 G • CHOLESTEROL 0 MG • SODIUM 238 MG • 72% CALORIES FROM FAT

Side-Dish Salads

FIVE SALADS
Four Ingredients

H *ere are five very simple salads, each calling for only four ingredients. Determine the proportions according to taste, and embellish if you'd like, in any way you'd like.*

Fennel and Orange

Toss together

Chopped fennel

Thinly sliced Vidalia onions

Fresh orange slices

Extra virgin olive oil

Beet and Dill

Combine

Shredded steamed or roasted beets

Plain nonfat yogurt

Chopped scallions

Minced fresh dill

Potato and Chive

Combine

Chopped boiled potatoes

Pureed avocado

Plain nonfat yogurt

Minced fresh chives

Tomato and Mozzarella

Lay on a plate

Sliced ripe tomatoes

Top with

Thinly sliced fresh mozzarella or shaved
    Parmesan cheese

Shredded fresh basil

Extra virgin olive oil

Spinach and Pine Nut

Toss together

Baby spinach

Toasted pine nuts (see Note, page 122)

Fresh orange juice

Walnut oil (just a drop)

SIDE-DISH SALAD BASICS

The difference between a salad you serve on the side and one you serve as a main course may be only a matter of size. But it may also be that side-dish salads, while varied and delicious, aren't substantial enough for dinner unless you serve them with another salad or an entrée of some kind.

• Use fresh ingredients. This is essential for simple salads that are lightly dressed, when there's little to mask the "distinctive taste" of aging produce.

• Make sure the salad's seasoning complements the main course—a Southwest-spiced (cumin and cilantro) corn salad with tacos, for example, or cooling Cucumber Raita (yogurt, scallions, and chives) with curry.

• Balance the ingredients in the whole meal, avoiding repetition. For example, if the main course has a yogurt sauce, serve a salad with a vinaigrette-style dressing. If the entrée calls for cheese, make a salad that does not.

• Consider the colors. A variety of colors, including varying shades of a single color, indicates a range of nutrients. If your main course is heavy on greens and grains, consider a tomato salad. If it's a tomato-based entrée, try mixed greens. If your salad plate is monochromatic, try spicing it up with grated carrot, radish slices, or shredded beets.

• Think in terms of textures. Crispy salads complement pasta entrées, soups, and stews; chewy marinated mushrooms go well with entrées featuring crispy ingredients, such as stir-fries.

ENDIVE, RADICCHIO, AND MUSHROOM SALAD

Serves 4

TOTAL TIME: ABOUT 10 MINUTES
TIME TO PREPARE: ABOUT 10 MINUTES
COOKING TIME: NONE
REFRIGERATION/FREEZING: REFRIGERATE UP TO 1 DAY. DO
  NOT FREEZE.

You'll love this in late autumn, when endive and radicchio are in season, and you welcome the warm taste of walnuts. Serve this with a hearty soup or with anything containing lentils.

3 Belgian endives

1 medium head radicchio

2 cups loosely packed sliced white button or
    cremini mushrooms

1/2 cup coarsely chopped walnuts

Juice of 1/2 lemon

1 tablespoon walnut oil

Salt and freshly ground black pepper to taste

Chop the endives and radicchio and place them in a large salad bowl. Add the mushrooms and walnuts and toss well.

Combine the lemon juice and walnut oil. Drizzle the mixture over the salad and toss gently. Season with salt and pepper. Serve right away.

PER SERVING: CALORIES 119 · PROTEIN 3 G · CARBOHYDRATE 7 G · FAT 9.8 G · CHOLESTEROL 0 MG · SODIUM 16.8 MG · 69% CALORIES FROM FAT · VERY GOOD SOURCE OF VITAMIN C; FOLACIN · GOOD SOURCE OF VITAMIN B₂

•

RADICCHIO WITH POTATOES AND CELERY

Serves 4

TOTAL TIME: ABOUT 25 MINUTES
TIME TO PREPARE: ABOUT 5 MINUTES
COOKING TIME: 20 MINUTES
DO AHEAD: YOU CAN MAKE THE DRESSING UP TO 2 DAYS AHEAD. COVER AND REFRIGERATE.
REFRIGERATION/FREEZING: REFRIGERATE UP TO 2 DAYS. DO NOT FREEZE.

*O*rdinarily celery strikes me as nature's flawed first draft of the far more flavorful fennel. But in this dish, it's just right in crunchy contrast to the tender potatoes.

2 medium Yukon Gold or red potatoes
2 large eggs
1 head radicchio, torn
2 celery stalks, thinly sliced
2 teaspoons Dijon mustard
½ cup loosely packed whole fresh parsley leaves
Juice of 1 lemon
2 tablespoons extra virgin olive oil
Salt and freshly ground black pepper to taste

Bring the potatoes with water to cover to a boil in a large pot, and boil the potatoes in their skins until you can just pierce them with a fork, about 2 minutes. Drain, and let them cool. Slice the potatoes ⅓ inch thick. Meanwhile, hard boil the eggs (see page 65).

Slice one of the eggs in half. Remove the yolk and set it aside. Slice the egg white and the remaining whole egg. Arrange the sliced egg, potatoes, radicchio, and celery on 4 serving plates.

With a hand mixer or a compact food processor, combine the reserved egg yolk, mustard, parsley, lemon juice, and olive oil into a smooth sauce. Drizzle over the salads. Season with salt and pepper.

PER SERVING: CALORIES 165 · PROTEIN 3.5 G · CARBOHYDRATE 17 G · FAT 9.6 G · CHOLESTEROL 106 MG · SODIUM 65 MG · 51% CALORIES FROM FAT · OUTSTANDING SOURCE OF VITAMIN C · GOOD SOURCE OF VITAMIN B₆; FOLACIN

SALAD OF BABY ARTICHOKES AND SHIITAKE MUSHROOMS

Serves 4

TOTAL TIME: ABOUT 3 HOURS, 50 MINUTES, INCLUDING
   TIME TO CHILL
TIME TO PREPARE: ABOUT 40 MINUTES, INCLUDING TIME
   TO SAUTÉ
COOKING TIME: 10 MINUTES
DO AHEAD: YOU CAN PREPARE THE ARTICHOKES UP TO 2
   DAYS IN ADVANCE. REFRIGERATE UNTIL READY TO USE.
REFRIGERATION/FREEZING: REFRIGERATE UP TO 1 DAY. DO
   NOT FREEZE.

*W*ell, they sure looked pretty in the produce department. But now that you've
brought them home, you'll be darned if
you know what to do with those adorable baby artichokes. You can't eat them raw, and they're too small
to steam, peel, or stuff. The solution is salad, especially this one, with chewy fresh shiitake mushrooms.

Juice of 1 lemon
2 pounds baby artichokes, trimmed
1 tablespoon extra virgin olive oil
1 garlic clove, thinly sliced
2 scallions, white part only, chopped
2 tablespoons minced fresh parsley
¼ red bell pepper, cored, seeded, and thinly
   sliced
1 teaspoon grated lemon zest
8 ounces shiitake mushrooms, cleaned, trimmed,
   and sliced
2 teaspoons white wine vinegar
Salt and freshly ground black pepper to taste

Place the lemon juice in a nonreactive
saucepan (such as enamel). Add the artichokes
and toss well. Add water to cover the artichokes and bring to a simmer over medium
heat. Simmer gently until the artichokes are
tender enough to pierce through the center
with a paring knife, about 7 minutes. Using a
slotted spoon, transfer the artichokes to a plate
and let them cool.

In a medium skillet, heat the oil over
medium-high heat. Add the garlic and swish
the slices through the oil until they start to
turn golden brown. Remove the garlic and discard. Add the scallions, parsley, red pepper,
and lemon zest and sauté until soft, about 10
minutes. Add the mushrooms and stir to coat
with the vegetables. Add the vinegar and continue cooking, stirring often, until the mushrooms are cooked through, about 6 minutes.
Remove the mixture from the heat.

Cut the artichokes in half or, if large
enough, quarters. Put them into a mixing bowl
and add the mushroom mixture. Toss well, and

chill for at least 3 hours before serving. Season with salt and pepper to serve.

PER SERVING: CALORIES 220 • PROTEIN 10 G • CARBOHYDRATE 45 G • FAT 4 G • CHOLESTEROL 0 MG • SODIUM 222 MG • 14% CALORIES FROM FAT • OUTSTANDING SOURCE OF VITAMIN C; FOLACIN • VERY GOOD SOURCE OF VITAMINS B₂, B₃, B₆; IRON, CALCIUM • GOOD SOURCE OF ZINC

•

GRILLED PORTOBELLO MUSHROOMS ON MESCLUN

Serves 4

TOTAL TIME: 3 HOURS, 25 MINUTES, TO 6 HOURS, 25 MINUTES, INCLUDING TIME TO MARINATE
TIME TO PREPARE: ABOUT 15 MINUTES
COOKING TIME: ABOUT 10 MINUTES
DO AHEAD: YOU CAN MARINATE THE MUSHROOMS UP TO 1 DAY IN ADVANCE. REFRIGERATE, COVERED, UNTIL READY TO USE.
REFRIGERATION/FREEZING: REFRIGERATE OVERNIGHT. DO NOT FREEZE.

I*t's always tempting to refer to mushrooms as "meaty," but this may be mystifying or repugnant to the growing number of people who've been vegetarian since birth. So, how to describe a vegetable (fungus, really) that can be as big as a beach umbrella and is as porous as eggplant but far more firm? That gets juicy when grilled, and is fun to chew? That complements mesclun and tastes terrific topped with finely shaved Parmesan?*

2 tablespoons extra virgin olive oil
3 tablespoons balsamic vinegar
2 scallions, including greens, minced
1 shallot, minced
1 tablespoon minced fresh basil, or 1 teaspoon crumbled dried basil
1 tablespoon minced fresh oregano, or 1 teaspoon crumbled dried oregano
10 ounces portobello mushroom caps, wiped clean and thickly sliced
4 cups mesclun
Salt and freshly ground black pepper to taste
Finely shaved Parmesan cheese, for garnish (optional and encouraged)

In a glass or earthenware bowl or baking dish, combine the olive oil, vinegar, scallions, shallot, basil, and oregano. Whisk well to mix. Add the mushroom caps and stir well to coat with the oil mixture. Cover with plastic wrap and refrigerate for 3 to 6 hours, stirring occasionally.

To grill, heat a charcoal, gas, or stovetop grill. When the grill is hot, add the mushrooms and drizzle with the marinade. Cover and cook until tender and cooked through, about 6 minutes. (It may be more depending on the thickness of the mushrooms and the heat of your grill.) Turn the mushrooms to cook the other side briefly, about 3 minutes.

To broil, heat the broiler. Lay the mushrooms on the broiler tray and drizzle with the marinade. Place the tray in the broiler about 1½ inches from the heat. Broil until the mushrooms soften, about 4 minutes. Turn the mushrooms over to broil the other side until tender, about 4 minutes more.

Distribute the mesclun evenly on serving plates. Place several grilled mushroom slices on top. Season with salt and pepper, and top with several slivers of shaved Parmesan, if you'd like.

PER SERVING: CALORIES 96 • PROTEIN 2.5 G • CARBOHYDRATE 7.14 G • FAT 7.2 G • CHOLESTEROL 0 MG • SODIUM 7.36 MG • 63% CALORIES FROM FAT • VERY GOOD SOURCE OF VITAMIN B₂ • GOOD SOURCE OF VITAMINS B₃, C; FOLACIN

COOL CUCUMBER-POTATO SALAD

Serves 4

TOTAL TIME: ABOUT 20 MINUTES, NOT INCLUDING TIME TO
   COOK THE POTATOES AND BEETS
TIME TO PREPARE: ABOUT 20 MINUTES
COOKING TIME: NONE
REFRIGERATION/FREEZING: REFRIGERATE UP TO 3 DAYS. DO
   NOT FREEZE.

M*ix this in the morning, give it a few
hours to chill, and you'll have the most
refreshing lunch you can imagine.*

1 large cucumber, peeled, seeded, and chopped
   (see page 526)
2 scallions, white part plus 1 inch of greens,
   chopped
1 pound medium waxy potatoes, such as Yukon
   Gold, cut into bite-sized pieces (see page 534)
2 tablespoons minced fresh chives
1/2 pound beets, steamed or baked, peeled and
   chopped (see page 518; optional)
1/2 cup low-fat cottage cheese
2/3 cup plain nonfat yogurt
1 tablespoon fresh lemon juice
Salt and freshly ground black pepper to taste

In a large mixing bowl, combine the cucumber,
scallions, potatoes, chives, and beets, if using.

   In a food processor or blender, or in a bowl
with an immersion blender, combine the cottage cheese, yogurt, and lemon juice until
smooth. Pour over the potato mixture and stir
well. Season with salt and pepper. Serve at
room temperature, or chill and serve cold.

PER SERVING: CALORIES 170 • PROTEIN 8.5 G • CARBOHYDRATE 34 G • FAT 0 G •
CHOLESTEROL 1.6 MG • SODIUM 182 MG • 3% CALORIES FROM FAT • OUTSTANDING
SOURCE OF VITAMIN C • VERY GOOD SOURCE OF VITAMIN B₆; FOLACIN • GOOD
SOURCE OF VITAMINS B₁, B₂, B₃

QUICK FRESH CORN SALAD

Serves 4

TOTAL TIME: ABOUT 15 MINUTES
TIME TO PREPARE: ABOUT 2 MINUTES
COOKING TIME: 8 TO 10 MINUTES
REFRIGERATION/FREEZING: REFRIGERATE UP TO 2 DAYS. DO
   NOT FREEZE.

Q*uick, fresh, and good, this salad takes
roughly two minutes of your precious
summer time. If you don't have chives,
just double the amount of scallion greens, cutting it
finely with kitchen shears, if you have them, and a
knife if you don't.*

4 ears of corn
1 scallion, including greens, chopped
8 cherry tomatoes, halved
1/4 cup minced fresh chives
1 cup plain nonfat yogurt
Salt and freshly ground black pepper to taste

Bring a large pot of water to a boil. Add the
corn and let the water return to a boil. Cover
the pot, turn off the heat, and leave the corn
for 8 to 10 minutes. (If you're using an electric
stove, take the pot off the burner.) Transfer the
corn to a plate to let it cool. (Or cook the corn
in the microwave according to the directions
on page 526.)

   Scrape the kernels off the cobs into a large
mixing bowl. Add the scallion, tomatoes, and
chives, and toss well. Add the yogurt and stir
thoroughly. Season with salt and pepper. Serve
at room temperature, or chill and serve cold.

PER SERVING: CALORIES 140 • PROTEIN 6.8 G • CARBOHYDRATE 29 G • FAT 1.7 G •
CHOLESTEROL 0 MG • SODIUM 53.5 MG • 10% CALORIES FROM FAT • VERY GOOD
SOURCE OF VITAMINS B₁, C • GOOD SOURCE OF VITAMINS B₂, B₃; FOLACIN

CORN AND RED PEPPER SALAD WITH CARAMELIZED SWEET ONIONS

Serves 6

TOTAL TIME: ABOUT 1 HOUR
TIME TO PREPARE: 10 MINUTES
COOKING TIME: ABOUT 50 MINUTES
DO AHEAD: YOU CAN COOK AND SCRAPE THE CORN UP TO 3 DAYS IN ADVANCE. REFRIGERATE, WRAPPED.
REFRIGERATION/FREEZING: REFRIGERATE, WRAPPED, UP TO 3 DAYS. DO NOT FREEZE.

*Y*ou get only one day to eat corn at its best, and that's the day it's been picked, a vexing fact of nature that defies vacuum packs and flash freezers. I have known this for years, yet all summer every summer I stop daily at each produce stand in my area and buy an armload of ears. I'd need a silo if it weren't for salads like this, calling for corn that's not necessarily just picked (and the *Incredible Corn Soup* on page 179).

6 ears of corn
2 teaspoons extra virgin olive oil
1 Vidalia or red onion, thinly sliced
1 tablespoon balsamic vinegar
2 red bell peppers, roasted, peeled, and chopped (see page 534)
¼ cup minced fresh basil
Salt and freshly ground black pepper to taste

Bring a large pot of water to a boil. Add the corn and let the water return to a boil. Cover the pot, turn off the heat, and leave the corn for 8 to 10 minutes. (If you're using an electric stove, take the pot off the burner.) Transfer the corn to a plate to let it cool. (Or cook the corn in the microwave according to directions on page 526.)

Meanwhile, heat the oil in a large skillet over medium heat, swirling the pan to coat the bottom. Add the onion, reduce the heat to medium, and sauté, stirring often, until the onion turns a light caramel color, about 40 minutes. Add the vinegar, raise the heat to medium-high, and stir until the liquid evaporates, about 1 minute. Turn off the heat.

Scrape the kernels off the cobs into a large mixing bowl. Add the onion, peppers, and basil. Toss well and season with salt and pepper. Serve at room temperature, or chill and serve cold.

PER SERVING: CALORIES 155 • PROTEIN 4.4 G • CARBOHYDRATE 32.9 G • FAT 3.14 G • CHOLESTEROL 0 MG • SODIUM 21.6 MG • 16% CALORIES FROM FAT • VERY GOOD SOURCE OF VITAMIN C • GOOD SOURCE OF VITAMINS B₁, B₃; FOLACIN

●

SPICY CORN SALAD WITH JALAPEÑO PEPPERS

Serves 4

TOTAL TIME: ABOUT 3 HOURS, 30 MINUTES, INCLUDING TIME TO CHILL
TIME TO PREPARE: 25 MINUTES
COOKING TIME: 8 TO 10 MINUTES
DO AHEAD: YOU CAN ROAST THE PEPPERS UP TO 3 DAYS IN ADVANCE. YOU CAN MAKE THE DRESSING UP TO 1 WEEK IN ADVANCE.
REFRIGERATION/FREEZING: REFRIGERATE UP TO 3 DAYS. DO NOT FREEZE.

While delicious freshly made, this salad tastes even better the next day. Credit the complex seasonings, which need time to mingle and meld.

Salad

6 ears of corn

2 jalapeño peppers, roasted and peeled (see page 534)

2 scallions, including greens, minced

⅓ cup minced fresh cilantro

1½ cups cherry tomatoes, halved

Dressing

½ ripe avocado, sliced

1 teaspoon Dijon mustard

1 small garlic clove, crushed

2 tablespoons fresh lemon juice

½ cup nonfat buttermilk or plain nonfat yogurt

¼ cup nonfat or reduced-fat sour cream

2 teaspoons ground cumin

For the Salad

Bring a large pot of water to a boil. Add the corn and let the water return to a boil. Cover the pot, turn off the heat, and leave the corn for 8 to 10 minutes. (If you're using an electric stove, take the pot off the burner.) Transfer the corn to a plate to let it cool. (Or cook the corn in the microwave according to the directions on page 526.)

Scrape the corn kernels off the cobs into a large mixing bowl. Add the peppers, scallions, cilantro, and cherry tomatoes and toss well.

For the Dressing

In a food processor, combine the avocado, mustard, garlic, lemon juice, buttermilk or yogurt, sour cream, and cumin. Process until smooth.

Add the dressing to the salad and toss. Cover with plastic wrap and chill for at least 3 hours before serving.

PER SERVING: CALORIES 104 • PROTEIN 3 G • CARBOHYDRATE 20.5 G • FAT 2.7 G • CHOLESTEROL 5.1 MG • SODIUM 7.5 MG • 21% CALORIES FROM FAT • OUTSTANDING SOURCE OF VITAMIN C • GOOD SOURCE OF VITAMINS A, B₁, B₆

CITRUS-MARINATED ASPARAGUS WITH SESAME SEEDS AND PINE NUTS

Serves 4

TOTAL TIME: ABOUT 1 HOUR, INCLUDING TIME TO CHILL
TIME TO PREPARE: ABOUT 35 MINUTES, INCLUDING TIME
   TO BLANCH AND SAUTÉ
COOKING TIME: 4 MINUTES
REFRIGERATION/FREEZING: REFRIGERATE UP TO 3 DAYS. DO
   NOT FREEZE.

I*f you took all of the asparagus that grew in one season and laid it end to end . . . you'd eventually wonder what on earth you were doing and decide to cook it with pine nuts and sesame seeds for a real treat instead.*

1 pound asparagus, trimmed and pared

1 tablespoon extra virgin olive oil

2 scallions, white part plus 1 inch of greens,
   minced

1 shallot, minced

1 garlic clove, minced

2 tablespoons minced fresh cilantro

1 tablespoon grated peeled fresh ginger

½ cup fresh orange juice

2 tablespoons fresh lemon juice

1 tablespoon low-sodium soy sauce

1 tablespoon sesame seeds, toasted (see Note,
   page 122)

1 tablespoon pine nuts, toasted (see Note,
   page 122)

Put a rack or a steamer basket on the bottom of a large saucepan.

Add water until it almost touches the rack. Bring the water to a boil. Add the asparagus, cover the pot, and steam over medium heat until the asparagus is bright green and crisp, about 2 to 7 minutes, depending on the size.

Heat the oil in a small skillet over medium-high heat. When it's hot, add the scallions, shallot, garlic, cilantro, and ginger. Reduce the heat to medium and sauté, stirring often, until the vegetables are soft, about 7 minutes. Stir in the orange juice, lemon juice, and soy sauce. Bring the mixture to a simmer over medium-high heat, and continue simmering until it's reduced by a third, about 4 minutes. Remove from the heat.

Place the asparagus in a glass or earthenware bowl. Add the sauce and toss well. Add the sesame seeds and pine nuts and toss again. Chill thoroughly, about 40 minutes. Toss well before serving.

PER SERVING: CALORIES 136 • PROTEIN 5.5 G • CARBOHYDRATE 13.7 G • FAT 8.4 G • CHOLESTEROL 0 MG • SODIUM 262 MG • 50% CALORIES FROM FAT • OUTSTANDING SOURCE OF VITAMIN C • GOOD SOURCE OF VITAMINS B₁, B₂, B₃, B₆; CALCIUM

CHILLED FENNEL IN CITRUS MARINADE

Serves 4

TOTAL TIME: ABOUT 20 MINUTES
TIME TO PREPARE: ABOUT 15 MINUTES
COOKING TIME: 5 MINUTES
REFRIGERATION/FREEZING: REFRIGERATE UP TO 4 DAYS. DO NOT FREEZE.

Call it fennel perfected; sautéing tempers the licorice taste, and citrus brings out the tang in this vegetable. Serve it with any rich entrée, for a sweet, crunchy contrast.

1 tablespoon extra virgin olive oil
1 large fennel bulb, without leafy fronds, thinly sliced
1 tablespoon fresh lemon juice
2 tablespoons fresh orange juice
Salt and freshly ground black pepper to taste

Heat the oil in a medium, nonreactive skillet over medium heat. When it's hot, add the fennel, turn down the heat to medium-low, and sauté until it begins to soften, about 7 minutes. Add the lemon and orange juices. Stir well, cover, and let the fennel steam until soft, but not mushy, about 5 minutes. Season with salt and pepper. Transfer to a glass or earthenware bowl and refrigerate. Serve chilled or at room temperature.

PER SERVING: CALORIES 69 • PROTEIN 1.4 G • CARBOHYDRATE 9.4 G • FAT 3.6 G • CHOLESTEROL 0 MG • SODIUM 59 MG • 43% CALORIES FROM FAT • VERY GOOD SOURCE OF VITAMIN C

•

SAVORY FRESH PEACH SALAD

Serves 4

TOTAL TIME: ABOUT 3 HOURS, 15 MINUTES, INCLUDING TIME TO CHILL
TIME TO PREPARE: ABOUT 15 MINUTES
COOKING TIME: NONE
DO AHEAD: THIS DISH CAN BE MADE UP TO 2 DAYS IN ADVANCE. REFRIGERATE, COVERED, UNTIL READY TO USE.
REFRIGERATION/FREEZING: REFRIGERATE UP TO 2 DAYS. DO NOT FREEZE.

You do this, too; I know you do: you bring home the most beautiful peaches you've ever seen, arrange them in a bowl, and put off eating them until they're no longer ornamental. Trouble is, by then they're no longer desirable either. Having done this before, you swear on your life not to do it again. But then . . . you're at the farmer's market, and well . . .

What you need is a way to have your fruit and eat it, too. And this side-dish salad comes pretty close, making good use of "bad" peaches.

1 cup plain nonfat yogurt
2 teaspoons fresh lemon juice
2 teaspoons honey
1 teaspoon Dijon mustard
2 large fresh peaches, peeled and chopped (see page 107)
1 celery stalk, chopped
1 tablespoon sesame seeds, toasted (see Note, page 122)
2 tablespoons minced fresh parsley
1 tablespoon minced fresh cilantro
2 tablespoons minced onions
4 dried apricots, minced

In a small bowl or measuring cup, combine the yogurt, lemon juice, honey, and mustard.

In a large mixing bowl, toss together the peaches, celery, sesame seeds, parsley, cilantro, onions, and apricots. Add the yogurt mixture and toss again. Chill for at least 3 hours before serving.

PER SERVING: CALORIES 110 • PROTEIN 4.8 G • CARBOHYDRATE 21 G • FAT 1.4 G • CHOLESTEROL 1.1 MG • SODIUM 75.5 MG • 11% CALORIES FROM FAT • GOOD SOURCE OF VITAMINS B₂, C; CALCIUM

•

EGGPLANT SALAD WITH RED BELL PEPPER

Serves 4

TOTAL TIME: ABOUT 30 MINUTES
TIME TO PREPARE: 10 MINUTES
COOKING TIME: ABOUT 20 MINUTES
DO AHEAD: YOU CAN BROIL, PEEL, AND SEED THE EGGPLANT 2 DAYS IN ADVANCE. REFRIGERATE, WRAPPED.
REFRIGERATION/FREEZING: REFRIGERATE UP TO 2 DAYS. DO NOT FREEZE.

You'll love this served on pita bread, along with fresh spinach and Orange-Vinaigrette-Style Dressing (see page 119).

1 large eggplant
3 tablespoons hot water
1 tablespoon tahini
⅓ cup plain nonfat yogurt
1 teaspoon ground cumin
1 teaspoon paprika
2 tablespoons minced fresh cilantro
1 red bell pepper, roasted, peeled, and sliced into ⅓-inch strips (see page 534)
¼ cup crumbled feta cheese (optional)

Heat the broiler. Prick the eggplant with a fork in 4 places, and place it under the broiler 2 inches from the heat until the skin buckles, 6 to 9 minutes. Turn it over and continue to broil until the skin buckles on the other side, 5 to 7 minutes more. If any part is still firm and smooth, turn the eggplant again so that the part in question is directly under the broiler and broil until the entire eggplant has buckled, about 5 minutes per side. Remove the eggplant and let it cool.

Meanwhile, in a small mixing bowl combine the hot water, tahini, yogurt, cumin, paprika, and cilantro, and stir until smooth. When the eggplant is cool enough to handle, cut off the ends, peel, and remove as many of the seeds as possible. Chop the pulp coarsely, and stir into the yogurt mixture. Add the pepper and the feta cheese, if desired, and mix well. Serve at room temperature, or chill and serve cold.

PER SERVING: CALORIES 118 • PROTEIN 5.7 G • CARBOHYDRATE 12.7 G • FAT 5.8 G • CHOLESTEROL 14 MG • SODIUM 192 MG • 42% CALORIES FROM FAT • OUT-STANDING SOURCE OF VITAMINS A, C • GOOD SOURCE OF VITAMINS B₁, B₂, B₆; CALCIUM, FOLACIN

CHOPPED CAPONATA
A Zesty Eggplant Salad
Serves 4

TOTAL TIME: ABOUT 4 HOURS, INCLUDING TIME TO CHILL
TIME TO PREPARE: ABOUT 30 MINUTES, INCLUDING TIME
  TO SAUTÉ
COOKING TIME: ABOUT 20 MINUTES
DO AHEAD: THE EGGPLANT CAN BE PREPARED UP TO 2 DAYS
  IN ADVANCE.
REFRIGERATION/FREEZING: REFRIGERATE UP TO 4 DAYS. DO
  NOT FREEZE.

Proper caponata, the genuine Sicilian thing, calls for many more ingredients than mine, each cooked separately and combined for a dish that brought one Italian writer "to the antechamber of the terrestrial paradise" (or so he said). While this may not transport you quite as far, it's refreshing and yummy, and much easier to make.

1 medium eggplant

2 teaspoons extra virgin olive oil

1 shallot, minced

1 small onion, chopped

1 garlic clove, minced

2 tablespoons minced fresh basil

2 tablespoons minced fresh parsley

1 tomato, peeled, seeded, and chopped
  (see page 544)

2 teaspoons balsamic vinegar

¼ cup minced oil-cured olives (optional)

1 teaspoon capers (optional)

Salt and freshly ground black pepper to taste

Heat the broiler. Prick the eggplant with a fork in 4 places, and place it under the broiler, 2 inches from the heat, until the skin buckles, 6 to 9 minutes. Turn it over and continue to broil until the skin buckles on the other side, 5 to 7 minutes more. If any part is still firm and smooth, turn the eggplant again so that the part in question is directly under the broiler and broil until the entire eggplant has buckled, about 5 minutes per side. Remove the eggplant and let it cool.

Meanwhile, heat the oil in a small skillet over medium heat. When it is hot, add the shallot, onion, garlic, basil, and parsley. Reduce the heat to medium and sauté, stirring often, until the vegetables have softened, about 10 minutes.

When the eggplant is cool enough to handle, cut off the ends, peel, and remove as many of the seeds as possible. Chop the pulp coarsely and transfer it to a large mixing bowl. Stir in the shallot mixture, along with the tomato, vinegar, and the olives and capers, if using. Season with salt and pepper. Chill, covered, for at least 3 hours, and serve cold.

PER SERVING: CALORIES 48 • PROTEIN 1.1 G • CARBOHYDRATE 6.4 G • FAT 2.4 G • CHOLESTEROL 0 MG • SODIUM 6 MG • 42% CALORIES FROM FAT • GOOD SOURCE OF VITAMIN C

COOL AND SPICY EGGPLANT SALAD WITH ROASTED GARLIC, GINGER, AND MINT

Serves 4

TOTAL TIME: ABOUT 4 HOURS, 25 MINUTES, INCLUDING TIME TO CHILL

TIME TO PREPARE: ABOUT 25 MINUTES, INCLUDING TIME TO SAUTÉ

COOKING TIME: ABOUT 1 HOUR

DO AHEAD: THIS DISH TASTES BEST MADE THE DAY BEFORE YOU SERVE IT. REFRIGERATE.

REFRIGERATION/FREEZING: REFRIGERATE UP TO 4 DAYS. DO NOT FREEZE.

Yet another delicious demonstration of how versatile eggplant can be. You'll be pummeling this dish with spices, so give it a day to absorb the shock.

4 garlic cloves, unpeeled

1 large eggplant, peeled and sliced into ½-inch-thick rounds

1 teaspoon ground cumin

½ teaspoon ground coriander

1 ripe medium tomato, chopped

¼ cup minced fresh cilantro

2 tablespoons minced fresh mint

2 teaspoons grated peeled fresh ginger

1 tablespoon fresh lemon juice

2 tablespoons fresh orange juice

1½ tablespoons extra virgin olive oil

½ teaspoon paprika

Salt to taste

Heat the oven to 450°F.

Wrap the garlic in foil in a single bundle, and place it directly on the oven rack. Roast until it's tender, about 30 minutes. At the same time, place the eggplant slices in a single layer on a lightly oiled nonstick baking sheet and bake until tender, about 20 minutes. Remove from the oven and let the garlic and eggplant cool.

Meanwhile put the cumin and coriander in a heavy skillet over medium heat. Stirring often, toast the spices until they just start to brown, about 7 minutes. Watch closely to make sure they don't burn.

Coarsely chop the eggplant and put it in a large mixing bowl along with the toasted spices. Peel the roasted garlic and mash it with a fork. Stir it in with the eggplant. Add the tomato, cilantro, mint, ginger, lemon juice, orange juice, olive oil, and paprika. Toss well. Season with salt.

Cover and refrigerate for at least 3 hours before serving. This salad tastes best the day after it's made.

PER SERVING: CALORIES 95 • PROTEIN 1.9 G • CARBOHYDRATE 11 G • FAT 5.6 G • CHOLESTEROL 0 MG • SODIUM 9.2 MG • 49% CALORIES FROM FAT • VERY GOOD SOURCE OF VITAMIN C

BEET AND VIDALIA ONION SALAD

Serves 4

TOTAL TIME: 1 HOUR, 6 MINUTES
TIME TO PREPARE: ABOUT 6 MINUTES
COOKING TIME: 1 HOUR
DO AHEAD: YOU CAN COOK THE BEETS UP TO 1 WEEK IN
    ADVANCE. REFRIGERATE, WRAPPED.
REFRIGERATION/FREEZING: REFRIGERATE UP TO 3 DAYS. DO
    NOT FREEZE.

S*weet, crisp, cool, nippy, zippy, brisk, and
zesty, this salad is so lively you practically
have to wrestle it to the table.*

½ pound beets, scrubbed
1 orange
1 Vidalia onion, quartered and thinly sliced
1 scallion, white part only, thinly sliced
⅓ cup reduced-fat or nonfat sour cream
2 tablespoons minced fresh mint
2 tablespoons minced fresh chives
2 teaspoons fresh lemon juice

Heat the oven to 425°F.

With a paring knife, carve an **X** at both the
root end and the stem end of each beet. Then
wrap each in a single layer of aluminum foil.
Bake until tender, about 1 hour. Unwrap the foil
and let the beets cool. (Or, bake in the microwave as directed on page 519.)

When the beets are cool enough to handle,
peel away the skin and chop them as finely—
or as coarsely—as you'd like.

Grate a tablespoon of zest from the orange
and squeeze out the juice. Discard the peel.

In a mixing bowl, combine the onion, scallion, orange juice and zest, sour cream, mint,
chives, and lemon juice. Add the beets and toss

well to coat with the dressing. Serve at room
temperature or refrigerate and serve chilled.

PER SERVING: CALORIES 71 • PROTEIN 3.1 G • CARBOHYDRATE 16 G • FAT 0 G •
CHOLESTEROL 0 MG • SODIUM 59 MG • 3% CALORIES FROM FAT • OUTSTANDING
SOURCE OF VITAMIN C • VERY GOOD SOURCE OF FOLACIN

•

ORANGE-AND-CILANTRO BEAN SALAD

Serves 4

TOTAL TIME: 20 MINUTES, NOT INCLUDING TIME TO COOK
    THE BEANS
TIME TO PREPARE: ABOUT 20 MINUTES
COOKING TIME: NONE
DO AHEAD: THE DRESSING CAN BE MADE UP TO 3 DAYS IN
    ADVANCE. REFRIGERATE UNTIL READY TO USE.
REFRIGERATION/FREEZING: REFRIGERATE UP TO 3 DAYS. DO
    NOT FREEZE.

C*itrusy cilantro accents the affinity between
black beans and orange in this sweet and
tangy salad. In other words, they all taste
really, really good together.*

1½ cups cooked black runner beans or black
    beans, drained and rinsed
1 navel orange, peeled, sectioned, and cut into
    bite-sized pieces
2 cups cherry tomatoes, halved or quartered,
    depending on size
2 scallions, white part only, chopped
¼ cup minced fresh cilantro
4 oil-cured green olives, minced

Dressing
1 tablespoon extra virgin olive oil
Juice of 1 lime
1 teaspoon Dijon mustard

In a glass or earthenware salad bowl, combine the beans, orange, tomatoes, scallions, cilantro, and olives. Toss well.

For the Dressing

Whisk together the olive oil, lime juice, and mustard. Pour over the salad and toss again. Serve at once.

PER SERVING: CALORIES 167 • PROTEIN 7.1 G • CARBOHYDRATE 26 G • FAT 4.6 G • CHOLESTEROL 0 MG • SODIUM 119 MG • 24% CALORIES FROM FAT • OUTSTANDING SOURCE OF VITAMIN C • VERY GOOD SOURCE OF VITAMIN B₁; FOLACIN • GOOD SOURCE OF IRON

•

RASPBERRY-CANNELLINI SUCCOTASH

Serves 4

TOTAL TIME: ABOUT 3 HOURS, 30 MINUTES, INCLUDING TIME TO CHILL, NOT INCLUDING TIME TO COOK THE BEANS

TIME TO PREPARE: ABOUT 25 MINUTES, INCLUDING TIME TO SAUTÉ

COOKING TIME: 8 TO 10 MINUTES

DO AHEAD: THIS DISH CAN BE MADE UP TO 3 DAYS IN ADVANCE. REFRIGERATE, COVERED, UNTIL READY TO USE.

REFRIGERATION/FREEZING: REFRIGERATE UP TO 3 DAYS. DO NOT FREEZE.

The word "succotash" derives from the Narraganset tribe's word for "whatever's in the stew pot." And in Narraganset, and many other native tongues, for that matter, "whatever," loosely translated, means "corn."

In this case, the corn is combined with cannellini, the biggest, firmest, and most flavorful of white beans; fresh raspberries; and a mild mustard-based dressing.

4 large ears of corn

1 tablespoon extra virgin olive oil

1½ cups chopped red onions

1 tablespoon minced fresh thyme, or 1 teaspoon crumbled dried thyme

2 teaspoons raspberry vinegar

1 teaspoon Dijon mustard

1½ cups cooked cannellini beans, drained and rinsed

1 cup fresh raspberries

Salt and freshly ground black pepper to taste

Bring a large pot of water to a boil. Add the corn and let the water return to a boil. Cover the pot, turn off the heat, and leave the corn for 8 to 10 minutes. (If you're using an electric stove, take the pot off the burner.) Transfer the corn to a plate to let it cool. (Or cook the corn in the microwave according to the directions on page 526.)

In a small skillet, heat the olive oil over medium heat. Add the onions and thyme and sauté until the onions soften, about 7 minutes. Add the raspberry vinegar and the mustard, and stir until the liquid evaporates, about 1 minute. Turn off the heat.

Scrape the kernels off the cobs into a mixing bowl. Add the beans and raspberries. Add the onion mixture, season with salt and pepper, and toss well. Refrigerate, covered, until chilled through, about 3 hours. Toss again before serving.

PER SERVING: CALORIES 265 • PROTEIN 10.7 G • CARBOHYDRATE 48 G • FAT 5.4 G • CHOLESTEROL 0 MG • SODIUM 36.2 MG • 17% CALORIES FROM FAT • OUTSTANDING SOURCE OF FOLACIN • VERY GOOD SOURCE OF VITAMINS B₁, C • GOOD SOURCE OF VITAMIN B₆; IRON, ZINC

•

CUCUMBER AND BULGUR WHEAT WITH FRESH HERBS

Serves 4

TOTAL TIME: ABOUT 4 HOURS, 10 MINUTES, INCLUDING
   TIME TO SOAK THE BULGUR AND CHILL
TIME TO PREPARE: ABOUT 25 MINUTES
COOKING TIME: 30 MINUTES
REFRIGERATION/FREEZING: REFRIGERATE UP TO 3 DAYS. DO
   NOT FREEZE.

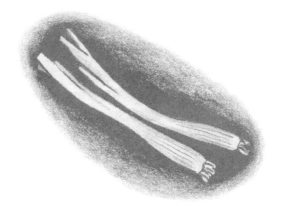

You'd think that bulgur wheat would weigh down this salad or at least blunt the taste. Not a bit; it chimes right in with everything else for a dish that's cool as . . . a cucumber, of course.

¾ cup water

⅔ cup bulgur wheat

2 cups plain nonfat yogurt

2 large cucumbers, peeled and seeded
   (see page 526)

2 scallions, including greens, minced

¼ cup finely minced fresh cilantro

¼ cup finely minced fresh chives

¼ cup finely minced fresh mint

¼ cup finely minced fresh dill

Salt and freshly ground black pepper to taste

Bring the water to a boil in a saucepan. Add the bulgur wheat and let the water return to a boil. Cover and remove from the heat. Let the bulgur sit, covered, for 30 minutes. Pour the bulgur into a sieve and press it with the back of a wooden spoon to squeeze out the excess water.

Pour the bulgur into a sieve and, using the back of a wooden spoon, press out as much water as possible. Transfer the bulgur to a large serving bowl.

Add the yogurt, cucumbers, scallions, cilantro, chives, mint, dill, salt and pepper, and stir thoroughly. Cover with plastic wrap and refrigerate at least 3 hours before serving. Serve cold.

PER SERVING: CALORIES 209 • PROTEIN 12 G • CARBOHYDRATE 41 G • FAT 0 G • CHOLESTEROL 2 MG • SODIUM 100 MG • 4% CALORIES FROM FAT • VERY GOOD SOURCE OF VITAMIN B₂; CALCIUM • GOOD SOURCE OF VITAMINS B₁, B₃, B₆, B₁₂, C; FOLACIN, IRON, ZINC

•

CANNELLINI BEAN AND SPINACH SALAD

Serves 4

TOTAL TIME: ABOUT 20 MINUTES, NOT INCLUDING TIME TO
   COOK THE BEANS OR ROAST THE PEPPER
TIME TO PREPARE: 20 MINUTES
COOKING TIME: NONE
DO AHEAD: YOU CAN ROAST THE PEPPER UP TO 3 DAYS IN
   ADVANCE, AND BOIL THE BEANS 1 WEEK AHEAD. REFRIG-
   ERATE UNTIL READY TO USE.

Start with dry cannellini beans and this simple side dish will be sensational. The beans will burst into being plump, creamy, and almost nutty. You can use canned beans, too, if they're not mushy and you rinse them well.

2 cups cooked cannellini beans, drained and
   rinsed
1 small red bell pepper, roasted, peeled, and
   finely chopped (see page 534)
6 oil-cured black olives, minced
3 cups loosely packed shredded fresh spinach
1 tablespoon extra virgin olive oil
Juice of ½ lemon
½ teaspoon ground cumin
Salt and freshly ground black pepper to taste

In a mixing bowl, combine the beans, bell pepper, olives, and spinach. In a separate bowl,
whisk together the olive oil, lemon, and cumin.
Pour the dressing evenly over the bean mixture
and toss well. Season with salt and pepper.
Serve at room temperature.

PER SERVING: CALORIES 160 • PROTEIN 8.8 G • CARBOHYDRATE 23 G • FAT 4.7 G •
CHOLESTEROL 0 MG • SODIUM 94.7 MG • 25% CALORIES FROM FAT • OUTSTANDING
SOURCE OF VITAMIN C; FOLACIN • VERY GOOD SOURCE OF VITAMIN A; IRON •
GOOD SOURCE OF VITAMINS B₁, B₆

TABBOULEH
A Wheat Salad
Serves 4

TOTAL TIME: ABOUT 40 MINUTES
TIME TO PREPARE: ABOUT 10 MINUTES
COOKING TIME: 30 MINUTES
REFRIGERATION/FREEZING: REFRIGERATE, COVERED, UP TO 5
DAYS. DO NOT FREEZE.

This Middle Eastern wheat salad is a genuine classic, dating back to 2000 B.C.
Believe me, it hasn't been around this long
simply because it's nourishing. It is also delicious. A
dollop of yogurt is traditional, but not required.

1¼ cups water
1 cup bulgur wheat
½ cup tightly packed minced fresh parsley
1½ tablespoons extra virgin olive oil
2 teaspoons fresh lemon juice
2 scallions, white part only, minced
2 tablespoons minced fresh mint (if fresh isn't
   available, omit the mint altogether; don't
   substitute dried)
1 medium tomato, finely chopped
1 cucumber, peeled, seeded, and minced (see
   page 526)
Salt and freshly ground black pepper to taste
Plain nonfat yogurt, for garnish (optional)

In a medium saucepan, bring the water to a
boil. Stir in the bulgur wheat. Let the water
come to a second boil, then *immediately* remove
from the heat. Let it sit for 30 minutes without
lifting the lid. Pour the bulgur into a sieve and
press it with the back of a wooden spoon to
squeeze out the excess water.
   Transfer the bulgur to a glass or earthenware serving bowl. Toss with the parsley, olive

oil, lemon juice, scallions, mint, if using, tomato, cucumber, and salt and pepper. Serve at room temperature, or cover and refrigerate for at least 3 hours, and serve chilled, topped with yogurt, if you'd like.

PER SERVING: CALORIES 187 • PROTEIN 5.2 G • CARBOHYDRATE 31 G • FAT 5.7 G • CHOLESTEROL 0 MG • SODIUM 15.8 MG • 26% CALORIES FROM FAT • VERY GOOD SOURCE OF VITAMIN C • GOOD SOURCE OF VITAMINS B₃, B₆; FOLACIN, IRON

Make It Your Own

Bulgur is a sturdy grain, so you can heap plenty of additional ingredients into tabbouleh and other bulgur salads without overwhelming the wheat. Always add the dressing while the bulgur is warm; it will absorb the flavors better.

🍃 Make a fruit and nut tabbouleh with approximately 1 cup chopped fresh fruit such as grapes, oranges, peaches, apricots, or apples or dried fruits such as raisins, prunes, apricots, and figs and 2 tablespoons chopped walnuts or toasted almonds (see page 56). Dress the salad with ¼ cup orange juice and 1 tablespoon extra virgin olive oil.

🍃 Add about 1½ cups cooked lentils, chickpeas, or white beans to the basic recipe for a lunch or light dinner entrée.

🍃 Use your favorite vinaigrette as a dressing instead of the oil and lemon juice.

🍃 In the winter, add ½ cup reconstituted sun-dried tomatoes and ½ cup sliced roasted red pepper (see page 534).

🍃 Make an olive tabbouleh using ½ cup cured olives of various colors. Add ¼ cup crumbled goat cheese or feta cheese and plenty of additional parsley. Dress with 2 tablespoons fresh lemon juice and 1 tablespoon extra virgin olive oil.

ORANGE-SESAME TABBOULEH

Serves 4

TOTAL TIME: ABOUT 40 MINUTES
TIME TO PREPARE: ABOUT 10 MINUTES
COOKING TIME: 30 MINUTES
DO AHEAD: THIS DISH CAN BE MADE UP TO 5 DAYS IN ADVANCE. REFRIGERATE, COVERED, UNTIL READY TO USE.
REFRIGERATION/FREEZING: REFRIGERATE UP TO 5 DAYS. DO NOT FREEZE.

A zesty little salad that's great with grilled foods. It improves with time, so you can make it midweek and enjoy it all weekend.

1¼ cups water
1 cup bulgur wheat
½ cup tightly packed minced fresh parsley
1 tablespoon extra virgin olive oil
2 teaspoons fresh lemon juice
2 scallions, white part only, minced
1 medium tomato, finely chopped
1 tablespoon sesame seeds, toasted (see Note, page 122)
1 tablespoon grated orange zest

Bring the water to a boil in a saucepan. Add the bulgur wheat and let the water return to a boil. Cover and remove from the heat. Let the bulgur sit, covered, for 30 minutes. Pour the bulgur into a sieve and press it with the back of a wooden spoon to squeeze out the excess water.

Transfer the bulgur to a serving bowl and add the parsley, olive oil, lemon juice, scallions, tomato, sesame seeds, and orange zest. Toss well and serve at room temperature.

PER SERVING: CALORIES 176 • PROTEIN 5.2 G • CARBOHYDRATE 30 G • FAT 5 G • CHOLESTEROL 0 MG • SODIUM 14.6 MG • 24% CALORIES FROM FAT • GOOD SOURCE OF VITAMINS B₃, C

Main-Course Salads

SUMMER MARKET SALAD

Serves 4

TOTAL TIME: 30 MINUTES
TIME TO PREPARE: 30 MINUTES
COOKING TIME: NONE
DO AHEAD: YOU CAN MAKE THE DRESSING UP TO 4 DAYS IN
    ADVANCE. COVER AND REFRIGERATE.
REFRIGERATION/FREEZING: REFRIGERATE FOR 1 DAY. DO
    NOT FREEZE.

This salad is not the product of inspiration as much as total confusion. I can't shop rationally in the summertime, when I love everything in stock. So I buy it all and deal with the consequences back in the kitchen.

Dressing

⅓ cup plus 2 tablespoons vegetable broth (see
    page 167)
2 tablespoons tahini
1 tablespoon fresh lemon juice
1 tablespoon fruit vinegar, such as raspberry,
    blueberry, strawberry, or mango
1 scallion, including greens, minced

6 cups mesclun or lettuce of any kind

Vegetables (all or any combination)

2 cups cherry tomatoes, halved or quartered,
    depending on size
2 cups chopped asparagus, steamed but crisp
    (see page 516)
2 cups sugar snap peas or snow peas, steamed
    but crisp (see page 533)
1½ cups cooked corn kernels

2 cups halved or quartered (depending on size)
    steamed new potatoes (see page 534)

For the Dressing

Whisk together the vegetable broth, tahini, lemon juice, vinegar, and scallion.

In a salad bowl, toss together the mesclun and all of the vegetables you've chosen for your salad. Pour on the dressing, and fold it gently into the salad. Serve at room temperature, or chill and serve cold.

PER SERVING: CALORIES 155 • PROTEIN 7 G • CARBOHYDRATE 24 G • FAT 5.7 G • CHOLESTEROL 0 MG • SODIUM 28.8 MG • 29% CALORIES FROM FAT • OUTSTANDING SOURCE OF VITAMIN C; FOLACIN • VERY GOOD SOURCE OF VITAMINS A, B₁ • GOOD SOURCE OF VITAMINS B₂, B₃, B₆; CALCIUM, IRON, ZINC

MAIN-COURSE SALAD BASICS

Ever kicked yourself for inviting guests when you didn't have the energy to entertain them? Ever think about shirking? Consider salad a solution? After all, your guests can't expect too much if you say that's what you're serving.

Alas, alack, and so on; salad isn't an easy out. A salad you make for lunch or

dinner should contain all of the elements of a good meal, which takes some planning and preparation.

Flavors: The ingredients should blend well and balance one another. No single flavor should dominate. If you have a strong ingredient, such as broccoli or feta cheese, make sure the other components can compete.

Colors: A variety of colors indicates a range of nutrients, and makes the salad look good.

Textures: A meal feels more satisfying when it includes a variety of textures. And when you add crispy ingredients along with tender ones, you can be sure you're getting some fiber.

Protein: Substantial sources of protein include eggs, tofu, legumes, or cheese. You can fortify the salad with a protein and mineral-rich dressing made with nonfat yogurt, tofu, or low-fat cottage or ricotta cheese.

Hearty Grains: Brown rice, bulgur wheat, barley, and wheat berries add flavor and bulk. Nuts complement and amplify the flavor of the grains—but use them sparingly, because they're fatty.

Whole Wheat Bread: Torn into small pieces and lightly toasted, wheat bread makes a wholesome alternative to commercial croutons, which may be fried and/or oversalted.

Although you need variety and substance, keep it simple. Once you get going, it can be hard to restrain yourself, but remember that a handful of well-considered, good ingredients can be better than an indiscriminate pile of whatever happens to be at hand.

●

LENTIL SALAD WITH MINCED VEGETABLES

Serves 4

TOTAL TIME: ABOUT 1 HOUR, 5 MINUTES
TIME TO PREPARE: ABOUT 25 MINUTES
COOKING TIME: 40 MINUTES
REFRIGERATION/FREEZING: REFRIGERATE UP TO 2 DAYS. DO NOT FREEZE.

L*entils bring their own earthy seasoning to this salad, which calls for a minimum of other ingredients.*

2 whole cloves

½ onion

1 cup uncooked lentils, rinsed

3 fresh sage leaves, minced, or 1 tablespoon crumbled dried sage

¼ cup red wine vinegar

2 cups water

1 tablespoon extra virgin olive oil

2 leeks, white part only, washed and chopped

2 carrots, peeled and chopped

2 celery stalks, chopped, or ½ small fennel bulb, without leafy fronds, chopped

Stick the cloves into the onion half. Place them in a heavy medium saucepan. Add the lentils, sage, vinegar, and water. Cover and bring to a simmer over medium heat. Simmer until the lentils are tender, about 40 minutes.

Meanwhile, heat the oil in a skillet over medium heat and sauté the leeks, carrots, and celery or fennel until softened, about 10 minutes.

Place a sieve over a bowl and strain the lentils, reserving the cooking broth.

Place the lentils on serving plate, and spoon the vegetables around them. Drizzle 2 tablespoons of the cooking liquid over the top and serve warm or at room temperature.

PER SERVING: CALORIES 243 • PROTEIN 14.8 G • CARBOHYDRATE 39 G • FAT 4 G • CHOLESTEROL 0 MG • SODIUM 49 MG • 14% CALORIES FROM FAT • OUTSTANDING SOURCE OF VITAMIN A; FOLACIN • VERY GOOD SOURCE OF VITAMINS B₆, C; IRON • GOOD SOURCE OF VITAMIN B₁, ZINC

•

LEMON-SPIKED LENTIL SALAD

Serves 4

TOTAL TIME: 50 MINUTES
TIME TO PREPARE: 10 MINUTES
COOKING TIME: 40 MINUTES
REFRIGERATION/FREEZING: REFRIGERATE UP TO 4 DAYS. DO
   NOT FREEZE.

L*emon gives its customary lift to this supper salad, balancing some heavy flavors with a taste that's sharp and light.*

Lentils

1 cup uncooked lentils, rinsed

1 onion, chopped

1 bouquet garni, containing rosemary, bay leaf, and tarragon (see page 558)

2 whole cloves

2½ cups water

2 tablespoons minced red onions

2 tablespoons minced dry-packed (not in oil) sun-dried tomatoes

2 teaspoons crumbled dried basil

2 teaspoons crumbled dried oregano

1 teaspoon extra virgin olive oil with lemon (see Note), or 1 teaspoon extra virgin olive oil plus 1 tablespoon fresh lemon juice

½ cup loosely packed crumbled feta cheese

6 cups mixed salad greens

For the Lentils

In a medium saucepan, combine the lentils, onion, bouquet garni, cloves, and water. Bring to a boil over high heat. Cover, turn down the heat to medium-low, and simmer until the lentils are tender and all of the water has been absorbed, about 40 minutes. Remove and discard the bouquet garni and the cloves.

In a glass or earthenware bowl, combine the red onions, sun-dried tomatoes, basil, oregano, olive oil, and lemon juice, if using. Add the lentils and toss gently to coat them with the oil and herbs. Add the feta cheese and toss again to distribute it evenly throughout.

Serve warm or at room temperature over mixed salad greens.

Note: For information on flavored oils, see mail-order information on page 596.

PER SERVING: CALORIES 240 • PROTEIN 16 G • CARBOHYDRATE 32.4 G • FAT 6 G • CHOLESTEROL 12.6 MG • SODIUM 213 MG • 22% CALORIES FROM FAT • OUTSTANDING SOURCE OF FOLACIN • VERY GOOD SOURCE OF VITAMINS B₁, C; IRON • GOOD SOURCE OF VITAMINS A, B₆; CALCIUM, ZINC

•

SUPPER FRUIT SALAD

Serves 4

TOTAL TIME: ABOUT 30 MINUTES, NOT INCLUDING TIME TO
   COOK WHEAT BERRIES
TIME TO PREPARE: ABOUT 30 MINUTES
COOKING TIME: 8 TO 10 MINUTES
REFRIGERATION/FREEZING: REFRIGERATE UP TO 3 DAYS. DO
   NOT FREEZE.

A reviewer once dismissed a book of mine without testing a thing in it, saying only that "the recipes look too unusual." Well, here's another shocker for her: a main-course salad calling for wheat berries, fresh fruit, and avocado dressing.

Now, eccentricity is not a trait I admire for its own sake, and it is possible to go too far. But when a "weird" dish is as good as this one, you can can convention.

3 or 4 ears of corn
1 cup cooked wheat berries (see page 579)
2 cups cooked chickpeas, drained and rinsed
2 cups loosely packed shredded green cabbage
¼ cup minced red onions
¼ cup minced fresh cilantro
¼ cup minced fresh chives
¼ cup minced fresh parsley
1 cup fresh blueberries
1 cup sliced fresh strawberries
¼ cup raisins

Dressing

¼ avocado
1 tablespoon fresh lemon juice
¼ cup reduced-fat or nonfat sour cream
½ cup nonfat or low-fat buttermilk

Bring a large pot of water to a boil. Add the corn and let the water return to a boil. Cover the pot, turn off the heat, and leave the corn for 8 to 10 minutes. (If you're using an electric stove, take the pot off the burner.) Transfer the corn to a plate to let it cool. (Or cook the corn in the microwave according to the directions on page 526.)

Scrape the kernels off the cobs into a large salad bowl. Add the wheat berries, chickpeas, cabbage, onions, cilantro, chives, parsley, blueberries, strawberries, and raisins, and toss well.

For the Dressing

In a food processor or blender, combine the avocado, lemon juice, sour cream, and buttermilk.

Process until smooth. Pour the dressing evenly over the salad and toss well. Serve at room temperature, or cover and refrigerate, and serve chilled.

PER SERVING: CALORIES 439 • PROTEIN 18.2 G • CARBOHYDRATE 86.4 G • FAT 6.8 G • CHOLESTEROL 1 MG • SODIUM 85.6 MG • 13% CALORIES FROM FAT • OUTSTANDING SOURCE OF VITAMIN C; FOLACIN • VERY GOOD SOURCE OF VITAMINS B₁, B₃, B₆; IRON, ZINC • GOOD SOURCE OF VITAMIN A; CALCIUM

CURRIED EGG SALAD

Serves 4

TOTAL TIME: ABOUT 2 HOURS, 45 MINUTES, INCLUDING
   TIME TO CHILL
TIME TO PREPARE: ABOUT 10 MINUTES
COOKING TIME: 15 MINUTES
DO AHEAD: YOU CAN MAKE THE DRESSING UP TO 4 DAYS
   AHEAD. REFRIGERATE UNTIL READY TO USE.
REFRIGERATION/FREEZING: REFRIGERATE UP TO 2 DAYS. DO
   NOT FREEZE.

Creamy and crunchy, sweet and savory, this salad could be the best way ever to eat hard-boiled eggs.

4 large eggs
2 cups small new potatoes (about 10)

Dressing
1 small garlic clove, grated
1 tablespoon grated peeled fresh ginger
2 tablespoons minced fresh cilantro
1 tablespoon fresh lemon juice
2 teaspoons honey
2 teaspoons Dijon mustard
⅔ cup plain nonfat yogurt
1 tablespoon curry powder

2 cups cherry tomatoes
2 celery stalks, trimmed and minced
1 small Granny Smith apple, minced
2 tablespoons slivered almonds, toasted (see
   page 56)
¼ cup raisins

For the Eggs and the Potatoes
To hard boil the eggs, place the eggs on the bottom of a deep saucepan. Add enough water to cover. Bring the water to a boil over medium-high heat. Cover the saucepan and remove from the heat. Let the eggs sit for 15 minutes. Drain and let cool water run over them to stop the cooking process. Peel.

To boil the potatoes, fill a medium saucepan with enough water to cover them. Bring to a boil over high heat. Add the potatoes, cover the pan, and lower the heat to medium. Boil until the potatoes are tender, about 10 minutes. Drain and let cool.

For the Dressing
In a medium mixing bowl, stir together the garlic, ginger, cilantro, lemon juice, honey, mustard, yogurt, and curry powder.

Chop the hard-boiled eggs and place them in a salad bowl. If the potatoes are larger than walnuts, cut them into halves or quarters before adding them to the bowl. Similarly, if the cherry tomatoes are larger than walnuts, cut them into halves or quarters before adding them to the bowl, too.

Toss in the celery, apple, almonds, and raisins.

Pour the dressing over the salad and mix gently but thoroughly. Cover and chill thoroughly before serving, about 2 hours.

PER SERVING: CALORIES 220 • PROTEIN 11 G • CARBOHYDRATE 28.9 G • FAT 7.9 G • CHOLESTEROL 213 MG • SODIUM 152 MG • 31% CALORIES FROM FAT • VERY GOOD SOURCE OF VITAMINS B₂, C • GOOD SOURCE OF VITAMINS A, B₆, B₁₂; FOLACIN, CALCIUM, IRON

RICE SALAD WITH SNOW PEAS, RED BEANS, AND SWEET CORN

Serves 4

TOTAL TIME: 3 HOURS, 40 MINUTES, INCLUDING TIME TO CHILL
TIME TO PREPARE: 40 MINUTES, INCLUDING TIME TO SAUTÉ
COOKING TIME: NONE
REFRIGERATION/FREEZING: REFRIGERATE UP TO 3 DAYS. DO NOT FREEZE.

You don't need a separate dressing for this substantial salad, which you season by tossing sautéed onions, garlic, and peppers with the rest of the ingredients.

1 tablespoon extra virgin olive oil
1 red onion, chopped
1 red bell pepper, cored, seeded, and chopped
1 yellow or orange bell pepper, cored, seeded, and chopped
2 teaspoons ground cumin
1 teaspoon ground coriander
3 tablespoons minced fresh chives
3 tablespoons minced fresh basil
3 tablespoons minced fresh parsley
2 teaspoons balsamic vinegar
2 cups cooked long-grain white or brown rice
4 cooked ears of corn (see page 526)
2 cups loosely packed snow peas, steamed until tender-crisp (see page 509)
2 cups cooked kidney beans, drained and rinsed
Salt and freshly ground black pepper to taste

Heat the oil in a medium skillet over medium-high heat, swirling the pan to coat the bottom. Add the onion, red pepper, yellow or orange pepper, cumin, coriander, chives, basil, and parsley. Sauté over medium heat until the onion softens, about 10 minutes. Add the vinegar, and stir until most of the liquid evaporates, about 2 minutes.

Transfer the mixture to a large mixing bowl. Stir in the rice, and scrape the corn kernels off the cob into the bowl. Add the snow peas and beans and toss well. Season with salt and pepper. Chill, covered, for at least 3 hours, and toss well before serving.

PER SERVING: CALORIES 420 • PROTEIN 17 G • CARBOHYDRATE 80 G • FAT 6.7 G • CHOLESTEROL 0 MG • SODIUM 33 MG • 13% CALORIES FROM FAT • OUTSTANDING SOURCE OF VITAMINS B_1, C; FOLACIN • VERY GOOD SOURCE OF VITAMINS A, B_3, B_6; IRON • GOOD SOURCE OF ZINC

•

ASPARAGUS SALAD WITH BELL PEPPERS AND EGGS

Serves 4 as a side dish; 2 as a main dish

TOTAL TIME: 1 HOUR, 10 MINUTES, INCLUDING TIME TO CHILL, NOT INCLUDING TIME TO ROAST THE PEPPERS
TIME TO PREPARE: ABOUT 20 MINUTES
COOKING TIME: ABOUT 5 MINUTES
DO AHEAD: YOU CAN PREPARE THE PEPPERS UP TO 3 DAYS IN ADVANCE. REFRIGERATE UNTIL READY TO USE.
REFRIGERATION/FREEZING: REFRIGERATE UP TO 2 DAYS. DO NOT FREEZE.

F ine ribbons of frittata and skinny steamed asparagus make a spectacular sight, and a smashing good salad for lunch or a light supper.

1 pound skinny asparagus, trimmed

1 ½ tablespoons extra virgin olive oil

1 large egg

2 tablespoons minced fresh parsley

Salt and freshly ground black pepper to taste

1 small red bell pepper, roasted, peeled, and sliced into thin strips (see page 534)

1 small yellow bell pepper, roasted, peeled, and sliced into thin strips (see page 534)

1 scallion, white part only, minced

½ teaspoon capers

2 teaspoons fresh lemon juice

2 tablespoons minced fresh basil

2 tablespoons minced fresh chives

2 teaspoons balsamic vinegar

Steam the asparagus by placing ¼ inch water in a skillet or wide saucepan. Bring the water to a simmer over medium-high heat, lay the asparagus in the pan—in a single layer if possible—cover, and steam until the asparagus turns bright green, about 12 minutes. (Or use the microwave method in the box above.) Transfer spears to a plate and refrigerate right away.

Brush an 8-inch nonstick omelette pan with 1 teaspoon of the olive oil. Heat the pan over medium heat. Meanwhile, in a small bowl, beat the egg lightly, adding the parsley, and salt and pepper. Pour the egg into the pan, turn the heat down to medium-low, and cook until it's set, about 2 minutes. Using your fingers, gently flip it over to lightly brown the other

MY FAVORITE METHOD: MICROWAVE ASPARAGUS

Trim the stems and stand the stalks tips up in an inch of water in a 2-cup Pyrex measuring cup. Cover with a damp paper towel and microwave for 2 minutes. Repeat for 1 more minute if not cooked enough.

side, about 1 minute. Transfer the frittata to a plate and refrigerate.

In a glass or ceramic bowl, combine the red and yellow bell peppers, scallion, and capers. Add the asparagus and lemon juice and toss well. Place the mixture in the refrigerator until thoroughly chilled, about 40 minutes.

Slice the frittata into thin strips (about ⅓ inch wide). Add them to the asparagus mixture. Toss in the minced basil and chives. Combine the balsamic vinegar and the remaining olive oil in a cup or small bowl. Add this dressing to the salad and toss thoroughly. Serve right away.

PER SERVING: CALORIES 225 • PROTEIN 9.8 G • CARBOHYDRATE 21 G • FAT 13.4 G • CHOLESTEROL 106 MG • SODIUM 41.9 MG • 49% CALORIES FROM FAT • OUTSTANDING SOURCE OF VITAMINS A, C; FOLACIN • VERY GOOD SOURCE OF VITAMINS B₁, B₂ • GOOD SOURCE OF VITAMIN B₃; IRON, ZINC

SWIFT, DELICIOUS BEAN SALAD

Serves 4

TOTAL TIME: ABOUT 30 MINUTES, NOT INCLUDING TIME TO
  COOK THE BEANS
TIME TO PREPARE: ABOUT 30 MINUTES, INCLUDING TIME
  TO SAUTÉ
COOKING TIME: NONE
REFRIGERATION/FREEZING: REFRIGERATE UP TO 4 DAYS. DO
  NOT FREEZE.

Even canned beans taste terrific this way, but if you have time to boil dried organic beans, they'll be even better (see Shop from Home).

1 1/2 tablespoons extra virgin olive oil
1 garlic clove, thinly sliced
2 tablespoons minced fresh basil
1/4 cup minced fresh parsley
1 large ripe tomato, chopped (but not peeled or
  seeded)
1 teaspoon capers
2 teaspoons balsamic vinegar
2 cups cooked chickpeas or cannellini beans,
  drained and rinsed
Salt and freshly ground black pepper to taste

Heat the oil in a medium skillet over medium-high heat. When it is hot, add the garlic, Turn the heat down to medium-low and, using a wooden spoon, swish the garlic through the oil. As soon as it starts to turn golden, about 3 minutes, lift the garlic out and discard it. Add the basil, parsley, tomato, and capers, and stir until the tomato starts to break down into pulp, about 5 minutes. Add the vinegar, stir well, and remove from the heat.

Place the beans in a glass or earthenware serving bowl. Add the tomato mixture and toss well. Season with salt and pepper. Serve at room temperature or cover with plastic wrap, refrigerate, and serve chilled.

PER SERVING: CALORIES 189 • PROTEIN 7.7 G • CARBOHYDRATE 24.9 G • FAT 7.3 G • CHOLESTEROL 0 MG • SODIUM 10.4 MG • 34% CALORIES FROM FAT • VERY GOOD SOURCE OF FOLACIN • GOOD SOURCE OF VITAMIN C; IRON

●

COLD TERIYAKI-STYLE NOODLE SALAD

Serves 4

TOTAL TIME: ABOUT 4 HOURS, 30 MINUTES, INCLUDING
  TIME TO MARINATE AND CHILL, NOT INCLUDING TIME TO
  MAKE THE BROTH OR STEAM THE VEGETABLES
TIME TO PREPARE: ABOUT 45 MINUTES, INCLUDING TIME
  TO SAUTÉ
COOKING TIME: ABOUT 10 MINUTES
DO AHEAD: YOU CAN MARINATE THE TOFU OVERNIGHT,
  COVERED AND REFRIGERATED.
REFRIGERATION/FREEZING: REFRIGERATE UP TO 2 DAYS. DO
  NOT FREEZE.

Teriyaki has a deep, rich flavor that's hard to take straight, but becomes luscious when you add ginger, garlic, and orange or pineapple juice. The noodles make for a chewy, filling main-course salad that looks like a lot of work, but is in fact simple.

1 tablespoon low-sodium soy sauce
1/2 cup fresh orange juice or pineapple juice
1 tablespoon honey
4 scallions, white part plus 1 inch of greens,
  sliced
2 tablespoons grated peeled fresh ginger
2 garlic cloves, grated
1/2 pound reduced-fat firm tofu

¼ cup Broth for Far Eastern–Flavored Dishes
(see page 168), Light Mushroom Broth (see
page 168), or vegetable broth

1 large leek, white part plus 1 inch of greens,
washed and julienned

1 large carrot, peeled and julienned

3 cups mixed steamed vegetables such as snow
peas, shredded cabbage, broccoli florets (see
pages 533, 521, and 519)

3 cups cooked linguine, made according to
package directions

In a glass or earthenware baking dish, combine
the soy sauce, orange or pineapple juice,
honey, half the scallions, half the ginger, and
half the garlic. Mix well. Cut the tofu into ⅓-
inch cubes. Add the tofu to the marinade,
cover with plastic wrap, and marinate for 40
minutes, turning over halfway through.

Bring the broth to a boil in a wok over
medium-high heat. Add the leek, carrot, and
the remaining scallions, ginger, and garlic.
Lower the heat to medium and sauté until soft,
about 2 minutes. Add the tofu in its marinade
and toss constantly until the tofu is coated with
the other ingredients.

Add the steamed vegetables. Toss well to
combine. Toss with the cooked pasta and
refrigerate until thoroughly chilled, about 3
hours.

PER SERVING: CALORIES 330 • PROTEIN 19.3 G • CARBOHYDRATE 52.4 G • FAT 6 G
• CHOLESTEROL 0 MG • SODIUM 1671 MG • 16% CALORIES FROM FAT • OUTSTAND-
ING SOURCE OF VITAMINS A, C; IRON • VERY GOOD SOURCE OF VITAMIN B₁;
FOLACIN • GOOD SOURCE OF VITAMINS B₂, B₃, B₆; ZINC

•

TAHINI TABBOULEH

Serves 4

TOTAL TIME: ABOUT 50 MINUTES, INCLUDING TIME TO
SOAK
TIME TO PREPARE: 10 MINUTES
COOKING TIME: 40 MINUTES
DO AHEAD: YOU CAN MAKE THE TAHINI DRESSING UP TO 2
DAYS IN ADVANCE. REFRIGERATE UNTIL READY TO USE.
REFRIGERATION/FREEZING: REFRIGERATE UP TO 3 DAYS. DO
NOT FREEZE.

A creamy yogurt dressing with the smoky
taste of tahini binds a slew of fresh vegetables in a sensational salad.

1 ¼ cups water

1 cup bulgur wheat

2 ears of corn

½ pound asparagus, stems trimmed and chopped

2 zucchini, chopped

½ pound sugar snap peas

Juice of 1 lemon

1 tablespoon balsamic vinegar

1 tablespoon tahini

¾ cup plain nonfat yogurt or soft tofu, beaten
until smooth

½ cup minced fresh parsley

4 scallions, including greens, chopped

½ pound cherry tomatoes, halved if larger than
marbles

Salt and freshly ground black pepper to taste

Bring the water to a boil in a small saucepan.
Add the bulgur wheat and let the water return
to a boil. Cover and remove the bulgur from
the heat. Let it sit, covered, for 30 minutes.
Pour the bulgur into a sieve and press it with
the back of a wooden spoon to squeeze out the
excess water.

Meanwhile, bring a large pot of water to a boil. Add the corn and let the water return to a boil. Cover the pot, turn off the heat, and leave the corn for 8 to 10 minutes. (If you're using an electric stove, take the pot off the burner.) Transfer the corn to a plate and let it cool. (Or cook the corn in the microwave according to directions on page 526.) Steam the asparagus, zucchini, and snap peas (see pages 516, 541, and 533 for steaming directions).

In a large mixing bowl, whisk together the lemon juice, balsamic vinegar, tahini, and yogurt or tofu. Stir in the bulgur, parsley, and scallions. Add the steamed vegetables and cherry tomatoes, and season with salt and pepper. Toss well and serve at room temperature.

PER SERVING: CALORIES 312 • PROTEIN 15.4 G • CARBOHYDRATE 61 G • FAT 4.2 G • CHOLESTEROL 0 MG • SODIUM 725 MG • 11% CALORIES FROM FAT • OUTSTANDING SOURCE OF VITAMINS B₁, C; FOLACIN • VERY GOOD SOURCE OF VITAMINS B₂, B₃, B₆; CALCIUM, IRON • GOOD SOURCE OF ZINC

Panzanellas

PANZANELLA

Serves 4

TOTAL TIME: 50 MINUTES, INCLUDING TIME TO SOAK BREAD
TIME TO PREPARE: ABOUT 20 MINUTES
COOKING TIME: NONE
REFRIGERATION/FREEZING: REFRIGERATE UP TO 1 DAY. DO NOT FREEZE.

This is the kind of recipe it kills food writers to offer. We're so sanctimonious about fresh ingredients, warning you off canned foods and giving detailed instructions for inspecting produce to the point where you may be too paranoid to shop. Then, suddenly, here's a bunch of salads that not only call for stale bread, but for drenching it in dressing long before the dish is to be served. Moreover, I'm saying, it's delicious on the day it's made and on the next.

Panzanella means "little swamp," referring to the, uh, rather particular texture of the salad, which can be made in a number of ways. The common component is bread.

¹⁄₃ cup water
1 tablespoon balsamic vinegar
3 cups packed bread chunks, crusts removed
1 small red onion, chopped
2 celery stalks, trimmed and chopped
1 cucumber, peeled, seeded, and chopped (see page 526)
¹⁄₄ cup minced fresh basil
¹⁄₄ cup minced fresh parsley
8 black olives, chopped
12 cherry tomatoes, halved
3 tablespoons extra virgin olive oil
Salt and freshly ground black pepper to taste

In a bowl, combine the water and the vinegar. Add the bread and soak for 30 minutes.

In a large salad bowl, combine the onion, celery, cucumber, basil, parsley, olives, tomatoes, and olive oil. Squeeze the excess moisture from the bread, add it to the salad, and toss well. Season with salt and pepper. Serve at room temperature.

PER SERVING: CALORIES 201 • PROTEIN 3.7 G • CARBOHYDRATE 20 G • FAT 12 G • CHOLESTEROL 0 MG • SODIUM 219 MG • 53% CALORIES FROM FAT • VERY GOOD SOURCE OF VITAMIN C • GOOD SOURCE OF VITAMIN B₁; FOLACIN, IRON

Make It Your Own

You may find that the basic Panzanella inspires you to improvise. The principle is so simple, you can spin off successfully in many directions. For additional guidelines for composing your own, see the various panzanella recipes that follow.

WHAT TO ADD AND WHEN TO ADD IT

Bread. Use a bread that blends well with the other ingredients, neither dominating the salad nor disappearing under the lettuce and dressing. Remove as much of the crust as possible before you soak the bread for the salad, and wring it out well before tossing with the other ingredients. For big chunky salads, use a hearty whole wheat bread; use pita or a lighter bread when the mix is more delicate. Herb breads work well in simple panzanellas made only with chopped tomatoes dressed with extra virgin olive oil and balsamic vinegar. Crusty rolls and bagels won't do because they won't absorb enough dressing to blend with the rest of the salad and will be tough to chew. Keep the proportion of bread to salad roughly 1 cup of bread chunks to 2 cups of other ingredients.

Dressing. Choose a dressing that complements the bread you're using. While any dressing will work with a good basic white bread, you may want to stick with extra virgin olive oil and balsamic vinegar when you're using herb bread. Creamier dressings complement whole wheat bread, which can taste coarse when tossed with a vinegar-based dressing.

Cheese. You can toss the grated and shredded cheese of your choice into the salad, using about ¼ cup cheese to 1 cup of bread, or melt cheese onto the bread before you add it to the mix: Heat the oven to 375°F. Spread the bread chunks in an even layer on a nonstick cookie sheet. Sprinkle the bread with the cheese, and bake until just melted, about 5 to 7 minutes. Instead of soaking the bread before adding it to the salad, toss it in right away. Mix the salad thoroughly, let it sit briefly to blend the flavors, and serve.

Pesto. Dot the bread chunks with pesto (see page 280) and melt as directed for cheese above. Do not soak the bread.

Other Ingredients. Panzanellas are supposed to be soggy, so you're free to throw in anything without regard for its withering effect on other ingredients. Try sliced roasted peppers, chopped cured olives, sliced marinated artichoke hearts, chopped oil-packed sun-dried tomatoes, and coarsely chopped fresh herbs.

CAESAR-STYLE SUMMERTIME PANZANELLA

Serves 4 as a side dish; 2 as a main dish

TOTAL TIME: ABOUT 25 MINUTES, INCLUDING TIME TO
   COOK THE EGG OR VEGETABLES
TIME TO PREPARE: 18 MINUTES
COOKING TIME: ABOUT 7 MINUTES
DO AHEAD: YOU CAN MAKE THE DRESSING UP TO 1 DAY IN
   ADVANCE. REFRIGERATE UNTIL READY TO USE.

Not your typical Caesar salad, but what is? Once defined as romaine lettuce tossed with raw egg, anchovy, and Parmesan cheese, today's Caesars come with lobster and kombu, or spinach and Swiss. So why not with these ingredients, too?

Dressing

¼ cup grated Parmesan cheese

½ cup plain nonfat yogurt

¼ cup nonfat buttermilk

2 tablespoons fresh lemon juice

1 tablespoon balsamic vinegar

2 teaspoons low-sodium soy sauce

1 teaspoon Dijon mustard

1 soft-boiled large egg (see page 65)

1 head romaine lettuce, torn into bite-sized
   pieces

3 cups bite-sized day-old bread chunks, lightly
   toasted

2 cups cherry tomatoes, halved or quartered,
   depending on size

2 cups sugar snap peas or snow peas, steamed
   (see page 509)

2 cooked ears of corn (see page 526)

For the Dressing

In a food processor or blender, combine the cheese, yogurt, buttermilk, lemon juice, vinegar, soy sauce, mustard, and soft-boiled egg. Process until smooth.

In a large salad bowl, toss together the lettuce, bread, tomatoes, and peas. Scrape the corn kernels off the cob into the bowl. Pour on the dressing and toss again to coat thoroughly. Let the salad sit for 5 minutes to allow the bread to absorb the dressing. Toss well again and serve.

PER SERVING (AS A SIDE DISH): CALORIES 326 • PROTEIN 18 G • CARBOHY-
DRATE 54.7 G • FAT 6.26 G • CHOLESTEROL 59.9 MG • SODIUM 472 MG • 16% CALO-
RIES FROM FAT • OUTSTANDING SOURCE OF VITAMIN C; FOLACIN • VERY GOOD
SOURCE OF VITAMINS A, B₂, B₃; CALCIUM, IRON • GOOD SOURCE OF VITAMIN B₆;
ZINC

SOUTHWEST PANZANELLA

Serves 4 as a side dish; 2 as a main dish

TOTAL TIME: ABOUT 1 HOUR, 45 MINUTES, INCLUDING TIME TO CHILL, NOT INCLUDING TIME TO COOK THE CHICKPEAS
TIME TO PREPARE: ABOUT 35 MINUTES
COOKING TIME: 8 TO 10 MINUTES
REFRIGERATION/FREEZING: REFRIGERATE UP TO 1 DAY. DO NOT FREEZE.

This variation on the "little swamp" theme features sourdough bread and those ever-appealing Southwest seasonings: fresh chilies, cilantro, cumin, and corn.

3 ears of corn
2 teaspoons red wine vinegar
¼ teaspoon grated garlic
½ cup water
3 cups packed sourdough bread chunks, crusts removed
1 cup chopped red onions
½ cup chopped Anaheim chili or jalapeño pepper
½ cup minced fresh cilantro
1 tablespoon fresh lime juice
2 cups cooked chickpeas, drained and rinsed
½ avocado, chopped
3 large firm ripe tomatoes, chopped, or 10 cherry tomatoes, halved
1 cucumber, peeled and seeded (see page 526)
⅓ cup grated Monterey Jack cheese
⅓ cup grated cheddar cheese
2 teaspoons ground cumin
2 teaspoons chili powder
1 tablespoon extra virgin olive oil

Bring a large pot of water to a boil. Add the corn and let the water return to a boil. Cover the pot, turn off the heat, and leave the corn for 8 to 10 minutes. (If you're using an electric stove, take the pot off the burner.) Transfer the corn to a plate to let it cool. (Or cook the corn in the microwave according to the directions on page 526.)

In a large bowl, combine the red wine vinegar and garlic with the water. Add the bread and toss well with your hands. Set aside.

In a large salad bowl, combine the onions, chili or pepper, cilantro, lime juice, chickpeas, avocado, tomatoes, cucumber, Jack cheese, and cheddar cheese. Scrape the corn kernels off the cob into the bowl, and add the cumin and chili powder. Toss well.

Squeeze excess moisture from the bread, add it to the salad, and toss again. Drizzle the olive oil over the salad, and toss again. Cover and refrigerate for at least an hour. Toss thoroughly before serving.

PER SERVING: CALORIES 514 • PROTEIN 21.2 G • CARBOHYDRATE 75 G • FAT 18.2 G • CHOLESTEROL 18.8 MG • SODIUM 265 MG • 30% CALORIES FROM FAT • OUTSTANDING SOURCE OF VITAMINS B₁, C; FOLACIN • VERY GOOD SOURCE OF VITAMINS A, B₂, B₃, B₆; CALCIUM, IRON, ZINC

GREEK-STYLE PANZANELLA

Serves 4 as a side dish; 2 as a main dish

TOTAL TIME: ABOUT 1 HOUR, 25 MINUTES, INCLUDING
TIME TO CHILL
TIME TO PREPARE: ABOUT 25 MINUTES
COOKING TIME: NONE
REFRIGERATION/FREEZING: REFRIGERATE UP TO 1 DAY. DO
NOT FREEZE.

With the addition of feta cheese and olives, the basic bread salad becomes fabulous main-course material.

2 cups packed bread chunks, crusts removed

2 teaspoons red wine vinegar

¼ cup water

1 red onion, chopped

2 celery stalks, chopped

10 cherry tomatoes, halved

1 cucumber, peeled, seeded, and chopped (see
page 526)

10 Greek olives, chopped

½ cup crumbled feta cheese

1 tablespoon minced fresh oregano, or 1
teaspoon crumbled dried oregano

2 tablespoons minced fresh parsley

2 tablespoons extra virgin olive oil

Place the bread in a large bowl. In a measuring cup combine the vinegar with the water. Pour evenly over the bread, and toss well so all of the bread is moistened. Squeeze out as much liquid as possible, and tilt the bowl to drain it, being careful not to dump the bread out, too.

Add the onion, celery, tomatoes, cucumber, olives, feta, oregano, and parsley. Toss well. Drizzle the olive oil over the salad and toss thoroughly. Chill for at least an hour, and toss again just before serving.

PER SERVING: CALORIES 235 • PROTEIN 7.4 G • CARBOHYDRATE 18.6 G • FAT 15.4 G • CHOLESTEROL 27.8 MG • SODIUM 542 MG • 57% CALORIES FROM FAT • VERY GOOD SOURCE OF VITAMINS B₂, C; CALCIUM • GOOD SOURCE OF VITAMINS A, B₁, B₆; FOLACIN, IRON

Raitas

Not quite salad, not quite salsa, raitas straddle the space between side dish and condiment. A cooling accompaniment for curries, raita can be spooned right on the dish, or eaten as a chaser.

BEET RAITA

Makes about 3 cups

TOTAL TIME: 2 HOURS, INCLUDING TIME TO BAKE THE
BEETS AND CHILL
TIME TO PREPARE: 10 MINUTES
COOKING TIME: 50 MINUTES
REFRIGERATION/FREEZING: REFRIGERATE UP TO 3 DAYS. DO
NOT FREEZE.

Refreshing and sweet, it's wonderful with grilled foods and with all kinds of curries (especially My Favorite Chickpeas, page 360).

2 medium beets

1 medium waxy potato, such as Yukon Gold

1½ cups plain nonfat yogurt

1 Vidalia onion or 2 scallions, including greens,
minced

½ teaspoon grated garlic

2 tablespoons minced fresh dill

2 tablespoons minced fresh cilantro
1 tablespoon fresh lemon juice
Salt and freshly ground black pepper to taste

Heat the oven to 425°F.

Wrap the unpeeled beets in foil. Bake the beets until tender, about 50 minutes, depending on size. Unwrap and slip off the peel. (Or bake them in the microwave; see page 519.)

Meanwhile, fill a medium saucepan with enough water to cover the potatoes. Bring to a boil over high heat, add the potatoes, cover, and lower the heat to medium. Boil the potatoes until tender, about 10 minutes. Drain and peel.

In a glass or ceramic mixing bowl, combine the yogurt, onion or scallions, garlic, dill, cilantro, lemon juice, beets, and potato. Season with salt and pepper. Cover and refrigerate until chilled through, about 1 hour. Serve cold.

PER SERVING (½ CUP): CALORIES 72 • PROTEIN 4.5 G • CARBOHYDRATE 13.5 G • FAT 0 G • CHOLESTEROL 1.1 MG • SODIUM 61.5 MG • 3% CALORIES FROM FAT • GOOD SOURCE OF VITAMIN C; CALCIUM

TOMATO RAITA

Makes about 1½ cups

TOTAL TIME: 1 HOUR, 10 MINUTES, INCLUDING THE TIME
   TO CHILL
TIME TO PREPARE: 10 MINUTES
COOKING TIME: NONE
REFRIGERATION/FREEZING: REFRIGERATE UP TO 3 DAYS,
   COVERED. DO NOT FREEZE.

D*ill will make it tangy, mint will make it, well, minty, while parsley would bring a subtle bite. Serve this with Potato Curry (see page 356) or Coconut Curry (see page 358).*

2 large ripe tomatoes, peeled, seeded, and
   chopped (see page 544)
½ teaspoon grated garlic
2 scallions, white parts plus 1 inch of greens,
   chopped
2 tablespoons minced fresh dill, mint, or parsley
1 cup plain nonfat yogurt
Salt and freshly ground black pepper to taste

In a glass or ceramic mixing bowl, combine the tomatoes, garlic, scallions, dill, mint, or parsley, and yogurt. Season with salt and pepper. Chill for 1 hour and serve cold.

PER SERVING (¼ RECIPE): CALORIES 66 • PROTEIN 4.5 G • CARBOHYDRATE 11 G • FAT 0 G • CHOLESTEROL 1.1 MG • SODIUM 56.8 MG • 7% CALORIES FROM FAT • VERY GOOD SOURCE OF VITAMIN C • GOOD SOURCE OF VITAMIN B₂; CALCIUM

SPINACH RAITA

Makes about 3 cups; serves 6

TOTAL TIME: ABOUT 3 HOURS, 15 MINUTES, INCLUDING
   TIME TO CHILL
TIME TO PREPARE: ABOUT 5 MINUTES
COOKING TIME: ABOUT 10 MINUTES
REFRIGERATION/FREEZING: REFRIGERATE UP TO 2 DAYS.
   DO NOT FREEZE.

More substantial than most raitas, this one can double as a side dish and condiment. Serve it with Grilled Fresh Corn and Chickpea Patties (see page 460) and curries.

10 ounces fresh spinach, thoroughly washed, steamed, and chopped (see page 539)
1 medium waxy potato, such as Yukon Gold, boiled until just cooked through, peeled, and finely diced (see page 534)
1 scallion, including greens, minced
1½ cups plain nonfat yogurt
1 teaspoon whole mustard seeds
½ teaspoon grated garlic
1 tablespoon minced fresh mint
1 tablespoon minced fresh parsley
1 teaspoon ground cumin
1 tablespoon fresh lime or lemon juice

In a glass or ceramic mixing bowl, combine the spinach, potato, scallion, yogurt, mustard seeds, garlic, mint, parsley, cumin, and lime or lemon juice. Cover and refrigerate until chilled through, about 3 hours. Serve cold.

PER SERVING (½ CUP): CALORIES 70.4 • PROTEIN 5.6 G • CARBOHYDRATE 11.9 G • FAT 0 G • CHOLESTEROL 1.1 MG • SODIUM 86.6 MG • 6% CALORIES FROM FAT • VERY GOOD SOURCE OF VITAMINS A, B₂, C; FOLACIN • GOOD SOURCE OF VITAMINS B₂, B₆; CALCIUM

CUCUMBER RAITA

Makes 3 cups; serves 6

TOTAL TIME: ABOUT 3 HOURS, 10 MINUTES, INCLUDING
   TIME TO CHILL
TIME TO PREPARE: ABOUT 10 MINUTES
COOKING TIME: NONE
REFRIGERATION/FREEZING: REFRIGERATE UP TO 4 DAYS. DO
   NOT FREEZE.

Spicy seasonings and crisp, cooling cucumbers make this raita uniquely refreshing. Serve it with curries and grilled food of all kinds.

½ teaspoon grated garlic
3 scallions, including greens, chopped
¼ cup minced fresh chives
¼ cup minced fresh cilantro
2 tablespoons minced fresh parsley
2 teaspoons ground cumin
1 teaspoon whole mustard seeds
2 tablespoons fresh lemon juice
1 cup plain nonfat yogurt
2 large cucumbers, peeled, seeded, and minced (see page 526)

In a blender or food processor, combine the garlic, scallions, chives, cilantro, parsley, cumin, mustard seeds, lemon juice, yogurt, and cucumbers. Process in short pulses until evenly distributed, about 10 pulses. Refrigerate until well chilled, about 3 hours.

PER SERVING (½ CUP): CALORIES 53.9 • PROTEIN 4.31 G • CARBOHYDRATE 9.1 G • FAT 0 G • CHOLESTEROL 1 MG • SODIUM 50.2 MG • 7% CALORIES FROM FAT • VERY GOOD SOURCE OF VITAMIN C • GOOD SOURCE OF VITAMIN B₂; CALCIUM

•

Relishes

PEACH AND LENTIL RELISH

Makes about 3 cups; serves 6

TOTAL TIME: ABOUT 3 HOURS, 15 MINUTES, INCLUDING
TIME TO CHILL, NOT INCLUDING TIME TO ROAST THE
PEPPER
TIME TO PREPARE: ABOUT 35 MINUTES, INCLUDING TIME
TO SAUTÉ
COOKING TIME: ABOUT 30 MINUTES
REFRIGERATION/FREEZING: REFRIGERATE UP TO 3 DAYS. DO
NOT FREEZE.

We don't have much say over how history represents us (or whether it does at all, for that matter), and so Luccullus (110–56 B.C.) who'd had a busy and triumphant career as a general, comes down to us mostly as a glutton and buffoon, famous for the fact that he'd divided his house into dining rooms that he used according to how much money he'd spent on a particular meal. Presumably his guests knew where they stood with ole Lucky by the time they were seated.

His grander meals were extravagant beyond anything his fellow Romans had enjoyed and occasionally featured foods no one had seen before, including peaches, which he'd brought back from a campaign in the East, and which have grown in southern Italy ever since.

Serve this luscious relish with grilled tofu or either of the "burgers" on pages 460 and 461.

2 teaspoons extra virgin olive oil
1 large red onion, thinly sliced
2 whole cloves
¼ cup minced fresh parsley
2 tablespoons minced fresh basil
Pinch ground cinnamon
1 teaspoon minced fresh sage (optional)
2 large fresh peaches, peeled and chopped (see page 107)
1 tablespoon fresh lemon juice
1 tablespoon balsamic vinegar
2 teaspoons tomato paste
½ cup uncooked lentils, rinsed
2 tablespoons currants
1½ cups water
1 yellow or orange bell pepper, cored, seeded, roasted, peeled, and thinly sliced (see page 534)

Heat the olive oil in a large skillet over medium heat. Add the onion, cloves, parsley, basil, cinnamon, and sage, if using, and sauté until the onion is soft and limp, about 15 minutes.

Add the peaches, lemon juice, and vinegar, and stir until almost all of the liquid has evaporated, about 2 minutes. Add the tomato paste and stir until it's thoroughly blended, about 4 minutes. Stir in the lentils, currants, and water. Cover and bring to a simmer over medium-high heat. Reduce the heat to medium-low and simmer until the lentils are tender and the water has been absorbed, about 30 minutes. Transfer to a mixing bowl, remove the cloves, stir in the bell pepper, cover, and refrigerate until thoroughly chilled, about 3 hours.

PER SERVING (½ CUP): CALORIES 107 • PROTEIN 5.5 G • CARBOHYDRATE 18.9 G • FAT 1.8 G • CHOLESTEROL 0 MG • SODIUM 18.8 MG • 14% CALORIES FROM FAT • OUTSTANDING SOURCE OF VITAMIN C • VERY GOOD SOURCE OF FOLACIN • GOOD SOURCE OF IRON

LEEK AND FENNEL RELISH

Serves 4 to 6

TOTAL TIME: ABOUT 3 HOURS, 15 MINUTES, INCLUDING
   TIME TO CHILL
TIME TO PREPARE: ABOUT 15 MINUTES
COOKING TIME: INCLUDED IN TIME TO PREPARE
REFRIGERATION/FREEZING: REFRIGERATE UP TO 4 DAYS. DO
   NOT FREEZE.

The sort of thing that makes you want to take a hatchet to your stove and quit cooking forever occurred when I invited about twelve people for a late-summer supper. I'd prepared a dozen dishes over several days and presented what was—in my modest estimation—a humdinger of a dinner. But the guests said little about the appetizers and main course, and raved *about this relish—a mere condiment! There's a lesson in simplicity here, but I'm still too sore to acknowledge it.*

1 tablespoon canola or vegetable oil
3 large leeks, white part only, washed and thinly
   sliced
1 fennel bulb, without leafy fronds, coarsely
   chopped
¼ cup minced fresh parsley
1 tablespoon fresh lemon juice
1 teaspoon Dijon mustard
½ cup plain nonfat yogurt
Salt and freshly ground black pepper to taste

Heat the oil in a skillet over medium-high heat. When it is hot, add the leeks, fennel, and parsley. Reduce the heat to medium and sauté, stirring often, until the leeks are soft, about 7 minutes. (The fennel should still be crunchy.)

Remove the mixture from the heat and transfer it to a medium glass or earthenware bowl. Let it cool completely. Stir in the lemon juice, mustard, and yogurt. Season with salt and pepper. Cover and chill for at least 3 hours.

PER SERVING (½ CUP): CALORIES 50 • PROTEIN 1.7 G • CARBOHYDRATE 5.8 G • FAT 2.4 G • CHOLESTEROL 0 MG • SODIUM 49.6 MG • 42% CALORIES FROM FAT • GOOD SOURCE OF VITAMIN C

Salsas

TOMATO SALSA

Makes about 3 cups; serves 8

TOTAL TIME: ABOUT 15 MINUTES, NOT INCLUDING TIME TO
   ROAST THE PEPPER
TIME TO PREPARE: 15 MINUTES
COOKING TIME: NONE
DO AHEAD: YOU CAN ROAST THE PEPPERS UP TO 3 DAYS IN
   ADVANCE. REFRIGERATE UNTIL READY TO USE.
REFRIGERATION/FREEZING: REFRIGERATE UP TO 5 DAYS. DO
   NOT FREEZE.

Try it with Chili (see page 352) and on the Tortilla-Style Frittata (see page 389), or bottle this delicious salsa and give it to your friends.

4 cups cherry tomatoes, halved
1 garlic clove, crushed
4 scallions, including greens, chopped
2 jalapeño peppers, roasted and peeled (see page
   534)
½ cup minced fresh cilantro
2 teaspoons ground cumin
1 teaspoon chili powder
Cayenne pepper to taste (optional)

In a food processor or blender place the tomatoes, garlic, scallions, jalapeños, cilantro, cumin, chili powder, and cayenne, if using. Process in short pulses until finely chopped and well combined, about 6 pulses. Be careful not to overdo it, or the mixture will liquefy. Serve at room temperature, or cover and refrigerate until ready to use.

PER SERVING (ABOUT ⅓ CUP): CALORIES 34 • PROTEIN 1.4 G • CARBOHYDRATE 7 G • FAT 0 G • CHOLESTEROL 0 MG • SODIUM 101 MG • 15% CALORIES FROM FAT • OUTSTANDING SOURCE OF VITAMIN C • GOOD SOURCE OF VITAMIN A

Make It Your Own

WHAT TO ADD AND WHEN TO ADD IT

🌢 Substitute yellow cherry tomatoes for all or some of the tomatoes.

🌢 Add sun-dried tomatoes (red or yellow) that you've reconstituted in water to cover, then drained and minced.

🌢 Reconstitute a dried chipotle pepper, mince it, and add it to the basic salsa.

🌢 Add chopped cured green olives.

PLUM SALSA

Makes about 1½ cups; serves 6

TOTAL TIME: ABOUT 3 HOURS, 15 MINUTES, INCLUDING TIME TO CHILL, NOT INCLUDING TIME TO ROAST THE PEPPER
TIME TO PREPARE: ABOUT 15 MINUTES
COOKING TIME: NONE
DO AHEAD: YOU CAN ROAST THE PEPPER UP TO 3 DAYS IN ADVANCE. REFRIGERATE UNTIL READY TO USE.
REFRIGERATION/FREEZING: REFRIGERATE UP TO 4 DAYS. DO NOT FREEZE.

Perhaps the best thing that could happen to grilled tofu (see page 456), or any grilled dish. This salsa is also delicious with Baked Beans (page 368) or Grain-Filled Onions (page 365).

4 large red or purple plums
½ cup chopped red onions
1 red bell pepper, roasted and peeled (see page 534)
1 jalapeño pepper or Anaheim chili, seeded
¼ cup minced fresh cilantro
2 teaspoons fresh lemon juice
Salt and freshly ground black pepper to taste

Fill a saucepan with water and bring it to a boil. Plunge the plums into the water, let it return to a boil, and wait 20 seconds. Drain the plums. When the plums are cool enough to handle, remove the skin and chop the fruit.

In a food processor or blender, place the plums and the onions, bell pepper, chili, cilantro, and lemon juice. Process in short pulses until chunky. Season with salt and pepper. Cover and chill thoroughly, about 3 hours, before serving.

PER SERVING (¼ CUP): CALORIES 25.9 • PROTEIN 0 G • CARBOHYDRATE 6 G • FAT 0 G • CHOLESTEROL 0 MG • SODIUM 62.8 MG • 8% CALORIES FROM FAT • VERY GOOD SOURCE OF VITAMIN C

1 yellow or orange bell pepper, cored, seeded
  and quartered
½ poblano chili, Anaheim chili, ancho chili, or
  jalapeño pepper, seeded and quartered
2 large ripe mangoes, peeled and cut from the pit
1 lime, peeled, white pith removed, and
  quartered

Place the garlic, mint, cilantro, scallions,
onion, tomato, tomatillo, bell pepper, chili,
mangoes, and lime in a blender or food processor and process in short pulses until chunky
and well combined.

PER SERVING (¼ **CUP**): CALORIES 79.5 • PROTEIN 1.8 G • CARBOHYDRATE 19.6 G
• FAT 0 G • CHOLESTEROL 0 MG • SODIUM 7.8 MG • 5% CALORIES FROM FAT • OUT-
STANDING SOURCE OF VITAMIN C • VERY GOOD SOURCE OF VITAMIN A • GOOD
SOURCE OF VITAMIN B₆

MANGO SALSA

Makes about 1½ cups; serves 6

TOTAL TIME: 10 MINUTES
TIME TO PREPARE: 10 MINUTES
COOKING TIME: NONE
REFRIGERATION: REFRIGERATE UP TO 4 DAYS.

Mangoes used to be too precious for any purpose other than eating one sweet slice at a time. To dilute them with other foods would've been like making mimosas with Dom Perignon. But mango supplies are up, prices are down, and I now toss them into salads, smoothies, and condiments like this, to serve with grilled foods and chili.

½ teaspoon grated garlic
½ cup fresh mint leaves
½ cup fresh cilantro leaves
2 scallions, including greens, chopped
1 red onion, quartered
1 ripe tomato, quartered and seeded (but not
  peeled)
1 tomatillo, husked and quartered

The Home Salad Bar

Make It Your Own

Your appetite may help you make a more satisfying salad than a recipe that's been set down
by someone else. Besides, it's more fun to have
a free hand with the salad bowl than to follow
precise directions. Here are some sets of compatible ingredients to guide you as you go.

🌿 *Greens.* Spinach and Bibb

🌿 *Herbs.* Minced fresh or crumbled dried
oregano

🌿 *Raw Vegetables.* Sliced mushrooms, thinly
sliced red onions

🌿 *Extras.* Toasted pine nuts, orange slices,
sliced black olives, crumbled feta cheese

🌿 *Dressing.* Orange-Sesame Dressing (see
page 121)

Greens. Shredded cabbage

Herbs. Minced fresh mint

Raw Vegetables. Diced cucumber, shredded carrots, minced scallions

Extras. Toasted sesame seeds or slivered almonds

Dressing. Dressing for Tahini Tabbouleh (see page 149)

Greens. Romaine

Herbs. Minced fresh basil and parsley

Legumes. Chickpeas

Extras. Steamed artichoke hearts, grated lemon zest, finely grated garlic

Dressing. Vinaigrette-Style Dressing (see page 117)

Greens. Mesclun

Herbs. Minced fresh cilantro

Raw Vegetables. Chopped red onions, shredded carrots, chopped celery

Steamed Vegetables. Shredded beets, cauliflower florets

Legumes. Cooked pinto beans or kidney beans

Grains. Cooked wheat berries or brown rice

Dressing. Multipurpose Creamy Dressing (see page 119)

Greens. Bibb

Herbs. Minced fresh mint

Grains. Cooked brown rice

Fresh Fruits. Sliced bananas, sliced strawberries, blueberries

Dried Fruits. Currants, cherries

Extras. Toasted almonds, unsweetened coconut

Dressing. Plain nonfat yogurt mixed with honey and fresh lemon juice

SOUPS IN MEAL PLANNING •

 SOUP MENUS • BROTHS •

VEGETABLE SOUPS • CREAM OF VEGETABLE

SOUPS • BEAN SOUPS •

 CHILLED SOUPS • FRUIT SOUPS

S O U P S

It's anyone's guess why soup is called *soup*. In the Middle Ages, "soup" referred to a chunk of bread placed in the bottom of a tureen to sop up the broth that was poured over it. Somehow, the broth became known as the "sop" or "soup" rather than the bread. And then the word splintered off again to become "supper," suggesting that from early on soup was often served as a meal.

Like salad, soup can be a simple starter, a light lunch, or a substantial supper. And like salad, it lends itself to improvisation. To be honest, I rarely follow soup recipes to the letter. Whenever I set out to reproduce a favorite spinach, lentil, or cream of carrot soup, I tend to end up following a whim and making it differently. In the pages ahead you'll find recipes that you can follow with confidence, and basic formulas, which you can adapt to your taste for your own signature soups.

Soups in Meal Planning

Some hearty soups can provide nearly 100 percent of your daily values for a number of vitamins, minerals, and nutrients. Even less substantial soups can contribute plenty, rounding out the nutritional content of a salad, sandwich, or substantial main course.

EARLY SPRING MINESTRONE (PAGE 196)
40% daily value for protein
210% daily value for vitamin A
103% daily value for vitamin C
49% daily value for folacin
29% daily value for vitamin B$_1$
22% daily value for vitamin B$_2$
42% daily value for iron
19% daily value for zinc

BAKED BEAN SOUP (PAGE 191)
34% daily value for protein
17% daily value for vitamin A
99% daily value for vitamin C
63% daily value for folacin
33% daily value for vitamin B$_1$
30% daily value for iron
13% daily value for zinc

CHILLED SPINACH AND HERB SOUP (PAGE 203)
24% daily value for protein
80% daily value for vitamin A
67% daily value for vitamin C
61% daily value for folacin
32% daily value for vitamin B$_2$
37% daily value for calcium
20% daily value for iron
11% daily value for zinc

(LIGHTLY) CURRIED SPLIT PEA SOUP (PAGE 195)
43% daily value for protein
54% daily value for folacin
26% daily value for iron
17% daily value for zinc

BULGUR AND RED LENTIL SOUP (PAGE 199)
58% daily value for protein
21% daily value for vitamin A
30% daily value for vitamin C
85% daily value for folacin
38% daily value for iron
24% daily value for zinc

Soup Menus

Incredible Corn Soup (page 179)
Grilled Vegetable Pockets (page 462)
Sorbet (page 489)

Cold Curried Peach Soup (page 208)
Asparagus Salad (page 146)
Soft and Chewy Dinner Rolls (page 408)

Winter Tomato-Wheat Berry Soup (page 197)
Lemon-Spiked Lentil Salad (page 143)
Fruit Soufflé (page 497)

Baked Bean Soup (page 191)
Beet and Vidalia Onion Salad (page 136)
Wheat Berry Bread (page 400)

Cherry Borscht (page 208)
Grilled Tofu in Mideast Marinade (page 456)
Lavosh (page 412)

Bulgur and Red Lentil Soup (page 199)
Baba Ghanouj (page 220)
Pita Bread (page 414)

Chickpea and Rosemary Passata (*page 192*)
Panzanella (*page 150*)

Broths

QUICK, EASY INFUSIONS

Makes 4 cups

TOTAL TIME: 40 MINUTES
TIME TO PREPARE: 10 MINUTES
COOKING TIME: 30 MINUTES TO SIMMER
REFRIGERATION/FREEZING: UP TO 4 DAYS/FREEZE UP TO
    6 MONTHS.

If you need a basic broth and have none on hand, you can boil up a simple infusion in thirty minutes with a handful of common ingredients.

2 large onions, peeled and quartered
2 large leeks, including greens, washed and sliced
4 shallots, peeled and quartered, or 8 scallions, including greens, chopped
2 large carrots, scrubbed and thickly sliced, or 2 large potatoes, scrubbed and quartered
2 celery stalks, including leaves, chopped, or 2 fennel bulbs, including leafy fronds, quartered
½ to 1 cup fresh parsley stems (optional)
1 teaspoon whole black peppercorns (optional)
4 cups water

Put the ingredients in the water, cover the pot, bring the mixture to a boil over high heat, then turn down the heat and simmer for 30 to 50 minutes. Strain the broth through a colander or sieve, and discard the vegetables. For a thicker broth, press the vegetables against the side of the colander and squeeze out the pulp.

MULTIPURPOSE VEGETABLE BROTH

Makes 1 gallon

TOTAL TIME: 1 HOUR, 40 MINUTES
TIME TO PREPARE: 10 MINUTES
COOKING TIME: 1 HOUR, 30 MINUTES
REFRIGERATION/FREEZING: REFRIGERATE UP TO 4 DAYS.
    FREEZE UP TO 6 MONTHS.

This is what's meant by "vegetable broth" in the recipes throughout this book. You'll want to keep plenty in stock so you can readily prepare the many dishes that call for it.

1 gallon water
1 pound onions (3 or 4 medium), peeled and quartered
2 pounds leeks (about 4 medium), white part only, washed and sliced
1 pound celery stalks (about 5 medium), including leaves, coarsely chopped
1 pound carrots (about 6 medium), scrubbed, trimmed, and coarsely chopped
1 pound potatoes (about 4 medium), unpeeled, scrubbed, and quartered
1 pound sweet potatoes (about 2 medium), unpeeled, scrubbed, and quartered (optional)
½ pound turnips (3 or 4 medium), scrubbed and quartered
1 cup parsley stems, tied in a bundle with twine (save the leaves for another use)
2 bay leaves
1 bouquet garni, containing 2 tablespoons dried thyme, 1 tablespoon fennel seeds, 1 tablespoon crumbled dried sage (see page 558)

Pour the water into a large pot, along with the onions, leeks, celery, carrots, potatoes, sweet potatoes, turnips, parsley stems, bay leaves, and bouquet garni. Cover and bring to a boil over medium-high heat. Lower the heat to medium-low, and let the broth simmer, covered, for 1 hour and 30 minutes.

Remove the bouquet garni. Pour the broth through a colander or sieve, and discard the vegetables. Transfer the broth to storage containers.

For a thicker, stronger broth, press the vegetables against the side of the colander or sieve to squeeze through as much pulp as possible. Transfer to storage containers. Stir the broth well before using it in recipes.

BROTH BASICS

Making broth is a lot like doing laundry. It's drudgery, but you have to do it. Of course you can buy commercial broth, but if you read the label on most brands, you may decide against it. Moreover, few taste as good as what you can make yourself.

Sometimes it doesn't matter all that much whether you use homemade broth or one from a can or bouillon cube. Even

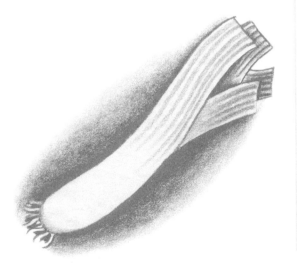

water may do. But often, good broth is essential, adding a layer of flavor to foods that would be bland without it.

TO MAKE A GOOD BROTH

• Use pure, clean water. Taste and smell your water before you begin. If you detect chlorine or anything unpleasant, switch to bottled spring water.

• Use fresh, robust vegetables and herbs. When you make broth, you're leeching the flavor from the raw ingredients. If the vegetables are rotting, you'll taste it.

• Give it time. Let the broth simmer for at least an hour and steep for an hour after that. Or make your broth in a pressure cooker, as I do. It takes half the time and tastes twice as strong. Follow instructions in owner's manual.

• Keep things in proportion, not adding too much of any one ingredient (unless this is intentional, as it would be for mushroom broth, for example). If a single flavor, such as celery, dominates the broth, it may have the same effect on the final dish. Use the proportions given in the basic recipes that follow as a guide.

Here's how to handle the nastiest part of the process, transferring the broth from the cooking pot to a container for storage: Place a large bowl in your sink. Make sure it's steady. Place a colander or large strainer over the bowl. Ideally, the colander should fit neatly into the rim of the container. Take the broth off the stove and, using both hands, pour it squarely into the center of the colander. Let the vegetables fall into the colander, too. Use the back of a spoon

to press the vegetables against the colander, pushing through as much of the vegetable pulp as you'd like to thicken the broth. If you want a thin broth, skip that step and just let the liquid run through until it stops dripping. Discard the vegetables (or puree them for baby food).

Once you've strained the broth, you can divide it into smaller containers. Freeze whatever you won't be using within a week. Refrigerate the rest, tightly covered. Since you'll probably need different amounts of broth for different purposes, store it in containers of various sizes, from ice-cube trays to one-quart yogurt cartons.

LIGHT BASIC VEGETABLE BROTH

Makes about 1 quart

TOTAL TIME: 1 HOUR, 5 MINUTES
TIME TO PREPARE: 5 MINUTES
COOKING TIME: 1 HOUR
REFRIGERATION/FREEZING: REFRIGERATE UP TO 4 DAYS.
   FREEZE UP TO 6 MONTHS.

A simple broth that you can simmer up swiftly for soups, risottos, and sauces. It's not quite as full-bodied as the broth on page 165, but it will serve you well in a pinch.

4 cups water
4 large carrots, scrubbed, trimmed, and cut into
   1-inch chunks
2 leeks, white part plus 2 inches of greens,
   washed and chopped
1 large onion, peeled and quartered
1 shallot, peeled and quartered
1 celery stalk, including leaves, coarsely chopped
2 bay leaves

Put the water in a large saucepan or stockpot. Add the carrots, leeks, onion, shallot, celery, and bay leaves. Bring the broth to a boil over high heat. Cover and turn down the heat to medium-low, and simmer for 1 hour. Strain through a fine sieve, pressing the vegetables through the mesh into the broth, if desired. Transfer the broth to storage containers.

•

LIGHT MUSHROOM BROTH

Makes about 4 cups

TOTAL TIME: 1 HOUR, 5 MINUTES
TIME TO PREPARE: 5 MINUTES
COOKING TIME: 1 HOUR
REFRIGERATION/FREEZING: REFRIGERATE UP TO 4 DAYS.
    FREEZE UP TO 6 MONTHS.

This broth makes a rich-tasting base for mushroom soups, sauces, and risottos, enhancing the flavor in the final dish.

4 cups water
6 scallions, white part plus 1 inch of greens, sliced
One 1-inch piece fresh ginger, peeled and thinly sliced
2 garlic cloves, sliced
1 medium onion, sliced
1 leek, white part plus 1 inch of greens, washed and sliced
4 dried porcini mushrooms

In a large saucepan or a stockpot, combine the water, scallions, ginger, garlic, onion, leek, and porcini. Bring to a boil over high heat. Cover, turn down the heat to medium-low, and simmer 1 hour. Strain through a fine sieve, saving the mushrooms for another use. Discard the remaining vegetables. Transfer the broth to storage containers.

•

BROTH FOR FAR EASTERN–FLAVORED DISHES

Makes about 4 cups

TOTAL TIME: 50 MINUTES
TIME TO PREPARE: 5 MINUTES
COOKING TIME: 45 MINUTES
REFRIGERATION/FREEZING: REFRIGERATE UP TO 4 DAYS.
    FREEZE UP TO 6 MONTHS.

This is the broth to use to season stir-fries and to make Mild Miso Soup (see page 173).

4 cups water
6 scallions, white part plus 2 inches of greens, chopped
4 dried shiitake mushrooms
One 1-inch piece fresh ginger, peeled and thinly sliced
2 garlic cloves, crushed
¼ cup minced fresh cilantro

In a saucepan, combine the water, scallions, mushrooms, ginger, garlic, and cilantro. Bring to a boil over high heat. Cover, turn down the heat to medium-low, and simmer 45 minutes. Strain through a fine sieve, saving the mushrooms for another use. Discard the remaining vegetables. Transfer the broth to storage containers.

HARRIED COOKS NEED TO KNOW

Q. How can you tell when you need good broth and when you can get away with one from a can or a bouillon cube, or when you can do without one altogether?

A. You need a good broth when the recipe calls for the following:

• Grains steeped in broth (risotto, for example). The flavor of the broth infuses the grain, seasoning the entire dish.

• Only a handful of ingredients, including broth (Sweet and Simple Borscht, see page 184, for example). The flavor of the broth will come through, and you'll want it to be good.

• Custom-flavored broth to season the dish (stir-fries, for example).

You can get away with canned or reconstituted broth when the recipe calls for the following:

• A lot of strong ingredients. In such a case, the broth is meant to bolster the taste without asserting its own flavor. If there's enough seasoning in the dish, you may even be able to use water instead.

• Using a small amount of broth, such as the amount called for to replace oil when you sweat vegetables rather than sauté them (see "The Basic Methods," page 512). But if the rest of the dish calls for more broth, you might as well use a good one at this stage, too.

TENDER SOUP DUMPLINGS

Serves 6

TOTAL TIME: ABOUT 50 MINUTES, INCLUDING TIME TO
  SOAK BREAD
TIME TO PREPARE: 15 MINUTES
COOKING TIME: ABOUT 35 MINUTES
REFRIGERATION/FREEZING: DO NOT REFRIGERATE OR
  FREEZE.

A simple way to add flavor and substance to any savory soup. For a quick, light soup supper dish, cook the dumplings as directed, in vegetable broth instead of water, and eat the dumplings with the broth!

2 cups tightly packed day-old French or
  sourdough bread chunks, crusts removed
⅔ cup milk, approximately
1 large egg white, lightly beaten
⅔ cup unbleached all-purpose flour
1 tablespoon grated Parmesan cheese
1 tablespoon minced fresh parsley

Place the bread chunks in a large mixing bowl. Squeezing it into the bread with your hands, add enough milk to thoroughly soak the bread. Let the bread sit 10 minutes to absorb the milk.

Still working with your hands, add the egg white and blend it into the bread mixture.

Switching to a wooden spoon, stir in the flour, Parmesan, and parsley.

Fill a large saucepan with water and bring it to a boil over high heat. Wet your hands and break off no more than 1 tablespoon of dough. Roll it into a ball and place it on a plate. Repeat the above procedure with the rest of the dough, wetting your hands as often as necessary to keep the dough from sticking to them.

Drop the balls, 5 to 8 at a time, into the boiling water. When they rise to the surface, about 2 to 3 minutes, let them boil 1 minute longer. Remove them with a slotted spoon and transfer them to a plate covered with a paper towel to drain before adding to soups.

PER SERVING: CALORIES 94 • PROTEIN 4.2 G • CARBOHYDRATE 17 G • FAT 0 G • CHOLESTEROL 1.6 MG • SODIUM 93.3 MG • 8% CALORIES FROM FAT

•

FLAVOR KICK

Makes about 4 cups

TOTAL TIME: 1 HOUR, 10 MINUTES
TIME TO PREPARE: 20 MINUTES, INCLUDING TIME TO SAUTÉ
COOKING TIME: ABOUT 50 MINUTES
REFRIGERATION/FREEZING: REFRIGERATE UP TO 3 DAYS.
  FREEZE UP TO 6 MONTHS.

Richer than ordinary vegetable broth, this highly concentrated vegetable reduction is meant to approximate the savory meat stocks and demi-glaces that better chefs depend on for extra dimensions of flavor. It takes time to prepare, but the effort required is not outrageous, given the effect this has on foods. Plus it freezes well, so you can make a lot at once to have on hand. Use it in place of ordinary broth for more robust flavor. Or use it to bolster the flavor of commercial broth, in the following proportions: When a recipe calls for 1 cup of broth, use ¾ cup broth and ¼ cup Flavor Kick. If the recipe calls for 2 cups of broth, use 1½ cups broth and ½ cup Flavor Kick.

Freeze it in small portions—¼ to ½ cup—so you can add as much or as little as you like in the months ahead. You can also pour it into ice-cube trays, freeze, then transfer the cubes to Ziploc bags, so you can use them like bouillon cubes, one at a time.

1 teaspoon extra virgin olive oil
1 large carrot, scrubbed, trimmed, and
  chopped
2 celery stalks, including leaves, chopped
1 large leek, including greens, washed and
  chopped
1 large onion, chopped
1 shallot, minced
1 garlic clove, minced
1 tablespoon tomato paste
¼ cup red wine
1 bay leaf
2 teaspoons crumbled dried thyme
2 cups vegetable broth
2 cups plus 1 tablespoon water
1 tablespoon arrowroot or cornstarch

Heat the olive oil over medium heat in a large nonstick saucepan. Add the carrot, celery, leek, onion, shallot, and garlic, and sauté until the onion is soft, about 8 minutes.

Stir in the tomato paste to blend thoroughly with the vegetables. Still stirring, add the red wine, and let the mixture simmer until most of it has evaporated, about 7 minutes.

Add the bay leaf, thyme, vegetable broth,

and 2 cups of the water. Let the broth simmer until it's reduced by half, about 40 minutes.

Blend the arrowroot or cornstarch with the remaining tablespoon of water in a cup or small bowl. Stir the mixture into the broth, and continue to simmer and stir until it's thick enough to coat the back of a wooden spoon. Strain through a fine sieve, discard the vegetables, and refrigerate until ready to use. Or transfer to small containers and freeze.

Vegetable Soups

RED OR YELLOW BELL PEPPER SOUP

Serves 4

TOTAL TIME: ABOUT 1 HOUR, 10 MINUTES, NOT INCLUD-
ING TIME TO ROAST THE PEPPERS OR TO MAKE THE BROTH
TIME TO PREPARE: 30 MINUTES, INCLUDING TIME TO SAUTÉ
COOKING TIME: 40 MINUTES
DO AHEAD: YOU CAN ROAST THE PEPPERS UP TO 3 DAYS IN
ADVANCE. KEEP WRAPPED AND REFRIGERATED UNTIL
READY TO USE. YOU CAN MAKE THE VEGETABLE BROTH
UP TO 6 MONTHS IN ADVANCE, KEEPING IT FROZEN UNTIL
READY TO USE.
REFRIGERATION/FREEZING: REFRIGERATE UP TO 3 DAYS.
FREEZE UP TO 3 MONTHS.

At the port of his hometown, Rapallo, Christopher Columbus is commemorated with a statue that has him, like anyone lucky enough to stand on that spot, staring out to sea. The difference between Columbus and you or me is that he would be thinking of sailing out into the blue, while we would be happy to take in the view, then retreat to the portside café for cappuccino.

In any event, Columbus sailed forth in search of Indian peppercorns and, losing his way, found him- self in South America, where he discovered chili pep- pers. He brought them home, where—too hot for most tastes—they were not a hit. He would have done better with sweet bell peppers, which trailed the chilies by a couple of centuries. The Europeans ate them up, so to speak, in dishes such as this soup, which comes from Tuscany.

1 tablespoon extra virgin olive oil
1 medium onion, chopped
2 celery stalks, including leaves, chopped
2 carrots, scrubbed, trimmed, and chopped
¼ cup minced fresh parsley
2 tablespoons minced fresh basil, or 2 teaspoons crumbled dried basil
2 medium boiling potatoes, peeled and quartered
4 red or yellow bell peppers, roasted, peeled, and sliced (see page 534)
4 cups vegetable broth (see page 165)

Heat the oil in a large, heavy saucepan over medium-high heat. Add the onion, celery, car-

rots, parsley, and basil, and sauté until the vegetables are soft and limp, about 15 minutes. Add the potatoes and peppers, and stir to coat with the vegetables.

Pour in the vegetable broth. Bring to a boil, turn down the heat to medium-low, cover, and simmer until the potatoes and peppers are soft enough to puree, about 40 minutes. Using an immersion blender or a food processor, puree the soup. Return it to the pot, if necessary, and heat gently before serving.

PER SERVING: CALORIES 128 • PROTEIN 2.6 G • CARBOHYDRATE 22.7 G • FAT 3.7 G • CHOLESTEROL 0 MG • SODIUM 24.9 MG • 25% CALORIES FROM FAT • OUTSTANDING SOURCE OF VITAMINS A, C • VERY GOOD SOURCE OF VITAMIN B₆ • GOOD SOURCE OF VITAMIN B₁; FOLACIN

TOMATO AND RICE SOUP

Serves 4

TOTAL TIME: 1 HOUR, 15 MINUTES, NOT INCLUDING TIME
    TO MAKE THE BROTH
TIME TO PREPARE: 45 MINUTES, INCLUDING TIME TO SAUTÉ
COOKING TIME: 30 MINUTES
DO AHEAD: YOU CAN MAKE THE VEGETABLE BROTH UP TO 6
    MONTHS IN ADVANCE, KEEPING IT FROZEN UNTIL READY
    TO USE.
REFRIGERATION/FREEZING: REFRIGERATE UP TO 3 DAYS.
    FREEZE UP TO 6 MONTHS.

Thanks to their proximity to the rice paddies of the Po Valley, the Milanese put rice in everything. And thanks to that, we have this soup, which I adapted from a recipe published in Milan.

2 teaspoons extra virgin olive oil
1 onion, chopped
1 celery stalk, trimmed and chopped
1 carrot, peeled and chopped
1 garlic clove, crushed and minced
¼ cup minced fresh basil
2 pounds tomatoes, peeled, seeded, and chopped
    (see page 544)
½ cup long-grain or medium-grain white rice
3 cups vegetable broth (see page 165)
Salt and freshly ground black pepper to taste

Heat the oil in a large saucepan or a stockpot over medium-high heat. When it is hot, add the onion, celery, carrot, garlic, and basil. Sauté, stirring often, until the vegetables are soft, about 10 minutes.

Add the tomatoes and cook, stirring often, until they simmer down into a thick sauce, about 10 minutes. Puree the mixture using an immersion blender or food processor. Return it to the heat.

Stir in the rice and vegetable broth. Bring to a boil over medium-high heat. Cover, reduce the heat to medium-low, and simmer until the rice has cooked, about 20 minutes. If the soup is too thick, add more vegetable broth or water until it's the consistency you want. Season with salt and pepper. Serve hot.

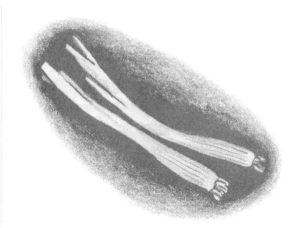

PER SERVING: CALORIES 177 • PROTEIN 4.4 G • CARBOHYDRATE 34.8 G • FAT 3.2 G • CHOLESTEROL 0 MG • SODIUM 37.9 MG • 16% CALORIES FROM FAT • OUTSTANDING SOURCE OF VITAMINS A, C • VERY GOOD SOURCE OF VITAMIN B₁ • GOOD SOURCE OF VITAMINS B₃, B₆; FOLACIN, IRON

•

MILD MISO SOUP

Serves 4

TOTAL TIME: ABOUT 40 MINUTES
TIME TO PREPARE: FEWER THAN 10 MINUTES
COOKING TIME: 30 MINUTES

A warm accompaniment to Nori Rolls (see page 370) or any stir-fry supper. It also goes well with Quick Cold Sesame Noodles (page 298) and the Soba on page 296.

3 cups water
6 scallions, including greens, chopped
6 dried shiitake mushrooms
6 wafer-thin slices peeled fresh ginger
1 large carrot, peeled and thinly sliced
2 tablespoons yellow or red miso (see Note)
½ cup cubed firm tofu (optional)

Put the water in a large saucepan. Add three-fourths of the scallions, reserving the rest. Add the mushrooms, ginger, and carrot. Bring to a boil over medium-high heat, cover, and turn the heat down to medium-low. Simmer until the vegetables are soft, about 30 minutes.

Strain the broth through a fine sieve. Remove the mushrooms from the sieve and reserve. Discard the remaining vegetables. Return the broth to the saucepan over low heat. Thinly slice the mushrooms and add them to the broth along with the remaining scallions. Stir in the miso thoroughly, never allowing the mixture to boil. Stir in the tofu, if you'd like. Serve warm.

Note: Red miso has a richer flavor than yellow, which is slightly sweet.

PER SERVING: CALORIES 95 • PROTEIN 7 G • CARBOHYDRATE 11.4 G • FAT 3.4 G • CHOLESTEROL 0 MG • SODIUM 329 MG • 29% CALORIES FROM FAT • OUTSTANDING SOURCE OF VITAMIN A • VERY GOOD SOURCE OF IRON

•

GOLDEN ONION SOUP

Serves 4

TOTAL TIME: ABOUT 1 HOUR, NOT INCLUDING TIME TO
MAKE THE BROTH
TIME TO PREPARE: ABOUT 40 MINUTES, INCLUDING TIME
TO SAUTÉ
COOKING TIME: ABOUT 20 MINUTES
EQUIPMENT: OVENPROOF SOUP BOWLS
DO AHEAD: YOU CAN MAKE THE SOUP WITHOUT THE BREAD
AND CHEESE UP TO 3 DAYS IN ADVANCE. COVER AND
REFRIGERATE. ADD THE BREAD AND CHEESE, AND BROIL AS
DIRECTED. YOU CAN MAKE THE VEGETABLE BROTH UP TO
6 MONTHS IN ADVANCE, KEEPING IT FROZEN UNTIL READY
TO USE.
REFRIGERATION/FREEZING: ONCE YOU'VE ADDED THE BREAD
AND CHEESE, THE SOUP WON'T KEEP. REFRIGERATE WITH-
OUT THE BREAD AND CHEESE UP TO 3 DAYS, OR FREEZE IT
UP TO 6 MONTHS. THAW, REHEAT, THEN ADD THE BREAD
AND CHEESE AND BROIL AS DIRECTED.

Our apartment in Paris was around the corner from Pied de Couchon, the restaurant that serves the most famous onion soup in France, big, bready, and boozy, a rich caramel color, with cheese that stretches clear to the ceiling. As good as it is, the soup was not the main attraction for me. I went for Oscar, the eponymous pig. Nattily dressed in a red bandana, Oscar spends his days on a lead, wandering from the perimeter of the outdoor seating section to his very own shed beside the shellfish stand.

I haven't tried to duplicate the soup that's served at Pied de Couchon. Mine is lighter in most respects, but the flavor is robust nonetheless (and the cheese is as much fun to stretch with your spoon).

1 tablespoon canola or vegetable oil
4 large onions, thinly sliced
Pinch sugar
1 tablespoon balsamic vinegar
4 cups vegetable broth (see page 165)
4 thick slices day-old French or sourdough
    bread, crusts removed
½ cup grated Parmesan or Gruyère cheese

Heat the oil in a large saucepan over medium-high heat. When it is hot, add the onions. Reduce the heat to medium and sauté, stirring often, until the onions are very soft and limp, about 30 minutes. Add the sugar and balsamic vinegar, and continue sautéing, stirring often, until the onions turn caramel brown, about 10 minutes more.

Pour the broth into the saucepan, and bring the mixture to a boil over medium-high heat. Reduce the heat to medium-low, and simmer gently to allow the broth to absorb the flavor of the onions, about 20 minutes.

Heat the broiler.

While the soup is simmering, toast the bread.

When the soup is done, spoon it into 4

ovenproof soup bowls. Top each serving with a slice of toast and sprinkle evenly with grated cheese. Place the bowls on a baking sheet and carefully place them under the broiler, watching constantly until the cheese is bubbly, about 1 to 2 minutes. Serve right away.

PER SERVING: CALORIES 215 • PROTEIN 9.1 G • CARBOHYDRATE 27 G • FAT 8.1 G • CHOLESTEROL 9.8 MG • SODIUM 389 MG • 34% CALORIES FROM FAT • VERY GOOD SOURCE OF CALCIUM • GOOD SOURCE OF VITAMIN C

•

BARLEY SOUP WITH ZUCCHINI

Serves 4

TOTAL TIME: ABOUT 1 HOUR, 45 MINUTES, INCLUDING TIME TO SOAK THE MUSHROOMS, BUT NOT INCLUDING TIME TO MAKE THE BROTH
TIME TO PREPARE: 25 MINUTES, INCLUDING TIME TO SAUTÉ
COOKING TIME: 45 TO 50 MINUTES
DO AHEAD: YOU CAN MAKE THE VEGETABLE BROTH UP TO 6 MONTHS IN ADVANCE, KEEPING IT FROZEN UNTIL READY TO USE.
REFRIGERATION/FREEZING: REFRIGERATE UP TO 3 DAYS. FREEZE UP TO 6 MONTHS.

W hen mealtime conversation flags, it's always fun to have some little-known facts to share about the food. Let's say you happen to be eating this soup when the room goes silent. Amaze your family and friends with the following barley trivia:

1. "Barley" shares a root word with "barn."

2. In ancient Greece, gladiators made such a big deal about getting their strength from this grain they were called barley eaters.

3. The Romans preferred wheat and used barley to feed their prisoners. Not, however, prepared like this:

1 ounce dried porcini mushrooms (about 1 cup loosely packed)
1 tablespoon extra virgin olive oil
1 onion, chopped
1 leek, white part only, washed and chopped
¼ cup minced fresh parsley
2 teaspoons grated peeled fresh ginger
2 cups sliced white button mushrooms
½ cup pearl barley
4 cups vegetable broth (see page 165)
1 large zucchini, sliced into rounds
Salt and freshly ground black pepper to taste

Soak the dried porcini in warm water to cover until soft, about 30 minutes.

Heat the oil in a large saucepan over medium-high heat. When it is hot, add the onion, leek, parsley, and ginger. Reduce the heat to medium and sauté, stirring often, until the vegetables are soft, about 7 minutes. Drain the porcini, reserving the soaking liquid. Stir them into the saucepan along with the button mushrooms. Sauté until the button mushrooms are just cooked through, about 5 minutes.

Add the barley, vegetable broth, and reserved porcini soaking liquid. Cover and simmer on medium-low until the barley has cooked, about 30 minutes. Add the zucchini and continue simmering 15 to 20 minutes. Season with salt and pepper.

PER SERVING: CALORIES 179 • PROTEIN 6.5 G • CARBOHYDRATE 30 G • FAT 4.2 G • CHOLESTEROL 0 MG • SODIUM 12.3 MG • 21% CALORIES FROM FAT • VERY GOOD SOURCE OF VITAMIN C • GOOD SOURCE OF VITAMINS B₂, B₃, B₆; FOLACIN, IRON

Cream of Vegetable Soups

The "cream" in "cream of vegetable soups" often refers to heavy cream, which can make up more than half the dish. The soups taste very good, but for all the fat and calories involved, you might as well have an ice-cream sundae for supper.

Here, "cream" doesn't refer to an ingredient, but to the consistency of soups made with pureed vegetables and broth, thickened with pureed potatoes and evaporated skim milk. Made this way, they are as delicious and far more nourishing than the old-style soups.

Just about any vegetable will make for a luscious low-fat version of classic cream soup. Because the flavor of the soup comes entirely from the vegetables you choose, be sure to pick the best. Shop with an open mind. If you had your heart set on cream of mushroom soup, but find the mushrooms are all moldy, check out the spinach or carrots instead.

CREAM OF CAULIFLOWER SOUP

Serves 4

TOTAL TIME: ABOUT 1 HOUR, NOT INCLUDING TIME TO MAKE THE BROTH
TIME TO PREPARE: ABOUT 10 MINUTES
COOKING TIME: ABOUT 50 MINUTES
DO AHEAD: YOU CAN MAKE THE VEGETABLE BROTH UP TO 6 MONTHS IN ADVANCE, KEEPING IT FROZEN UNTIL READY TO USE.
REFRIGERATION/FREEZING: REFRIGERATE UP TO 3 DAYS. FREEZE UP TO 3 MONTHS.

4 cups vegetable broth (see page 165)
1 large onion, thinly sliced
1 large leek, white part and 2 inches of greens, washed and sliced
2 pounds (about 4 cups) chopped cauliflower
1 pound potatoes, preferably Yukon Gold, peeled and sliced
Salt and freshly ground black pepper to taste
2 teaspoons cornstarch (optional)
1/2 cup evaporated skim milk or nonfat buttermilk (optional)

Pour 1/2 cup of the vegetable broth into a large saucepan or stockpot. Bring to a boil over medium-high heat. Add the onion and leek. Reduce the heat to medium, and simmer, stirring often, until the liquid has almost entirely evaporated, and the vegetables are very soft, about 7 minutes.

Add the remaining vegetable broth, the chopped cauliflower, and potatoes. Bring to a boil over medium-high heat. Cover, reduce the heat to medium-low, and simmer until the cauliflower and potatoes are tender enough to puree, about 40 minutes.

Using an immersion blender or food processor, puree the mixture. Return it to the heat, on low. Season with salt and pepper. Serve hot, or cover, refrigerate, and serve chilled.

For a thicker, richer-tasting soup, stir the cornstarch into ¼ cup of the evaporated milk or buttermilk to make a thick paste. Stir the remaining evaporated milk or buttermilk into the soup, then slowly stir in the paste. Continue stirring until the soup has thickened, about 7 minutes.

Alternatively, let the soup cool until it stops steaming. Pour ½ cup of soup into a separate bowl and stir in the cornstarch. Add the evaporated milk or buttermilk and whisk well to get rid of lumps. Whisking constantly, pour the mixture into the soup pot. To serve warm, heat slowly on medium-low, taking care not to boil or the soup will curdle. To serve cold, chill thoroughly, at least 4 hours.

PER SERVING: CALORIES 180 • PROTEIN 7.7 G • CARBOHYDRATE 39.9 G • FAT 0 G • CHOLESTEROL 0 MG • SODIUM 82.2 MG • 3% CALORIES FROM FAT • OUTSTANDING SOURCE OF VITAMINS B₆, C; FOLACIN • GOOD SOURCE OF VITAMINS B₁, B₂, B₃; IRON

•

SIMPLE SOOTHING MUSHROOM SOUP

Serves 4

TOTAL TIME: ABOUT 40 MINUTES
TIME TO PREPARE: ABOUT 20 MINUTES
COOKING TIME: ABOUT 20 MINUTES
REFRIGERATION/FREEZING: REFRIGERATE UP TO 3 DAYS. DO NOT FREEZE.

I t is simple; it is soothing; it is, in short, sensational. Serve it with a light entrée, such as spinach salad or with a cheese frittata.

2 teaspoons extra virgin olive oil or canola oil
2 scallions, white part only, chopped
10 ounces firm mushrooms, such as white button, portobello, or cremini, thinly sliced
1 pound white or red potatoes, peeled and diced
2 tablespoons minced fresh dill, or 2 teaspoons crumbled dried dill
1 teaspoon paprika
Salt and freshly ground black pepper to taste
Plain nonfat yogurt or reduced-fat or nonfat sour cream (optional), for garnish
Minced fresh parsley, for garnish

Heat the oil in a large saucepan over medium heat. When it's hot, add the scallions. Reduce the heat to medium and sauté, stirring often, until the scallions have softened, about 7 minutes. Add the mushrooms and continue to sauté until they soften and begin to give up liquid, about 7 minutes more. Add the potatoes and dill and stir well to mix.

Add just enough water to cover, stir again, raise the heat to medium, and bring to a gentle simmer. Cover the saucepan, reduce the heat to medium-low, and simmer until the potatoes are soft enough to puree, about 15 minutes.

Puree the soup by transferring the mixture to a food processor or blender and processing in short pulses until it's thick and creamy. Or use an immersion blender in the saucepan to achieve the same effect. Return the soup to medium heat. Season with the paprika and the salt and pepper. Stir well and add a dollop of yogurt or sour cream, if you'd like. Sprinkle with parsley, and serve hot.

PER SERVING: CALORIES 130 • PROTEIN 4 G • CARBOHYDRATE 24.3 G • FAT 2.6 G • CHOLESTEROL 0 MG • SODIUM 11.1 MG • 18% CALORIES FROM FAT • OUTSTANDING SOURCE OF VITAMIN C • VERY GOOD SOURCE OF VITAMINS B₂, B₃ • GOOD SOURCE OF VITAMINS B₁, B₆; IRON

FRESH TOMATO SOUP WITH CILANTRO PISTOU

Serves 4

TOTAL TIME: ABOUT 50 MINUTES
TIME TO PREPARE: 40 MINUTES, INCLUDING TIME TO MAKE
    THE PISTOU AND SAUTÉ
COOKING TIME: ABOUT 10 MINUTES
REFRIGERATION/FREEZING: REFRIGERATE UP TO 3 DAYS. DO
    NOT FREEZE.

Pistou" and "pesto" refer to a paste featuring ground fresh herbs, used to season pasta or, as in this instance, soup. Until recently you'd have been safe in assuming that the herb in question was basil. Anyone making that assumption today is in for a shock on the order of finding that Baskin & Robbins has commandeered the pesto market, using herbs as varied as rosemary and cilantro!

6 ripe tomatoes, peeled, seeded, and chopped
    (see page 544)
2 teaspoons canola or vegetable oil
1 red onion, chopped
1 garlic clove, minced
3 tablespoons minced fresh cilantro
2 tablespoons minced fresh basil, or 2 teaspoons
    crumbled dried basil
1 teaspoon ground cumin
Salt and freshly ground black pepper to taste
1 recipe Cilantro Pistou (recipe follows)

Using a food processor, blender, or immersion blender, puree the tomatoes in spurts. Take care not to overdo it, or the mixture will be too thin.

Heat the oil in a large skillet over medium-high heat, swirling the pan to coat the bottom. Add the onion, garlic, cilantro, basil, and cumin, and sauté until the onion is soft, about

12 minutes. Add the pureed tomatoes, and bring to a simmer. Turn the heat down to medium, and simmer until the mixture reduces by about about a third, about 10 minutes. Meanwhile, make the Cilantro Pistou.

Season the soup with salt and pepper and serve warm, stirring the Cilantro Pistou into the soup just before serving, or pass it at the table to be spooned into each soup bowl to taste.

PER SERVING (SOUP ONLY): CALORIES 62 • PROTEIN 1.7 G • CARBOHYDRATE 9.1 G • FAT 3 G • CHOLESTEROL 0 MG • SODIUM 17.9 MG • 38% CALORIES FROM FAT • OUTSTANDING SOURCE OF VITAMIN C • GOOD SOURCE OF VITAMIN A

Cilantro Pistou

Serves 4

TOTAL TIME: ABOUT 3 MINUTES
TIME TO PREPARE: ABOUT 3 MINUTES
COOKING TIME: NONE
REFRIGERATION/FREEZING: REFRIGERATE UP TO 4 DAYS.
    FREEZE UP TO 3 MONTHS.

You'll find additional pestos in the pasta chapter. Like the others, this pesto is good on pasta. And, try it on corn, too.

1 teaspoon grated garlic
1 teaspoon corn or canola oil
¼ cup tightly packed minced fresh cilantro
2 tablespoons minced fresh basil
¼ cup plus 2 tablespoons grated Parmesan cheese

Place the garlic, oil, cilantro, basil, and cheese in a small blender cup, a mini–food processor, or a mortar and combine to make a paste.

PER SERVING (PISTOU): CALORIES 43 • PROTEIN 2.8 G • CARBOHYDRATE 1.3 G • FAT 3 G • CHOLESTEROL 4.9 MG • SODIUM 117 MG • 62% CALORIES FROM FAT

•

INCREDIBLE CORN SOUP

Serves 4

TOTAL TIME: ABOUT 1 HOUR, 15 MINUTES, NOT INCLUD-
ING TIME TO MAKE THE BROTH

TIME TO PREPARE: 35 MINUTES, INCLUDING TIME TO SAUTÉ

COOKING TIME: 8 TO 10 MINUTES TO COOK THE CORN, 30
MINUTES TO SIMMER

DO AHEAD: YOU CAN MAKE THE VEGETABLE BROTH UP TO 6
MONTHS IN ADVANCE, KEEPING IT FROZEN UNTIL READY
TO USE.

REFRIGERATION/FREEZING: REFRIGERATE UP TO 2 DAYS. DO
NOT FREEZE.

You can see how things escalate. Someone creates a recipe for Corn Soup, so you make one for Very Good Corn Soup. Then someone else comes out with Excellent Corn Soup, and the next thing you know, you're calling yours "incredible." In this case, it happens to be apt.

The moral? Modesty is no virtue when it would be misleading.

3 ears of corn

2 teaspoons canola oil

1 sweet onion, such as Vidalia, chopped

1 leek, white part only, chopped

4 scallions, white part only, chopped

1 tablespoon grated peeled fresh ginger

2 tablespoons minced fresh basil

1 tablespoon minced fresh mint

1 medium russet potato, peeled and chopped

2 cups vegetable broth (see page 165)

Salt and freshly ground black pepper to taste

Bring a large pot of water to a boil. Add the corn and let the water return to a boil. Cover the pot, turn off the heat, and leave the corn for 8 to 10 minutes. (If you're using an electric stove, take the pot off the burner.) Transfer the corn to a plate to let it cool. (Or cook the corn in the microwave according to the directions on page 526.)

Heat the oil in a large saucepan over medium-high heat. When it is hot, add the onion, leek, scallions, ginger, basil, and mint. Reduce the heat to medium and sauté, stirring often, until the vegetables are soft, about 12 minutes.

Scrape the corn off the cob and stir in the kernels along with the potato. Add the vegetable broth and bring to a gentle boil over medium-high heat. Reduce the heat to medium-low, cover, and simmer until the potato is soft enough to puree and the liquid has reduced to just cover the other ingredients, about 30 minutes.

Puree the mixture using an immersion blender or a food processor. Return it to the heat. Warm it through, season with salt and pepper, and serve hot.

PER SERVING: CALORIES 189 • PROTEIN 5.4 G • CARBOHYDRATE 37.8 G • FAT 3.9 G • CHOLESTEROL 0 MG • SODIUM 26.4 MG • 17% CALORIES FROM FAT • VERY GOOD SOURCE OF VITAMIN B₁; FOLACIN • GOOD SOURCE OF VITAMINS B₃, B₆; IRON

CREAMY HERB SOUP

Serves 4

TOTAL TIME: ABOUT 1 HOUR, 5 MINUTES, NOT INCLUDING TIME TO COOK THE EGGS FOR THE GARNISH OR TO MAKE THE BROTH
TIME TO PREPARE: 30 MINUTES
COOKING TIME: 35 MINUTES
DO AHEAD: YOU CAN MAKE THE VEGETABLE BROTH UP TO 6 MONTHS IN ADVANCE, KEEPING IT FROZEN UNTIL READY TO USE. YOU CAN BOIL THE EGGS UP TO 3 DAYS IN ADVANCE. REFRIGERATE UNTIL READY TO USE.
REFRIGERATION/FREEZING: REFRIGERATE UP TO 3 DAYS. DO NOT FREEZE.

For a while it was getting farcical; you couldn't order anything short of dessert that didn't include arugula, a bitter green that was suddenly, inexplicably chic a short time ago. But now the fad's died down, and we can take it where it works or leave it when it doesn't. It happens to work splendidly here, where, sautéed and simmered, it mellows and melds with leeks, scallions, and chives.

2 teaspoons canola or vegetable oil
1 leek, white part plus 1 inch of greens, washed and chopped
6 scallions, including greens, minced
1/2 cup minced fresh parsley
1/2 cup minced fresh chives
2 cups watercress, chopped
4 cups arugula, chopped
1 1/2 pounds potatoes, peeled and diced
4 cups vegetable broth (see page 165)
1 tablespoon cornstarch
1 cup plain nonfat yogurt, at room temperature
Salt and freshly ground black pepper to taste
2 hard-boiled large eggs (see page 65), for garnish

Heat the oil in a large saucepan over medium-high heat. When it is hot, add the leek, scallions, parsley, chives, watercress, and arugula. Cover, reduce the heat to medium-low, and simmer until the vegetables are soft, about 8 minutes.

Stir in the potatoes and vegetable broth. Bring to a simmer over medium-high heat. Reduce the heat to medium-low, cover, and simmer until the potatoes are tender enough to puree, about 20 minutes. Remove from the heat. Puree the mixture using an immersion blender or food processor. If using a food processor, return the soup to the saucepan.

Stir the cornstarch into 1/4 cup of the yogurt in a cup or small bowl. Add 2 tablespoons of the hot soup to the mixture and stir well. Add another 2 tablespoons of soup, then pour the yogurt-soup mixture into the saucepan. Slowly stir in the rest of the yogurt. Heat slowly over low heat, to prevent separating, stirring until the mixture thickens, about 5 minutes. (To be safer, transfer the soup to a double boiler and cook with the water barely simmering.) Don't let the mixture boil. Season with salt and pepper and serve right away, or refrigerate, covered, for several hours and serve cold.

Chop the hard-boiled eggs and sprinkle an even portion over each serving.

PER SERVING: CALORIES 272 • PROTEIN 12.3 G • CARBOHYDRATE 45.6 G • FAT 5.3 G • CHOLESTEROL 108 MG • SODIUM 117 MG • 17% CALORIES FROM FAT • OUTSTANDING SOURCE OF VITAMIN C • VERY GOOD SOURCE OF VITAMINS A, B₂, B₆; FOLACIN, CALCIUM • GOOD SOURCE OF VITAMINS B₁, B₃, B₁₂; IRON

•

BUTTERNUT SQUASH SOUP

Serves 4

TOTAL TIME: ABOUT 45 MINUTES, NOT INCLUDING TIME TO MAKE THE BROTH

TIME TO PREPARE: 20 MINUTES

COOKING TIME: 25 MINUTES

DO AHEAD: YOU CAN MAKE THE VEGETABLE BROTH UP TO 6 MONTHS IN ADVANCE, KEEPING IT FROZEN UNTIL READY TO USE.

REFRIGERATION/FREEZING: REFRIGERATE UP TO 3 DAYS. FREEZE UP TO 6 MONTHS.

Every fall the weekly food sections fill up with recipes pairing butternut squash with apples, as if it were heretical to do anything else with it. Don't get me wrong; this recipe is not simply a reaction to the overplay of that combination. And even if it were, it's hard to see what harm there is when defiance inspires something this delicious.

2 cups vegetable broth (see page 165)

2 shallots, minced

2 whole cloves

2 teaspoons ground ginger

2 teaspoons ground cinnamon

1 teaspoon ground nutmeg

2 pounds butternut squash (about 2 medium), peeled, seeded, and chopped

One 12-ounce can evaporated skim milk

2 teaspoons cornstarch or arrowroot

1 tablespoon maple syrup

Pour ⅓ cup of the broth into a large saucepan. Add the shallots, and bring the broth to a simmer over medium-high heat. Turn the heat down to medium and continue to simmer, stirring often, until the shallots are soft, about 7 minutes. Stir in the cloves, ginger, cinnamon, and nutmeg. Add the remaining broth and the squash. Turn the heat up to medium-high, and bring the mixture to a gentle boil. Cover, turn the heat down to medium-low, and simmer until the squash is tender enough to puree, about 10 minutes.

Fish out the cloves and discard them. Using an immersion blender, puree the mixture. (Alternatively, transfer the mixture to a food processor, puree, and return it to the saucepan.)

In a small bowl, combine ⅓ cup of the evaporated skim milk with the cornstarch or arrowroot, stirring well. Stir the mixture into the soup, along with the rest of the milk. Turn the heat up to medium, and stir constantly until the soup is thickened, about 5 minutes. Add the maple syrup, stir well, and serve hot.

PER SERVING: CALORIES 174 • PROTEIN 8.5 G • CARBOHYDRATE 37 G • FAT 0.658 G • CHOLESTEROL 3.06 MG • SODIUM 108 MG • 3% CALORIES FROM FAT • OUTSTANDING SOURCE OF VITAMINS A, C • VERY GOOD SOURCE OF CALCIUM • GOOD SOURCE OF VITAMINS B₁, B₂, B₃, B₆; FOLACIN

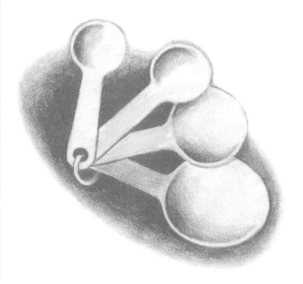

CREAM OF FRESH TOMATO SOUP

Serves 4

TOTAL TIME: ABOUT 1 HOUR, 5 MINUTES
TIME TO PREPARE: ABOUT 50 MINUTES, INCLUDING TIME
   TO SAUTÉ
COOKING TIME: 20 MINUTES
DO AHEAD: YOU CAN PEEL AND CHOP THE TOMATOES UP TO
   3 DAYS IN ADVANCE. REFRIGERATE UNTIL READY TO USE.
REFRIGERATION/FREEZING: REFRIGERATE UP TO 3 DAYS. DO
   NOT FREEZE.

Yes, it's delicious, but please don't make it before its time, i.e., late summer when tomatoes are finally truly in season. The flavor hinges on perfectly ripe tomatoes.

2 teaspoons canola or vegetable oil

1 sweet onion, such as Vidalia, thinly sliced

2 bay leaves

3 pounds fresh tomatoes, peeled, seeded, and
   chopped (see page 544)

2 teaspoons cornstarch

1/2 cup evaporated skim milk

Salt and freshly ground black pepper to taste

Heat the oil in a large saucepan over medium-high heat. When it's hot, add the onion and bay leaves. Reduce the heat to medium and sauté, stirring often, until the onion is soft and translucent, about 7 minutes.

Turn up the heat to medium-high and pour in the tomatoes. Stir until they start to bubble, about 2 minutes. Turn down the heat to medium-low, cover, and simmer gently until the tomatoes thicken, about 20 minutes.

Remove the bay leaves and discard. Puree the tomatoes with an immersion blender or food processor. If you use a food processor, transfer the soup back to the saucepan.

In a small bowl, stir the cornstarch into the evaporated skim milk. Make sure they're well blended. Stirring constantly with a whisk, pour the milk mixture into the tomatoes. Place over medium-low heat and whisk until thick and smooth, about 6 minutes. Season with salt and pepper. Serve hot.

PER SERVING: CALORIES 135 • PROTEIN 5.6 G • CARBOHYDRATE 23.7 G • FAT 3.5 G • CHOLESTEROL 1.15 MG • SODIUM 68.4 MG • 21% CALORIES FROM FAT • OUT-STANDING SOURCE OF VITAMIN C • VERY GOOD SOURCE OF VITAMIN A • GOOD SOURCE OF VITAMINS B₁, B₂, B₃, B₆; FOLACIN, CALCIUM

•

CLASSIC LEEK AND POTATO SOUP WITH WATERCRESS

Serves 4

TOTAL TIME: ABOUT 45 MINUTES
TIME TO PREPARE: 25 MINUTES
COOKING TIME: 20 MINUTES
REFRIGERATION/FREEZING: REFRIGERATE UP TO 3 DAYS.
   FREEZE UP TO 6 MONTHS.

When something's tiresome, we say it's cliché. When it's good, it's a classic. Take leek and potato soup. It will be tinkered with forever, but the basic combo will never be abandoned.

4 large leeks, white part only, washed and thinly
   sliced

1 pound white or red potatoes, peeled and thinly
   sliced

4 cups watercress, coarsely chopped

1 cup nonfat or low-fat buttermilk (optional)

Salt and freshly ground black pepper to taste

In a large saucepan, combine the leeks, potatoes, and watercress. Add enough water to cover by 1 inch. Bring to a gentle boil over medium-high heat. Cover, lower the heat to medium-low, and simmer until the leeks and potatoes are soft enough to puree, about 20 minutes.

Using an immersion blender or a food processor or blender, puree the soup in short spurts, taking care not to overdo it, or the soup will be too thin. If you use a food processor or blender, transfer the soup back to the saucepan.

If you'll be adding buttermilk, stir it in now. To serve the soup hot, return it to the stove and warm it very gently over low heat, about 5 minutes, stirring often to prevent curdling. Don't let it boil. Season with salt and pepper. To serve cold, cover and refrigerate for at least 3 hours until it is chilled through.

PER SERVING: CALORIES 194 • PROTEIN 7 G • CARBOHYDRATE 41.4 G • FAT 1 G • CHOLESTEROL 2.14 MG • SODIUM 110 MG • 5% CALORIES FROM FAT • OUTSTANDING SOURCE OF VITAMIN C • VERY GOOD SOURCE OF VITAMIN B₆; FOLACIN, IRON • GOOD SOURCE OF VITAMINS A, B₁, B₂, B₃; CALCIUM

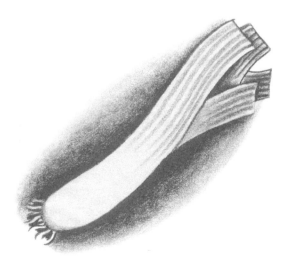

CREAMY SPINACH SOUP

Serves 4

TOTAL TIME: ABOUT 30 MINUTES, NOT INCLUDING TIME TO MAKE THE BROTH
TIME TO PREPARE: ABOUT 30 MINUTES, INCLUDING TIME TO SAUTÉ
COOKING TIME: INCLUDED IN TIME TO PREPARE
REFRIGERATION/FREEZING: REFRIGERATE UP TO 3 DAYS.

Buttermilk adds body and bite to this tangy, nourishing, anytime soup. Grit-free spinach is essential. Wash it well, rinsing each leaf. Or save time and spring for ready-washed spinach.

2 teaspoons extra virgin olive oil
1 medium onion, chopped
1 ½ pounds fresh spinach, washed and torn
1 tablespoon brown rice flour (see Note) or unbleached all-purpose flour
½ cup vegetable broth (see page 165) or water
1 large egg yolk
½ cup nonfat buttermilk
Pinch ground nutmeg
Salt and freshly ground black pepper to taste

Heat the oil in a large saucepan over medium heat. When it's hot, add the onion. Reduce the heat to medium and sauté, stirring often, until the onion is soft and translucent, about 7 minutes. Add the spinach and the flour, and cook until the spinach is wilted, about 3 minutes. Add the vegetable broth or water and stir well. Remove from the heat.

Using an immersion blender or a food processor, puree the spinach mixture. If you use a food processor, return the puree to the saucepan.

In a mixing bowl, whisk together the egg yolk and buttermilk. Whisk into the spinach mixture. Gently heat on medium-low, stirring often, until the mixture has thickened and is warm throughout, about 5 minutes. Don't let the soup boil or it will curdle. Sprinkle with nutmeg and season with salt and pepper.

Note: See mail-order information (page 596) for sources of brown rice flour.

PER SERVING: CALORIES 104 • PROTEIN 7.1 G • CARBOHYDRATE 11.8 G • FAT 4.51 G • CHOLESTEROL 54.3 MG • SODIUM 169 MG • 35% CALORIES FROM FAT • OUTSTANDING SOURCE OF VITAMINS A, C; FOLACIN • VERY GOOD SOURCE OF VITAMINS B₂, B₆; CALCIUM, IRON • GOOD SOURCE OF VITAMIN B₁

•

SWEET AND SIMPLE BORSCHT

Serves 4

TOTAL TIME: 1 HOUR, 10 MINUTES, NOT INCLUDING TIME TO MAKE THE BROTH

TIME TO PREPARE: 20 MINUTES

COOKING TIME: 40 MINUTES

DO AHEAD: YOU CAN MAKE THE VEGETABLE BROTH UP TO 6 MONTHS IN ADVANCE, KEEPING IT FROZEN UNTIL READY TO USE.

REFRIGERATION/FREEZING: REFRIGERATE UP TO 3 DAYS. FREEZE UP TO 6 MONTHS.

Beets aren't for everyone, as a particular check-out clerk reminds me every time I buy them. She recoils when she sees them moving toward her on the belt, and punches in the price code muttering "like totally yucky," avoiding eye contact as if this beet thing of mine might be contagious.

So I offer this soup for beet lovers only. The flavor of the vegetable is barely diluted by broth, so it's bound to please only those disposed toward it from the start.

4 medium beets (about 1 pound), scrubbed and halved

2 medium potatoes (about 1 pound), preferably Yukon Gold, peeled and quartered

2 cups vegetable broth (see page 165)

Plain nonfat yogurt or reduced-fat or nonfat sour cream, for garnish

Place the beets and potatoes in a large saucepan with enough water to cover. Bring them to a boil over medium-high heat, cover, lower the heat to medium-low, and let them simmer until the beets have cooked through, about 40 minutes.

Using a slotted spoon, remove the beets and transfer them to a cutting board. Discard the cooking water. When they are cool enough to handle, strip off the peels and throw them away. Chop the beets and put them in a food processor, along with the potatoes and broth. Puree in short pulses, taking care not to overdo it and make the soup too watery.

Return the soup to the saucepan and heat gently until it is warmed through. Serve hot, topped with a dollop of yogurt or sour cream.

Or refrigerate the soup for at least 4 hours and serve it chilled, also with yogurt or sour cream.

PER SERVING: CALORIES 129 • PROTEIN 4.9 G • CARBOHYDRATE 27.8 G • FAT 0 G • CHOLESTEROL 0 MG • SODIUM 68.7 MG • 2% CALORIES FROM FAT • OUTSTANDING SOURCE OF VITAMIN C • GOOD SOURCE OF VITAMIN B6; FOLACIN

•

PUREED ASPARAGUS SOUP

Serves 4

TOTAL TIME: ABOUT 35 MINUTES, NOT INCLUDING TIME TO MAKE THE BROTH

TIME TO PREPARE: 15 MINUTES

COOKING TIME: 20 MINUTES

DO AHEAD: YOU CAN MAKE THE VEGETABLE BROTH UP TO 6 MONTHS IN ADVANCE, KEEPING IT FROZEN UNTIL READY TO USE.

REFRIGERATION/FREEZING: REFRIGERATE UP TO 2 DAYS. FREEZE UP TO 6 MONTHS.

People have eaten asparagus at least as far back as the pharaohs, sometimes even because they liked the taste. But there were other reasons, too, which a Roman physician ticked off with the zeal of a patent medicine salesman, claiming it "alleviates inflammation of the stomach, excites lechery, is good for the sight and pain in the eyes, soothes the stomach gently, and is good for pain in the kidneys, stomach and intestines."

Whether or not asparagus is such a panacea, serving it this way resolves the problem of whether it should be eaten with fingers or fork. Hand out the spoons.

1 1/2 pounds asparagus, trimmed, pared, and cut into thirds

1 shallot, sliced

2 large potatoes, preferably Yukon Gold, peeled and sliced

4 cups vegetable broth (see page 165)

6 fresh mint leaves

1 teaspoon grated lemon zest

Salt and freshly ground black pepper to taste

Minced fresh chives, for garnish

Minced scallion greens, for garnish

In a large saucepan combine the asparagus, shallot, potatoes, vegetable broth, mint, and lemon zest. Bring them to a boil over medium-high heat. Cover, reduce the heat to medium-low, and simmer until the potatoes are tender enough to puree, about 20 minutes.

Puree the soup with an immersion blender or in a food processor. If using a food processor, transfer the soup back to the saucepan. Heat the soup to warm it through. Season with salt and pepper and garnish each serving with a sprinkle of chives and scallion greens.

PER SERVING: CALORIES 88.9 • PROTEIN 5.25 G • CARBOHYDRATE 19.2 G • FAT 0 G • CHOLESTEROL 0 MG • SODIUM 7.69 MG • 4% CALORIES FROM FAT • OUTSTANDING SOURCE OF VITAMIN C; FOLACIN • VERY GOOD SOURCE OF VITAMINS B1, B6 • GOOD SOURCE OF VITAMINS A, B2, B3; IRON

ZUCCHINI PASSATA

Serves 4

TOTAL TIME: ABOUT 35 MINUTES
TIME TO PREPARE: ABOUT 10 MINUTES, INCLUDING TIME
   TO SAUTÉ
COOKING TIME: ABOUT 20 MINUTES
REFRIGERATION/FREEZING: REFRIGERATE UP TO 3 DAYS. DO
   NOT FREEZE.

I would have thought that zucchini is too watery and weak to support an entire soup. I would have been wrong. This soup is surprisingly substantial and full of flavor.

2 teaspoons extra virgin olive oil
1 leek, white part only, washed and thinly sliced
2 large zucchini, peeled
2 tablespoons water
2 cups nonfat buttermilk
1 tablespoon cornstarch
1 large egg yolk
Salt and freshly ground black pepper to taste

Heat the oil in a large saucepan over medium heat. When it's hot, add the leek. Reduce the heat to medium and sauté, stirring often, until the leek is soft and limp, about 7 minutes. Meanwhile, slice the zucchini, then quarter the slices. Add them to the leeks, along with the water. Continue to cook over medium heat until the zucchini slices are tender all the way through, about 10 minutes. Remove from the heat. Puree the zucchini, either with an immersion blender or by transferring the soup to a food processor. If you use a food processor, return the puree to the saucepan.

Stir 1⅔ cups of the buttermilk into the puree. In a mixing bowl, whisk together the remaining ⅓ cup buttermilk, cornstarch, and egg yolk. Whisk the mixture into the saucepan and heat gently over medium-low, stirring often, until the soup is thickened and warm, about 10 minutes. Don't let the soup boil, or it will curdle. Season with salt and pepper.

PER SERVING: CALORIES 129 • PROTEIN 6.7 G • CARBOHYDRATE 16 G • FAT 4.8 G • CHOLESTEROL 57 MG • SODIUM 141 MG • 33% CALORIES FROM FAT • VERY GOOD SOURCE OF VITAMIN C; CALCIUM • GOOD SOURCE OF VITAMINS B₁, B₂, B₆; FOLACIN

•

APPLE-TURNIP SOUP

Serves 4

TOTAL TIME: 1 HOUR
TIME TO PREPARE: 20 MINUTES
COOKING TIME: 40 MINUTES
REFRIGERATION/FREEZING: REFRIGERATE UP TO 3 DAYS.
   FREEZE UP TO 6 MONTHS.

When people can't tell what they're eating, it could be that the food is overdone, old, or just poorly prepared. Remember the "mystery meat" served at camp? But sometimes a little enigma's a wonderful thing, as you'll see when you serve this soup. Your guests will dip in their spoons over and over, teased by a taste they clearly enjoy but can't pin down.

Two tips: Don't substitute fresh apples (you'll end up with applesauce). And use pressed apple juice if you can, the pulpy kind labeled "Not from concentrate" or sold in jugs at country stores in autumn.

½ cup loosely packed dried apples
1 onion, preferably Vidalia, chopped
1 celery stalk, trimmed and chopped
3 large turnips, peeled and diced
3 cups apple juice, preferably fresh pressed
Plain nonfat yogurt, for garnish (optional)

Place the apples, onion, celery, turnips, and apple juice in a large saucepan. Bring the mixture to a simmer over medium-high heat. Reduce the heat to medium-low, cover, and simmer until all of the vegetables and the dried fruit are soft enough to puree, about 40 minutes.

Puree with an immersion blender or in a food processor. If using a food processor, transfer the soup back to the saucepan. Return to the heat and warm through. Serve with a dollop of yogurt if you'd like.

PER SERVING: CALORIES 145 • PROTEIN 1.7 G • CARBOHYDRATE 35.5 G • FAT 0 G • CHOLESTEROL 0 MG • SODIUM 94.2 MG • 2% CALORIES FROM FAT • OUTSTANDING SOURCE OF VITAMIN C • GOOD SOURCE OF VITAMIN B₆

•

S W E E T C A R R O T
S O U P

Serves 4

TOTAL TIME: ABOUT 1 HOUR, 5 MINUTES
TIME TO PREPARE: ABOUT 10 MINUTES
COOKING TIME: ABOUT 55 MINUTES
REFRIGERATION/FREEZING: YOU CAN REFRIGERATE THE
   SOUP UP TO 3 DAYS. REHEAT GENTLY, OVER A DOUBLE
   BOILER OR VERY LOW HEAT. DO NOT FREEZE.

This soup works so well because carrot and apricot bring each other into balance: The apricots sweeten the carrots, while the carrots make the apricots mellow.

½ cup dried apricots
1 onion, chopped
4 large carrots, peeled and sliced
2 cups fresh orange juice
1 bay leaf
1 tablespoon grated peeled fresh ginger

½ tablespoon cornstarch
1 cup evaporated skim milk

Place the apricots, onion, carrots, orange juice, bay leaf, and ginger in a large saucepan. If the juice doesn't cover the carrots, add enough water to bring the liquid level up to cover by an inch.

Bring the mixture to a simmer over medium-high heat. Reduce the heat to medium-low, cover, and simmer until the carrots are soft enough to puree, about 50 minutes. Check the liquid level often, adding water to cover by an inch as needed.

Discard the bay leaf. Puree the mixture with an immersion blender or in a food processor. If using a food processor, transfer the soup back to the saucepan. Return to the stove, on medium-low heat.

Stir the cornstarch into the evaporated skim milk in a small bowl, and whisk the mixture into the soup. Continue whisking until the soup is thick and creamy, about 5 minutes. Serve hot.

PER SERVING: CALORIES 167 • PROTEIN 3.8 G • CARBOHYDRATE 39 G • FAT 0 G • CHOLESTEROL 0 MG • SODIUM 46.2 MG • 3% CALORIES FROM FAT • OUTSTANDING SOURCE OF VITAMINS A, C • GOOD SOURCE OF VITAMINS B₁, B₆; FOLACIN

Bean Soups

YOUR BASIC HEARTWARMING BLACK BEAN SOUP

Serves 4

TOTAL TIME: 50 MINUTES, NOT INCLUDING TIME TO SOAK
   THE BEANS, COOK THE EGGS, OR ROAST THE PEPPER
TIME TO PREPARE: 5 MINUTES
COOKING TIME: 45 MINUTES
DO AHEAD: YOU CAN COOK THE BEANS UP TO 1 WEEK IN
   ADVANCE. YOU CAN BOIL THE EGGS FOR THE GARNISH UP
   TO 3 DAYS IN ADVANCE. REFRIGERATE BOTH UNTIL READY
   TO USE.
REFRIGERATION/FREEZING: REFRIGERATE UP TO 3 DAYS.
   FREEZE UP TO 6 MONTHS.

*S*tart with the plumpest, glossiest dry beans
you can find, and you'll enjoy a wonderful
full-bodied soup with fathoms of flavor. Garnishes are optional for color and zest.

4 cups black beans, picked over, rinsed, and
      soaked 6 hours (for quick soaking method,
      see page 565)
2 large onions, quartered
2 garlic cloves, crushed
4 large celery stalks, trimmed and cut into 4
      pieces
2 bay leaves
Salt and freshly ground black pepper to taste

Garnishes (Optional)
2 hard-boiled large eggs (see page 65), diced
Minced fresh parsley
Chopped roasted red pepper (see page 534)
Grated orange zest
Minced scallions

Drain the beans and place them in a large
saucepan along with the onions, garlic, celery,
and bay leaves. Add water to cover by 2 inches.
Bring to a boil over high heat. Turn the heat
down to medium-low, cover, and simmer gently until the beans are soft, about 45 minutes.
Remove the bay leaves and puree the mixture
with an immersion blender or a food processor.
If using a food processor, transfer the mixture
back to the saucepan. Season with salt and
pepper. Serve hot, topped with the eggs, parsley, red peppers, orange zest, and/or scallions.

PER SERVING: CALORIES 228 • PROTEIN 13.3 G • CARBOHYDRATE 43.9 G • FAT 1 G
• CHOLESTEROL 0 MG • SODIUM 69 MG • 4% CALORIES FROM FAT • OUTSTANDING
SOURCE OF VITAMIN A; FOLACIN • VERY GOOD SOURCE OF VITAMIN B₁ • GOOD
SOURCE OF VITAMINS B₆, C; IRON, ZINC

BEAN SOUP BASICS

Think about the meal you've enjoyed most in your life, and I'll bet what comes to mind isn't the fanciest, the most expensive, or one that you anticipated weeks in advance. Chances are the meal you remember is memorable because it was deeply satisfying. It may not have been a big deal, but it was the right thing at the right time.

For me, the right time was around 1:00 P.M. on New Year's Day. I'd spent the morning playing ice hockey on a pond in New Hampshire, where the temperature was close to zero. If I'd ever been hungrier heading for a meal, I couldn't remember when that might have been. And if I'd ever been more satisfied by one, I wasn't aware of that, either. The right thing turned out to be the bowl of black bean soup (see page 188) I had for lunch. It was utterly plain, garnished simply with a hard-boiled egg. I have yet to enjoy a meal more.

Most bean soups are substantial and nourishing enough for supper—put a salad together from prepared packaged greens or the supermarket salad bar, add bread, and you're set.

• Don't use canned beans for soup unless the recipe calls for a lot of other things. Canned beans (drained and rinsed) are fine in minestrone, for example. But when beans are the main ingredient, you'll prefer the taste and texture of beans you've boiled yourself.

• Make sure the beans are thoroughly cooked, or they won't puree smoothly.

• It's easy to season bean soups because beans themselves are so flavorful. Even if the recipe calls for broth, you might not need any if, instead of throwing it out, you substitute an equal amount of the water you used to cook the beans.

BEAN SOUP SEASONINGS

Here are some justly enduring combinations and dependably delicious blends of beans, spices, and herbs.

Black Beans
Orange, cumin, coriander, and cilantro
Onion, carrot, celery, and bay leaf

Cannellini Beans and Chickpeas
Onion, garlic, and rosemary
Onion, fennel, tomato, and basil

Kidney Beans and Pinto Beans
Onion, garlic, tomato, cumin, and chili
powder

Lentils and Split Peas
Onion, thyme, and bay leaf
Garlic, ginger, cumin, coriander, and curry
powder

Navy Beans and Great Northern Beans
Onion, celery, and sage

HIGHLY SPICED BLACK BEAN SOUP

Serves 4

TOTAL TIME: ABOUT 1 HOUR, 10 MINUTES, NOT INCLUD-
ING TIME TO COOK THE BEANS
TIME TO PREPARE: 15 MINUTES, INCLUDING TIME TO SAUTÉ
COOKING TIME: ABOUT 55 MINUTES
DO AHEAD: YOU CAN COOK THE BEANS UP TO 1 WEEK IN
ADVANCE. REFRIGERATE UNTIL READY TO USE.
REFRIGERATION/FREEZING: REFRIGERATE UP TO 3 DAYS.
FREEZE UP TO 6 MONTHS.

Black beans have so much good flavor of their own, you really have to lay on the spices to season them at all. Given time to steep, this soup takes on a complex taste that's citrusy, winy, and hard to pin down.

1 tablespoon canola or vegetable oil

2 garlic cloves, minced

1 large onion, chopped

2 celery stalks, including leaves, chopped

2 carrots, peeled and chopped

¼ cup minced fresh cilantro

1 tablespoon ground cumin

2 teaspoons ground coriander

1 teaspoon paprika

1 teaspoon crumbled dried oregano

2 bay leaves

3 cups cooked black beans, drained and
    rinsed

1 tablespoon fresh lemon juice

Salt and freshly ground black pepper to taste

Heat the oil in a large saucepan over medium-high heat. When it is hot, add the garlic, onion, celery, carrots, cilantro, cumin, coriander, paprika, oregano, and bay leaves. Reduce the heat to medium, and sauté, stirring often, until the vegetables have softened, about 10 minutes.

Stir in the black beans, lemon juice, and enough water to cover by 2 inches. Bring the soup to a boil over medium-high heat. Cover, reduce the heat to medium-low, and simmer until the water reduces to the point where it barely covers the beans, about 45 to 55 minutes. Check the water level, adding more if the soup is cooking down rapidly. Remove the bay leaves and puree the soup with an immersion blender or in a food processor. If using a food processor, transfer the soup back to the saucepan. Reheat before serving. Season with salt and pepper, and serve hot.

PER SERVING: CALORIES 237 • PROTEIN 12.6 G • CARBOHYDRATE 39 G • FAT 4.2 G • CHOLESTEROL 0 MG • SODIUM 33 MG • 16% CALORIES FROM FAT • OUTSTANDING SOURCE OF VITAMIN A; FOLACIN • VERY GOOD SOURCE OF VITAMIN B₁ • GOOD SOURCE OF VITAMINS B₆, C; IRON, ZINC

BAKED BEAN SOUP

Serves 4 to 6

TOTAL TIME: 40 MINUTES, NOT INCLUDING TIME TO MAKE
   THE BEANS
TIME TO PREPARE: 10 MINUTES
COOKING TIME: 30 MINUTES
DO AHEAD: YOU CAN MAKE THE BEANS UP TO 3 DAYS IN
   ADVANCE. REFRIGERATE UNTIL READY TO USE.
REFRIGERATION/FREEZING: REFRIGERATE UP TO 3 DAYS.
   FREEZE UP TO 6 MONTHS.

B lame backyard barbecues for the fact that baked beans will always and forever be a side dish. Certain traditions become natural laws; we see those beans on the plate and start looking for the main course. This soup is a masterful compromise with convention. It calls for baked beans, tastes like baked beans, but looks more like supper (especially when you serve it with bread and a salad).

1 recipe Baked Beans (see page 214)
2 cups peeled, seeded, and chopped tomatoes
   (see page 544)
1 large onion, chopped
2 large celery stalks, including leaves, chopped
3 cups water

Combine the beans, tomatoes, onion, and celery in a large saucepan. Add the water. Bring to a simmer over medium-high heat. Reduce the heat to low, cover, and continue to simmer gently, stirring often, until the onion and celery are soft enough to puree, about 30 minutes.

   Puree the soup with an immersion blender or in a food processor or blender. If using a food processor or blender, transfer the soup back to the saucepan. Reheat just before serving.

PER SERVING (¼ RECIPE): CALORIES 363 • PROTEIN 15.4 G • CARBOHYDRATE 76.2 G • FAT 1.9 G • CHOLESTEROL 0 MG • SODIUM 82.8 MG • 5% CALORIES FROM FAT • OUTSTANDING SOURCE OF VITAMIN C; FOLACIN • VERY GOOD SOURCE OF VITAMINS B₁, B₆; IRON • GOOD SOURCE OF VITAMINS A, B₂, B₃; ZINC

CHUNKY CHICKPEA SOUP

Serves 4

TOTAL TIME: 2 HOURS, 30 MINUTES, NOT INCLUDING TIME
   TO MAKE THE BROTH
TIME TO PREPARE: 30 MINUTES, INCLUDING TIME TO SAUTÉ
COOKING TIME: 2 HOURS
DO AHEAD: YOU CAN SOAK THE CHICKPEAS UP TO 3 DAYS
   IN ADVANCE. REFRIGERATE UNTIL READY TO USE.
REFRIGERATION/FREEZING: REFRIGERATE UP TO 3 DAYS.
   FREEZE UP TO 6 MONTHS.

S alvation on snow days.

1 ½ cups dried chickpeas
2 teaspoons extra virgin olive oil
2 medium onions, chopped
2 celery stalks, chopped (reserve the leaves for
   the bouquet garni)
2 medium carrots, peeled and chopped
3 garlic cloves, peeled
4 cups vegetable broth (see page 165)
1 bouquet garni, containing 6 celery leaves and
   1 tablespoon crumbled dried herbes de
   Provence (see page 559)
1 bay leaf
¼ teaspoon white pepper
Salt to taste

Bring 4 cups of water to a boil in a large saucepan. Add the chickpeas and let the water return to a boil. Cover, and turn off the heat. (If you're using an electric stove, take the saucepan off the burner, or the water will continue to boil.) Let the chickpeas sit, covered, for an hour.

   Heat the oil in a large nonstick saucepan over medium heat. Add the onions, celery, carrots, and garlic and sauté over medium-low heat until the vegetables have softened, about 12 minutes.

Drain the chickpeas and add them to the saucepan. Add the vegetable broth, bouquet garni, and bay leaf and bring to a simmer over medium-high heat. Cover, and lower the heat to medium-low. Let the soup simmer until the chickpeas have cooked through, about 1 hour.

Transfer the mixture to a food processor, in small batches, if necessary, and process in pulses until the chickpeas are well chopped, and the soup is thick. Take care not to puree it; the soup should be chunky.

Return the soup to the saucepan, stir in the pepper, and heat gently over low heat. Season with salt, and serve hot.

PER SERVING: CALORIES 336 • PROTEIN 15.8 G • CARBOHYDRATE 55.2 G • FAT 6.9 G • CHOLESTEROL 0 MG • SODIUM 50 MG • 18% CALORIES FROM FAT • OUT-STANDING SOURCE OF VITAMIN A; FOLACIN • VERY GOOD SOURCE OF VITAMINS B₁, B₆, C; IRON • GOOD SOURCE OF VITAMIN B₂; CALCIUM, ZINC

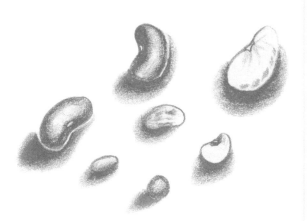

CHICKPEA AND ROSEMARY PASSATA

Serves 4

TOTAL TIME: 40 MINUTES, NOT INCLUDING TIME TO MAKE THE BROTH OR THE CHICKPEAS
TIME TO PREPARE: 10 MINUTES
COOKING TIME: 30 MINUTES
DO AHEAD: YOU CAN COOK THE CHICKPEAS UP TO 1 WEEK IN ADVANCE. WRAP AND REFRIGERATE UNTIL READY TO USE. YOU CAN MAKE THE VEGETABLE BROTH UP TO 6 MONTHS IN ADVANCE, KEEPING IT FROZEN UNTIL READY TO USE. WHILE REHEATING, STIR AND DILUTE WITH ADDITIONAL VEGETABLE BROTH BEFORE SERVING.
REFRIGERATION/FREEZING: REFRIGERATE UP TO 3 DAYS. FREEZE UP TO 6 MONTHS.

A*n eloquent case for simplicity. This soup, though spare, is substantial and delicious.*

4 large sprigs rosemary
1 cup Light Basic Vegetable Broth (see page 167)
3 cups freshly cooked chickpeas (see page 565; do not use canned for this recipe)
Salt and freshly ground black pepper to taste

Place the rosemary and broth in a saucepan and heat over medium-high heat. Simmer gently for 15 minutes. Turn off the heat and let the rosemary steep for 15 minutes more.

Add the chickpeas and puree with an immersion blender or in a food processor. If using a food processor, transfer the soup back to the saucepan. Season with salt and pepper. Heat over medium heat before serving, stirring often.

PER SERVING: CALORIES 207 • PROTEIN 11 G • CARBOHYDRATE 34.7 G • FAT 3.4 G • CHOLESTEROL 0 MG • SODIUM 9.4 MG • 15% CALORIES FROM FAT • OUTSTAND-ING SOURCE OF FOLACIN • VERY GOOD SOURCE OF IRON • GOOD SOURCE OF VITAMIN B₁; ZINC

CHILI BEAN SOUP

Serves 4

TOTAL TIME: 1 HOUR, 15 MINUTES, NOT INCLUDING TIME
    TO COOK THE BEANS
TIME TO PREPARE: 45 MINUTES, INCLUDING TIME TO SAUTÉ
COOKING TIME: 30 MINUTES
REFRIGERATION/FREEZING: REFRIGERATE UP TO 3 DAYS.
    FREEZE UP TO 6 MONTHS.

This is not a recipe to share with the chili purists you know, who, as noted elsewhere, can be dangerous when provoked. They might consider making soup of their favorite dish a desecration akin to, I don't know, putting it in calzone (see page 419).

1 tablespoon canola or vegetable oil

1 large onion, chopped

1 garlic clove, minced

2 tomatillos, husked and diced

¼ cup minced fresh cilantro

1 tablespoon chili powder

2 teaspoons crumbled dried oregano

1 teaspoon ground cumin

Pinch cayenne pepper

1 tablespoon red wine vinegar or balsamic
    vinegar

3 cups cooked kidney or pinto beans, drained
    and rinsed

2 cups chopped peeled fresh tomatoes (see page
    544), or canned chopped tomatoes

2 tablespoons stone-ground cornmeal

1 cup water

Heat the oil in a large saucepan over medium-high heat. When it is hot, add the onion, garlic, tomatillos, cilantro, chili powder, oregano, cumin, and cayenne. Reduce the heat to medium and sauté, stirring often, until the onion is soft, about 7 minutes. Add the vinegar and stir until most of the moisture has evaporated, about 3 minutes.

Add the beans, tomatoes, cornmeal, and water. Stir well. Bring the soup to a gentle boil over medium-high heat. Cover, turn down the heat to low, and simmer gently, stirring often, until it is thickened, about 30 minutes.

Puree with an immersion blender or in a food processor. If using a food processor, transfer the soup back to the saucepan. Reheat before serving.

PER SERVING: CALORIES 260 • PROTEIN 13.6 G • CARBOHYDRATE 63.2 G • FAT 5.1 G • CHOLESTEROL 0 MG • SODIUM 33.7 MG • 17% CALORIES FROM FAT • OUTSTANDING SOURCE OF VITAMIN C; FOLACIN • VERY GOOD SOURCE OF VITAMIN B_1; IRON • GOOD SOURCE OF VITAMINS A, B_3, B_6; ZINC

•

PASTA E FAGIOLI

Serves 4 to 6

TOTAL TIME: ABOUT 1 HOUR, 30 MINUTES, NOT INCLUD-
ING TIME TO ROAST THE PEPPERS, COOK THE BEANS, OR
MAKE THE BROTH
TIME TO PREPARE: 40 MINUTES, INCLUDING TIME TO SAUTÉ
COOKING TIME: ABOUT 50 MINUTES
DO AHEAD: YOU CAN ROAST THE PEPPERS UP TO 3 DAYS IN
ADVANCE. KEEP THEM WRAPPED AND IN THE REFRIGERA-
TOR UNTIL READY TO USE. YOU CAN MAKE THE VEG-
ETABLE BROTH UP TO 6 MONTHS IN ADVANCE, KEEPING IT
FROZEN UNTIL READY TO USE.
REFRIGERATION/FREEZING: REFRIGERATE UP TO 3 DAYS.
FREEZE UP TO 3 MONTHS.

If you want an example of a genuine misnomer, consider "authentic Italian cooking." It's not only a misnomer, it's an absurdity; Italy wasn't even a country until relatively recently, so the concept of a national cuisine is necessarily contrived. Moreover, the food in Liguria—on Italy's northwest coast—has much more in common with what's eaten in neighboring France than with what's served in Trieste, to the northeast. And then there's the popular guide to restaurants in Milan, which says that the most common foreign food served in that city is Tuscan.

All this by way of saying there is no definitive version of dishes that have been identified as "Italian." I've seen pasta e fagioli made with penne and white beans and with farfalle and kidney beans. Sometimes there are greens in it, sometimes not. Have fun with the basic formula, only take care not to overcook the pasta.

1 tablespoon extra virgin olive oil
1 large onion, chopped
2 garlic cloves, minced
2 leeks, white part only, washed and chopped

1 fennel bulb, including leafy fronds, chopped, or 4 celery stalks, including leaves, chopped
1 red bell pepper, roasted, peeled, and chopped (see page 534)
1 yellow bell pepper, roasted, peeled, and chopped (see page 534)
1/2 cup minced fresh basil, or 1 1/2 tablespoons crumbled dried basil
1/4 cup minced fresh parsley
2 tablespoons minced fresh rosemary
1 tablespoon balsamic vinegar
2 cups fresh or canned tomato puree
3 cups vegetable broth (see page 165)
2 cups cooked cannellini beans, scarlet runner beans, chickpeas, or kidney beans, drained and rinsed
2 cups dried short pasta, such as penne or farfalle, cooked until not quite done (there should still be some white in the center when you bite into it)
2 cups tightly packed chopped collard greens
Salt and freshly ground black pepper to taste

Heat the oil in a large saucepan or stockpot over medium-high heat. When it is hot, add the onion, garlic, leeks, fennel or celery, red bell pepper, yellow bell pepper, basil, parsley, and rosemary. Reduce the heat to medium and sauté, stirring often, until the vegetables are soft, about 10 minutes. Add the balsamic vine-gar and stir until most of it evaporates, about 3 minutes.

Stir in the tomato puree and vegetable broth. Bring to a boil over medium-high heat. Reduce the heat to medium-low, cover, and simmer until the soup has thickened, about 50 minutes. Stir in the beans, the pasta, and the collards. Cover and continue cooking until the pasta is cooked al dente, and the collards turn bright green, about 4 minutes more. Season with salt and pepper, and serve hot.

•

(L I G H T L Y)   C U R R I E D S P L I T   P E A   S O U P

Serves 4

TOTAL TIME: ABOUT 40 MINUTES
TIME TO PREPARE: 20 MINUTES, INCLUDING TIME TO SAUTÉ
COOKING TIME: 20 MINUTES
REFRIGERATION/FREEZING: REFRIGERATE UP TO 3 DAYS.
    FREEZE UP TO 6 MONTHS.

A*t times throughout her career, a food writer is expected to come up with recipes for things she really hates. This situation reminds me of the story about Mozart, who accepted a commission to write a piece for the flute, an instrument he claimed to detest. The result was arguably the most magnificent music ever written for that instrument.*

I am no more fond of split peas than Mozart was of the flute. And while I can't claim this is the best split pea soup you'll ever have, I can hope it's a contender.

2 teaspoons canola or vegetable oil
1 large onion, chopped
1 garlic clove, minced
1 tablespoon grated peeled fresh ginger
2 celery stalks, trimmed and chopped

1 Granny Smith apple, peeled, seeded, and chopped
¼ cup minced fresh cilantro
1 tablespoon curry powder
2 teaspoons ground cumin
2 teaspoons whole mustard seeds
1 teaspoon ground coriander
1 teaspoon ground turmeric
1½ cups yellow or green split peas
1 tablespoon fresh lemon juice
Salt and freshly ground black pepper to taste

Heat the oil in a medium saucepan over medium-high heat. When it is hot, add the onion, garlic, ginger, celery, apple, cilantro, curry powder, cumin, mustard seeds, coriander, and turmeric. Reduce the heat to medium and sauté, stirring often, until the vegetables have softened, about 10 minutes.

Stir in the split peas. Add enough water to cover by 2 inches. Bring to a boil over medium-high heat. Reduce the heat to medium-low, cover, and simmer until the split peas are soft enough to puree, about 20 minutes. (Squeeze one with your fingernail to be sure the core is soft and cooked through.)

Puree with an immersion blender or in a food processor. If using a food processor, transfer the soup back to the saucepan. Return to low heat. Stir in the lemon juice and season with salt and pepper. Serve hot.

•

EARLY SPRING MINESTRONE

Serves 4

TOTAL TIME: ABOUT 2 HOURS, 15 MINUTES, NOT INCLUD-
ING TIME TO COOK THE BEANS OR TO MAKE THE BROTH
TIME TO PREPARE: 1 HOUR, 15 MINUTES, INCLUDING TIME
TO SAUTÉ
COOKING TIME: 1 HOUR
REFRIGERATION/FREEZING: REFRIGERATE UP TO 3 DAYS.
FREEZE UP TO 6 MONTHS.

Minestre, minestrini, minestrone. *So goes the declension of soups in Italian, from spare broth (minestre), to very basic vegetable (minestrini), to a virtual stew pot of produce, legumes, and pasta (minestrone).*

Here's one for that time of year when seasonal vegetables overlap—as artichokes head out, and new potatoes come in. It's one of the better ways I know to make the best of the old and the most of the new (and an excellent supper, besides).

1 tablespoon extra virgin olive oil
1 large onion, chopped
1 large leek, white part plus 2 inches of greens, washed and thinly sliced
2 garlic cloves, minced
1 fennel bulb, without leafy fronds, or 4 celery stalks, trimmed and thinly sliced
4 large carrots, peeled and chopped
2 medium turnips, peeled and chopped
2 medium potatoes, peeled and chopped
4 medium artichokes, pared, trimmed, and quartered (see page 514)
¼ cup minced fresh parsley
1 tablespoon crumbled dried oregano
1 tablespoon crumbled dried basil
2 bay leaves
½ cup pearl barley

1 cup chopped peeled fresh tomatoes (see page 544), or canned chopped tomatoes
2 cups cooked cannellini beans, drained and rinsed
8 cups vegetable broth (see page 165)
Salt and freshly ground black pepper to taste
Grated Parmesan or Asiago cheese, for garnish (optional)

Heat the oil in a stockpot or large saucepan over medium-high heat. When it's hot, add the onion, leek, garlic, fennel or celery, and carrots. Reduce the heat to medium and sauté, stirring often, until the vegetables have softened, about 10 minutes.

Stir in the turnips, potatoes, artichokes, parsley, oregano, basil, bay leaves, barley, tomatoes, and beans. Stir well. Add the vegetable broth and bring to a boil over medium-high heat. Cover, reduce the heat to medium-low, and simmer until the barley is cooked and the artichokes and potatoes are tender enough to pierce with a fork, about 1 hour. Season with salt and pepper. Serve sprinkled with grated cheese, if you'd like.

PER SERVING: CALORIES 449 • PROTEIN 17.9 G • CARBOHYDRATE 87.9 G • FAT 4.8 G • CHOLESTEROL 0 MG • SODIUM 179 MG • 9% CALORIES FROM FAT • OUT-STANDING SOURCE OF VITAMINS A, C; FOLACIN, IRON • VERY GOOD SOURCE OF VITAMINS B₁, B₃, B₆; CALCIUM • GOOD SOURCE OF VITAMIN B₂; ZINC

Make It Your Own

You can make minestrone with anything you like—provided no single vegetable dominates the dish (that rules out broccoli or brussels sprouts, which tend to be overwhelming). Not that the ingredients should be bland, but they should blend with the others, absorbing and contributing flavor in equal measure with the rest.

WHAT TO ADD AND WHEN TO ADD IT

🖉 Add any seasonal vegetable that looks good on the day you shop, such as green beans, okra, fresh peas.

🖉 Substitute parsnips or rutabagas for the turnips.

🖉 Make an alphabet soup by substituting alphabet noodles for the barley. Add the noodles to the soup for the final eight to ten minutes of cooking.

🖉 Substitute chickpeas, lima beans, or navy beans for the cannellini beans.

•

WINTER TOMATO–
WHEAT BERRY SOUP

Serves 4

TOTAL TIME: 1 HOUR, 40 MINUTES, TO 2 HOURS, NOT
  INCLUDING TIME TO SOAK THE BEANS AND THE WHEAT
  BERRIES
TIME TO PREPARE: 20 MINUTES, INCLUDING TIME TO SAUTÉ
COOKING TIME: 1 HOUR, 20 MINUTES, TO 1 HOUR, 40
  MINUTES
DO AHEAD: YOU MUST SOAK THE WHEAT BERRIES
  OVERNIGHT.
REFRIGERATION/FREEZING: REFRIGERATE UP TO 4 DAYS.
  FREEZE INDEFINITELY.

L*ike "granola" and "sprouts," "wheat berry" used to be an adjective, as in "She's one of those wheat berry, sprouts, and granola types." This wasn't supposed to be flattering, although it should have been. I'd imagine that a Wheat Berry Type would be someone who thinks good food should be fun, who goes in for wheat in its sweetest, chewiest form, and who'll make this soup for you whenever you want it.*

1 cup kidney beans, soaked overnight and drained
    (for quick soaking method, see page 565)
3 cups water
2 teaspoons extra virgin olive oil
1 large onion, chopped
2 large leeks, white part only, washed and chopped
3 celery stalks, or 1 small fennel bulb, without
    leafy fronds, chopped
1 cup wheat berries, soaked overnight and drained
1 medium potato, peeled and diced
2 cups chopped peeled fresh tomatoes (see page
    544), or canned chopped tomatoes
1 bouquet garni, containing three 3-inch sprigs
    rosemary (see page 558)
Salt and freshly ground black pepper to taste

Put the beans in a medium saucepan with the water. Cover and bring to a boil over medium-high heat. Turn down the heat and simmer until the beans are tender, 40 minutes to 1 hour. Don't drain the beans.

Heat the olive oil in a separate large saucepan over medium-high heat. Turn down the heat to medium-low and sauté the onion, leeks, and celery or fennel, stirring often, until they're soft, about 10 minutes. Stir in the beans and their cooking water. Add the wheat berries, potato, tomatoes, and the rosemary bundle. Cover and simmer gently over low heat until the wheat berries are swollen and tender, about 40 minutes. Stir occasionally to keep the vegetables from sticking to the pot. If the soup is too thick, add as much water as necessary to reach a consistency you like. Season with salt and pepper.

PER SERVING: CALORIES 300 • PROTEIN 14.2 G • CARBOHYDRATE 57 G • FAT 3.4 G • CHOLESTEROL 0 MG • SODIUM 54.9 MG • 10% CALORIES FROM FAT • OUTSTANDING SOURCE OF VITAMIN C; FOLACIN • VERY GOOD SOURCE OF VITAMINS B₁, B₆; IRON • GOOD SOURCE OF VITAMINS B₂, B₃; CALCIUM, ZINC

WINTER GARDEN SOUP

Serves 4

TOTAL TIME: ABOUT 50 MINUTES, NOT INCLUDING TIME TO
COOK THE BEANS OR TO MAKE THE BROTH
TIME TO PREPARE: ABOUT 10 MINUTES
COOKING TIME: ABOUT 40 MINUTES
DO AHEAD: YOU CAN COOK THE BEANS UP TO 1 WEEK IN
ADVANCE. WRAP AND REFRIGERATE. OR YOU CAN MAKE
THE SOUP WITHOUT THE BREAD, AND REFRIGERATE IT FOR
2 DAYS, ADDING THE BREAD JUST BEFORE SERVING.
REFRIGERATION/FREEZING: REFRIGERATE UP TO 2 DAYS.
YOU CAN MAKE THE SOUP WITHOUT THE BREAD AND
FREEZE IT FOR UP TO 3 MONTHS. THAW AND ADD THE
BREAD WHILE HEATING.

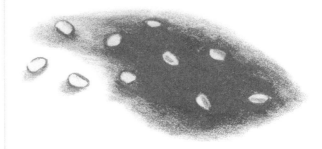

W*hen it gets to be that time of year when
it feels as if winter will last forever,
make this soup, and you may not
mind if it goes on for a while longer.*

1 tablespoon extra virgin oil

2 medium onions, chopped

1 garlic clove, minced

4 cups loosely packed shredded green or red
cabbage

2 large turnips, peeled and diced

2 medium potatoes, peeled and chopped

2 teaspoons crumbled dried herbes de Provence

1 cup canned chopped tomatoes, including juice

6 cups vegetable broth (see page 165)

2 cups cooked white beans, such as cannellini,
drained and rinsed

2 cups loosely packed whole wheat bread
chunks, crusts removed

Salt and freshly ground black pepper to taste

Grated Gruyère or Parmesan cheese, for garnish
(optional)

Heat the oil in a medium skillet over medium-high heat. When it is hot, add the onions and garlic. Reduce the heat to medium and sauté, stirring often, until the onions have softened, about 7 minutes. Add the cabbage, turnips, potatoes, and herbes de Provence, and stir well to mix. Stir in the tomatoes and their juice. Add the vegetable broth and beans. Bring the soup to a boil over medium-high heat. Cover, reduce the heat to medium-low, and simmer until the potatoes are cooked through, about 15 minutes. Add the bread and continue cooking until the soup is very thick, about 10 more minutes. Season with salt and pepper, and sprinkle with grated cheese, if you'd like.

PER SERVING: CALORIES 267 • PROTEIN 13.2 G • CARBOHYDRATE 47.2 G • FAT
4.6 G • CHOLESTEROL 0 MG • SODIUM 251 MG • 15% CALORIES FROM FAT • OUT-
STANDING SOURCE OF VITAMIN C • VERY GOOD SOURCE OF FOLACIN, IRON •
GOOD SOURCE OF VITAMINS B₁, B₂, B₆; CALCIUM

•

BULGUR AND RED LENTIL SOUP

Serves 4 to 6

TOTAL TIME: ABOUT 1 HOUR, 15 MINUTES, NOT INCLUD-
ING TIME TO SOAK THE BEANS OR TO MAKE THE BROTH
TIME TO PREPARE: 40 MINUTES, INCLUDING TIME TO SAUTÉ
COOKING TIME: 20 MINUTES
REFRIGERATION/FREEZING: REFRIGERATE UP TO 3 DAYS.

We expect Mother Nature to hold herself to higher standards than cut-rate car dealers, but every once in a while, she pulls a bait and switch. Consider red lentils. You buy them because they're peachy pink, thinking "Gee, won't they look pretty on the plate." You get them home, toss them on to cook, and the minute they hit the heat, you find you've been had. They're now the color of mustard and turning rapidly to mush.

Red lentils won't decorate your dish, but they will season it. They taste less like ordinary lentils than like peppery split peas and are particularly good with the sharp sort of herbs you'll use in this piquant soup.

2 teaspoons olive oil

2 medium onions, thinly sliced

1/3 cup minced fresh cilantro

1/4 cup minced fresh dill, or 2 tablespoons crumbled dried dill

1/4 cup minced fresh chives

1 cup uncooked red lentils

1/2 cup bulgur wheat

4 cups water, or 2 cups water plus 2 cups vegetable broth (see page 165)

1 cup cooked chickpeas, drained and rinsed

2 cups torn fresh spinach or beet greens

1 1/2 cups plain nonfat yogurt

Heat the olive oil in a large heavy saucepan. Add the onions, cilantro, dill, and chives, and sauté over medium-low heat, stirring often, until the onions are so soft they're close to melting, about 20 minutes. It's essential to let the onions sauté long enough to become very sweet.

Add the lentils and bulgur and stir to coat them with the herbs, about 1 minute. Add the water and broth, if using, stir well, and bring the soup to a simmer over medium-high heat. Cover, lower the heat to medium-low, and cook until the bulgur and lentils are tender, about 20 minutes. Add the chickpeas and the spinach or beet greens, and stir until the leaves turn bright green, about 2 minutes.

Remove the soup from the heat and let it cool for 10 to 15 minutes, stirring it occasionally to help it along. Put the yogurt in a large mixing bowl. Add 1 tablespoon of the hot soup, and stir well. Add another spoonful, and stir. Continue to transfer the soup into the yogurt, gradually increasing the amount of soup as you go until you've blended two-thirds of it with the yogurt. Stir well, and transfer the yogurt mixture to the rest of the soup in the saucepan. Heat carefully over low heat, stirring to warm through.

PER SERVING (1/4 RECIPE): CALORIES 374 • PROTEIN 26 G • CARBOHYDRATE 63 G • FAT 3.5 G • CHOLESTEROL 1.65 MG • SODIUM 103 MG • 8% CALORIES FROM FAT • OUTSTANDING SOURCE OF FOLACIN • VERY GOOD SOURCE OF VITAMINS A, B₁, B₂, B₆, C; CALCIUM, IRON • GOOD SOURCE OF VITAMIN B₃

Chilled Soups

COLD CREAM OF BROCCOLI SOUP

Serves 4

TOTAL TIME: ABOUT 1 HOUR, PLUS 4 HOURS TO CHILL, BUT NOT INCLUDING TIME TO MAKE THE BROTH
TIME TO PREPARE: ABOUT 10 MINUTES
COOKING TIME: ABOUT 47 MINUTES
REFRIGERATION/FREEZING: REFRIGERATE, COVERED, UP TO 3 DAYS. FREEZE UP TO 3 MONTHS.

Everyone needs a good subterfuge from time to time. That goes double for anyone trying to serve broccoli to someone determined to reject it. At the risk of promoting underhanded, deceptive, and manipulative behavior, I offer this soup, and the following advice: when they ask you what's in it, change the subject until they're done.

4 cups vegetable broth (see page 165)
1 large onion, thinly sliced
1 large leek, white part and 2 inches of greens, washed and sliced
4 cups chopped fresh broccoli (about 2 pounds)
1 pound potatoes, preferably Yukon Gold, peeled and sliced
½ cup nonfat or low-fat buttermilk
1 tablespoon fresh lemon juice
Salt and freshly ground black pepper to taste
2 tablespoons minced fresh chives, for garnish

Pour ½ cup of the vegetable broth into a large saucepan or stockpot. Bring to a boil over medium-high heat. Add the onion and leek. Reduce the heat to medium, and simmer, stirring often, until the liquid has almost entirely evaporated, and the vegetables are very soft, about 7 minutes.

Add the remaining vegetable broth, the broccoli, and potatoes. Bring to a boil over medium-high heat. Cover, reduce the heat to medium-low, and simmer until the broccoli and potatoes are tender enough to puree, about 40 minutes.

Using an immersion blender or food processor, puree the mixture. Let the soup cool to room temperature. Whisk the buttermilk and lemon juice into the soup. Cover and chill thoroughly, at least 4 hours. Season with salt and pepper, and garnish with chives.

PER SERVING: CALORIES 166 • PROTEIN 6.6 G • CARBOHYDRATE 36 G • FAT 0 G • CHOLESTEROL 1.07 MG • SODIUM 67.6 MG • 4% CALORIES FROM FAT • OUTSTANDING SOURCE OF VITAMIN C • VERY GOOD SOURCE OF VITAMIN B₆; FOLACIN • GOOD SOURCE OF VITAMINS A, B₁, B₂, B₃; CALCIUM, IRON

CHILLED SOUP BASICS

Cold-weather meals are easy. Just make something warm and hearty enough, and everyone's happy.

But summer food is a different story. No one may want much of anything other than ice cream, which could be fine with you—until your mother's voice harkens from the distance, "No dessert until you've had your dinner." As always, she's right.

Chilled soups are the solution. Refreshing and filling, they're simple for you and appetizing for everyone.

• The most refreshing cold soups call for light ingredients, such as cucumber, yogurt, buttermilk, fresh fruit, and tangy seasonings such as dill, mint, cilantro, and curry powder.

• For an easy, creamy cold soup, make any

creamed vegetable soup according to the basic recipe on page 176, omitting the milk. Let it cool, then stir in a cup of yogurt or buttermilk. Chill for at least three hours.

• To thicken and chill a soup, run the soup through the blender with chipped ice just before serving. Serve immediately or the soup will get runny. Or you can chill and thicken cold soup in an ice-cream maker, running it in the machine for several minutes until it reaches the temperature and consistency you want.

•

CHILLED CREAM OF CARROT SOUP WITH GINGER AND LIME

Serves 4

TOTAL TIME: 3 HOURS, 55 MINUTES, INCLUDING TIME TO CHILL, BUT NOT INCLUDING TIME TO MAKE THE BROTH
TIME TO PREPARE: 15 MINUTES, INCLUDING TIME TO SAUTÉ
COOKING TIME: ABOUT 40 MINUTES
DO AHEAD: YOU CAN MAKE THE VEGETABLE BROTH UP TO 6 MONTHS IN ADVANCE, KEEPING IT FROZEN UNTIL READY TO USE.
REFRIGERATION/FREEZING: REFRIGERATE UP TO 3 DAYS.

1 pound carrots, peeled and sliced

1 sweet onion, such as Vidalia, thinly sliced

1 bay leaf

2 to 4 cups vegetable broth, as needed (see page 165)

1 teaspoon unsalted butter or canola or vegetable oil

1 shallot, minced

2 scallions, white part only, minced

2 teaspoons grated peeled fresh ginger

1 teaspoon cornstarch

1/2 cup evaporated skim milk

2 tablespoons fresh orange juice

1 tablespoon fresh lime juice

1 teaspoon maple syrup

Plain nonfat yogurt, for garnish

Place the carrots, onion, and bay leaf in a large saucepan. Add 2 cups of the vegetable broth. Cover and simmer over medium heat, adding more broth to keep the carrots well covered throughout, until you can pierce the carrots easily with a fork, about 30 minutes.

Puree the mixture with an immersion blender or in a food processor. Process until smooth, and set aside.

Melt the butter or heat the oil in a separate large saucepan. Add the shallot, scallions, and ginger, and sauté over medium-low heat until softened, about 4 minutes. Stir in the pureed carrots.

Combine the cornstarch and evaporated milk in a small bowl. Whisk it into the carrot mixture and heat gently, stirring with the whisk, until the soup has thickened and warmed through, about 7 minutes. Remove from the heat, and stir in the orange juice, lime juice, and maple syrup.

Spoon into soup bowls and top each serving with a dollop of yogurt. To serve cold, refrigerate for 3 hours.

PER SERVING: CALORIES 114 • PROTEIN 4.3 G • CARBOHYDRATE 22 G • FAT 1.3 G • CHOLESTEROL 3.7 MG • SODIUM 78.9 MG • 10% CALORIES FROM FAT • OUTSTANDING SOURCE OF VITAMIN A • VERY GOOD SOURCE OF VITAMIN C • GOOD SOURCE OF VITAMINS B₁, B₂, B₆; CALCIUM

•

GAZPACHO

Serves 4

TOTAL TIME: 10 MINUTES, NOT INCLUDING TIME TO ROAST
THE PEPPERS OR GARLIC, COOK THE EGG, OR MAKE THE
DUMPLINGS OR THE BROTH
TIME TO PREPARE: 10 MINUTES
COOKING TIME: NONE
DO AHEAD: YOU CAN BOIL THE EGG AND/OR ROAST THE
PEPPERS UP TO 3 DAYS IN ADVANCE. WRAP AND REFRIGER-
ATE UNTIL READY TO USE.
REFRIGERATION/FREEZING: REFRIGERATE UP TO 3 DAYS.
FREEZE UP TO 6 MONTHS.

*C*onnoisseurs of the soup are bound to wonder where the green peppers are in my version. The answer is, they're not. I don't like
the way they dominate every dish they go into and I
won't have the rest of the good ingredients bullied in
that way. But if you'd miss them otherwise, use green
peppers in place of or in addition to the red and yellow called for here.

4 medium ripe tomatoes, peeled, seeded, and
    chopped (see page 544)
1 red bell pepper, roasted, peeled, and chopped
    (see page 534)

1 small yellow or orange bell pepper, roasted,
    peeled, and chopped (see page 534)
1 large cucumber, peeled, seeded, and chopped
    (see page 526)
4 scallions, including greens, minced
1 small red or Vidalia onion, chopped
½ fennel bulb without leafy fronds, or 2 celery
    stalks, including leaves, chopped
1 small garlic clove, minced
3 tablespoons minced fresh basil
3 tablespoons minced fresh parsley
1 teaspoon extra virgin olive oil
2 teaspoons balsamic vinegar
1 cup vegetable broth (see page 165)
1 teaspoon low-sodium soy sauce

Garnishes (Choose One Group;
Optional)
1 slice French bread or sourdough toast
1 roasted garlic clove (see page 529)
1 hard-boiled large egg (see page 65)
1 tablespoon fresh lime juice

1 recipe Tender Soup Dumplings (see page 169)
1 small cucumber, peeled, seeded, and chopped
    (see page 526)
1 tablespoon fresh lime juice

In a food processor or blender, place the tomatoes, red bell pepper, yellow or orange bell
pepper, cucumber, scallions, onion, fennel or
celery, garlic, basil, parsley, olive oil, balsamic
vinegar, vegetable broth, and soy sauce.
Process in short spurts to puree, about 10
spurts.

If using the garnish, just before serving, rub
the bread or toast with the garlic and cut it into
small pieces. Chop the egg. Distribute both

evenly among the servings. Sprinkle each serving with a bit of the lime juice.

Or just before serving, place an equal amount of dumplings and cucumber into each serving. Sprinkle each serving with a bit of the lime juice.

PER SERVING (WITHOUT GARNISH): CALORIES 86 • PROTEIN 3.3 G • CARBO-HYDRATE 17 G • FAT 1.8 G • CHOLESTEROL 0 MG • SODIUM 103 MG • 17% CALORIES FROM FAT • OUTSTANDING SOURCE OF VITAMIN C • VERY GOOD SOURCE OF VIT-AMIN A • GOOD SOURCE OF VITAMINS B₁, B₆; FOLACIN, IRON

•

CHILLED SPINACH AND HERB SOUP

Serves 4

TOTAL TIME: ABOUT 20 MINUTES, INCLUDING TIME TO CHILL
TIME TO PREPARE: 20 MINUTES
COOKING TIME: NONE
REFRIGERATION/FREEZING: REFRIGERATE UP TO 3 DAYS.

*Y*ou may have fresh herbs, mild buttermilk, and the best intentions in the world, but the success of this soup hinges entirely on thoroughly washed spinach.

That wasn't the note I'd intended to write for this recipe. I was going to wax rhapsodic, celebrating the soup's zip and zest. But my husband reminded me what happened the first time I served it: grit got hopelessly in the way. Now I buy spinach that's been washed and wrapped, and suggest you do the same.

1 pound fresh spinach leaves, washed and
   steamed (see page 539)
2 tablespoons minced fresh oregano
2 tablespoons minced fresh basil
2 tablespoons minced fresh mint

2 tablespoons minced fresh chives
2 tablespoons minced fresh dill
2 tablespoons minced fresh parsley
2 scallions, white part plus 2 inches of greens,
   minced
1 tablespoon cornstarch
3 cups nonfat buttermilk or nonfat plain yogurt
¼ cup plain nonfat yogurt
Salt and freshly ground black pepper to taste

Put the steamed spinach, oregano, basil, mint, chives, dill, parsley, scallions, cornstarch, buttermilk, and yogurt in a food processor and puree. Heat gently over a double boiler, stirring constantly, until thickened, about 10 minutes. Or heat over very low direct heat, stirring constantly and taking great care not to boil, about 5 minutes, or the soup will separate. Cover and refrigerate until chilled through. Season with salt and pepper.

PER SERVING: CALORIES 121 • PROTEIN 10.6 G • CARBOHYDRATE 17 G • FAT 2.1 G • CHOLESTEROL 6.7 MG • SODIUM 297 MG • 15% CALORIES FROM FAT • OUTSTAND-ING SOURCE OF VITAMINS A, C; FOLACIN • VERY GOOD SOURCE OF VITAMIN B₂; CALCIUM, IRON • GOOD SOURCE OF VITAMINS B₁, B₆; ZINC

•

Fruit Soups

COLD CHERRY SOUP

Serves 4

TOTAL TIME: ABOUT 4 HOURS, INCLUDING TIME TO CHILL
TIME TO PREPARE: 20 MINUTES
COOKING TIME: ABOUT 40 MINUTES
EQUIPMENT: CHERRY PITTER
REFRIGERATION/FREEZING: REFRIGERATE UP TO 3 DAYS.
    FREEZE UP TO 6 MONTHS.

One rule of thumb governing utensil purchases is to consider the cost of the item in relation to how often you'll use it. Since cherry season is so short, a pitter scores pretty low on the price-use ratio. But the formula is badly flawed, not taking into account how this gadget affects your life when you put it to use. By that reckoning, if owning a cherry pitter moved you to make this soup just once a year, it'd be worth the ten dollars or so you can expect to pay for it.

1 cup loosely packed dried apples

2 pounds cherries, chopped

1 tablespoon cornstarch

2 cups nonfat buttermilk

2 tablespoons fresh lime juice

Place the dried apples and cherries in a medium saucepan with water to cover by an inch. Bring to a simmer over medium-high heat. Cover and reduce the heat to medium-low. Simmer until the apples and cherries are soft enough to puree, about 30 minutes.

Puree with a food processor or immersion blender and return to low heat. Transfer ¼ cup of the puree to a separate bowl and whisk in the cornstarch until the mixture is smooth.

Whisking constantly, pour the cornstarch mixture into the saucepan. Continue whisking until the mixture thickens, about 7 minutes. Turn off the heat and let the mixture cool to room temperature.

Stir in the buttermilk, cover, and chill thoroughly, at least 3 hours. Ladle the soup into 4 soup bowls and sprinkle each serving with lime juice.

PER SERVING: CALORIES 253 • PROTEIN 6.9 G • CARBOHYDRATE 54.6 G • FAT 3.3 G • CHOLESTEROL 4.29 MG • SODIUM 140 MG • 11% CALORIES FROM FAT • VERY GOOD SOURCE OF VITAMINS B₂, C • GOOD SOURCE OF VITAMIN B₁: CALCIUM

FRUIT SOUP BASICS

The difference between fruit soup and a fruit shake or smoothie is that some part of the soup is cooked before the whole thing is chilled and served. Also, some fruit soups include savory ingredients, such as onions and celery, to temper the sweetness and allow the true fruit flavor to come through (for example, the Strawberry Soup on page 206, and the Apple-Turnip Soup on page 186).

• Make a base for your soup by plumping dried fruit in fruit juice. The combination sweetens the soup and thickens it. Choose a dried fruit that complements the fresh fruit you'll be using. Dried apricots, peaches, apples, and pears go well with fresh peaches, mangoes, strawberries, and cantaloupe. Stay away from prunes and figs, which may over-power the other ingredients.

• The fruit juice should complement the fresh and dried fruits, also. Apple and orange juice make good bases for peach or strawberry soup. Apple juice is also a good base for cherry soup. Try either orange or pineapple juice when you're making can-taloupe soup or mango soup.

• To make the soup, prepare whatever fresh fruit you'll be using by peeling, seed-ing, and chopping it. (See below for direc-tions.) Place the fresh fruit along with dried fruit in a nonreactive saucepan. Use about 4 cups fresh and ½ cup dried fruit for a 4-serving soup.

Add enough fruit juice to cover the fruit by several inches, about 1 cup.

Bring the juice to a simmer over medium-high heat. Cover and reduce the heat to medium-low. Simmer until the fruit is plump, and tender enough to puree.

Puree using an immersion blender or food processor.

• To prepare peaches, nectarines, cherries, or plums for soup, bring a large pot of water to a boil. Plunge the fruit in, bring to a second boil, and let the fruit boil for thirty seconds. Remove the fruit with a slotted spoon and transfer to a colander. Place under cold running water to cool. Slip off the skin. Remove the pits, chop, and puree using an immersion blender or food processor.

• You can further thicken a fruit soup with cornstarch. After you've pureed the fruit and juice, place ¼ cup in a small bowl and return the rest of the mixture to the saucepan. Stir about 2 teaspoons of corn-starch into the reserved puree, then whisk it into the soup in the saucepan. Continue whisking as you heat the soup gently over medium-low heat. When it thickens, remove it from the heat and let it cool. (The soup will thicken more when it cools.) Cover and chill thoroughly before serving.

• Add a tablespoon of fresh lemon or lime juice to any fruit soup for accent.

• For a tangy, more substantial soup, whisk in a cup or two of nonfat buttermilk, plain yogurt, or soft tofu before chilling.

• Garnish cold fruit soups with minced fresh mint and/or unsweetened coconut if you'd like, or bit of complementary chopped fruit.

STRAWBERRY SOUP

Serves 4

TOTAL TIME: ABOUT 3 HOURS, 30 MINUTES, INCLUDING
  TIME TO CHILL
TIME TO PREPARE: ABOUT 5 MINUTES
COOKING TIME: ABOUT 20 MINUTES
REFRIGERATION/FREEZING: REFRIGERATE UP TO 3 DAYS. DO
  NOT FREEZE.

Sweet, creamy, and cool, this soup, were it not for the savory touch of onion, could easily be dessert. But, as it is, you'll want to serve it as a first course.

½ cup dried apricots or dried peaches
1 small Vidalia onion, thinly sliced
2 quarts fresh strawberries, hulled and sliced
1½ cups fresh orange juice or apple juice
1 tablespoon cornstarch or arrowroot
2 cups nonfat buttermilk or plain nonfat
    yogurt
1 tablespoon fresh lime juice

Place the apricots or peaches, onion, and strawberries in a large saucepan. Add the juice and bring to a boil over medium-high heat. Reduce the heat, cover, and simmer gently until the dried fruit is plump and soft, about 20 minutes.

Remove the mixture from the heat. Puree with an immersion blender or food processor. Return the puree to medium-low heat. Place the cornstarch or arrowroot in a small bowl and add ¼ cup of the soup. Stir until smooth. Slowly whisk the mixture into the soup, and continue stirring until thickened, about 5 minutes. Remove the soup from the heat.

Let the soup cool completely, about 30 minutes. (You can speed it along by filling a large bowl with ice cubes, then transferring the soup to a bowl that will fit inside it. Place the whole thing in the refrigerator, and stir often.)

When the soup is cool, whisk in the buttermilk or yogurt and the lime juice. Chill thoroughly, about 2½ hours, and serve cold.

PER SERVING: CALORIES 252 • PROTEIN 10.03 G • CARBOHYDRATE 53.3 G • FAT 1.39 G • CHOLESTEROL 2.2 MG • SODIUM 99.8 MG • 5% CALORIES FROM FAT • OUTSTANDING SOURCE OF VITAMIN C • VERY GOOD SOURCE OF VITAMIN B₂; FOLACIN, CALCIUM • GOOD SOURCE OF VITAMINS A, B₁, B₆, B₁₂; IRON, ZINC

•

COLD APRICOT SOUP

Serves 4

TOTAL TIME: ABOUT 3 HOURS, 35 MINUTES, INCLUDING
  TIME TO CHILL
TIME TO PREPARE: 10 MINUTES
COOKING TIME: 20 MINUTES
REFRIGERATION/FREEZING: REFRIGERATE UP TO 3 DAYS.
  FREEZE UP TO 6 MONTHS.

Fresh apricots don't keep well, so when you see yours slipping past their prime, quick! Into this soup. Dried apricots sweeten them up and boost their flavor, while lemon juice and ginger shock them back to life.

2 pounds ripe fresh apricots
½ cup dried apricots
1 tablespoon fresh lemon juice
1 teaspoon sugar or honey
1 cup nonfat or low-fat buttermilk
Pinch ground ginger

Bring about 4 inches of water to a boil in a large pot. Add the fresh apricots, bring to a second boil, and remove the apricots with a slotted spoon after 40 seconds. When they are cool enough to handle, peel, slice, and remove the pits.

Place the dried apricots in a saucepan and add water to cover. Bring to a simmer over medium-high heat. Cover, reduce the heat to medium-low, and simmer until the apricots are soft, about 20 minutes. Drain and allow them to cool for 5 minutes.

Place the dried apricots in a food processor or blender, and puree. Add the fresh apricots and puree. Add the lemon juice, sugar or honey, buttermilk, and ginger, and process until smooth.

Transfer the soup to a glass bowl, cover, and refrigerate until thoroughly chilled, about 3 hours. Serve cold.

PER SERVING: CALORIES 177 • PROTEIN 5.8 G • CARBOHYDRATE 39.5 G • FAT 1.5 G • CHOLESTEROL 2.1 MG • SODIUM 68.2 MG • 7% CALORIES FROM FAT • OUTSTANDING SOURCE OF VITAMIN A • GOOD SOURCE OF VITAMIN B₂; CALCIUM, IRON

•

CANTALOUPE SOUP
Serves 4

TOTAL TIME: ABOUT 4 HOURS, 5 MINUTES, INCLUDING TIME TO CHILL
TIME TO PREPARE: ABOUT 20 MINUTES
COOKING TIME: ABOUT 30 MINUTES
REFRIGERATION/FREEZING: REFRIGERATE UP TO 3 DAYS. DO NOT FREEZE.

*P*ick a less-than-perfect melon? Your secret's safe in this revivifying soup, where dried apricots compensate for almost any flaw.

3 cups plus 2 tablespoons fresh orange juice
⅓ cup loosely packed dried apricots

2 teaspoons cornstarch
1 ripe cantaloupe, cut from the rind, seeded, and chopped
2 tablespoons fresh lime juice
1 cup nonfat buttermilk or plain nonfat yogurt

In a heavy nonreactive saucepan (enamel is ideal for this), bring 3 cups of the orange juice to a simmer. Add the apricots and continue simmering until they are very soft, about 30 minutes. Remove from the heat and let them cool about 15 minutes. Transfer the apricots and juice to a food processor or blender, and puree. Return the puree to the saucepan.

In a cup or small bowl, combine the cornstarch and the remaining 2 tablespoons of orange juice to make a thick paste. Stir this into the puree and heat gently over medium heat, stirring often, until the mixture is thickened, about 15 minutes. Remove from the heat and transfer to a large glass or earthenware bowl.

Puree the cantaloupe in a food processor or blender. Stir the puree into the orange juice–apricot mixture, along with the lime juice and buttermilk or yogurt. Cover the soup and chill it thoroughly before serving, at least 3 hours.

PER SERVING: CALORIES 183 • PROTEIN 4.9 G • CARBOHYDRATE 40 G • FAT 1.3 G • CHOLESTEROL 2.1 MG • SODIUM 79 MG • 6% CALORIES FROM FAT • OUTSTANDING SOURCE OF VITAMINS A, C • VERY GOOD SOURCE OF FOLACIN • GOOD SOURCE OF VITAMINS B₁, B₂, B₆; CALCIUM

•

CHERRY BORSCHT

Serves 4

TOTAL TIME: ABOUT 5 HOURS, 10 MINUTES, INCLUDING
   TIME TO CHILL
TIME TO PREPARE: 20 MINUTES
COOKING TIME: ABOUT 50 MINUTES
DO AHEAD: YOU CAN PIT THE CHERRIES AND/OR COOK THE
   BEETS UP TO 3 DAYS IN ADVANCE. REFRIGERATE UNTIL
   READY TO USE.
EQUIPMENT: CHERRY PITTER
REFRIGERATION/FREEZING: REFRIGERATE UP TO 3 DAYS. DO
   NOT FREEZE.

*T*he taste of Bing cherries blends seamlessly
with beets for the ideal midsummer soup,
full of flavor and rich in color.

4 large beets, scrubbed
1 pound cherries, pitted
1 teaspoon fresh lemon juice or raspberry vinegar
1 cup plain nonfat yogurt
¼ cup reduced-fat or nonfat sour cream

In a large saucepan simmer the beets in water
to cover over medium heat until they're tender
enough to pierce with a knife, about 40 minutes. Drain the beets, reserving 1 cup of the
cooking liquid. Set the beets aside to cool.

Put the cherries in a medium saucepan
along with the reserved beet-cooking liquid.
Bring to a simmer over medium-high heat, and
simmer until the cherries are very soft, about
10 minutes. Add the lemon juice or vinegar and
simmer for 2 minutes more.

Peel and quarter the beets. Place them in a
food processor along with the cherries and
cooking liquid. Puree the mixture and transfer
to a large bowl. Refrigerate the soup until it's
thoroughly chilled, about 3 hours. In a separate
mixing bowl, blend together the yogurt and
sour cream, and stir them into the beet and
cherry puree before serving.

PER SERVING: CALORIES 147 • PROTEIN 6.7 G • CARBOHYDRATE 30 G • FAT 1.2 G •
CHOLESTEROL 1.1 MG • SODIUM 95.3 MG • 7% CALORIES FROM FAT • GOOD
SOURCE OF VITAMINS B₂, C; FOLACIN, CALCIUM

•

COLD CURRIED PEACH SOUP

Serves 4

TOTAL TIME: 5 HOURS, INCLUDING TIME TO CHILL
TIME TO PREPARE: 40 MINUTES, INCLUDING TIME TO SAUTÉ
COOKING TIME: 20 MINUTES
REFRIGERATION/FREEZING: REFRIGERATE UP TO 3 DAYS. DO
   NOT FREEZE.

*P*eaches and curry have an affinity that this
soup exploits to luscious effect. It's a great
start to any grilled supper.

2 teaspoons unsalted butter
1 cup chopped red onions

2 teaspoons grated peeled fresh ginger

2 teaspoons grated garlic

2 tablespoons minced fresh basil

2 tablespoons minced fresh cilantro

2 teaspoons curry powder

1 whole clove

1 tablespoon fresh lemon juice

2 teaspoons brown sugar

1 large ripe tomato, peeled, seeded, and chopped (see page 544)

4 large peaches (about 1½ pounds), peeled and chopped

1½ tablespoons unsweetened coconut, toasted (see Note)

1 cup nonfat buttermilk or nonfat plain yogurt (optional)

Melt the butter in a saucepan over medium-high heat, swirling the pan to coat the bottom. Add the onions, ginger, garlic, basil, cilantro, curry powder, and clove, reduce the heat to medium-low, and sauté, stirring often, until the onions are soft, about 12 minutes. Add the lemon juice and stir until most of the liquid has evaporated, about 2 minutes.

Stir in the brown sugar, tomato, and peaches. Cover and let simmer, stirring often, until the peaches are so soft they seem to be melting, about 20 minutes. Remove from the heat.

Discard the clove. Using a food processor or immersion blender, puree the soup. Strain it by pouring it through a sieve, pushing the pulp against the sieve with the back of a wide wooden spoon.

Stir in the coconut. Cover the soup and chill it thoroughly, at least 4 hours. Stir in the buttermilk or yogurt, if desired. Serve cold.

Note: To toast coconut, spread the coconut out in an even layer over a piece of foil on a baking sheet and bake at 300° F. until the coconut turns golden brown, about 3 minutes.

PER SERVING: CALORIES 131 • PROTEIN 5 G • CARBOHYDRATE 22 G • FAT 3.4 G • CHOLESTEROL 6.28 MG • SODIUM 52 MG • 22% CALORIES FROM FAT • VERY GOOD SOURCE OF VITAMIN C • GOOD SOURCE OF VITAMIN B₂; CALCIUM

STARTERS AND SIDE DISHES

I'll bet most restaurateurs secretly wish that their floors would open and swallow up people like me who order appetizers for dinner. If only they understood it's not that we're cheap, but that we're more intrigued by the first courses than by the entrées.

You can mix and match the following small dishes and starters to make an entire meal out of them. The only trick involved is getting everything to balance out: flavors, textures, colors, and nutritional content. Here are some tips to help you:

Write down each dish you want to serve. Now picture the meal on the plate. Is there something green, red, yellow, tan? What about the texture? Is there something grainy, leafy, smooth, chewy? Next consider seasonings. Is there something tangy, something mild? If one dish is spicy, is there something cool to tame it?

If all of this mixing and matching makes your head spin, just serve any of the following dishes as a first course, or on the side of a soup, salad, or substantial entrée.

STARTERS AND SIDE DISHES IN MEAL

PLANNING • STARTER AND SIDE

DISH MENUS • SAVORY SIDE DISHES •

MASHED POTATOES • POTATO GRATINS •

SAVORY SOUFFLÉS • TERRINES • SAVORY

 FLANS • FILLED THINGS •

BEAN SPREADS • SAVORY VEGETABLE

PANCAKES • RICES AND PILAFS •

CROSTINI • CROSTINI SPREADS

Starters and Side Dishes in Meal Planning

When you make a meal of small dishes, you can cover the full range of vitamins, minerals, and nutrients, preparing something high in calcium and vitamin D, something high in antioxidants, and something high in protein, fiber, and minerals. And when you serve them as accompaniments, you can use them to round out the nutritional content of the entrée. You don't even have to think this through; chances are that once you've balanced flavors, colors, and textures, you'll have balanced vitamins and nutrients, too.

SPICY SPINACH NUGGETS WITH
COOLING CHIVE SAUCE (PAGE 216)
20% daily value for protein
58% daily value for vitamin A
74% daily value for vitamin C
47% daily value for folacin
25% daily value for vitamin B_2
20% daily value for iron
10% daily value for zinc

KIDNEY BEAN HUMMUS (PAGE 254)
30% daily value folacin
10% daily value for vitamin C
14% daily value for vitamin B_1
20% daily value for iron
10% daily value for zinc

SAVORY CARROT FLAN (PAGE 245)
21% daily value for protein
325% daily value for vitamin A
36% daily value for vitamin C
23% daily value for vitamin B_2
23% daily value for calcium

SWEET POTATO SOUFFLÉ (PAGE 232)
25% daily value for protein
145% daily value for vitamin A
24% daily value for vitamin C
26% daily value for vitamin B_2
18% daily value for calcium

CARROT-SPINACH TERRINE (PAGE 237)
32% daily value for protein
266% daily value for vitamin A
37% daily value for vitamin C
31% daily value for folacin
23% daily value for vitamin B_2
22% daily value for iron

Starter and Side Dish Menus

Baba Ghanouj (*page 220*)
Hummus (*page 254*)
Tabbouleh (*page 139*)
Spinach Strudel (*page 437*)

Artichokes and Mushrooms in Lemon-Mustard
Sauce (*page 225*)
Your Basic Heartwarming Black Bean Soup
(*page 188*)

Fresh Tomato Soup with Cilantro Pistou
(*page 178*)
Tamale-Style Fresh Corn Nuggets (*page 246*)

Cucumber and Bulgur Wheat
with Fresh Herbs (*page 138*)
Spicy Spinach Nuggets with Cooling Chive
Sauce (*page 216*)

(Lightly) Curried Split Pea Soup (*page 195*)
Asparagus-Potato Puffs (*page 222*)
Savory Baked Corn Cakes (*page 257*)
with Caramelized Vidalia Onions (*page 224*)

Strawberry Soup (*page 206*)
Carrot-Spinach Terrine (*page 237*)
Fresh Herb-Filled Tomatoes (*page 252*)
Early Spring Minestrone (*page 196*)
Parsnip and Apple Terrine (*page 236*)

Savory Carrot Flan (*page 245*)
Simple Baked Artichokes (*page 213*)
Creamy Rice with Potatoes and Leek (*page 259*)

Rolled Roasted Red Peppers (*page 249*)
Kidney Bean Hummus (*page 254*)
Curried Creamed Eggplant (*page 222*)
Lavosh (*page 412*)

Morels with Spinach and Cream (*page 215*)
Baked Stuffed Artichokes with Mushrooms
(*page 252*)
Bulgur Wheat with Spinach, Raisins, and
Pine Nuts (*page 262*)
Mixed greens with Creamy Chive Dressing
(*page 120*)

Sweet Potato Soufflé (*page 232*)
Chili Rice (*page 260*)
Quick Crunchy Collards (*page 218*)

Savory Side Dishes

SIMPLE BAKED ARTICHOKES

Serves 4

TOTAL TIME: ABOUT 40 MINUTES
TIME TO PREPARE: 10 MINUTES
COOKING TIME: 30 MINUTES
DO AHEAD: YOU CAN MAKE THIS DISH UP TO 3 DAYS IN
 ADVANCE. REFRIGERATE UNTIL READY TO USE.
REFRIGERATION/FREEZING: REFRIGERATE UP TO 3 DAYS. DO
 NOT FREEZE.

I f you were to challenge the assertion that baking
fresh artichokes is ever simple, I'd have to con-
cede. "Simple" here refers to the spare seasonings
—meant only to bring out the artichoke's own
flavor—and to the kind of pleasure it provides.

Juice of ¹/₂ lemon
4 large artichokes
1 tablespoon crumbled dried herbes de Provence
1 tablespoon plus 1 teaspoon extra virgin olive
 oil
Salt and freshly ground black pepper to taste

Heat the oven to 350° F.

Fill a glass bowl large enough to hold the artichokes with cold water and add the lemon juice.

Clean the artichokes by trimming off the stems and pulling away the outer layer of tough leaves. When you get to the tender inner leaves, trim off the spiky tops with kitchen shears. Spread the inner layers open as wide as possible and pull out the prickly center. Drop each into the lemon water as it's done.

In a small mixing bowl combine the herbes de Provence, olive oil, and salt and pepper. Cut 4 large pieces of aluminum foil. Drain the artichokes well and place each in the center of a piece of foil. Distributing the herb mixture evenly, rub it onto the artichokes, reaching between the leaves.

Wrap each artichoke in the foil. Place the artichokes in a shallow roasting pan and bake until tender, about 30 minutes.

PER SERVING: CALORIES 90 • PROTEIN 4.1 G • CARBOHYDRATE 13.4 G • FAT 3.5 G • CHOLESTEROL 0 MG • SODIUM 114 MG • 31% CALORIES FROM FAT • VERY GOOD SOURCE OF VITAMIN C • GOOD SOURCE OF FOLACIN

•

BAKED BEANS

Serves 4

TOTAL TIME: ABOUT 1 HOUR, 20 MINUTES, NOT INCLUD-
ING TIME TO COOK THE BEANS
TIME TO PREPARE: 20 MINUTES
COOKING TIME: 1 HOUR
DO AHEAD: YOU CAN MAKE THIS DISH UP TO 3 DAYS IN
ADVANCE. REFRIGERATE UNTIL READY TO USE.
REFRIGERATION/FREEZING: REFRIGERATE UP TO 5 DAYS
FREEZE UP TO 6 MONTHS.

There's some dispute over whether Native Americans introduced the concept to the Pilgrims, or if New England sea captains brought the idea back from North Africa. Whatever. The Puritans loved baked beans, but ate them anyway—which isn't to say they didn't take self-denial seriously. Just that it only went so far.

3 cups cooked navy beans, Jacobs cattle beans,
    or buckskin beans, rinsed and drained (for
    sources of cattle and buckskin beans, see
    mail-order information, page 596)
4 cups chopped peeled fresh tomatoes (see page
    544) or canned tomato puree
1 large onion, chopped
1 garlic clove, minced
3 tablespoons dark brown sugar
3 tablespoons molasses or maple syrup
1 tablespoon cider vinegar
2 teaspoons Dijon mustard
Salt and freshly ground black pepper to taste

Heat the oven to 350° F.

In a large covered baking dish, combine the beans, tomatoes, onion, garlic, brown sugar, molasses or maple syrup, vinegar, mustard, and salt and pepper. Mix well.

Bake, covered, until the sauce is thick and clinging to the beans, about 1 hour. Stir well before serving.

PER SERVING: CALORIES 217 • PROTEIN 9.3 G • CARBOHYDRATE 45.2 G • FAT 1 G • CHOLESTEROL 0 MG • SODIUM 37.4 MG • 4% CALORIES FROM FAT • OUTSTANDING SOURCE OF VITAMIN C • VERY GOOD SOURCE OF VITAMIN B₁; FOLACIN • GOOD SOURCE OF IRON

•

MORELS WITH SPINACH AND CREAM

Serves 4

TOTAL TIME: ABOUT 1 HOUR, 5 MINUTES, TO 1 HOUR, 15 MINUTES, INCLUDING TIME TO SOAK THE MUSHROOMS

TIME TO PREPARE: ABOUT 35 MINUTES, INCLUDING TIME TO SAUTÉ

COOKING TIME: ABOUT 5 MINUTES

DO AHEAD: YOU CAN MAKE THIS DISH UP TO 2 DAYS AHEAD, AND SERVE CHILLED.

REFRIGERATION/FREEZING: REFRIGERATE UP TO 2 DAYS. DO NOT FREEZE.

*M*orels grow in northern Michigan, where they are Big Trouble. Discovering a morel patch is something like winning the lottery and affects lives in much the same way: making sane men paranoid and setting siblings into the kind of rivalry that reflects well on Cain and Abel. In divorce cases, rights to a morel patch are more hotly contested than child custody, I'm told, and during prime season, people have been known to patrol their patch armed to the teeth against pilferers.

Lest hyperbole become reality, I won't say this is a dish to die for. But it's certainly scrumptious. Serve over toast, mashed potatoes, polenta (see page 324), or pasta.

6 dried morels

2 teaspoons unsalted butter

1 large leek, white part only, washed and sliced

1 large scallion, white part and 1 inch of greens, sliced

1 cup thickly sliced fresh mushrooms, such as cremini, shiitake, or portobello

6 fresh morels, sliced crosswise into 4 slices each

1 tablespoon white wine, or 2 teaspoons white wine vinegar

1 tablespoon light cream

3 tablespoons reduced-fat or nonfat sour cream

1 cup loosely packed torn fresh spinach

Minced fresh tarragon, for garnish (if fresh tarragon isn't available, omit it; don't substitute dried)

Place the dried morels in a shallow bowl and add warm water to cover. Set aside for 30 to 40 minutes, until soft. Strain the liquid and discard. Slice the mushrooms crosswise, making small rings.

Melt the butter in a medium skillet. Add the leek and scallion, and sauté, stirring often, until softened, about 7 minutes. Add the fresh mushrooms and the fresh and dried morels and sauté, stirring often, until soft, about 6 minutes. Raise the heat to medium-high, and add the wine or vinegar. Stir constantly, loosening any vegetables that may be sticking to the pan. Turn off the heat.

Combine the cream and sour cream in a small bowl. Stir the mixture into the skillet. Turn the heat to low, and add the spinach, stirring until the leaves turn bright green, about 2 minutes. Top with fresh tarragon, if available.

PER SERVING: CALORIES 76 • PROTEIN 3 G • CARBOHYDRATE 8.9 G • FAT 3.4 G • CHOLESTEROL 9.3 MG • SODIUM 297 MG • 39% CALORIES FROM FAT • GOOD SOURCE OF VITAMINS A, C; FOLACIN, IRON

SPICY SPINACH NUGGETS WITH COOLING CHIVE SAUCE

Serves 4

TOTAL TIME: ABOUT 40 MINUTES

TIME TO PREPARE: ABOUT 40 MINUTES

COOKING TIME: INCLUDED IN TIME TO PREPARE

DO AHEAD: YOU CAN ASSEMBLE THE NUGGETS UP TO 2 DAYS BEFORE COOKING THEM. YOU CAN ALSO MAKE THE SAUCE UP TO 3 DAYS IN ADVANCE. KEEP BOTH WRAPPED AND REFRIGERATED UNTIL READY TO USE.

REFRIGERATION/FREEZING: REFRIGERATE UP TO 2 DAYS. DO NOT FREEZE.

D*on't you love the sound of this dish? And if you find the* name *appealing, just wait until you taste it.*

Spinach Nuggets

1 pound fresh spinach, thoroughly cleaned

3 teaspoons extra virgin olive oil

4 scallions, white part plus 1 inch of greens, chopped

2 tablespoons minced fresh mint

½ cup minced fresh parsley

2 teaspoons ground cumin

2 teaspoons paprika

1 teaspoon ground cinnamon

1 tablespoon tomato paste

1 large egg, separated

¼ cup unbleached all-purpose flour

Cooling Chive Sauce

1 cucumber, peeled, seeded, and minced (see page 526)

3 tablespoons minced fresh chives

¼ cup minced fresh cilantro

¼ teaspoon minced garlic

1 cup plain nonfat yogurt

Salt and freshly ground black pepper to taste

To make the Spinach Nuggets

Rinse the spinach—even if it's been washed—leaving the leaves damp. Place them in a large skillet on medium-high heat. Cover and let the spinach steam until it turns bright green, about 3 minutes. Remove from the heat, uncover, and set aside to cool.

Heat 2 teaspoons of the oil in a small skillet over medium-high heat. Add the scallions, mint, parsley, cumin, paprika, and cinnamon. Lower the heat and sauté over medium heat until the scallions have softened, about 8 minutes. Stir in the tomato paste and continue cooking for 3 minutes, stirring constantly to blend thoroughly. Remove from the heat.

Squeeze the excess moisture from the spinach, and chop it coarsely. Place it in a mixing bowl along with the scallion mixture. Add the egg yolk and mix with your hands until everything's well combined. Shape the mixture into 8 balls of equal size.

Place the flour on a plate, and put the egg white into a shallow bowl. Dip each spinach ball into the flour, and then into the egg white.

Place the remaining teaspoon of olive oil in a nonstick skillet, and heat it over medium heat. Swirl the pan to coat it evenly with the oil. Add the spinach balls and sauté until lightly browned, tossing constantly to cook evenly.

To make the Cooling Chive Sauce

Combine the cucumber, chives, cilantro, garlic, and yogurt in a food processor or blender.

Process in short pulses until chunky. Season with salt and pepper.

Top the nuggets with the sauce, or pass on the side.

PER SERVING: CALORIES 156 • PROTEIN 9.1 G • CARBOHYDRATE 19.2 G • FAT 5.3 G • CHOLESTEROL 54.4 MG • SODIUM 159 MG • 30% CALORIES FROM FAT • OUT-STANDING SOURCE OF VITAMINS A, C; FOLACIN. • VERY GOOD SOURCE OF VITA-MIN B₂; CALCIUM, IRON • GOOD SOURCE OF VITAMINS B₁, B₆; ZINC

•

SWEET ONIONS WITH ASPARAGUS SPEARS

Serves 4

TOTAL TIME: ABOUT 50 MINUTES
TIME TO PREPARE: ABOUT 18 MINUTES
COOKING TIME: ABOUT 30 MINUTES
EQUIPMENT: CHARCOAL OR STOVETOP GRILL (OPTIONAL)
DO AHEAD: YOU CAN PREPARE THE ONION-WRAPPED
    ASPARAGUS 1 DAY IN ADVANCE. REFRIGERATE UNTIL
    READY TO GRILL OR BROIL.
REFRIGERATION/FREEZING: REFRIGERATE OVERNIGHT. DO
    NOT FREEZE.

Two seasonal sensations meet to make a third. Serve this with something simple, such as Frittatas (page 383).

4 large Vidalia or other sweet onions, peeled
1 pound slender asparagus, trimmed
¼ cup extra virgin olive oil
2 tablespoons fresh orange juice
2 tablespoons minced fresh basil
1 scallion, white part only, minced

In a large saucepan over medium-high heat, bring enough water to cover the onions to a boil. Add the onions and boil until they're soft but still retain their shape, about 20 minutes. Drain and set aside to cool. Bring another pot of water to boil over medium-high heat and blanch the asparagus in boiling water, for about 30 seconds, then drain and dunk in cold water to stop the cooking. Set aside.

In a mixing bowl, combine the olive oil, orange juice, basil, and scallion.

Heat your grill or broiler.

Using a sharp paring knife, slice the outer layer off one of the onions in one piece, cutting from top to bottom, so that you can unravel it. Place the layer horizontally on your work surface. (The ends may curl toward the center; hold them flat while you proceed.) Place 3 or 4 asparagus spears on top, vertically, and roll up the onion layer so that it holds them snugly in the center, with the tips and the stems sticking out on either end. When you reach the smaller layers, start cutting from another onion. Continue stripping away layers of the onions and wrapping asparagus until you've used up one or the other.

Brush each asparagus roll with the olive oil mixture. Grill over hot coals or cook under the broiler, turning after 3 to 4 minutes, until the onions have browned, about 6 to 8 minutes in all.

PER SERVING: CALORIES 91 • PROTEIN 4.5 G • CARBOHYDRATE 19.8 G • FAT 0 G • CHOLESTEROL 0 MG • SODIUM 7.4 MG • 4% CALORIES FROM FAT • OUTSTANDING SOURCE OF VITAMIN C; FOLACIN • GOOD SOURCE OF VITAMINS B₁, B₂

•

ROASTED FRESH TOMATOES

Serves 6

TOTAL TIME: ABOUT 30 MINUTES
TIME TO PREPARE: ABOUT 8 MINUTES
COOKING TIME: ABOUT 20 MINUTES
DO AHEAD: YOU CAN ROAST THE TOMATOES UP TO 3 DAYS
    IN ADVANCE. REFRIGERATE UNTIL READY TO USE.
REFRIGERATION/FREEZING: REFRIGERATE UP TO 3 DAYS. DO
    NOT FREEZE.

Wait for the height of tomato season for this, then savor every bite, as a hot or cold side dish or as a topping for Crostini (see page 263), Risotto (see page 304), Gnocchi (see page 316), or Pasta (see page 270).

2 pounds tomatoes
1 tablespoon extra virgin olive oil
1 garlic clove, grated
½ cup loosely packed shredded fresh basil
Salt and freshly ground black pepper to taste

Heat the oven to 425°F.

Core the tomatoes with a paring knife. If the tomatoes are small or Romas, cut them in half. Squeeze gently to get rid of the seeds. If they're medium or large, cut them into quarters, and squeeze gently to eliminate the seeds.

Place the oil, garlic, and basil in a glass or earthenware bowl. Add the tomatoes and toss to coat with the oil and herbs. Placing them skin side up, transfer the tomatoes to a glass or earthenware baking dish or a Pyrex pie plate.

Bake until the skin darkens, caramelizing to a deep glossy brown, about 20 minutes. Season with salt and pepper.

PER SERVING: CALORIES 60 • PROTEIN 1.7 G • CARBOHYDRATE 9 G • FAT 2.8 G • CHOLESTEROL 0 MG • SODIUM 14.8 MG • 38% CALORIES FROM FAT • OUTSTANDING SOURCE OF VITAMIN C • GOOD SOURCE OF VITAMIN A; IRON

QUICK CRUNCHY COLLARDS

Serves 4

TOTAL TIME: ABOUT 10 MINUTES
TIME TO PREPARE: ABOUT 10 MINUTES
COOKING TIME: INCLUDED IN PREPARATION TIME

In the antebellum South you, and your guests, knew you had made it when you could afford to serve a meal without vegetables . . . when you could fill your plate with so much "real" food—meat, bread, grits, and gravy—that you didn't need those nasty greens to take up space. Slaves, of course, couldn't eat so "well." They had to make do with what they grew. And since many grew collards, they did just fine. Perhaps the most nutritious green, collards contain abundant vitamins and minerals that seem to have spared the slaves some of the dietary deficiencies that afflicted their masters.

Strong and sharp when raw, collards become sweet as they cook. Here they're steamed just long enough to get rid of the bite, while staying crisp.

10 ounces collard greens, well rinsed and
  coarsely chopped
2 scallions, white part plus 2 inches of greens,
  chopped
1 tablespoon sesame seeds, toasted (see Note,
  page 122)
2 teaspoons fresh lemon juice

In a large saucepan, bring 2 inches of water to a
boil. Add the collards, cover, and cook until
they turn bright green, about 3 minutes. Immediately lift the collards out with a slotted spoon
and transfer to a colander. Shake the water out
as thoroughly as you can.

In a large glass or earthenware bowl, combine the scallions, sesame seeds, and lemon
juice. Add the collards, stir thoroughly, and
serve right away.

PER SERVING: CALORIES 37 • PROTEIN 1.6 G • CARBOHYDRATE 6.2 G • FAT 1.2 G •
CHOLESTEROL 0 MG • SODIUM 15.4 MG • 27% CALORIES FROM FAT • VERY GOOD
SOURCE OF VITAMINS A, C

•

SPINACH WITH POTATOES, FENNEL, AND PINE NUTS

Serves 4

TOTAL TIME: ABOUT 40 MINUTES, NOT INCLUDING TIME TO
  MAKE THE BROTH
TIME TO PREPARE: ABOUT 25 MINUTES, INCLUDING TIME
  TO SAUTÉ
COOKING TIME: ABOUT 13 MINUTES
REFRIGERATION/FREEZING: REFRIGERATE UP TO 3 DAYS. DO
  NOT FREEZE.

E vidently, a lot of people get depressed in
  midautumn, when the days get markedly
  shorter. I tend to cheer up, however, since

suppertime—and the chance to enjoy seasonal
dishes such as this soothing combination of spinach,
potatoes, and fennel—comes that much sooner. Try
this with Tomato and Rice Soup (see page 172).

1 tablespoon extra virgin olive oil
1 medium onion, chopped
1 leek, white part only, washed and sliced
1 fennel bulb, without leafy fronds, chopped
1 cup vegetable broth (see page 165)
4 medium Yukon Gold or red potatoes, sliced
1 pound fresh spinach, washed and torn
Pinch saffron threads or powder
1/2 cup nonfat sour cream or soft tofu
2 tablespoons pine nuts, toasted (see Note,
  page 122)
Salt and freshly ground black pepper to taste

Heat the oil in a large, deep skillet over
medium-high heat. When it's hot, add the
onion, leek, and fennel. Reduce the heat to
medium-low and sauté, stirring often, until the
vegetables have softened, about 12 minutes. If
they start to stick, add 1 tablespoon of the vegetable broth.

Add the potatoes and the rest of the vegetable broth. Cover and simmer over medium
heat until the potatoes are just cooked
through, about 10 minutes. Stir in the spinach,
saffron, sour cream or tofu, and pine nuts, until
well blended. Cover and simmer until the
spinach has cooked, about 3 minutes. Season
with salt and pepper.

PER SERVING: CALORIES 220 • PROTEIN 13.4 G • CARBOHYDRATE 18.6 G • FAT
13.9 G • CHOLESTEROL 0 MG • SODIUM 128 MG • 49% CALORIES FROM FAT • OUT-
STANDING SOURCE OF VITAMINS A, C; FOLACIN, IRON • VERY GOOD SOURCE OF
VITAMINS B1, B6; CALCIUM • GOOD SOURCE OF VITAMINS B2, B3; ZINC

•

BABA GHANOUJ

Makes about 1 cup, serves 4

TOTAL TIME: ABOUT 20 MINUTES
TIME TO PREPARE: ABOUT 3 MINUTES
COOKING TIME: ABOUT 15 TO 20 MINUTES
DO AHEAD: YOU CAN PREPARE THE EGGPLANT PUREE UP TO
    2 DAYS IN ADVANCE. REFRIGERATE UNTIL READY TO USE.
REFRIGERATION/FREEZING: WRAP AND REFRIGERATE UP TO 5
    DAYS. DO NOT FREEZE.

When, at fifteen, I told my mother I would no longer eat beef, she started looking for clues that I'd signed on with some cult. Finding none, she blamed my friends. When I told her that not one of them intended to go vegetarian, she turned the blame on herself. "It was the meat loaf, wasn't it?" She tried bribery ("I'll make you some shish kebab"). She tried threats ("I'll make you some okra"). She tried inconvenience ("You can cook for yourself from now on"). Eventually, in the spirit of conciliation, she tried baba ghanouj.

It was hard for my mother to accept my decision because the dinner table had been our common ground; it seemed to her I was walling off my portion, shutting her out by refusing what she would provide for me. But when I showed an interest in Middle Eastern cuisine—big with vegetarians back then—we found there was plenty we could share. This eggplant and tahini dish, for example, was just coming into vogue in the mainstream, but my mother, who is Armenian, had eaten it her whole life. Serve it as a spread on toasted pita or as a sandwich filling, rolled in Lavosh (see page 412) with tomatoes and sprouts.

1 large eggplant
1 garlic clove, grated
One 2-inch piece fresh ginger, peeled and grated
¼ cup plus 1 tablespoon minced fresh cilantro
1½ teaspoons ground cumin
Pinch paprika
2 tablespoons fresh lemon juice
1 tablespoon tahini
½ cup plain nonfat yogurt (optional)
1 tablespoon sesame seeds, toasted (see Note, page 122) for garnish

Heat the broiler.

Place the whole eggplant underneath, about 2 inches from the heat source. When the top has buckled, turn twice more to cook all sides, between 5 and 7 minutes for each side. Remove with a long-tined fork. Let it cool thoroughly on a plate.

Meanwhile, combine the garlic, ginger, ¼ cup cilantro, cumin, paprika, lemon juice, tahini, and yogurt, if using, in a glass or earthenware bowl. Peel the eggplant and scrape away as many of the seeds as possible. Coarsely chop the flesh and add it to the tahini mixture. Blend well.

Sprinkle with the sesame seeds and 1 tablespoon cilantro.

PER SERVING: CALORIES 52 • PROTEIN 1.8 G • CARBOHYDRATE 7.3 G • FAT 2.4 G • CHOLESTEROL 0 MG • SODIUM 4.3 MG • 38% CALORIES FROM FAT

VARIATION: For a more substantial sandwich filling or spread, add 1 cup cooked white beans or chickpeas along with the eggplant. Puree the mixture to make it perfectly smooth.

BAKED ARTICHOKES AND POTATOES

Serves 4

Artichokes suit those of a phlegmatic and melancholy disposition.

—Louis Lemery, Treatise on Food, 1745

TOTAL TIME: ABOUT 1 HOUR, 10 MINUTES, NOT INCLUDING TIME TO MAKE THE BROTH
TIME TO PREPARE: ABOUT 25 MINUTES
COOKING TIME: 40 TO 45 MINUTES
DO AHEAD: YOU CAN PARE AND QUARTER THE ARTICHOKES UP TO 1 DAY AHEAD. REFRIGERATE, IN A GLASS BOWL WITH WATER AND LEMON JUICE AS DIRECTED BELOW.
REFRIGERATION/FREEZING: REFRIGERATE UP TO 3 DAYS. DO NOT FREEZE.

1 pound potatoes, preferably Yukon Gold
4 large artichokes
Juice of 1 lemon
2 tablespoons fine dried bread crumbs
1 garlic clove, grated
1 tablespoon extra virgin olive oil
¼ cup grated Parmesan cheese
2 tablespoons minced fresh parsley
1 cup vegetable broth (see page 165)

Heat the oven to 350° F.

Peel the potatoes and slice them into thin rounds. Set them aside for the moment.

Fill a glass bowl with enough cold water to hold the artichokes, and add the lemon juice. Cut the stem off an artichoke and then cut the very bottom off the stem. Peel the coarse outer layer from the stem and slice the stem into thin rounds. Place them in the bowl of lemon water. Peel away the tough, dark-colored outer leaves of the artichoke. When you get to the bright, tender inner leaves, trim the spiky tips with kitchen shears. Cut the artichoke in half lengthwise and scoop out the purple leaves and the light green fuzz in the center. Cut each half in half again. As soon as you've cleaned and quartered it, place the artichoke in the lemon water. Repeat with each artichoke.

In a mixing bowl, combine the bread crumbs and garlic. Pour the olive oil evenly over the bottom of an 8-inch square baking dish. Place a layer of potatoes on top, then top with a layer of well-drained artichokes. Repeat until you've used up all of each. Sprinkle with the bread crumb mixture, then top with the cheese and parsley. Pour the vegetable broth evenly over all.

Cover the dish loosely with foil and bake until tender, about 35 to 40 minutes. Remove the foil and continue to bake until the top is golden brown, about 5 minutes more.

PER SERVING: CALORIES 226 • PROTEIN 9.7 G • CARBOHYDRATE 38 G • FAT 5.7 G • CHOLESTEROL 4.9 MG • SODIUM 265 MG • 21% CALORIES FROM FAT • OUTSTANDING SOURCE OF VITAMIN C • VERY GOOD SOURCE OF VITAMIN B6; FOLACIN • GOOD SOURCE OF VITAMINS B1, B3; CALCIUM

CURRIED CREAMED EGGPLANT

Serves 4

TOTAL TIME: ABOUT 30 TO 35 MINUTES
TIME TO PREPARE: ABOUT 15 MINUTES, INCLUDING TIME TO SAUTÉ
COOKING TIME: ABOUT 15 TO 20 MINUTES
DO AHEAD: YOU CAN BROIL AND CHOP THE EGGPLANT UP TO 2 DAYS IN ADVANCE.
REFRIGERATION/FREEZING: REFRIGERATE UP TO 3 DAYS. DO NOT FREEZE.

A *light, tangy puree that's good warm or cold. Serve over rice or scoop with pita bread.*

2 pounds miniature or Japanese eggplants

1 ½ teaspoons canola or vegetable oil

1 onion, chopped

6 garlic cloves, minced

2 teaspoons grated peeled fresh ginger

¼ teaspoon whole fennel seeds

2 teaspoons ground cumin

¼ cup canned tomato puree

⅓ cup nonfat or low-fat buttermilk or plain nonfat yogurt

Heat the broiler.

Place the whole eggplants underneath, about 2 inches from the heat source. When the top has buckled, turn them twice more to cook all sides, between 5 and 7 minutes for each side. Remove with a long-tined fork. Let them cool thoroughly on a plate.

Meanwhile, heat the oil in a medium skillet over medium-high heat. Add the onion, garlic, ginger, fennel seeds, and cumin, and sauté over medium heat until the onion is soft, about 7 minutes. Add the tomato puree, and stir until it reduces and thickens, about 3 minutes. Transfer to a large mixing bowl and set aside to cool.

When the eggplants are cool enough to handle, cut off the stem end, and peel away the skin. Discard as many seeds as you can without tossing away the flesh. Chop the pulp and stir it into the bowl with the tomato mixture. Add the buttermilk or yogurt 1 tablespoon at a time, allowing the temperature to adjust so the mixture won't curdle.

Serve at room temperature or chilled.

PER SERVING: CALORIES 110 • PROTEIN 4.0 G • CARBOHYDRATE 21 G • FAT 2.3 G • CHOLESTEROL 0 MG • SODIUM 92.3 MG • 18% CALORIES FROM FAT • VERY GOOD SOURCE OF VITAMIN C • GOOD SOURCE OF VITAMINS B₁, B₆; FOLACIN

•

ASPARAGUS-POTATO PUFFS

Serves 6

TOTAL TIME: ABOUT 1 HOUR, 35 MINUTES
TIME TO PREPARE: 20 MINUTES
COOKING TIME: 1 HOUR, 15 MINUTES
DO AHEAD: YOU CAN MAKE THE DOUGH UP TO 2 DAYS IN ADVANCE. REFRIGERATE UNTIL READY TO USE.
REFRIGERATION/FREEZING: REFRIGERATE UP TO 3 DAYS. FREEZE UP TO 2 MONTHS.

D *on't you hate it when you rave over your hostess's incredible main course, only to have her smile dismissively and chirp, "Oh, it's nothing"? Wouldn't you love to be able to irk your guests in just the same way? Only you know very well that if you were to spend all day making an elaborate meal, you'd take credit for every second.*

This dish looks elegant and tastes like the culmination of weeks at a culinary academy. But, when it

comes to the amount of effort involved, you can truly say, "It's nothing."

4 medium potatoes, preferably Yukon Gold

8 slender asparagus spears

⅓ cup nonfat or low-fat buttermilk

¼ cup minced fresh parsley

2 tablespoons minced fresh chives or scallion greens

2 large eggs, lightly beaten

¼ cup grated Gruyère cheese

⅓ cup unbleached all-purpose flour

1½ teaspoons baking powder

In a large saucepan over medium-high heat, bring enough water to a boil to cover the potatoes. Boil the potatoes in their skins until cooked through, about 40 minutes. Drain and set aside until cool enough to handle. Peel and roughly slice.

Fill a large saucepan with water and bring it to a boil.

At the same time, fill a large bowl with cold water and ice cubes, and line a colander with paper towels.

Plunge the asparagus spears into the boiling water. The moment they turn bright green, about 30 to 45 seconds, remove them with a slotted spoon and transfer them to the ice water, to stop the cooking, about 15 seconds, then transfer to the colander to drain. Chop the spears and set aside.

Heat the oven to 375° F. Squirt 6 cups in a muffin tin or 6 custard cups with nonstick spray, or grease them lightly with canola oil.

In a large mixing bowl, mash the potatoes with the buttermilk, parsley, chives or scallion greens, eggs, and cheese. In a separate bowl, combine the flour and baking powder with a long-tined fork. Stir thoroughly into the potato mixture. Add the asparagus and stir to distribute it well.

Spoon an equal amount of the potato mixture into each prepared cup. Bake until puffy and golden brown, about 30 minutes. Serve hot.

PER SERVING: CALORIES 260 • PROTEIN 14 G • CARBOHYDRATE 33.7 G • FAT 8.2 G • CHOLESTEROL 92 MG • SODIUM 211 MG • 28% CALORIES FROM FAT • OUTSTANDING SOURCE OF IRON • VERY GOOD SOURCE OF VITAMINS B₆, C; CALCIUM • GOOD SOURCE OF VITAMINS A, B₁, B₂, B₃; ZINC

VARIATIONS: Substitute 1 cup chopped broccoli for the asparagus, and ¼ cup grated cheddar cheese for the Gruyère; substitute 1 cup fresh or frozen chopped spinach for the asparagus, and 2 tablespoons Parmesan cheese for the Gruyère; or substitute 1 cup minced peeled carrots for the asparagus.

CARAMELIZED VIDALIA ONIONS

Serves 4

TOTAL TIME: ABOUT 35 MINUTES
TIME TO PREPARE: ABOUT 35 MINUTES, INCLUDING TIME
   TO SAUTÉ
COOKING TIME: INCLUDED IN TIME TO PREPARE
REFRIGERATION/FREEZING: REFRIGERATE UP TO 3 DAYS. DO
   NOT FREEZE.

It's obvious why certain foods became sacred in various parts of the world. Corn in South America and rice in Asia, for example, are essential crops, worshiped for their fundamental role in life. Less obvious is why the Egyptians deemed onions holy enough to entomb with the pharaohs.

Maybe there wasn't anything sacred about it. Maybe Ramses and Tut, not trusting to chance, just wanted to be sure they'd have onions in the after-world. If there are onions in heaven, I'm sure they're made like this—sautéed to the brink of melting, where they become astonishingly sweet. Serve them over Savory Baked Corn Cakes (see page 257),

Oven-Baked Leek and Fennel Pancakes (see page 258), or with grilled foods of all kind.

2 teaspoons extra virgin olive oil
2 Vidalia onions, thinly sliced
2 teaspoons balsamic vinegar
1 teaspoon Dijon mustard
Salt and freshly ground pepper to taste

Heat a large nonstick skillet over medium-high heat. Add the oil and swirl to coat the bottom. Add the onions, and reduce the heat to medium. Sauté, stirring often, until the onions soften, about 7 minutes. Reduce the heat to low, and continue to sauté until the onions are so tender they seem to be melting, about 20 minutes. Add the balsamic vinegar and mustard, raise the heat to medium, and stir until the liquid evaporates, about 2 minutes.

Season with salt and pepper, transfer to a serving bowl, and let cool to room temperature.

Serve at room temperature or chilled.

PER SERVING: CALORIES 48 • PROTEIN 0 G • CARBOHYDRATE 6.5 G • FAT 2.3 G • CHOLESTEROL 0 MG • SODIUM 2.2 MG • 42% CALORIES FROM FAT

NOW TRY THIS: Along with the onions, add one of the following pairs: 2 tablespoons minced fresh mint and 2 tablespoons minced fresh parsley; 2 tablespoons minced fresh basil and 2 tablespoons minced fresh parsley; a pinch crumbled dried thyme and 2 teaspoons apricot preserves (It may seem strange, but fruit preserves blend beautifully with long-cooked onions.); or a pinch crumbled dried thyme and 2 teaspoons strawberry preserves.

ARTICHOKES AND MUSHROOMS IN LEMON-MUSTARD SAUCE

Serves 4

TOTAL TIME: 35 MINUTES
TIME TO PREPARE: 35 MINUTES, INCLUDING TIME TO SAUTÉ
COOKING TIME: INCLUDED IN TIME TO PREPARE
REFRIGERATION/FREEZING: DO NOT REFRIGERATE OR
   FREEZE.

To anyone accustomed to seeing just two types of artichokes, large and small, the markets in Italy at a certain time of year would seem to be hosting a botanical freak show. That's when purple artichokes, long-stemmed artichokes, gargantuan artichokes and minuscule, are bought in armloads by women who seem to know what to do with them, and to be in a rush to get it done. The show has a short run over there, and home cooks want to use up the first batch and come back for more before they're gone.

We don't have to have the same sense of urgency, thanks to California, which keeps us in artichokes all year long. But if I were you, I wouldn't wait long to try them done this way.

4 large artichokes, trimmed, quartered, and fuzzy
   center removed (see page 514)
Juice of 4 lemons
1 tablespoon extra virgin olive oil
4 scallions, white part only, chopped
1 garlic clove, minced
2 tablespoons minced fresh parsley
1 pound firm mushrooms, such as cremini, white
   button, or portobello, sliced
¼ cup red wine vinegar
2 large egg yolks
1 teaspoon Dijon mustard
Salt and freshly ground black pepper to taste

Place the artichokes in a large glass bowl. Sprinkle with one-fourth of the lemon juice and set them aside.

Heat the olive oil in a large skillet over medium-high heat. Add the scallions, garlic, and parsley, and sauté until soft, about 8 minutes. Add the mushrooms, wine vinegar, and artichokes, and stir well. Cover, reduce the heat to medium-low, and cook, lifting the cover to stir often, until the artichokes and mushrooms are cooked through, about 7 minutes. Transfer to a mixing bowl and set aside to cool just until it's no longer steaming.

Combine the remaining lemon juice with the egg yolks and mustard. Stir into the cooled mushroom mixture, season with salt and pepper, and serve right away.

PER SERVING: CALORIES 165 • PROTEIN 8.4 G • CARBOHYDRATE 22.3 G • FAT 6.7 G • CHOLESTEROL 0 MG • SODIUM 141 MG • 33% CALORIES FROM FAT • OUTSTANDING SOURCE OF VITAMIN C • VERY GOOD SOURCE OF VITAMINS B₂, B₃; FOLACIN • GOOD SOURCE OF VITAMINS B₁, B₆; ZINC

GRILLED MUSHROOMS AND SOUR CREAM

Serves 4

TOTAL TIME: ABOUT 20 MINUTES
TIME TO PREPARE: ABOUT 10 MINUTES
COOKING TIME: ABOUT 10 MINUTES

Heap them on sourdough, and serve them with soup. Or spread them lightly on toast for heavenly crostini.

2 tablespoons extra virgin olive oil
1 tablespoon fresh lemon juice
2 teaspoons grated lemon zest
2 teaspoons balsamic vinegar
2 tablespoons minced fresh parsley
½ teaspoon grated garlic
Salt and freshly ground black pepper to taste
1 pound portobello mushrooms, thickly sliced
¼ cup nonfat or reduced-fat sour cream
2 tablespoons minced fresh chives

Heat a grill, stovetop grill, or broiler.

In a bowl, combine the olive oil, lemon juice, lemon zest, vinegar, parsley, garlic, and salt and pepper. Brush the mushroom slices with the mixture. Place them on the hot grill or stovetop grill or under the broiler until the mushrooms soften and brown, about 6 minutes. Turn them and brown the other side, about 4 minutes.

Transfer them to a mixing bowl and stir in the sour cream and chives. Serve warm or at room temperature.

PER SERVING: CALORIES 60 • PROTEIN 3.5 G • CARBOHYDRATE 7.5 G • FAT 2.7 G • CHOLESTEROL 0 MG • SODIUM 15.8 MG • 36% CALORIES FROM FAT • VERY GOOD SOURCE OF VITAMIN B₂ • GOOD SOURCE OF VITAMIN B₃

Mashed Potatoes

MASHED POTATOES

Serves 6

TOTAL TIME: ABOUT 50 MINUTES, NOT INCLUDING TIME TO MAKE THE BROTH
TIME TO PREPARE: ABOUT 10 MINUTES
COOKING TIME: ABOUT 40 MINUTES
REFRIGERATION/FREEZING: REFRIGERATE UP TO 3 DAYS. DO NOT FREEZE.

The emphasis is on the spuds when made as follows—a novel concept for a dish that is often gooped up beyond recognition. Since you actually taste the potatoes, choose the best (organically grown, sprout free) when you make them like this.

1 cup vegetable broth (see page 165), approximately
6 medium russet or Yukon Gold potatoes, peeled and sliced ⅓ inch thick
1½ cups low-fat cottage cheese
½ cup nonfat milk or plain nonfat yogurt
2 tablespoons minced fresh chives (optional)
Salt and freshly ground black pepper to taste

Pour 2 inches of vegetable broth into a medium saucepan, and place the potato slices in a steamer basket that fits into the pan, or into a sieve that will be sufficiently suspended above the broth.

Cover and bring the broth to a boil over medium-high heat. Reduce the heat to low, and steam the potatoes until they're cooked through, about 40 minutes. Check the level of the broth often, adding more as necessary and adjusting the heat to keep it at a simmer.

Meanwhile, in a food processor or blender, combine the cottage cheese and milk or yogurt. Process until smooth.

Transfer the potatoes to a large mixing bowl and mash them coarsely with the back of a wooden spoon or a potato masher. Add the cottage cheese mixture and continue mashing until it's thoroughly incorporated. Season with chives, if you'd like, and salt and pepper.

PER SERVING: CALORIES 137 • PROTEIN 10 G • CARBOHYDRATE 22.7 G • FAT 0 G • CHOLESTEROL 2.8 MG • SODIUM 247 MG • 5% CALORIES FROM FAT • VERY GOOD SOURCE OF VITAMIN C • GOOD SOURCE OF VITAMIN B₆

Make It Your Own

The basic recipe is just the beginning. . . .

WHAT TO ADD AND WHEN TO ADD IT

🌿 *Leeks.* Slice four leeks and add only the white part to the potatoes before you steam them. Once they've steamed, mash the potatoes and leeks together, and continue as in the basic recipe.

🌿 *Other Vegetables.* You can use the same "steam along" method with other vegetables, such as peeled and sliced rutabagas, turnips, beets, onions, celery, fennel, shredded cabbage, and chopped spinach. Use about 1 cup of chopped vegetables for each batch of mashed potatoes, and make sure that vegetable is thoroughly cooked when the potato is done.

🌿 *Garlic.* Roast garlic cloves (see page 529), and mash one into the potatoes after they've steamed, adding more to taste. Season with minced flat-leaf parsley.

🌿 *Cheeses.* Once you've pureed the cottage cheese and milk, add the grated or shredded cheese of your choice, and process again to blend. Start with 1 tablespoon, adding more to taste. Mash into hot potatoes as directed in the basic recipe. Mix and match cheeses with the vegetables listed above. For example, cheddar and cabbage or rutabagas, Gruyère and spinach, Parmesan and fennel.

🌿 *Pesto.* A little basil or olive pesto (see page 280) goes a long way. Mash in about 2 teaspoons along with the cottage cheese mixture, adding more to taste.

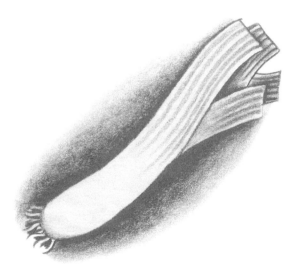

MASHED SWEET POTATOES

Serves 6

TOTAL TIME: ABOUT 30 MINUTES, INCLUDING TIME TO
COOL THE POTATOES, BUT NOT INCLUDING TIME TO
MAKE THE BROTH
TIME TO PREPARE: ABOUT 5 MINUTES
COOKING TIME: ABOUT 15 MINUTES
REFRIGERATION/FREEZING: REFRIGERATE UP TO 2 DAYS. DO
NOT FREEZE.

These simple, scrumptious sweet potatoes taste more like the filling for pumpkin pie than a vegetable dish providing 400 percent of your daily value for vitamin A.

2 tablespoons grated peeled fresh ginger

1 whole clove

4 medium sweet potatoes, peeled and sliced

1/3 cup vegetable broth (see page 165) or water

1/3 cup low-fat cottage cheese or part-skim ricotta cheese

2 tablespoons nonfat milk

1 tablespoon maple syrup

1 teaspoon ground cinnamon

Pinch ground nutmeg

In a large, heavy saucepan, combine the ginger, clove, sweet potatoes, and vegetable broth or water. Cover and bring to a boil over medium-high heat. Turn down the heat and simmer until the potatoes are soft, about 15 minutes. Remove from the heat. Using a slotted spoon, transfer the potatoes to a large mixing bowl. Discard the cooking water and clove. Let the sweet potatoes cool just until they stop steaming, about 10 minutes.

Meanwhile, combine the cottage cheese or ricotta and the milk in a food processor or blender, and puree until smooth. Mash into the cooled potato mixture with a potato masher or the back of a wooden spoon. Mash in the maple syrup, cinnamon, and nutmeg. Serve warm.

PER SERVING: CALORIES 129 • PROTEIN 3.4 G • CARBOHYDRATE 28 G • FAT 0 G • CHOLESTEROL 0 MG • SODIUM 67 MG • 3% CALORIES FROM FAT • OUTSTANDING SOURCE OF VITAMIN A • VERY GOOD SOURCE OF VITAMIN C • GOOD SOURCE OF VITAMINS B₂, B₆

Potato Gratins

POTATO GRATIN

Serves 6

TOTAL TIME: ABOUT 45 MINUTES, NOT INCLUDING TIME TO
MAKE THE BROTH
TIME TO PREPARE: ABOUT 20 MINUTES, INCLUDING TIME
TO SAUTÉ
COOKING TIME: ABOUT 25 MINUTES
DO AHEAD: YOU CAN MAKE THE MASHED POTATOES UP TO
2 DAYS IN ADVANCE. REFRIGERATE UNTIL READY TO USE.
REFRIGERATION/FREEZING: REFRIGERATE UP TO 2 DAYS. DO
NOT FREEZE.

Whether the French Revolution succeeded in elevating the masses is the subject of ongoing debate, but it certainly gave prestige to the potato. Their reign threatened by the shortage of grain, Louis XVI and Marie Antoinette put their potato patch under guard so thieves would assume the crop was precious, make off with the spuds, and sell them to the desperately hungry mobs. It was their hope that, once full, the people would lose their appetite for revolution.

But the starving subjects didn't need a royal ruse to get them to eat potatoes. They needed a good recipe. In their desperation for bread, the French tried to use potato flour in place of wheat flour. But potato flour has no gluten, and the results were awful.

When the people finally gave up on the bread and resorted to preparing potatoes in other ways, they found that far from satisfying their hunger for power, potatoes gave them the strength to seize it.

Today I think it's safe to say that nobody doesn't like potatoes in at least one form or another: baked, mashed, steamed, fried, souffléed, gratinéed . . .

2 teaspoons extra virgin olive oil

2 shallots, minced

1 garlic clove, minced

2 pounds potatoes, preferably Yukon Gold, peeled and sliced

½ cup vegetable broth (see page 165), approximately

¼ cup minced fresh parsley

3 tablespoons grated Parmesan cheese

Salt and freshly ground black pepper to taste

Heat the oil in a large skillet over medium-high heat. When it's hot, add the shallots and garlic, reduce the heat to medium-low, and sauté until the shallots have softened, about 6 minutes. Add the potatoes and vegetable broth. Cover and continue to cook over medium-low until the potatoes are soft enough to mash with the back of a spoon, about 20 minutes. Add more broth if necessary to prevent sticking.

Heat the broiler. Lightly grease an 8-inch gratin dish or baking dish or squirt with non-stick spray.

Mash the potatoes coarsely with the back of a spoon. Stir in the parsley. Place the potato mixture in the dish in a smooth, even layer. Sprinkle with Parmesan. Broil until the top is golden brown, about 3 minutes. Season with salt and pepper.

PER SERVING: CALORIES 165 • PROTEIN 4 G • CARBOHYDRATE 31 G • FAT 2.6 G • CHOLESTEROL 2.4 MG • SODIUM 68 MG • 14% CALORIES FROM FAT • VERY GOOD SOURCE OF VITAMINS B₆, C • GOOD SOURCE OF VITAMINS B₁, B₃

Make It Your Own

The flavor of the basic gratin is so subtle, you can alter it easily and in many different ways.

WHAT TO ADD AND WHEN TO ADD IT

Rosemary. This herb is one of the best seasonings for potatoes, but don't use it straight, or it'll overwhelm the dish. Instead, steep it in the vegetable broth, then add the broth to the potatoes. Here's how: Heat the vegetable broth called for in the basic recipe, add three large sprigs of rosemary, and simmer gently over medium heat for fifteen minutes. Discard the rosemary and proceed with the recipe.

Complementary Herbs and Cheeses. Replace the parsley and Parmesan in the basic recipe with chives and cheddar; caraway seeds and Havarti; thyme and Gruyère; or Monterey Jack cheese with jalapeño peppers.

Seasoned Bread Crumbs. For a crispy topping and extra flavor, sprinkle the top of the gratin with ⅔ cup soft bread crumbs, mixed with ¼ cup minced fresh herbs of your choice. (Dot with a teaspoon of cut-up unsalted butter if you'd like.) Broil as directed in the basic recipe, until the topping is golden and toasted.

Sautéed Chopped or Sliced Aromatic Vegetables. Stir about 1 cup of vegetables such as leeks, onions, and shallots into the potato mixture just before you transfer it to the gratin dish or baking dish. Broil as directed in the basic recipe.

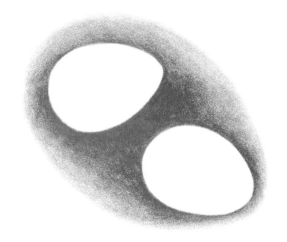

Savory Soufflés

SPINACH SOUFFLÉ
A Basic Soufflé

Serves 4

TOTAL TIME: ABOUT 40 MINUTES, NOT INCLUDING TIME TO
  MAKE THE WHITE SAUCE
TIME TO PREPARE: ABOUT 10 MINUTES
COOKING TIME: ABOUT 30 MINUTES
EQUIPMENT: 8-INCH SOUFFLÉ DISH
DO AHEAD: YOU CAN MAKE THE WHITE SAUCE UP TO 3
  DAYS IN ADVANCE. COVER AND REFRIGERATE. STIR WELL
  BEFORE USING, THINNING WITH ADDITIONAL MILK IF
  NECESSARY.

S erve this mild-flavored soufflé with a rich-
  tasting soup, such as *Simple Soothing Mushroom* (see page 177).

4 cups fresh spinach, washed and chopped, or
  one 10-ounce package frozen chopped
  spinach, thawed and squeezed dry
1 recipe Light All-Purpose White Sauce (see
  page 279)
½ cup grated Parmesan cheese
2 large egg yolks
4 large egg whites

Heat the oven to 425° F. Squirt the soufflé dish with nonstick spray, or grease lightly with unsalted butter.

In a mixing bowl, combine the spinach, white sauce, cheese, and egg yolks. Whisk to blend thoroughly.

In another bowl, beat the egg whites until stiff. Fold them into the spinach mixture until just blended.

Pour into the prepared soufflé dish. Bake until puffy and golden, about 30 minutes. Serve immediately.

PER SERVING: CALORIES 172 • PROTEIN 16.6 G • CARBOHYDRATE 11.8 G • FAT 6.6 G • CHOLESTEROL 119 MG • SODIUM 416 MG • 35% CALORIES FROM FAT • OUTSTANDING SOURCE OF VITAMIN A; CALCIUM • VERY GOOD SOURCE OF VITAMIN B2 • GOOD SOURCE OF VITAMINS B6, B12, C; FOLACIN, ZINC

SAVORY SOUFFLÉ BASICS

Soufflés are sensitive. Served promptly—as soon as they're done—they're stunning. Wait a second too long, and they're sunk. Instead of the cloudlike dish you'd planned, you've got a concave calamity, and a lot of explaining to do.

Timing is the only trick involved in making a good soufflé. The rest is a simple matter of whipping egg whites and folding them into a cheese sauce or vegetable puree.
• Let the egg whites come to room temperature before beating them (but don't leave them out for more than an hour). Beat them until they're stiff, but not dry. In other words, they should form peaks that look like stiff shaving cream, not foam, on the ends of your beaters.
• Fold the whites into the filling so that they're fully incorporated (the color and texture of the mixture should be even).

Don't give in to the inevitable temptation to stir, or the soufflé will be tough and heavy.

• Give your oven time to heat to the correct temperature before you put in the soufflé. In most cases this will take about fifteen minutes.

• Bake the mixture in a soufflé dish—a round dish with straight sides—choosing the proper size for the amount you'll be baking. For each cup of filling, you need 1½- to 2-cup capacity. So, for 3 to 4 cups of filling, you need one 6-cup mold or three 2-cup molds.

• Butter the soufflé dish well, or squirt it with nonstick spray; it will help the filling rise evenly.

• Bake the soufflé in the middle or lower third of your oven. First remove the upper rack so the risen soufflé won't mash against it.

• Don't open the oven door to check the soufflé until at least three-fourths of the cooking time has passed, or it will collapse. Serve it immediately.

• Do-ahead tip: You can make the filling up to three days in advance, keeping it and

CONFOUNDED COOKS WANT TO KNOW

Q. What do you mean by "fold"?

A. Folding has been described as "gently stirring," but this is not correct. "Stirring" implies a circular motion, while folding involves something more like a lift and tuck. To fold, use a rubber spatula or large plastic spoon. With the spatula or spoon, scoop up a portion of the beaten egg whites, about a sixth of the total amount. Then gently tilt the spatula and tuck it into the mixture receiving the whites. Gently bring the spatula up and over, as if turning the pages of a book. Repeat, gently lifting the mixture from the bottom of the bowl, and "folding" it over the whites until you can't see any white. Repeat, adding the whites in equal portions until you've transferred all of them and the mixture is light. Resist the temptation to stir, or you'll deflate the whites.

the reserved egg whites covered and refrigerated. (Don't beat the eggs until you're about to make the soufflé.) Bring the filling and egg whites to room temperature before proceeding with the recipe.

Make It Your Own

At the crudest level, a soufflé is a puree of whatever you please that's had air pumped into it via egg whites. The only tricks are restraining yourself from checking on it during the first fifteen minutes, using ingredients that are flavorful but not too heavy (they'll weigh down the mixture), and getting it to the table before it collapses.

WHAT TO ADD AND WHEN TO ADD IT

✒ *Vegetable/Potato Puree.* In place of spinach in the basic recipe, steam 1 cup any firm fresh vegetable (such as broccoli, asparagus, carrots) over vegetable broth and steam or boil a medium peeled potato (about ¼ pound). Drain the vegetable and potato, and puree along with about 1 tablespoon of any herbs you'd like. Beat in the egg yolks and cheese if desired; whip the whites, and proceed from there as directed in the basic recipe.

✒ *Cheese.* Beat the grated or shredded cheese of your choice into the basic mixture in place of the Parmesan before folding in the egg whites. Use only between 1 tablespoon and ¼ cup of cheese. More may weigh down the soufflé.

✒ *Pureed Dried Fruits.* See "Desserts," page 466.

SWEET POTATO SOUFFLÉ

Serves 4

TOTAL TIME: 1 HOUR, 20 MINUTES
TIME TO PREPARE: 10 MINUTES
COOKING TIME: 1 HOUR, 10 MINUTES
EQUIPMENT: FOUR 8-OUNCE SOUFFLÉ DISHES (OPTIONAL)
DO AHEAD: YOU CAN MAKE THE SWEET POTATO PUREE UP TO 3 DAYS IN ADVANCE. REFRIGERATE UNTIL READY TO USE.

Only the Parmesan makes the difference between this side dish and dessert. Serve it when you want something sweet for lunch or a light supper.

2 large sweet potatoes
¼ cup evaporated skim milk
2 large egg yolks
¼ cup grated Parmesan cheese
1 teaspoon grated orange zest
2 teaspoons maple syrup
Pinch ground cloves
Pinch ground cinnamon
Pinch ground nutmeg
4 large egg whites

Heat the oven to 425° F. Coat four 8-ounce soufflé dishes or one 4-cup soufflé dish with nonstick spray or grease lightly with unsalted butter.

Bake the potatoes until they're tender enough to mash, about 40 minutes. Reduce the oven temperature to 400° F.

When the potatoes are cool enough to handle, peel and mash them in a mixing bowl with the evaporated skim milk and egg yolks. Add the Parmesan, orange zest, maple syrup, cloves, cinnamon, and nutmeg, and stir well.

In another bowl, whip the egg whites to stiff peaks. Fold them into the sweet potato mixture until just blended. Bake until puffy and golden, about 30 minutes. Serve right away.

PER SERVING: CALORIES 178 • PROTEIN 9.9 G • CARBOHYDRATE 23.8 G • FAT 4.6 G • CHOLESTEROL 112 MG • SODIUM 204 MG • 24% CALORIES FROM FAT • OUTSTANDING SOURCE OF VITAMIN A • VERY GOOD SOURCE OF VITAMINS B2, C • GOOD SOURCE OF VITAMIN B6; CALCIUM

Terrines

BROCCOLI AND CHEDDAR TERRINE
A Basic Terrine
Serves 8

TOTAL TIME: ABOUT 1 HOUR, 30 MINUTES
TIME TO PREPARE: ABOUT 10 MINUTES, INCLUDING TIME
    TO SAUTÉ
COOKING TIME: 1 HOUR, 20 MINUTES
DO AHEAD: YOU CAN STEAM AND PUREE THE VEGETABLES
    UP TO 2 DAYS IN ADVANCE. REFRIGERATE UNTIL READY
    TO USE.
REFRIGERATION/FREEZING: REFRIGERATE UP TO 3 DAYS.
    FREEZE UP TO 3 MONTHS.

I*t's interesting how some ideas persist long after they've become obsolete. For instance, the notion that terrines are difficult predates the food processor, which has eliminated most of the work involved, making them easy to prepare. Lovely looking and easy to serve, terrines—loaves of pureed vegetables, served in slices or as a spread—make ideal party and picnic food.*

4 cups loosely packed chopped broccoli
1 cup chopped peeled medium-starch or starchy
    potatoes, such as russet or Yukon Gold
2 teaspoons canola or vegetable oil, or unsalted
    butter

1 large onion, chopped
1 tablespoon balsamic vinegar
1 large egg, lightly beaten
1 large egg white
1 cup fine dried bread crumbs or cooked grain,
    such as brown rice or fine bulgur wheat
½ cup shredded sharp cheddar cheese

Heat the oven to 425°F. Squirt an 8½ × 4½-inch loaf pan with nonstick spray or grease lightly with unsalted butter.

Put a rack or a steamer basket on the bottom of a large saucepan. Add water until it almost touches the rack. Bring the water to a boil.

Add the broccoli, cover the pot, and steam until bright green and cooked but still crisp in the center, about 4 minutes for florets, 8 minutes for stems, and 10 to 12 minutes for a full head. Drain and transfer the broccoli to a food processor. Return the rack or steamer basket to the saucepan.

If the water has evaporated, add fresh water to the saucepan until it almost touches the rack, and bring to a boil.

Add the potatoes, cover the pan, turn the heat down to medium-low, and let the potatoes steam until tender, about 15 minutes. Check the water level often, adding more as it evaporates. Drain and add them to the food processor. Process the vegetables just to puree, taking care not to liquefy.

Heat the oil or melt the butter in a large skillet over medium-high heat. Add the onion, reduce the heat to medium-low, and sauté until it's soft, about 7 minutes. Add the balsamic vinegar, turn up the heat to medium-high, and continue cooking and stirring until the vinegar has evaporated, about 2 minutes. Transfer the ingredients to a large mixing bowl.

Stir in the vegetable puree, egg, egg white, bread crumbs or cooked grain, and cheese. Mix thoroughly.

Pour the terrine mixture into the prepared pan. Place the pan inside a deep baking dish. Pour water into the outer dish until it comes halfway up the pan. Bake until the terrine is firm and a knife inserted in the center comes out clean, about 50 minutes, checking the water level and adding more as necessary to maintain it.

Let the terrine cool on a rack, then cover and refrigerate it to chill through. Run a wet knife around the rim to loosen it, place a plate over the top of the terrine, and using both hands, flip the pan and invert the terrine onto the plate. Slice it with a wet knife and serve cool or at room temperature.

PER SERVING: CALORIES 134 • PROTEIN 6.4 G • CARBOHYDRATE 16.7 G • FAT 4.9 G • CHOLESTEROL 34 MG • SODIUM 180 MG • 33% CALORIES FROM FAT • OUTSTANDING SOURCE OF VITAMIN C • GOOD SOURCE OF VITAMINS A, B1, B2, FOLACIN, CALCIUM

TERRINE BASICS

• Starchy vegetables such as carrots, potatoes, and turnips make firm terrines. If you're using a softer vegetable, such as broccoli (in the basic recipe), cauliflower, spinach, or mushrooms, include a starchy vegetable for texture. Choose a starchy vegetable with a neutral flavor (such as a potato) or a with a flavor that complements the main ingredient. Carrots go well with spinach, for example; turnip complements cauliflower, and parsnips give a nice bite to mushrooms.

• Steam the vegetables thoroughly, making sure they're soft enough to puree. Steam them rather than cook them in water, because you don't want any excess moisture in the mix. Puree the vegetables well but not until liquefied; smooth texture assures even flavor.

• Cook the terrine in a water bath so it will bake evenly and turn out smooth. Direct heat gives it a hard crust, makes the top crack, and leaves the inside runny.

• The basic recipe makes a relatively firm loaf that slices neatly. To make a spreadable pâté, omit the bread crumbs or cooked grain. You may have to bake it longer, up to thirty minutes more. Test often after the time given, inserting a slender paring knife into the terrine until it comes out clean. Without the grain, the terrine will spread more easily and taste more of the main ingredient.

• You can make individual terrines by dividing this mixture among six custard cups or ramekins. Cook in a water bath as described in the basic recipe, and cool as directed.

Make It Your Own

You have a lot of leeway when you make terrines. But there are two fundamental rules: (1) the flavors should blend; (2) the ingredients should be firm, not watery.

WHAT TO ADD AND WHEN TO ADD IT

Vegetables. Puree any steamed vegetable you'd like, provided it doesn't liquefy in the process. (For extra flavor, steam it over vegetable broth.) If the puree is watery, let it sit in a sieve to drain. Meanwhile, boil or bake starchy potatoes (1 cup chopped peeled potatoes for 2 cups vegetable puree). Puree the potatoes and blend them with the vegetable puree to give it body.

Hard Cheese. Match the cheese to the vegetable, using Gruyère for spinach terrines, for example, Asiago cheese for artichoke terrines, Parmesan for asparagus, and cheddar for broccoli.

Soft Cheese. For additional, sweet flavor and a denser texture, add 1 cup nonfat ricotta cheese to the basic recipe. Just make sure the ricotta isn't watery. If it looks runny to you, let it sit in a sieve to drain for twenty minutes before you add it to your terrine mixture. You can use soft tofu instead, as long as it's fresh. Line a sieve with paper towel and let the tofu drain for thirty minutes.

Grains. Use 1 cup cooked bulgur in place of bread crumbs or rice as a binder. Or cook ½ cup couscous according to package directions, and use that instead.

Aromatic Vegetables and Herbs. Substitute 1 cup chopped leeks (white part only) or 4 minced shallots for the onion in the basic recipe. Or use half onion and half leeks or shallots. Season your terrine with herbs that complement the other ingredients, making sure to mince them (if fresh) or crumble them (if dried) well and to stir them in thoroughly so they're evenly distributed. For guidance and inspiration in choosing complementary herbs (if you don't have any strong preferences already), you can look at other recipes that call for whatever you're using as the main ingredient, and use the same seasoning. Check the ingredients for the Classic Leek and Potato Soup with Watercress (see page 182), for example, and you'll find that it's seasoned with chives. This combination works very well in a terrine, too.

•

PARSNIP AND APPLE TERRINE

Serves 8

TOTAL TIME: 4 HOURS, 40 MINUTES, INCLUDING TIME TO
   CHILL
TIME TO PREPARE: 10 MINUTES, INCLUDING TIME TO SAUTÉ
COOKING TIME: ABOUT 1 HOUR, 30 MINUTES
DO AHEAD: YOU CAN MAKE THE APPLE-PARSNIP PUREE UP
   TO 3 DAYS IN ADVANCE. REFRIGERATE UNTIL READY TO
   USE.
REFRIGERATION/FREEZING: REFRIGERATE UP TO 3 DAYS.
   FREEZE UP TO 3 MONTHS. LET THAW AT ROOM
   TEMPERATURE.

*W*e named our son for a good friend
whom, I thought until recently, I knew
pretty well. We've cooked for each
other throughout fifteen years and are—or so I
thought—kindred spirits when it comes to food. But
then he happened to say something that put our
friendship in a whole new light. The subject was
parsnips. He loves them, he said. "Buttered, roasted,
you name it. Just love 'em." Suddenly there was a
chasm between us; how well could I have known
someone who loves parsnips? Then, I thought, it had
been years since I'd had one, so maybe I like
parsnips, too.

To be honest, I don't—at least not on their own.
But puree them, then bake them with apples and
cheese, and I'll eat parsnips with pleasure.

1 pound parsnips, peeled and sliced
1 cup loosely packed dried apples
2 teaspoons unsalted butter or canola oil
1 small white onion, chopped
1 tablespoon minced fresh dill, or 1 teaspoon
   crumbled dried dill
1 cup low-fat cottage cheese
⅓ cup shredded cheddar cheese
1 cup loosely packed dried bread crumbs

Place the parsnips and dried apples in a large
saucepan. Add water to cover by 2 inches.
Bring to a boil over medium-high heat. Reduce
the heat to medium-low. Cover and simmer
until the parsnips are tender enough to puree,
about 30 to 40 minutes. Drain thoroughly and
let them cool.

Meanwhile, melt the butter or heat the oil
in a small skillet over medium-high heat. When
it is hot, add the onion and dill. Reduce the
heat to medium and sauté, stirring often, until
the onion is soft, about 7 minutes. Remove
from the heat.

Heat the oven to 425°F. Lightly grease an
8½ × 4½-inch loaf pan or squirt it with nonstick spray.

Puree the parsnips and apples with an
immersion blender or in a food processor. Add
the onion, cottage cheese, cheddar cheese, and
bread crumbs. Process again until smooth.

Pour the mixture into the prepared pan.
Cover loosely with aluminum foil.

Place the pan inside a deep baking dish. Pour water into the outer dish until it comes halfway up the pan. Bake until the terrine is firm and a knife inserted in the center comes out clean, about 50 minutes. Check the water level often, adding more as necessary to maintain it.

Transfer the terrine to a cooling rack. When it's cool, cover it with plastic wrap and refrigerate for at least three hours. To serve, insert a wet knife between the terrine and the side of the pan, and run it all the way around. Place a plate over the top of the terrine, and using both hands, flip the pan and invert the terrine onto the plate.

PER SERVING: CALORIES 160 • PROTEIN 7 G • CARBOHYDRATE 25 G • FAT 3.6 G • CHOLESTEROL 8.7 MG • SODIUM 263 MG • 20% CALORIES FROM FAT • GOOD SOURCE OF VITAMIN C; FOLACIN, CALCIUM

•

CARROT-SPINACH TERRINE

Serves 6

TOTAL TIME: 4 HOURS, 35 MINUTES, INCLUDING TIME TO CHILL

TIME TO PREPARE: ABOUT 15 MINUTES, INCLUDING TIME TO SAUTÉ

COOKING TIME: 1 HOUR, 20 MINUTES

DO AHEAD: YOU CAN MAKE THE CARROT-APRICOT PUREE UP TO 3 DAYS IN ADVANCE. REFRIGERATE UNTIL READY TO USE.

REFRIGERATION/FREEZING: REFRIGERATE UP TO 3 DAYS. FREEZE UP TO 3 MONTHS. LET THAW AT ROOM TEMPERATURE.

Some recipes are easy to decipher; you can tell at a glance how the final dish will taste. This isn't one of them. The combination of carrots, spinach, and cheese is easy enough to imagine. The apricots are the wild card here.

In fact it's the apricots that make this dish. The cheddar buffers the sugar in them, and the onion softens their bite, so only the pure flavor remains to blend with the rest. Just make sure to soak them until they are pulpy, and puree them thoroughly before you proceed.

1 pound carrots, peeled and sliced

1 cup loosely packed dried apricots

2 teaspoons unsalted butter or canola oil

1 small white onion, chopped

2 scallions, white part plus 2 inches of greens, chopped

4 cups fresh spinach, washed and chopped, or one 10-ounce package frozen chopped spinach, thawed and squeezed dry

2 teaspoons crumbled dried oregano

1 cup loosely packed dried bread crumbs

¼ cup grated Parmesan cheese

2 large eggs

1 cup low-fat cottage cheese

⅓ cup shredded cheddar cheese

Place the carrots and dried apricots in a large saucepan. Add water to cover by 2 inches. Bring to a boil over medium-high heat. Reduce the heat to medium-low. Cover and simmer until the carrots are tender enough to puree, about 30 minutes. Drain thoroughly and let them cool.

Meanwhile, melt 1 teaspoon of the butter or heat 1 teaspoon of the oil in a small skillet over medium-high heat. When it is hot, add the onion. Reduce the heat to medium and sauté, stirring often, until the onion is soft, about 7 minutes. Transfer to a small bowl and set aside.

Heat the oven to 425°F. Lightly grease an

8½ × 4½-inch loaf pan or squirt it with non-stick spray.

Heat the remaining butter or oil in a medium skillet over medium-high heat. When it is hot, add the scallions. Reduce the heat to medium and sauté, stirring often, until the scallions are soft, about 5 minutes. Add the spinach and oregano, and stir well until the spinach, if raw, turns bright green. If using thawed frozen spinach, stir to combine it with the scallions.

Transfer the mixture to a food processor, along with half of the bread crumbs and the Parmesan cheese. Process in short spurts until well combined, about 6 to 8 spurts. Don't let the processor run steadily or the mixture will liquefy.

Transfer the spinach mixture to a bowl and set aside.

Place the carrots and apricots in the food processor and puree, processing until smooth. Add the eggs, cottage cheese, cheddar cheese, remaining bread crumbs, and onion. Process in short spurts to combine thoroughly, about 6 to 8 spurts.

Spread half of the spinach on the bottom of the prepared pan. Spread the carrot-apricot mixture on top, and spread the remaining spinach mixture over that. Cover loosely with foil.

Place the pan inside a deep baking dish. Pour water into the outer dish until it comes halfway up the pan. Bake until the terrine is firm and a knife inserted in the center comes out clean, about 50 minutes. Check the water level often, adding more as necessary to maintain it. Cool completely on a rack. Cover and refrigerate until chilled through, about 3 hours.

To serve, insert a wet knife between the terrine and the side of the pan, and run it all the way around. Place a plate over the top of the terrine, and using both hands, flip the pan and invert the terrine onto the plate.

PER SERVING: CALORIES 260 • PROTEIN 14 G • CARBOHYDRATE 37 G • FAT 7 G • CHOLESTEROL 50 MG • SODIUM 490 MG • 24% CALORIES FROM FAT • OUTSTANDING SOURCE OF VITAMIN A • VERY GOOD SOURCE OF VITAMINS B₂, C; FOLACIN, CALCIUM, IRON • GOOD SOURCE OF VITAMINS B₁, B₃, B₆

•

BAKED RATATOUILLE TERRINE

Serves 8

TOTAL TIME: ABOUT 1 HOUR, 35 MINUTES, NOT INCLUDING TIME TO ROAST THE PEPPERS
TIME TO PREPARE: 35 MINUTES, INCLUDING TIME TO SAUTÉ
COOKING TIME: ABOUT 1 HOUR
EQUIPMENT: 8-INCH SOUFFLÉ DISH
DO AHEAD: YOU CAN ROAST THE PEPPERS UP TO 2 DAYS IN ADVANCE. YOU CAN ALSO ASSEMBLE THE DISH UP TO 3 DAYS IN ADVANCE. REFRIGERATE UNTIL READY TO USE.
REFRIGERATION/FREEZING: REFRIGERATE UP TO 3 DAYS. DO NOT FREEZE.

A *neat, compact way to serve ratatouille. Put it out for buffets and pack it up for picnics.*

1 large eggplant, peeled and diced

Coarse salt (optional)

1 tablespoon extra virgin olive oil

1 large onion, sliced

4 garlic cloves, minced

½ cup shredded fresh basil

¼ cup minced fresh parsley

1 tablespoon balsamic vinegar

1 pound tomatoes, peeled, seeded, and chopped
    (see page 544)

1 red bell pepper, roasted and peeled (see page 534)

1 yellow bell pepper, roasted and peeled (see page 534)

⅓ cup chopped oil-cured black olives

2 teaspoons capers

3 medium zucchini, sliced paper thin

1 cup crumbled feta cheese

2 cups bread chunks, crusts removed

Heat the oven to 425°F. Butter the soufflé dish.

If the eggplant has few seeds, it won't need salting. If the eggplant is seedy, sprinkle it with salt, and place it in a colander lined with paper towels. Set aside while you continue with the next steps

Heat the olive oil in a large, heavy skillet over medium-high heat. Add the onion, garlic, basil, and parsley, and sauté over medium heat until the onion is soft, about 7 minutes. Add the balsamic vinegar, turn up the heat to medium-high, and stir until most of the liquid has evaporated, about 1 minute. Add the egg-plant and stir to mix with the onion. Add the tomatoes, bell peppers, olives, and capers, and stir well. Simmer, uncovered, until the tomatoes have cooked down and the mixture is very thick, about 20 minutes.

Line the prepared soufflé dish with the zucchini slices, covering the bottom and sides, overlapping the pieces so the dish is entirely covered. Sprinkle the feta cheese over the zucchini on the bottom of the dish. Spoon the vegetable mixture on top. Cover evenly with the bread.

Place the dish inside a large baking pan. Pour water into the outer pan so it comes halfway up the soufflé dish. Cover the soufflé dish loosely with foil, and bake until the terrine has set, about 40 minutes, removing the foil 5 minutes before the end of the cooking time.

Let the soufflé dish cool on a rack for 10 minutes. Invert a serving plate and place it on top of the soufflé dish. Holding both together, flip the dishes so that the soufflé dish is inverted on the serving plate. Carefully lift the soufflé dish. Serve at room temperature, or wrap and refrigerate for about 3 hours, and serve chilled.

PER SERVING: CALORIES 175 • PROTEIN 7.5 G • CARBOHYDRATE 17 G • FAT 9.4 G • CHOLESTEROL 27.6 MG • SODIUM 431 MG • 46% CALORIES FROM FAT • OUTSTANDING SOURCE OF VITAMIN C • VERY GOOD SOURCE OF VITAMIN B₂ • GOOD SOURCE OF VITAMINS A, B₁, B₆ FOLACIN, CALCIUM

MUSHROOM PÂTÉ

Serves 6 to 8

TOTAL TIME: ABOUT 3 HOURS, 15 MINUTES, INCLUDING
TIME TO CHILL
TIME TO PREPARE: ABOUT 15 MINUTES, INCLUDING TIME
TO SAUTÉ
COOKING TIME: INCLUDED IN TIME TO PREPARE
DO AHEAD: YOU CAN COOK THE BULGUR UP TO 3 DAYS IN
ADVANCE. COVER AND REFRIGERATE UNTIL READY TO
USE.
REFRIGERATION/FREEZING: REFRIGERATE UP TO 4 DAYS. DO
NOT FREEZE.

I realize that devotees of true pâté—the kind that calls for goose livers—resent the use of "pâté" in reference to anything else. I'd agree if there were deception involved, if the use of the word was meant to suggest that the food in question tastes like the original. But I'm forced to use "pâté" for lack of another word to describe this delectable mushroom-sesame puree that's packed into a mold and served as a spread.

½ cup bulgur wheat

2 teaspoons canola or vegetable oil

4 scallions, white part and 2 inches of greens,
    chopped

8 ounces firm fresh mushrooms, such as cremini,
    white button, or portobello, sliced

1 tablespoon balsamic vinegar

2 tablespoons tahini

Place the bulgur in a small saucepan. In a separate sauce pan, bring ¾ cup of water to a boil. Pour the boiling water over the bulgur, cover, and let rest while you proceed with the recipe.

Meanwhile, heat the oil in a medium skillet over medium-high heat. When it is hot, add the scallions. Reduce the heat to medium and sauté, stirring often, until the scallions are soft, about 5 minutes. Stir in the mushrooms. Add the vinegar and keep stirring until the mushrooms color and soften, about 6 minutes. Remove from the heat.

Strain any moisture from the bulgur through a fine sieve, then place the bulgur and tahini in a food processor. Process until smooth. Using a slotted spoon, add the mushrooms to the mixture in the food processor. Process until smooth.

Transfer the mixture to a 6-inch loaf pan or 2-cup mold. Pat it in firmly. Cover with plastic wrap and refrigerate at least 3 hours.

PER SERVING: CALORIES 98 • PROTEIN 3.4 G • CARBOHYDRATE 12.7 G • FAT 4.6 G
• CHOLESTEROL 0 MG • SODIUM 6.21 MG • 39% CALORIES FROM FAT

Savory Flans

SAVORY FLAN

Serves 4

TOTAL TIME: ABOUT 1 HOUR
TIME TO PREPARE: ABOUT 5 MINUTES
COOKING TIME: ABOUT 55 MINUTES
REFRIGERATION/FREEZING: REFRIGERATE UP TO 3 DAYS. DO
   NOT FREEZE.

Each flan is meant to be a bit of highly concentrated flavor. Because the basic flan tastes of nothing, whatever you add will permeate the dish.

½ cup evaporated skim milk
½ cup nonfat milk
½ cup nonfat dry milk
2 large eggs, lightly beaten
1 large egg yolk
Filling (see "Make It Your Own")

Heat the oven to 450° F. Squirt four 6-inch custard cups with nonstick spray or grease lightly with unsalted butter.

Whisk together the evaporated skim milk, nonfat milk, and nonfat dry milk. Beat in the eggs and egg yolk. Whisk in the filling until smooth.

Pour the mixture into the custard cups, filling the cups halfway. Place the cups in a large shallow baking pan and pour water into the pan so that it comes halfway up the sides of the custard cups. Cover loosely with foil and bake until the flans are firm and a knife inserted in the center of one of the custard cups comes out clean, about 50 minutes, adding more water to the outer pan as necessary. If the tops still seem moist, remove the foil and continue baking until they're dry, about 5 minutes more. To unmold, see unmolding instructions for Fresh Corn Custard (page 249). Serve hot or at room temperature, or chill thoroughly for about 3 hours and serve cold.

PER SERVING: CALORIES 142 • PROTEIN 12.7 G • CARBOHYDRATE 13.3 G • FAT 4 G • CHOLESTEROL 164 MG • SODIUM 166 MG • 26% CALORIES FROM FAT • VERY GOOD SOURCE OF VITAMINS B₂, B₁₂; CALCIUM • GOOD SOURCE OF VITAMIN A; ZINC

Make It Your Own

Anything you add to the basic mixture will infuse the flan with flavor.

WHAT TO ADD AND WHEN TO ADD IT

Grated Cheese. Once you've made the basic flan mixture, whisk in 2 tablespoons to ¼ cup any cheese you'd like, from mild cheddar to strong Gruyère. Use a ladle to spoon the mixture into the custard cups, or the cheese will settle in the mixing bowl instead of blending evenly into the flans.

Fresh Vegetables. Steam 2 cups of any chopped vegetable of your choice (such as artichokes, asparagus, broccoli, carrots, and spinach) in vegetable broth or water. Blot away any moisture and puree. If the puree seems watery and thin, add ½ cup fine dried bread crumbs and/or the same amount of grated cheese. If you think you should add the bread crumbs but you're not sure, go ahead and toss them in. They won't affect the flavor of the flan.

Herbs. Add 2 tablespoons finely minced fresh herbs, or 2 teaspoons crumbled dried herbs, to the basic recipe, choosing seasonings that complement the other ingredients.

MUSHROOM FLAN

Serves 6

TOTAL TIME: ABOUT 1 HOUR, 10 MINUTES
TIME TO PREPARE: ABOUT 15 MINUTES, INCLUDING TIME
   TO SAUTÉ
COOKING TIME: ABOUT 50 TO 55 MINUTES
REFRIGERATION/FREEZING: REFRIGERATE UP TO 3 DAYS. DO
   NOT FREEZE.

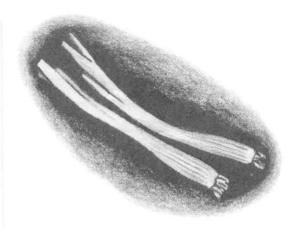

A creamy, smooth, soothing autumn side dish. Try it with Pasta e Fagioli (see page 194) or Classic Leek and Potato Soup with Watercress (see page 182).

2 teaspoons extra virgin olive oil

2 scallions, white part plus 2 inches of green, chopped

1 shallot, chopped

¼ cup minced fresh parsley

1 pound cremini, portobello, or white button mushrooms, sliced

2 tablespoons balsamic vinegar or dry white wine

½ cup shredded Gruyère cheese

½ cup evaporated skim milk

½ cup nonfat milk

½ cup nonfat dry milk

2 large eggs, lightly beaten

1 large egg yolk

Heat the oven to 450°F. Squirt six 6-inch custard cups with nonstick spray or grease lightly with unsalted butter.

Heat the oil in a medium nonstick skillet over medium-high heat. When it's hot, add the scallions, shallot, and parsley. Reduce the heat to medium and sauté, stirring often, until the vegetables have softened, about 7 minutes.

Stir in the mushrooms to coat with the vegetables. Add the vinegar or wine and con-tinue stirring until the mushrooms are very soft, about 10 minutes.

Transfer the mixture to a food processor or blender along with the cheese. Process in short pulses until the mixture is dense and evenly colored, about 8 pulses.

Whisk together the evaporated skim milk, nonfat milk, and nonfat dry milk. Beat together the eggs and egg yolk, and add to the milk mixture. Whisk in the mushroom mixture.

Pour the mixture into the custard cups, fill-ing the cups halfway. Place the cups in a large shallow baking pan and pour water into the pan so that it comes halfway up the sides of the custard cups. Cover loosely with foil and bake until the flans are firm and a knife inserted in the center of one of the custard cups comes out clean, about 50 minutes, adding more water to the outer pan as necessary. If the tops still seem moist, remove the foil and continue baking until they're dry, about 5 minutes more. Serve hot or at room temperature, or chill thor-oughly for about 3 hours and serve cold.

PER SERVING: CALORIES 170 • PROTEIN 13 G • CARBOHYDRATE 14 G • FAT 7.4 G • CHOLESTEROL 120 MG • SODIUM 147 MG • 38% CALORIES FROM FAT • OUTSTAND-ING SOURCE OF VITAMIN B₂ • VERY GOOD SOURCE OF CALCIUM • GOOD SOURCE OF VITAMINS A, B₁, B₃, B₆, B₁₂, C; FOLACIN, IRON

SUN-DRIED TOMATO FLAN

Serves 4

TOTAL TIME: ABOUT 5 HOURS, INCLUDING TIME TO SOAK
THE TOMATOES AND CHILL
TIME TO PREPARE: ABOUT 5 MINUTES
COOKING TIME: ABOUT 50 TO 55 MINUTES
REFRIGERATION/FREEZING: REFRIGERATE UP TO 3 DAYS. DO
NOT FREEZE.

Sharp and sweet, this flan goes well with subtle dishes such as Artichoke Risotto (see page 315) or Artichoke and Mushroom Savory Pie (see page 434).

2 cups dry-packed (not in oil) sun-dried tomatoes
¼ cup minced fresh basil
¼ cup grated Parmesan cheese

½ cup evaporated skim milk
½ cup nonfat milk
½ cup nonfat dry milk
2 large eggs, lightly beaten
1 large egg yolk

Place the tomatoes in water to cover until soft, about 1 hour.

Heat the oven to 450°F. Squirt four 6-inch custard cups with nonstick spray or lightly grease with unsalted butter.

Drain the tomatoes well, dabbing with paper towels to absorb as much water as possible. In a food processor or blender, puree them with the basil and cheese.

Whisk together the evaporated skim milk, nonfat milk, and nonfat dry milk. Beat together the eggs and egg yolk, and add to the milk mixture. Stir in the tomato mixture.

Pour the mixture into the custard cups, filling the cups halfway. Place the cups in a large shallow baking pan and pour water into the pan so that it comes halfway up the sides of the custard cups. Cover loosely with foil and bake until the flans are firm and a knife inserted in the center of one of the custard cups comes out clean, about 50 minutes, adding more water to the outer pan as necessary. If the tops still seem moist, remove the foil and continue baking until they're dry, about 5 minutes more. Serve hot or at room temperature, or chill for about 3 hours and serve cold.

PER SERVING: CALORIES 230 • PROTEIN 18 G • CARBOHYDRATE 27 G • FAT 6.6 G •
CHOLESTEROL 169 MG • SODIUM 835 MG • 25% CALORIES FROM FAT • OUTSTAND-
ING SOURCE OF CALCIUM • VERY GOOD SOURCE OF VITAMINS A, B₂, C • GOOD
SOURCE OF VITAMINS B₁, B₃, B₆, B₁₂; FOLACIN, ZINC

SPINACH FLAN

Serves 4

TOTAL TIME: ABOUT 4 HOURS, INCLUDING TIME TO CHILL
TIME TO PREPARE: ABOUT 5 MINUTES
COOKING TIME: ABOUT 50 TO 55 MINUTES
REFRIGERATION/FREEZING: REFRIGERATE UP TO 3 DAYS. DO
   NOT FREEZE.

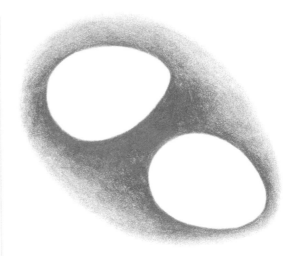

I ts smooth texture and subtle flavor make this flan an ideal accompaniment to heartier dishes such as *Winter Tomato—Wheat Berry Soup* (see page 197), and *Stewed Beans with Potatoes and Olives* (see page 332).

4 cups fresh spinach, washed and chopped, or
   one 10-ounce package frozen chopped
   spinach
2 tablespoons grated Parmesan cheese
1 teaspoon crumbled dried oregano
Pinch ground nutmeg
½ cup evaporated skim milk
½ cup nonfat milk
½ cup nonfat dry milk
2 large eggs, lightly beaten
1 large egg yolk

Heat the oven to 450° F. Squirt four 6-inch custard cups with nonstick spray or lightly grease with unsalted butter.

If you're using fresh spinach, steam it until it turns bright green (see page 539). Drain it thoroughly and blot it dry. If using frozen spinach thaw it and squeeze it dry by placing in a fine sieve and pushing against the mesh with the back of a spoon.

In a food processor or blender, puree the spinach, cheese, oregano, and nutmeg.

Whisk together the evaporated skim milk, nonfat milk, and nonfat dry milk. Beat together the eggs and egg yolk, and add to the milk mixture. Whisk in the spinach mixture.

Pour the mixture into the custard cups, filling the cups halfway. Place the cups in a large, shallow baking pan and pour water into the pan so that it comes halfway up the sides of the custard cups. Cover loosely with foil and bake until the flans are firm and a knife inserted in the center of one of the custard cups comes out clean, about 50 minutes, adding more water to the outer pan as necessary. If the tops still seem moist, remove the foil and continue baking until they're dry, about 5 minutes more. Serve hot or at room temperature, or chill thoroughly for about 3 hours and serve cold.

PER SERVING: CALORIES 148 • PROTEIN 13 G • CARBOHYDRATE 12.5 G • FAT 4.9 G • CHOLESTEROL 166 MG • SODIUM 217 MG • 30% CALORIES FROM FAT • VERY GOOD SOURCE OF VITAMINS A, B₂; CALCIUM • GOOD SOURCE OF VITAMIN B₁₂; FOLACIN, ZINC

SAVORY CARROT FLAN

Serves 4

TOTAL TIME: ABOUT 4 HOURS, 35 MINUTES, INCLUDING TIME TO CHILL
TIME TO PREPARE: ABOUT 5 MINUTES
COOKING TIME: ABOUT 1 HOUR, 30 MINUTES
REFRIGERATION/FREEZING: REFRIGERATE UP TO 3 DAYS. DO NOT FREEZE.

This elegant side dish is just *savory enough to serve with supper. Any sweeter, and it would have to be dessert.*

1 pound carrots, peeled and sliced
2 bay leaves
1 small onion, sliced
1 tablespoon grated peeled fresh ginger
¼ cup fresh orange juice
1 teaspoon maple syrup
Pinch ground nutmeg
Pinch ground cinnamon
Pinch crumbled dried marjoram
½ cup evaporated skim milk
¼ cup nonfat dry milk
1 large egg
1 large egg white

Heat the oven to 375°F. Squirt a 1-quart baking dish with nonstick spray or lightly grease with unsalted butter.

Place the carrots, bay leaves, onion, ginger, and orange juice in a medium saucepan. Add water to cover the vegetables by about 1 inch. Cover and simmer over medium heat until you can pierce the carrots easily with a fork, about 30 minutes. Check often, adding more water as necessary to prevent burning. Drain any liquid that remains. Remove and discard the bay leaves.

Transfer the contents of the saucepan to a food processor.

Add the maple syrup, nutmeg, cinnamon, marjoram, evaporated milk, dry milk, egg, and egg white. Process until smooth.

Pour the mixture into the baking dish. Place this dish in a larger dish. Pour water into the larger dish so that it comes halfway up the sides of the smaller.

Bake for 1 hour, until firm and a knife inserted in the center of the flan comes out clean, adding more water to the larger dish as it evaporates. Serve hot or at room temperature, or chill thoroughly for about 3 hours and serve cold.

PER SERVING: CALORIES 151 • PROTEIN 9.3 G • CARBOHYDRATE 25.5 G • FAT 1 6 G • CHOLESTEROL 55.9 MG • SODIUM 147 MG • 10% CALORIES FROM FAT • OUTSTANDING SOURCE OF VITAMIN A • VERY GOOD SOURCE OF VITAMINS B₂, C; CALCIUM • GOOD SOURCE OF VITAMINS B₁, B₆

Filled Things

TAMALE-STYLE FRESH CORN NUGGETS

Serves 4 to 6

TOTAL TIME: ABOUT 1 HOUR, 40 MINUTES
TIME TO PREPARE: ABOUT 30 MINUTES
COOKING TIME: ABOUT 1 HOUR, 10 MINUTES
DO AHEAD: YOU CAN MAKE THE FILLING OF YOUR CHOICE
   UP TO 3 DAYS IN ADVANCE. REFRIGERATE UNTIL READY
   TO USE. YOU CAN ALSO MAKE THE CORNMEAL MIXTURE
   UP TO 2 DAYS IN ADVANCE. REFRIGERATE UNTIL READY
   TO USE.
REFRIGERATION/FREEZING: REFRIGERATE UP TO 4 DAYS.
   FREEZE UP TO 6 MONTHS.

Saying they're "tamale style" rather than "tamales" is one way to avoid having to apologize for the fact that these are not in any way authentic. Authentic tamales call for a special kind of cornmeal, a tub of lard, and a month of Sundays. It's a lot of time and trouble for something you eat in one bite, and which is packed with fat and few redeeming nutrients.

These borrow those aspects of real tamales that lend themselves to a dish that's not only delicious, but fast and wholesome, too.

3 ears of corn
1 cup stone-ground cornmeal
1 teaspoon sugar
1 teaspoon ground cumin
Pinch cayenne pepper
2 tablespoons nonfat or low-fat buttermilk or
   plain nonfat yogurt
1 recipe Bean Filling, Sweet Potato Filling, or
   Cheese Filling (recipes follow) or Kidney
   Bean Hummus (see page 254)

Husks from 6 ears of corn (remove carefully so
   leaves remain intact)

Garnishes (optional)
Nonfat or reduced-fat sour cream
Chopped avocados
Minced fresh cilantro
Basic Tomato Salsa (see page 158)

Scrape off the corn kernels, place them in a food processor, and process in short pulses to puree, about 6 pulses. (The texture will be coarse.)

Add the cornmeal, sugar, cumin, cayenne, and buttermilk or yogurt. Pulse again until the ingredients are well combined, about 6 pulses.

Transfer the corn mixture to a mixing bowl. Add the filling of your choice and stir to blend thoroughly.

Fill a wide saucepan with water and bring it to a boil. Add the toughest corn husks (the tender inner husks won't have to be parboiled) and simmer gently until softened, about 3 minutes. Drain and let them cool.

When they are cool enough to handle, place 2 husks on a flat surface, one on top of the other, to make an X. Place a spoonful of stuffing in the center. Start with the bottom husk and fold the ends of both husks over to form a square packet. Place it seam side down. Cut a long thin strip of aluminum foil and wrap it around the packet to secure it. Set it aside while you repeat this with the remaining husks and filling.

Place a rack in the bottom of a large saucepan or stockpot. Add water until it nearly touches the rack. Place the tamales on top, stacking them if necessary. Bring the water to a boil over medium-high heat. Cover, reduce the heat to medium-low, and simmer until the tamales are firm to the touch, about 1 hour. Check the water level often, taking care to pour additional water down the side of the pan so you won't submerge the tamales when you replenish it.

Remove the tamales with tongs and let them cool until you can handle them. Unwrap and serve them garnished with sour cream, avocados, minced cilantro, and salsa, if desired.

Bean Filling
Serves 4 to 6

1 recipe Refried Bean Puree (see page 256)
⅓ cup shredded cheddar cheese

Combine the bean spread and the cheese. Stir thoroughly.

Sweet Potato Filling
Serves 4 to 6

2 medium sweet potatoes
3 tablespoons nonfat or reduced-fat sour cream
1 tablespoon maple syrup
½ teaspoon ground cinnamon
½ teaspoon ground ginger

In a large, heavy saucepan, combine the sweet potatoes and water to cover and bring to a boil over medium-high heat. Turn down the heat and simmer until the potatoes are soft, about 15 minutes. Remove from the heat. Using a slotted spoon, transfer the potatoes to a large

mixing bowl. Discard the cooking water. Let the sweet potatoes cool just until they stop steaming, about 10 minutes.

Mash the sweet potatoes with a long-tined fork, incorporating the sour cream as you do. Add the maple syrup, cinnamon, and ginger, and continue mashing to blend thoroughly.

Cheese Filling
Serves 4 to 6

⅓ cup shredded cheddar cheese
⅓ cup shredded Monterey Jack cheese with jalapeño peppers or Monterey Jack cheese plus 2 teaspoons minced peeled roasted jalapeño peppers (see page 534)
¼ cup minced fresh cilantro

Mix together the cheddar cheese, Jack cheese, jalapeños if using, and cilantro.

PER SERVING (WITH BEAN FILLING): CALORIES 250 • PROTEIN 10.3 G • CARBO-HYDRATE 43.2 G • FAT 5.2 G • CHOLESTEROL 6.7 MG • SODIUM 116 MG • 18% CALO-RIES FROM FAT • VERY GOOD SOURCE OF VITAMIN C; FOLACIN • GOOD SOURCE OF VITAMINS A, B₁, B₆; IRON, ZINC

PER SERVING (WITH SWEET POTATO FILLING): CALORIES 280 • PROTEIN 6.7 G • CARBOHYDRATE 62 G • FAT 2.1 G • CHOLESTEROL 0 MG • SODIUM 46.6 MG • 70% CALORIES FROM FAT • OUTSTANDING SOURCE OF VITAMIN A • VERY GOOD SOURCE OF VITAMIN C • GOOD SOURCE OF FOLACIN, IRON

PER SERVING (WITH CHEESE FILLING): CALORIES 218 • PROTEIN 6.9 G • CAR-BOHYDRATE 39.5 G • FAT 5 G • CHOLESTEROL 10 MG • SODIUM 86.5 MG • 19% CALORIES FROM FAT • GOOD SOURCE OF VITAMINS B₁, B₃

•

FRESH CORN CUSTARD WITH POLENTA CRUST

Serves 4

TOTAL TIME: ABOUT 1 HOUR, 35 MINUTES
TIME TO PREPARE: 35 MINUTES
COOKING TIME: 1 HOUR, 10 MINUTES
DO AHEAD: YOU CAN MAKE THE POLENTA UP TO 4 DAYS IN ADVANCE. REFRIGERATE UNTIL READY TO USE.
REFRIGERATION/FREEZING: REFRIGERATE UP TO 2 DAYS.

You wouldn't think that patriotism had much to do with produce, but then you'd be surprised. Patrick Henry criticized Thomas Jefferson for preferring foreign foods to those of his own country. As far as Jefferson was concerned, it was as irrelevant to discuss food in a political context as it would have been to discuss politics in terms of the weather.

Presumably Henry would have had to eat his words if he'd gone to Paris while Jefferson was ambassador to France. In his garden in the heart of that city, the Sage of Monticello grew sweet corn from home.

Meanwhile, across the border, cornmeal had become far more popular in Italy than it was among former Europeans in the States, who preferred to eat corn fresh. This sensational fresh-corn-filled polenta calls for both.

Polenta

1 ½ cups water
¼ cup stone-ground cornmeal
Pinch crumbled dried oregano
¼ teaspoon salt

2 ears of corn
2 large eggs, lightly beaten
1 ½ cups nonfat milk

½ cup finely grated cheddar or Monterey Jack cheese
¼ teaspoon salt
2 tablespoons minced seeded jalapeño peppers (optional)

To make the Polenta

Bring the water to a boil in a large, heavy saucepan over high heat. Pour the cornmeal into the water in a steady stream, and stir briskly with a whisk. Turn the heat down to medium-high and continue whisking. When the mixture thickens enough to coat the whisk, switch to a wooden spoon. Continue stirring until the polenta is thick enough to pull away from the pot, about 25 minutes. Stir in the oregano and salt. Set aside to cool.

Bring a large pot of water to a boil. Add the corn and let the water return to a boil. Cover the pot, turn off the heat, and leave the corn for 8 to 10 minutes. (If you're using an electric stove, take the pot off the burner.) Transfer the corn to a plate to let it cool. (Or cook the corn in the microwave according to the directions on page 526.)

Heat the oven to 350° F.

Scrape the kernels from the corncobs into a bowl. In a separate mixing bowl, beat together the eggs, milk, cheese, and salt.

Butter four 6-inch custard cups. When the polenta has stopped steaming, but is still warm, spoon a quarter of it into the bottom of each custard cup. Using a piece of plastic wrap, press the polenta to cover the bottom of the cups in an even layer. Give the milk mixture a stir, and pour it into the cups, filling each no more than halfway.

Add an equal amount of corn to each cup. Add the jalapeños, if desired.

Place the cups in a baking dish large enough to hold them. Add water to the outer dish so that it comes halfway up the sides of the custard cups. Cover loosely with aluminum foil. Bake until firm and a knife inserted in the center comes out clean, about 50 minutes. Remove the foil and brown the tops, about 10 minutes.

To unmold, let the custards cool to room temperature on a rack. Run a small spatula or butter knife around each custard, and carefully invert each on a plate. Serve at room temperature or cover and refrigerate, and serve chilled.

PER SERVING: CALORIES 196 • PROTEIN 11.7 G • CARBOHYDRATE 20.7 G • FAT 8.12 G • CHOLESTEROL 123 MG • SODIUM 492 MG • 36% CALORIES FROM FAT • VERY GOOD SOURCE OF VITAMIN B₂, CALCIUM • GOOD SOURCE OF VITAMINS A, B₁, B₁₂, C; FOLACIN

MICROWAVE POLENTA: Put the water and cornmeal into a deep microwavable bowl. With the bowl uncovered, microwave at full power for 6 minutes. Whisk well, then return the uncovered bowl to the microwave for another 6 minutes. Whisk again, cover with a damp paper towel, and return for another 6 minutes. Whisk again. If necessary, continue in 3-minute spurts until the polenta is thick enough to pull away from the bowl. Stir in the oregano and salt, and set aside to cool. Continue as in the main recipe.

ROLLED ROASTED RED PEPPERS

Serves 4

TOTAL TIME: ABOUT 30 MINUTES
TIME TO PREPARE: 10 MINUTES
COOKING TIME: 20 MINUTES
DO AHEAD: YOU CAN ROAST THE PEPPERS AND/OR ASSEMBLE THE DISH UP TO 2 DAYS IN ADVANCE. REFRIGERATE UNTIL READY TO COOK.
REFRIGERATION/FREEZING: REFRIGERATE UP TO 2 DAYS. DO NOT FREEZE.

Provided you use fresh ingredients, this dish comes with an iron-clad guarantee: you can't ruin it, it's going to be good.

¼ cup minced fresh parsley
1 cup nonfat or part-skim ricotta cheese
½ cup crumbled feta cheese
¼ cup minced oil-cured black olives
2 large red bell peppers, roasted and peeled (see page 534)

Heat the oven to 350°F.

Combine the parsley, ricotta cheese, feta cheese, and olives in a mixing bowl.

Cut each pepper half in half lengthwise, so you'll have 8 wide strips.

Spread an equal amount of the cheese mixture on each pepper, leaving a ½-inch margin at the bottom and top.

Roll up each pepper and place it on a baking sheet. Bake for 20 minutes, until the filling is golden brown.

PER SERVING: CALORIES 148 • PROTEIN 13.8 G • CARBOHYDRATE 7.1 G • FAT 7.1 G • CHOLESTEROL 27.4 MG • SODIUM 385 MG • 43% CALORIES FROM FAT • OUTSTANDING SOURCE OF VITAMINS A, C • GOOD SOURCE OF CALCIUM

SPRING ROLLS WITH PEANUT SAUCE

Serves 4

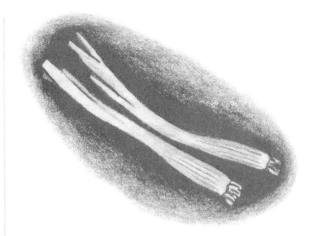

TOTAL TIME: ABOUT 40 MINUTES, INCLUDING TIME TO
  MAKE THE SAUCE
TIME TO PREPARE: ABOUT 20 MINUTES
COOKING TIME: ABOUT 20 MINUTES
DO AHEAD: YOU CAN MAKE THE SAUCE UP TO 5 DAYS IN
  ADVANCE. REFRIGERATE UNTIL READY TO USE.

S oft spring-roll wrappers dressed with addic-
tive peanut sauce hold a simple crunchy filling for a dish that's great with Mild Miso
Soup (see page 173) or as a prelude to a curry or
stir-fry.

One 2-ounce package bean thread noodles
    (available at Asian-specialty stores and in the
    Asian-specialty section of some
    supermarkets)
1 tablespoon rice vinegar
1 teaspoon sugar
1 scallion, including greens, minced
1 large carrot, peeled and shredded
1 cup loosely packed bean sprouts or pea shoots
¼ cup minced fresh basil
¼ cup minced fresh cilantro
2 tablespoons minced fresh mint
Sixteen 8-inch round rice wrappers (1 package)
    (available at Asian-specialty stores and in the
    Asian-specialty section of some
    supermarkets)
2 cups loosely packed shredded tender lettuce,
    such as Boston, Bibb, or mesclun
1 recipe Peanut Sauce for Spring Rolls . . . and
    More (recipe follows), at room temperature

In a large saucepan, bring about 3 cups of water to a boil. Add the bean threads and remove the pan from the heat. Let it sit for 15 minutes, until the noodles are soft. In a small bowl combine the rice vinegar and sugar. Drain the noodles and cut them coarsely into 2-inch pieces with kitchen shears. Toss them with the vinegar and sugar.

In a mixing bowl, combine the scallion, carrot, sprouts or pea shoots, basil, cilantro, and mint. Fill a pie plate with warm water. Place one rice wrapper in the water and let it soak until it's very soft and pliable and translucent, about 1 minute. Do not soak it too long, or it will tear.

Remove the wrapper and place it on a work surface. Blot it dry with a paper towel. Put another wrapper in the water while you fill this one.

Place a single layer of shredded lettuce over the surface. Sprinkle with the vegetable and herb mixture and add a layer of bean thread noodles.

Enclose the filling by folding the wrapper's sides, top, and bottom over it, then rolling up the spring roll. Let it sit seam side down while you remove the other wrapper from the water and blot it dry. Place the filled spring roll in the center of the fresh wrapper, and fold the outer wrapper around the spring roll the way you did the first, giving the roll a double wrapping, making it easier to handle. Dampen a paper towel, squeeze out the excess water, and drape it over the rolls as you finish them.

Repeat with 14 more wrappers, making a total of 8 rolls.

Serve with peanut sauce drizzled on top.

•

PEANUT SAUCE FOR SPRING ROLLS . . . AND MORE

Serves 4

TOTAL TIME: ABOUT 20 MINUTES, NOT INCLUDING TIME TO MAKE THE BROTH
TIME TO PREPARE: ABOUT 2 MINUTES
COOKING TIME: ABOUT 7 TO 20 MINUTES
REFRIGERATION/FREEZING: REFRIGERATE UP TO 5 DAYS. FREEZE UP TO 1 YEAR.

*Y*ou'll love this sauce over steamed or grilled vegetables, pasta, and salad greens, too!

1 cup Broth for Far Eastern–Flavored Dishes (see page 168) or vegetable broth (see page 165)
1 onion, thinly sliced
1 garlic clove, minced
1 tablespoon grated peeled fresh ginger
2 ripe tomatoes, peeled, seeded, and chopped (see page 544), or ½ cup canned chopped tomatoes

2 tablespoons creamy peanut butter (with no added oil, sugar, or salt)
1 tablespoon low-sodium soy sauce
1 teaspoon honey
Pinch red pepper flakes

In a medium saucepan, bring ⅓ cup of the broth to a boil.

Add the onion, garlic, and ginger. Reduce the heat to medium-low and simmer, stirring often, until the liquid has nearly evaporated and the onion is very soft, about 10 minutes.

Stir in the tomatoes, peanut butter, soy sauce, honey, and pepper flakes. Add the remaining broth and let it simmer, stirring often, until the sauce is thickened, about 7 to 10 minutes.

PER SERVING: CALORIES 80 • PROTEIN 3.2 G • CARBOHYDRATE 9 G • FAT 4.2 G • CHOLESTEROL 0 MG • SODIUM 225 MG • 44% CALORIES FROM FAT • VERY GOOD SOURCE OF VITAMIN C

FRESH HERB-FILLED TOMATOES

Serves 4

TOTAL TIME: ABOUT 40 MINUTES, NOT INCLUDING TIME TO
   MAKE THE BROTH
TIME TO PREPARE: ABOUT 20 MINUTES, INCLUDING TIME
   TO SAUTÉ
COOKING TIME: ABOUT 20 MINUTES
REFRIGERATION/FREEZING: REFRIGERATE UP TO 2 DAYS. DO
   NOT FREEZE.

Thomas Jefferson loved tomatoes and tried to persuade his fellow farmers to cultivate them, with no luck at all. Most Americans of European extraction believed they were poisonous and wouldn't touch them. In fact, Americans didn't get over their fear of tomatoes until the Italians arrived en masse at the turn of the century, bringing tomato-based dishes that were just too good to ignore.

4 large firm ripe tomatoes

2 teaspoons extra virgin olive oil

2 Vidalia onions, thinly sliced

¼ cup minced fresh parsley

2 tablespoons minced fresh oregano

¼ cup minced fresh basil

2 tablespoons minced fresh tarragon

1 tablespoon balsamic vinegar

½ cup vegetable broth (see page 165) or water

¼ cup grated Asiago or Parmesan cheese, or
   crumbled ricotta salata

Heat the oven to 425°F.

Slice off the top ¼ inch of each tomato. Scoop out the pulp with a spoon. Separate as many of the seeds as possible from the pulp. Discard the seeds, reserving the pulp.

Heat the oil in a medium skillet over medium-high heat. When it's hot, add the onions, parsley, oregano, basil, and tarragon. Reduce the heat to medium and sauté, stirring often, until the onions are soft and limp, about 12 minutes.

Add the balsamic vinegar and stir until most of it has evaporated, about 2 minutes. Stir in the tomato pulp and continue to cook, stirring often, until it thickens into a dense sauce, about 6 minutes.

Spoon the tomato-herb mixture into the hollowed tomatoes. Pour an inch of vegetable broth or water into an 8-inch baking pan, and place the tomatoes inside. Sprinkle the tomatoes evenly with the grated or crumbled cheese. Bake until the tomatoes are soft and the cheese is bubbly, about 20 minutes. Serve hot. Serve leftovers cold or at room temperature.

PER SERVING: CALORIES 157 • PROTEIN 5.2 G • CARBOHYDRATE 15.5 G • FAT 9.3 G • CHOLESTEROL 4.9 MG • SODIUM 137 MG • 50% CALORIES FROM FAT • OUTSTANDING SOURCE OF VITAMIN C • GOOD SOURCE OF VITAMINS A, B₁, B₆; FOLACIN, CALCIUM

•

BAKED STUFFED ARTICHOKES WITH MUSHROOMS

Serves 4

TOTAL TIME: ABOUT 1 HOUR, 15 MINUTES, NOT INCLUDING TIME TO MAKE THE BROTH
TIME TO PREPARE: 40 MINUTES, INCLUDING TIME TO SAUTÉ
COOKING TIME: ABOUT 35 MINUTES
REFRIGERATION/FREEZING: REFRIGERATE UP TO 2 DAYS. DO
   NOT FREEZE.

In the latest English-language edition of the food encyclopedia Larousse Gastronomique, there's this curious juxtaposition of two facts: "[The artichoke] was reputed to be an aphrodisiac, and women were often forbidden to eat it. Catherine de Médicis, who was fond of artichokes, encouraged their cultivation in France." It's not clear whether linking those sentences was meant as a comment on Catherine's character, or whether the editor simply missed the implications in his rush to make note, once again, of her transforming influence on French cuisine.

4 large artichokes

1 lemon

2 teaspoons extra virgin olive oil

1 small onion, chopped

2 garlic cloves, minced

¼ cup minced fresh parsley

1 pound firm mushrooms, such as portobello or
    cremini, sliced

2 tablespoons white wine

¼ cup dried bread crumbs

Pinch ground nutmeg

Salt and freshly ground black pepper to taste

¼ cup vegetable broth (see page 165)

Strip the tough, dark outer leaves off the artichokes. Turn each on its side and use a heavy knife to cut off the top third. Trim the stem so each artichoke can stand upright. Grate 1 tablespoon of zest from the lemon and set it aside. Squeeze the juice from the lemon into a large nonreactive saucepan. Add the artichokes and enough water to cover. Cover the pan and bring the water to a gentle boil over medium-high heat. Lower the heat to medium-low and simmer until the artichokes are just tender, 12 to 15 minutes, depending on their size. Be careful not to overcook, or they will fall apart. Lift the artichokes out and let drain upside down and cool.

Heat the oven to 425°F.

In a large skillet, heat the oil over medium-high heat. Add the onion, garlic, parsley, and zest. Stir well and sauté until the onion is soft and limp, about 7 minutes. Add the mushrooms and sauté until they're soft and just cooked through, about 7 minutes. Add the wine and sauté until most of it evaporates, about 3 minutes. Turn off the heat.

Transfer the mushroom mixture to a mixing bowl and stir in the bread crumbs, nutmeg, and salt and pepper.

Spread the leaves of each artichoke away from the center. Pull the sharp, slick leaves out of the cavity and, using a teaspoon, scrape off the fuzzy choke. Place an equal amount of mushroom mixture into each artichoke cavity. Place them in a baking dish along with the broth. Cover loosely with foil and bake 20 minutes, until the filling is firm.

PER SERVING: CALORIES 152 • PROTEIN 7.8 G • CARBOHYDRATE 26.4 G • FAT 3.3 G • CHOLESTEROL 0 MG • SODIUM 176 MG • 18% CALORIES FROM FAT • VERY GOOD SOURCE OF VITAMINS B₂, B₃, C; FOLACIN • GOOD SOURCE OF VITAMINS B₁, B₆; ZINC

Bean Spreads

HUMMUS VARIATIONS
Basic Hummus

Serves 4

TOTAL TIME: ABOUT 5 MINUTES
TIME TO PREPARE: ABOUT 5 MINUTES
COOKING TIME: NONE
REFRIGERATION/FREEZING: REFRIGERATE UP TO 5 DAYS.
FREEZE UP TO 6 MONTHS.

One way to account for the appeal of hummus is to note that it's an acceptable adult alternative to peanut butter. But then that wouldn't acknowledge that hummus—sesame-flavored chickpea spread seasoned with garlic and lemon—is delicious in its own right.

1 small garlic clove, peeled
2 tablespoons minced fresh cilantro
2 tablespoons minced fresh parsley
2 tablespoons fresh lemon juice
1 tablespoon tahini
2 cups cooked chickpeas, drained and rinsed
2 teaspoons ground cumin
Pinch paprika
1 tablespoon sesame seeds, toasted (optional; see Note, page 122)

Combine the garlic, cilantro, parsley, lemon juice, tahini, chickpeas, cumin, and paprika in a food processor or blender. Blend until smooth. Sprinkle with toasted sesame seeds, if you'd like.

PER SERVING: CALORIES 165 • PROTEIN 8.2 G • CARBOHYDRATE 24.6 G • FAT 4.5 G • CHOLESTEROL 0 MG • SODIUM 8.86 MG • 24% CALORIES FROM FAT • VERY GOOD SOURCE OF FOLACIN • GOOD SOURCE OF VITAMINS B₁, C; IRON, ZINC

Kidney Bean Hummus

Serves 4

TOTAL TIME: ABOUT 5 MINUTES
TIME TO PREPARE: ABOUT 5 MINUTES
COOKING TIME: NONE
REFRIGERATION/FREEZING: REFRIGERATE UP TO 5 DAYS.
FREEZE UP TO 6 MONTHS.

This Southwest-style variation tastes terrific spread on flour tortillas or baked taco chips.

1 small garlic clove, peeled
¼ cup minced fresh cilantro
2 tablespoons fresh lemon juice
1 tablespoon fresh lime juice
1 tablespoon tahini
2 cups cooked kidney beans, drained and rinsed
2 teaspoons ground cumin
1 teaspoon chili powder
Pinch cayenne pepper
2 tablespoons minced scallion greens, for garnish

Combine the garlic, cilantro, lemon juice, lime juice, tahini, kidney beans, cumin, chili powder, and cayenne pepper in a food processor or blender. Blend until smooth. Sprinkle with the scallion greens.

PER SERVING: CALORIES 145 • PROTEIN 8.7 G • CARBOHYDRATE 22.9 G • FAT 2.9 G • CHOLESTEROL 0 MG • SODIUM 9.6 MG • 17% CALORIES FROM FAT • VERY GOOD SOURCE OF FOLACIN, IRON • GOOD SOURCE OF VITAMINS B₁, C; ZINC

BEAN SPREAD BASICS

Everything has to be called something, I guess, and while I haven't thought of a better one, "bean spread" is too narrow a name for a preparation that can also be a dip, a stuffing for vegetables, and a filling for pastas, tortillas, and vegetable sushi. But given the options ("puree" sounds too thin, and "paste" we last ate in preschool), we'll settle for "spread," mindful that it's only partly descriptive, not all inclusive.

THE PRINCIPLES

• The flavor of the spread depends on the type of bean you use and the herbs and spices you puree with it. To work out compatible combinations, think of bean dishes you've enjoyed, or find a recipe for a bean dish that appeals to you (for example, Highly Spiced Black Bean Soup, page 190, and Chunky Chickpea Soup, page 191). Chances are the beans and seasonings in those dishes blend well as a spread, too. Generally, kidney and pinto beans go well with Southwest/Mexican seasonings, such as chili powder, cumin, and cilantro; chickpeas, tahini, and cumin make a classic Middle Eastern dish; and lentils are delicious pureed with ginger and curry spices.

• Try to use good dried beans that you boil yourself, rather than canned beans. Beans are the dominant ingredient, and the dish will be better in the end if you start with the best.

• Make sure the beans are thoroughly cooked. They don't release their flavor until they're at the soft stage. And on a more practical level, you can't puree them if they're still hard.

• Drain the beans thoroughly, reserving about ½ cup of the cooking water. As you puree the beans with the other ingredients, add as much of the reserved cooking water as you need to get the consistency you want. If you want a very thick spread, you may end up not adding any.

• For lighter spreads, puree the beans with yogurt, soft tofu, or fruit juice. For richer spreads, puree the beans with peanut butter, tahini, almond butter, or cashew butter (use no more than 1 tablespoon for each 2 cups of cooked beans, and dilute the mixture with fresh lemon juice, orange juice, or reserved bean liquid).

• You can keep most bean spreads, covered and refrigerated, up to five days. Spreads that include cheese or other dairy products have a shorter shelf life, about two days.

RED LENTIL SPREAD

Serves 4

TOTAL TIME: ABOUT 55 MINUTES, INCLUDING TIME TO SIT
TIME TO PREPARE: ABOUT 5 MINUTES
COOKING TIME: ABOUT 20 MINUTES
REFRIGERATION/FREEZING: REFRIGERATE UP TO 5 DAYS.
   FREEZE UP TO 6 MONTHS

Red lentils are never to be confused with—or used in place of—lentils that are green or black. They have a much softer (read "mushy") consistency and a faint flavor that benefits from a slew of spices, such as those used here. Try this spread on pita bread, served alongside soup or curry.

2 teaspoons canola or vegetable oil
1/2 garlic clove, grated
One 1-inch piece fresh ginger, peeled and grated
2 tablespoons minced fresh cilantro
2 teaspoons ground cumin
1/2 teaspoon ground turmeric
1 cup uncooked red lentils, rinsed
1 1/3 cups water, approximately
1 tablespoon fresh lemon juice

Heat the oil in a small saucepan over medium-high heat. When it's hot, add the garlic, ginger, cilantro, cumin, and turmeric. Reduce the heat to medium-low and sauté, stirring often, until the garlic starts to toast, about 3 minutes. Stir in the lentils along with the water. Bring to a boil over medium-high heat. Reduce the heat to medium-low, cover, and cook until the lentils have cooked through and all of the water has been absorbed, about 20 minutes. Check often after 10 minutes to make sure they aren't sticking. If so, add another 1/4 cup water, stir, cover, and continue cooking.

Mash the lentils with the back of a wooden spoon. Stir in the lemon juice. Let the spread sit at least 30 minutes at room temperature before serving.

PER SERVING: CALORIES 126 • PROTEIN 9.1 G • CARBOHYDRATE 19 G • FAT 1.9 G • CHOLESTEROL 0 MG • SODIUM 4.6 MG • 14% CALORIES FROM FAT • VERY GOOD SOURCE OF FOLACIN • GOOD SOURCE OF VITAMIN B₁; IRON

•

REFRIED BEAN PUREE

Serves 4

TOTAL TIME: ABOUT 20 MINUTES, NOT INCLUDING TIME TO
   COOK THE BEANS
TIME TO PREPARE: ABOUT 20 MINUTES, INCLUDING TIME
   TO SAUTÉ
COOKING TIME: INCLUDED IN TIME TO PREPARE
REFRIGERATION/FREEZING: REFRIGERATE UP TO 5 DAYS.
   FREEZE UP TO 6 MONTHS.

Serve this Southwest-style spread as a dip or as a filling for roasted bell peppers (see page 534). You can also toss it with hot pasta, and top with grated Cheddar cheese.

2 teaspoons canola or vegetable oil
1 red onion, finely chopped
3 garlic cloves, minced
2 scallions, white part only, minced
1/2 red bell pepper, cored, seeded, and minced
1/2 jalapeño pepper, cored, seeded, and minced
2 teaspoons ground cumin
2 teaspoons crumbled dried oregano
Cayenne pepper to taste
2 teaspoons tomato paste
2 cups cooked pinto or kidney beans, drained
   and rinsed

Heat the oil in a medium skillet over medium-high heat, swirling the pan to coat the bottom.

Add the onion, garlic, scallions, bell pepper, jalapeño pepper, cumin, oregano, and cayenne pepper. Reduce the heat to medium and sauté, stirring often, until the vegetables have softened, about 15 minutes.

Stir in the tomato paste and the beans, and stir well to combine. Transfer the mixture to a food processor and process, starting with short pulses, then running at 2 long spurts (about 30 seconds each, depending on the strength of your machine) to make a dense puree.

PER SERVING: CALORIES 164 • PROTEIN 7.9 G • CARBOHYDRATE 27.8 G • FAT 2.8 G • CHOLESTEROL 0 MG • SODIUM 25.9 MG • 15% CALORIES FROM FAT • OUTSTANDING SOURCE OF VITAMIN C; FOLACIN • GOOD SOURCE OF VITAMIN B; IRON

Savory Vegetable Pancakes

S A V O R Y   B A K E D
C O R N   C A K E S

Serves 4

TOTAL TIME: ABOUT 25 MINUTES, NOT INCLUDING TIME TO PREPARE THE ONIONS
TIME TO PREPARE: ABOUT 10 MINUTES
COOKING TIME: 14 TO 16 MINUTES
DO AHEAD: YOU CAN MAKE THE BATTER UP TO 2 DAYS IN ADVANCE. REFRIGERATE UNTIL READY TO USE.
REFRIGERATION/FREEZING: REFRIGERATE UP TO 3 DAYS. FREEZE UP TO 6 MONTHS.

One summer, we had a four-year-old next door who fell in love with my husband. She was over every day, up to five times a day, asking to see him. Once she caught me while I was making supper and went to inspect the corn cakes cooling on the counter. "Which one will Simon have?" she wanted to know. I pointed to the largest. "Can I have a bite of it?"

As a rule, four-year-olds aren't the most adven-turesome eaters, so I was happy that she asked, and flattered when she wanted more.

4 ears of corn
1 scallion, white part and 1 inch of greens, chopped
2 large eggs, lightly beaten
2 tablespoons unbleached all-purpose flour
½ teaspoon salt
1 recipe Caramelized Vidalia Onions (see page 224), for garnish
Reduced-fat or nonfat sour cream, for garnish

Heat the oven to 375° F.

Bring a large pot of water to a boil. Add the corn and let the water return to a boil. Cover the pot, turn off the heat, and leave the corn for 8 to 10 minutes. (If you're using an electric stove, take the pot off the burner.) Transfer the corn to a plate to let it cool. (Or cook the corn in the microwave according to the directions on page 526.)

Let the corn cool, and scrape off the kernels. In a food processor, combine the corn, scallion, eggs, flour, and salt. Process in short pulses until the corn is finely minced, taking care not to liquefy.

Drop the batter, 3 tablespoons at a time, onto a nonstick baking sheet. Bake in the center of the oven until lightly browned on the edges, about 10 minutes. Turn the cakes with a spatula, and continue to bake until browned on the bottom, 4 to 6 minutes longer. Serve warm, topped with Vidalia onions and sour cream.

PER SERVING: CALORIES 139 • PROTEIN 6.1 G • CARBOHYDRATE 23.4 G • FAT 3.5 G • CHOLESTEROL 106 MG • SODIUM 312 MG • 21% CALORIES FROM FAT • GOOD SOURCE OF VITAMINS B₁, B₂, C; FOLACIN

Make It Your Own

You can substitute other vegetables and/or seasonings for the leeks, and fennel in the basic recipe, provided the ingredients you choose aren't too watery.

WHAT TO ADD AND WHEN TO ADD IT

☞ *Vegetables*. Using the Oven-Baked Leek and Fennel Pancakes recipe as a guide, substitute 4 cups of any chopped vegetable for the leek and fennel and proceed from there, sautéing, pureeing, and baking as directed.

☞ *Cheese*. Substitute a cheese that complements the main ingredient. Gruyère goes well with carrots, for example, and Parmesan or Asiago with asparagus.

☞ *Herbs*. Similarly, substitute complementary herbs. With carrots and Gruyère, you might want to use sage. Try mint with asparagus and Parmesan.

☞ *Flour*. You can alter the flavor of the pancakes by using different kinds of flour. Instead of all-purpose flour, try brown rice flour, which tastes faintly nutty, or oat flour, which is sweet. (If you can't find them where you shop, see the mail-order information, page 596.) Start by using the amount specified in the basic recipe. If the batter doesn't hold together, add 1 tablespoon more at a time until it does. If the pancakes turn out too heavy, cut back by a tablespoon or so next time.

OVEN-BAKED LEEK AND FENNEL PANCAKES

Serves 4

TOTAL TIME: ABOUT 35 MINUTES
TIME TO PREPARE: ABOUT 20 MINUTES, INCLUDING TIME TO SAUTÉ
COOKING TIME: ABOUT 15 MINUTES
DO AHEAD: YOU CAN MAKE THE LEEK AND FENNEL MIXTURE UP TO 2 DAYS IN ADVANCE. REFRIGERATE UNTIL READY TO BAKE.
REFRIGERATION/FREEZING: REFRIGERATE UP TO 3 DAYS. DO NOT FREEZE.

While the typical—that is, fried—potato pancake can be pasty, greasy, and bland, the basic idea has lots of promise, which this recipe fulfills. It calls for blanching vegetables with complementary ingredients and baking, rather than frying them for a dish to accompany hearty soups, salads, or light entrées. This basic combination includes leek and fennel, but you can vary it as you'd like, following the guidelines in "Make It Your Own."

2 teaspoons extra virgin olive oil
2 large leeks, white part only, washed and thinly sliced
1 fennel bulb, without leafy fronds, chopped
3 tablespoons water, approximately
1 large egg, lightly beaten
½ cup reduced-fat or nonfat sour cream
½ cup unbleached all-purpose flour
¼ cup shredded cheddar cheese
1 tablespoon minced fresh chives

Heat the oil in a medium skillet over medium-high heat. When it's hot, add the leeks and fennel. Reduce the heat to medium and sauté, stirring often, until the vegetables soften, about

7 minutes. As they start to stick, add the water and stir well to keep the vegetables from burning. Add more water if necessary, and continue to sauté until the leeks and fennel are soft enough to puree. Remove them from the heat and let them cool for 10 minutes. Heat the oven to 375°F.

Meanwhile, in a mixing bowl, beat together the egg, sour cream, and flour to form a smooth paste.

Puree the leek and fennel mixture either by transferring it to a food processor or blender and processing in short pulses until smooth and thick or by running an immersion blender inside the skillet to achieve the same effect.

Stir the leek-fennel puree, cheddar cheese, and chives into the flour mixture until smooth, making a batter the consistency of a milk shake.

Drop the batter, 2 tablespoons at a time, onto a nonstick baking sheet or a baking sheet that's been lightly coated with canola oil or nonstick spray, leaving about 2 inches between each pancake. Bake until the bottom is golden brown and the top has set, about 15 minutes.

Remove the pancakes with a spatula and serve them hot.

PER SERVING: CALORIES 192 • PROTEIN 8.4 G • CARBOHYDRATE 26 G • FAT 6.2 G • CHOLESTEROL 60.4 MG • SODIUM 121 MG • 29% CALORIES FROM FAT • VERY GOOD SOURCE OF VITAMIN C • GOOD SOURCE OF VITAMINS A, B₁, B₂; FOLACIN, CALCIUM

Rices and Pilafs

CREAMY RICE WITH POTATOES AND LEEK

Serves 4

TOTAL TIME: ABOUT 50 MINUTES
TIME TO PREPARE: ABOUT 30 MINUTES, INCLUDING TIME
   TO SAUTÉ
COOKING TIME: 20 MINUTES
REFRIGERATION/FREEZING: REFRIGERATE UP TO 2 DAYS. DO
   NOT FREEZE.

Risotto is wonderful, but it's not always practical, which is probably a good thing. If everyone had enough time to stand over a stove and stir for thirty to forty minutes at a go, who knows what kind of trouble they'd get into? Anyway, here's one for the pragmatists—a dish as creamy and flavorful as any conventional risotto, demanding less supervision and stamina.

1 tablespoon extra virgin olive oil
1 large leek, white part only, washed and sliced
2 medium potatoes, preferably Yukon Gold, peeled and diced
2 teaspoons balsamic vinegar or dry white wine
1 cup arborio or short-grain rice
2½ to 3 cups water
¼ cup grated Asiago, Fontina, or Parmesan cheese
Salt and freshly ground black pepper to taste

Heat the oil in a large saucepan over medium-high heat. When it's hot, add the leek. Reduce the heat to medium and sauté, stirring often, until the leek is soft and limp, about 7 minutes. Add the potatoes and stir well. Add the balsamic vinegar or wine and the rice, and stir again to mix. Pour in 2½ cups of the water. Bring to a boil over medium-high heat. Reduce the heat to medium-low, cover, and simmer until almost all of the liquid has been absorbed, about 20 minutes. (If the liquid is absorbed before the rice has cooked—that is, if the rice is still firm in the center—add ½ cup more water.) Remove the rice from the heat and stir in the cheese. Replace the cover and let the rice sit 5 minutes. Season with salt and pepper, and serve right away.

PER SERVING: CALORIES 202 • PROTEIN 5.4 G • CARBOHYDRATE 32.8 G • FAT 5.5 G • CHOLESTEROL 4.92 MG • SODIUM 126 MG • 24% CALORIES FROM FAT

•

CHILI RICE

Serves 4

TOTAL TIME: 45 MINUTES TO 1 HOUR, 5 MINUTES, DEPENDING ON THE RICE USED, NOT INCLUDING TIME TO ROAST THE PEPPER OR COOK THE BEANS
TIME TO PREPARE: 25 MINUTES, INCLUDING TIME TO SAUTÉ
COOKING TIME: 20 TO 40 MINUTES
DO AHEAD: YOU CAN ROAST THE PEPPERS UP TO 2 DAYS IN ADVANCE. REFRIGERATE UNTIL READY TO USE.
REFRIGERATION/FREEZING: REFRIGERATE UP TO 3 DAYS. FREEZE UP TO 3 MONTHS.

This chili's in the rice rather than on top of it. Make it a day or so ahead, and serve it with Tortilla-Style Frittata (page 389), Tamale-Style Fresh Corn Nuggets (page 246), or a cold soup or salad.

2 teaspoons extra virgin olive oil or canola oil
4 scallions, white part only, minced
1 celery stalk, including leaves, chopped
1 garlic clove, minced
1 Anaheim chili or jalapeño pepper, roasted, peeled, and chopped (see page 534)
2 teaspoons crumbled dried oregano
2 teaspoons ground cumin
2 teaspoons chili powder
1 cup long-grain white or brown rice
1 tablespoon red wine vinegar or balsamic vinegar
½ cup peeled chopped fresh tomatoes or canned chopped tomatoes
1½ to 2 cups water
1½ cups cooked kidney or black beans, drained and rinsed
Salt and freshly ground black pepper to taste

Heat the oven to 325°F.

Heat the oil in a large ovenproof saucepan over medium-high heat. When it's hot, add the scallions, celery, garlic, chili or jalapeño pepper, oregano, cumin, and chili powder. Reduce the heat to medium and sauté, stirring often, until the vegetables have softened, about 7 minutes. Stir in the rice and vinegar, and continue to cook until most of the liquid has been absorbed, about 2 minutes. Stir in the tomatoes and 1½ cups water (2 cups if you're using brown rice).

Bring to a boil over medium-high heat. Cover and place in the oven until the rice is cooked and all of the liquid has been absorbed, about 20 minutes for white rice, 40 minutes for brown. Stir in the beans and heat through. Season with salt and pepper.

PER SERVING: CALORIES 267 • PROTEIN 8 G • CARBOHYDRATE 51 G • FAT 3.4 G • CHOLESTEROL 0 MG • SODIUM 153 MG • 12% CALORIES FROM FAT • VERY GOOD SOURCE OF VITAMIN B₁; IRON • GOOD SOURCE OF VITAMIN B₃, C; FOLACIN

BULGUR WHEAT PILAF WITH COOL MINT SAUCE

Serves 4

TOTAL TIME: ABOUT 50 MINUTES
TIME TO PREPARE: ABOUT 20 MINUTES, INCLUDING TIME
    TO SAUTÉ
COOKING TIME: 30 MINUTES
DO AHEAD: YOU CAN MAKE THE SAUCE UP TO 3 DAYS IN
    ADVANCE. REFRIGERATE UNTIL READY TO USE.
REFRIGERATION/FREEZING: REFRIGERATE UP TO 3 DAYS. DO
    NOT FREEZE.

My grandfather seemed to be breaking all the rules regarding dinner when he filled his pilafs with sweet things such as cinnamon, raisins, currants, prunes, dried apricots, and nuts. At some point he explained it was "traditional" to make rice and bulgur wheat that way, inadvertently suggesting you can get away with anything if there's tradition behind it. And so I sought out other traditions that permitted sweets with supper, finding fruit soup and noodle pudding among others.

Here's the pilaf that set me off on the search.

2 teaspoons extra virgin olive oil
1 large onion, chopped
1 teaspoon ground cinnamon
2 tablespoons currants
2 teaspoons pine nuts, toasted (see Note, page 122)
1 cup bulgur wheat
1¼ cups water

Mint Sauce
½ teaspoon minced garlic
¼ cup minced fresh mint
1½ cups plain nonfat yogurt

Heat the olive oil in a medium, heavy saucepan over medium-high heat, swirling the pan to coat the bottom. Add the onion and cinnamon. Reduce the heat to medium and sauté, stirring often, until the onion has softened, about 7 minutes. Add the currants, pine nuts, and bulgur, and stir to coat with the onion, about 1 minute. Add the water. Bring to a simmer over medium-high heat, cover, reduce the heat to low, and let the bulgur steam for 15 minutes.

Meanwhile, to make the sauce, combine the garlic, mint, and yogurt in a mixing bowl. Stir thoroughly to blend.

Turn off the heat, and let the bulgur rest for 15 minutes before lifting the lid. Fluff with a fork and serve with a drizzle of the sauce.

PER SERVING: CALORIES 230 • PROTEIN 10.5 G • CARBOHYDRATE 41 G • FAT 4 G • CHOLESTEROL 1.6 MG • SODIUM 79 MG • 15% CALORIES FROM FAT • VERY GOOD SOURCE OF CALCIUM • GOOD SOURCE OF ZINC

BULGUR WHEAT WITH SPINACH, RAISINS, AND PINE NUTS

Serves 4

TOTAL TIME: ABOUT 35 MINUTES
TIME TO PREPARE: 20 MINUTES, INCLUDING TIME TO SAUTÉ
COOKING TIME: 15 MINUTES
DO AHEAD: YOU CAN MAKE THIS DISH UP TO 3 DAYS IN ADVANCE. REFRIGERATE UNTIL READY TO USE.
REFRIGERATION/FREEZING: REFRIGERATE UP TO 3 DAYS. FREEZE UP TO 3 MONTHS.

So sweet and crunchy, it's practically confectionary. Serve it whenever you want a refreshing contrast to something spicy, or a lively sidekick for something mild.

2 teaspoons extra virgin olive oil

4 scallions, white part only, minced

2 tablespoons pine nuts, toasted (see Note, page 122)

1 teaspoon ground cumin

1 teaspoon ground cinnamon

¼ teaspoon ground allspice

¼ cup raisins

4 cups loosely packed chopped fresh spinach, or one 10-ounce package frozen chopped spinach, thawed and squeezed dry

1 cup bulgur wheat

1⅔ cups water

Salt and freshly ground black pepper to taste

Plain nonfat yogurt, for garnish (optional)

Heat the oil in a large, deep skillet over medium-high heat. When it's hot, add the scallions, pine nuts, cumin, cinnamon, and allspice. Reduce heat to medium. Sauté, stirring often, until the scallions are soft, about 6 minutes. Add the raisins, spinach, and bulgur. Stir well.

Pour in the water. Bring to a simmer over medium-high heat. Cover, reduce the heat to low, and simmer gently until the bulgur has cooked and the water has been absorbed, about 15 minutes. Season with salt and pepper, and serve each portion with a dollop of yogurt, if you'd like.

PER SERVING: CALORIES 259 • PROTEIN 9.7 G • CARBOHYDRATE 39 G • FAT 10.3 G • CHOLESTEROL 0 MG • SODIUM 53 MG • 32% CALORIES FROM FAT • VERY GOOD SOURCE OF VITAMINS A, C; FOLACIN, IRON • GOOD SOURCE OF VITAMINS B₂, B₃, B₆; ZINC

Crostini

At one time, crostini were simply croutons, slivers of toast added to soups. Then some Tuscan was inspired to top the croutons with chopped liver. And if you order crostini in Florence today, that's what you'll get. But elsewhere, the definition has broadened to include bite-sized pieces of toast topped with just about anything.

Make It Your Own

When topping crostini, keep in mind that you're meant to eat them in one or two bites, and consider how a given combination will taste the moment it hits your tongue. Also, the topping shouldn't be runny, and the base should be sturdy enough to hold what's on top, but not to chip your teeth.

WHAT TO ADD AND WHEN TO ADD IT

✐ *Toast.* Choose simple, unseasoned breads, such as baguettes, rye, sourdough, or whole wheat. The flavor of "fancier" breads may detract from the topping.

To prepare the bread, heat the oven to 350° F. Slice the bread about ¼ inch thick. Trim away the crust. Flatten each slice with a rolling pin, then cut out circles with a biscuit cutter, or slice the bread into bite-sized squares. Place them in a single layer on a baking sheet, and put them in the oven until toasted, about three minutes. Check after one minute to make sure the slices don't burn.

✑ *Crackers and Pitas.* For these and fat-free crackers and tortilla chips, bagel chips and toasted mini pitas, choose neutral flavors such as plain, rye, or wheat. Again, seasonings could clash with your topping or dilute the flavor.

✑ *Polenta (Baked Cornmeal Squares).* See page 324 for suggestions for preparing polenta crostini.

✑ *Potato.* Heat the oven to 425° F. Slice an unpeeled medium-waxy or waxy potato (Yukon Gold or red round or white round) into rounds ⅓ inch thick. Place them in a single layer on a nonstick baking sheet. Bake until the tops turn golden brown and begin to buckle, about 8 minutes. Using a spatula, turn them over to brown the other side, about 3 minutes.

✑ *Toppings.* Top each piece of toast with about 1 tablespoon minced roasted red, yellow, or orange bell peppers (see page 534) with or without capers; chopped fresh tomatoes, olive oil, and finely grated smoked mozzarella; or Caramelized Vidalia Onions (see page 224). Or cut a garlic clove in half and rub the toasted bread with the cut side, then drizzle it with olive oil and fresh lemon juice, and sprinkle with a combination of minced fresh parsley and basil. Try Chopped Caponata (see page 134), Basic Hummus (see page 254), Baba Ghanouj (see page 220), Red Lentil Spread

PSSST . . .

No time to make a topping? You can still create crostini—by combining prepared, store-bought products. Try tapenade on crackers; marinated artichoke hearts (mince them); goat cheese or fresh diced mozzarella drizzled with olive oil; crumbled feta cheese and minced cured black olives; and oil-packed sun-dried tomatoes (drain well and blot excess oil). Find a good brand of ready-made hummus and baba ghanouj to spread on toasted wedges of pita bread.

(see page 256), Peach and Lentil Relish (see page 157), Crostini Spreads (see page 264), Kidney Bean Hummus (see page 254), chopped mixed cured olives, Grilled Mushrooms and Sour Cream (see page 226), salsa (see pages 158 to 160), pestos, especially olive (see page 274), Curried Egg Salad (see page 145), or artichokes in lemon (chop the artichokes well).

✑ *Focaccia and Pizza.* Focaccia and pizza become crostini when you cut them into bite-sized pieces. (See pages 416 and 425 for recipes.)

Crostini Spreads

FETA AND CHIVE

Serves 12

TOTAL TIME: ABOUT 8 HOURS, 5 MINUTES, INCLUDING
  TIME TO MAKE THE STRAINED YOGURT
TIME TO PREPARE: ABOUT 5 MINUTES
COOKING TIME: NONE
DO AHEAD: YOU CAN MAKE THE YOGURT BASE UP TO 3
  DAYS IN ADVANCE. REFRIGERATE UNTIL READY TO USE.
REFRIGERATION/FREEZING: REFRIGERATE UP TO 3 DAYS.

1 cup Strained Yogurt (see page 102)
½ cup nonfat or reduced-fat cream cheese
1 cup crumbled feta cheese
¼ cup minced fresh chives
1 scallion, including greens, minced

In a food processor or blender, process the
yogurt, cream cheese, feta cheese, chives, and
scallion in short pulses until well combined,
about 5 pulses. Then process steadily until
smooth, about 10 seconds.

PER SERVING: CALORIES 117 • PROTEIN 10 G • CARBOHYDRATE 7.9 G • FAT 4.5 G •
CHOLESTEROL 23 MG • SODIUM 405 MG • 36% CALORIES FROM FAT • VERY GOOD
SOURCE OF VITAMIN B₂, CALCIUM • GOOD SOURCE OF VITAMIN B₁₂

•

HONEY MUSTARD

Serves 8

Exclusively for sliced potatoes, this chive-sea-
soned spread is wonderful on steamed baby
spuds. Simply, steam the smallest potatoes
you can find, chill them, and then slice off the tops
and dab the potatoes with this spread. To make them
stand upright on a serving tray, cut a slice from the
bottom so they rest flat.

1 cup Strained Yogurt (see page 102)
½ cup nonfat or reduced-fat cream cheese
½ teaspoon Dijon mustard
1 teaspoon honey
1 scallion, including greens, chopped
¼ cup minced fresh chives
2 teaspoons fresh lemon juice

In a food processor or blender, process the
yogurt, cream cheese, mustard, honey, scallion,
chives, and lemon juice in short pulses until
well combined, about 5 pulses. Then process
steadily until smooth, about 10 seconds.

PER SERVING: CALORIES 98 • PROTEIN 11.2 G • CARBOHYDRATE 11.5 G • FAT 0 G •
CHOLESTEROL 7.1 MG • SODIUM 268 MG • 2% CALORIES FROM FAT • VERY GOOD
SOURCE OF CALCIUM

•

AVOCADO
CILANTRO

Serves 8

Really good on sourdough, tortilla chips, or
toasted pita.

1 cup Strained Yogurt (see page 102)
½ cup nonfat or reduced-fat cream cheese
½ avocado
2 scallions, including greens, chopped
¼ cup minced fresh cilantro
2 teaspoons green salsa (see brand preferences,
  page 595)
1 teaspoon fresh lemon juice
1 teaspoon fresh lime juice
2 teaspoons ground cumin

In a food processor or blender, process the yogurt, cream cheese, avocado, scallions, cilantro, salsa, lemon juice, lime juice, and cumin in short pulses until well combined, about 5 pulses. Then process steadily until smooth, about 10 seconds.

PER SERVING: CALORIES 115 • PROTEIN 11.4 G • CARBOHYDRATE 11.7 G • FAT 2.1 G • CHOLESTEROL 7.1 MG • SODIUM 266 MG • 17% CALORIES FROM FAT • VERY GOOD SOURCE OF CALCIUM

•

PESTO AND SUN-DRIED TOMATO

Serves 8

1 cup Strained Yogurt (see page 102)

½ cup nonfat or reduced-fat cream cheese

2 tablespoons basil pesto (see page 280, or brand preferences, page 595)

2 dry-packed (not in oil) sun-dried tomatoes, reconstituted (soak in warm water to cover for 20 minutes, drain, and blot dry)

1 teaspoon capers

2 tablespoons grated Parmesan or Asiago cheese

In a food processor or blender, process the yogurt, cream cheese, pesto, tomatoes, capers, and cheese in short pulses until well combined, about 5 pulses. Then process steadily until smooth, about 10 seconds.

PER SERVING: CALORIES 117 • PROTEIN 12 G • CARBOHYDRATE 11 G • FAT 2.1 G • CHOLESTEROL 8.7 MG • SODIUM 318 MG • 18% CALORIES FROM FAT • VERY GOOD SOURCE OF CALCIUM

•

BELL PEPPER, BASIL, AND SMOKED CHEESE

Serves 10

1 cup Strained Yogurt (see page 102)

½ cup nonfat or reduced-fat cream cheese

1 red bell pepper, roasted, peeled, and chopped (see page 534)

1 yellow bell pepper, roasted, peeled, and chopped (see page 534)

¼ cup minced fresh basil

½ cup nonfat or part-skim ricotta cheese

¼ cup grated smoked mozzarella or provolone cheese

In a food processor or blender, process the yogurt, cream cheese, peppers, basil, ricotta, and mozzarella or provolone in short pulses until well combined, about 5 pulses. Then process steadily until smooth, about 10 seconds.

PER SERVING: CALORIES 102 • PROTEIN 11 G • CARBOHYDRATE 10.3 G • FAT 1.1 G • CHOLESTEROL 8 MG • SODIUM 240 MG • 10% CALORIES FROM FAT • VERY GOOD SOURCE OF VITAMINS A, C; CALCIUM

PASTA, RISOTTO, GNOCCHI, AND MORE

Anyone who orders pasta, gnocchi, or risotto for dinner in Italy quickly learns this isn't done. These are first courses, and if you order them for dinner, the waiter will stand there and wait for you to choose an entrée—either fish, meat, or a substantial vegetable dish, such as eggplant Parmesan. If you don't, he may regard you with contempt for the rest of the meal. Clearly you—an American—are insufficiently interested in food. What he interprets as your poor appetite is a blow to his national pride. You may feel you've ordered enough, but he feels insulted. Since he's the one in charge here, shortly, you'll regret not having asked for the eggplant.

While I object to certain things Americans have done with pasta (such as put it in cans) we're right to serve it for supper. Same goes for gnocchi and risotto. They are substantial, versatile, and easy to prepare. Above all, they make everybody happy, and no meal need do much more than that.

PASTA IN MEAL PLANNING •

PASTA MENUS • PASTA PANTRY •

 FRESH PASTA • PASTA TOPPINGS

• ONE-DISH PASTAS • FILLED PASTAS

 • RISOTTOS • GNOCCHI •

DUMPLINGS • POLENTA

Pasta in Meal Planning

A well-prepared main-course pasta dish or risotto can contain a full complement of vitamins, minerals, and nutrients; a starter or side-dish pasta can supplement or balance an entrée's nutritional content. You'll cover more ground if you manage to avoid serving too much of a single ingredient—cheese, for example. If you're serving a pasta with cheese as the main course, serve a starter or side dish without any. You'll get more pleasure out of the cheese, and you'll avoid the additional fat you'd get from double dipping. Here's what you dish out along with delicious pastas:

LENTILS WITH SPINACH RAGOUT
(PAGE 282)
51% daily value for protein
240% daily value for vitamin A
88% daily value for vitamin C
94% daily value for folacin
45% daily value for iron

SWEET BLACK BEANS ON
WHOLE WHEAT PENNE (PAGE 289)
36% daily value for protein
52% daily value for vitamin C
40% daily value for folacin
28% daily value for vitamin B_1
25% daily value for iron
15% daily value for zinc

ARTICHOKE RISOTTO (PAGE 315)
103% daily value for vitamin A
43% daily value for vitamin C

23% daily value for folacin
24% daily value for vitamin B_6
26% daily value for iron
14% daily value for calcium

BELL PEPPER RISOTTO (PAGE 313)
64% daily value for vitamin A
206% daily value for vitamin C

BAKED EGGS ON POLENTA WITH SPINACH
(PAGE 327)
27% daily value for protein
59% daily value for vitamin A
33% daily value for vitamin C
41% daily value for folacin
26% daily value for vitamin B_2
18% daily value for iron

SWISS CHARD (OR SPINACH)-RICOTTA
GNOCCHI (PAGE 320)
37% daily value for protein
36% daily value for vitamin A
800% daily value for vitamin C
62% daily value for folacin
16% daily value for calcium

Pasta Menus

30-MINUTE MEALS
Gnochetti with Spinach and Ricotta Salata
(*page 296*)
Mesclun with Vinaigrette-Style Dressing
(*page 117*)

Gnochetti with Spinach and Ricotta Salata
(*page 296*)
Endive, Radicchio, and Mushroom Salad
(*page 124*)

Simplest Fresh Tomato Sauce (*page 278*) on
Spaghetti with grated parmesan
Fennel and Orange Salad (*page 123*)

Bell Pepper and Fresh Tomato Sauce (*page 281*)
on penne
Beet and Vidalia Onion Salad (*page 136*)

Creamy Spinach Soup (*page 183*)
Lovely Lentil Sauce (*page 283*) on linguine
Your Own Sourdough Bread (*page 410*)

Mild Miso Soup (*page 173*)
Quick Cold Sesame Noodles (*page 298*)
Mango Cream (*page 496*)

Sweet and Simple Borscht (*page 184*)
Pierogi (*page 323*)
Potato Rye Bread with Caraway (*page 402*)

Chilled Fennel in Citrus Marinade (*page 132*)
Baked Fresh Lasagna with Asparagus Cream
(*page 303*)
Hearth-warming Homemade Bread (*page 393*)

Butternut Squash Soup (*page 181*)
Sweet Black Beans on Whole Wheat Penne
(*page 289*)
Wheat Berry Bread (*page 400*)

Chilled Cream of Carrot Soup with
Ginger and Lime (*page 201*)
Baked Eggs on Polenta with Spinach (*page 327*)

Red or Yellow Bell Pepper Soup (*page 171*) with
Tender Soup Dumplings (*page 169*)
Artichoke Risotto (*page 315*)

Creamy Herb Soup (*page 180*)
Mushroom Risotto (*page 311*)

Cream of Cauliflower Soup (*page 176*)
Radicchio Risotto (*page 310*)

Cold Cream of Broccoli Soup (*page 200*)
Fresh Corn Risotto (*page 312*)

Apple-Turnip Soup (*page 186*)
Pumpkin Gnocchi (*page 319*) with Lovely
Lentil Sauce (*page 283*)

Spinach-Ricotta Gnocchi (*page 320*)
Simplest Fresh Tomato Sauce (*page 278*)
Panzanella (*page 150*)

Baby spinach with Orange-Sesame Dressing
(*page 121*)
Beet Drop Dumplings (*page 321*)

Pasta Pantry

You'll find my brand-name recommendations for most of these items on page 595. If you can't find what you want where you shop, see the mail-order information on page 596.

Extra virgin olive oil

Balsamic vinegar

Long pastas (any two): spaghetti, linguine, fettuccine, tagliatelle, capellini (angel hair), perciatelli

Short pastas (any two): penne, penne rigate, gnocchetti, ziti, orecchiette, farfalle (bow ties), radiatore

Shell-shaped pastas: large seashells, medium seashells

Short whole wheat pastas (imported brand only): penne, rigatoni

Legumes: lentilles du Puy, chickpeas, cannellini beans, black runner beans, kidney beans

Cornmeal (for polenta)

Tomatoes in a carton or can

Arborio rice

Spices and herbs, including dried basil, fennel seeds, and oregano

In the Refrigerator

Cured olives

Parmesan cheese

Asiago cheese

Ricotta cheese

Ricotta salata

Mozzarella cheese

Onions

Garlic

Leeks

Shallots

Fresh basil

Frozen artichoke hearts

Fresh Pasta

PASTA

Serves 6

TOTAL TIME: ABOUT 1 HOUR, 30 MINUTES, INCLUDING TIME TO CHILL THE DOUGH
TIME TO PREPARE: ABOUT 50 MINUTES
COOKING TIME: ABOUT 3 MINUTES
EQUIPMENT: PASTA MACHINE AND GROOVED ROLLER FOR RAVIOLI
REFRIGERATION/FREEZING: REFRIGERATE THE FRESH PASTA UP TO 5 DAYS, WRAPPED IN PLASTIC, OR WRAP IT FIRST IN PLASTIC, THEN IN FOIL, AND FREEZE UP TO 5 MONTHS. DO NOT THAW BEFORE COOKING FROZEN FRESH PASTA.

¾ cup semolina flour

¾ cup unbleached all-purpose flour

1 teaspoon salt, preferably coarse salt

3 large egg whites

If you're using a food processor or a Mixmaster, put the semolina and all-purpose flour and the salt in the work bowl with the metal blade (food processor) or paddle (Mixmaster). Turn on the machine and slowly pour in the egg whites. As soon as the dough clumps together, turn off the machine. Remove the dough and knead it by hand until it's smooth. The dough should be very firm, but pliable enough to knead. If it's too stiff, add water, 1 teaspoon at a time, until you get the right consistency. If it's too soft, add flour 1 tablespoon at a time until it's firm enough.

Once the dough is smooth, shape it into a ball and cover it loosely with a damp paper towel. Wrap a piece of plastic wrap over that and refrigerate it for 30 minutes before proceeding to roll and shape.

To roll with a hand-crank machine, tear off a quarter of the dough and dust it lightly with all-purpose flour. Pat it with your hands to flatten it slightly, then feed it into your machine, with the feed slot set at its widest. Roll it through, dusting it lightly again. Reset the feed slot to the next width, and roll it through again. Continue rolling and tightening the slot until the pasta is as thin as you'd like. Be careful not to overdo it, or the dough will tear.

If you're making lasagna, cut the sheets of dough to size to fit your pan, and proceed to layer it immediately. You won't have to cook the pasta first; it's fresh and thin enough to cook while the lasagna bakes.

For ravioli, place one sheet on a flour-dusted work surface. Drop the filling by the tablespoon, spacing it 2 inches apart. Cover with a second sheet of dough. Use a grooved roller to cut the ravioli into squares. To cook, proceed with the recipe you're using.

For noodles, simply run the dough through the setting for spaghetti, fettuccine, or capellini. Let the pasta dry for 15 minutes before cooking in boiling water for about 3 minutes.

If you're using an automatic pasta maker, follow the directions that came with the machine.

PER SERVING: CALORIES 122 • PROTEIN 4.9 G • CARBOHYDRATE 24 G • FAT 0 G • CHOLESTEROL 0 MG • SODIUM 383 MG • 2% CALORIES FROM FAT

FRESH PASTA BASICS

Unless you're waging a determined campaign for martyrdom, don't even think about mixing pasta dough by hand. Kneading the eggs and flour to the right consistency is tough going, the kind of thing that can make you sweat and—if it's your custom—swear, but that a food processor or Mixmaster can do neatly and swiftly, without having a fit.

Once you've made the dough, you have to roll it out. Again, you can do this by hand, but a machine sure helps. I use a simple hand-crank model.

The dough will taste best if you make it with a combination of semolina flour and unbleached all-purpose flour. (If you can't find semolina where you shop, see mail-order information, page 596.) Pasta made at home with whole wheat flour tends to be coarse, but if you want to use it, try adding ¼ cup whole wheat in place of an equal amount of the semolina in the basic recipe.

If you're making lasagna or ravioli, have your filling fully prepared before you make the pasta. You don't have to boil the pasta for the lasagna beforehand. Just bake it according to the lasagna recipe you're using, and it will cook during that process.

If you're making noodles rather than lasagna or ravioli, cut the dough according to the directions that come with your machine, then dry it by laying it one layer thick on a kitchen towel in a cool, airy spot. If you're going to be storing it, make sure it's completely dry, then wrap it tightly in a plastic bag and refrigerate for up to five days.

Or wrap it first in plastic, then in foil, and freeze it for up to five months. Don't defrost it before you boil it.

Fresh pasta, whether just made or allowed to dry, cooks much more quickly than commercial dried pasta, usually in under three minutes if just made and under five if frozen. Start testing for doneness after one minute for fresh, two minutes for frozen.

Make It Your Own

You can season your pasta dough to complement or enhance the flavor in your sauce. Be careful not to add too much to the dough, or it may buckle or tear.

WHAT TO ADD AND WHEN TO ADD IT

Lemon Zest. Add 1 tablespoon finely grated zest when you mix the dough.

Spinach. Add 1 tablespoon finely minced, well-drained, cooked spinach when you mix the dough. Add 2 tablespoons additional unbleached all-purpose flour to compensate for the extra moisture. Spinach adds more color than flavor to the dough.

Beets. Add 1 tablespoon cooked, thoroughly pureed beets when you mix the dough. Add 2 tablespoons additional unbleached all-purpose flour to compensate for the extra moisture. Like spinach, beets add more color than flavor to the dough.

🍃 *Saffron*. Dissolve ¼ teaspoon in 1 teaspoon hot water. Let it cool. Add it when you mix the dough. Add 2 tablespoons additional unbleached all-purpose flour to compensate for the extra moisture.

🍃 *Basil or Other Herbs*. Add 1 tablespoon finely minced fresh herbs when you mix the dough.

Pasta Toppings

FIVE-INGREDIENT TOPPINGS

Glance at the ingredients, and you'll know how each of these swift, simple sauces will taste. Use fresh produce and herbs, if possible, but you'll do fine with whatever you have on hand at home.

Tomato and Herb Topping
Serves 4

TOTAL TIME: ABOUT 40 MINUTES
TIME TO PREPARE: ABOUT 25 MINUTES, INCLUDING TIME TO SAUTÉ
COOKING TIME: ABOUT 15 MINUTES
DO AHEAD: YOU CAN PEEL, SEED, AND CHOP THE TOMATOES UP TO 3 DAYS IN ADVANCE. REFRIGERATE UNTIL READY TO USE.
REFRIGERATION/FREEZING: REFRIGERATE UP TO 3 DAYS. FREEZE UP TO 6 MONTHS.

2 teaspoons extra virgin olive oil
2 large leeks, white part only, washed and chopped
4 scallions, including greens, chopped
4 large ripe tomatoes, peeled, seeded, and chopped (see page 544), or one 16-ounce can or carton chopped tomatoes

1 tablespoon minced fresh oregano or 1½ teaspoons crumbled dried oregano

Heat the oil in a medium skillet over medium-high heat. When hot, add the leeks and scallions. Reduce the heat to medium and sauté, stirring often, until the vegetables are soft and limp. Add the tomatoes and oregano, and cook over medium heat until the tomatoes reduce to a pulpy sauce, about 15 minutes.

PER SERVING: CALORIES 100 • PROTEIN 2.7 G • CARBOHYDRATE 18 G • FAT 3 G • CHOLESTEROL 0 MG • SODIUM 30.8 MG • 25% CALORIES FROM FAT • OUTSTANDING SOURCE OF VITAMIN C • GOOD SOURCE OF VITAMINS A, B₁, B₆; FOLACIN

VARIATION: To serve as a main course for four, add 2 cups cooked, drained, and rinsed chickpeas or cannellini beans and/or ½ cup grated Asiago or Parmesan cheese.

Basil and Olive Topping

Serves 2

TOTAL TIME: ABOUT 10 MINUTES
TIME TO PREPARE: ABOUT 10 MINUTES
COOKING TIME: INCLUDED IN TIME TO PREPARE

2 teaspoons extra virgin olive oil
1 garlic clove, thinly sliced
1 cup minced oil-cured olives
¼ cup minced fresh basil
¼ cup grated Pecorino, Parmesan, or Asiago
   cheese

Heat the oil in a medium skillet over medium-high heat. When it is hot, add the garlic clove, reduce the heat to medium-low and swish the garlic through the oil until it starts to color, about 10 seconds. As soon as it turns golden, remove and discard it. Toss the olives and basil into the oil and stir well to coat. Remove from the heat. Toss with freshly cooked, drained pasta and the cheese.

PER SERVING: CALORIES 146 • PROTEIN 5.9 G • CARBOHYDRATE 1.7 G • FAT 13.2 G • CHOLESTEROL 9.8 MG • SODIUM 1169 MG • 80% CALORIES FROM FAT • VERY GOOD SOURCE OF CALCIUM

Snow Pea and Smoked Mozzarella Topping

Serves 2

TOTAL TIME: ABOUT 10 MINUTES
TIME TO PREPARE: ABOUT 10 MINUTES, INCLUDING TIME
   TO SAUTÉ
COOKING TIME: INCLUDED IN TIME TO PREPARE

2 teaspoons extra virgin olive oil
1 small onion, minced
¼ cup minced fresh parsley
2 cups loosely packed snow peas
¼ cup grated smoked mozzarella

Heat the oil in a medium skillet over medium-high heat. When it is hot, add the onion and parsley. Reduce the heat to medium and sauté, stirring often, about 7 minutes. Add the snow peas and stir until they turn bright green, about 1 minute. Remove from the heat and toss with freshly cooked, drained pasta and the mozzarella.

PER SERVING: CALORIES 156 • PROTEIN 8.5 G • CARBOHYDRATE 14.9 G • FAT 7.3 G • CHOLESTEROL 7.6 MG • SODIUM 85.7 MG • 41% CALORIES FROM FAT • OUTSTANDING SOURCE OF VITAMIN C • VERY GOOD SOURCE OF FOLACIN, IRON • GOOD SOURCE OF VITAMINS B₁, B₂

Sun-Dried Tomato and Fresh Ricotta Topping

Serves 2

TOTAL TIME: ABOUT 15 MINUTES, INCLUDING TIME TO
   SOAK THE TOMATOES
TIME TO PREPARE: ABOUT 5 MINUTES
COOKING TIME: INCLUDED IN TIME TO PREPARE

6 dry-packed (not in oil) sun-dried tomatoes
2 teaspoons extra virgin olive oil
1 garlic clove, thinly sliced
2 tablespoons minced fresh basil

½ cup part-skim ricotta cheese (don't use nonfat, it doesn't have enough body or flavor)

Place the sun-dried tomatoes in a bowl. Pour boiling water over them and let them sit until they soften, about 10 minutes. Drain, chop, and set them aside.

Heat the oil in a small skillet over medium-high heat. When it is hot, add the garlic clove, reduce the heat to medium-low, and swish the garlic slices through the oil until they start to color, about 40 seconds. As soon as they turn golden, remove and discard them. Add the tomatoes and basil and stir to coat with the oil and heat through, about 2 minutes. Remove from the heat and toss with freshly cooked, drained pasta and the ricotta.

PER SERVING: CALORIES 107 • PROTEIN 7.6 G • CARBOHYDRATE 5.9 G • FAT 6.1 G • CHOLESTEROL 19 MG • SODIUM 102 MG • 51% CALORIES FROM FAT • GOOD SOURCE OF VITAMIN C; CALCIUM

Zucchini and Ricotta Salata Topping
Serves 2

TOTAL TIME: ABOUT 10 MINUTES
TIME TO PREPARE: ABOUT 10 MINUTES, INCLUDING TIME TO SAUTÉ
COOKING TIME: INCLUDED IN TIME TO PREPARE

2 teaspoons extra virgin olive oil
4 scallions, including greens, minced
1 medium zucchini, diced
2 tablespoons minced fresh basil
½ cup crumbled ricotta salata

Heat the oil in a medium skillet over medium-high heat. When it is hot, add the scallions and sauté until they're soft, about 7 minutes. Add the zucchini and basil, and sauté until the zucchini is just cooked through, about 2 to 3 minutes. Remove from the heat and toss with freshly cooked, drained pasta and the ricotta salata.

PER SERVING: CALORIES 142 • PROTEIN 8.29 G • CARBOHYDRATE 7.8 G • FAT 9.5 G • CHOLESTEROL 19 MG • SODIUM 83 MG • 58% CALORIES FROM FAT • VERY GOOD SOURCE OF CALCIUM • GOOD SOURCE OF VITAMINS A, C; FOLACIN

PASTA TOPPING BASICS

Like musical notes, the eligible ingredients for pasta toppings lend themselves to recombination, apparently without end. And as with musical notes, some combinations are better than others. Here are some guidelines for good composition.

• Opposites do not attract when pasta is concerned; more often than not, like goes better with like. For fine pasta such as angel hair and spaghettini, use a simple light fresh tomato sauce, saving the heartier sauces for sturdier noodles, such as linguine and fettuccine. Use heavier sauces on dense, short pastas, too, such as orecchiette and penne, and lighter sauces on the more delicate kind such as farfalle (bow ties) and ditalini.

• Go easy on the sauce so you can taste the pasta. Toss light sauces such as simple fresh tomato sauce with the pasta before serving. For heavier sauces, dish the pasta on to serving plates and spoon the sauce on top.

• Serve pasta on plates or in shallow bowls. If you serve it in regular bowls, the sauce will sink to the bottom.

• If you're using a flavored pasta, top it with a mild sauce so that the flavor of the pasta can come through. And match the flavor of the sauce to the pasta. For example, tomato and basil sauce on lemon pasta isn't a great idea. But a white sauce with Parmesan would be wonderful.

Make It Your Own

While it's nice to be known for a lovely smile and a charming personality, nothing beats having a good pasta sauce to your name.

WHAT TO ADD AND WHEN TO ADD IT

Herbs and Spices. When you change the seasoning, you change the sauce. Switch from basil and oregano to cilantro and cumin, and a Mediterranean-style sauce becomes southwestern. If using spices and dried herbs, add them at the beginning, when you sauté the aromatic vegetables, such as onion and garlic. If you're using minced fresh herbs, add half at the beginning when you sauté, then stir in the rest at the end.

Wine or Vinegar. These ingredients give a subtle, tangy undertaste to sauces. After you've sautéed the aromatic vegetables, add a splash of red or white wine or seasoned vinegar. For a change or if you don't want to open a bottle of wine, try substituting a seasoned vinegar for the wine, using half as much as the amount of wine called for. Similarly, if the recipe calls for vinegar, add wine instead, doubling the amount.

Cheeses. When a sauce calls for grated cheese, experiment with different varieties, switching from Parmesan to Asiago or Fontina, or cheddar to Gruyère or Emmentaler. Taste the cheese before you add it to be sure you want that particular flavor in the dish.

Thickened Soup. Follow your favorite soup recipe, using less water or broth than called for. Or prepare it as directed and cook it down until the soup is thick enough for sauce.

Salads. Any vegetable salad—especially those with creamy dressings—can become a pasta salad. If your salad includes lettuce, use about half as much as you'd use if you were

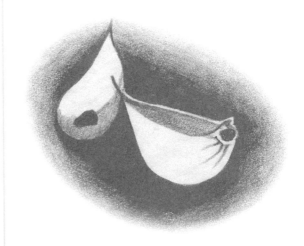

serving it on its own and chop it very fine. Lentil and bean salads work well, too. To serve, rinse just-cooked short pasta with cold water before tossing it with the salad. (Rinsing keeps the pasta from sticking together.)

·

LIGHT BÉCHAMEL
Serves 4

TOTAL TIME: ABOUT 10 MINUTES
TIME TO PREPARE: ABOUT 10 MINUTES
COOKING TIME: INCLUDED IN TIME TO PREPARE
REFRIGERATION/FREEZING: DO NOT REFRIGERATE OR FREEZE

Béchamel sauce is such a staple in northern Italy that when recipes call for it, they don't bother telling how it should be made, saying only "Prepare a béchamel in the usual way."

Their usual way would start with a few tablespoons of butter, and end with a cup or so of cream. It would involve constant stirring on top of the stove and precise timing that, frankly, makes me nervous.

My usual way is easier and lighter, calling for a dab of butter, skim milk, and a swift pass through the microwave.

2 teaspoons unsalted butter
1 tablespoon unbleached all-purpose flour
½ cup evaporated skim milk
½ cup nonfat milk
Salt and freshly ground black pepper to taste
Pinch ground nutmeg (optional)
2 tablespoons grated Parmesan, Asiago, Gruyère, or sharp cheddar cheese (optional)

Place the butter in a deep microwave-proof bowl. Melt it on high power, about 15 seconds. Whisk in the flour, then return the bowl to the microwave for 15 seconds. Give the mixture another stir with the whisk and return it to the microwave for 15 seconds.

Whisk in the evaporated skim milk and nonfat milk, and return the mixture to the microwave for 30 seconds. Stir and microwave at 30-second intervals until you have a thick sauce. Season with salt and pepper, adding nutmeg and/or grated cheese, if you'd like.

PER SERVING: CALORIES 60 · PROTEIN 3.6 G · CARBOHYDRATE 6.6 G · FAT 2 G · CHOLESTEROL 6.9 MG · SODIUM 52.7 MG · 31% CALORIES FROM FAT · GOOD SOURCE OF CALCIUM

Poached Egg with Spinach and Béchamel
Serves 1

1 English muffin (see page 78)
½ cup steamed spinach (see page 540)
2 tablespoons Light Béchamel
¼ cup low-fat cottage cheese
1 poached large egg (see page 62)

Split and toast the English muffin. Meanwhile, stir together the spinach and 1½ tablespoons of the béchamel sauce. Spread both toasted muffin halves with the cottage cheese and top with the spinach-béchamel sauce. Split the poached egg in half and place one half of the egg on each muffin half and drizzle with additional sauce.

·

SPICY FRESH TOMATO SAUCE

Serves 4

TOTAL TIME: ABOUT 25 MINUTES
TIME TO PREPARE: ABOUT 25 MINUTES, INCLUDING TIME
  TO SAUTÉ
COOKING TIME: INCLUDED IN TIME TO PREPARE
DO AHEAD: YOU CAN PEEL, SEED, AND CHOP THE TOMA-
  TOES UP TO 3 DAYS IN ADVANCE. REFRIGERATE UNTIL
  READY TO USE.
REFRIGERATION/FREEZING: REFRIGERATE UP TO 3 DAYS.
  FREEZE UP TO 6 MONTHS.

Cilantro, cumin, and jalapeño pepper give the sauce a southwestern taste. Serve it over pasta or with Fresh Corn Risotto (see page 312): make a well in the risotto, and fill with sauce.

2 teaspoons canola oil
1 large onion, chopped
2 garlic cloves, minced
3 tablespoons minced fresh cilantro
2 tablespoons minced fresh basil
1 jalapeño pepper, seeded, and chopped
2 teaspoons ground cumin
6 fresh tomatoes, peeled, seeded, and chopped
    (see page 544), or 4 cups canned chopped
    tomatoes
Salt and freshly ground black pepper to taste

Heat the oil in a large skillet over medium-high heat, swirling the pan to coat the bottom. Add the onion, garlic, cilantro, basil, jalapeño, and cumin, and sauté, stirring often, until the onion is soft, about 12 minutes. Add the tomatoes and continue to cook until they break down into a thick sauce, about 7 minutes.

Using a food processor or immersion blender, puree the sauce in short spurts. Be careful not to overdo it, or the sauce will be too thin. Season with salt and pepper.

PER SERVING: CALORIES 76 • PROTEIN 2.1 G • CARBOHYDRATE 12 G • FAT 2.9 G • CHOLESTEROL 0 MG • SODIUM 80 MG • 31% CALORIES FROM FAT • OUTSTANDING SOURCE OF VITAMIN C • GOOD SOURCE OF VITAMINS A, B₆

•

SIMPLEST FRESH TOMATO SAUCE

Serves 4

TOTAL TIME: 25 MINUTES
TIME TO PREPARE: 25 MINUTES
COOKING TIME: INCLUDED IN TIME TO PREPARE
DO AHEAD: YOU CAN PEEL, SEED, AND CHOP THE TOMA-
  TOES UP TO 3 DAYS IN ADVANCE. REFRIGERATE UNTIL
  READY TO USE.
REFRIGERATION/FREEZING: REFRIGERATE UP TO 4 DAYS.
  FREEZE UP TO 6 MONTHS.

Everyone has a secret for "the best" tomato sauce. Some say it's the tomatoes, some the quality of the olive oil, while others say it's a matter of cooking it quickly on very high heat. I endorse all three.

1 tablespoon extra virgin olive oil
1 large garlic clove, thinly sliced
1½ pounds fresh tomatoes (see Note), peeled,
    seeded, and chopped (see page 544)
2 tablespoons minced fresh basil, or 2 teaspoons
    crumbled dried basil
Salt and freshly ground black pepper to taste

Heat the oil in a medium skillet over medium-high heat. When it's hot, add the garlic. Reduce the heat to medium-low and swish the garlic slices through the oil until the slices begin to color, about 40 seconds. Remove the garlic from the oil with a slotted spatula or a fork and discard them. Swiftly pour the tomatoes into the hot oil, add the crumbled dried basil if using, and cook until the tomatoes reduce into a thick sauce, about 10 minutes. Stir in the minced fresh basil, if using. Remove the sauce from the heat, and season with salt and pepper.

You can leave it chunky, or puree it with an immersion blender, or in a food processor. (Don't overdo it, or the sauce will be watery.)

Note: The tomatoes must be ripe to burstin', so to speak, more red than orange, with no black spots.

PER SERVING: CALORIES 68 • PROTEIN 1.6 G • CARBOHYDRATE 8.6 G • FAT 3.9 G • CHOLESTEROL 0 MG • SODIUM 15.7 MG • 47% CALORIES FROM FAT • OUTSTANDING SOURCE OF VITAMIN C • GOOD SOURCE OF VITAMIN A

LIGHT ALL-PURPOSE WHITE SAUCE

Serves 4

TOTAL TIME: ABOUT 15 MINUTES, NOT INCLUDING TIME TO MAKE THE BROTH
TIME TO PREPARE: 15 MINUTES
COOKING TIME: INCLUDED IN TIME TO PREPARE
REFRIGERATION/FREEZING: REFRIGERATE UP TO 2 DAYS. BEFORE SERVING, HEAT GENTLY, WHISKING IN ADDITIONAL VEGETABLE BROTH TO RESTORE ORIGINAL CONSISTENCY. DO NOT BOIL.

*L*ighter than béchamel, this sauce isn't meant to be served straight. Season it with herbs, cheeses, or vegetable puree, and pour it over pasta, rice, or egg dishes.

2 cups vegetable broth (see page 165)
1 tablespoon cornstarch or arrowroot
½ cup evaporated skim milk
½ cup nonfat milk
Salt and freshly ground white pepper to taste

Bring the vegetable broth to a boil in a medium saucepan over medium-high heat. Reduce the heat to medium-low, keeping it at a simmer.

In a small bowl, mix the cornstarch or arrowroot with 2 tablespoons of the evaporated milk to make a thick paste. Stir it into the broth along with the rest of the evaporated milk and the nonfat milk, and whisk until the sauce thickens, about 7 minutes.

Season with salt and pepper.

PER SERVING: CALORIES 45 • PROTEIN 3.5 G • CARBOHYDRATE 6.9 G • FAT 0 G • CHOLESTEROL 1.7 MG • SODIUM 52.6 MG • 3% CALORIES FROM FAT • GOOD SOURCE OF CALCIUM

•

PESTO

Serves 4

TOTAL TIME: ABOUT 5 MINUTES
TIME TO PREPARE: ABOUT 5 MINUTES
COOKING TIME: NONE
DO AHEAD: YOU CAN TOAST THE PINE NUTS UP TO 1 WEEK
   IN ADVANCE. REFRIGERATE UNTIL READY TO USE.
REFRIGERATION/FREEZING: REFRIGERATE, COVERED, FOR UP
   TO 5 DAYS. FREEZE UP TO 5 MONTHS. TO FREEZE, DIVIDE
   THE PESTO INTO SMALL PORTIONS SO YOU WON'T HAVE
   TO DEFROST A WHOLE BATCH WHEN YOU NEED ONLY A
   BIT. YOU CAN FREEZE IT IN ICE CUBE TRAYS, THEN TRANS-
   FER THE CUBES TO ZIPLOC BAGS.

Philosophers, theologians, and you and I may debate why we're here for years on end, and never reach a conclusion that satisfies us all. But I bet we could swiftly and unanimously resolve any question regarding the reason basil was put on this earth: pesto. While it's a splendid seasoning for anything with tomatoes, and an asset to chili and curry, nothing you can do with this heady herb rivals pesto.

4 garlic cloves
2 tablespoons pine nuts, toasted (see Note,
   page 122)
2 cups packed fresh basil leaves
3 tablespoons extra virgin olive oil
2 tablespoons grated Parmesan, Pecorino, or
   Asiago cheese

Place the garlic, pine nuts, basil, oil, and cheese in a blender or food processor. Process in short spurts to combine, then process with the motor running to make a smooth paste.

PER SERVING: CALORIES 114 • PROTEIN 1.6 G • CARBOHYDRATE 1.3 G • FAT 11.7 G • CHOLESTEROL 2.4 MG • SODIUM 59.4 MG • 90% CALORIES FROM FAT

NOW DECIDE HOW YOU'LL USE IT

• Toss it with freshly cooked pasta. (Don't drain the pasta thoroughly; leave some of the pasta cooking water to thin the pesto.)
• Spread it on pizza dough, scatter shredded mozzarella on top, and bake 8 to 10 minutes, or until golden brown.
• Swirl it into vegetable soup or risotto for added seasoning.
• When making a frittata, place a spoonful of pesto in the skillet, pour the egg mixture on top, stir well, and cook according to the basic Frittata recipe (see page 68).
• Spread it on bread, toast the bread, and cut into croutons to toss with salad greens or stir into soup.
• Use it to stuff mushroom caps. Fill white mushroom caps with pesto and broil until bubbly.
• Blend with reduced-fat or nonfat sour cream and use it to top baked potatoes.
• Toss pesto with cubed red or white potatoes, place them in a roasting pan, and place in an oven at 400° F. until done, about twenty-five minutes.

Make It Your Own

You can substitute a number of herbs for the basil, replace the pine nuts with nuts of another kind, and try various combinations of cheeses and herbs.

WHAT TO ADD AND WHEN TO ADD IT
🌿 Walnuts. These can take the place of pine nuts in the Pesto recipe.

✒ *Mint and Parmesan.* Add mint and Parmesan in the same proportions as the basil and cheese in the basic recipe.

✒ *Cilantro and Asiago.* Substitute for the basil and Parmesan in the basic recipe in the same proportions. Add 1 teaspoon grated lemon zest for lift, if you'd like.

✒ *Parsley and Pecorino.* Try this combination in the same proportions as the basil and cheese in the basic recipe.

✒ *Olives, Basil, and Parmesan.* Use ½ cup minced olives with the 2 cups of basil; omit the nuts with this combination, or the pesto will be too heavy. Add 1 teaspoon capers if you'd like a mild, tangy taste.

•

BELL PEPPER AND FRESH TOMATO SAUCE

Serves 4

TOTAL TIME: 25 MINUTES
TIME TO PREPARE: 25 MINUTES, INCLUDING TIME TO SAUTÉ
COOKING TIME: INCLUDED IN TIME TO PREPARE
DO AHEAD: YOU CAN ROAST THE PEPPERS AND PEEL, SEED, AND CHOP THE TOMATOES UP TO 3 DAYS IN ADVANCE. REFRIGERATE BOTH UNTIL READY TO USE.
REFRIGERATION/FREEZING: REFRIGERATE UP TO 3 DAYS. FREEZE UP TO 6 MONTHS.

Saffron's nice, but not necessary in a fresh seasonal sauce, which you can make in minutes. For a complete meal, toss it with pasta and grated cheese. If you want something even more substantial, throw in some garbanzo beans or white beans—canned or boiled yourself—as well.

2 teaspoons extra virgin olive oil
1 shallot, minced
1 garlic clove, minced
2 yellow or orange bell peppers or one of each, roasted, peeled, and chopped (see page 534)
¼ cup minced fresh basil, or 1 tablespoon crumbled dried basil
2 teaspoons white wine vinegar
½ pound fresh tomatoes, peeled, seeded, and chopped (see page 544) or 1 cup canned tomatoes
Pinch powdered saffron (optional)
Salt and freshly ground black pepper to taste
Grated Parmesan, Asiago, Romano, or Fontina cheese, for garnish (optional)

Heat the oil in a large skillet over medium-high heat, swirling the pan to coat the bottom. Add the shallot, garlic, peppers, and basil. Reduce the heat to medium and sauté, stirring often, until the shallot softens, about 7 minutes.

Raise the heat to medium-high and add the vinegar, stirring until it evaporates, about 1 minute. Add the tomatoes, reduce the heat to medium, and cook, stirring constantly, until the tomatoes break down into a pulpy sauce, about 6 minutes. Stir in the saffron, if using, and season with salt and pepper. Top with the grated cheese of your choice, if you'd like.

PER SERVING: CALORIES 45 • PROTEIN 0 G • CARBOHYDRATE 5.8 G • FAT 2.4 G • CHOLESTEROL 0 MG • SODIUM 4.1 MG • 45% CALORIES FROM FAT • OUTSTANDING SOURCE OF VITAMIN C • VERY GOOD SOURCE OF VITAMIN A

•

A QUARTET OF
LENTIL RAGOUTS

When you consider that people have cooked with lentils since Neolithic times, you have to wonder whether you can do anything with them that some cave dwelling ancestor didn't try some seven thousand years ago. To claim originality with one of the world's oldest foods is to stand on shaky ground.

When it comes to describing the following sauces, it's safe enough to say that each is very good, and markedly distinct.

Lentils with Spinach
Serves 4

TOTAL TIME: ABOUT 1 HOUR
TIME TO PREPARE: ABOUT 30 MINUTES, INCLUDING TIME
   TO SAUTÉ
COOKING TIME: ABOUT 30 MINUTES
REFRIGERATION/FREEZING: REFRIGERATE UP TO 3 DAYS.
   FREEZE UP TO 6 MONTHS.

Serve this rich, chunky sauce over short pasta, such as ziti, penne rigate, or radiatore, or spoon it over rice, and top with Parmesan cheese.

2 teaspoons extra virgin olive oil
1 large onion, sliced
4 garlic cloves, minced
4 carrots, peeled and chopped
2 large leeks, white part plus 2 inches of greens,
   washed and chopped
3 large celery stalks, including leaves, chopped,
   or 1 fennel bulb, including leafy fronds,
   coarsely chopped
3 cups chopped fresh spinach or Swiss chard
2 cups water
1 cup canned chopped tomatoes, including juice
1 cup uncooked lentils, preferably lentilles du
   Puy
½ cup minced fresh parsley
Salt and freshly ground black pepper to taste

Heat the oil in a large skillet over medium heat. When it's hot, add the onion, garlic, carrots, leeks, and celery or fennel. Sauté, stirring often, until the vegetables are soft and limp, about 20 minutes.

Stir in the spinach or chard and cook, stirring, until the mixture turns bright green, about 2 minutes more.

Add the water, tomatoes, and lentils. Stir well, cover, and simmer for 30 minutes over medium-low heat, until the lentils are cooked through. Stir in the parsley and season with salt and pepper.

PER SERVING: CALORIES 353 • PROTEIN 23 G • CARBOHYDRATE 53 G • FAT 7.2 G • CHOLESTEROL 9.8 MG • SODIUM 344 MG • 18% CALORIES FROM FAT • OUTSTANDING SOURCE OF VITAMINS A, C; FOLACIN, IRON • VERY GOOD SOURCE OF VITAMINS B₁, B₂, B₆; CALCIUM • GOOD SOURCE OF VITAMIN B₃; ZINC

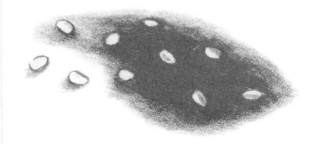

Light Lemony Lentil Sauce

Serves 4

TOTAL TIME: ABOUT 1 HOUR, 5 MINUTES, NOT INCLUDING
TIME TO MAKE THE BROTH
TIME TO PREPARE: ABOUT 25 MINUTES, INCLUDING TIME
TO SAUTÉ
COOKING TIME: 40 MINUTES
DO AHEAD: YOU CAN PEEL AND CHOP THE TOMATOES UP TO
3 DAYS IN ADVANCE. REFRIGERATE UNTIL READY TO USE.
REFRIGERATION/FREEZING: REFRIGERATE UP TO 3 DAYS.
FREEZE UP TO 6 MONTHS.

*Lemon makes this sauce taste lighter than most others
made with lentils. Serve it over spaghetti, spaghettini,
or rice.*

1 tablespoon extra virgin olive or canola oil

1 large onion, chopped

2 garlic cloves, minced

1 carrot, peeled and chopped

1 celery stalk, chopped

1 1/2 cups peeled, seeded, and chopped fresh
  tomatoes (see page 544) or canned chopped
  tomatoes

2 cups vegetable broth (see page 165)

1 cup uncooked lentils, rinsed

Juice of 1 lemon

1 tablespoon white wine vinegar

2 teaspoons low-sodium soy sauce

2 teaspoons crumbled dried basil

2 teaspoons crumbled dried oregano

2 teaspoons crumbled dried thyme

Salt and freshly ground black pepper to taste

Heat the oil in a large, wide saucepan over
medium heat. Add the onion, garlic, carrot,
and celery, and sauté over medium-low heat,
stirring often, until soft, about 15 minutes.

Stir in the tomatoes, vegetable broth,
lentils, lemon juice, vinegar, soy sauce, basil,
oregano, and thyme. Turn up the heat to
medium-high and bring the sauce to a simmer.
Lower the heat to medium-low, cover, and simmer gently until the lentils are tender and most
of the moisture is gone, about 40 minutes. Season with salt and pepper.

PER SERVING: CALORIES 236 • PROTEIN 15 G • CARBOHYDRATE 37 G • FAT 4.1 G •
CHOLESTEROL 0 MG • SODIUM 162 MG • 15% CALORIES FROM FAT • OUTSTANDING
SOURCE OF VITAMINS A, C; FOLACIN • VERY GOOD SOURCE OF VITAMIN B6; IRON

Lovely Lentil Sauce

Serves 4

TOTAL TIME: ABOUT 1 HOUR, 5 MINUTES, NOT INCLUDING
TIME TO MAKE THE BROTH
TIME TO PREPARE: ABOUT 25 MINUTES, INCLUDING TIME
TO SAUTÉ
COOKING TIME: ABOUT 40 MINUTES
DO AHEAD: YOU CAN PEEL, SEED, AND CHOP THE TOMA-
TOES UP TO 3 DAYS IN ADVANCE. REFRIGERATE UNTIL
READY TO USE.
REFRIGERATION/FREEZING: REFRIGERATE UP TO 3 DAYS.
FREEZE UP TO 6 MONTHS.

*Serve this simple, full-flavored sauce over gnocchi or
short pasta such as gnocchetti, orecchiette, or penne
rigate.*

2 teaspoons extra virgin olive oil

1 onion, chopped

1 garlic clove, minced

1/4 cup minced fresh parsley

2 fresh sage leaves, minced, or 1 teaspoon
  crumbled dried sage

2 cups peeled, seeded, and chopped fresh tomatoes
  (see page 544) or canned chopped tomatoes

2 whole cloves

2/3 cup uncooked lentils, preferably lentilles du
  Puy

1 1/4 cups vegetable broth (see page 165) or
  water, approximately

Salt and freshly ground black pepper to taste

Heat the oil in a large skillet over medium-high heat. When it's hot, add the onion, garlic, parsley, and sage. Reduce the heat to medium and sauté, stirring often, until the onion is soft and limp, about 12 minutes. Add the tomatoes and cloves, and continue cooking, stirring often, until the tomatoes cook down into a thick sauce, about 10 minutes.

Stir in the lentils and the vegetable broth or water. Bring to a simmer over medium-high heat. Reduce the heat to medium-low, cover, and simmer gently until the lentils are tender and the liquid has been absorbed, about 30 minutes. If the liquid has been absorbed but the lentils are still hard at the center, add ¼ to ½ cup more broth or water and continue cooking over medium-low heat until the lentils are soft. Remove the cloves before serving. Season with salt and pepper.

PER SERVING: CALORIES 160 • PROTEIN 10 G • CARBOHYDRATE 25 G • FAT 2.9 G • CHOLESTEROL 0 MG • SODIUM 14.3 MG • 16% CALORIES FROM FAT • OUTSTANDING SOURCE OF VITAMIN C; FOLACIN • VERY GOOD SOURCE OF IRON • GOOD SOURCE OF VITAMIN B₁

•

Rich, Savory Lentil Ragout

Serves 6 as a starter or side dish,
or 4 as a main course

TOTAL TIME: 1 HOUR, 20 MINUTES, NOT INCLUDING TIME
TO MAKE FLAVOR KICK OR THE BROTH
TIME TO PREPARE: 30 MINUTES, INCLUDING TIME TO SAUTÉ
COOKING TIME: 50 MINUTES
REFRIGERATION/FREEZING: REFRIGERATE UP TO 3 DAYS.
FREEZE UP TO 6 MONTHS.

Enhanced with Flavor Kick, it's the richest of these ragouts. Serve it with bulgur or barley or on whole wheat penne.

1 tablespoon extra virgin olive oil
2 cups chopped onions
2 large leeks, white part only, washed and chopped
2 large celery stalks, trimmed and chopped
2 large carrots, peeled and chopped
3 garlic cloves, minced
1 tablespoon crumbled dried oregano
2 teaspoons ground cinnamon
2 whole cloves
1 tablespoon tomato paste
2 tablespoons red wine vinegar
1 cup uncooked lentils, rinsed
¼ cup Flavor Kick (see page 170) plus 3 cups vegetable broth (see page 165), or 3¼ cups vegetable broth

Heat the olive oil in a large, deep skillet over medium-high heat. Add the onions, leeks, celery, carrots, garlic, oregano, cinnamon, and cloves, and sauté over medium heat until the vegetables are soft, about 15 minutes.

Add the tomato paste and vinegar, and stir to blend. Stir in the lentils, Flavor Kick, and vegetable broth. Turn up the heat to medium-high, and bring the sauce to a simmer. Cover and turn down the heat to medium-low, and cook until the lentils are soft and most of the liquid has been absorbed, about 50 minutes.

PER SERVING (¼ RECIPE): CALORIES 286 • PROTEIN 16.2 G • CARBOHYDRATE 49 G • FAT 4.2 G • CHOLESTEROL 0 MG • SODIUM 82.3 MG • 13% CALORIES FROM FAT • OUTSTANDING SOURCE OF VITAMIN A; FOLACIN • VERY GOOD SOURCE OF VITAMINS B₁, B₆; IRON • GOOD SOURCE OF VITAMINS B₂, B₃; CALCIUM, ZINC

•

TOMATO AND MUSHROOM RAGOUT

Serves 4

TOTAL TIME: ABOUT 55 MINUTES
TIME TO PREPARE: ABOUT 30 MINUTES, INCLUDING TIME
   TO SAUTÉ
COOKING TIME: ABOUT 25 MINUTES
DO AHEAD: YOU CAN PEEL, SEED, AND CHOP THE TOMATOES
   UP TO 3 DAYS IN ADVANCE. REFRIGERATE UNTIL READY
   TO USE.
REFRIGERATION/FREEZING: REFRIGERATE UP TO 3 DAYS.
   FREEZE UP TO 6 MONTHS.

Certain words just send me. "Porridge" is one; "ragout" is another. They're Big Woolly Blanket foods, thick, warm, and consoling. Serve this one over freshly cooked sturdy pasta, such as radiatore, or try it on polenta (see page 324).

2 teaspoons extra virgin olive oil
1 onion, chopped
2 garlic cloves, minced
1 teaspoon crumbled dried herbes de Provence
   (see page 559)
½ teaspoon whole fennel seeds
½ pound portobello, or other firm mushrooms,
   such as cremini, chopped
1 tablespoon balsamic vinegar

4 fresh medium tomatoes, peeled, seeded, and
   chopped (see page 544)
Salt and freshly ground black pepper to taste

Heat the oil in a large skillet over medium-high heat, swirling the pan to coat the bottom. Add the onion, garlic, herbes de Provence, and fennel seeds and sauté until the onion is soft and translucent, about 7 minutes.

Add the mushrooms, turn the heat down to medium, and continue to sauté, stirring often, until they're cooked through and they've given up most of their liquid, about 12 minutes. Stir in the balsamic vinegar, raise the heat to medium-high, and keep stirring until the liquid evaporates, about 4 minutes. Add the tomatoes, stir well, and cook until the tomatoes break down into a very thick sauce, about 20 minutes. Stir often to prevent sticking. Season with salt and pepper.

PER SERVING: CALORIES 76 • PROTEIN 2.7 G • CARBOHYDRATE 12 G • FAT 2.9 G • CHOLESTEROL 0 MG • SODIUM 14.7 MG • 31% CALORIES FROM FAT • OUTSTANDING SOURCE OF VITAMIN C • GOOD SOURCE OF VITAMINS B₁, B₂, B₃, B₆

THREE-MUSHROOM SAUCE

Serves 6 as a starter or side dish, or
4 as a main course

TOTAL TIME: 1 HOUR, 20 MINUTES, INCLUDING TIME TO
SOAK THE MUSHROOMS
TIME TO PREPARE: 40 MINUTES, INCLUDING TIME TO SAUTÉ
COOKING TIME: 40 MINUTES
REFRIGERATION/FREEZING: REFRIGERATE UP TO 3 DAYS.
FREEZE UP TO 6 MONTHS.

Fresh mushrooms alone would be perfectly wonderful, but dried porcini boost the taste of this wintertime sauce into another dimension. Serve this sauce over a thick-cut pasta, such as fettuccine, tagliatelle, or penne.

1 ounce dried porcini mushrooms

⅔ cup warm water

1 tablespoon unsalted butter or extra virgin olive oil

2 leeks, white part plus 1 inch of greens, washed and sliced

4 scallions, white part plus 1 inch of greens, sliced

2 shallots, minced

1 tablespoon balsamic vinegar

3 tablespoons minced fresh dill

3 cups sliced mixed fresh mushrooms, such as shiitake, portobello, white button

1 tablespoon arrowroot or cornstarch

½ cup evaporated skim milk

⅓ cup finely diced Taleggio or Muenster cheese

Soak the dried mushrooms in the warm water until they are soft, about 40 minutes.

Drain and reserve the water. Chop the porcini coarsely.

Heat the butter or oil in a large, deep skillet over medium heat. Add the leeks, scallions, and shallots, and turn down the heat to medium-low. Sauté the vegetables until they are soft, stirring often, about 10 minutes.

Add the vinegar, turn up the heat to medium-high, and cook, stirring constantly, until the liquid has evaporated, about 3 minutes.

Add the dill and the porcini and fresh mushrooms, and continue to cook, stirring constantly until the mushrooms darken and begin to release liquid, about 3 minutes. Stir in half the reserved soaking water. Add the arrowroot or cornstarch to the remaining soaking water, blend well with a fork, and add to the mushroom mixture along with the evaporated milk.

Turn up the heat to medium-high and stir constantly until the sauce thickens, about 7 minutes. Lower the heat to medium-low and add the Taleggio or Muenster, and continue to stir until the cheese has melted and blended evenly throughout.

PER SERVING (¼ RECIPE): CALORIES 180 • PROTEIN 9.3 G • CARBOHYDRATE 22 G • FAT 6.4 G • CHOLESTEROL 17.8 MG • SODIUM 116 MG • 31% CALORIES FROM FAT • VERY GOOD SOURCE OF VITAMINS B₂, C; CALCIUM, IRON • GOOD SOURCE OF VITAMINS A, B₃, B₆; FOLACIN

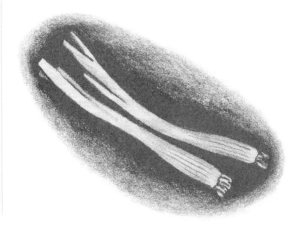

CHUNKY SAFFRON-BEAN SAUCE

Serves 4

TOTAL TIME: ABOUT 1 HOUR
TIME TO PREPARE: ABOUT 50 MINUTES, INCLUDING TIME
  TO SAUTÉ
COOKING TIME: 10 MINUTES
DO AHEAD: YOU CAN MAKE THE BEANS UP TO 1 WEEK IN
  ADVANCE. YOU CAN MAKE THE SAFFRON PASTE UP TO 4
  DAYS AHEAD. REFRIGERATE BOTH UNTIL READY TO USE.
REFRIGERATION/FREEZING: REFRIGERATE UP TO 3 DAYS.
  FREEZE UP TO 6 MONTHS.

This big *saffron-seasoned sauce lives up to its billing only if you boil the beans yourself. Canned beans are too mushy to be "chunky." This is wonderful over ricotta-stuffed pasta shells (page 301).*

2 teaspoons extra virgin olive oil

1 medium white or yellow onion, chopped

1 large red onion, chopped

1 carrot, peeled and chopped

1 celery stalk, trimmed and chopped

2 teaspoons crumbled dried basil

2 teaspoons crumbled dried oregano

1 teaspoon whole fennel seeds

2 cups chopped peeled fresh tomatoes (see page
    544), or canned chopped tomatoes,
    including juice

2 cups cooked mixed assorted beans, such as
    chickpeas, kidney, navy, black and/or pinto
    beans, drained and rinsed

2 cups chopped fresh spinach, or one 10-ounce
    package frozen chopped spinach, thawed
    and squeezed dry

1 recipe Saffron Seasoning Paste (recipe follows)

In a large skillet, heat the olive oil over medium heat. Add the onions, carrot, celery, basil, oregano, and fennel seeds and sauté until the vegetables are soft, about 14 minutes.

Stir in the tomatoes and beans, and simmer over medium-low, until the tomatoes cook down, and the sauce is thick, about 10 minutes. Meanwhile, make the Saffron Seasoning Paste. Stir in the spinach until everything's well combined.

Turn off the heat and stir in the Saffron Seasoning Paste. Let the sauce sit for 7 to 10 minutes before serving.

PER SERVING: CALORIES 216 • PROTEIN 10 G • CARBOHYDRATE 35.6 G • FAT 4.9 G • CHOLESTEROL 0 MG • SODIUM 57.8 MG • 19% CALORIES FROM FAT • OUTSTANDING SOURCE OF VITAMINS A, C; FOLACIN, CALCIUM • VERY GOOD SOURCE OF IRON • GOOD SOURCE OF VITAMINS B₁, B₂, B₆; ZINC

Saffron Seasoning Paste

Makes about 3 tablespoons

1 garlic clove, unpeeled

Generous pinch powdered saffron

2 tablespoons minced fresh basil, or 1 tablespoon
    crumbled dried basil

2 tablespoons nonfat sour cream

Heat a toaster oven or regular oven to 425°F. Wrap the garlic in foil and place it on a baking sheet. Bake until it's soft, about 15 minutes. Unwrap and let it cool.

Using your fingers, squeeze the garlic clove into a small bowl, and mash it with the saffron and basil. Stir in the sour cream to make a smooth, evenly colored paste.

One-Dish Pastas

ARTICHOKES, MUSHROOMS, AND POTATOES WITH WHOLE WHEAT PASTA

Serves 4

TOTAL TIME: ABOUT 1 HOUR, 55 MINUTES
TIME TO PREPARE: ABOUT 1 HOUR, 15 MINUTES, INCLUD-
ING TIME TO COOK THE ARTICHOKES AND SAUTÉ
COOKING TIME: ABOUT 25 MINUTES TO SIMMER, ABOUT 15
MINUTES TO COOK THE PASTA
DO AHEAD: YOU CAN PREPARE THE ARTICHOKES UP TO 2
DAYS AHEAD. REFRIGERATE UNTIL READY TO USE.
REFRIGERATION/FREEZING: REFRIGERATE UP TO 3 DAYS. DO
NOT FREEZE.

The poet T. S. Eliot wrote that April is the cruelest month, but I say it's February. Winter's tiresome already, but not nearly over, and there's little of anything good to eat. There are the first artichokes and mushrooms and potatoes, however, which may be enough to bridge the gap until spring.

4 medium artichokes, trimmed, quartered, and pared (see page 514), or one 10-ounce package frozen artichokes, thawed
1 tablespoon extra virgin olive oil
2 shallots, minced
4 scallions, white part plus 2 inches of greens, chopped
2 cups loosely packed sliced white button, cremini, or portobello mushrooms
1 tablespoon balsamic vinegar
2 cups canned chopped tomatoes, drained
2 teaspoons capers
2 medium potatoes, preferably Yukon Gold, peeled and sliced 1/3 inch thick
12 ounces dried whole wheat spaghetti
1/4 cup grated Asiago or Parmesan cheese, for garnish

If you're using fresh artichokes, bring enough water to cover the artichokes to a boil in a large saucepan. Add the artichokes, and let the water return to a boil. Cover the saucepan, reduce the heat to medium-low, and simmer until the artichokes are tender enough to pierce with a fork, about 15 minutes.

Meanwhile, heat the oil in a large skillet over medium-high heat. When it's hot, add the shallots and scallions. Reduce the heat to medium and sauté, stirring often, until the vegetables are soft, about 7 minutes. Add the mushrooms and continue cooking until they color and begin to give up liquid, about 6 minutes. Stir in the vinegar, tomatoes, capers, potatoes, and cooked fresh or thawed frozen artichokes, and bring to a simmer.

Cover and reduce the heat to low. Cook, stirring often, until the potatoes have cooked through, about 20 minutes. Meanwhile, prepare the spaghetti according to the package directions. Drain.

Serve the sauce over the hot whole wheat spaghetti, sprinkled with the cheese.

PER SERVING: CALORIES 342 • PROTEIN 12.6 G • CARBOHYDRATE 60 G • FAT 6.8 G • CHOLESTEROL 6.1 MG • SODIUM 71.3 MG • 18% CALORIES FROM FAT • OUTSTANDING SOURCE OF VITAMIN C • VERY GOOD SOURCE OF VITAMINS B₁, B₂, B₃, B₆; FOLACIN • GOOD SOURCE OF CALCIUM, IRON, ZINC

SWEET BLACK BEANS ON WHOLE WHEAT PENNE

Serves 4

TOTAL TIME: ABOUT 1 HOUR, NOT INCLUDING TIME TO COOK THE BEANS

TIME TO PREPARE: ABOUT 45 MINUTES, INCLUDING TIME TO SAUTÉ

DO AHEAD: YOU CAN MAKE THE BEANS UP TO 1 WEEK IN ADVANCE. REFRIGERATE UNTIL READY TO USE.

REFRIGERATION/FREEZING: REFRIGERATE UP TO 3 DAYS. FREEZE UP TO 6 MONTHS.

Black beans on whole wheat pasta" sounds like one of those coarse, punishing dishes from the days when some vegetarians seemed to believe that the best diet comprised foods that taste bad. In fact this dish represents how far we've come since then. Here, and in current vegetarian cooking overall, sophisticated seasonings and produce, fresh dried legumes, and good pasta make vegetarianism a rich cuisine, not just a way of life.

1 tablespoon extra virgin olive oil

1 onion, chopped

1 fennel bulb, without leafy fronds, chopped, or
   3 celery stalks, trimmed and chopped

½ small red bell pepper, cored, seeded, and
   chopped

¼ cup loosely packed minced fresh cilantro

2 tablespoons minced fresh parsley

2 teaspoons ground cumin

1 teaspoon ground coriander

1 tablespoon balsamic vinegar

¼ cup fresh orange juice

2 cups cooked black beans, preferably black
   runner beans, drained and rinsed

12 ounces dried whole wheat penne

Heat the oil in a large skillet over medium-high heat. When it's hot, add the onion, fennel or celery, red pepper, cilantro, parsley, cumin, and coriander. Reduce the heat to medium and sauté, stirring often, until the vegetables have softened, about 12 minutes. Add the vinegar and stir until most of it has evaporated, about 2 minutes. Add the orange juice and stir until it reduces slightly, about 3 minutes. Stir in the beans, lower the heat to medium-low, and cook, stirring often, for 5 minutes.

Meanwhile, prepare the penne according to the package directions. Drain the pasta and toss it with the bean mixture. Serve warm, room temperature, or cold as a salad.

PER SERVING: CALORIES 348 • PROTEIN 16 G • CARBOHYDRATE 64 G • FAT 5 G • CHOLESTEROL 0 MG • SODIUM 35 MG • 12% CALORIES FROM FAT • OUTSTANDING SOURCE OF VITAMIN C; FOLACIN • VERY GOOD SOURCE OF VITAMIN B₁; IRON • GOOD SOURCE OF ZINC

PASTA WITH ROASTED FRESH TOMATO

Serves 6

TOTAL TIME: ABOUT 10 MINUTES, NOT INCLUDING TIME TO ROAST THE TOMATOES

TIME TO PREPARE: ABOUT 3 MINUTES

COOKING TIME: ABOUT 7 MINUTES TO COOK THE PASTA

DO AHEAD: YOU CAN ROAST THE TOMATOES UP TO 2 DAYS IN ADVANCE. COVER AND REFRIGERATE.

REFRIGERATION/FREEZING: REFRIGERATE UP TO 2 DAYS. DO NOT FREEZE.

So swift, so simple, so good.

1 cup part-skim ricotta cheese (don't use nonfat for this; it doesn't have enough body)

¼ cup grated Parmesan cheese, plus additional for garnish (optional)

2 tablespoons minced fresh oregano, or 1 tablespoon crumbled dried oregano

1 recipe Roasted Fresh Tomatoes (see page 218)

1 pound dried short pasta, such as penne or farfalle

In a large glass or ceramic mixing bowl, combine the ricotta, ¼ cup Parmesan, and oregano. Set aside. Chop the roasted tomatoes, and set them aside, too.

Cook the pasta according to the package directions. Drain, and toss well with the ricotta mixture and roasted tomatoes.

Serve hot, with additional Parmesan, if you'd like.

PER SERVING: CALORIES 255 • PROTEIN 14 G • CARBOHYDRATE 40 G • FAT 4.8 G • CHOLESTEROL 3.2 MG • SODIUM 95 MG • 17% CALORIES FROM FAT • OUTSTANDING SOURCE OF VITAMIN C • VERY GOOD SOURCE OF VITAMINS B₁, B₃; IRON • GOOD SOURCE OF VITAMINS A, B₂; CALCIUM

CHILLED ORECCHIETTE WITH PESTO AND FRESH TOMATO

Serves 6 as a starter or side dish, or 4 as a main dish

TOTAL TIME: 3 HOURS, 20 MINUTES, INCLUDING TIME TO CHILL, BUT NOT INCLUDING TIME TO COOK THE PASTA

TIME TO PREPARE: ABOUT 20 MINUTES

COOKING TIME: INCLUDED IN TIME TO PREPARE

DO AHEAD: YOU CAN MAKE THE PESTO UP TO 1 WEEK IN ADVANCE. REFRIGERATE UNTIL READY TO USE.

REFRIGERATION/FREEZING: REFRIGERATE UP TO 3 DAYS. DO NOT FREEZE.

Orecchiette (little ears) is the perfect pasta for pesto. It's short and thick, with shallow "bowls" to cup the sauce.

Pesto

1 cup fresh basil leaves

¼ cup fresh flat-leaf parsley

1 small garlic clove, quartered

1 tablespoon extra virgin olive oil

2 teaspoons fresh lemon juice

¼ cup grated Parmesan cheese

1 tomato, peeled, seeded, and chopped (see page 544)

¼ cup minced oil-cured black olives

2 tablespoons capers

3 cups cooked orecchiette pasta

To make the Pesto

Combine the basil, parsley, garlic, olive oil, lemon juice, and Parmesan in a blender or a compact food processor. Process in short spurts until the ingredients are thoroughly combined. Continue processing steadily for 1 minute to make a paste.

Scrape the pesto into a mixing bowl, and add the tomato, olives, and capers. Stir well. Add the pasta and toss until it's thoroughly coated.

Refrigerate until chilled through, at least 3 hours. Toss again before serving.

PER SERVING (¼ RECIPE): CALORIES 197 • PROTEIN 7.4 G • CARBOHYDRATE 27 G • FAT 6.5 G • CHOLESTEROL 4.9 MG • SODIUM 216 MG • 30% CALORIES FROM FAT • VERY GOOD SOURCE OF VITAMIN C • GOOD SOURCE OF VITAMIN B₁: CALCIUM, IRON

•

SHORT PASTA WITH SPINACH, RAISINS, AND CHICKPEAS

Serves 4 as a starter or side dish, or 2 as a main dish

TOTAL TIME: ABOUT 40 MINUTES
TIME TO PREPARE: ABOUT 30 MINUTES, INCLUDING TIME TO SAUTÉ
COOKING TIME: 10 MINUTES TO COOK THE PASTA
REFRIGERATION/FREEZING: REFRIGERATE UP TO 2 DAYS. DO NOT FREEZE.

It's a shame about Henry VIII. Not just the bit about the wives, but one of the things that happened as a consequence. When, in a huff over his divorce decree, the king quit the Catholic Church, he also abandoned Lent. Once it was no longer necessary to give up meat for forty days each year, the English dropped fresh produce from their diet, or went on to prepare it so poorly, you almost wish they had. Meanwhile, the French and Italians, who stuck with the Church, developed scores of vegetable entrées for sustenance throughout the long "fasting" season.

Evidently their stomachs are not as strong as their faith; giving up meat can't be much of a penance with dishes like this to replace it.

2 teaspoons extra virgin olive oil
1 small white onion, minced
2 cups loosely packed shredded fresh spinach
2 tablespoons chopped walnuts
2 tablespoons raisins
1 cup cooked chickpeas, drained and rinsed
12 ounces dried short pasta, such as small shells, orecchiette, or gnocchetti
⅔ cup nonfat or part-skim ricotta cheese

Heat the oil in a large skillet over medium-high heat. When it's hot, add the onion. Reduce the heat to medium and sauté, stirring often, until the onion is soft and limp, about 8 minutes. Add the spinach, walnuts, raisins, and chickpeas, and stir until the spinach wilts, about 3 minutes. Remove from the heat.

Meanwhile, make the pasta according to the package directions. While the pasta is cooking, puree the ricotta cheese in a food processor or blender, making it smooth and creamy. Stir it into the skillet. Drain the pasta in a colander, then toss the pasta into the skillet and stir well with a wooden spoon to coat with the sauce.

PER SERVING (½ RECIPE): CALORIES 292 • PROTEIN 15 G • CARBOHYDRATE 44 G • FAT 6.3 G • CHOLESTEROL 0 MG • SODIUM 27.3 MG • 19% CALORIES FROM FAT • VERY GOOD SOURCE OF FOLACIN • GOOD SOURCE OF VITAMINS A, B₁, B₂, B₃, B₆, C; IRON

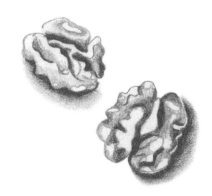

BROCCOLI RABE WITH LINGUINE

Serves 4

TOTAL TIME: ABOUT 30 MINUTES

TIME TO PREPARE: 20 MINUTES, INCLUDING TIME TO SAUTÉ

COOKING TIME: 10 MINUTES

REFRIGERATION/FREEZING: REFRIGERATE UP TO 2 DAYS. DO NOT FREEZE.

When I lived in Milan I bought my produce from a couple named Anna and Tomasso. Anna grew up in Puglia and was dying to go back to visit. But Tomasso didn't want any part of it, so she returned only in memories, most of which concerned food, and involved comparisons unfavorable to the merchandise for sale at her own stand. The cauliflower in Puglia were much bigger, the melons much sweeter, the eggplant firmer, she said. She also gave me cooking tips, which were particularly helpful when it came to fixing what's called cima *in Italy and broccoli rabe over here. This sharp, leafy vegetable, something like a cross between broccoli and chard, is delicious done up the way Anna described: sautéed in olive oil, seasoned with hot pepper flakes, and tossed with pasta.*

1 tablespoon extra virgin olive oil

1 garlic clove, minced

¼ cup minced fresh parsley

1 pound broccoli rabe, chopped

3 tablespoons minced dry-packed (not in oil) sun-dried tomatoes

¼ cup chopped oil-cured black olives

½ cup nonfat or part-skim ricotta

¼ cup grated Parmesan cheese

1 teaspoon red pepper flakes

12 ounces linguine

In a large skillet with a cover, heat the olive oil over medium-high heat. Add the garlic and parsley and sauté, stirring constantly, until the garlic starts to color, about 3 minutes.

Add the broccoli rabe, lower the heat to medium-low, cover, and cook, lifting the cover occasionally to stir, until the broccoli rabe turns bright green, 3 to 4 minutes. Remove from the heat.

In a large mixing bowl, combine the sun-dried tomatoes, olives, ricotta, Parmesan, and red pepper flakes. Add the broccoli rabe and stir to combine thoroughly.

Cook the pasta according to the package directions. Drain, and toss well with the broccoli mixture.

PER SERVING: CALORIES 133 • PROTEIN 8.3 G • CARBOHYDRATE 7.1 G • FAT 8.7 G • CHOLESTEROL 14.4 MG • SODIUM 284 MG • 56% CALORIES FROM FAT • OUT-STANDING SOURCE OF VITAMIN C • VERY GOOD SOURCE OF CALCIUM • GOOD SOURCE OF VITAMINS A, B₂; FOLACIN

FRESH ARTICHOKES ON PASTA

Serves 4 as a starter or side dish, or 2 as a main dish

TOTAL TIME: ABOUT 1 HOUR
TIME TO PREPARE: 45 MINUTES, INCLUDING TIME TO SAUTÉ
COOKING TIME: 10 MINUTES TO COOK THE PASTA
DO AHEAD: YOU CAN COOK THE ARTICHOKES UP TO 2
DAYS AHEAD. REFRIGERATE UNTIL READY TO USE.
REFRIGERATION/FREEZING: REFRIGERATE UP TO 3 DAYS. DO
NOT FREEZE.

Artichokes were one of the many foods Catherine de Médicis brought with her to France when she moved there from Tuscany to marry the Dauphin. She was known to have eaten so many on one occasion that she suffered debilitating stomachaches for months afterward.

I can relate, and haven't yet worked out how to resist the impulse to overdo it on the artichokes. Instead, I try to channel that impulse into dishes such as this, where it will serve the greater good—that is, my family and friends.

2 lemons
2 large artichokes
2 teaspoons extra virgin olive oil
1 shallot, minced
1 garlic clove, minced
2 tablespoons dry white wine
¼ cup minced fresh parsley
12 ounces dried long or short pasta, such as
  spaghetti, fusilli, or farfalle
¼ cup grated Parmesan cheese
Salt and freshly ground black pepper to taste

Fill a nonreactive saucepan with water and add the juice of 1 lemon. Cut away the stems of the artichokes and snap off all of the tough outer leaves. Once you reach the light green, tender, leaves, cut each artichoke in half lengthwise. With a melon scoop, paring knife, or teaspoon, scoop out the fuzz at the center. Cut the artichoke into quarters lengthwise. Put the artichokes in the saucepan and bring the water to a simmer over medium-high heat. Cover and cook until they are tender enough to pierce with a fork, about 15 minutes. Drain the artichokes thoroughly in a colander. In a large glass or ceramic bowl, grate 1 tablespoon zest and squeeze 1 tablespoon lemon juice from remaining lemon. Add the artichokes and toss well.

Heat the oil in a large skillet over medium-high heat. When it is hot, add the shallot and garlic. Reduce the heat to medium and sauté, stirring, until the garlic starts to color, about 40 seconds. Add the wine, parsley, and remaining lemon zest from the second lemon. Stir until half of the liquid evaporates, about 2 minutes. Add the quartered artichokes and stir well.

Meanwhile, cook the pasta according to the package directions. Drain and toss with the cheese and artichoke mixture. Season with salt and pepper. Serve right away.

PER SERVING (½ RECIPE): CALORIES 172 • PROTEIN 7.7 G • CARBOHYDRATE 25 G • FAT 4.6 G • CHOLESTEROL 4.9 MG • SODIUM 177 MG • 24% CALORIES FROM FAT • VERY GOOD SOURCE OF VITAMIN C • GOOD SOURCE OF VITAMIN B₁: FOLACIN, CALCIUM, IRON

ANGEL-HAIR PASTA WITH ASPARAGUS AND CHERRY TOMATOES

Serves 4 as a starter or side dish, or
2 as a main dish

TOTAL TIME: ABOUT 35 MINUTES
TIME TO PREPARE: 25 MINUTES, INCLUDING TIME TO SAUTÉ
REFRIGERATION/FREEZING: REFRIGERATE OVERNIGHT. DO
NOT FREEZE.

Cooking with cherry tomatoes is like getting permission to cheat on a test. You can't peel them, so you're spared that much trouble by default. Buy them ripe; if they're opaque orange, they'll be too tart. If they're full, rich red, soft but not squishy, they'll be perfect.

2 teaspoons extra virgin olive oil

1 garlic clove, minced

1 shallot, minced

2 tablespoons minced fresh parsley

2 tablespoons minced fresh mint

2 cups chopped cherry tomatoes

1 ½ cups asparagus tips (cut from approximately
    1 pound of whole asparagus; stems reserved
    for another use, such Asparagus Frittata,
    page 385)

12 ounces dried angel-hair pasta (capellini)

¼ cup grated Parmesan cheese, for garnish

Salt and freshly ground black pepper to taste

Heat the oil in a medium skillet over medium-high heat. When it's hot, add the garlic, shallot, parsley, and mint. Reduce the heat to medium and sauté, stirring often, until the shallot has softened, about 6 minutes. Add the cherry tomatoes and cook, stirring often, until the tomatoes cook down into a pulpy sauce, about 7 minutes. Stir in the asparagus tips, cover, and let them cook until they're bright green and just cooked through, about 3 minutes (maybe longer if the tips are thick). Remove from the heat.

Meanwhile, cook the pasta according to the package directions. Drain in a colander, and toss with the sauce. Distribute the pasta evenly on serving plates and sprinkle each serving with cheese. Season with salt and pepper.

PER SERVING (½ RECIPE): CALORIES 156 • PROTEIN 7.1 G • CARBOHYDRATE 22 G • FAT 4.8 G • CHOLESTEROL 4.9 MG • SODIUM 124 MG • 27% CALORIES FROM FAT • VERY GOOD SOURCE OF VITAMIN C; FOLACIN • GOOD SOURCE OF VITAMINS B₁, B₂, B₃; CALCIUM, IRON

CHILLED PASTA SALAD WITH FRESH TOMATOES, CHICKPEAS, OLIVES, AND FETA CHEESE

Serves 6 as a starter or side dish, or
4 as a main dish

TOTAL TIME: ABOUT 3 HOURS, 30 MINUTES, INCLUDING
TIME TO CHILL, BUT NOT INCLUDING TIME TO COOK THE
CHICKPEAS
TIME TO PREPARE: ABOUT 25 MINUTES
COOKING TIME: INCLUDED IN TIME TO PREPARE
DO AHEAD: YOU CAN MAKE THIS UP TO 1 DAY IN ADVANCE.
REFRIGERATE UNTIL READY TO USE.
REFRIGERATION/FREEZING: REFRIGERATE UP TO 2 DAYS. DO
NOT FREEZE.

Beautiful women and specialty food merchants have more in common than you might imagine. A good-looking girl, no matter how clever or charming, must always suspect that her looks are her main draw, while a handsome grocer with a fine selection of olives and cheese may never know whether the women who come by his shop are there to see him or to check out his stock.

In Ken's case, it's both. Ken is Adonis and Epicurus rolled into one, and you can find him at a strip mall in Darien, Connecticut. Just get on line. It forms at nine on Saturday morning as women of all ages wait to be flirted into buying Tallegio, Roblouchon, or Montrachet nonpareil, here or anywhere I know of outside Italy or France. Old hands know they can have more time with Ken if they get into the olives, which give him special pride. He'll insist that you sample them, and he'll stand there with you, with just the right words to describe how they taste.

And so it happens that my refrigerator, like hundreds across Fairfield County, holds lots and lots of olives at any given time, but not, as the expression goes, "more than I know what to do with." For instance:

1 tablespoon extra virgin olive oil
1 garlic clove, thinly sliced
¼ cup minced fresh basil
1 pound tomatoes, peeled, seeded, and chopped (see page 544)
2 cups cooked chickpeas, drained and rinsed
⅓ cup chopped oil-cured black Greek or niçoise-style olives
½ cup crumbled feta cheese
2 teaspoons capers
6 cups cooked short pasta, such as penne rigate, farfalle, or radiatore

In a small skillet, heat the olive oil over medium heat. Add the garlic and swish it through the oil until it starts to color, about 3 minutes. Remove and discard it. Add the basil and stir well to flavor the oil. Remove the skillet from the heat.

In a mixing bowl, combine the tomatoes, chickpeas, olives, feta cheese, and capers. Add the pasta and the basil oil, and toss well. Chill for at least 3 hours. Toss again before serving.

PER SERVING (¼ RECIPE): CALORIES 444 • PROTEIN 18.3 G • CARBOHYDRATE 62 G • FAT 14.5 G • CHOLESTEROL 27.4 MG • SODIUM 594 MG • 29% CALORIES FROM FAT • OUTSTANDING SOURCE OF FOLACIN • VERY GOOD SOURCE OF VITAMINS B₁, C; CALCIUM, IRON • GOOD SOURCE OF VITAMINS B₂, B₃, B₆; ZINC

GNOCHETTI WITH SPINACH AND RICOTTA SALATA

Serves 4

TOTAL TIME: ABOUT 25 MINUTES
TIME TO PREPARE: ABOUT 5 MINUTES
COOKING TIME: ABOUT 20 MINUTES
REFRIGERATION/FREEZING: REFRIGERATE UP TO 3 DAYS.
   FREEZE UP TO 5 MONTHS.

Ricotta salata is ricotta cheese that's been drained, dried, and hardened just enough to crumble. It's best in simple sauces because its delicate flavor is easily overwhelmed.

2 teaspoons extra virgin olive oil
2 large leeks, white part only, washed and
   chopped
4 scallions, white part only, minced
2 teaspoons white wine vinegar
1 small yellow pepper, roasted, peeled, and diced
   (see page 534)
2 cups torn fresh spinach
3 cups dried gnocchetti
½ cup crumbled ricotta salata

In a medium skillet, heat the olive oil over medium heat. When it is hot, add the leeks and scallions, and sauté over medium-low until soft, about 7 minutes. Add the vinegar, turn up the heat to medium-high, and stir until most of the liquid has evaporated. Turn down the heat to medium-low. Add the yellow pepper and the spinach, and stir just until the spinach turns bright green, about 2 minutes. Remove from the heat.

Meanwhile, prepare the gnocchetti according to the package directions. Drain, then toss with the leek mixture. Add the cheese and toss thoroughly again. Serve right away.

PER SERVING: CALORIES 252 • PROTEIN 9.8 G • CARBOHYDRATE 38 G • FAT 25 G • CHOLESTEROL 15.5 MG • SODIUM 63.3 MG • 25% CALORIES FROM FAT • OUTSTANDING SOURCE OF VITAMINS A, C • VERY GOOD SOURCE OF FOLACIN, IRON • GOOD SOURCE OF VITAMINS B₁, B₂, B₃, B₆; CALCIUM

•

ORANGE-SESAME-TEMPEH SOBA

Serves 4

TOTAL TIME: ABOUT 1 HOUR, 45 MINUTES, TO 3 HOURS,
   45 MINUTES, INCLUDING TIME TO MARINATE THE TEMPEH
   AND SOAK THE MUSHROOMS
TIME TO PREPARE: ABOUT 25 MINUTES, INCLUDING TIME
   TO SAUTÉ
EQUIPMENT: WOK
DO AHEAD: MARINATE THE TEMPEH UP TO 4 HOURS BEFORE
   CONTINUING WITH THE RECIPE.
REFRIGERATION/FREEZING: REFRIGERATE UP TO 2 DAYS. DO
   NOT FREEZE.

Having more than come to terms with tofu, I'm still not sold on tempeh. Even forgetting that fermented soybeans aren't the most mouth-watering concept, and that the stuff looks like an allergic reaction, I find it tastes too strong to be as versatile as tofu, and that taste isn't all that inspiring for me.

So why cook with it at all? Because it's there, and it's nourishing, and it can even, in the right context, such as this, taste very good.

1 cup fresh orange juice
2 tablespoons low-sodium soy sauce
1 tablespoon rice vinegar
1 tablespoon honey
2 garlic cloves, minced

1 tablespoon sesame seeds, toasted (see Note, page 122)

2 tablespoons grated peeled fresh ginger

2 scallions, including greens, minced

2 leeks, white part only, minced

⅓ cup minced fresh cilantro

1 pound tempeh, cut into 1-inch cubes

4 dried shiitake mushrooms

½ cup warm water

1 tablespoon canola or vegetable oil

1 shallot, minced

2 tablespoons minced fresh basil

6 fresh shiitake mushrooms, sliced

½ pound asparagus, trimmed, pared, and chopped

1 tablespoon cornstarch

14 ounces soba noodles

In a large glass or earthenware bowl, combine the orange juice, soy sauce, vinegar, honey, half of the garlic, sesame seeds, half of the ginger, half of the scallions, half of the leeks, and half of the cilantro. Add the tempeh, and stir well to coat. Cover with plastic wrap and refrigerate for 1 to 3 hours.

Place the dried shiitake mushrooms in a small bowl and add the warm water. Dunk the mushrooms several times with your hands to moisten them, then set them aside until they are soft, about 20 minutes.

Heat the oil in a wok over medium-high heat. When it's hot, add the shallot and basil along with the remaining garlic, ginger, scallions, leeks, and cilantro. Reduce the heat to medium-low and stir until the vegetables have seasoned the oil, about 2 minutes. Remove the dried shiitakes from the soaking liquid, reserving the liquid. Chop the dried mushrooms and add them to the wok along with the fresh mushrooms. Toss well. Drain the tempeh, saving the marinade, and add the tempeh to the wok. Stir for 2 minutes, to coat with the other ingredients.

Add the tempeh marinade to the wok. Stir in the asparagus, and keep stirring until it turns bright green, about 3 minutes. Stir the cornstarch into the mushroom soaking liquid, and add the mixture to the wok. Stir until the sauce in the wok thickens, about 3 to 4 minutes. Turn off the heat.

Meanwhile, prepare the soba noodles according to the package directions. Drain, and serve at once, topped with the hot tempeh mixture.

PER SERVING: CALORIES 498 • PROTEIN 31.5 G • CARBOHYDRATE 70 G • FAT 14 G • CHOLESTEROL 0 MG • SODIUM 490 MG • 24% CALORIES FROM FAT • OUTSTANDING SOURCE OF VITAMINS B₃, C; FOLACIN • VERY GOOD SOURCE OF VITAMINS B₁, B₂, B₆, B₁₂; IRON, ZINC • GOOD SOURCE OF VITAMIN A; CALCIUM

QUICK COLD SESAME NOODLES

Serves 4 as a starter or side dish, or
2 as a main dish

TOTAL TIME: 3 HOURS, 25 MINUTES, INCLUDING TIME TO
  CHILL
TIME TO PREPARE: 15 MINUTES
COOKING TIME: 10 MINUTES
REFRIGERATION/FREEZING: REFRIGERATE OVERNIGHT. DO
  NOT FREEZE.

Given the current paper shortage, I hate to waste yet more space on the fallacy that Marco Polo discovered pasta in China and subsequently introduced it to Italy. If those who insist on this version of events would simply consult the source, they'd find that Polo "discovered" that people in China ate pasta, just as the folks back in Venice did. I don't know why everyone's so concerned with which country influenced the other, when it's possible that each came to pasta independently at roughly the same time.

But there's no doubt which influence dominates here. Don't be alarmed by the peanut butter; there's just a bit, and it buffers the tahini, which would taste too strong without it.

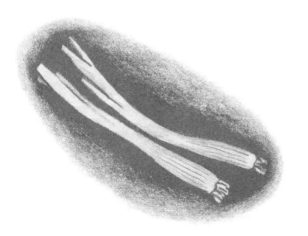

1 small garlic clove, grated
2 teaspoons grated peeled fresh ginger
1 scallion, including greens, chopped
1 tablespoon unsalted peanut butter
1 tablespoon tahini
1 teaspoon low-sodium soy sauce
1 tablespoon rice vinegar
1 tablespoon sesame seeds, toasted (see Note,
    page 122)
2 tablespoons hot water
8 ounces soba noodles or dried linguine

Place the garlic, ginger, scallion, peanut butter, tahini, soy sauce, rice vinegar, sesame seeds, and hot water in a food processor. Process until smooth. Transfer sauce to a large mixing bowl.

Cook the soba noodles or linguine according to the package directions. Drain, rinse with cold water (this keeps the noodles from sticking together), and toss with the sauce. Refrigerate until chilled through, at least 3 hours. Toss again before serving.

PER SERVING (½ RECIPE): CALORIES 241 • PROTEIN 10.5 G • CARBOHYDRATE 30.5 G • FAT 10.6 G • CHOLESTEROL 0 MG • SODIUM 208 MG • 37% CALORIES FROM FAT • GOOD SOURCE OF VITAMINS B1, B2; FOLACIN, IRON, ZINC

Filled Pastas

EARLY SPRING RAVIOLI

Serves 4

TOTAL TIME: ABOUT 2 HOURS, INCLUDING TIME TO MAKE
THE PASTA, BUT NOT INCLUDING TIME TO MAKE THE
BROTH
TIME TO PREPARE: ABOUT 1 HOUR, 45 MINUTES
COOKING TIME: 15 MINUTES
EQUIPMENT: PASTA MACHINE AND GROOVED ROLLER
(OPTIONAL)
DO AHEAD: YOU CAN MAKE THE PASTA UP TO 5 DAYS IN
ADVANCE. REFRIGERATE UNTIL READY TO USE. YOU CAN
PREPARE THE TOMATO SAUCE OR VEGETABLE BROTH UP
TO 6 MONTHS IN ADVANCE. FREEZE UNTIL READY TO USE.
REFRIGERATION/FREEZING: REFRIGERATE UP TO 3 DAYS.
FREEZE UP TO 6 MONTHS.

*P*asta machines make it easier, but the process
of rolling, cutting, and stuffing ravioli is still
an act of love. A good filling and apprecia-
tive guests make it all worthwhile. I'm happy to help
with the first, hoping that this delicious mix of aromatic vegetables and lemon-accented cheese will take
care of the rest for you.

Filling

2 teaspoons extra virgin olive oil
1 medium onion, finely chopped
1 medium carrot, finely chopped
1 leek, white part only, washed and finely
    chopped
1/2 fennel bulb, without leafy fronds, finely
    chopped, or 1 large celery stalk, trimmed
    and finely chopped
2 cups torn fresh spinach
1 tablespoon grated lemon zest
2/3 cup nonfat or part-skim ricotta cheese

1/4 cup grated Parmesan cheese
Freshly ground black pepper

1 recipe Pasta (see page 270), or 1 small package
    (about 16) wonton wrappers
1 recipe Simplest Fresh Tomato Sauce (see
    page 278), or 2 cups vegetable broth (see
    page 165)

To make the Filling

Heat the oil in a medium skillet over medium-
high heat. When it's hot, add the onion, carrot,
leek, and fennel or celery. Reduce the heat to
medium and sauté, stirring often, until the vegetables are soft, about 12 minutes. Add the
spinach and continue sautéing until the leaves
have wilted, about 2 minutes. Remove from the
heat.

Stir in the lemon zest, ricotta, and Parmesan. Mix well and season with pepper to taste.

If you're using fresh pasta, shape the ravioli
according to the directions on page 300, or follow the package directions for wonton wrappers. Fill the ravioli with spring mixture and
simmer them in water to cover, until done,
about 3 minutes. Drain and top with hot
tomato sauce. Or simmer them in the vegetable broth and serve with the broth. Either
way, serve immediately.

PER SERVING: CALORIES 143 • PROTEIN 8.9 G • CARBOHYDRATE 11 G • FAT 7.6 G •
CHOLESTEROL 17.4 MG • SODIUM 208 MG • 46% CALORIES FROM FAT • OUTSTAND-
ING SOURCE OF VITAMIN A • VERY GOOD SOURCE OF VITAMIN C; FOLACIN, CAL-
CIUM • GOOD SOURCE OF VITAMIN B₂

FILLED PASTA BASICS

One of the misconceptions Americans have about the way Italians eat is that they have fresh pasta all the time. In fact fresh pasta is a treat in Italy, as it is over here, more often served in restaurants than at home. Moreover, the fillings aren't fancy, and the sauces are spare. They keep it simple on principle: once you've taken the trouble to put fresh pasta on the table, you should be able to taste it.

THE (OTHER) PRINCIPLES

• When you're making lasagna with fresh pasta you don't have to cook the pasta before you fill it, as you do when you use dried noodles. It will cook thoroughly as it bakes. Fresh ravioli also cooks quickly. Check it after three minutes.

• Add flavor to your ravioli by simmering it in broth rather than cooking it in water. You can serve it in a little of the broth instead of sauce.

• Choose sauces and fillings that complement one another and won't obscure the taste of the pasta. Pair a light sauce with a light filling, and a richer sauce with a heavier filling. For example, if you're filling your pasta with fresh spring vegetables, top it with a light tomato sauce or with a drizzle of lemon juice and extra virgin olive oil. If you're loading the lasagna with baked eggplant and several cheeses, spoon a hearty ragout on top.

• Make sure your filling isn't watery, or the dish will be runny and the pasta may get gummy in the juices. If you use ratatouille, for example, drain the excess juice thoroughly before layering the lasagna. If you're using frozen spinach or chard, squeeze it as dry as possible. You can do this by putting the thawed vegetable in a sieve and pressing it against the side with the back of a spoon. And if you're using a soft cheese like ricotta or cottage cheese, include an absorbent binder such as bread crumbs and/or a dry cheese, such as Parmesan. (Use approximately ½ cup fine soft bread crumbs with each cup of soft cheese.)

• Don't cook fresh green vegetables such as asparagus, peas, and broccoli thoroughly before you add them to lasagna, or they may be mushy once the dish is done. Just blanch them (see page 502). However, since ravioli cooks quickly, the vegetables should be cooked through when you seal them in the pasta.

• When you're making ravioli, be sure to seal the pasta firmly around the filling, or you may lose the filling when it cooks. Don't overstuff the pasta, and leave a wide margin around the filling, about ¼ inch, so you can press the pasta together for a tight seal.

FILLINGS FOR LARGE SHELL-SHAPED PASTA

Easy Cheese Filling

Serves 4

TOTAL TIME: 20 MINUTES
TIME TO PREPARE: 5 MINUTES
COOKING TIME: ABOUT 15 MINUTES TO COOK THE PASTA
REFRIGERATION/FREEZING: REFRIGERATE UP TO 4 DAYS. DO
NOT FREEZE.

The simplest thing you can do with pasta and legitimately call it supper. Top with a hearty sauce, such as one of the lentil sauces (see pages 282 to 285), Tomato and Mushroom Ragout (see page 285), or Simplest Fresh Tomato Sauce (see page 278).

4 cups nonfat or part-skim ricotta cheese
¹/₂ cup grated Parmesan cheese
16 large dried pasta shells, such as seashells,
    manicotti, or cannelloni

In a food processor or blender, combine the ricotta and Parmesan. Process until smooth.

Cook the pasta according to the package directions. Fill the pasta with the cheese mixture, and bake according to the package directions.

PER SERVING: CALORIES 257 • PROTEIN 41 G • CARBOHYDRATE 12.5 G • FAT 3.7 G • CHOLESTEROL 9.8 MG • SODIUM 233 MG • 14% CALORIES FROM FAT • GOOD SOURCE OF CALCIUM

Spinach Filling

Serves 4

TOTAL TIME: ABOUT 20 MINUTES
TIME TO PREPARE: 3 MINUTES
COOKING TIME: ABOUT 15 MINUTES TO COOK THE PASTA
REFRIGERATION/FREEZING: REFRIGERATE UP TO 4 DAYS. DO
NOT FREEZE.

4 cups nonfat or part-skim ricotta cheese
1 cup shredded part-skim mozzarella or
    Monterey Jack cheese
¹/₂ cup grated Parmesan cheese
One 10-ounce package frozen chopped spinach,
    thawed and squeezed dry
¹/₄ teaspoon ground nutmeg
16 large dried pasta shells, such as seashells,
    manicotti, or cannelloni

In a food processor or blender, combine the ricotta, mozzarella or Jack cheese, Parmesan cheese, spinach, and nutmeg. Process until smooth.

Cook the pasta according to the package directions. Fill the pasta with the spinach mixture, and bake according to the package directions.

PER SERVING: CALORIES 353 • PROTEIN 51 G • CARBOHYDRATE 16 G • FAT 8.7 G • CHOLESTEROL 25 MG • SODIUM 434 MG • 23% CALORIES FROM FAT • OUTSTANDING SOURCE OF VITAMIN A; CALCIUM • VERY GOOD SOURCE OF VITAMIN C; FOLACIN • GOOD SOURCE OF VITAMIN B₂; ZINC

Other Fillings for Shells
Refried Bean Puree (see page 256)

LASAGNA WITH STEWED VEGETABLES

Serves 6

TOTAL TIME: ABOUT 1 HOUR, 40 MINUTES, NOT INCLUD-
ING TIME TO ROAST THE PEPPERS OR COOK THE BEANS
TIME TO PREPARE: ABOUT 35 MINUTES
COOKING TIME: ABOUT 1 HOUR
EQUIPMENT: PASTA MACHINE (OPTIONAL)
DO AHEAD: YOU CAN ROAST THE PEPPERS UP TO 2 DAYS IN
ADVANCE. YOU CAN ALSO MAKE THE SAUCE UP TO 2
DAYS IN ADVANCE. REFRIGERATE UNTIL READY TO USE.
REFRIGERATION/FREEZING: REFRIGERATE UP TO 3 DAYS.
FREEZE UP TO 2 MONTHS.

I have made the Parmesan optional so vegans can enjoy this delicious dish, which is splendid with or without cheese. If it seems like a big job to handle at one go, take two days to prepare it, using the do-ahead guidelines above.

4 miniature or Japanese eggplants

2 teaspoons extra virgin olive oil

1 onion, chopped

2 garlic cloves, minced

1 large red bell pepper, roasted, peeled, and
    chopped (see page 534)

1 large yellow bell pepper, roasted, peeled, and
    chopped (see page 534)

2 zucchini or summer squash, minced

¼ cup minced fresh basil

2 tablespoons minced fresh oregano, or 1
    tablespoon crumbled dried oregano

2 tablespoons balsamic vinegar

1 pound firm tofu, cut into 1-inch cubes

1 cup cooked robust, flavorful beans, such as
    cannellini, runner, or kidney, drained and
    rinsed

½ cup mixed oil-cured pitted olives, chopped

2 teaspoons capers

1 cup chopped peeled fresh tomatoes (see page
    544), or canned chopped tomatoes,
    including juice

¼ cup grated Parmesan cheese (optional)

1 recipe Pasta, rolled and cut for lasagna (see
    page 270), or 12 large wonton or spring-roll
    wrappers

Heat the oven to 425°F. Squirt a baking sheet with nonstick spray. Slice the eggplants into rounds ¼ inch thick and lay them in a single layer on the baking sheet. Bake in the center of the oven until soft, 7 to 10 minutes. Turn the slices and cook them briefly on the other side just to color, about 2 minutes. Remove and lower the oven to 375°F.

Heat the oil in a large skillet over medium-high heat. When it is hot, add the onion, garlic, bell peppers, zucchini or summer squash, basil, and oregano. Reduce the heat to medium and sauté, stirring often, until the vegetables have softened, about 10 minutes. Add the balsamic vinegar, turn up the heat to medium-high, and stir until it has evaporated, about 2 minutes.

Add the tofu, beans, olives, capers, and tomatoes and continue cooking, stirring often, until the tomatoes thicken and reduce, about 7 minutes. Stir in the eggplant slices and the Parmesan, if you'd like. Turn off the heat.

Squirt 6 custard cups or an 8-inch baking dish with nonstick spray. If using the custard cups, place a single sheet of pasta or a wonton or spring-roll wrapper on your work surface. Turn a cup upside down onto the pasta and run a knife around the rim to cut out a circle. Repeat until you've cut 12 circles. Place a spoonful of the vegetable mixture at the bottom of each cup. Cover with a round of pasta. Place a heaping spoonful or two of vegetables over that and cover with another round. Finish with a thick layer of vegetables.

If using a baking dish, spread a thin layer of the vegetables over the bottom. Cover with a layer of pasta. Top with more vegetables, then place another layer of pasta on top. Finish with a thick layer of vegetables.

Cover the cups or baking dish with aluminum foil and bake, covered, for 40 minutes. Remove the foil and continue baking for 10 minutes. Remove the lasagna from the oven and let it sit 15 minutes before inverting each cup onto a serving plate, or cutting the pan-baked lasagna into squares.

PER SERVING: CALORIES 245 • PROTEIN 19 G • CARBOHYDRATE 23.7 G • FAT 10.4 G • CHOLESTEROL 3.2 MG • SODIUM 253 MG • 35% CALORIES FROM FAT • OUTSTANDING SOURCE OF VITAMIN C; IRON • VERY GOOD SOURCE OF VITAMINS A, B₁; FOLACIN, CALCIUM • GOOD SOURCE OF VITAMINS B₂, B₆; ZINC

•

BAKED FRESH LASAGNA WITH ASPARAGUS CREAM

Serves 4

TOTAL TIME: ABOUT 1 HOUR, 20 MINUTES, NOT INCLUDING TIME TO MAKE PASTA
TIME TO PREPARE: ABOUT 1 HOUR
COOKING TIME: 20 MINUTES TO BAKE
EQUIPMENT: PASTA MACHINE (OPTIONAL)
REFRIGERATION/FREEZING: REFRIGERATE, UNCOOKED, 1 DAY. FREEZE UP TO 6 MONTHS.

Lasagna, as most Americans know it, is thick slabs of pasta, plastered with sauce and cheese, and baked until the noodles crinkle. It's a dish sons beg their mothers to make, then brag about to their friends. But this isn't all there is to lasagna. When it's made with fresh pasta, it must be layered with much lighter ingredients, as it is in this delectable dish.

2 pounds asparagus, trimmed
2 cups nonfat or part-skim ricotta cheese
2 teaspoons extra virgin olive oil
1 shallot, minced
2 tablespoons grated lemon zest
1 recipe Pasta, rolled and cut for lasagna (see page 270), or 8 large wonton or spring-roll wrappers
½ cup grated Parmesan cheese
1 teaspoon unsalted butter

Set aside half the asparagus and cut the rest into quarters. Cook the cut asparagus by heating 2 inches of water in a medium saucepan. When the water has come to a boil, add the cut asparagus, cover, and simmer gently until it is soft enough to puree, about 6 to 10 minutes, depending on the thickness of the stalks.

Remove the asparagus from the water and puree it in a food processor or blender, taking care not to overdo it, or the asparagus will liquefy. Add the ricotta and process until you have a thick cream of uniform color.

Heat the oil in a medium skillet over medium-high heat. When it is hot, add the shallot and lemon zest. Reduce the heat to medium and sauté, stirring often just to season the oil and soften the shallot, about 3 minutes.

Chop the remaining asparagus. Add it to the skillet, and stir until it turns bright green, about 4 minutes. Turn off the heat.

Heat the oven to 350°F.

Lightly grease an 8-inch gratin dish or baking dish or squirt with nonstick spray. Place a layer of pasta or the wonton wrappers on the bottom. (If using wonton wrappers, overlap them slightly to avoid cracks.) Spread a third of the asparagus cream on top. Place a layer of the sautéed asparagus over it, and sprinkle with a third of the grated Parmesan. Repeat with 2 more layers, ending with the last of the asparagus cream, sautéed asparagus, and Parmesan. Cut the butter into tiny pieces and distribute them evenly over the top.

Bake until the top is browned and bubbly, about 20 minutes.

PER SERVING: CALORIES 392 • PROTEIN 34.5 G • CARBOHYDRATE 46.7 G • FAT 19 G • CHOLESTEROL 49.8 MG • SODIUM 245 MG • 19% CALORIES FROM FAT • OUTSTANDING SOURCE OF VITAMIN C; FOLACIN • VERY GOOD SOURCE OF VITAMINS B₁, B₂; CALCIUM, IRON • GOOD SOURCE OF VITAMINS A, B₃, B₄; ZINC

•

Risottos

RISOTTO WITH HERBS
A Basic Risotto
Serves 4

TOTAL TIME: 50 MINUTES, NOT INCLUDING TIME TO MAKE THE BROTH
TIME TO PREPARE: 50 MINUTES
COOKING TIME: INCLUDED IN TIME TO PREPARE
REFRIGERATION/FREEZING: REFRIGERATE UP TO 2 DAYS. DO NOT FREEZE.

Here's a risotto to learn from, and to make time and again once you've got it down. It has lots of flavor, but no substantial protein source, so serve it as a first course or as a side dish with a hearty soup or salad.

4 cups vegetable broth (see page 165)
1 tablespoon extra virgin olive oil
2 shallots, minced
¼ cup minced mixed fresh herbs, such as oregano and basil, parsley and mint, or sage and thyme
1 cup arborio or carnaroli rice
¼ cup dry white wine
¼ cup grated Parmesan cheese, or more, if you'd like

Pour the vegetable broth into a large saucepan and bring it to a simmer over medium heat. Turn down the heat to medium low, keeping the broth at a simmer.

Meanwhile, heat the oil in a separate heavy saucepan over medium-high heat, swirling the pan to coat the bottom. Reduce the heat to medium-low. Add the shallots and minced herbs and stir until the herbs wilt and the shallots soften, about 6 minutes. Add the rice and stir to coat with the herbs, about 1 minute.

Using a ladle, add about 1 cup of the hot broth to the rice. Stir constantly over medium heat until the broth has been absorbed, about 5 minutes. Add another ladleful and keep stirring until this, too, has been absorbed.

Continue the process, adding broth about ½ cup at a time and stirring until the rice kernels are plump and no longer chalk white in the center. The risotto should look like creamy rice pudding, and the kernels should be nice and chewy. This should take 25 to 30 minutes altogether. Finally, stir in the wine and the grated Parmesan. Continue stirring until there's no liquid left on the surface and the cheese is well distributed throughout. Serve right away.

PER SERVING: CALORIES 245 • PROTEIN 6.2 G • CARBOHYDRATE 39 G • FAT 5.5 G • CHOLESTEROL 4.9 MG • SODIUM 121 MG • 22% CALORIES FROM FAT • GOOD SOURCE OF VITAMINS B₁, B₃; CALCIUM, IRON

RISOTTO BASICS

Even the simplest food can become silly if it gets trendy enough. Look what's happened to pizza. It started as lovely, fresh flat bread topped with tomatoes and herbs. Now it's a dumping ground for everything from bacon, lettuce, and tomatoes to pineapple and Spam.

Risotto seems headed in the same direction, as chefs too confident in their own creativity destroy the integrity of a dish that is best as a showcase for a *single* ingredient. A good risotto features one dominant flavor, with complementary seasonings added just for support. And while it's known —inexplicably—as a tricky dish, there's nothing complicated about it, as you'll see when you run down these basics, and as you'll affirm when you make it yourself.

• Use arborio or carnaroli rice. No other rice has the right starch content for risotto. Other rices will be too gummy, too mushy, or too firm.

• If you're going to be making risotto often, it's worth getting an enamel saucepan, such as those made by Le Creuset or Chantal. The rice won't stick as it cooks, and the pans are easy to clean.

• Use a good vegetable broth. The grains absorb every drop and all of the flavor in it. The better the broth, the better the risotto.

• Keep your broth, or whatever liquid you're adding, at a low simmer before it's added to the risotto. This helps the rice cook more evenly.

• You don't have to stand over the pot and stir every second, but make sure you stir often enough to keep the rice from sticking together or to the pan. Stir well every time you add broth and about every 2 minutes between additions. After a while, you'll develop a stirring pattern that works well for you.

• Serve the risotto right away, or it will become gummy. While leftover risotto is rarely good on its own, you can use it in other dishes, such as frittatas (see page 383) and filled vegetables (see page 361).

Make It Your Own

Don't barrage the basic recipe with additional ingredients; remember: the best risotto tastes intensely of one flavor.

❧ *Vegetables.* After you've sautéed the aromatic vegetables, such as the shallot, onion, and leeks, and just before you add the rice, add 1 cup of a finely chopped vegetable of your choice. Look through some of the recipes in this section for examples and guidelines.

❧ *Herbs.* Substitute any minced fresh herb, adding it as directed in the basic recipe. If you're using dried herbs, use half as much as the amount given for fresh.

❧ *Vegetable or Fruit Juice.* You can use tomato juice, carrot juice, apple juice, or orange juice in combination or in place of broth, provided the flavors complement the other ingredients. For example, you could use half tomato juice in Risotto with Fresh Tomato and Basil (see page 307) and half or all orange juice in Sweet Potato Risotto (see page 308). You'll need more juice than broth because the acid in the juice blocks absorption. Count on 5 cups of juice for each cup of rice.

❧ *Milk.* For a richer-tasting risotto, substitute 1 cup of milk for 1 cup of the broth. This works well in heartier risottos such as sweet potato. You'll notice that the Fresh Corn Risotto (see page 312) calls for milk exclusively. Milk conveys the true corn flavor far better than broth.

❧ *Vinegars.* For a lovely tang, substitute half as much vinegar (balsamic, red wine, white wine, herb, or fruit) for the amount of wine called for in the recipe (for example, instead of 2 tablespoons of wine, use 1 tablespoon vinegar).

❧ *Cheeses.* Substitute any grated cheese you'd like for the Parmesan, provided it goes with the rest of the ingredients. Any cheese would work

in the basic recipe, Risotto with Herbs (see page 304), while in the recipe for tomato-basil risotto (see page 307) you'd want to use either Parmesan, as specified, or another pungent Italian cheese such as Asiago, Pecorino, or Fontina. For the Fresh Corn Risotto (see page 312), cheddar is a natural choice, but Monterey Jack or Monterey Jack with jalapeños is delicious, too.

❧ *Sauce.* You can make a substantial main course of risotto by spooning the rice onto individual serving dishes, making a well in the center of each portion, and filling it with a hearty pasta sauce such as one of the lentil ragouts (see pages 282 to 285).

✎ *Filled Vegetables.* Use risotto to fill vegetables (see page 362). Try Bell Pepper Risotto (see page 313) in cored bell peppers; Artichoke Risotto (see page 315) in steamed, scooped-out artichokes; Sweet Potato Risotto (see page 308) in baked, scooped-out acorn squash.

RISOTTO WITH FRESH TOMATO AND BASIL

Serves 6 as a starter or side dish, or
4 as a main dish

TOTAL TIME: 50 MINUTES, NOT INCLUDING TIME TO MAKE
THE BROTH
TIME TO PREPARE: 50 MINUTES
COOKING TIME: INCLUDED IN TIME TO PREPARE
REFRIGERATION/FREEZING: REFRIGERATE UP TO 2 DAYS. DO
NOT FREEZE.

If summer had nothing else to recommend it, fresh basil and native tomatoes might be enough, especially in simple dishes such as this.

4 cups vegetable broth (see page 165)
1 tablespoon extra virgin olive oil
1 garlic clove, sliced
2 shallots, minced
½ cup torn fresh basil leaves
2 ripe tomatoes, peeled, seeded, and chopped
(see page 544)
1 cup arborio or carnaroli rice
¼ cup grated Parmesan cheese, or more, if you'd
like

Pour the vegetable broth into a large saucepan and bring it to a simmer over medium heat. Turn down the heat to medium-low, keeping the broth at a simmer.

Meanwhile, heat the oil in a separate heavy saucepan over medium-high heat, swirling the pan to coat the bottom. Add the garlic, and swish it through the oil to season it. When the garlic begins to color, about 40 seconds, remove and discard it. Add the shallots and basil and stir until the basil wilts and the shallots soften, about 6 minutes. Add the tomatoes and cook, stirring constantly, until they break down into a thick sauce, about 5 minutes. Add the rice and stir to coat with the tomatoes, about 1 minute.

Using a ladle, add about 1 cup of hot broth. Stir constantly over medium heat until the broth has been absorbed by the rice, about 5 minutes. Add another ladleful and keep stirring until this, too, has been absorbed.

Continue the process, adding broth about ½ cup at a time and stirring until the rice kernels are plump and no longer chalk white in the center. The risotto should look like creamy rice pudding, and the kernels should be nice and chewy. This should take 25 to 30 minutes altogether. Finally, stir in the final ¼ cup of broth and the grated Parmesan. Continue stirring until there's no liquid left on the surface and the cheese is well distributed throughout.

PER SERVING (¼ RECIPE): CALORIES 250 • PROTEIN 6.8 G • CARBOHYDRATE 42 G • FAT 5.8 G • CHOLESTEROL 4.9 MG • SODIUM 126 MG • 21% CALORIES FROM FAT • GOOD SOURCE OF VITAMINS B₁, B₃, C; CALCIUM, IRON

SWEET POTATO RISOTTO

Serves 6 as a starter or side dish, or
4 as a main dish

TOTAL TIME: ABOUT 45 MINUTES
TIME TO PREPARE: ABOUT 45 MINUTES
COOKING TIME: INCLUDED IN TIME TO PREPARE
REFRIGERATION/FREEZING: Refrigerate up to 2 days. Do
NOT FREEZE.

If you think you don't like sweet potatoes, try this once, and I'll bet you change your mind. Sweet potatoes are so nourishing, it's worth finding a way to enjoy them, and you may find none better than this creamy, cinnamon-spiked risotto.

4 cups vegetable broth (see page 165)
2 teaspoons unsalted butter
1 small onion, minced
1 medium sweet potato, peeled and chopped
1 cup arborio or carnaroli rice
2 tablespoons grated Parmesan cheese
Pinch ground nutmeg
Pinch ground cinnamon
Salt and freshly ground black pepper to taste

Pour the vegetable broth into a large saucepan and bring it to a simmer over medium heat. Turn down the heat to medium-low, keeping the broth at a simmer.

Meanwhile, in a medium, heavy saucepan, melt the butter over medium heat. Add the onion and sauté until it's soft, about 7 minutes. Add the sweet potato and stir until it begins to soften, about 6 minutes. Add the rice and stir to coat with the vegetables, about 1 minute.

Using a ladle, add about 1 cup of hot broth. Stir constantly over medium heat until the broth has been absorbed, about 5 minutes.

Add another ladleful and keep stirring until this, too, has been absorbed.

Continue the process, adding broth about ½ cup at a time and stirring, until the rice kernels are plump and no longer chalk white in the center. The risotto should look like creamy rice pudding, and the kernels should be nice and chewy. This should take 25 to 30 minutes altogether. Finally, stir in the final ladleful of broth and the grated Parmesan. Continue stirring until there's no liquid left on the surface and the cheese is well distributed throughout. Stir in the nutmeg and cinnamon. Season with salt and pepper, and serve right away.

PER SERVING (¼ RECIPE): CALORIES 248 • PROTEIN 5.4 G • CARBOHYDRATE 48 G • FAT 3.3 G • CHOLESTEROL 7.6 MG • SODIUM 66 MG • 12% CALORIES FROM FAT • OUTSTANDING SOURCE OF VITAMIN A • VERY GOOD SOURCE OF VITAMIN B₂ • GOOD SOURCE OF VITAMINS B₃, B₆, C; IRON

S P I N A C H   R I S O T T O

Serves 6 as a starter or side dish, or
4 as a main dish

TOTAL TIME: ABOUT 40 MINUTES
TIME TO PREPARE: ABOUT 40 MINUTES
COOKING TIME: INCLUDED IN TIME TO PREPARE
REFRIGERATION/FREEZING: REFRIGERATE UP TO 2 DAYS. DO
 NOT FREEZE.

Risotto tends to amplify the flavor of its main
ingredient; this dish tastes more like spinach
than spinach alone.

4 cups vegetable broth (see page 165)
2 teaspoons unsalted butter, or 2 teaspoons extra
 virgin olive oil
2 shallots, minced
4 scallions, white part only, minced
1 tablespoon minced fresh oregano, or 1½
 teaspoons crumbled dried oregano
1 cup arborio or carnaroli rice
2 cups finely chopped fresh spinach
3 tablespoons dry white wine, or 1 tablespoon
 white wine vinegar

¼ cup grated Parmesan cheese
2 tablespoons pine nuts, toasted (see Note, page
 122; optional)

Pour the vegetable broth into a large saucepan
and bring it to a simmer over medium heat.
Turn down the heat to medium-low, keeping
the broth at a simmer.

Meanwhile, melt the butter or heat the oil
in a medium, heavy saucepan. Sauté the shallots, scallions, and oregano until the shallots
and scallions soften, about 6 minutes. Add the
rice and the spinach and stir to coat with the
vegetables, about 1 minute. Add the wine or
vinegar and continue stirring until the liquid
evaporates, about 1 minute.

Using a ladle, add about 1 cup of hot
broth. Stir constantly over medium heat until
the broth has been absorbed, about 5 minutes.
Add another ladleful and keep stirring until
this, too, has been absorbed.

Continue the process, adding broth about
½ cup at a time and stirring until the rice kernels are plump and no longer chalk white in
the center. The risotto should look like creamy
rice pudding, and the kernels should be nice
and chewy. This should take 25 to 30 minutes
altogether. Finally, stir in the final ladleful of
broth and the grated Parmesan. Continue stirring until there's no liquid left on the surface
and the cheese is well distributed throughout.
Stir in the pine nuts, if you'd like, and serve
right away.

PER SERVING (¼ RECIPE): CALORIES 261 • PROTEIN 7.3 G • CARBOHYDRATE
41 G • FAT 5.7 G • CHOLESTEROL 14.3 MG • SODIUM 160 MG • 21% CALORIES FROM
FAT • GOOD SOURCE OF VITAMINS B₁, B₃, C; CALCIUM, IRON

RADICCHIO
RISOTTO

Serves 6 as a starter or side dish, or
4 as a main dish

TOTAL TIME: ABOUT 50 MINUTES, NOT INCLUDING TIME TO
MAKE THE BROTH
TIME TO PREPARE: ABOUT 50 MINUTES
COOKING TIME: INCLUDED IN TIME TO PREPARE
REFRIGERATION/FREEZING: REFRIGERATE UP TO 2 DAYS. DO
NOT FREEZE.

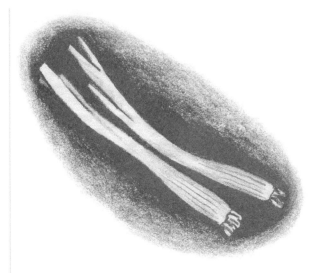

I can only compare what happens in Milanese
markets when radicchio season starts with what
goes on over here when fresh native corn comes
in. I didn't get why a salad green should cause a sensation until I learned what you can do with it. Raw,
radicchio is sharp and crisp. Cooked, it has the flavor of light red wine, and unlike most lettuces, which
just go limp, radicchio melts nicely into soups, pasta
sauces, and, of course, risotto.

4 cups vegetable broth (see page 165)
1 tablespoon unsalted butter
2 shallots, minced
2 cups shredded radicchio
1 cup arborio or carnaroli rice
¼ cup dry white wine
¼ cup grated Parmesan cheese
Salt and freshly ground black pepper to taste

Pour the vegetable broth into a large saucepan
and bring it to a simmer over medium heat.
Turn down the heat to medium-low, keeping
the broth at a simmer.

Meanwhile, in a medium, heavy saucepan,
melt the butter over medium heat. Add the
shallots and sauté until soft, about 7 minutes.
Add the radicchio and stir until it darkens and
goes limp, about 4 minutes. Add the rice and

stir to coat with the vegetables, about 1
minute. Pour in the wine, raise the heat to
medium-high, and stir until most of it has
evaporated, about 3 minutes.

Using a ladle, add about 1 cup of hot
broth. Stir constantly over medium heat until
the broth has been absorbed, about 5 minutes.
Add another ladleful and keep stirring until
this, too, has been absorbed.

Continue the process, adding broth about
½ cup at a time and stirring until the rice kernels are plump and no longer chalk white in
the center. The risotto should look like creamy
rice pudding, and the kernels should be nice
and chewy. This should take 25 to 30 minutes
altogether. Finally, stir in the final ladleful of
broth and the grated Parmesan. Continue stirring until there's no liquid left on the surface
and the cheese is well distributed throughout.
Season with salt and pepper.

PER SERVING (¼ RECIPE): CALORIES 244 • PROTEIN 6.4 G • CARBOHYDRATE
39 G • FAT 5.1 G • CHOLESTEROL 12 MG • SODIUM 125 MG • 20% CALORIES FROM
FAT • GOOD SOURCE OF VITAMINS B₁, B₃; CALCIUM, IRON

MUSHROOM
RISOTTO

Serves 6 as a starter or side dish, or 4 as a main dish

TOTAL TIME: ABOUT 50 MINUTES, NOT INCLUDING TIME TO
MAKE THE BROTH
TIME TO PREPARE: ABOUT 50 MINUTES
COOKING TIME: INCLUDED IN TIME TO PREPARE
DO AHEAD: YOU CAN MAKE THE BROTH UP TO 6 MONTHS IN
ADVANCE. FREEZE UNTIL READY TO USE.
REFRIGERATION/FREEZING: REFRIGERATE UP TO 2 DAYS. DO
NOT FREEZE.

If you like cream of mushroom soup, you may like this even more. It has the same strong mushroom taste and a similarly soothing consistency, but you can sink your teeth into it, too, which intensifies the pleasure.

4 cups Light Mushroom Broth (see page 168) or
    vegetable broth (see page 165)
2 teaspoons unsalted butter
3 scallions, white part only, minced
1 shallot or small red or white onion, minced
1 cup chopped mixed mushrooms (see Note)
1 cup arborio rice
1 tablespoon balsamic or red wine vinegar
2 tablespoons grated Parmesan cheese

Pour the broth into a large saucepan and bring it to a simmer over medium heat. Turn down the heat to medium-low, keeping the broth at a simmer.

Meanwhile, melt the butter in a medium, heavy saucepan over medium heat, and sauté the scallions and shallot or onion until softened, about 6 minutes. Add the mushrooms and continue sautéing until they darken and begin to release their liquid. Add the rice and stir to coat with the vegetables, about 1 minute. Turn up the heat to medium-high and add the vinegar. Stir until the liquid has evaporated, about 1 minute.

Using a ladle, add about 1 cup of hot broth. Stir constantly over medium heat until the broth has been absorbed, about 5 minutes. Add another ladleful and keep stirring until this, too, has been absorbed.

Continue the process, adding broth about ½ cup at a time and stirring until the rice kernels are plump and no longer chalk white in the center. The risotto should look like creamy rice pudding, and the kernels should be nice and chewy. This should take 25 to 30 minutes altogether. Finally, stir in the final ladleful of broth and the grated Parmesan. Continue stirring until there's no liquid left on the surface and the cheese is well distributed throughout.

Note: You can use a combination of fresh and dried mushrooms. If you use dried, soak them for at least 30 minutes in warm water to cover. Drain the water and substitute for part of the broth.

PER SERVING (¼ RECIPE): CALORIES 239 • PROTEIN 7 G • CARBOHYDRATE 42.2 G • FAT 4.3 G • CHOLESTEROL 10 MG • SODIUM 122 MG • 16% CALORIES FROM FAT • VERY GOOD SOURCE OF VITAMIN B₁ • GOOD SOURCE OF VITAMINS B₂, B₃, C; CALCIUM, IRON

FRESH CORN RISOTTO

Serves 6 as a starter or side dish, or
4 as a main dish

TOTAL TIME: ABOUT 1 HOUR, 50 MINUTES
TIME TO PREPARE: ABOUT 50 MINUTES
COOKING TIME: ABOUT 1 HOUR TO COOK AND STEEP THE
   CORN
REFRIGERATION/FREEZING: REFRIGERATE OVERNIGHT. DO
   NOT FREEZE.

W*hat? No broth? Milk carries the flavor far more effectively. It won't taste like corn without it.*

4 ears of corn

4 cups (1 quart) nonfat milk

1 tablespoon unsalted butter

1 cup chopped red onions

1 cup arborio rice

Salt and freshly ground black pepper to taste

Bring a large pot of water to a boil. Add the corn and let the water return to a boil. Cover the pot, turn off the heat, and leave the corn for 8 to 10 minutes. (If you're using an electric stove, take the pot off the burner.) Transfer the corn to a plate to let it cool. (Or cook the corn in the microwave according to the directions on page 526.)

Scrape the corn kernels into a bowl, reserving the cobs. Transfer the kernels to a food processor or blender, and process in short spurts until roughly chopped.

Break the cobs in half and place them in a large, heavy saucepan. Add the milk and bring it to a simmer over medium heat. Let the milk simmer for 10 minutes, turn off the heat, cover, and let the cobs steep for 40 minutes. Remove and discard the corncobs. Heat the milk again over medium-low heat, keeping it just below a simmer.

Melt the butter in a medium, heavy saucepan over medium-high heat, swirling the pan to coat the bottom. Add the onions and sauté until they are softened, about 8 minutes. Add the corn kernels and rice and stir to coat with the onions, about 1 minute.

Add 1 cup of hot milk to the rice, and stir constantly over medium heat until most of it is absorbed, about 5 minutes. Continue adding milk about ½ cup a time and stirring until the rice kernels are plump and no longer chalk white in the center. The risotto should look like creamy rice pudding, and the kernels should be nice and chewy. Serve right away.

PER SERVING (¼ RECIPE): CALORIES 427 • PROTEIN 17.2 G • CARBOHYDRATE 81 G • FAT 5.5 G • CHOLESTEROL 12.2 MG • SODIUM 153 MG • 11% CALORIES FROM FAT • OUTSTANDING SOURCE OF VITAMIN B₁ • VERY GOOD SOURCE OF VITAMINS A, B₂, B₃, C; FOLACIN • GOOD SOURCE OF VITAMINS B₆, B₁₂; CALCIUM, IRON, ZINC

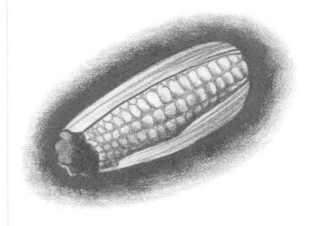

BELL PEPPER RISOTTO

Serves 6 as a starter or side dish, or
4 as a main dish

TOTAL TIME: ABOUT 1 HOUR, NOT INCLUDING TIME TO
MAKE THE BROTH
TIME TO PREPARE: ABOUT 1 HOUR
COOKING TIME: INCLUDED IN TIME TO PREPARE
REFRIGERATION/FREEZING: REFRIGERATE UP TO 2 DAYS. DO
NOT FREEZE.

Superlatives in cookbooks can be cliché, and some aren't based entirely on fact. But this risotto really is supremely delicious. Really.

4 cups vegetable broth (see page 165)
1 tablespoon unsalted butter or extra virgin olive
    oil
2 shallots, minced
1 carrot, peeled and minced
1 celery stalk, trimmed and minced
1 red bell pepper, cored, seeded, and diced
1 yellow or orange bell pepper, cored, seeded,
    and diced
1 cup arborio rice
¼ cup dry white wine, or 1 tablespoon good-
    quality white wine vinegar
⅓ cup grated Parmesan cheese

Pour the vegetable broth into a large saucepan and bring it to a simmer over medium heat. Turn down the heat to medium-low, keeping the broth at a simmer.

Meanwhile, melt the butter or heat the oil in a medium, heavy saucepan over medium-high heat, swirling the pan to coat the bottom. Add the shallots, carrot, celery, and bell peppers, and sauté until they're softened, about 10 minutes. Add the rice and the wine or vinegar and stir until most of the liquid has evaporated, 2 to 5 minutes.

Using a ladle, add about 1 cup of hot broth. Stir constantly over medium heat until the broth has been absorbed, about 5 minutes. Add another ladleful and keep stirring until this, too, has been absorbed.

Continue the process, adding broth about ½ cup at a time and stirring until the rice kernels are plump and no longer chalk white in the center. The risotto should look like creamy rice pudding, and the kernels should be nice and chewy. It should take 25 to 30 minutes altogether. Finally, stir in the final ladleful of broth and the grated Parmesan. Continue stirring until there's no liquid left on the surface and the cheese is well distributed throughout.

PER SERVING (¼ RECIPE): CALORIES 278 • PROTEIN 7.8 G • CARBOHYDRATE 45 G • FAT 6.3 G • CHOLESTEROL 6.4 MG • SODIUM 174 MG • 21% CALORIES FROM FAT • OUTSTANDING SOURCE OF VITAMINS A, C • VERY GOOD SOURCE OF VITAMIN B₁ • GOOD SOURCE OF VITAMINS B₃, B₆; CALCIUM, IRON

ASPARAGUS RISOTTO WITH LEMON AND MINT

Serves 6 as a starter or side dish, or 4 as a main dish

TOTAL TIME: 1 HOUR, 10 MINUTES, NOT INCLUDING TIME
   TO MAKE THE BROTH
TIME TO PREPARE: 40 MINUTES
COOKING TIME: 30 MINUTES TO SIMMER THE ASPARAGUS
REFRIGERATION/FREEZING: REFRIGERATE UP TO 2 DAYS. DO
   NOT FREEZE.

Some seasonings are more inspired than others. Think of basil and garlic (especially with tomatoes); nutmeg and cinnamon (with pumpkin or sweet potatoes); and lemon, Parmesan, and mint, with asparagus, as follows.

½ pound asparagus

4 cups Light Basic Vegetable Broth (see page
   167) or vegetable broth (see page 165)

1 tablespoon unsalted butter

2 shallots, minced

2 tablespoons minced fresh mint

1 tablespoon minced fresh basil

1 teaspoon grated lemon zest

1 cup arborio rice

2 tablespoons white wine, or 1 tablespoon white
   wine vinegar

¼ cup grated Parmesan cheese

Cut off the tips of the asparagus and set them aside. Chop the stems and put them in a large saucepan. Add the broth, cover, and simmer over medium-low heat for 30 minutes. Strain the broth, discarding the asparagus stems. Return the broth to the saucepan and bring it back to a simmer.

Melt the butter in a medium, heavy saucepan. Sauté the shallots, mint, basil, and lemon zest until the shallots soften, about 6 minutes. Add the rice and stir to coat with the herbs, about 1 minute. Add the wine or vinegar and continue stirring until the liquid evaporates, about 1 minute.

Using a ladle, add about 1 cup of hot broth. Stir constantly over medium heat until the broth has been absorbed, about 5 minutes. Add another ladleful and keep stirring until this, too, has been absorbed.

Continue the process, adding broth about ½ cup at a time and stirring until the rice kernels are plump and no longer chalk white in the center. The risotto should look like creamy rice pudding, and the kernels should be nice and chewy. This should take 25 to 30 minutes altogether. Finally, stir in the final ladleful of broth and the reserved asparagus tips. Continue stirring until the tips are bright green and there's no liquid left on the surface, about 3 to 5 minutes. Add the grated Parmesan and stir until the cheese is well distributed throughout. Serve right away.

PER SERVING (¼ RECIPE): CALORIES 219 • PROTEIN 7.3 G • CARBOHYDRATE 40.8 G • FAT 2.3 G • CHOLESTEROL 4.9 MG • SODIUM 121 MG • 10% CALORIES FROM FAT • VERY GOOD SOURCE OF VITAMIN B₁; FOLACIN • GOOD SOURCE OF VITAMINS B₃, C; CALCIUM, IRON

ARTICHOKE RISOTTO

Serves 6 as a starter or side dish, or 4 as a main dish

TOTAL TIME: ABOUT 2 HOURS, 10 MINUTES
TIME TO PREPARE: 1 HOUR, 10 MINUTES
COOKING TIME: 1 HOUR
REFRIGERATION/FREEZING: REFRIGERATE UP TO 2 DAYS. DO
    NOT FREEZE.

You need fresh artichokes for this recipe, which calls for making a broth from the outer leaves. The broth gives an intense flavor to the rice, fortifying the taste of the hearts and the stems.

Juice of 1 lemon
2 large artichokes
1 large onion
2 carrots, peeled and chopped
2 leeks, white part plus 2 inches of greens,
    washed and chopped
1 large potato, peeled and quartered
1 tablespoon extra virgin olive oil
1 small onion, minced
1 cup arborio rice
2 tablespoons dry white wine or balsamic vinegar
2 tablespoons grated Parmesan cheese
Pinch ground nutmeg
Salt and freshly ground black pepper to taste

Fill a glass bowl large enough to hold the artichokes with cold water. Add half of the lemon juice and set aside.

Place 5 cups of water in a large pot and add the remaining lemon juice.

Cut the stem off each artichoke. Trim the very bottom of the stem, then pare away the coarse outer layer. Slice the stem into thick rounds, and place them in the bowl of water.

Pull all of the leaves off the artichokes and place them in the large pot of water. Using a sharp paring knife, slice the remaining portion in half and carve out the spiky leaves in the center. Using a melon scoop or teaspoon, scoop out the fuzz. When you're done, you should have two smooth, shallow bowls. Place them in the bowl of water along with the stems.

To the large pot with the artichoke leaves, add the large onion, the carrots, leeks, and potato. Bring to a boil, cover, lower the heat to medium-low, and simmer for 1 hour. Strain the broth. Discard the vegetables and return the broth to the pot. Keep it hot over low heat.

In a large, heavy saucepan, heat the oil over medium heat. Add the minced small onion and sauté until soft, about 6 minutes. Drain the artichoke stems and hearts, cut them into quarters, and add them to the saucepan. Stir just to season, about 2 minutes. Add the rice and stir to coat with the vegetables, about 1 minute. Pour in the wine or vinegar, raise the heat to medium-high, and stir until most of it has evaporated, about 2 minutes.

Using a ladle, add about 1 cup of hot broth. Stir constantly over medium heat until the broth has been absorbed, about 5 minutes. Add another ladleful and keep stirring until this, too, has been absorbed.

Continue the process, adding broth about ½ cup at a time and stirring until the rice kernels are plump and no longer chalk white in the center. The risotto should look like creamy rice pudding, and the kernels should be nice and chewy. This should take 25 to 30 minutes altogether. Finally, stir in a final ladleful of broth, the grated Parmesan, and nutmeg. Season with salt and pepper. Continue stirring until there's no liquid left on the surface and the cheese is well distributed throughout.

PER SERVING (¼ RECIPE): CALORIES 339 • PROTEIN 9.2 G • CARBOHYDRATE 66 G • FAT 5.0 G • CHOLESTEROL 2.4 MG • SODIUM 146 MG • 13% CALORIES FROM FAT • OUTSTANDING SOURCE OF VITAMINS A, C • VERY GOOD SOURCE OF VITAMINS B₁, B₆ FOLACIN, IRON • GOOD SOURCE OF VITAMIN B₃; CALCIUM

Gnocchi

GNOCCHI
Basic Potato Dumplings

Serves 6

TOTAL TIME: ABOUT 2 HOURS, 15 MINUTES, INCLUDING TIME TO CHILL THE DOUGH
TIME TO PREPARE: ABOUT 15 MINUTES
COOKING TIME: ABOUT 5 MINUTES
DO AHEAD: YOU CAN MAKE THE DOUGH UP TO 3 DAYS IN ADVANCE. REFRIGERATE UNTIL READY TO USE.
REFRIGERATION/FREEZING: REFRIGERATE THE GNOCCHI UP TO 3 DAYS. FREEZE UP TO 5 MONTHS. DO NOT THAW BEFORE COOKING FROZEN GNOCCHI.

Top these gems simply with *Simplest Fresh Tomato Sauce* (see page 278), or lemon zest, minced parsley, and Parmesan cheese.

2 pounds starchy potatoes (4 medium), such as
    russet or Yukon Gold
1 large egg, lightly beaten
Pinch ground nutmeg (optional)
2 to 3 cups unbleached all-purpose flour
½ teaspoon salt

Heat the oven to 425° F. Bake the potatoes until tender, about 50 minutes, or bake in the microwave (see page 536). When they are cool enough to handle, peel and mash them well with a potato masher in a large mixing bowl. Add the egg, nutmeg, and ½ cup flour, knead-ing the ingredients in with your hands. Continue adding flour ½ cup at a time, until the mixture becomes too stiff to mix anymore.

Shape the dough into a ball, wrap it in wax paper or plastic, and refrigerate it for at least an hour and up to 1 day.

Fill a large saucepan or stockpot with water, and bring it to a boil. Meanwhile, divide the dough into 6 equal parts. Rolling the dough between your palms or on a smooth, clean countertop, make each part into a rope about 1 inch thick. Cut the ropes into pieces about 1 inch long.

When the water starts to boil, add the salt. Add the gnocchi about 5 to 8 at a time, and simmer until they rise to the surface, about 3 minutes, being very careful not to let the water come to a fast boil. Let them cook 1 minute longer, then scoop them out with a slotted spoon and transfer to paper towels to drain. Repeat this process until all the gnocchi are cooked. Serve right away.

PER SERVING: CALORIES 332 • PROTEIN 11.3 G • CARBOHYDRATE 68 G • FAT 1.5 G • CHOLESTEROL 35.5 MG • SODIUM 198 MG • 4% CALORIES FROM FAT • OUTSTANDING SOURCE OF VITAMIN C • VERY GOOD SOURCE OF VITAMINS B₁, B₂, B₃, B₆; IRON • GOOD SOURCE OF FOLACIN

GNOCCHI BASICS

Gnocchi are dumplings made from potatoes or ricotta cheese. However, the word "gnocchi" means "lumps," and the dish has gotten its share of them over the years. For instance, I was challenged once to explain the difference between gnocchi and cannonballs. While it's true that they can go down like lead projectiles, gnocchi can also be great fun to eat—a firm, chewy form of pasta, excellent with sauce or tossed with cheese and baked.

• For potato gnocchi, use dry-fleshed potatoes such as russets. Waxy-fleshed red or white boiling potatoes are too soft—they don't contain enough starch—and will absorb so much flour that the gnocchi will be heavy and tough.

• Bake, steam, or microwave the potatoes; don't boil them. Boiling makes them watery and prone to absorb too much flour.

• Use a good all-purpose flour. You'll find my brand recommendations on page 595. Don't use whole wheat flour, which makes mealy gnocchi.

• If you adapt the basic recipe, adding minced vegetables or seasonings, be sure the extra ingredients aren't bulky or watery, or the gnocchi may fall apart while they cook. See more about this below.

• Cook all types of gnocchi in plenty of water, giving each lots of room. If you crowd the pot, they'll cook unevenly.

• Remove the gnocchi 1 minute after they've risen to the surface. Undercooked, they taste pasty; cooked too long, they may explode.

Make It Your Own

Like fresh pasta, gnocchi can be seasoned with additional ingredients. No matter what you add, the flavor will be subtle, buffered by the potato.

WHAT TO ADD AND WHEN TO ADD IT

✐ *Cheese.* Add ¼ cup of any grated cheese—especially Parmesan—to the potatoes in the basic recipe. If you switch to cheddar, you can add minced fresh cilantro, too, and serve the gnocchi topped with Spicy Fresh Tomato Sauce (see page 278) or Tomato Salsa (see page 158). If you switch to Swiss cheese, you can serve the gnocchi in a bowl of Multipurpose Vegetable Broth (see page 165) with shredded fresh spinach.

✐ *Herbs.* Add any minced fresh or crumbled dried herb to the basic mixture, ideally one that complements the sauce or topping you'll be using. Add no more than 2 tablespoons finely minced herbs or 1 tablespoon well-crumbled dried herbs.

✐ *Pureed Vegetables.* Steam ½ cup chopped vegetable (any vegetable that isn't watery, such as asparagus, beets, broccoli, chard, spinach) until very tender. Blot it dry, then puree and stir it into the basic mixture. Add an extra ½ cup flour to compensate for the additional moisture. If the dough is still too soft to roll into ropes, add more flour 1 tablespoon at a time until you can shape the gnocchi.

✐ *Sauces.* Serve basic Gnocchi with your favorite pasta sauce, whether it's one you've made yourself or—we won't tell anyone—bought at the prepared-foods counter where you shop.

✐ *Bake It.* For a gnocchi casserole, make the basic recipe, and drain the gnocchi well. Heat the oven to 425°F. and place the gnocchi in a baking dish. Pour the sauce over them and sprinkle with the cheese of your choice. Tomato sauce and shredded mozzarella always work, but you can make a Southwest version by using Spicy Fresh Tomato Sauce and shredded Jack with jalapeños. Bake until bubbly, about 15 minutes. And do experiment with different sauces.

CARROT GNOCCHI

Serves 6

TOTAL TIME: ABOUT 1 HOUR, 35 MINUTES, INCLUDING
   TIME TO CHILL THE DOUGH
TIME TO PREPARE: 30 MINUTES
COOKING TIME: ABOUT 5 MINUTES
DO AHEAD: YOU CAN MAKE THE DOUGH 1 DAY IN
   ADVANCE. REFRIGERATE UNTIL READY TO USE. YOU CAN
   PREPARE THE POTATOES AND CARROTS UP TO 3 DAYS IN
   ADVANCE. REFRIGERATE UNTIL READY TO USE.
REFRIGERATION/FREEZING: REFRIGERATE UP TO 2 DAYS. DO
   NOT FREEZE.

Consistency matters most in gnocchi, which should be firm and chewy but not like leather; good flavor is a bonus. You'll have the best of both if you start with dry, starchy potatoes, such as russets, and carrots that are fresh and crisp.

1 pound potatoes, russet or Yukon Gold
1 ½ pounds carrots (about 4 large) or frozen,
   defrosted
1 large egg, lightly beaten
Pinch ground ginger
2 to 3 cups unbleached all-purpose flour
½ teaspoon salt

Heat the oven to 425°F. Bake the potatoes until tender, about 50 minutes, or bake in the microwave (see page 536). When they are cool enough to handle, peel and mash them well with a potato masher.

Meanwhile, put a rack or a steamer basket on the bottom of a large saucepan. Add water until it almost touches the rack. Bring to a boil. Add the carrots, cover the pot, and steam over medium heat until tender, about 8 to 10 minutes, mash with a potato masher, and set aside to cool.

Put the potatoes, carrot puree, egg, ginger, and 1 cup of flour in a large mixing bowl and mix with your hands until everything's well combined. Continue adding flour ¼ cup at a time if necessary to make a stiff dough. Shape the dough into a ball, wrap it in wax paper or plastic, and refrigerate it for at least an hour and up to 1 day.

Bring a large pot of water to a boil. Meanwhile, divide the dough into 6 equal parts. Rolling the dough between your palms or on a smooth, clean countertop, make each part into a rope about 1 inch thick. Cut the ropes into pieces about 1 inch long.

When the water starts to boil, add the salt. Add the gnocchi about 5 to 8 at a time, and cook until they rise to the surface, about 3 minutes. Let them cook 1 minute longer, then scoop them out with a slotted spoon and transfer them to a paper towel to drain. Repeat this process until all the gnocchi are cooked. Serve right away.

PER SERVING: CALORIES 262 • PROTEIN 9.2 G • CARBOHYDRATE 50 G • FAT 2.2 G • CHOLESTEROL 71 MG • SODIUM 221 MG • 8% CALORIES FROM FAT • OUTSTANDING SOURCE OF VITAMIN A • VERY GOOD SOURCE OF VITAMINS B₁, B₂, B₃, C • GOOD SOURCE OF VITAMIN B₆; FOLACIN, IRON

PUMPKIN GNOCCHI

Serves 6

TOTAL TIME: ABOUT 1 HOUR, 45 MINUTES
TIME TO PREPARE: ABOUT 15 MINUTES
COOKING TIME: ABOUT 1 HOUR, 30 MINUTES
DO AHEAD: YOU CAN MAKE THE DOUGH UP TO 3 DAYS IN
   ADVANCE. REFRIGERATE UNTIL READY TO USE.
REFRIGERATION/FREEZING: REFRIGERATE THE GNOCCHI UP
   TO 3 DAYS. FREEZE UP TO 5 MONTHS. DO NOT THAW
   BEFORE COOKING FROZEN GNOCCHI.

You won't want to drown the distinct pumpkin flavor, so serve these with Light Bechamel sauce and a speck of Parmesan (see page 277), or one of the lentil sauces (see pages 282 to 285). Use the pulp from fresh pumpkin; canned pumpkin puree is too thin.

1 pound peeled seeded fresh pumpkin, cut into
   2-inch chunks
1 pound russet potatoes
2 to 3 cups unbleached all-purpose flour
   (depending on the texture of the pumpkin; if
   it's watery you'll need more flour)
1 large egg, lightly beaten
Pinch ground cinnamon
Pinch ground nutmeg
½ teaspoon salt

Heat the oven to 425°F. Squirt a baking pan with a nonstick baking spray, and bake the pumpkin and potatoes, uncovered, until tender all the way through, about 40 minutes for the pumpkin and 50 for the potatoes. Alternatively, cook each separately in the microwave. (For microwave directions, see page 536.)

When they are cool enough to handle, peel the potatoes. In a large mixing bowl, mash the potatoes together with the pumpkin with a potato masher. Use your hands to knead in the flour, the egg, cinnamon, and nutmeg.

Shape the dough into a ball, wrap it in wax paper or plastic, and refrigerate it for at least an hour and up to 3 days.

Fill a large saucepan or stockpot with water, and bring it to a boil. Meanwhile, divide the dough into 6 equal parts. Rolling the dough between your palms or on a smooth, clean countertop, make each part into a rope about 1 inch thick. Cut the ropes into pieces about 1 inch long.

When the water starts to boil, add the salt. Add the gnocchi, about 5 to 8 at a time, and cook until they rise to the surface, about 3 minutes. Let them cook 1 minute longer, then scoop them out with a slotted spoon and transfer them to paper towels to drain. Repeat the process until all the gnocchi are cooked. Serve right away.

PER SERVING: CALORIES 201 • PROTEIN 6.3 G • CARBOHYDRATE 41.3 G • FAT 1.2 G • CHOLESTEROL 35.5 MG • SODIUM 194 MG • 6% CALORIES FROM FAT • OUTSTANDING SOURCE OF VITAMIN A • VERY GOOD SOURCE OF VITAMINS B₁, C • GOOD SOURCE OF VITAMINS B₂, B₃, B₆; IRON

SWEET POTATO DROP GNOCCHI

Serves 4

TOTAL TIME: ABOUT 2 HOURS, 10 MINUTES, INCLUDING
   TIME TO CHILL THE DOUGH
TIME TO PREPARE: 15 MINUTES
COOKING TIME: ABOUT 55 MINUTES
DO AHEAD: PREPARE THE DOUGH UP TO 3 DAYS IN
   ADVANCE. REFRIGERATE UNTIL READY TO USE.
REFRIGERATION/FREEZING: REFRIGERATE UP TO 3 DAYS. DO
   NOT FREEZE.

Pardon the pun, but you don't have to knock yourself out for these gnocchi. Just drop the dough into boiling water, drain, and serve on the side in place of potatoes. Top these with the Lovely Lentil Sauce (see page 283), or drizzle with extra virgin olive oil and some fresh lemon juice, or dust with grated Parmesan cheese.

1 large sweet potato
2 cups unbleached all-purpose flour
1 large egg, lightly beaten
1/2 teaspoon ground cinnamon
Pinch ground nutmeg
1/2 teaspoon salt

Heat the oven to 425°F. Bake the sweet potato until tender, about 50 minutes, or bake in the microwave (see page 536). When it is cool enough to handle, peel and mash it with a potato masher. Add the flour, egg, cinnamon, and nutmeg and mix with your hands until well combined. Shape the dough into a ball, wrap it in wax paper or plastic, and refrigerate it for at least an hour and up to 1 day.

Fill a large saucepan or stockpot with water, and bring it to a boil.

When the water starts to boil, add the salt. Using 2 spoons, scoop up about 2 tablespoons of dough with one, and scrape it off into the pot with the other. Cooking no more than 5 to 8 gnocchi at a time, wait for them to rise to the surface, about 3 minutes. Let them cook 1 minute longer, then scoop them out with a slotted spoon and transfer them to paper towels to drain. Repeat this process until all the gnocchi are cooked. Serve them right away.

PER SERVING: CALORIES 216 • PROTEIN 6.3 G • CARBOHYDRATE 45.3 G • FAT 0 G • CHOLESTEROL 0 MG • SODIUM 286 MG • 2% CALORIES FROM FAT • OUTSTANDING SOURCE OF VITAMIN A • VERY GOOD SOURCE OF VITAMIN B₂ • GOOD SOURCE OF VITAMINS B₃, C; IRON

•

SWISS CHARD (OR SPINACH)–RICOTTA GNOCCHI

Serves 4

TOTAL TIME: ABOUT 25 MINUTES
TIME TO PREPARE: ABOUT 5 MINUTES
COOKING TIME: ABOUT 5 MINUTES
DO AHEAD: YOU CAN MAKE THE DOUGH UP TO 2 DAYS IN
   ADVANCE. REFRIGERATE UNTIL READY TO USE.
REFRIGERATION/FREEZING: REFRIGERATE THE GNOCCHI UP
   TO 3 DAYS. DO NOT FREEZE.

If dumplings are tempting, but making the dough from mashed potatoes is daunting, you'll want to try these gnocchi, which involve nothing more than combining ricotta, egg, chard or spinach, and Parmesan; rolling the mixture into balls with your hands; and dropping the gnocchi into a pot of boiling water. Serve sprinkled with fresh lemon juice or with Simplest Tomato Sauce (see page 278). They're subtle and slightly sweet, creamy, and soothing.

1 cup nonfat or part-skim ricotta cheese

1 cup unbleached all-purpose flour, plus
additional for dusting

4 cups fresh Swiss chard or spinach, thoroughly
cleaned and chopped, or one 10-ounce
package frozen chopped Swiss chard or
spinach, thawed and squeezed dry

1 large egg, lightly beaten

2 tablespoons grated Parmesan cheese

Pinch ground nutmeg

1 lemon

In a large mixing bowl, combine the ricotta, flour, chard or spinach, egg, Parmesan, and nutmeg. Grate 1 teaspoon of zest from the lemon, and stir it into the mixture. Squeeze the juice from the lemon and set aside.

Flour your hands and roll the mixture into walnut-sized balls.

Bring a large pot of water to a boil. Add the gnocchi about 5 to 8 at a time and boil until they rise to the surface, about 3 minutes. Let them boil for 1 minute longer, then scoop them out with a slotted spoon and transfer to paper towels to drain. Repeat this process until all the gnocchi are cooked. Sprinkle with the reserved lemon juice and serve.

PER SERVING: CALORIES 420 • PROTEIN 16.7 G • CARBOHYDRATE 11.2 G • FAT 3.2 G • CHOLESTEROL 37.1 MG • SODIUM 97 MG • 5% CALORIES FROM FAT • OUT-STANDING SOURCE OF VITAMIN C; FOLACIN • VERY GOOD SOURCE OF VITAMINS A, B₁, B₂, B₆ • GOOD SOURCE OF VITAMIN B₃; CALCIUM, IRON

•

Dumplings

BEET DROP DUMPLINGS

Serves 6

TOTAL TIME: 1 HOUR, 35 MINUTES, INCLUDING TIME TO
CHILL THE DOUGH
TIME TO PREPARE: 10 MINUTES
COOKING TIME: ABOUT 55 MINUTES
DO AHEAD: COOK THE BEETS UP TO 3 DAYS IN ADVANCE.
REFRIGERATE UNTIL READY TO USE. MAKE THE DOUGH 1
DAY IN ADVANCE. REFRIGERATE UNTIL READY TO USE.
REFRIGERATION/FREEZING: REFRIGERATE UP TO 2 DAYS. DO
NOT FREEZE.

So, you think you don't like beets? Take a bite of these. Flour and egg blunt that beety edge for crimson-colored dumplings that are chewy and just sweet. Try them topped with plain yogurt, diced cucumber, and chives.

2 medium beets (about ½ pound)

4 starchy potatoes (about 1 pound), such as
russet or Idaho

1 large egg, lightly beaten

1¼ to 2 cups unbleached all-purpose flour, plus
more if needed

2 teaspoons grated orange zest

Heat the oven to 425° F. Wrap the unpeeled beets in foil. Bake the beets and potatoes until tender, about 50 minutes, depending on size. Unwrap the beets and slip off the peel. When the potatoes are cool enough to handle, peel and mash together with the beets. When they are well combined, add the egg, ¾ cup flour, and zest, kneading with your hands if the mixture becomes too hard to manage with a spoon. If necessary, add more flour, 2 tablespoons at a time, for a firm dough. Cover with plastic wrap and refrigerate for at least 30 minutes.

Bring a large pot of water to a boil. Lightly flour your hands. For each dumpling, scoop up 2 heaping tablespoons of the beet mixture and roll it into a ball in your palms. Drop it into the water. Cook 5 or 6 dumplings at a time, taking care not to crowd the pot.

When the dumplings rise to the surface, after about 3 minutes, let them boil for 1 minute more, then with a slotted spoon transfer them to a plate lined with paper towels. They will no longer be perfectly round, which is fine. Repeat this process until all the dumplings are cooked. Let them drain for several minutes before serving.

PER SERVING: CALORIES 196 • PROTEIN 6.4 G • CARBOHYDRATE 39.9 G • FAT 1.2 G • CHOLESTEROL 35.5 MG • SODIUM 27.7 MG • 6% CALORIES FROM FAT • VERY GOOD SOURCE OF VITAMINS B₁, C • GOOD SOURCE OF VITAMINS B₂, B₃, B₆; FOLACIN, IRON

MUSHROOM DUMPLINGS

Serves 4

TOTAL TIME: ABOUT 1 HOUR, 35 MINUTES, INCLUDING TIME TO SOAK THE BREAD, BUT NOT INCLUDING TIME TO MAKE THE BROTH
TIME TO PREPARE: ABOUT 50 MINUTES, INCLUDING TIME TO SAUTÉ
COOKING TIME: 5 MINUTES
DO AHEAD: YOU CAN SHAPE THE DUMPLINGS UP TO 2 DAYS AHEAD. REFRIGERATE UNTIL READY TO USE.
REFRIGERATION/FREEZING: REFRIGERATE, UNCOOKED, UP TO 2 DAYS. DO NOT FREEZE.

There are more straightforward ways to eat mushrooms, and easier ways to prepare them. But these dumplings are delicious (and the fact that you bothered will flatter your guests).

1 ½ cups bread chunks, crusts removed
4 dried porcini mushrooms
⅔ cup warm nonfat milk
2 teaspoons extra virgin olive oil
1 large onion, chopped
8 ounces portobello or other firm fresh
    mushrooms, such as cremini, chopped
2 teaspoons crumbled dried oregano
1 large egg, lightly beaten
¼ cup plus 2 tablespoons unbleached all-
    purpose flour
1 teaspoon salt
½ cup vegetable broth (see page 165)
½ cup nonfat or reduced-fat sour cream

In a mixing bowl, soak the bread and the porcini in the milk for 40 minutes, or until the porcini are soft.

Meanwhile, heat the oil in a large skillet over medium-high heat. When it is hot, add the onion. Reduce the heat to medium and sauté, stirring often, until the onion is soft and translucent, about 7 minutes. Add the fresh mushrooms and oregano, and sauté until the mushrooms are cooked through and have given up most of their liquid, about 7 minutes.

Remove the mixture from the heat and transfer it to a food processor. Process in short spurts to make a dense puree. Transfer to a mixing bowl.

Squeeze the excess milk out of the bread and porcini. Mince the porcini and add them along with the bread to the mushroom mixture. Add the egg and flour and mix well with your hands.

Bring water to boil in a large pot. Meanwhile, moisten your hands and shape the mushroom mixture into golf-ball-sized dumplings. When the water's at a boil, add the salt, then add as many dumplings as you can without crowding them. Keeping the water at a simmer, reducing the heat if it's boiling rigorously, cook the dumplings until they rise to the surface, between 3 and 4 minutes. Let them cook for 1 minute longer. If they stick to the bottom, prod them gently with a wooden spoon. Remove the dumplings with a slotted spoon and let them drain on a plate covered with a paper towel.

While the dumplings are cooking, combine the vegetable broth and sour cream in a saucepan, and heat gently over medium-low heat, taking care not to boil. Spoon the sauce over the dumplings and serve.

PER SERVING: CALORIES 417 • PROTEIN 16.4 G • CARBOHYDRATE 76.8 G • FAT 4.8 G • CHOLESTEROL 54 MG • SODIUM 1196 MG • 10% CALORIES FROM FAT • OUTSTANDING SOURCE OF VITAMINS B₁, B₂ • VERY GOOD SOURCE OF VITAMIN B₃, IRON • GOOD SOURCE OF FOLACIN

•

P I E R O G I

Serves 4

TOTAL TIME: 2 HOURS, 30 MINUTES, INCLUDING TIME TO CHILL DOUGH
TIME TO PREPARE: ABOUT 1 HOUR, 15 MINUTES
COOKING TIME: ABOUT 15 MINUTES
DO AHEAD: YOU CAN MAKE THE DOUGH AND/OR THE FILLING UP TO 3 DAYS IN ADVANCE. REFRIGERATE UNTIL READY TO USE.
REFRIGERATION/FREEZING: REFRIGERATED, UNCOOKED, UP TO 3 DAYS. FREEZE UP TO 6 MONTHS.

Adapting dishes that have a strong ethnic identity is a touchy business. Inevitably, you are treading on sacred ground, mocking tradition, and insulting someone's grandmother—quite possibly your own. But if you want to be sane and slim, you've got to do it.

According to custom, pierogi, a sort of Polish ravioli, is served in enough butter to keep a cow in business for a year, which is about how long it takes to make it. Here you streamline the process and skim off some calories, with delicious results.

2 cups unbleached all-purpose flour, plus more
    as needed
1 large egg, lightly beaten
½ cup water
2 medium russet potatoes
½ cup nonfat milk
1 large leek, white part only, sliced
½ cup diced havarti cheese
½ teaspoon caraway seeds (optional)
2 teaspoons unsalted butter or canola oil
1 large onion, thinly sliced
4 cups shredded green cabbage
2 teaspoons crumbled dried oregano

In a food processor, combine the 2 cups of flour, egg, and water in short pulses to form a dough that's soft but not sticky. Add more flour 2 tablespoons at a time if necessary to reach the proper consistency. Roll the dough into a ball, transfer to a bowl, cover with plastic wrap, and refrigerate for at least an hour before using.

Meanwhile, bake the potatoes in a conventional oven, or in the microwave (see page 536). When cool enough to handle, peel off the skin and place in a large mixing bowl. Heat the milk in a heavy, medium saucepan over medium heat. Add the leek, stirring until it softens, about 10 minutes. Drain off the milk. Add the leek to the potatoes, and mash together with a potato masher or the back of a wooden spoon. Add the cheese and the caraway, if using, and continue mashing until well combined.

Roll out the dough on a lightly floured surface about 1/16 inch thick (in other words, very thin). Using a 4-inch biscuit cutter, cut out 14 rounds.

Place a heaping teaspoon of filling in the center of the round. Wet your fingertip and run it around the edge of the dough. Fold the top over the filling, and press along the bottom edge to seal. Repeat until you've used up all of the filling or the dough.

Fill a large pot with water and bring to a gentle boil over medium-high heat. Add 4 or 5 pierogi at a time and boil for 5 minutes, or until they rise to the surface. Remove with a slotted spoon and place on paper towels to drain. Repeat until all of the pierogi are cooked.

Melt the butter in a large skillet. Sauté the onion until it is soft and translucent, about 7 minutes. Add the cabbage and oregano, stir, cover, and steam until just tender, about 5 minutes. Add the pierogi and stir gently to heat through and coat with vegetables, about 3 minutes. Serve right away.

PER SERVING: CALORIES 625 • PROTEIN 15.5 G • CARBOHYDRATE 70.6 G • FAT 9.1 G • CHOLESTEROL 74.3 MG • SODIUM 141 MG • 19% CALORIES FROM FAT • OUTSTANDING SOURCE OF VITAMINS B₁, C • VERY GOOD SOURCE OF VITAMINS B₂, B₃, B₆; FOLACIN, CALCIUM, IRON • GOOD SOURCE OF VITAMIN A; ZINC

Polenta

POLENTA

Serves 6 as a starter or side dish, or 4 as a main dish

TOTAL TIME: ABOUT 30 TO 40 MINUTES, NOT INCLUDING TIME TO MAKE THE BROTH
TIME TO PREPARE: ABOUT 30 TO 40 MINUTES
COOKING TIME: INCLUDED IN TIME TO PREPARE
REFRIGERATION/FREEZING: THE POLENTA WILL BECOME FIRM WHEN IT'S CHILLED. TO REFRIGERATE, POUR IT INTO A SMOOTH LAYER IN A SHALLOW BAKING PAN, AND COVER WITH PLASTIC WRAP. REFRIGERATE UP TO 4 DAYS. DO NOT FREEZE.

You will not find "cornmeal mush" on many restaurant menus, but it may be there just the same. It would be called "polenta," a name that's meant to be more appetizing. I'm not so sure it is, though. After all, "cornmeal mush" is perfectly descriptive, and suggests something simple, warm, and toasty. Moreover, the foreign name "polenta" sounds intimidating, indicating, perhaps, that fixing this dish requires some special skill. But go on and call it cornmeal mush, so you'll know there's nothing to it.

4 cups water or Light Basic Vegetable Broth (see page 167)
1 cup stone-ground cornmeal
Salt to taste

In a large saucepan, bring the water or broth to a boil over medium-high heat. Sprinkle in the cornmeal in a steady stream with one hand while whisking with the other. Lower the heat to medium, and whisk until the polenta is so thick it pulls away from the pan and resists further stirring, 30 to 40 minutes. Season with salt.

Or combine the cornmeal and the water or broth in a large saucepan. Bring to a boil over medium-high heat, stirring often. Once it comes to a boil, reduce the heat to medium and continue as above.

PER SERVING: CALORIES 110 · PROTEIN 2.4 G · CARBOHYDRATE 23.5 G · FAT 1.1 G · CHOLESTEROL 0 MG · SODIUM 10.7 MG · 9% CALORIES FROM FAT

MICROWAVE METHOD: Place the water or broth and cornmeal in a 2-quart microwave-proof mixing bowl. On full power, bring the mixture to a boil, about 4 minutes; remove and stir. Return it to the microwave on full power for 4 minutes; remove and stir again. Continue cooking at full power, removing and stirring, at 6-minute intervals, until the polenta pulls away from the side and resists further stirring. Season with salt.

POLENTA BASICS

Prima patria, poi polenta ("First our country, then polenta") was the rallying cry of one of several eighteenth-century Italian societies devoted to the greater glory of cornmeal mush. While Americans couldn't harvest wheat fast enough, the Italians were planting our native corn and enjoying it in ways we'd never imagined.

• Stone-ground cornmeal has a true corn taste that you won't get from the quick-cooking kind. Save instant cornmeal for sprinkling on your baking stone when you make bread or pizza.

• You need more liquid to cook cornmeal than most other grains, a ratio of at least 4:1. Be sure to use enough, or the polenta will be dry and lumpy.

• There aren't any shortcuts to making good polenta; you have to stir it often to get the ideal consistency. Some people swear by the pressure cooker, but when it comes to polenta, I only end up swearing at mine. I have yet to figure out how to regulate the time and temperature to get it just right. And quick-cooking polenta is no solution, either; it's been precooked, losing flavor in the process.

• The most effective way to prevent lumps is to cook the polenta over a double boiler. It will take a while longer, but you won't have to stir as often. Follow the basic recipe, putting the ingredients in the top of a double boiler instead of a saucepan. Keep the bottom of the boiler adequately full and bubbling away. Stir thoroughly with a whisk every five minutes at the start of cooking, every three as it thickens, and constantly toward the end, until it's thick enough to resist you.

Make It Your Own

You can serve polenta straight off the stove, while it's still soft, making a well in the center and filling it with vegetables and sauce. Or you can pour it into a baking pan, let it set, then slice it and top like pizza or toast.

WHAT TO ADD AND WHEN TO ADD IT

🖉 *Cheese.* There are at least two ways to add the cheese of your choice to polenta. Stir up to

WHAT NOW?

You can serve the polenta hot off the stove as a side dish, topped with anything you might put on pasta, such as freshly grated cheese, tomato sauce, and so on, or you might just spoon over it the juices or sauce from your entrée.

Or you can make crostini. Pour the hot polenta into a nonstick baking pan in a layer about 1 inch thick. Let it chill.

Heat the oven to 350°F.

Bake the polenta until it begins to brown, about 15 minutes. When it is firm, cut it into bite-sized squares.

Brush the squares lightly with extra virgin olive oil and top with anything you'd put on crostini (see pages 264 to 265).

Or brush the squares lightly with extra virgin olive oil, top with minced fresh basil and grated Parmesan cheese, and grill over charcoal or brown under the broiler. You can use fresh rosemary sprigs in place of the basil and cheese. Or you can substitute fresh minced cilantro and grated sharp cheddar for both.

²⁄₃ cup grated cheese into the pan with the polenta when it's just about cooked.

Or pour half of the just-cooked polenta into a shallow nonstick baking dish in an even layer. Cover with a layer of grated or shredded cheese, then spread the remaining polenta evenly on top. Bake in a 350°F. oven until bubbly and brown, about fifteen minutes. Let the polenta sit seven minutes before cutting it into squares and serving.

✎ *Sun-dried Tomatoes and Cheese.* Just before the polenta is done, stir in about ¼ cup grated Parmesan cheese and ¼ cup to ½ cup minced sun-dried tomatoes. Season with a generous pinch each of dried basil and dried oregano. Serve in bowls.

Or take this a step further by pouring the polenta into a nonstick baking dish and letting it cool until it's no longer steaming. Cover with a layer of grated mozzarella, and broil until the cheese is bubbly, about 1½ minutes.

✎ *Milk.* You can make sweet Polenta Porridge for breakfast by cooking the polenta in milk and sweetening it with molasses just before it's done (see the recipe on page 54). You can use the same mixture to make a sort of breakfast crostini. Just pour it into a shallow nonstick baking pan, cover, and chill overnight. Heat the oven to 350°F., and brown the polenta, about fifteen minutes. Top with syrup or honey and fresh fruit.

✎ *Olive Oil and Herbs.* Pour just-cooked polenta onto a nonstick baking sheet and let it cool completely. Brush it lightly with extra virgin olive oil combined with one finely minced small garlic clove. Brown under the broiler, about one minute, and sprinkle with minced fresh basil.

✐ *Scrambled Eggs with Herbs.* Heat the oven to 350°F. Pour the polenta onto a nonstick baking sheet and bake until it's browned, about fifteen minutes. Cut it into rectangles and top with scrambled eggs garnished with the minced fresh herbs of your choice. Or serve the toasted polenta instead of bread on the side.

•

BAKED EGGS ON POLENTA WITH SPINACH

Serves 4

TOTAL TIME: ABOUT 35 MINUTES
TIME TO PREPARE: ABOUT 25 MINUTES
COOKING TIME: 8 MINUTES TO BAKE
DO AHEAD: YOU CAN LAYER THE POLENTA AND SPINACH THE DAY BEFORE. KEEP REFRIGERATED UNTIL READY TO BAKE WITH EGGS.
REFRIGERATION/FREEZING: DO NOT REFRIGERATE OR FREEZE.

My husband and I met—entirely by chance—in a restaurant. Consequently, good food is more than incidental to our marriage; a bad meal has the weight of a bad omen. Afterward we are nice to each other in a cordial, cautious kind of way.

With the volume of testing I do, we're bound to eat a bad meal from time to time. The stakes are particularly high when I have to make polenta. Simon hates polenta, and the fact that he grew up in Italy doesn't necessarily make it ironic. He's from Florence, polenta is from Lombardy, and you can't expect a Tuscan to tuck into polenta any more than you'd expect your cousin from New Hampshire to hanker after grits.

So the night I made this dish, I was prepared to swap Simon's portion for a plate of pasta. I ended up putting back the pasta instead. "But you hate polenta," I said. "Not your polenta," he replied. What a guy.

And, by the way, what a dish.

2¼ cups water
¼ teaspoon salt
½ cup stone-ground cornmeal
¼ cup grated cheese, such as Parmesan, Gruyère, cheddar, or smoked mozzarella
4 cups fresh spinach, washed, coarsely chopped, and cooked (see page 539), or one 10-ounce package frozen chopped spinach, thawed and squeezed dry
4 large eggs

Bring the water to a boil in a large saucepan over medium-high heat. Add the salt, then sprinkle in the cornmeal in an even stream, whisking constantly. Keeping the mixture at a brisk boil, continue whisking until it thickens to the consistency of oatmeal, about 25 minutes. Whisk in the cheese and remove it from the heat.

Heat the oven to 350°F. Spread the spinach evenly over the bottom of an 8-inch square baking pan. Spread the cornmeal mixture evenly on top. Using a spoon, make four 2-inch indentations in the surface, evenly spaced several inches apart. Break the eggs and plop each into an indentation.

Bake, uncovered, until the egg whites have set and the yolk is firm but not solid, about 8 minutes.

PER SERVING: CALORIES 174 • PROTEIN 12.1 G • CARBOHYDRATE 15 G • FAT 7.6 G • CHOLESTEROL 217 MG • SODIUM 241 MG • 39% CALORIES FROM FAT • OUTSTANDING SOURCE OF VITAMIN A; FOLACIN • VERY GOOD SOURCE OF VITAMINS B₂, C • GOOD SOURCE OF VITAMINS B₁, B₆, B₁₂; CALCIUM, IRON

ONE-DISH DINNERS

When dinner is a collection of small dishes—salads, soups, or starters—which of them you call the entrée is an arbitrary matter.

But when you serve one of the following, there's no mistaking the main course. These are substantial dishes that sit squarely in the center of the table. Each calls for filling combinations of fresh produce, grains, and legumes and is a meal in itself.

 ONE-DISH DINNERS IN MEAL

PLANNING • ONE-DISH DINNER MENUS

• STEWS AND CASSEROLES • CHILIS •

CURRIES • FILLED VEGETABLES • NORI

ROLLS • STIR-FRIES •

SAVORY CHEESECAKES • EGG DISHES

One-Dish Dinners in Meal Planning

Most of the dishes in this section provide a substantial share of critical daily values, sometimes more than 100 percent for particular vitamins, minerals, and nutrients, for example:

SPRING GARDEN TORTILLAS (PAGE 355)
61% daily value for protein
41% daily value for vitamin A
239% daily value for vitamin C
38% daily value for vitamin B_2
38% daily value for vitamin B_3
37% daily value for vitamin B_6
53% daily value for iron
33% daily value for calcium
25% daily value for zinc

POTATO-FENNEL STEW WITH MIXED BEANS AND TOFU (PAGE 336)
69% daily value protein
33% daily value for vitamin A
222% daily value for vitamin C
62% daily value for folacin
92% daily value for iron

LENTIL AND MUSHROOM STEW (PAGE 340)
56% daily value for protein
54% daily value for vitamin A
40% daily value for vitamin C
23% daily value for vitamin B_3
22% daily value for vitamin B_6
80% daily value for iron
30% daily value for calcium
20% daily value for zinc

CHICKPEAS AND STEAMED VEGETABLES IN PEANUT SAUCE (PAGE 337)
35% daily value for protein
16% daily value for vitamin A
80% daily value for vitamin C
68% daily value for folacin
18% daily value for vitamin B_6
26% daily value for iron
17% daily value for zinc

MOO-SHU MUSHROOMS (PAGE 374)
51% daily value for protein
54% daily value for vitamin A
40% daily value for vitamin C
23% daily value for vitamin B_3
22% daily value for vitamin B_6
80% daily value for iron
30% daily value for calcium
20% daily value for zinc

CABBAGE-FILLED CABBAGE STIR-FRY
(PAGE 376)
105% daily value for vitamin A
160% daily value for vitamin C
55% daily value for folacin
30% daily value for vitamin B6
27% daily value for iron
19% daily value for calcium

One-Dish Dinner Menus

30-MINUTE MEALS
Black Beans with Orange and Saffron
(page 341)
Mixed salad greens with Creamy Chive
Dressing (page 120)

Cabbage-Filled Cabbage Stir-Fry (page 376)
Rice
Quick Fresh Corn Salad (page 128)

Tortilla-Style Frittata (page 389)
Tomato Salsa (page 158)
Mixed greens with Avocado-Buttermilk
Dressing (page 120)

Apple-Turnip Soup (page 186)
Couscous (page 338)
Lavosh (page 412)
Fig Glace (page 488)

Sweet and Simple Borscht (page 184)
Mushroom Fricassee with Eggs (page 381)
Rice
Carrot Cake (page 474)

My Favorite Chickpeas (page 360)
Cucumber Raita (page 156) or Beet Raita
(page 154)
Rice
Naan (page 415)
Sorbet (page 489)

Butternut Squash Soup (page 181)
Grain-Filled Onions (page 365)
Potato-Fennel Stew with Mixed Beans and
Tofu (page 336)
Maple-Apple-Cranberry Crumble (page 479)

Mild Miso Soup (page 173)
Nori Rolls (page 370)
Mixed greens with That Japanese Dressing
(page 122)
Mango Cream (page 496)

Cream of Fresh Tomato Soup (page 182)
Spinach Savory Cheesecake (page 381)
Torta di Budino di Riso Integrale (page 482)

Potato Curry (page 356)
Red Lentil Spread (page 256)
Beet Raita (page 154)
Basmati or jasmati rice
Swift Chapati-Style Flat Bread (page 412)
Lemon-Berry Pudding (page 495)

Classic Leek and Potato Soup with Watercress
(page 182)
Chilled Filled Spinach Rolls (page 369)
Medium-grain brown rice
Soft and Chewy Dinner Rolls (page 408)
Sweet-Potato-Biscuit Strawberry Shortcake
(page 481)

Stews and Casseroles

STEWED BEANS WITH POTATOES AND OLIVES

Serves 6

TOTAL TIME: ABOUT 45 MINUTES, NOT INCLUDING TIME TO
COOK THE BEANS
TIME TO PREPARE: ABOUT 25 MINUTES, INCLUDING TIME
TO SAUTÉ
COOKING TIME: ABOUT 20 MINUTES
REFRIGERATION/FREEZING: REFRIGERATE UP TO 3 DAYS.
FREEZE UP TO 6 MONTHS.

This is one of my favorite fallback dishes, calling for ingredients I always have on hand (or can speed through the express lane) and tasting, reliably, delicious.

6 new potatoes
1 tablespoon extra virgin olive oil
2 large onions, chopped
1 garlic clove, minced
2 tablespoons minced fresh oregano, or 1
    tablespoon crumbled dried oregano
2 tablespoons dry white wine
2 cups fresh or canned chopped tomatoes
1½ cups cooked chickpeas, drained and rinsed
1½ cups cooked white beans, drained and rinsed
8 oil-cured black olives, pitted, or a combination
    of black and green olives
2 teaspoons capers
¼ to ⅓ cup crumbled feta cheese (optional)
Salt and freshly ground black pepper to taste

In a large pot bring enough water to cover the potatoes to a boil. Add the potatoes and gently simmer until they're just cooked through, about 10 minutes. Lift the potatoes out with a slotted spoon and let them cool.

Heat the oil in a large skillet over medium-high heat. When it's hot, add the onions, garlic, and oregano. Reduce the heat to medium and sauté, stirring often, until the onions are soft and limp, about 8 minutes. Add the wine and stir until most of the liquid has evaporated, about 4 minutes.

Stir in the tomatoes, and cook, stirring often, until they start to thicken, about 5 minutes. Add the chickpeas, white beans, olives, and capers. Cut the potatoes into quarters and add them, too. Cover and continue cooking, stirring occasionally, until the sauce is very thick, about 10 minutes. Stir in the feta, if using. Season with salt and pepper.

PER SERVING: CALORIES 310 • PROTEIN 12.3 G • CARBOHYDRATE 56.9 G • FAT 4.5 G • CHOLESTEROL 0 MG • SODIUM 147 MG • 13% CALORIES FROM FAT • OUTSTANDING SOURCE OF VITAMIN C • VERY GOOD SOURCE OF VITAMIN B₆: FOLACIN, IRON • GOOD SOURCE OF VITAMINS B₁, B₃: ZINC

SPEEDY SUMMER CASEROLE

Serves 4

TOTAL TIME: ABOUT 1 HOUR, 30 MINUTES, INCLUDING
TIME TO DRAIN THE EGGPLANT
TIME TO PREPARE: ABOUT 10 MINUTES
COOKING TIME: ABOUT 50 MINUTES
DO AHEAD: YOU CAN MAKE THE CASSEROLE, UNCOOKED,
UP TO 3 DAYS IN ADVANCE. REFRIGERATE UNTIL READY
TO USE.
REFRIGERATION/FREEZING: REFRIGERATE UP TO 2 DAYS. DO
NOT FREEZE.

Summer's four basic food groups: tomato, olives, basil, and cheese. Serve a cold soup to start and you'll be set.

1 eggplant, unpeeled, sliced into ⅓-inch-thick
     rounds
Coarse salt
1 large ripe tomato, thinly sliced
3 hard-boiled large eggs (see page 65), sliced
½ cup shredded fresh mozzarella or Havarti
     cheese
1 cup fresh bread crumbs
½ cup grated Parmesan cheese
1 garlic clove, chopped
2 tablespoons minced fresh basil
2 tablespoons minced fresh parsley
¼ cup minced oil-cured black olives
1 tablespoon extra virgin olive oil

If the eggplant contains a lot of seeds, sprinkle the slices liberally with salt and leave them to drain for 30 minutes in a colander lined with paper towels.

Heat the oven to 425°F. Squirt an 8-inch baking dish with nonstick spray or lightly grease with unsalted butter. Lightly rinse the eggplant, just to remove the surface salt, if using, and pat it dry. Spread the slices in a single layer on a nonstick baking sheet and bake until soft, about 25 minutes. Remove the eggplant from the oven, but leave the heat on.

Transfer the slices to the prepared baking dish, covering the bottom evenly with them, overlapping if necessary. Top with the tomato slices. Distribute the eggs and the mozzarella or Havarti cheese evenly on top.

In a mini–food processor or blender, combine the bread crumbs, Parmesan, garlic, basil, parsley, and olives. Process in short spurts to combine. Sprinkle evenly over the casserole, and drizzle the olive oil over that.

Cover loosely with foil and bake for 15 minutes. Remove the foil and continue baking until the topping has browned and the cheese has melted, about 10 minutes. Let the casserole sit for 10 minutes before serving. Serve hot or at room temperature. Serve leftovers cold.

PER SERVING: CALORIES 300 • PROTEIN 20.3 G • CARBOHYDRATE 16.6 G • FAT 17.4 G • CHOLESTEROL 184 MG • SODIUM 552 MG • 51% CALORIES FROM FAT • OUT-STANDING SOURCE OF CALCIUM • VERY GOOD SOURCE OF VITAMIN B₂ • GOOD SOURCE OF VITAMINS A, B₆, B₁₂; FOLACIN, IRON, ZINC

LENTIL TERRINES WITH MIXED-VEGETABLE SAUCE

Serves 6

TOTAL TIME: ABOUT 2 HOURS, 30 MINUTES, INCLUDING TIME TO SOAK THE BREAD CRUMBS, BUT NOT INCLUDING TIME TO MAKE THE BROTH

TIME TO PREPARE: ABOUT 1 HOUR, INCLUDING TIME TO SAUTÉ

COOKING TIME: ABOUT 1 HOUR

DO AHEAD: YOU CAN MAKE THE UNCOOKED TERRINES UP TO 3 DAYS IN ADVANCE. REFRIGERATE UNTIL READY TO USE.

REFRIGERATION/FREEZING: REFRIGERATE, UNCOOKED, UP TO 3 DAYS. DO NOT FREEZE.

This is the kind of dish that gives food writers a bad name. The ingredients and instructions run on and on, as if everyone can—or cares to—spend as much time in the kitchen as we who get paid for it. I feel your pain.

But I can also anticipate your pleasure if you're able to set aside two hours or so for something this special: savory lentil pâté on top of creamy chard, topped with a chunky vegetable sauce.

Terrines

1 cup fine dried white or whole wheat bread crumbs

²⁄₃ cup nonfat milk

2 teaspoons extra virgin olive oil

1 small onion, chopped

2 large zucchini, chopped

1 tablespoon crumbled dried thyme

1 cup uncooked lentils, preferably lentilles de Puy (if you can't find them where you shop, see mail-order information, page 596), rinsed

1½ cups water, plus more as needed

2 large egg whites

Vegetable Sauce

2 teaspoons extra virgin olive oil

1 shallot, chopped

2 carrots, peeled and diced

½ red or yellow bell pepper, cored, seeded, and diced

2 cups cherry tomatoes, halved if larger than marbles

1 medium potato, peeled and finely diced

12 asparagus spears, trimmed and chopped

¼ cup dry white wine

2 cups loosely packed sugar snap peas

Chard Sauce

1 tablespoon cornstarch

2 cups vegetable broth (see page 165)

½ cup evaporated skim milk

1 pound Swiss chard, washed, stemmed, and coarsely chopped

¼ cup grated Parmesan or Asiago cheese

½ cup loosely packed shredded part-skim mozzarella cheese

Pinch ground nutmeg

Salt and freshly ground black pepper to taste

For the Terrines

In a small bowl, soak the bread crumbs in the milk for 30 minutes.

Meanwhile, heat the oil in a medium skillet over medium-high heat. When it is hot, add the onion, zucchini, and thyme. Reduce the heat to medium and sauté, stirring often, until the onion softens, about 7 minutes. Add the lentils and stir to coat well with the vegetables. Stir in the water, raise the heat to medium-high, and bring it to a simmer. Reduce the heat to medium-low, cover, and simmer until the

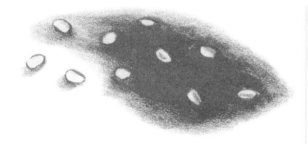

lentils are soft and the water has been absorbed, about 30 minutes. Check occasionally, adding more water if necessary.

Heat the oven to 425°F.

Squeeze the milk out of the bread crumbs. Place the bread crumbs in a food processor or blender. Drain any excess water from the lentils, and add the mixture to the food processor or blender, along with the egg whites. Process in short pulses to puree and blend, about 6 pulses. Take care not to overdo it, or the ingredients will liquefy.

Squirt six 6-inch custard cups or ramekins with nonstick spray or grease lightly with olive oil. Distribute the lentil mixture evenly among the cups. Place them in a large baking dish. Add water to the larger dish so that it comes halfway up the sides of the custard cups. Bake until the terrines are set, about 25 minutes. Transfer to a cooling rack, and let them sit for 10 minutes.

For the Vegetable Sauce

Heat the oil in a medium skillet over medium-high heat. When it is hot, add the shallot, carrots, red or yellow pepper, and cherry tomatoes. Reduce the heat to medium and sauté, stirring often, until the vegetables soften, about 7 minutes. Add the potato, asparagus, and wine, and cook, stirring often, until the potato is tender, about 10 minutes. Add the sugar snap peas and cook until they are bright green, about 1 minute more. Remove from the heat.

For the Chard Sauce

Stir the cornstarch into 2 tablespoons of the vegetable broth to make a thick paste. Set it aside. In a medium saucepan on medium heat, combine the remaining vegetable broth and the evaporated skim milk. Stir well to blend. Add the cornstarch mixture, and continue stirring until the sauce thickens, about 5 minutes. Add the chard and stir until it turns bright green, about 3 minutes.

Add the Parmesan or Asiago and mozzarella to the chard sauce and stir well until the cheeses have melted, about 1 minute. Season with nutmeg and salt and pepper, and spoon an equal amount of sauce onto the center of 4 serving plates.

Run a butter knife around the rim of each terrine and turn them out onto the serving plates on top of the sauce. Spoon the chopped vegetable mixture in a ring around each one, also placing a bit on top. Serve right away.

PER SERVING: CALORIES 467 • PROTEIN 32 G • CARBOHYDRATE 59 G • FAT 12 G • CHOLESTEROL 27.2 MG • SODIUM 615 MG • 23% CALORIES FROM FAT • OUTSTANDING SOURCE OF VITAMINS A, C; FOLACIN, CALCIUM • VERY GOOD SOURCE OF VITAMINS B₁, B₂, B₆; ZINC

POTATO-FENNEL STEW WITH MIXED BEANS AND TOFU

Serves 4

TOTAL TIME: ABOUT 1 HOUR, 35 MINUTES, NOT INCLUD-
ING TIME TO ROAST THE PEPPERS, COOK THE BEANS, OR
MAKE THE BROTH
TIME TO PREPARE: ABOUT 35 MINUTES, INCLUDING TIME
TO SAUTÉ
COOKING TIME: ABOUT 1 HOUR
REFRIGERATION/FREEZING: REFRIGERATE UP TO 3 DAYS.
FREEZE UP TO 4 MONTHS.

It often happens that people who aren't vegetarian don't feel comfortable with those who are until they know where they stand on tofu. Having been on both sides, I would advise that if you're a vegetarian in that situation, affect indifference or even disdain. If you express enthusiasm, you won't be understood.

You have to admit that tofu, on the face of it, is not very appetizing. "Bean Curd" just doesn't have the same ring as "pâté de foie gras" or "chicken pot-pie." So just give the skeptics some time. Or, better yet, give them this.

2 teaspoons extra virgin olive oil
1 onion, chopped
1 large fennel bulb, including leafy fronds, chopped
1 large leek, white part plus 1 inch of greens, washed and chopped
¼ cup minced fresh parsley
2 tablespoons minced fresh rosemary
2 teaspoons whole fennel seeds
2 tablespoons balsamic vinegar
1 red bell pepper, roasted and peeled (see page 534)
1 yellow bell pepper, roasted and peeled (see page 534)

1 pound fresh tomatoes, peeled and chopped (see page 544) or 2½ cups canned chopped tomatoes
1 pound firm tofu, cubed
1 cup cooked cannellini beans, drained and rinsed
1 cup cooked black runner beans, drained and rinsed
Large pinch powdered saffron
2 cups vegetable broth (see page 165)
2 cups tiny new potatoes, scrubbed
Salt and freshly ground black pepper to taste

Heat the oil in a large skillet over medium-high heat. When it's hot, add the onion, fennel, leek, parsley, rosemary, and fennel seeds. Reduce the heat to medium and sauté, stirring often, until the vegetables are soft and limp, about 10 minutes. Add the balsamic vinegar and stir until most of it has evaporated, about 2 minutes.

Stir in the red and yellow bell peppers and tomatoes. Continue cooking until the tomatoes simmer down into a thick sauce, about 7 minutes. Stir in the tofu and beans.

Dissolve the saffron in the broth and add it to the the skillet along with the potatoes, stirring gently to avoid crumbling the tofu. Bring to a simmer, cover, reduce the heat to medium-low, and simmer gently, stirring occasionally, for 50 minutes, until the stew is thick and the potatoes are cooked through. Season with salt and pepper.

PER SERVING: CALORIES 472 • PROTEIN 31 G • CARBOHYDRATE 65.5 G • FAT 13.5 G • CHOLESTEROL 0 MG • SODIUM 74.4 MG • 24% CALORIES FROM FAT • OUT-STANDING SOURCE OF VITAMIN C; FOLACIN, IRON • VERY GOOD SOURCE OF VIT-AMIN A; ZINC

●

CHICKPEAS AND VEGETABLES STEAMED IN PEANUT SAUCE

Serves 4

TOTAL TIME: 30 MINUTES, NOT INCLUDING TIME TO MAKE
  THE BROTH OR STEAM THE VEGETABLES
TIME TO PREPARE: ABOUT 20 MINUTES
COOKING TIME: ABOUT 6 MINUTES
EQUIPMENT: WOK
DO AHEAD: YOU CAN MAKE THE BROTH MONTHS IN
  ADVANCE IF YOU KEEP IT FROZEN, 4 DAYS IN ADVANCE IF
  YOU REFRIGERATE IT.
REFRIGERATION/FREEZING: REFRIGERATE UP TO 2 DAYS. DO
  NOT FREEZE.

Nothing can spoil a meal like nostalgia. You can get so caught up in recalling how good something was, you miss out on the merits of the food in front of you. You'd think that yesteryear's tomatoes were uniformly glorious, big as pumpkins, and red as the setting sun. I would love to hear someone say, "I hated the tomatoes I got as a kid. They were, like, Day-Glo orange and all mealy inside."

In appreciation of the here and now, there's no comparison between the overprocessed peanut butter I had growing up and what we can get today, which is basically spreadable peanuts. And it's that good stuff that makes this sauce possible. Serve this over hot rice.

1 shallot
2 scallions, including greens
1 onion or leek
½ green poblano chili
1 red bell pepper
4 garlic cloves
2 tablespoons grated peeled fresh ginger
¼ cup minced fresh basil
¼ cup minced fresh mint
¼ cup minced fresh cilantro
1 tablespoon low-sodium soy sauce
1 teaspoon sugar
½ tablespoon tomato paste
2 tablespoons peanut butter (with no added oil,
  sugar, or salt)
2 tablespoons grated unsweetened coconut
1 cup Broth for Far Eastern–Flavored Dishes (see
  page 168) or vegetable broth (see page 165)
1 tablespoon cornstarch
2 teaspoons canola or vegetable oil
3 cups cooked chickpeas, drained and rinsed
2 cups steamed vegetables, such as broccoli
  florets, cabbage, carrots, snow peas, and/or
  asparagus (see pages 514 to 546)

In a food processor, combine the shallot, scallions, onion or leek, chili, red pepper, garlic, ginger, basil, mint, and cilantro, pulsing until you get a chunky consistency. Transfer the mixture to a bowl and set aside.

Add the soy sauce, sugar, tomato paste, peanut butter, and coconut to the food processor. Process to make a thick paste. Add the broth and cornstarch and process again to blend.

Heat a wok or large skillet over medium-high heat. Add the oil and swirl to coat the bottom and sides. Add the shallot and herb mixture, and toss quickly to season the oil, about 3 minutes. Add the chickpeas and steamed vegetables, and toss again to season and heat through, about 3 minutes. Add the broth mixture and stir until thickened and everything's thoroughly mixed, about 2 minutes.

PER SERVING: CALORIES 334 • PROTEIN 15.6 G • CARBOHYDRATE 46.6 G • FAT 11.3 G • CHOLESTEROL 0 MG • SODIUM 244 MG • 29% CALORIES FROM FAT • OUTSTANDING SOURCE OF VITAMIN C; FOLACIN • VERY GOOD SOURCE OF IRON • GOOD SOURCE OF VITAMINS A, B₁, B₂, B₃, B₆; ZINC

NOW TRY THIS: Make a marinade with ¼ cup low-sodium soy sauce; 1 tablespoon grated peeled fresh ginger; 1 garlic clove, minced; 1 teaspoon sugar; and 1 scallion, white part and 1 inch of greens; minced. Marinate 1 cup firm tofu for at least 30 minutes. Add it instead of the chickpeas, following the directions in the main recipe.

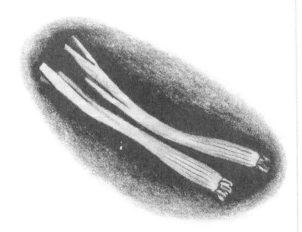

COUSCOUS
A Mediterranean Stew
Serves 4

TOTAL TIME: ABOUT 1 HOUR, NOT INCLUDING TIME TO ROAST THE PEPPERS, COOK THE CHICKPEAS, OR MAKE THE BROTH
TIME TO PREPARE: ABOUT 25 MINUTES
COOKING TIME: ABOUT 35 MINUTES
DO AHEAD: YOU CAN COOK THE CHICKPEAS UP TO 1 WEEK IN ADVANCE. YOU CAN ROAST THE PEPPERS UP TO 3 DAYS IN ADVANCE. REFRIGERATE UNTIL READY TO USE.
REFRIGERATION/FREEZING: REFRIGERATE UP TO 3 DAYS. FREEZE UP TO 2 MONTHS.

I know it's wrong, and potentially cruel, to invite guests to dinner for the purpose of performing an experiment. But certain occasions lend themselves to this breach of etiquette. I'm thinking of the time I made dinner for a friend whose doctor had prescribed a no-fat diet. His wife generously offered to bring something for him so I could serve the other guests whatever I pleased. But I wanted to see whether I could work within my friend's restrictions and make everyone happy with the very same meal.

Well, they drained the Apple-Turnip Soup (see page 186) and totally cleaned the Couscous platter. Dessert was Chocolate-Cherry Sorbet (see page 491), which nobody declined.

1 eggplant, stem and root end removed, thinly sliced
1 pound tiny new potatoes, scrubbed
½ cup vegetable broth (see page 165), plus more as needed
2 tablespoons balsamic vinegar
1 large onion, chopped
2 shallots, minced
2 tablespoons grated peeled fresh ginger
¼ cup minced fresh basil
2 teaspoons ground cumin

2 teaspoons ground coriander

1 teaspoon ground cinnamon

½ teaspoon powdered saffron

2 red bell peppers, roasted, peeled, and thinly sliced (see page 534)

1 yellow bell pepper, roasted, peeled, and thinly sliced (see page 534)

3 cups cooked chickpeas, drained and rinsed

1½ cups chopped peeled fresh tomatoes (see page 544), or canned chopped tomatoes

¼ cup currants

1½ cups uncooked quick-cooking couscous

Salt and freshly ground black pepper to taste

Cucumber Raita (see page 156; optional)

Heat the oven to 425°F.

Squirt a nonstick baking sheet with nonstick spray. Place the eggplant slices in a single layer and bake until tender, about 15 minutes, depending on the thickness of the slices. Remove them from the oven and let them cool.

While the eggplant is baking, bring a pot of water to a boil, add the potatoes, reduce the heat to medium, and simmer until they're tender, about 10 minutes. Drain and set aside.

In a large skillet, bring the broth and vinegar to a simmer over medium-high heat. Add the onion, shallots, ginger, basil, cumin, coriander, cinnamon, and saffron, turn down the heat to medium, and simmer until the liquid has reduced to almost nothing, about 10 minutes. (Make sure there's some liquid left, or the vegetables will burn.)

Stir in the peppers and chickpeas and mix well. Add the tomatoes and continue cooking and stirring until reduced to a thick sauce, about 5 minutes. Stir in the currants, eggplant slices, and potatoes. Reduce the heat to low,

cover, and simmer just to let the flavors bind, about 7 minutes. Check the liquid level, adding broth 2 tablespoons at a time if necessary to prevent burning.

Meanwhile prepare the couscous. Place the couscous in a large saucepan. In a medium saucepan bring 1¾ cups water to a boil. Pour the water over the couscous, cover, and let sit for 20 minutes. Fluff with a fork before serving. Transfer it to a serving platter. Make a deep well in the center and empty the skillet into it. Season with salt and pepper, and serve with Cucumber Raita as a condiment, if you'd like.

PER SERVING: CALORIES 420 • PROTEIN 18.4 G • CARBOHYDRATE 83.9 G • FAT 4.3 G • CHOLESTEROL 0 MG · SODIUM 44.7 MG • 9% CALORIES FROM FAT • OUT-STANDING SOURCE OF VITAMINS A, B₆, C; FOLACIN, IRON • VERY GOOD SOURCE OF VITAMIN B₁; CALCIUM, ZINC

LENTIL AND MUSHROOM STEW

Serves 6

TOTAL TIME: ABOUT 2 HOURS, 30 MINUTES
TIME TO PREPARE: ABOUT 40 MINUTES
COOKING TIME: ABOUT 1 HOUR, 15 MINUTES
REFRIGERATION/FREEZING: REFRIGERATE UP TO 3 DAYS. DO NOT FREEZE.

This luscious, bone-warming stew tastes best several hours to several days after you've made it, once the tofu has had time to absorb the rich, earthy flavors of the porcini and lentils. Serve it over rice or barley.

1 ounce dried porcini mushrooms

2 large onions

1 whole clove

1 cup uncooked lentils, preferably lentilles du Puy, rinsed

1 bay leaf

2 teaspoons extra virgin olive oil

2 garlic cloves, minced

2 leeks, white part only, washed and chopped

¼ cup minced fresh parsley

2 teaspoons ground cumin

1 teaspoon crumbled dried summer savory

1 teaspoon ground cinnamon

2 tablespoons balsamic vinegar, approximately

8 ounces fresh cremini or portobello mushrooms, sliced

2 parsnips, peeled and thickly sliced

1 tablespoon brown rice flour or unbleached all-purpose flour

1 pound firm tofu, cut into 1-inch cubes

Place the porcini in a small bowl. Add hot water to cover and set aside until the mushrooms are soft, about 30 minutes.

Chop one of the onions and set it aside. Cut the remaining onion into quarters. Stick the clove into 1 quarter, and place all 4 pieces in a large saucepan. Add the lentils and bay leaf. Add water to cover by 1½ inches. Bring to a boil over medium-high heat. Cover, reduce the heat to medium-low, and simmer until the lentils are tender, about 30 minutes.

Meanwhile, heat the oil in a medium skillet over medium-high heat. When it's hot, add the chopped onion, garlic, leeks, parsley, cumin, savory, and cinnamon. Reduce the heat to medium and sauté, stirring often, until the vegetables are soft, about 7 minutes. Add the balsamic vinegar and continue stirring until most of it has evaporated, about 2 minutes. Stir in the fresh mushrooms and parsnips and continue sautéing until they're soft, about 10 minutes. If the vegetables start to stick, add more balsamic vinegar 1 teaspoon at a time, scrape, and stir.

Drain the porcini through a fine sieve, reserving the water. Chop them and add them to the pan. Sprinkle the mixture with the flour and stir well.

Drain the lentils, discarding the liquid, clove, and bay leaf. Add them to the mushroom mixture. Stir well to blend.

Stir in the mushroom soaking liquid, and continue stirring until the sauce thickens, about 5 minutes. Add the tofu, and stir well to coat. Cover and simmer over low heat until the flavors of the stew permeate the tofu, about 45 minutes. Stir gently and let the stew sit for 15 minutes before serving.

PER SERVING: CALORIES 340 • PROTEIN 25 G • CARBOHYDRATE 45 G • FAT 9.1 G • CHOLESTEROL 0 MG • SODIUM 32.7 MG • 23% CALORIES FROM FAT • OUTSTANDING SOURCE OF FOLACIN, IRON • VERY GOOD SOURCE OF VITAMINS B₁, B₂, B₆, C; CALCIUM, ZINC • GOOD SOURCE OF VITAMIN B₃

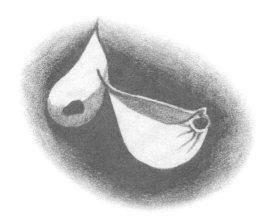

BLACK BEANS WITH ORANGE AND SAFFRON

Serves 4

TOTAL TIME: ABOUT 30 MINUTES, NOT INCLUDING TIME TO ROAST THE PEPPERS OR COOK THE BEANS

TIME TO PREPARE: ABOUT 30 MINUTES, INCLUDING TIME TO SAUTÉ

COOKING TIME: INCLUDED IN TIME TO PREPARE

DO AHEAD: YOU CAN ROAST THE PEPPERS UP TO 3 DAYS IN ADVANCE. REFRIGERATE UNTIL READY TO USE.

REFRIGERATION/FREEZING: REFRIGERATE UP TO 2 DAYS. FREEZE UP TO 6 MONTHS.

In the Middle Ages, the upwardly mobile flaunted their spice shelves, using the precious contents liberally and indiscriminately. The point wasn't to season their food well, but to show they could afford to do it.

While I have never served something expensive for its own sake, I have been known not to serve certain foods because they're too cheap; I don't want my guests to think I scrimped on their supper. This was my problem with beans. Everyone knows beans are cheap, and no matter what you do with them, they're still beans and they're still cheap—unless you season them with saffron. Saffron is an exceedingly expen-sive spice, but affordable nonetheless, since a pinch goes a long, long way. Like most saffron-seasoned dishes, this tastes best the day after you make it— hot, cold, or room temperature. Serve it over rice.

1 orange
2 teaspoons extra virgin olive oil
1 large onion, chopped
3 garlic cloves, minced
2 yellow or orange bell peppers, roasted, peeled, and chopped (see page 534)
1/2 cup minced fresh cilantro
2 teaspoons crumbled dried oregano
2 teaspoons ground cumin
2 teaspoons ground coriander
2 teaspoons tomato paste
1 tablespoon balsamic vinegar or red wine vinegar
1/4 teaspoon powdered saffron
3 cups cooked black beans, drained and rinsed

Grate 2 teaspoons of zest from the orange peel and then juice the orange, discarding the rest. Set aside.

Heat the oil in a large skillet over medium heat. Add the onion, garlic, peppers, cilantro, oregano, cumin, and coriander and sauté until the onion is soft and limp, about 10 minutes. Stir in the tomato paste and blend. Add the vinegar, turn up the heat to medium-high, and stir until the liquid evaporates, about 2 minutes. Add the orange juice and zest and the saffron. Stir until the mixture thickens, about 2 minutes.

Stir in the beans and heat through, about 3 minutes.

PER SERVING: CALORIES 317 • PROTEIN 17.7 G • CARBOHYDRATE 56.7 G • FAT 3.9 G • CHOLESTEROL 0 MG • SODIUM 29.4 MG • 11% CALORIES FROM FAT • OUTSTANDING SOURCE OF VITAMIN C; FOLACIN • VERY GOOD SOURCE OF IRON, ZINC

SPICY TOFU WITH EGGPLANT AND PEPPERS

Serves 4

TOTAL TIME: ABOUT 2 HOURS, INCLUDING TIME TO PRESS THE TOFU

TIME TO PREPARE: ABOUT 30 MINUTES, INCLUDING TIME TO SAUTÉ

COOKING TIME: ABOUT 1 HOUR

DO AHEAD: YOU CAN ROAST THE PEPPERS UP TO 3 DAYS IN ADVANCE. REFRIGERATE UNTIL READY TO USE.

REFRIGERATION/FREEZING: REFRIGERATE UP TO 2 DAYS. FREEZE UP TO 3 MONTHS.

*W*e all know someone who won't touch tofu. Try this one on him, and you may give a slight boost to soybean shares. Seasoned with garlic, curry spices, and sweet bell peppers, it's best served over plain boiled rice or soba noodles.

1 pound firm tofu

1 large eggplant, peeled and chopped

Coarse salt

1 tablespoon canola or vegetable oil

1 onion, chopped

2 scallions, white part only, chopped

3 garlic cloves, minced

One 1-inch piece fresh ginger, peeled and grated

1 red bell pepper, roasted, peeled, and chopped (see page 534)

1 yellow bell pepper, roasted, peeled, and chopped (see page 534)

1 jalapeño pepper, cored, seeded, and minced

2 teaspoons whole mustard seeds, toasted (see page 56)

¼ cup torn fresh basil

¼ cup fresh cilantro

2 teaspoons ground cumin

1 teaspoon ground coriander

1 teaspoon ground turmeric

1 tablespoon curry powder

1 tablespoon tomato paste

1 tablespoon fresh lemon juice

Salt and freshly ground black pepper to taste

Place the tofu in a pie plate. Cover with several sheets of paper towel, and put a heavy pot on top. Set aside for at least an hour. When it has been pressed, discard the liquid and cut the tofu into small (½-inch) cubes.

Line a colander with paper towels and place the eggplant inside. Sprinkle with salt, and toss gently. Set aside for 30 minutes.

Heat the oil in a large, heavy skillet over medium-high heat. Add the onion, scallions, garlic, and ginger. Lower the heat to medium, and sauté until soft, about 8 minutes. Rinse the eggplant lightly, just enough to get the salt off the surface, and pat it dry with fresh paper towels. Add to the skillet along with the bell peppers, jalapeño pepper, mustard seeds, basil, cilantro, cumin, coriander, turmeric, curry powder, tomato paste, lemon juice, and pressed

tofu. Sauté, stirring often, until the eggplant is cooked through, about 7 minutes. Season with salt and pepper.

•

RATATOUILLE
A Vegetable Stew
Serves 4

TOTAL TIME: 1 HOUR, 30 MINUTES, INCLUDING TIME TO DRAIN THE EGGPLANT
TIME TO PREPARE: 20 MINUTES, INCLUDING TIME TO SAUTÉ
COOKING TIME: 40 MINUTES
DO AHEAD: YOU CAN ROAST THE PEPPERS UP TO 3 DAYS IN ADVANCE. REFRIGERATE UNTIL READY TO USE.
REFRIGERATION/FREEZING: REFRIGERATE, COVERED, UP TO 4 DAYS. FREEZE UP TO 6 MONTHS.

*H*ere's where you get into real trouble with the food authorities. Authentic ratatouille isn't a stew at all, but a combination of vegetables, each cooked separately and united for serving. It is a method I would recommend only to die-hard procrastinators looking for something to do for the sake of putting off doing something else.

The results you'll get with this technique (endorsed, incidentally, by Larousse) will make you wonder why anyone would bother with a more complicated approach. Perhaps it could be better. But that won't cross your mind.

2 medium eggplants, sliced into ¼-inch-thick
  rounds
Coarse salt (optional)
1 tablespoon extra virgin olive oil

2 onions, sliced
1 fennel bulb, without leafy fronds, chopped
  (optional)
4 garlic cloves, crushed
1 red bell pepper, roasted, peeled, and sliced
  (see page 534)
1 yellow bell pepper, roasted, peeled, and sliced
  (see page 534)
6 medium ripe tomatoes, peeled, seeded, and
  chopped (see page 544), or one 16-ounce
  can or carton chopped tomatoes
1 bouquet garni, containing basil, oregano, and
  thyme (see page 558)
2 firm zucchini, sliced into ½-inch-thick rounds
Salt and freshly ground black pepper to taste

Heat the oven to 425°F.

If the eggplant slices are full of seeds, sprinkle them with salt. Line a colander with paper towels, and place the eggplant inside to drain for 30 minutes. Rinse lightly, just to remove the salt from the surface. Blot dry with a paper towel. Place the eggplant in a single layer on a nonstick baking sheet and bake until light brown on top, about 10 minutes. Turn over to brown the other side, about 5 minutes. Remove from the oven.

Heat the oil in a large skillet over medium-high heat. When it is hot, add the onions, fennel, if using, and garlic. Reduce the heat to medium and sauté, stirring often, until the onions are soft and translucent, about 12 minutes. Stir in the bell peppers, eggplants, tomatoes, and bouquet garni. Cook at a gentle simmer over medium heat until the sauce thickens, about 30 minutes. Stir in the zucchini and cook until tender, about 3 minutes. Remove and discard the bouquet garni. Season with salt and pepper, and serve at room temperature or chilled.

Make It Your Own

You can alter the basic ratatouille recipe easily, using the vegetables and seasonings you love most.

WHAT TO ADD AND WHEN TO ADD IT

✐ *Cheese.* Stir in about 2 tablespoons grated Parmesan, Asiago, Pecorino, or Fontina or about ¼ cup crumbled feta cheese just before serving the ratatouille.

✐ *Beans.* Add 2 to 3 cups cooked cannellini beans, chickpeas, or any similar style bean (see pages 565 to 571).

✐ *Olives and/or Capers.* Stir in ⅓ cup assorted sliced cured olives and/or 2 teaspoons whole capers, drained, before serving the ratatouille.

✐ *Pesto.* Stir 1 tablespoon of Pesto (see page 280) or Cilantro Pesto (see page 281) into the ratatouille while it's still hot. Add more to taste.

✐ *Eggs.* Top each portion of ratatouille with a poached egg (see page 62), or add sliced hard-boiled eggs (see page 65) for a lunch or supper dish.

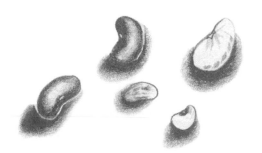

✐ *Polenta, pasta, or risotto.* Serve ratatouille over soft polenta or polenta squares (see page 324), or over pasta. You can also make a well in each serving of Risotto with Herbs, add a heaping spoonful of ratatouille, and then dust with grated cheese.

•

EGGPLANT, POTATO, AND SPINACH WITH AROMATIC HERBS

Serves 4

TOTAL TIME: ABOUT 1 HOUR, 55 MINUTES, NOT INCLUDING TIME TO COOK THE CHICKPEAS
TIME TO PREPARE: ABOUT 40 MINUTES, INCLUDING TIME TO SAUTÉ
COOKING TIME: ABOUT 15 MINUTES
DO AHEAD: YOU CAN PREPARE THE EGGPLANT UP TO 2 DAYS IN ADVANCE. REFRIGERATE UNTIL READY TO USE.
REFRIGERATION/FREEZING: REFRIGERATE UP TO 2 DAYS. DO NOT FREEZE.

Mellow eggplant puree tames some wild and zesty herbs in this one-dish dinner, which also includes chickpeas, potatoes, and yogurt. Serve it warm or cold, or over rice or egg noodles.

1 pound potatoes, preferably Yukon Gold
1 large eggplant
2 teaspoons extra virgin olive oil
1 leek, white part and 1 inch of greens, washed and thinly sliced
1 large onion, thinly sliced
2 scallions, white part and 1 inch of greens, thinly sliced
¼ cup minced fresh mint

¼ cup minced fresh cilantro

¼ cup minced fresh chives

¼ cup minced fresh basil, or 2 tablespoons crumbled dried basil

¼ cup minced fresh dill, or 1 tablespoon crumbled dried dill

2 tablespoons minced fresh oregano

1 tablespoon white wine or wine vinegar

2 cups loosely packed chopped fresh spinach, or one 10-ounce package frozen chopped spinach, thawed and squeezed dry

⅓ cup nonfat or low-fat buttermilk

⅓ cup plain nonfat yogurt

2 cups cooked chickpeas, drained and rinsed

Salt and freshly ground black pepper to taste

Heat the oven to 425°F.

Bake the potatoes until tender, about 50 minutes, or bake in the microwave (see page 536), and set aside to cool.

Heat the broiler.

Place the eggplant under the broiler, and broil until the skin buckles and chars, about 7 minutes. Turn to broil the other side, about 7 minutes. Transfer to a plate and let it cool. When the eggplant is cool enough to handle, cut off the stem end, and peel away the skin. Discard as many seeds as you can without tossing away the flesh. Chop the pulp and set it aside.

Heat the oil in a large nonstick skillet over medium-high heat, and swirl the pan to coat the bottom. Add the leek, onion, scallions, mint, cilantro, chives, basil, dill, and oregano, and sauté over medium heat until the vegetables are so tender they seem close to melting, about 20 minutes. Add the wine or vinegar, raise the heat to medium-high, and stir until

the liquid evaporates, about 1 minute. Reduce the heat to medium-low, add the fresh spinach, if using, and cook, stirring constantly, until the leaves have turned bright green, about 2 minutes. If using frozen spinach, stir until it is evenly incorporated with the sauce, about 1 minute. Add the eggplant pulp, and stir well.

Slice the potatoes, cut the slices in half, and stir them into the skillet. Turn off the heat.

Stir together the buttermilk and yogurt, and add them slowly (no more than a tablespoon at a time to start, gradually increasing the amount to ¼ cup) to the skillet, allowing the temperature to adjust so the mixture won't curdle. Stir in the chickpeas, and season with salt and pepper.

To serve, heat carefully over low heat, stirring until just warmed through. However, if you're as timid as I am about heating dishes that may curdle, you'll be glad to know that this dish is delicious at room temperature, and wonderful chilled.

PER SERVING: CALORIES 450 • PROTEIN 16.6 G • CARBOHYDRATE 87.5 G • FAT 5.3 G • CHOLESTEROL 1.0 MG • SODIUM 86 MG • 10% CALORIES FROM FAT • OUTSTANDING SOURCE OF VITAMINS B₆, C; FOLACIN • VERY GOOD SOURCE OF VITAMINS A, B₁, B₂; IRON • GOOD SOURCE OF ZINC

EGGPLANT BAKED WITH LENTILS

Serves 6

TOTAL TIME: ABOUT 2 HOURS, NOT INCLUDING TIME TO MAKE THE SAUCE

TIME TO PREPARE: ABOUT 40 MINUTES, INCLUDING TIME TO SAUTÉ

COOKING TIME: ABOUT 1 HOUR, 15 MINUTES

DO AHEAD: YOU CAN MAKE THE SAUCE UP TO 2 DAYS IN ADVANCE. YOU CAN MAKE THE LENTIL SAUCE UP TO 3 DAYS IN ADVANCE. REFRIGERATE UNTIL READY TO USE.

REFRIGERATION/FREEZING: REFRIGERATE UP TO 3 DAYS. DO NOT FREEZE.

I doubt I'll ever run out of things to do with eggplant. And if I do, I wouldn't mind starting all over with this, a rich-tasting casserole of lentils and cheese, seasoned with cinnamon and herbs.

2 medium eggplants, sliced but not peeled
Coarse salt
1 tablespoon extra virgin olive oil
1 large onion, chopped
1 garlic clove, minced

2 whole cloves
1 tablespoon crumbled dried oregano
1 tablespoon crumbled dried basil
2 teaspoons ground cinnamon
2 tablespoons balsamic vinegar
2 cups fresh or canned chopped tomatoes
1 cup uncooked lentils, preferably lentilles du Puy, picked over and rinsed
1 cup water
Salt and freshly ground black pepper to taste
1 recipe White Sauce with Jack Cheese (recipe follows)

Heat the oven to 425°F.

Spread the eggplant slices on a nonstick baking sheet (you'll probably need two), and sprinkle both sides liberally with coarse salt. Set aside for 30 minutes.

Meanwhile, heat the oil in a large skillet over medium heat. When it's hot, add the onion, garlic, cloves, oregano, basil, and cinnamon. Reduce the heat to medium and sauté, stirring often, until the onion is soft and limp, about 10 minutes. Add the balsamic vinegar and stir until most of the liquid has evaporated, about 3 minutes.

Stir in the tomatoes and lentils. Stir in the water. Turn up the heat to medium-high, bring the mixture to a gentle boil, cover, turn down the heat to medium-low, and simmer until the lentils are soft, about 30 minutes.

While the lentils are cooking, rinse the eggplant slices with cold water and pat them dry with fresh paper towels. Spread them on the baking sheets in a single layer, and bake until soft and cooked through, about 20 minutes. Remove from the oven. Turn down the oven heat to 350°F.

When the lentils are cooked, drain off any excess liquid, remove the cloves, and season with salt and pepper. Spread about ½ cup on the bottom of an 8-inch baking dish. Top with a layer of half the eggplant. Cover with half of the remaining lentil mixture, then top that with half of the cheese sauce. Repeat with the remaining ingredients.

Cover loosely with foil and bake for 35 minutes. Remove the foil and continue baking until the cheese is brown and bubbly, about 10 minutes more. Let cool on a rack for 10 minutes before cutting and serving.

PER SERVING: CALORIES 278 • PROTEIN 18.6 G • CARBOHYDRATE 32 G • FAT 9.7 G • CHOLESTEROL 17.9 MG • SODIUM 251 MG • 30% CALORIES FROM FAT • OUTSTANDING SOURCE OF FOLACIN • VERY GOOD SOURCE OF VITAMIN C; CALCIUM, IRON • GOOD SOURCE OF VITAMIN A; ZINC

•

WHITE SAUCE WITH JACK CHEESE

Serves 4

TOTAL TIME: ABOUT 15 MINUTES
TIME TO PREPARE: 15 MINUTES
COOKING TIME: INCLUDED IN TIME TO PREPARE
DO AHEAD: YOU CAN MAKE THIS SAUCE 2 DAYS AHEAD. REFRIGERATE UNTIL READY TO USE. BEFORE SERVING, HEAT GENTLY, WHISKING IN ADDITIONAL VEGETABLE BROTH TO RESTORE ORIGINAL CONSISTENCY. DO NOT BOIL.
REFRIGERATION/FREEZING: REFRIGERATE UP TO 3 DAYS. DO NOT FREEZE.

This is the Light All-Purpose White Sauce (see page 279), adapted for this recipe. You can also serve it over steamed vegetables, such as cauliflower and broccoli.

2 cups vegetable broth (see page 165)
1 tablespoon cornstarch or arrowroot
½ cup evaporated skim milk
½ cup nonfat milk
½ cup shredded Monterey Jack cheese
Salt and freshly ground black pepper to taste

Bring the vegetable broth to a boil in a medium saucepan over medium-high heat. Reduce the heat to medium-low, keeping the broth at a simmer.

In a small bowl, mix the cornstarch or arrowroot with 2 tablespoons of the evaporated milk to make a thick paste. Stir it into the broth along with the rest of the evaporated milk, nonfat milk, and Jack cheese, and whisk until the sauce thickens, about 5 minutes.

Season with salt and pepper.

PER SERVING: CALORIES 95 • PROTEIN 6.9 G • CARBOHYDRATE 6.9 G • FAT 4.4 G • CHOLESTEROL 14.3 MG • SODIUM 128 MG • 42% CALORIES FROM FAT • VERY GOOD SOURCE OF CALCIUM

CHEESE CREPE BUNDLES IN MINCED RATATOUILLE

Serves 6

TOTAL TIME: ABOUT 1 HOUR, 30 MINUTES
TIME TO PREPARE: ABOUT 1 HOUR
COOKING TIME: ABOUT 30 MINUTES
DO AHEAD: YOU CAN MAKE THE CREPES UP TO 2 DAYS IN ADVANCE, PUTTING WAX PAPER BETWEEN THEM TO KEEP THEM SEPARATE, COVERING WITH PLASTIC, AND REFRIGERATING. YOU CAN MAKE THE RATATOUILLE AND/OR MIX THE CHEESE FILLING UP TO 2 DAYS IN ADVANCE.
REFRIGERATION/FREEZING: DO NOT REFRIGERATE OR FREEZE.

Granted, cheese-filled crepes in ratatouille sauce isn't something you whip up in a flash; it's a lot to tackle at one go. But if you make the crepes two days ahead and the sauce the day before, it's simple to assemble and serve. Not incidentally, it looks spectacular and tastes superb.

Crepes

1 large egg
3 large egg whites
1 cup nonfat milk
Pinch salt
1 cup unbleached all-purpose flour

Cheese Filling

4 cups fresh chard or spinach, washed and coarsely chopped, or one 10-ounce package frozen chard or spinach, thawed and squeezed dry
1 cup nonfat or part-skim ricotta cheese
¼ cup grated Parmesan or Asiago cheese
Pinch ground nutmeg
Salt and freshly ground black pepper to taste

Ratatouille

4 miniature Japanese eggplants
1 tablespoon extra virgin olive oil
1 onion, minced
2 garlic cloves, minced
1 small red bell pepper, cored, seeded, and minced
1 small yellow bell pepper, cored, seeded, and minced
2 zucchini or summer squash, minced
¼ cup minced fresh basil
2 tablespoons minced fresh oregano, or 1 tablespoon crumbled dried oregano
2 tablespoons balsamic vinegar
2 cups peeled chopped fresh tomatoes (see page 544) or canned chopped tomatoes
Salt and freshly ground black pepper to taste

16 fresh chives (or 8 scallion greens, cut in half crosswise, each about 6 inches long)

For the Crepes

In a large mixing bowl, beat together the egg and egg whites, milk, salt, and flour. Pour the mixture through a fine sieve into another bowl. Let rest for 30 minutes.

Heat a 6-inch nonstick pan over medium-high heat. Pour 3 tablespoons of batter into the center of the pan and quickly swirl the pan to coat it evenly. Cook the crepe over medium heat until the bottom has set, about 40 seconds. Loosening the crepe with a nonmetallic implement (such as a small plastic knife or spatula), turn it over with your fingers and cook it until the other side has set, about 1 minute. Transfer the crepe to a plate, and stack the crepes, alternating each with a sheet of wax paper, as you finish them. Serve as soon as pos-

sible, or let them cool completely, wrap them in plastic with a sheet of wax paper between each crepe, and refrigerate or freeze.

For the Cheese Filling

If you're using fresh chard or spinach, put 1 inch of water in a saucepan. Bring it to a boil. Add the chard or spinach, cover, and remove it from the heat. Let the chard or spinach sit until bright green, about 3 minutes. Remove the pan's cover, transfer the chard or spinach to a colander, and let it cool. Squeeze out the excess water. Place the fresh or frozen chard or

spinach in a mixing bowl. Add the ricotta, Parmesan or Asiago, and nutmeg. Season with salt and pepper. Set aside in the refrigerator.

For the Ratatouille

Heat the oven to 425°F.

Slice the eggplants into rounds ¼ inch thick. Lay them in a single layer on a nonstick baking sheet and place them in the oven until they're soft, 7 to 10 minutes. Turn and cook them briefly on the other side just to color, about 2 minutes.

Heat the oil in a large skillet over medium-high heat. When it's hot, add the onion, garlic, bell peppers, zucchini or summer squash, basil, and oregano. Reduce the heat to medium and sauté, stirring often, until the vegetables have softened, about 10 minutes. Add the balsamic vinegar, turn up the heat to medium-high, and stir until it has evaporated, about 2 minutes.

Add the tomatoes and continue cooking, stirring often, until they thicken and reduce, about 7 minutes. Season with salt and pepper. Turn off the heat.

To assemble, place 2 tablespoons of the cheese filling in the center of each crepe. Bring the sides up to make a little sack. Tie a chive or scallion green around each to close. You should have between 8 and 12 bundles. Place the bundles in the skillet with the ratatouille, cover, and simmer until heated through, about 15 minutes. Serve right away.

PER SERVING: CALORIES 376 • PROTEIN 20.4 G • CARBOHYDRATE 54.2 G • FAT 9.7 G • CHOLESTEROL 87.6 MG • SODIUM 249 MG • 23% CALORIES FROM FAT • OUT-STANDING SOURCE OF VITAMIN C • VERY GOOD SOURCE OF VITAMIN A; CAL-CIUM, FOLACIN • GOOD SOURCE OF IRON

L E E K - A N D - O N I O N
P O T A T O   P I E

Serves 4

TOTAL TIME: ABOUT 2 HOURS, NOT INCLUDING TIME TO
    BAKE THE POTATOES
TIME TO PREPARE: 40 MINUTES, INCLUDING TIME TO SAUTÉ
COOKING TIME: ABOUT 1 HOUR
EQUIPMENT: 8-INCH SPRINGFORM PAN
DO AHEAD: YOU CAN MAKE THE CRUST UP TO 2 DAYS IN
    ADVANCE. PREPARE THE PIE UP TO 3 DAYS AHEAD.
REFRIGERATION/FREEZING: REFRIGERATE UP TO 3 DAYS.
    FREEZE INDEFINITELY.

Composers transpose music all the time, taking a piece meant for flute, for example, and reworking it for violin or piano. You can transpose recipes with similar success, taking ingredients for a much-loved soup, in this case, and putting them in a pie.

Crust

1 pound Yukon gold or russet-type potatoes

1 large egg, beaten

⅓ cup nonfat or part-skim ricotta cheese

1 tablespoon whole wheat flour

1 tablespoon unsalted butter or canola or
    vegetable oil

3 cups thinly sliced leeks, white part only (about
    2 large leeks)

2 cups thinly sliced onions

Pinch salt

1 large egg

1 large egg yolk

1 cup evaporated skim milk

1 tablespoon unbleached all-purpose flour

½ cup nonfat or reduced-fat sour cream

2 tablespoons minced fresh chives

For the Crust
Heat the oven to 425°F.

Bake the potatoes until tender, about 50 minutes, or bake in the microwave (see page 536).

Peel and mash the potatoes. Combine them with the egg, ricotta, and flour, mixing with your hands until you have a soft, pliant dough. Press the dough into the bottom of an 8-inch springform pan, and bake until it's firm but still springy, about 20 minutes. Take it out of the oven and let it cool. Don't turn off the oven.

In a large skillet or sauté pan, melt the butter or heat the oil. Add the leeks, onions, and salt, and sauté until very soft, about 15 minutes.

In a mixing bowl, beat together the egg and egg yolk, the evaporated skim milk, and flour. Make sure there are no lumps.

Spread the sour cream over the potato crust and sprinkle the chives evenly on top. Pour in the egg mixture, and place the pie in the oven. Bake until the filling has set, about 50 minutes. If the top starts to brown before the custard has set, cover the pie with foil and continue baking until a knife stuck into the center comes out clean. Let it sit 10 minutes before serving. Serve hot, room temperature, or cold.

PER SERVING: CALORIES 335 • PROTEIN 15.6 G • CARBOHYDRATE 52.7 G • FAT 7.8 G • CHOLESTEROL 161 MG • SODIUM 110 MG • 20% CALORIES FROM FAT • OUTSTANDING SOURCE OF VITAMIN C • VERY GOOD SOURCE OF VITAMINS B₂, B₄; FOLACIN, CALCIUM, IRON • GOOD SOURCE OF VITAMINS A, B₁, B₃, B₁₂; IRON

TANGY TOFU SAUCE FOR ASSORTED FRESH VEGETABLES

Serves 4

TOTAL TIME: ABOUT 40 MINUTES, NOT INCLUDING TIME TO COOK THE RICE OR PASTA, STEAM THE VEGETABLES, OR MAKE THE BROTH
TIME TO PREPARE: ABOUT 40 MINUTES
COOKING TIME: INCLUDED IN TIME TO PREPARE
REFRIGERATION/FREEZING: REFRIGERATE UP TO 3 DAYS. DO NOT FREEZE.

I t's hard to say whether this sauce is better in winter, served warm over barley, mushrooms, and tubers, or in summer, served chilled over snow peas, sweet corn, and rice. You may want to study the matter closely, making it often throughout the year.

2 teaspoons canola oil, or ¹/₂ cup vegetable broth (see page 165) plus 2 tablespoons balsamic vinegar

2 large onions, thinly sliced

1 tablespoon grated peeled fresh ginger, or 1 teaspoon ground ginger

¹/₄ cup minced fresh dill, or 1 tablespoon crumbled dried dill

¹/₂ pound extra-firm tofu, cut into 1-inch cubes

1 cup plain nonfat yogurt, at room temperature

1 tablespoon cornstarch

2 teaspoons paprika

1 teaspoon dry mustard

1 tablespoon low-sodium soy sauce

Freshly ground black pepper to taste

4 cups mixed steamed or boiled vegetables, such as broccoli florets, brussels sprouts, beets, cabbage, new potatoes, or spinach (see pages 514 to 546)

If using oil, heat it in a medium skillet over medium-high heat, swirling the pan to coat the bottom. Or combine the vegetable broth and balsamic vinegar in a medium saucepan and bring to a brisk simmer.

Add the onions, ginger, and dill, and sauté or sweat until the onions are limp, about 15 minutes.

In a food processor or blender, combine the tofu, yogurt, and cornstarch. Stir the mixture into the onion mixture, along with the paprika, dry mustard, and soy sauce. Gently heat over medium-low, stirring often, until heated through and thickened, about 10 minutes. Season with pepper, and serve hot or cold over steamed vegetables.

PER SERVING (SAUCE ONLY): CALORIES 240 • PROTEIN 18.3 G • CARBOHY-DRATE 25 G • FAT 7.5 G • CHOLESTEROL 1.1 MG • SODIUM 169 MG • 33% CALORIES FROM FAT • OUTSTANDING SOURCE OF VITAMIN B₂; IRON • VERY GOOD SOURCE OF VITAMIN B₁; CALCIUM • GOOD SOURCE OF VITAMINS B₆, C; FOLACIN, ZINC

Chilis

CHILI

Serves 4

TOTAL TIME: ABOUT 45 MINUTES, NOT INCLUDING TIME TO
COOK THE BEANS
TIME TO PREPARE: ABOUT 20 MINUTES, INCLUDING TIME
TO SAUTÉ
COOKING TIME: ABOUT 25 MINUTES
DO AHEAD: YOU CAN ROAST AND PEEL THE PEPPERS UP TO
3 DAYS IN ADVANCE. REFRIGERATE UNTIL READY TO USE.
REFRIGERATION/FREEZING: REFRIGERATE UP TO 3 DAYS.
FREEZE UP TO 6 MONTHS.

Chili, like politics and pennant races, is a subject that should not be broached in polite company. People who like chili tend to have passionate opinions about how it should be made and might prefer slugging it out to conceding that their recipe might not be the definitive one.

Passions run high the other way, too. When chili first caught on in this country, Mexicans couldn't express enough contempt for it. The editor of a 1959 Mexican dictionary gave it a good shot, though, defining chili as "a detestable food with a false Mexican title which is sold in the United States from Texas to New York." Meanwhile, Texans brag that it started in San Antonio, and Californians, New Mexicans, and folks from Arizona are eager to take credit for the regional riffs they've put on the dish.

2 teaspoons corn oil or canola or vegetable oil
1 large red or white onion, chopped
3 garlic cloves, minced
2 tomatillos, husked and chopped, or 3
  tablespoons green salsa (see brand
  recommendations, page 595)
1 jalapeño pepper, cored, seeded, and minced
1 red bell pepper, cored, seeded, and chopped

¼ cup minced fresh cilantro
1 ½ tablespoons chili powder
1 tablespoon ground cumin
2 teaspoons crumbled dried oregano
2 tablespoons balsamic or red wine vinegar
4 large ripe tomatoes, cored, seeded, and
  chopped (see page 544), or 2 cups canned
  or boxed chopped tomatoes
3 cups cooked kidney, black runner, pinto, or
  black turtle beans, drained and rinsed
½ cup shredded cheddar cheese (optional)

Garnishes (Optional)
Nonfat sour cream or Strained Yogurt (see
  page 102)
Minced fresh cilantro
Minced red onions

Heat the oil in a large skillet over medium-high heat. When it's hot, add the onion, garlic, tomatillos (but don't add salsa yet if using instead), jalapeño, red bell pepper, cilantro, chili powder, cumin, and oregano. Reduce the heat to medium and sauté, stirring often, until the vegetables are soft, about 7 minutes. Add the vinegar and stir until it's almost evaporated, about 3 minutes.

Add the tomatoes and the green salsa, if using. Stir well and simmer over medium-low until the sauce thickens, about 7 minutes. Stir in the beans, cover, and simmer until the mixture thickens further, about 20 minutes. Turn off the heat and let the chili sit at least an hour before reheating and serving. If you'll be keeping the chili for more than 2 hours before serving, refrigerate it once it's reached room temperature.

Stir in the cheese just before serving, if you'd like, or sprinkle it on the individual servings. Pass the sour cream or yogurt and additional cilantro and onions at the table, if desired.

PER SERVING: CALORIES 256 • PROTEIN 14 G • CARBOHYDRATE 45 G • FAT 3.8 G • CHOLESTEROL 0 MG • SODIUM 83.6 MG • 13% CALORIES FROM FAT • OUTSTANDING SOURCE OF VITAMIN C; FOLACIN • VERY GOOD SOURCE OF VITAMINS A, B₁, B₆; IRON • GOOD SOURCE OF VITAMINS B₂, B₃; ZINC

CHILI BASICS

Chili Pantry: Beans (especially black beans, chickpeas, kidney beans, pinto beans, and runner beans), ground cumin, chili powder, dried chilies (see box, page 535), dried oregano, cornmeal, canned or boxed tomatoes, medium-grain or long-grain rice, red wine vinegar, corn oil or canola oil, red and green salsas

In the Refrigerator: Onions, garlic, cilantro, tomatoes, tomatillos, scallions, chilies, bell peppers, avocados, sour cream or Strained Yogurt (see page 102), tortillas

• Use good, robust beans. See the guide on page 565 for choosing beans. If you can't find good fresh dried beans where you shop, you can get them by mail (see page 596). The better beans cost more than the kind you may be used to, but you'll find the flavor is so superior, you won't care. Besides, they may cost more than ordinary beans, but they're still inexpensive when you calculate price per serving.

• Make sure your spices and herbs are fresh. If they've been sitting around for more than six months, buy a new supply, preferably at a store with a fast turnover. Buy them in small portions, so they won't have a chance to go stale.

• Chili's complex flavors need time to meld. Whenever possible make the chili a few hours before serving and up to a day ahead.

• Adjust the heat to taste, starting with the amount of peppers and seasonings in the basic recipe and increasing to taste and tolerance.

Make It Your Own

If you're looking for a dish to call your own, chili is a good choice. Once you've made the base, you can build on it in any number of ways. See Chili, page 352, for a base that can be used with all of the following suggestions.

WHAT TO ADD AND WHEN TO ADD IT

✐ *Vegetables.* Once you've made the base, add fresh vegetables such as mushrooms, zucchini, fresh corn, sweet potatoes, new potatoes. Then add tomatoes and beans, according to the basic recipe. Play around with different types of beans as well. Keep in mind that the more vegetables you add to the chili, the longer you should let the dish sit so each ingredient can absorb the seasoning.

✐ *Tofu.* Add cubed extra-firm tofu once you've made the flavor base. Stir well to coat with the seasonings before you add the tomatoes. Because it takes a while for tofu to absorb flavors, chili made with tofu will taste best if you make it at least six hours before serving.

✐ *Tortillas.* Use the chili to make burritos by cooking it down over medium heat, stirring often, until it's very dense. Spoon the thickened chili into the center of a large flour tortilla. Fold the top and bottom of the tortilla to enclose the filling, then fold in one of the sides. Roll to encase it entirely. Serve garnished with guacamole, sour cream, salsa, and minced fresh cilantro.

Hollowed Vegetables for Stuffing. Use the chili to fill vegetables. Mix it with cooked rice and spoon it into hollowed-out bell peppers, tomatoes, and onions (see instructions for preparing vegetables for filling on page 362). If you'd like, top the stuffed vegetables with shredded cheddar or Jack cheese, cover loosely with foil, and bake at 350°F. until soft, about fifteen minutes.

Pasta. Cook the chili down over medium heat, stirring often, until it's very dense, and spoon it over pasta (especially corn pasta, which tastes like tortillas). Sprinkle with a combination of grated Parmesan cheese and grated sharp cheddar.

•

CHUNKY BEAN BURRITOS WITH SPICY TOMATO SAUCE

Serves 4

TOTAL TIME: ABOUT 1 HOUR, 20 MINUTES, NOT INCLUDING TIME TO ROAST THE PEPPER, COOK THE BEANS, OR MAKE THE SAUCE

TIME TO PREPARE: ABOUT 1 HOUR, INCLUDING TIME TO SAUTÉ

COOKING TIME: 20 MINUTES

DO AHEAD: YOU CAN ROAST THE PEPPERS UP TO 3 DAYS IN ADVANCE. YOU CAN MAKE THE TOMATO SAUCE UP TO 3 DAYS IN ADVANCE. REFRIGERATE BOTH UNTIL READY TO USE.

REFRIGERATION/FREEZING: REFRIGERATE UP TO 3 DAYS. FREEZE UP TO 6 MONTHS.

Some food critics have contempt for "crowd pleasers," as if there's something wrong with foods that simply make people happy. A dish has to be a little bit twisted to have their respect, and those lowlifes who fail to appreciate pineapple/mint/kombu coulis, for instance, have only themselves to blame.

I'm too insecure to take such a stand. I crave approval the way my crowd craves the flavors that make this dish so pleasing for them and rewarding for me.

2 teaspoons corn oil or canola oil

1 red onion, chopped

2 garlic cloves, minced

2 tablespoons minced fresh cilantro

2 tablespoons minced fresh basil, or 1 tablespoon crumbled dried basil

1 tablespoon minced fresh oregano, or 1 1/2 teaspoons crumbled dried oregano

1 tablespoon ground cumin

2 teaspoons chili powder

1 red bell pepper, roasted, peeled, and chopped (see page 534)

1 jalapeño pepper, cored, seeded, and minced

2 tomatillos, husked and chopped, or 3 tablespoons green salsa

2 ripe tomatoes, peeled, seeded, and chopped (see page 544)

1 pound extra-firm tofu, cut into bite-sized cubes

2 cups cooked kidney, black runner, or pinto beans

1 1/2 cups loosely packed shredded cabbage

1/2 cup grated cheddar or Monterey Jack cheese, or a mixture of both

1 recipe Spicy Fresh Tomato Sauce (see page 278)

4 large flour tortillas or Lavosh (see page 412)

Heat the oil in a large skillet over medium-high heat, swirling the pan to coat the bottom. Add the onion, garlic, cilantro, basil, oregano, cumin, chili powder, red bell pepper, jalapeño, and tomatillos, and sauté until the vegetables are soft, about 15 minutes. Add the tomatoes, and continue cooking until they break down and give up most of their liquid, about 10 minutes. Add the tofu and beans and sauté, stirring often, to coat with the vegetables and infuse with flavor, about 20 minutes. Stir in the cabbage and keep stirring until it cooks through, but is still crisp, about 5 minutes. Stir in the cheese, and remove from the heat.

Heat the tomato sauce. Place each tortilla or lavosh on a serving plate, and spoon an equal amount of the filling in the center. Fold in the sides and roll it up to enclose the filling, and top with tomato sauce.

PER SERVING: CALORIES 518 • PROTEIN 34.2 G • CARBOHYDRATE 55.7 G • FAT 20.7 G • CHOLESTEROL 14.9 MG • SODIUM 368 MG • 34% CALORIES FROM FAT • OUTSTANDING SOURCE OF VITAMINS B₁, C; FOLACIN, CALCIUM, IRON • VERY GOOD SOURCE OF VITAMINS A, B₂, B₆; ZINC • GOOD SOURCE OF VITAMIN B₃

•

SPRING GARDEN TORTILLAS

Serves 4

TOTAL TIME: ABOUT 35 MINUTES, NOT INCLUDING TIME TO COOK THE CHICKPEAS
TIME TO PREPARE: ABOUT 35 MINUTES, INCLUDING TIME TO SAUTÉ
COOKING TIME: INCLUDED IN TIME TO PREPARE
DO AHEAD: YOU CAN MAKE THE FILLING UP TO 3 DAYS IN ADVANCE. REFRIGERATE UNTIL READY TO USE.
REFRIGERATION/FREEZING: REFRIGERATE UP TO 3 DAYS. FREEZE UP TO 6 MONTHS.

A favorite excuse for sweeping up everything in the produce section in prime season, these tortillas taste fresh, wholesome, and, yes, full of spice.

2 teaspoons canola or vegetable oil
1 red onion, chopped
2 garlic cloves, minced
1 small green bell pepper, cored, seeded, and chopped
1 small red bell pepper, cored, seeded, and chopped
¼ cup minced fresh cilantro
1 tablespoon chili powder
2 teaspoons ground cumin
½ teaspoon cayenne pepper
¼ cup dry white wine
2 ears of corn
2 cups chopped peeled tomatoes (see page 544)
2 cups cooked chickpeas, drained and rinsed
2 zucchini, chopped
2 cups loosely packed asparagus tips, stems removed (see Note)
2 cups loosely packed sugar snap peas
½ cup shredded cheddar cheese
8 small flour tortillas

Garnishes (Optional)
Nonfat or reduced-fat sour cream
Tomato Salsa (see page 158), or store-bought salsa
Chopped avocado
Minced fresh cilantro

Heat the oil in a large, deep skillet over medium-high heat. When it's hot, add the onion, garlic, green and red peppers, cilantro, chili powder, cumin, and cayenne pepper. Reduce the heat to medium and sauté, stirring often, until the vegetables are soft, about 10 minutes. Add the wine, turn up the heat to medium-high, and stir until most of it has evaporated, about 3 minutes.

Scrape the kernels off the corncobs into the skillet. Stir in the tomatoes and chickpeas. Cook, stirring often, until the corn has turned deep yellow and the tomatoes have thickened, about 7 minutes. Add the zucchini, asparagus, and peas. Continue stirring just until the vegetables are cooked through and still crisp, 3 to 4 minutes. Remove the filling from the heat and stir in the cheese.

Place 2 tortillas on each of 4 serving plates and put an equal amount of the vegetable mixture on each one. Fold in the sides of each tortilla to cover the filling, then fold the top and bottom to enclose it like an envelope. Garnish with sour cream, salsa, avocado, and cilantro.

Note: You can use the asparagus stems in a frittata (see page 383) or a stir-fry (see page 374).

PER SERVING: CALORIES 660 • PROTEIN 27.5 G • CARBOHYDRATE 108 G • FAT 16.9 G • CHOLESTEROL 14.4 MG • SODIUM 488 MG • 22% CALORIES FROM FAT • OUTSTANDING SOURCE OF VITAMINS A, B₁, C; FOLACIN, IRON • VERY GOOD SOURCE OF VITAMINS B₂, B₃, B₆; CALCIUM, ZINC

Curries

POTATO CURRY
A Basic Vegetable Curry

Serves 4

TOTAL TIME: 45 MINUTES, NOT INCLUDING TIME TO COOK THE CHICKPEAS
TIME TO PREPARE: 45 MINUTES, INCLUDING TIME TO SAUTÉ
COOKING TIME: 7 TO 10 MINUTES
REFRIGERATION/FREEZING: REFRIGERATE UP TO 4 DAYS. FREEZE INDEFINITELY.

To stay credible, we food writers have to be ready to bluff our way through a question from time to time. You get better at this as you go along, so I can now speak—albeit briefly—with apparent authority on subjects beyond my grasp, such as sausage casings and the best way to cook okra (in reality I'm not sure there is one). But occasionally I'm thrown, as I was at the hair salon when my stylist asked me, "Why is it that curry I make at home never tastes like it does in the restaurants?"

I couldn't say what she might be doing wrong. Although the curries I made at home were delicious in their own right, I wasn't able to duplicate my favorite Indian restaurant dishes, either. I mumbled something about culture and genetics, before admitting I had no idea and promised to look into the matter. I did, and discovered that fresh spices account for the difference in taste. Most of us don't cook with those particular spices often enough to have them fresh, but even spices you've had for a while do a fine job seasoning dishes such as this curry with potatoes. (See page 595 for my spice brand recommendations.)

1 pound potatoes, preferably Yukon Gold
1 tablespoon peanut or vegetable oil
2 medium onions, chopped
6 garlic cloves, minced
2 tablespoons grated peeled fresh ginger
1 tablespoon ground cumin
2 teaspoons ground coriander
1 teaspoon curry powder
1 cup chopped peeled fresh tomatoes (see page 544) or canned chopped tomatoes
1 hot red pepper, roasted, peeled, and minced
3 cups cooked chickpeas, drained and rinsed
1 tablespoon lemon juice
¼ cup minced fresh cilantro
1 cup plain nonfat yogurt

In a medium saucepan, bring enough water to cover the potatoes to a boil. Add the potatoes and simmer over medium-high heat until you can pierce with a paring knife, about 7 minutes. Drain and cut into bite-sized pieces.

Meanwhile, heat the oil in a large skillet over medium-high heat. Add the onions, garlic, ginger, cumin, coriander, and curry powder. Reduce the heat to medium-low and sauté the ingredients until the onions are tender and limp, about 12 minutes.

Stir in the tomatoes, red pepper, chickpeas, lemon juice, and cilantro, cover, and let simmer over low heat until the tomatoes have cooked down, about 7 to 10 minutes. Add the potatoes, and stir to combine with the other ingredients. Turn off the heat, stir in the yogurt, cover, and let sit for 10 minutes before serving.

PER SERVING: CALORIES 428 • PROTEIN 18.7 G • CARBOHYDRATE 74.8 G • FAT 7.7 G • CHOLESTEROL 1.1 MG • SODIUM 72.8 MG • 16% CALORIES FROM FAT • OUTSTANDING SOURCE OF VITAMIN C; FOLACIN • VERY GOOD SOURCE OF VITAMINS B₁, B₆; CALCIUM, IRON, ZINC

CURRY BASICS

Curry Pantry: Ground cumin, curry powder, ground turmeric, ground coriander, ground ginger, cayenne pepper, coconut milk, canned or boxed tomatoes

In the Refrigerator: Fresh ginger, garlic, onions or scallions, cilantro, hot or sweet peppers, yogurt

• Use fresh spices. Spices lose flavor over time, so the longer you've had them on your shelf, the less you can rely on them. Buy them in small portions at a shop with a fast turnover, and replace the spices you use most often every six months. For optimum flavor, toast them lightly by placing the spice in a dry skillet over medium-low heat just until golden, stirring often to prevent burning.

• The flavors of garlic and ginger are essential to most curries. Always use fresh garlic and ginger. Dried, neither lends the right taste to the dish. To make sure the flavors blend throughout the dish, grate the ginger and garlic on the fine teeth of a cheese grater, rather than chopping or mincing them.

• Most curries taste best the day after they've been made, once the complex flavors have had a chance to meld.

Make It Your Own

Using the basic recipe as a guide, you can make your own house version of the dish.

WHAT TO ADD AND WHEN TO ADD IT

✐ *Fresh Vegetables.* Add 2 cups of any chopped steamed vegetable, or a mixture of vegetables, when you add the potatoes.

✐ *Tempeh or Tofu.* Substitute cubed tempeh or extra-firm tofu for the chickpeas.

✐ *Peppers and Spices.* For a milder curry, substitute an Anaheim chili or a red bell pepper for the hot red pepper. Experiment with brands of curry powder. Curry powder is a blend of spices, and different companies use different ingredients in different proportions, so that each brand has a distinct taste.

✐ *Yogurt or Buttermilk.* To cool down the curry or give it a light tang, stir in plain nonfat yogurt or buttermilk to taste before serving. Or pass a bowl of either at the table so your guests can help themselves.

✐ *Garnishes.* When you serve the curry, put out condiment bowls containing chopped peanuts or almonds, shredded dried coconut, raisins, sliced bananas, minced fresh cilantro, minced red onions, and raitas (see pages 558, 532, and 154).

•

COCONUT CURRY WITH POTATO, CAULIFLOWER, AND EGGS

Serves 4

TOTAL TIME: ABOUT 1 HOUR, NOT INCLUDING TIME TO STEAM THE VEGETABLES OR COOK THE EGGS
TIME TO PREPARE: 35 MINUTES, INCLUDING TIME TO SAUTÉ
COOKING TIME: INCLUDED IN TIME TO PREPARE
DO AHEAD: YOU CAN MAKE THE SAUCE UP TO 3 DAYS IN ADVANCE, ADDING THE STEAMED VEGETABLES BEFORE SERVING.
REFRIGERATION/FREEZING: REFRIGERATE UP TO 3 DAYS. FREEZE UP TO 6 MONTHS.

A little bit of coconut milk goes a long way toward making this dish. Coconut milk is expensive, so be sure to freeze what you don't use so you'll have it for next time.

4 garlic cloves, quartered
One 2-inch piece peeled fresh ginger, sliced
1 jalapeño pepper, seeded and quartered
½ cup loosely packed torn fresh basil
½ cup loosely packed fresh cilantro
2 teaspoons whole cumin seeds
2 teaspoons whole mustard seeds
2 teaspoons ground coriander
1 teaspoon ground cinnamon
½ teaspoon ground turmeric
1 tablespoon water
2 teaspoons canola or vegetable oil

1 large onion, chopped
1 tomato, peeled, seeded, and chopped (see page 544)
¼ cup coconut milk
¼ cup evaporated skim milk
1 tablespoon unsweetened coconut
1 tablespoon fresh lemon juice
2 large red potatoes, boiled but still firm (see page 537)
2 cups loosely packed cauliflower florets, steamed (see page 523)
2 cups loosely packed shredded green cabbage, steamed (see page 521)
4 hard-boiled large eggs (see page 65), chopped

In a food processor, place the garlic, ginger, jalapeño, basil, cilantro, cumin seeds, mustard seeds, coriander, cinnamon, and turmeric. Add the water, and process into a paste (the seeds will still be whole).

Heat the oil in a large skillet over medium-high heat, swirling the pan to coat the bottom. Add the paste and the onion, and sauté until the onion is soft, about 8 minutes. Stir in the tomato, coconut milk, evaporated skim milk, and coconut. Continue stirring over medium heat until the mixture is thickened, about 4 minutes.

Add the lemon juice, potatoes, cauliflower, cabbage, and eggs, and stir to coat well with the sauce. Turn off the heat, cover, and let rest for about 20 minutes. Turn up the heat to medium and stir thoroughly to heat through before serving.

PER SERVING: CALORIES 277 • PROTEIN 12.7 G • CARBOHYDRATE 32.8 G • FAT 11.9 G • CHOLESTEROL 214 MG • SODIUM 174 MG • 37% CALORIES FROM FAT • OUTSTANDING SOURCE OF VITAMIN C • VERY GOOD SOURCE OF VITAMINS B₂, B₆; FOLACIN • GOOD SOURCE OF VITAMIN A; CALCIUM, IRON, ZINC

PEANUT CURRY WITH SWEET POTATO AND COLLARD GREENS

Serves 4

TOTAL TIME: ABOUT 40 MINUTES, NOT INCLUDING TIME TO COOK THE BEANS

TIME TO PREPARE: ABOUT 20 MINUTES, INCLUDING TIME TO SAUTÉ

COOKING TIME: ABOUT 20 MINUTES

DO AHEAD: YOU CAN MAKE THE SAUCE UP TO 3 DAYS IN ADVANCE, ADDING THE VEGETABLES AND BEANS JUST BEFORE SERVING. REFRIGERATE UNTIL READY TO USE.

REFRIGERATION/FREEZING: REFRIGERATE UP TO 3 DAYS. FREEZE UP TO 6 MONTHS.

Serve this sensational curry over boiled rice, with Beet Raita (see page 154) and Naan (see page 415) or Pita Bread (see page 414) on the side.

2 teaspoons canola or vegetable oil

1 large onion, chopped

One 2-inch piece fresh ginger, peeled and grated

4 garlic cloves, minced

½ cup loosely packed minced cilantro,

1 red bell pepper, roasted, peeled, and chopped (see page 534)

1 jalapeño pepper, roasted, peeled, and chopped (see page 534)

1 tablespoon ground cumin

2 teaspoons whole mustard seeds

2 teaspoons ground coriander

1 teaspoon ground turmeric

1 teaspoon paprika

¼ teaspoon cayenne pepper, or more to taste

2 large tomatoes, peeled, seeded, and chopped (see page 544)

1 medium sweet potato, peeled and chopped

1 pound potatoes, preferably Yukon Gold, peeled and cut into bite-sized pieces

¼ cup coconut milk

2 tablespoons smooth peanut butter (with no added oil, sugar, or salt)

1 pound collard greens, stemmed and coarsely chopped

2 cups cooked beans, such as chickpeas, rattle-snake, or tongues of fire, drained and rinsed

Heat the oil in a large skillet over medium-high heat. When it's hot, add the onion, ginger, garlic, and cilantro. Reduce the heat to medium and sauté, stirring often, until the onion is soft and translucent, about 7 minutes. Add the bell pepper, jalapeño, cumin, mustard seeds, coriander, turmeric, paprika, and cayenne. Stir to blend. Stir in the tomatoes, sweet potato, and potatoes. Cover and let simmer over medium-low, until the potatoes have cooked through, about 15 minutes.

Combine the coconut milk and peanut butter, and stir until smooth. Add them to the skillet along with the collards and beans. Cook until the collards turn bright green, about 4 minutes. Cover and let the curry sit for 20 minutes before serving.

PER SERVING: CALORIES 419 • PROTEIN 14.7 G • CARBOHYDRATE 65.8 G • FAT 13.4 G • CHOLESTEROL 0 MG • SODIUM 81.3 MG • 27% CALORIES FROM FAT • OUTSTANDING SOURCE OF VITAMINS A, C; FOLACIN • VERY GOOD SOURCE OF VITAMINS B₂, B₆; IRON • GOOD SOURCE OF ZINC

MY FAVORITE CHICKPEAS

Serves 4

TOTAL TIME: ABOUT 30 MINUTES, NOT INCLUDING TIME TO COOK THE CHICKPEAS

TIME TO PREPARE: ABOUT 15 MINUTES, INCLUDING TIME TO SAUTÉ

COOKING TIME: 20 MINUTES

DO AHEAD: YOU CAN COOK THE CHICKPEAS UP TO 4 DAYS IN ADVANCE. REFRIGERATE UNTIL READY TO USE.

REFRIGERATION/FREEZING: REFRIGERATE UP TO 3 DAYS. DO NOT FREEZE.

When asked whether there'd been a single dish that had convinced me I could happily be a vegetarian, I cited the spicy chickpeas in Madhur Jaffrey's comprehensive World-of-the-East Vegetarian Cooking. A friend served them to me years ago, and my first taste was one of those transforming events—no chickpea's been safe from me since. This is my version of Jaffrey's superspeedy, ginger-and-garlicky dish. Yogurt and rice make it dinner.

2 teaspoons canola or vegetable oil

4 garlic cloves, grated

3 tablespoons grated peeled fresh ginger

1 tablespoon ground cumin

2 teaspoons ground coriander

1 teaspoon ground turmeric

¼ teaspoon cayenne pepper

1 cup fresh or canned tomato puree

2 cups cooked chickpeas, drained and rinsed

1 tablespoon fresh lemon juice

Heat the oil in a skillet over medium-high heat. When it's hot, turn down the heat to low and add the garlic, ginger, cumin, coriander, turmeric, and cayenne pepper. Sauté, stirring constantly, until everything is well combined and the mixture has a uniform color, about 4 minutes.

Stir in the tomato puree, turn the heat up to medium, and bring to a gentle simmer. Add the chickpeas, and bring to a second simmer. Cover, reduce the heat to low, and simmer until the mixture is thick, about 20 minutes.

Stir in the lemon juice and remove from the heat. Let the chickpeas sit 10 minutes before serving.

PER SERVING: CALORIES 257 • PROTEIN 12.2 G • CARBOHYDRATE 41.3 G • FAT 6.1 G • CHOLESTEROL 0 MG • SODIUM 19.2 MG • 21% CALORIES FROM FAT • OUTSTANDING SOURCE OF FOLACIN • VERY GOOD SOURCE OF VITAMIN C; IRON • GOOD SOURCE OF ZINC

CURIOUS COOKS WANT TO KNOW

Q. What *is* curry?

A. At one time curry was *kari*, a South Indian word for "sauce." Eventually it came to mean a sauce seasoned with a particular combination of spices (no one can say with certainty which spices), and then the spice mixture was being called curry as well. Before long the name attached to entire stews that were seasoned with it. And although curries as we know them can be hot, the original curry was not. Chilies came from South America and didn't reach India until the sixteenth century, when curry was already being cooked.

Filled Vegetables

BELL PEPPERS WITH DOUBLE-CORN FILLING

Serves 4

TOTAL TIME: ABOUT 1 HOUR, 25 MINUTES
TIME TO PREPARE: ABOUT 20 MINUTES
COOKING TIME: ABOUT 55 MINUTES
DO AHEAD: YOU CAN MAKE THE FILLING UP TO 3 DAYS IN
   ADVANCE. REFRIGERATE UNTIL READY TO USE.
REFRIGERATION/FREEZING: REFRIGERATE UP TO 3 DAYS. DO
   NOT FREEZE.

From the end of June to the middle of August, I put corn in practically everything, to the point where, not seeing it in the main course or salad, my husband gets nervous about dessert.

You don't need the freshest fresh corn for this dish, so you can enjoy it for weeks surrounding peak season.

4 large bell peppers of any color

4 ears of corn

¼ cup nonfat buttermilk

2½ cups water

½ cup stone-ground yellow cornmeal

1 jalapeño pepper, cored, seeded, and minced

⅓ cup shredded cheddar, Monterey Jack, or
   mozzarella cheese, or a combination of any
   of them

1 teaspoon ground cumin

Slice off the tops of the bell peppers, to make each into a cup. Pull out the core and the seeds. Stand the peppers upright in the bottom of a large saucepan or deep skillet. Add water so that it comes 1 inch up the sides of the pep-pers. Bring the water to a simmer over medium-high heat. Cover (if the skillet lid won't cover the peppers, make a tent out of foil), reduce the heat to medium-low, and simmer gently until the peppers are soft and pliable, but not mushy, about 10 minutes. Remove them with a slotted spoon or tongs, and let them cool.

Heat the oven to 425°F.

Meanwhile, scrape the kernels from the corncobs and place them in a food processor or blender, along with the buttermilk. Process in short pulses until the corn is finely chopped, about 8 pulses.

Place the water in a deep saucepan. Bring it to a boil over medium-high heat. Whisking constantly with one hand, sprinkle in the corn-meal with the other. Reduce the heat to medium and continue whisking until the mix-ture thickens to the consistency of Cream of Wheat, about 7 minutes. Stir in the corn mix-ture, jalapeño, cheese, and cumin, and con-tinue whisking until the mixture is bubbly, but still smooth, about 6 more minutes.

Spoon an equal amount of the corn-cornmeal mixture into each pepper. Place the peppers in a baking dish and cover the dish loosely with foil. Bake until the cheese is bub-bly, about 35 minutes. Remove the foil and bake to brown the tops, about 10 minutes more.

Let the peppers rest for 10 minutes before serving.

PER SERVING: CALORIES 254 • PROTEIN 9.8 G • CARBOHYDRATE 47 G • FAT 5.8 G • CHOLESTEROL 10.3 MG • SODIUM 167 MG • 19% CALORIES FROM FAT • OUTSTAND-ING SOURCE OF VITAMIN C • VERY GOOD SOURCE OF VITAMIN B₁; FOLACIN • GOOD SOURCE OF VITAMINS A, B₂, B₃, B₆; CALCIUM, IRON, ZINC

•

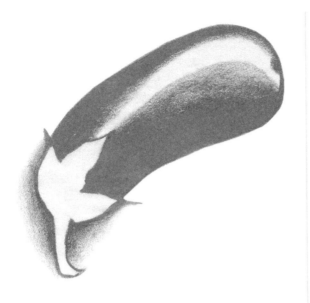

FILLED VEGETABLE BASICS

They'll tell you they're elegant; they'll tell you they're tasty. But no one else is going to name the *real* reason for making filled vegetables: you get to play with your food. In fact, you must. To fill vegetables, you have to carve and scoop and pat and smush. The results can be fabulous, and getting there is great good fun.

• The vegetable you're stuffing must be sturdy enough to contain the filling without leaking or collapsing. Among whole vegetables, try artichokes, bell peppers, eggplants, mushrooms, onions, turnips, squash (especially acorn squash, baby pumpkins, and zucchini), and tomatoes. For filled leafy vegetables, try cabbage (head and savoy), chard, and collards. You can use spinach, too, as long as you layer it at least four leaves thick (single leaves tear too easily). Ditto lettuces such as radicchio and Bibb.

• To prepare whole vegetables as deep cups for stuffing, slice off the top of the vegetable a half inch from the stem end. Hollow the vegetable out with a paring knife or melon scoop. Reserve the pulp if the recipe calls for it. If the vegetable has a hollow full of seeds—for example, acorn squash and bell peppers—scoop out the seeds and throw them away. (Onions and artichokes must be prepared in a special manner. See specific recipes for directions, page 365 for onions, page 214 for artichokes.)

• To make whole vegetables into shallow "boats" for stuffing, slice the vegetable in half lengthwise and carve out the seeds and/or pulp.

• To prepare zucchini or summer squash for stuffing, turn the vegetables into hollow tubes like this: Choose squash no longer than six inches. Cut off each end. Carve out the flesh with a melon scoop, making a hollow tube. Once you've filled the tubes with your stuffing, stand them upright to bake.

• Once you've prepared the cups, boats, or tubes, you have to soften them for stuffing. Heat the oven to 350°F. Stand the hollowed shells in a baking dish and pour enough vegetable broth or water into the dish to come halfway up the side of the vegetable. You can put bell peppers, tomatoes, or onions into a large nonstick muffin tin, instead, adding 1 tablespoon vegetable broth per muffin cup.

Cover the baking dish or muffin tin with foil and bake until the shells are soft and pliable, but not mushy. The timing will vary depending on the texture of the vegetable. Eggplants take about fifteen minutes, squash closer to forty. Remove the vegetables, let them rest until they're cool enough to handle, and stuff.

• To stuff leaves, prepare them by steaming the leaves in a wire basket steamer or a colander over boiling water until they're *just* tender and pliable, about fifteen seconds for spinach, three minutes for collards and chard, four minutes for savoy cabbage, and seven for cabbage. Watch the time, or they'll get too soft and tear. Let the leaves cool completely before you fill them.

When it comes time to stuff them, place the filling in the center of each leaf and fold the sides in around it to seal it like an envelope. Don't make bulging packages, because the filling often expands and may burst through the leaves.

Make It Your Own

Combine vegetables and fillings that serve one another, putting hearty, spicy fillings in flavorful shells (chili and rice in green peppers; spicy corn salad in red peppers). Similarly, fill more delicate shells with subtler stuffing (spinach

with sweet turtle beans, page 369, and yellow peppers with Red Lentil Spread, page 256). Keep an eye on the colors, too, choosing attractive combinations.

WHAT TO ADD AND WHEN TO ADD IT

🖉 *Salads.* Prepare vegetables to stuff with salads by steaming them until they're *just* cooked through (except tomatoes, which you can leave raw). Put panzanella in tomatoes, and tabbouleh in bell peppers or onions, for example.

🖉 *Cheese.* Mix grated hard cheese with bread crumbs and a softer cheese, such as ricotta or cottage cheese, in proportions of about 1 tablespoon grated cheese, ½ cup of bread crumbs, and 1 cup of soft cheese. Fill the prepared vegetable cups or boats, cover loosely with foil, and bake as directed on page 366. Remove the foil for the last 5 minutes of baking.

🖉 *Grains.* Make stuffings of pilafs or other grain dishes. For example, you can fill prepared spinach leaves with Couscous (see page 338), or put fruit and nut bulgur (see page 577) into red peppers.

🖉 *Legumes.* Use bean salads, stews, and purees to fill prepared vegetables. Try the Refried Bean Puree (see page 256) in green pepper boats, or Basic Hummus (see page 254) in eggplant. Or try the Lemon-Spiked Lentil Salad (see page 143) in hollowed tomatoes.

🖉 *Chopped Vegetables.* You can make fillings by sautéing chopped fresh vegetables with onions and herbs. Use sautéed mushrooms, dill, and chives to fill artichokes; chopped spinach sautéed with scallions and mixed with bread crumbs and grated cheese to fill mushrooms; shredded zucchini sautéed with onions to fill eggplant.

BAKED TURNIPS WITH APPLES AND CHEDDAR CHEESE

Serves 4

TOTAL TIME: ABOUT 1 HOUR, 10 MINUTES
TIME TO PREPARE: ABOUT 15 MINUTES
COOKING TIME: ABOUT 45 MINUTES
REFRIGERATION/FREEZING: REFRIGERATE UP TO 2 DAYS.
REHEAT WRAPPED IN FOIL. DO NOT FREEZE.

Turnips can be a bit bitter. Here's a great way to sweeten them up. This dish goes well with frittatas of all kinds, and with *Baked Beans* (see page 214) or a hearty soup, such as *Simple Soothing Mushroom Soup* (see page 177).

4 large turnips, about 3 inches in diameter
⅔ cup nonfat milk
2 leeks, white part only, washed and thinly sliced
1 cup loosely packed diced dried apples
⅔ cup low-fat cottage cheese
½ cup shredded sharp cheddar cheese

Heat the oven to 425°F.

Slice the ends off the turnips and peel them with a vegetable peeler. Wrap each in foil, place them in a baking dish or roasting pan, and bake until they're soft, about 30 minutes. Unwrap and let them cool. Turn the heat down to 375°F.

Meanwhile, heat the milk in a medium, deep skillet over medium heat, taking care not to let it boil. Add the leeks and stir constantly until they're soft and limp, about 6 minutes. Place the dried apples in a medium mixing bowl and pour the leek mixture on top. Let the mixture sit until the apples soften, about 10 minutes.

Using a paring knife or a teaspoon, scoop out the center of each turnip, leaving a shell about ½ inch thick. Place the pulp in a food processor along with the cottage cheese and the apple and leek mixture. Process in short spurts until well combined. (Don't expect a smooth puree; the apples will remain a bit chunky.) Add the cheddar cheese and process again to incorporate it.

Fill the turnip shells with the mixture and return them to the baking dish or roasting pan. Cover loosely with foil and bake them for 20 minutes, until the cheddar has melted and the filling has settled. Remove the foil and bake until bubbly, about 5 minutes more.

PER SERVING: CALORIES 210 • PROTEIN 11.8 G • CARBOHYDRATE 30.6 G • FAT 5.5 G • CHOLESTEROL 17.2 MG • SODIUM 373 MG • 23% CALORIES FROM FAT • OUTSTANDING SOURCE OF VITAMIN C • VERY GOOD SOURCE OF CALCIUM • GOOD SOURCE OF VITAMIN B₂; IRON

GRAIN-FILLED ONIONS

Serves 4

TOTAL TIME: ABOUT 2 HOURS, 5 MINUTES
TIME TO PREPARE: 15 MINUTES, INCLUDING TIME TO SAUTÉ
COOKING TIME: 1 HOUR, 50 MINUTES
DO AHEAD: YOU CAN MAKE THE FILLING IN ADVANCE, THEN
   WRAP AND REFRIGERATE UP TO 3 DAYS, OR FREEZE UP TO
   6 MONTHS.
REFRIGERATION/FREEZING: REFRIGERATE UP TO 3 DAYS. DO
   NOT FREEZE.

An old French proverb contends "Quand
oignon a trois pelures, hiver aura grande
froidure." In other words, when an onion
has three skins, the winter will be very cold. If it
turns out to be true, fill the onions with this hearty
stuffing and serve with Potato-Fennel Stew with
Mixed Beans and Tofu (see page 336).

4 large Vidalia or Spanish onions

2 teaspoons extra virgin olive oil

2 carrots, peeled and chopped

2 teaspoons ground cumin

1 teaspoon ground cinnamon

1 teaspoon ground coriander

1 cup barley

¼ cup currants

½ cup apricot preserves

Peel the onions and, using a sharp paring knife,
cut out the center of each, leaving a shell only
2 or 3 layers thick. (The centers won't come
out neatly; you'll probably have to hack away
at them. That's fine, as long as you manage to
leave the shells intact.) Coarsely chop the
onion you've cut from the centers, and set it
aside for now.

Place the shells on the bottom of a deep
saucepan, large enough to fit them without
crowding them. Add cold water to cover, turn
the heat to medium-high, and bring to a simmer. Simmer until the onion shells are soft and
pliant, but not mushy, about 30 minutes. Using
a slotted spoon, transfer the onions to a plate
to cool. Pour the cooking water into a measuring cup, and reserve.

Meanwhile, heat the oil in a heavy
saucepan over medium-high heat. When it's
hot, add the reserved chopped onions, carrots,
cumin, cinnamon, and coriander, reduce the
heat to medium-low and sauté, stirring often,
until the vegetables are soft and limp, about 7
minutes. Add the barley and currants, and stir
to coat with the vegetables and spices.

Add 3 cups of the reserved onion water. If
you don't have 3 cups, add as much fresh water
as necessary.

Bring the water to a simmer, cover the
saucepan, and turn down the heat to low. Cook
until all of the water has been absorbed, about
50 minutes.

Meanwhile, heat the oven to 400°F.

Fluff the barley with a fork, and distribute
it evenly among the onions. Place the onions
in a shallow baking dish with an inch of water,
and cover them tightly with foil. Bake until the
bottoms start to caramelize, about 20 minutes.

Meanwhile, heat the apricot preserves over
low heat in a small saucepan until they liquefy.

Remove the foil from the onions, brush
them all over with the apricot preserves, and
bake, uncovered, for 10 minutes more.

PER SERVING: CALORIES 300 • PROTEIN 7.7 G • CARBOHYDRATE 63.2 G • FAT
3.4 G • CHOLESTEROL 0 MG • SODIUM 24.3 MG • 10% CALORIES FROM FAT • OUT-
STANDING SOURCE OF VITAMIN A • VERY GOOD SOURCE OF VITAMIN C • GOOD
SOURCE OF VITAMINS B₁, B₃, B₆; FOLACIN, IRON, ZINC

STUFFED MINIATURE EGGPLANT WITH ZUCCHINI AND THREE CHEESES

Serves 4

TOTAL TIME: ABOUT 1 HOUR, 30 MINUTES, NOT INCLUD-
ING TIME TO MAKE THE BROTH

TIME TO PREPARE: ABOUT 30 MINUTES, INCLUDING TIME
TO SAUTÉ

COOKING TIME: ABOUT 55 MINUTES

DO AHEAD: YOU CAN HOLLOW OUT THE EGGPLANTS AND
PREPARE THE FILLING UP TO 2 DAYS IN ADVANCE. SPRIN-
KLE WITH FRESH LEMON JUICE, WRAP IN PLASTIC, AND
KEEP REFRIGERATED UNTIL READY TO USE. IT MAY DIS-
COLOR, BUT THE FLAVOR WON'T BE AFFECTED.

REFRIGERATION/FREEZING: REFRIGERATE UP TO 2 DAYS.

You might well think that baby eggplant is a bimbo vegetable; it's hard to imagine that anything that adorable can really be food. But it is. Sweeter than the big boys, it's more tender, too. And it's just the right shape for stuffing as follows.

8 miniature or Japanese eggplants

2 teaspoons extra virgin olive oil

1 garlic clove, minced

1 shallot, minced

2 tablespoons minced fresh basil, or 1 tablespoon
    crumbled dried basil

2 tablespoons minced fresh parsley

2 tablespoons minced fresh mint

1 medium zucchini, peeled and chopped

½ cup dried bread crumbs

½ cup vegetable broth (see page 165)

½ cup nonfat or part-skim ricotta cheese

¼ cup grated Gruyère cheese

1 large egg, lightly beaten

2 tablespoons grated Parmesan cheese

Cut off the root end of each eggplant, and using a small melon scoop or a paring knife, carefully gouge out the inside, leaving the shell intact. Set the shells aside and chop the pulp.

Heat the oil in a medium skillet over medium-high heat. When it's hot, add the garlic, shallot, basil, parsley, and mint. Reduce the heat to medium and sauté, just to season the oil, about 2 minutes. Add the chopped eggplant pulp, zucchini, and bread crumbs. Stir well to blend with the herbs. Add the vegetable broth, turn up the heat to medium-high, and bring to a simmer. Cover the skillet, reduce the heat to medium-low, and simmer until the eggplant and zucchini are soft enough to mash, about 15 minutes.

Using a slotted spoon, transfer the vegetables to a large mixing bowl, leaving the broth in the saucepan. Place the eggplant shells in the saucepan, cover, and simmer gently until the shells are soft, but not mushy, about 10 minutes.

Meanwhile, heat the oven to 350°F. Squirt an 8-inch baking dish with nonstick spray or lightly grease with unsalted butter.

Mash the zucchini-eggplant mixture with a

fork. Add the ricotta, Gruyère, and egg, and stir well to blend.

When the eggplant shells are soft, use a spoon to fill them with the cheese mixture. Place them upright in the prepared baking dish, cover with foil, and bake until the filling is set, about 25 minutes.

Remove the foil and sprinkle the tops with the Parmesan cheese. Continue baking, uncovered, until the cheese has melted, about 5 minutes.

PER SERVING: CALORIES 209 • PROTEIN 13.3 G • CARBOHYDRATE 23.2 G • FAT 7.6 G • CHOLESTEROL 63.1 MG • SODIUM 212 MG • 32% CALORIES FROM FAT • GOOD SOURCE OF VITAMIN C: FOLACIN, IRON

•

SPINACH-STUFFED TOMATOES

Serves 4

TOTAL TIME: ABOUT 45 MINUTES
TIME TO PREPARE: ABOUT 10 MINUTES
COOKING TIME: 35 MINUTES
DO AHEAD: YOU CAN MAKE THE FILLING UP TO 3 DAYS IN ADVANCE. REFRIGERATE UNTIL READY TO USE.
REFRIGERATION/FREEZING: REFRIGERATE UP TO 2 DAYS. DO NOT FREEZE.

One of those "light and jiffy" summer dishes you'll enjoy serving—and having—for lunch. Serve with Creamy Herb Soup (see page 180).

4 large firm ripe tomatoes
4 cups fresh spinach, washed and chopped, or one 10-ounce package frozen chopped spinach, thawed and squeezed dry
1 cup low-fat cottage cheese
¼ cup grated Parmesan cheese

½ cup dried bread crumbs
1 teaspoon crumbled dried oregano

Heat the oven to 425°F. Squirt an 8-inch baking dish with nonstick spray or lightly grease with unsalted butter.

Slice off the top ¼ inch of each tomato. Scoop out the pulp with a spoon. Separate as many of the seeds as possible from the pulp. Discard the seeds, reserving the pulp.

In a mixing bowl, combine the tomato pulp, spinach, cottage cheese, Parmesan, bread crumbs, and oregano.

Cover loosely with foil and bake until the tomatoes are soft and the filling has set, about 30 minutes. Remove the foil and return to the oven to brown the tops, about 5 minutes.

PER SERVING: CALORIES 158 • PROTEIN 13.9 G • CARBOHYDRATE 18.8 G • FAT 3.7 G • CHOLESTEROL 7.4 MG • SODIUM 509 MG • 21% CALORIES FROM FAT • OUTSTANDING SOURCE OF VITAMINS A, C • VERY GOOD SOURCE OF VITAMIN B₂: FOLACIN, CALCIUM • GOOD SOURCE OF IRON

BLACK BEANS IN BELL PEPPERS

Serves 4

TOTAL TIME: 50 MINUTES, NOT INCLUDING TIME TO COOK
THE BEANS

TIME TO PREPARE: ABOUT 25 MINUTES, INCLUDING TIME
TO SAUTÉ

COOKING TIME: 25 MINUTES

DO AHEAD: YOU CAN MAKE THE FILLING UP TO 3 DAYS IN
ADVANCE. REFRIGERATE UNTIL READY TO USE.

REFRIGERATION/FREEZING: REFRIGERATE UP TO 3 DAYS. DO
NOT FREEZE.

*Choose firm, jumbo peppers for this dish.
Flimsy peppers will fall apart, and you'll
lose precious filling, which you're sure to
regret when you reach your last bite and wish for
more.*

2 teaspoons canola or vegetable oil

1 large white onion, chopped

2 garlic cloves, minced

1 jalapeño pepper or Anaheim chili, cored,
    seeded, and minced

¼ cup minced fresh cilantro

2 teaspoons ground cumin

2 teaspoons chili powder

1 teaspoon crumbled dried oregano

2 teaspoons red wine vinegar

2 cups cooked black turtle beans, drained and
    rinsed

¼ cup shredded cheddar cheese

¼ cup grated Parmesan cheese

1 large firm red bell pepper, roasted and peeled
    (see page 534)

1 large firm yellow bell pepper, roasted and
    peeled (see page 534)

1 recipe Plum Salsa (see page 158) or Tomato
    Salsa (see page 159)

Heat the oven to 350°F. Squirt a shallow baking dish with nonstick spray or lightly grease with unsalted butter.

Heat the oil in a large skillet over medium-high heat, swirling the pan to coat the bottom. Add the onion, garlic, jalapeño or Anaheim chili, cilantro, cumin, chili powder, and oregano and sauté, stirring often, until the onion softens, about 8 minutes. Stir in the vinegar and beans. Reduce the heat to medium-low, cover the skillet, and cook, stirring often, until the beans are very tender, about 20 minutes. Using the back of a wooden spoon, mash the beans.

Transfer to a mixing bowl, and stir in the cheddar and Parmesan cheese. Fill each pepper half with an equal amount of the bean mixture and place in the prepared baking dish. Cover loosely with foil and bake until set, about 20 minutes. Remove the foil and return the peppers to the oven to brown the tops, about 5 minutes more. Serve with salsa.

PER SERVING: CALORIES 246 • PROTEIN 13.7 G • CARBOHYDRATE 33.3 G • FAT 7.5 G • CHOLESTEROL 12.4 MG • SODIUM 181 MG • 26% CALORIES FROM FAT • OUTSTANDING SOURCE OF VITAMIN C • VERY GOOD SOURCE OF VITAMIN A; FOLACIN, CALCIUM, IRON • GOOD SOURCE OF ZINC

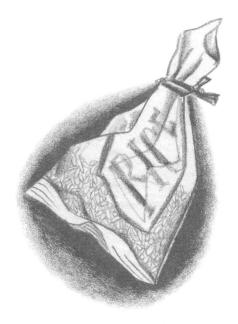

CHILLED FILLED
SPINACH ROLLS

Serves 4

TOTAL TIME: ABOUT 4 HOURS, 50 MINUTES, INCLUDING
  TIME TO CHILL
TIME TO PREPARE: ABOUT 50 MINUTES, INCLUDING TIME
  TO SAUTÉ
COOKING TIME: INCLUDED IN TIME TO PREPARE
DO AHEAD: YOU CAN MAKE THE FILLING UP TO 3 DAYS
  BEFORE YOU FILL THE ROLLS. REFRIGERATE UNTIL READY
  TO USE.
REFRIGERATION/FREEZING: REFRIGERATE UP TO 2 DAYS. DO
  NOT FREEZE.

The very thing that makes these fun to eat makes them a bit tricky to put together. The tender spinach, while a treat to bite into, is subject to tears when you roll it. But if you work with patience, layering the leaves and handling them with care, they'll turn out just fine. Serve with soup (Cold Cream of Broccoli, page 200; Creamy Herb, page 180; or Gazpacho, page 202) for a bracing summer supper. Note that this recipe calls for black

turtle beans, because they're small and sweet. They're the kind that works best in this dish, not too bulky in the leaves.

2 pounds fresh spinach, thoroughly cleaned and
   stems trimmed
2 teaspoons extra virgin olive oil
1 large onion, coarsely chopped
1 red bell pepper, cored, seeded, and chopped
¼ cup minced fresh basil
2 tablespoons minced fresh mint
¼ teaspoon ground cinnamon
2 teaspoons red wine vinegar
3 tablespoons currants
1 tomato, peeled, seeded, and chopped
   (see page 544)
1 cup cooked black turtle beans, drained
   and rinsed
1 cup cooked short-grain or medium-grain
   brown rice
Salt and freshly ground black pepper to taste
2 tablespoons fresh lemon juice

Bring 2 cups of water to a boil in a saucepan and cook the spinach leaves by placing them in a large bowl and pouring the water over them. Let them sit for 2 minutes, then carefully lift out the leaves and transfer them to a large plate lined with paper towels to drain.

Heat the oil in a medium skillet over medium-high heat, swirling the pan to coat the bottom. Add the onion, red bell pepper, basil, mint, and cinnamon, reduce the heat to medium, and sauté until the onion is soft and limp, about 20 minutes.

Add the vinegar, turn up the heat to medium-high, and stir until most of it evaporates, about 1 minute. Lower the heat to medium, add the currants and tomato, and stir until the tomato cooks down, about 4 minutes. Turn off the heat and stir in the beans and rice. Season with salt and pepper.

On a flat surface, lay 4 or 5 spinach leaves, overlapping them in such a way that they virtually form a crepe about 6 inches in diameter. This will be the casing for your filling. (Depending on the size and texture of the leaves, you may need more. If the leaves are small and tender, you may need as many as 8 to make a sturdy casing.)

Place about 3 tablespoons of filling in the lower third of the spinach leaves, and roll them up from the bottom, folding in the sides after the first roll. Once you've folded in the sides, the casing should seal itself as you continue to roll. Repeat with the remaining filling and spinach.

Chill the rolls for at least 4 hours. They're best the day after they've been made. Just before serving, drizzle with lemon juice. Serve cold.

PER SERVING: CALORIES 227 • PROTEIN 12.5 G • CARBOHYDRATE 39.2 G • FAT 4.9 G • CHOLESTEROL 0 MG • SODIUM 187 MG • 18% CALORIES FROM FAT • OUTSTANDING SOURCE OF VITAMINS A, C; FOLACIN, IRON • VERY GOOD SOURCE OF VITAMINS B₁, B₂, B₆; CALCIUM • GOOD SOURCE OF VITAMIN B₃; ZINC

Nori Rolls

NORI ROLLS
Vegetable Sushi
Serves 4

TOTAL TIME: 2 HOURS, 10 MINUTES, INCLUDING TIME TO MARINATE THE TOFU
TIME TO PREPARE: 1 HOUR, 30 MINUTES
COOKING TIME: ABOUT 40 MINUTES
DO AHEAD: YOU CAN MARINATE THE TOFU UP TO 2 DAYS IN ADVANCE. REFRIGERATE UNTIL READY TO USE.
REFRIGERATION/FREEZING: REFRIGERATE UP TO 1 DAY. DO NOT FREEZE.

¼ cup low-sodium soy sauce

2 teaspoons honey

1 teaspoon grated garlic

1 tablespoon grated peeled fresh ginger

1 pound extra-firm tofu, cut into ¼-inch-wide strips

2 cups short-grain brown rice

2 tablespoons rice vinegar

1 tablespoon extra-fine sugar

2 scallions, white part only, minced

2 tablespoons sesame seeds, toasted (see Note, page 122)

5 sheets sushi nori (available at Asian-specialty stores and in the Asian-specialty section of many supermarkets)

1 cup finely shredded carrots

10 fresh spinach leaves, steamed (see page 539) and squeezed dry

1½ cups alfalfa sprouts

In a deep, wide dish, such as a pie plate, combine the soy sauce, honey, garlic, and ginger. Add the tofu and let it marinate for at least an hour, turning it over halfway through.

Cook the rice according to package.

In a large glass or ceramic bowl, combine the rice vinegar and sugar. Add the hot rice in fourths, stirring the mixture well after each addition. Stir in the scallions and sesame seeds, and mix well to blend evenly.

For each roll, place a sheet of nori on a piece of wax paper so that the bottom edge of the nori lies along the bottom edge of the paper. Moisten your hands with cold water and place a handful of rice in the center of the nori, spread it out in a thin layer to fill the sheet evenly. Add more rice if necessary. Place 2 strips of tofu across the center of the nori, so they run the entire width of the sheet. Place a portion of carrots on top of the tofu and some spinach over that, finishing with some of the sprouts (use about a fifth of each filling ingredient). Start rolling the nori from the bottom by gripping the nori and the wax paper, and using the paper to help you make a tight roll.

Let the nori rest, seam side down, while you repeat the procedure with the remaining rice and nori. You should have 5 rolls.

To serve, wet the blade of a serrated knife, and cut the rolls into rounds about an inch thick. Serve at room temperature.

PER SERVING: CALORIES 364 • PROTEIN 19.6 G • CARBOHYDRATE 52.4 G • FAT 10.5 G • CHOLESTEROL 0 MG • SODIUM 1062 MG • 25% CALORIES FROM FAT • OUT-STANDING SOURCE OF VITAMIN A • VERY GOOD SOURCE OF VITAMINS B₁, B₃, B₆, C; FOLACIN, CALCIUM, ZINC

NORI ROLL BASICS

One of my favorite definitions of sushi nori appeared in, of all places, an Italian food magazine. Attempting to describe it for their readers, the editors compared sushi nori with *i nostri panini* (our sandwiches), an explanation I like because it suggests you can have a free hand in filling them.

• Use fresh nori (sheets of dried seaweed), which are more pliable and better tasting than nori that's gone stale. You can tell whether it's fresh by gently bending the package. If you can feel the sheets crinkle, it's too old.

• When preparing the rice, stir it into the vinegar mixture while the rice is still warm. When warm, the rice better absorbs the dressing.

• Just before filling and rolling, hold the nori briefly (about 5 seconds) above a low flame or an electric burner set on low. Heated, the nori is easier to roll, and there's less chance it will crack.

• You'll find it easier to spread the rice on the nori if you wet your hands first. Spread the grains in a single layer, or the rolls will be too thick.

• Wet the blade of a serrated knife before cutting the nori. Wet, the blade will slice more easily.

Make It Your Own

At their best sushi nori are small bundles of contrasts and contradictions: sweet sugar and tart vinegar, crunchy carrots and creamy tofu, tangy scallions and mild sesame. With that principle in mind, you can customize them as follows.

WHAT TO ADD AND WHEN TO ADD IT

Other Rices. Substitute different types of short-grain rice, including blends. Avoid long-grain rice, though, because it doesn't hold together well.

Vegetables. You can use any crispy fresh or steamed vegetable, as long as it's sliced thin enough to keep the roll from becoming too bulky. Try sliced avocado, shredded carrots, steamed slender asparagus spears, steamed French green beans, shredded beets, steamed snow peas, shredded zucchini, bean sprouts, and alfalfa sprouts. Add them after you've spread the rice on the nori, laying them in a horizontal strip in the center of the rice-spread nori.

Tempeh or Bean Purees. You can substitute sliced tempeh for the tofu in the basic recipe. Or spread the rice with a layer of pureed split peas, green lentils, chickpeas, or kidney beans before rolling it up.

Vinegar. Substitute fruit vinegar, such as raspberry or mango, for the rice vinegar in the dressing in the basic recipe.

•

SWEET BEET SUSHI

Serves 6

TOTAL TIME: 2 HOURS, 10 MINUTES, INCLUDING TIME TO MARINATE THE TOFU, BUT NOT INCLUDING TIME TO COOK THE BEETS
TIME TO PREPARE: 1 HOUR, 30 MINUTES
COOKING TIME: ABOUT 40 MINUTES
DO AHEAD: YOU CAN MARINATE THE TOFU UP TO 2 DAYS IN ADVANCE. REFRIGERATE UNTIL READY TO USE.
REFRIGERATION/FREEZING: REFRIGERATE UP TO 1 DAY. DO NOT FREEZE.

Beets make these rice-filled nori rolls pretty and sweet. They're also beautiful, especially during the winter holidays because the colors are so festive.

1 tablespoon grated peeled fresh ginger

2 tablespoons low-sodium soy sauce

2 teaspoons honey

2 medium beets, boiled (see page 518), peeled, and shredded (you can use a food processor with a fine shredding disk or the wide grates on a cheese grater)

2 tablespoons sesame seeds, toasted (see Note, page 122)

1 pound extra-firm tofu or tempeh, cut into ½-inch-wide strips

2 cups short-grain brown rice

3 tablespoons rice vinegar

1 tablespoon extra-fine sugar

1 scallion, white part only, minced

1 tablespoon wasabi powder (available at Asian-specialty stores and in the Asian-specialty section of many supermarkets)

1 tablespoon water, approximately

5 sheets sushi nori (available at Asian-specialty stores and in the Asian-specialty section of many supermarkets)

1 carrot, cut into matchsticks

1 1/2 cups alfalfa sprouts or pea shoots

In a deep, wide dish, such as a pie plate, combine the ginger, soy sauce, honey, beets, and sesame seeds. Add the tofu or tempeh and let it marinate for at least an hour, turning it over halfway through.

Cook the rice according to package directions.

In a large glass or ceramic bowl, combine the rice vinegar and sugar. Add the rice in fourths, stirring it well after each addition. Stir in the scallion and mix well to blend evenly.

In a small bowl, combine the wasabi powder with the water and mix to make a thick paste, adding more water if necessary to get the right consistency.

For each roll, place a sheet of nori on a piece of wax paper so that the short edge of the nori lies along the bottom edge of the paper. Moisten your hands with cold water and place a handful of rice in the center of the nori; spread it out to cover the sheet evenly. Add more rice if necessary. Using your finger, paint a strip of wasabi paste along the center of the nori, running horizontally all the way across

the rice. Place 2 or 3 strips of marinated tofu or tempeh directly on top, distributing a bit of the beet mixture over it. Place a portion of the carrot over the beets, and add some sprouts or pea shoots after that (use about a fifth of all the filling ingredients). Take care not to lay the filling on too thick, or you won't be able to roll up the nori. Start rolling the nori from the bottom by gripping the nori and the wax paper, and using the paper to help you make a tight roll. Tuck and roll, being careful not to roll the wax paper into the sushi.

Let the nori rest, seam side down, while you repeat the procedure with the remaining rice and nori. You should have 5 rolls.

To serve, wet the blade of a serrated knife, and cut the rolls into rounds about an inch thick. Serve at room temperature.

PER SERVING: CALORIES 390 • PROTEIN 18.6 G • CARBOHYDRATE 60 G • FAT 9.9 G • CHOLESTEROL 0 MG • SODIUM 312 MG • 22% CALORIES FROM FAT • OUTSTANDING SOURCE OF IRON • VERY GOOD SOURCE OF VITAMINS A, B$_1$, B$_3$, B$_6$; CALCIUM • GOOD SOURCE OF VITAMIN B$_2$; FOLACIN, ZINC

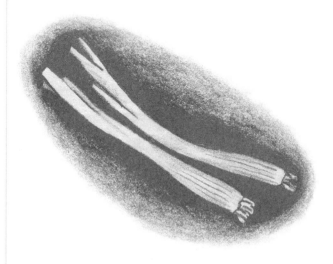

Stir-Fries

MOO-SHU MUSHROOMS

Serves 4

TOTAL TIME: ABOUT 2 HOURS, 15 MINUTES, INCLUDING
  TIME TO MARINATE
TIME TO PREPARE: ABOUT 30 MINUTES, INCLUDING TIME
  TO STIR-FRY
COOKING TIME: ABOUT 45 MINUTES
EQUIPMENT: WOK
DO AHEAD: YOU CAN MAKE THE MARINADE UP TO 3 DAYS
  IN ADVANCE, AND/OR MARINATE THE TOFU AND MUSH-
  ROOMS OVERNIGHT. REFRIGERATE UNTIL READY TO USE.
REFRIGERATION/FREEZING: REFRIGERATE UP TO 2 DAYS. DO
  NOT FREEZE.

Moo-shu pork was my favorite thing on the Chinese menu when I was a kid, mostly because it gave me a chance to eat with my hands without being scolded and sent to my room. Now I make this version at home and relish the hoisin-seasoned mushrooms as much as I used to enjoy licking the goo off my thumbs.

There's nothing difficult about this dish, as long as you assemble and organize your ingredients before you begin.

Marinade

3 tablespoons soy sauce
1 tablespoon rice wine
½ teaspoon sesame oil
1 pound extra-firm tofu, cut into ½-inch-wide
  strips
½ pound sliced mushrooms

Sauce

1⅓ cups water
2 scallions, white part plus 2 inches of greens,
  chopped

3 paper-thin slivers peeled fresh ginger
1 garlic clove, crushed
2 tablespoons minced fresh cilantro
6 dried shiitake mushrooms
1 tablespoon rice wine
1 tablespoon low-sodium soy sauce
1 teaspoon sesame oil
2 tablespoons cornstarch

Stir-Fry

2 teaspoons canola or vegetable oil
3 garlic cloves, minced
3 scallions, white part and 1 inch of greens, minced
1 tablespoon minced peeled fresh ginger
1 leek, white part plus 1 inch of greens, washed
  and julienned
1 carrot, peeled and julienned
2 cups shredded green cabbage

Romaine lettuce leaves or flat bread (see page
  114 and page 412)
Hoisin sauce
Cooked white rice

For the Marinade

Combine the soy sauce, rice wine, and sesame oil in a large shallow bowl or baking dish. Add the tofu and mushrooms and marinate, refrigerated, for an hour, turning occasionally.

For the Sauce

Combine the water, scallions, ginger, garlic, and cilantro in a medium saucepan and bring to a boil over medium-high heat. Cover, reduce the heat to medium-low, and simmer for 45 minutes. Strain, discarding the vegetables. Combine this broth with the shiitake mushrooms, rice wine, soy sauce, sesame oil, and cornstarch. At the end of the marinating time, drain the marinade. Set the tofu and mushrooms aside, and stir the marinade into the sauce. Set aside.

For the Stir-Fry

Heat a large wok. When it's hot, add the oil, and swirl the wok to coat the bottom and sides.

Add the garlic, scallions, and ginger, and toss to season the oil, about 1 minute. Add the leek, carrot, and cabbage, and toss well until the vegetables start to soften, about 2 minutes. With a slotted spoon, transfer the vegetables to a bowl. Add the tofu and mushrooms to the wok and toss well until the mushrooms have colored and the tofu is heated through, about 2 minutes.

Add the sauce and stir until it thickens, about 2 minutes. Return the leek, carrot, and cabbage to the wok and stir well to combine thoroughly, about 1 minute more.

Serve wrapped in romaine lettuce leaves or flat bread, topped with a dab of hoisin sauce and additional sauce from the stir-fry over a side portion of rice.

PER SERVING: CALORIES 303 • PROTEIN 23 G • CARBOHYDRATE 27.5 G • FAT 14.5 G • CHOLESTEROL 0 MG • SODIUM 852 MG • 39% CALORIES FROM FAT • OUTSTANDING SOURCE OF VITAMINS A, C; IRON • VERY GOOD SOURCE OF VITAMINS B₁, B₂, B₃, B₆; FOLACIN, CALCIUM, ZINC

STIR-FRY BASICS

Stir-frying was a fad a few years ago, and all kinds of claims were made for this way of cooking, notably that it's a snap—something to do after a hectic day at work. Not true. To make a good stir-fry you have to be organized and alert. Unless you arrange your ingredients before you leave in the morning, you may be too tired to assemble them when you get home at night. Save stir-frying for a weekend or a tranquil evening; you'll have more fun and a much better meal.

In Pantry: Soy sauce, mirin (rice wine) or sherry, sesame oil, hoisin sauce, dried shiitake mushrooms

In the Refrigerator: Garlic, fresh ginger, scallions, leeks, cilantro, carrots, snow peas, mushrooms

• Since the vegetables are cooked briefly, their true flavor will come through in the end. Consequently, you'll want the best (freshest) ingredients you can find.

• Ginger and garlic are fundamental stir-fry seasonings. Both must be fresh. The dried versions just don't work in the wok.

• Have all of your ingredients ready to go into the wok. Line them up in the order in which you'll be adding them, starting with the vegetables that need the most time to cook (such as mushrooms), and ending with those that need least (such as snow peas).

• There are several good brands of stir-fry sauces available, which may save you the trouble of making your own.

CABBAGE-FILLED CABBAGE STIR-FRY

Serves 4

TOTAL TIME: 30 MINUTES, NOT INCLUDING TIME TO MAKE THE BROTH
TIME TO PREPARE: 20 MINUTES, INCLUDING TIME TO STIR-FRY
COOKING TIME: ABOUT 5 MINUTES
EQUIPMENT: WOK
DO AHEAD: YOU CAN MAKE THE BROTH 6 MONTHS IN ADVANCE IF YOU KEEP IT FROZEN, 4 DAYS IN ADVANCE IF YOU REFRIGERATE IT.
REFRIGERATION/FREEZING: REFRIGERATE UP TO 2 DAYS. DO NOT FREEZE.

*C*risp, crunchy stir-fried cabbage inside crisp, crunchy steamed cabbage . . . can't you just feel how good it tastes? (Crunch, crunch!)

1 head green cabbage
1½ cups Broth for Far Eastern–Flavored Dishes (see page 168), Light Mushroom Broth (see page 168), or vegetable broth (see page 165)
1 tablespoon cornstarch
2 tablespoons low-sodium soy sauce
2 teaspoons rice wine
1 teaspoon sugar
1 tablespoon canola or vegetable oil
2 shallots, minced
3 garlic cloves, minced
2 tablespoons grated peeled fresh ginger
2 teaspoons grated lemon zest
6 scallions, white part and 1 inch of greens, chopped
2 leeks, white part and 1 inch of greens, washed and julienned
2 carrots, peeled and julienned
1 cup sliced fresh mushrooms, including shiitake, if possible
2 cups beans sprouts
1 cup cooked kidney, pinto or black turtle beans, drained and rinsed

Separate 8 to 10 leaves from the cabbage head. Bring an inch of water to a boil in a deep saucepan. Place the leaves inside and cover the pot. Steam until the leaves are pliable, about 4 minutes. Remove them with tongs or a slotted spoon and set them aside to cool. Chop enough of the remaining raw cabbage to make 2 cups.

In a small bowl or Pyrex measuring cup, combine the broth, cornstarch, soy sauce, rice wine, and sugar. Stir well and set aside, ideally within reach of your stove.

Heat a large wok over medium-high heat. Add the oil, and swish it around to coat the wok's bottom and sides. When the oil is hot, add the shallots, garlic, ginger, and lemon zest. Toss them quickly to season the oil, about 1 minute.

Add the scallions, leeks, carrots, and chopped cabbage, and toss again, for about 2 minutes, until the vegetables begin to soften.

Add the mushrooms, bean sprouts, and beans, and toss again to mix, about 1 minute.

Stir the broth–soy sauce mixture well, and pour it into the wok. Toss constantly until the sauce thickens, and everything's thoroughly mixed, about 2 minutes.

To serve, divide the reserved steamed cabbage leaves among four serving plates. Place a heap of filling in the center of each leaf. Roll it up to enclose the filling, or let your guests roll their own.

PER SERVING: CALORIES 243 • PROTEIN 9.9 G • CARBOHYDRATE 44.7 G • FAT 4.6 G • CHOLESTEROL 0 MG • SODIUM 274 MG • 16% CALORIES FROM FAT • OUTSTANDING SOURCE OF VITAMINS A, C; FOLACIN • VERY GOOD SOURCE OF VITAMINS B₁, B₆; IRON • GOOD SOURCE OF CALCIUM

Savory Cheesecakes

SAVORY CHEESECAKE

Serves 6

TOTAL TIME: ABOUT 4 HOURS, 5 MINUTES, INCLUDING
   TIME TO CHILL
TIME TO PREPARE: ABOUT 5 MINUTES
COOKING TIME: 1 HOUR TO BAKE
EQUIPMENT: 9-INCH SPRINGFORM PAN
REFRIGERATION/FREEZING: REFRIGERATE UP TO 3 DAYS. DO
   NOT FREEZE.

Assured of anonymity, ordinarily enthusiastic hosts will admit that brunch can be a problem. Who wants to get up in time to make an elaborate midday meal? When pressed, they'll confess: The temptation to run out for bagels can be hard to beat.

The alternative to falling back on the bakery is making the main dish the day before, preferably something that not only can be made ahead of time, but benefits from advanced preparation. Savory cheesecakes qualify on both counts. They need time to chill and to absorb the flavors from the vegetables and seasonings.

4 large eggs, lightly beaten
1 pound nonfat or part-skim ricotta cheese
½ cup nonfat sour cream
½ cup shredded cheddar, Monterey Jack, or
   mozzarella cheese
½ cup grated Parmesan cheese
3 tablespoons unbleached all-purpose flour

Place racks on the lowest rung and in the center of the oven. Heat the oven to 325°F.

In a large mixing bowl or in a food processor or blender, combine the eggs, ricotta, sour cream, cheddar, Jack, or mozzarella cheese, Parmesan, and flour. Blend the mixture until it's smooth. Pour into a 9-inch springform pan.

Place a baking pan of water on the rack set on the lowest rung of the oven. Put the cheesecake on the rack in the center of the oven and bake until it's golden brown and a knife inserted in the center comes out clean, about 1 hour.

Cool completely, then refrigerate at least 3 hours before serving.

PER SERVING: CALORIES 147 • PROTEIN 14 G • CARBOHYDRATE 7.5 G • FAT 6.5 G • CHOLESTEROL 151 MG • SODIUM 114 MG • 40% CALORIES FROM FAT • GOOD SOURCE OF VITAMINS A, B_2

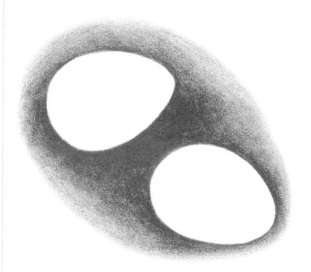

SAVORY CHEESECAKE
BASICS

• Because ricotta cheese is fundamental to the dish, you'll need a very good one. (You'll find recommendations on page 595.)
• Be sure your filling isn't runny. If you have doubts, let it drain in a sieve before adding it to the basic mixture. If you still have your doubts, add ½ cup unseasoned fine bread crumbs to each cup of filling.
• Bake the cheesecake in a springform pan. It will settle and become heavy if baked in a conventional cake pan, and you'll have a hard time getting it out to serve it.
• Bake until it's firm all the way through. Cool it thoroughly on a rack and chill well (at least four hours) before serving.

Make It Your Own

When using the basic recipe, you can have a fairly free hand with additional ingredients, provided they're not watery, which will make the dish runny, or too bulky, which will make it fall apart.

WHAT TO ADD AND WHEN TO ADD IT
Herbs. After you've blended the basic mixture, throw in a handful of minced chopped fresh basil, oregano, and parsley. In a food processor or blender, process in short spurts until they're evenly distributed. And/or lightly sauté ½ teaspoon garlic with 1 cup chopped onions, drain them thoroughly, and add them instead of, or along with, the herbs.
Cheeses. Change the cheeses for a different taste or to complement an additional ingredient. For a Southwest flavor, omit the Parmesan and mozzarella and add Monterey Jack with jalapeños, along with cheddar. Instead of plain mozzarella, add ½ cup shredded smoked mozzarella along with ½ cup drained reconstituted sun-dried tomatoes, and process with the basic mixture.

Vegetables. You can use any pureed, well-drained vegetable. Try ten ounces cooked fresh or defrosted and squeezed dry frozen chopped spinach added to the basic recipe along with a pinch of nutmeg and crumbled dried oregano. With the spinach, use any of the cheeses given in the basic recipe, or substitute Swiss for the cheddar, Jack, or mozzarella. Try steamed chopped broccoli, following the basic recipe, choosing cheddar as the cheese. Or use the recipes for Carrot and Cabbage Filling (see page 379) and Artichoke (see page 380) as guidelines for preparing your favorite vegetable as a filling.

CARROT AND CABBAGE CHEESECAKE

Serves 6

TOTAL TIME: ABOUT 4 HOURS, 35 MINUTES, INCLUDING TIME TO CHILL

TIME TO PREPARE: ABOUT 35 MINUTES, INCLUDING TIME TO SAUTÉ

COOKING TIME: 1 HOUR

EQUIPMENT: 9-INCH SPRINGFORM PAN

REFRIGERATION/FREEZING: REFRIGERATE UP TO 3 DAYS. DO NOT FREEZE.

2 teaspoons canola or vegetable oil

1 large carrot, peeled and grated

1 large onion, chopped

2 cups tightly packed shredded green cabbage

Salt and freshly ground black pepper to taste

1 recipe Savory Cheesecake, unbaked
   (see page 377)

Place racks on the lowest rung and in the center of the oven. Heat the oven to 325°F.

Heat the oil in a large skillet over medium-high heat. When it is hot, add the carrot, onion, and cabbage. Reduce the heat to medium and sauté, stirring often, until the vegetables are soft, about 20 minutes. Add salt and pepper. If the vegetables start to stick, stir in water 1 tablespoon at a time to prevent burning. (Make sure there's no water left in the pan when you add the vegetables to the Basic Savory Cheesecake mixture.)

Remove the mixture from the heat, and let it cool until it stops steaming.

Meanwhile, prepare the Savory Cheesecake mixture in a food processor. Transfer the cabbage mixture to the food processor and process in short pulses to combine, about 6 to 8 pulses. Pour the filling into a 9-inch spring-form pan.

Place a baking pan of water on a rack set on the lowest rung of the oven. Put the cheesecake on the rack in the center of the oven and bake until it's golden brown and a knife inserted in the center comes out clean, about 1 hour.

Cool completely, then refrigerate at least 3 hours before serving.

PER SERVING: CALORIES 245 • PROTEIN 23.1 G • CARBOHYDRATE 14 G • FAT 10.6 G • CHOLESTEROL 158 MG • SODIUM 278 MG • 39% CALORIES FROM FAT • OUT-STANDING SOURCE OF VITAMIN A • VERY GOOD SOURCE OF CALCIUM • GOOD SOURCE OF VITAMIN C

•

ARTICHOKE CHEESECAKE

Serves 6

TOTAL TIME: ABOUT 5 HOURS, INCLUDING TIME TO CHILL
TIME TO PREPARE: ABOUT 30 MINUTES
COOKING TIME: ABOUT 1 HOUR, 30 MINUTES
EQUIPMENT: 9-INCH SPRINGFORM PAN
REFRIGERATION/FREEZING: REFRIGERATE UP TO 3 DAYS. DO
   NOT FREEZE.

*I*f you don't have time to prepare fresh artichokes,
you'll be glad to know that this great entrée is
just as good with frozen hearts.

Juice of 1 lemon, if using fresh artichokes

2 large artichokes, pared, trimmed, and quartered
   (see page 514), or one 10-ounce package
   frozen artichoke hearts, defrosted

2 teaspoons extra virgin olive oil

2 scallions, white part only, minced

¼ cup minced fresh parsley

1 recipe Basic Savory Cheesecake, unbaked (see
   page 377)

If using fresh artichokes, fill a large saucepan with enough water to cover the artichokes, add the lemon juice, and bring to a boil. Add the artichokes and simmer until they're tender all the way through, about 30 minutes. Remove the artichokes and let them drain, reserving the cooking water. Skip this step if using defrosted artichoke hearts.

Place racks on the lowest rung and in the center of the oven. Heat the oven to 325°F.

Heat the oil in a large skillet over medium-high heat. When it's hot, add the scallions and parsley, lower the heat to medium-low, and sauté until the scallions are soft, about 5 minutes. Add the fresh or defrosted artichokes and sauté until you can mash the artichokes down with the back of a spoon, about 15 minutes. To prevent sticking, add the artichoke cooking water or fresh water, if using frozen artichokes, 2 tablespoons at a time, taking care not to add too much. (There should be no water in the pan when you add the artichokes to the cheese mixture.)

Remove the artichokes and scallions from the heat, transfer them to a mixing bowl, and let them cool until they're no longer steaming. Add the Basic Savory Cheesecake mixture and stir well to combine. Pour the mixture into a 9-inch springform pan. Place a baking pan of water on the rack set on the lowest rung of the oven. Put the cheesecake on the rack in the center of the oven and bake until it's golden brown and a knife inserted in the center comes out clean, about 1 hour.

Cool completely, then refrigerate at least 3 hours before serving.

PER SERVING: CALORIES 250 • PROTEIN 23.9 G • CARBOHYDRATE 14.4 G • FAT 10.6 G • CHOLESTEROL 158 MG • SODIUM 309 MG • 38% CALORIES FROM FAT • VERY GOOD SOURCE OF CALCIUM • GOOD SOURCE OF VITAMINS A, B₂, B₁₂, C; FOLACIN

SPINACH SAVORY CHEESECAKE

Serves 6

TOTAL TIME: ABOUT 4 HOURS, 5 MINUTES, INCLUDING
TIME TO CHILL
TIME TO PREPARE: ABOUT 5 MINUTES
COOKING TIME: 1 HOUR
EQUIPMENT: 9-INCH SPRINGFORM PAN
REFRIGERATION/FREEZING: REFRIGERATE UP TO 3 DAYS. DO
NOT FREEZE.

I t takes just five minutes to make a brunch entrée
that's so good you'd want to make it even if it
took four times as long.

10 ounces fresh spinach, washed and finely
chopped, or one 10-ounce package frozen
chopped spinach, thawed and squeezed dry
2 teaspoons crumbled dried oregano
Pinch ground nutmeg
1 recipe Basic Savory Cheesecake, unbaked (see
page 377)

Place racks on the lowest rung and in the center of the oven. Heat the oven to 325°F.

Add the spinach, oregano, and nutmeg to the Savory Cheesecake mixture in a food processor and process in short pulses to combine, about 6 to 8 pulses. Pour the filling into a 9-inch springform pan.

Place a baking pan of water on the rack set on the lowest rung of the oven. Put the cheesecake on the rack in the center of the oven and bake until it's golden brown and a knife inserted in the center comes out clean, about 1 hour.

Cool completely, then refrigerate at least 3 hours before serving.

PER SERVING: CALORIES 220 • PROTEIN 23.7 G • CARBOHYDRATE 11 G • FAT 9.1 G • CHOLESTEROL 158 MG • SODIUM 306 MG • 37% CALORIES FROM FAT • OUTSTANDING SOURCE OF VITAMIN A • VERY GOOD SOURCE OF VITAMINS B₂, C; FOLACIN, CALCIUM • GOOD SOURCE OF VITAMIN B₁₂

Egg Dishes

MUSHROOM FRICASSEE WITH EGGS

Serves 4

TOTAL TIME: ABOUT 30 MINUTES
TIME TO PREPARE: ABOUT 30 MINUTES, INCLUDING TIME
TO SAUTÉ
COOKING TIME: INCLUDED IN TIME TO PREPARE
REFRIGERATION/FREEZING: DO NOT REFRIGERATE OR
FREEZE.

F or those of us who don't want to have to decide
which of the many marvelous mushrooms to
buy—a dish that makes use of an assortment
limited only by what's available where you shop.

1 tablespoon extra virgin olive oil
3 scallions, white part only, minced
¼ cup minced fresh parsley
1 pound mixed mushrooms, such as portobello,
cremini, oyster, shiitake, sliced
⅓ cup nonfat sour cream
2 tablespoons minced fresh chives
1 tablespoon fresh lemon juice
4 large eggs
Salt and freshly ground black pepper to taste

Heat the oil in a large skillet over medium-high heat. When it is hot, add the scallions and parsley. Reduce the heat to medium and sauté, stirring often, until the scallions are soft, about 6 minutes. Add the mushrooms and sauté, stirring often, until they are cooked through, about 10 minutes. Stir in the sour cream, chives, and lemon juice and keep the mixture warm.

Rub a large nonstick skillet lightly with olive oil or squirt with nonstick spray. Heat the pan over medium-high heat. Break the eggs into the skillet, making sure they don't run together. (Depending on the size of your skillet, you may have to do this in several batches.) As soon as the white becomes firm, about 2 minutes, slide a spatula underneath it and fold it up over the yolk, making a little packet. Distribute the mushrooms among 4 serving bowls, top each with an egg, and serve right away. Season with salt and pepper.

PER SERVING: CALORIES 150 • PROTEIN 10 G • CARBOHYDRATE 9.1 G • FAT 8.8 G • CHOLESTEROL 212 MG • SODIUM 82.8 MG • 51% CALORIES FROM FAT • OUTSTANDING SOURCE OF VITAMIN B₂ • VERY GOOD SOURCE OF VITAMIN C • GOOD SOURCE OF VITAMINS A, B₁, B₆, B₁₂; FOLACIN, IRON, ZINC

•

SPINACH AND EGGS IN CHEESE SOUFFLÉ

Serves 2

TOTAL TIME: ABOUT 40 MINUTES
TIME TO PREPARE: ABOUT 30 MINUTES
COOKING TIME: ABOUT 10 MINUTES

As mentioned elsewhere, eggs have been under attack for some time, for reasons that aren't fully justified. Here's a volley from the other side: poached eggs and spinach under a blanket of golden cheese soufflé.

⅓ cup nonfat milk
⅓ cup evaporated skim milk
1 tablespoon cornstarch or arrowroot
1 large egg yolk
¼ cup grated Parmesan, sharp cheddar, or
    Gruyère cheese
2 large eggs
2 large egg whites

Salt and freshly ground black pepper to taste
2 cups loosely packed torn fresh spinach

Heat the oven to 400° F.

In a heavy saucepan, combine the nonfat and evaporated skim milk, and heat slowly over medium-low heat. Whisk in the cornstarch or arrowroot. Continue whisking until the mixture thickens, about 5 minutes. Remove from heat. Stir the egg yolk into the milk mixture. Add the cheese and mix well to blend.

Poach the 2 eggs by bringing 2 inches of water to a simmer in a medium, deep skillet. Add the eggs and let the water come back to a simmer. Cover the skillet and remove it from the heat. Let the eggs rest, covered, until the whites are set and the yolks looks opaque, about 3 minutes.

Meanwhile, whip the egg whites to form stiff peaks. Fold the whites swiftly but gently into the cheese sauce. Season with salt and pepper.

Spread the spinach over the bottom of an 8-inch gratin dish or baking dish. Pour half of

the sauce over the spinach. Place the poached eggs on top and cover with the remaining sauce. Bake until the sauce is golden brown, about 6 minutes. Serve right away.

PER SERVING: CALORIES 262 • PROTEIN 22 G • CARBOHYDRATE 11 G • FAT 14 G • CHOLESTEROL 440 MG • SODIUM 444 MG • 49% CALORIES FROM FAT • VERY GOOD SOURCE OF VITAMIN A • GOOD SOURCE OF FOLACIN

•

SUPPER FRITTATA

Serves 4

TOTAL TIME: ABOUT 20 MINUTES
TIME TO PREPARE: ABOUT 10 MINUTES, INCLUDING TIME TO SAUTÉ
COOKING TIME: ABOUT 10 MINUTES
REFRIGERATION/FREEZING: REFRIGERATE UP TO 3 DAYS.

Frittatas make fabulous free-style fast and easy suppers. Slice them into wedges or strips, and they're perfect party food. See page 68 in the breakfast section for several more variations.

1 tablespoon extra virgin olive oil or unsalted butter
1 small onion, chopped, or 2 tablespoons chopped shallots or scallions, white part only
1 tablespoon minced fresh herb(s), or 1 teaspoon crumbled dried herb(s), such as basil, oregano, thyme, tarragon, and/or mint
6 large eggs (see Note)
2 tablespoons to 1/3 cup grated or shredded cheese of your choice (optional)
Salt and freshly ground black pepper to taste

Place a rack in the upper third of the oven. Heat the oven to 350°F.

Heat the oil or melt the butter in a 12-inch ovenproof nonstick skillet over medium heat. Swirl the pan to distribute the oil or butter evenly over the bottom and sides. Sauté the onion, shallots, or scallions, and herb(s) until the vegetables are soft, about 7 minutes.

Break the eggs into a large bowl, and beat them lightly with a fork or whisk. If using cheese, whisk it in with the eggs at this time.

Pour the eggs into the skillet and stir lightly with a fork until they start to set, about 2 minutes. Once the bottom is firm and set to about 1/3 inch, use a thin, nonmetallic spatula to lift the edge of the frittata that's closest to you. Tilt the pan slightly toward you so that the uncooked egg runs underneath. Lower the edge and swirl the pan gently to distribute the egg evenly.

Continue cooking for about 40 seconds, then lift the edge again, repeating the procedure above until the top—while still not set—is no longer runny, about 4 minutes.

Place the skillet in the oven until the top of the frittata is set and dry to the touch, 2 to 4 minutes. Check each minute after two, because the frittata will turn tough if cooked too long.

Run a spatula around the edges to loosen the frittata, and invert it onto a serving plate. Season to taste with salt and pepper. Serve at once, let cool to room temperature, or refrigerate and serve chilled.

Note: To reduce the amount of fat and calories, you can use 4 whole eggs and 3 whites instead. The frittata may not be as moist as a result.

PER SERVING: CALORIES 143 • PROTEIN 9.6 G • CARBOHYDRATE 2.1 G • FAT 10.5 G • CHOLESTEROL 326 MG • SODIUM 95.7 MG • 67% CALORIES FROM FAT • GOOD SOURCE OF VITAMIN A, IRON

MUSHROOM
FRITTATA

Serves 4

TOTAL TIME: ABOUT 25 MINUTES
TIME TO PREPARE: ABOUT 15 MINUTES, INCLUDING TIME
   TO SAUTÉ
COOKING TIME: ABOUT 10 MINUTES
DO AHEAD: YOU CAN MAKE THE MUSHROOMS UP TO 3
   DAYS IN ADVANCE. REFRIGERATE UNTIL READY TO USE.
REFRIGERATION/FREEZING: REFRIGERATE UP TO 3 DAYS.

Use firm, fresh mushrooms for this frittata, and serve it with soup (especially Tomato and Rice Soup, see page 172). You'll also enjoy it with spinach salad or a salad with walnuts and radicchio.

1 tablespoon extra virgin olive oil
2 tablespoons minced scallions, white part only
2 tablespoons minced fresh parsley
½ pound cremini or portobello mushrooms, chopped
6 large eggs
3 tablespoons nonfat or reduced-fat sour cream
¼ cup shredded Havarti or Monterey Jack cheese
Salt and freshly ground black pepper to taste

Place a rack in the upper third of the oven. Heat the oven to 350° F.

Heat the oil in a 12-inch ovenproof non-stick skillet over medium heat. Swirl the pan to distribute the oil evenly over the bottom and sides. Sauté the scallions and parsley until the scallions are soft, about 7 minutes. Add the mushrooms and sauté until just cooked through, about 3 minutes.

Drain any excess water that may have accumulated in the pan, and spread the mushrooms in a single layer.

Lightly beat together the eggs, sour cream, and cheese in a mixing bowl.

Pour the eggs into the skillet, over the mushrooms, and stir lightly with a fork until they start to set, about 2 minutes. Once the bottom is firm and about ⅓ inch thick, use a thin, nonmetallic spatula to lift the frittata's edge closest to you. Tilt the pan slightly toward you so that the uncooked egg runs underneath. Lower the edge and swirl the pan gently to distribute the egg evenly.

Continue cooking for about 40 seconds, then lift the edge again, repeating the procedure above until the top—while still not set—is no longer runny, about 4 minutes.

Place the skillet in the oven until the top of the frittata is set and dry to the touch, 2 to 4 minutes. Check each minute after two, because the frittata will turn tough if cooked too long.

Run a spatula around the edges to loosen the frittata, and invert it onto a serving plate.

Season to taste with salt and pepper. Serve at once, let cool to room temperature, or refrigerate and serve chilled.

PER SERVING: CALORIES 218 • PROTEIN 14.9 G • CARBOHYDRATE 5 G • FAT 15.4 G • CHOLESTEROL 331 MG • SODIUM 181 MG • 63% CALORIES FROM FAT • OUTSTANDING SOURCE OF VITAMIN B₂ • VERY GOOD SOURCE OF VITAMIN A • GOOD SOURCE OF FOLACIN, CALCIUM, ZINC

•

ASPARAGUS FRITTATA

Serves 4

TOTAL TIME: ABOUT 25 MINUTES
TIME TO PREPARE: ABOUT 15 MINUTES
COOKING TIME: ABOUT 10 MINUTES
DO AHEAD: YOU CAN BLANCH THE ASPARAGUS UP TO 3 DAYS IN ADVANCE.
REFRIGERATION/FREEZING: REFRIGERATE UP TO 3 DAYS.

A good use for leftover asparagus, or the stems reserved from asparagus risotto. Of course, you should also consider buying asparagus expressly for this dish!

⅓ pound trimmed asparagus or leftover cooked asparagus
1 tablespoon extra virgin olive oil or unsalted butter
1 shallot, minced
1 tablespoon minced fresh mint, or 1 teaspoon crumbled dried mint
2 tablespoons minced fresh parsley
6 large eggs
3 tablespoons grated Parmesan cheese
Salt and freshly ground black pepper to taste

Place a rack in the upper third of the oven. Heat the oven to 350°F.

Fill a large saucepan with enough water to cover the asparagus and bring to a boil over high heat. At the same time fill a large bowl with cold water and ice cubes, and line a colander with paper towels. Plunge the asparagus into the boiling water. The moment they turn bright green, about 30 to 40 seconds, remove them with a slotted spoon and place them in the ice water for 15 seconds, to stop the cooking, then transfer to the colander to drain.

Meanwhile, heat the oil or melt the butter in a 12-inch ovenproof nonstick skillet over medium heat. Swirl the pan to distribute the oil evenly over the bottom and sides. Sauté the shallot, mint, and parsley until the shallot is soft, about 7 minutes. Add the asparagus and sauté just to coat with the shallot and herbs. Spread the asparagus in a single layer in the skillet.

Break the eggs into a bowl, and beat them lightly with a fork or whisk. Lightly beat in the cheese. Pour the eggs into the skillet, over the asparagus, and stir lightly with a fork until the eggs start to set, about 2 minutes. Once the bottom is firm and set to about ⅓ inch, use a thin, nonmetallic spatula to lift the frittata's edge closest to you. Tilt the pan slightly toward you so that the uncooked egg runs underneath. Lower the edge and swirl the pan gently to distribute the egg evenly.

Continue cooking for about 40 seconds, then lift the edge again, repeating the procedure above until the egg on top—while still not set—is no longer runny, about 4 minutes.

Place the skillet in the oven until the top of the frittata is set and dry to the touch, 2 to 4 minutes. Check each minute after two, because the frittata will turn tough if cooked too long.

Run a spatula around the edges to loosen the frittata, and invert it onto a serving plate. Season to taste with salt and pepper. Serve at once, let cool to room temperature, or refrigerate and serve chilled.

PER SERVING: CALORIES 176 • PROTEIN 12.6 G • CARBOHYDRATE 4.5 G • FAT 11.9 G • CHOLESTEROL 329 MG • SODIUM 186 MG • 61% CALORIES FROM FAT • VERY GOOD SOURCE OF VITAMINS A, B₂, C; FOLACIN • GOOD SOURCE OF VITAMINS B₆, B₁₂; CALCIUM

•

QUICK TORTILLAS WITH EGGS

Serves 4

TOTAL TIME: ABOUT 10 MINUTES, NOT INCLUDING TIME TO MAKE THE HUMMUS
TIME TO PREPARE: ABOUT 10 MINUTES
COOKING TIME: INCLUDED IN TIME TO PREPARE
DO AHEAD: YOU CAN MAKE THE HUMMUS UP TO 4 DAYS IN ADVANCE. REFRIGERATE UNTIL READY TO USE.
REFRIGERATION/FREEZING: DO NOT REFRIGERATE OR FREEZE.

A natural for Sunday supper. Make the hummus ahead, lay in a stack of tortillas, and it'll be just a few minutes till dinner's on.

4 large eggs

2 tablespoons water

4 whole wheat flour tortillas or Lavosh (see page 412)

1 recipe Kidney Bean Hummus (see page 254)

2 tablespoons nonfat sour cream

½ cup chopped avocado

Salsa, for garnish (optional)

¼ cup minced fresh cilantro, for garnish (optional)

Salt and freshly ground black pepper to taste

Squirt a large nonstick skillet with nonstick spray or lightly rub it with canola oil. Heat the skillet over medium heat. When it's hot, crack the eggs into it. As the whites set, add the water. Cook until the whites are firm and the yolks are still runny, about 4 minutes.

Meanwhile, spread each tortilla or lavosh with an equal portion of Kidney Bean Hummus. Spread the sour cream evenly on top, then cover with an even amount of avocado. Using a slotted spatula, slide an egg on top of each. Serve with a dash of salsa and a bit of cilantro, if you'd like. Season with salt and pepper, and serve right away.

PER SERVING: CALORIES 266 • PROTEIN 16.5 G • CARBOHYDRATE 30.4 G • FAT 10.2 G • CHOLESTEROL 213 MG • SODIUM 122 MG • 33% CALORIES FROM FAT • VERY GOOD SOURCE OF VITAMIN B₂; FOLACIN, IRON • GOOD SOURCE OF VITAMINS A, B₁, B₆, C; ZINC

NOW TRY THIS: Use Refried Bean Puree or one of the variations (see page 254) instead of Kidney Bean Hummus.

•

SUN-DRIED TOMATO AND BLACK OLIVE FRITTATA

Serves 4

TOTAL TIME: ABOUT 20 MINUTES
TIME TO PREPARE: ABOUT 10 MINUTES
COOKING TIME: ABOUT 10 MINUTES
REFRIGERATION/FREEZING: REFRIGERATE UP TO 3 DAYS.

Classic Mediterranean flavors make this frittata one you'll try and try again. Serve it with Red or Yellow Bell Pepper Soup (see page 171) or Chickpea and Rosemary Passata (see page 192).

1 tablespoon extra virgin olive oil
½ garlic clove, sliced
1 tablespoon minced fresh basil, or 1 teaspoon crumbled dried basil
1 tablespoon minced fresh oregano, or 1 teaspoon crumbled dried oregano
¼ cup minced dry-packed (not in oil) sun-dried tomatoes
3 tablespoons minced cured niçoise-style olives
6 large eggs
⅓ cup loosely packed crumbled feta cheese
Salt and freshly ground black pepper to taste

Place a rack in the upper third of the oven. Heat the oven to 350°F.

Heat the oil in a 12-inch ovenproof non-stick skillet over medium-low heat, then swish the garlic clove through the warm oil until the garlic begins to color. Remove the garlic and discard. Sauté the basil, oregano, sun-dried tomatoes, and olives until the tomatoes soften and begin to plump up, about 3 minutes. Spread the tomatoes and olives in a single layer in the pan.

Lightly beat together the eggs and the cheese in a mixing bowl (the mixture will be lumpy, which is fine). Pour the eggs into the pan, and stir lightly with a fork until they start to set, about 2 minutes. Once the bottom is firm and set to about ⅓ inch, use a thin, non-metallic spatula to lift the frittata's edge closest to you. Tilt the pan slightly toward you so that the uncooked egg runs underneath. Lower the edge and swirl the pan gently to distribute the egg evenly.

Continue cooking for about 40 seconds, then lift the edge again, repeating the procedure above until the top—while still not set— is no longer runny, about 4 minutes.

Place the skillet in the oven until the top of the frittata is set and dry to the touch, 2 to 4 minutes. Check each minute after two, because the frittata will turn tough if cooked too long.

Run a spatula around the edges to loosen the frittata, and invert it onto a serving plate. Season to taste with salt and pepper. Serve at once, let cool to room temperature, or refrigerate and serve chilled.

PER SERVING: CALORIES 198 • PROTEIN 12 G • CARBOHYDRATE 4.3 G • FAT 14.8 G • CHOLESTEROL 331 MG • SODIUM 380 MG • 67% CALORIES FROM FAT • VERY GOOD SOURCE OF VITAMIN B2 • GOOD SOURCE OF VITAMINS A, B12; FOLACIN, CALCIUM, IRON

SAVORY APPLE SOUFFLÉED FRITTATA

Serves 2

TOTAL TIME: ABOUT 20 MINUTES

TIME TO PREPARE: ABOUT 10 MINUTES, INCLUDING TIME
 TO SAUTÉ

COOKING TIME: ABOUT 10 MINUTES

REFRIGERATION/FREEZING: REFRIGERATE UP TO 3 DAYS. DO
 NOT FREEZE.

Cheddar cheese, apple, and cinnamon make
a sweet and savory (and simple!) springy
soufflé-style frittata. Serve it for brunch,
with fruit salad on the side.

2 large eggs, separated

2 tablespoons nonfat sour cream

2 tablespoons shredded sharp cheddar cheese

1 teaspoon unsalted butter or canola oil

2 tablespoons minced onion

⅓ cup diced peeled apples

½ teaspoon ground cinnamon

½ teaspoon ground cumin

Place a rack in the upper third of the oven and
heat the oven to 400°F.

In a mixing bowl, lightly beat the egg
yolks to blend them together. Stir in the sour
cream and cheddar cheese.

Melt the butter or heat the oil in a 7-inch
ovenproof nonstick skillet over medium heat.
When it's hot, swirl the pan to distribute it
evenly. Sauté the onions, apples, cinnamon,
and cumin until the onions and apples are soft,
about 6 minutes.

In another mixing bowl, beat the egg
whites until stiff but not dry. Gently fold the
whites into the yolk mixture.

Gently pour the egg mixture into the skillet and let it cook over medium heat until the
bottom and sides are set, about 5 minutes.
Transfer the skillet to the oven and bake until
the top of the frittata is set and golden brown,
3 to 4 minutes.

To loosen the frittata from the skillet, run a
plastic spatula around the rim. Lift the frittata
onto a serving plate. Do not invert it as you
would an ordinary frittata, or it will collapse.
Serve immediately.

PER SERVING: CALORIES 186 • PROTEIN 9.2 G • CARBOHYDRATE 12.5 G • FAT
11.4 G • CHOLESTEROL 231 MG • SODIUM 118 MG • 54% CALORIES FROM FAT •
GOOD SOURCE OF VITAMINS A, B₂, B₁₂

TORTILLA-STYLE FRITTATA

Serves 4

TOTAL TIME: ABOUT 20 MINUTES, NOT INCLUDING TIME TO
MAKE THE HUMMUS OR BEAN PUREE
TIME TO PREPARE: ABOUT 10 MINUTES
COOKING TIME: ABOUT 10 MINUTES
DO AHEAD: YOU CAN MAKE THE TOPPING UP TO 2 DAYS IN
ADVANCE. REFRIGERATE UNTIL READY TO USE.
REFRIGERATION/FREEZING: REFRIGERATE UP TO 3 DAYS. DO
NOT FREEZE.

This frittata is almost firm enough to be a pancake. Cornmeal and cheddar cheese make it dense and flavorful.

Tortilla

1 cup cooked fresh or defrosted frozen corn
    kernels

1 teaspoon stone-ground cornmeal

1 tablespoon nonfat or low-fat buttermilk or
    plain nonfat yogurt

1 large egg

2 tablespoons grated cheddar cheese

1 tablespoon minced scallion greens

¼ teaspoon ground cumin

Topping

2 tablespoons Kidney Bean Hummus (see page
    254), Refried Bean Puree (see page 256), or
    commercial bean spread (see preferred brands
    and mail-order information, page 595)

2 tablespoons plain nonfat yogurt

2 tablespoons minced fresh avocado, for garnish

1 small tomato, chopped, for garnish

Heat the oven to 325°F.

For the Tortilla

Place half the corn kernels in a compact food processor or blender. Add the cornmeal and buttermilk or yogurt and process in short spurts until the corn is chopped and everything's well blended.

Place the remaining kernels in a small mixing bowl and add the buttermilk or yogurt mixture. Whisk in the egg, cheese, scallion greens, and cumin.

Heat an 8-inch ovenproof nonstick skillet over medium heat. When it's hot, pour in the egg mixture. Swirl the pan so it spreads into an even layer. When the bottom has set, after about 4 to 5 minutes, place the skillet in the oven to set the top of the frittata, about 4 minutes.

Using a nonmetallic spatula, loosen the bottom and invert it onto a serving plate.

For the Topping

Spread the frittata with the Kidney Bean Hummus, puree, or spread, then with the yogurt. Distribute the avocado and tomato on top. Serve right away.

PER SERVING: CALORIES 102 • PROTEIN 5.3 G • CARBOHYDRATE 12 G • FAT 4.2 G • CHOLESTEROL 57 MG • SODIUM 89.8 MG • 35% CALORIES FROM FAT • GOOD SOURCE OF VITAMIN C; FOLACIN

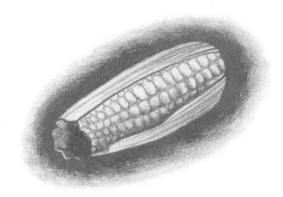

BREADS AND BREAD DISHES

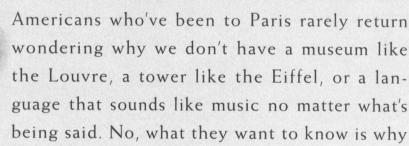

Americans who've been to Paris rarely return wondering why we don't have a museum like the Louvre, a tower like the Eiffel, or a language that sounds like music no matter what's being said. No, what they want to know is why the bread in Paris is so much better than ours.

Study the matter and you'll find that bad bread is part of our legacy. Domestic wheat was scarce until after the Civil War, and then, ever bent on progress, processors took pride in milling the life out of flour and making uniform, squishy, bland loaves with unnatural shelf lives.

At last, this trend is in reverse, and more stores and restaurants take pride in offering good breads made in small batches with premium ingredients. While being able to buy good bread is a treat, making it yourself is even better. Handling the dough (even if it's only briefly as you take it from a bread machine and shape it) is cathartic, and baking fills the house with what may be the world's most appetizing aroma.

BREAD IN MEAL PLANNING •

BREAD PANTRY • BREAD MENUS •

 BREADS • SOURDOUGH BREADS

• FLAT BREADS • PIZZAS • CALZONES •

FOCACCIA • CREPES • SAVORY

 PIES • PHYLLO • STRATAS AND

SAVORY BREAD PUDDINGS

Bread in Meal Planning

Although we tend to think of bread as something to accompany a meal, it can be a major ingredient, too. It's the foundation for pizza, the casing for calzone, a thickener for soup (page 198), and the principle ingredient in panzanella (page 154), savory french toast (page 442), and scrumptious stratas (page 440). It can provide vitamin B, zinc, fiber, and complex carbohydrates. Consider, for example:

SWEET AND CREAMY CARROT CALZONE (PAGE 422)
64% daily value for protein
325% daily value for vitamin A
72% daily value for vitamin C
27% daily value for folacin
57% daily value for vitamin B_1
40% daily value for vitamin B_2
31% daily value for iron
35% daily value for calcium

WHEAT BERRY BREAD (PAGE 400)
27% daily value for vitamin B_1
19% daily value for vitamin B_3
15% daily value for iron

GRAPE-NUTS BRAN BREAD (PAGE 406)
10% daily value for folacin
18% daily value for vitamin B_1
10% daily value for iron

STACKED CREPES WITH SOUFFLÉED SPINACH AND CHEESE (PAGE 432)
39% daily value for protein
49% daily value for vitamin A
23% daily value for vitamin C
33% daily value for folacin
29% daily value for calcium
19% daily value for iron
11% daily value for zinc

WINTER GARDEN SAVORY PIE (PAGE 436)
31% daily value for protein
66% daily value for vitamin C
31% daily value for folacin
30% daily value for vitamin B_1
24% daily value for vitamin B_2
21% daily value for vitamin B_6
20% daily value for iron
15% daily value for calcium

Bread Pantry

You'll find my brand-name recommendations for most of these items on page 595. If you can't find what you want where you shop, see the mail-order information on page 596.

All-purpose flour
Whole wheat flour
Semolina flour
Cornmeal, preferably stone-ground
Rye flour
Dry active yeast
Wheat berries
Rolled oats
Grape-Nuts cereal
Seeds (caraway, sesame, and poppy)
Salt
Sugar
Baking powder

Baking soda
Extra virgin olive oil
Barley-malt syrup
Dried herbs

In the Refrigerator
Plain nonfat yogurt
Low-fat cottage cheese
Nonfat milk
Phyllo dough (keep frozen)

Bread Menus

Raspberry-Cannellini Succotash *(page 137)*
Mushroom Crepes *(page 430)*

Tomato and Rice Soup *(page 172)*
Focaccia *(page 425)*
Mixed salad greens with Vinaigrette-Style Dressing *(page 117)*

Cayote Calzone *(page 421)*
Mixed salad greens
with Avocado-Buttermilk Dressing *(page 120)*

Pureed Asparagus Soup *(page 185)*
Torta di Pasqua *(page 438)*

Sweet Carrot Soup *(page 187)*
Winter Garden Savory Pie *(page 436)*

Barley Soup with Zucchini *(page 175)*
Whole Wheat Chickpea Bread *(page 403)*

Zucchini Passata *(page 186)*
Strata *(page 440)*

Breads

HEARTH-WARMING HOMEMADE BREAD

Makes 2 loaves; serves 16

TOTAL TIME: ABOUT 7 TO 24 HOURS, USING THE SPONGE METHOD; ABOUT 5 HOURS, USING THE STRAIGHT DOUGH METHOD. BOTH METHODS INCLUDE TIME FOR THE DOUGH TO RISE.
TIME TO PREPARE: ABOUT 50 MINUTES
COOKING TIME: 40 MINUTES
EQUIPMENT: BAKING STONE, BAKER'S PEEL (OPTIONAL)
FREEZING: FREEZE UP TO 3 MONTHS.

This bread is never disappointing, so it will build your confidence if you are just beginning to bake, and it will serve as a simple standby if you are already a pro.

You can make this bread using the "sponge" method, which involves making a batter, allowing it to ferment, then adding it to the final bread dough, or by the "straight" method, for which you skip the batter and just make the dough. The sponge method takes longer, but the bread tastes better, with a sweetish-sourdough flavor that's a product of time, not additional ingredients. And the longer you let the sponge ferment—up to twenty-four hours—the better the bread will taste.

2 cups warm water (98° to 115°F.)
1 tablespoon sugar
1 tablespoon (1 packet) dry active yeast
6 cups unbleached all-purpose flour (see page 581 for recommendations)
1 tablespoon salt
Cornmeal, for dusting

To make the bread with the sponge method, in a large mixing bowl, combine the water, sugar,

and yeast. Let the mixture sit until it turns creamy and tiny bubbles appear on the surface, about 5 to 7 minutes.

In a separate mixing bowl, whisk together 3 cups of the flour with the salt. Stir this flour mixture into the yeast mixture, and beat by hand or with the dough hook of a Mixmaster at low speed until very elastic. This will take about 100 strokes by hand, and about 2 minutes by machine. Scrape down the sides of the bowl, cover it with plastic wrap and a kitchen towel, and set it aside in a draft-free place to ferment until it has doubled in volume and become very bubbly, about 2 hours. For an enhanced flavor, let the dough sit up to 24 hours, if desired.

Beat down the batter, and stir in another cup of flour. Keep adding flour until the dough is stiff enough to handle. (If you're wearing rings, take them off now!) The dough will be sticky, but fight the temptation to add more flour until you've tried to work with it for a while. When people describe bread making as bliss, this is not the part they mean. Add flour

as necessary only to make it possible to shape the mess into a smooth, springy dough. Easier said than done, at first. But too much flour makes bread tough and tasteless. Go easy on the flour, and you'll be glad you struggled through this sticky stage.

You can bypass this mess entirely by using a Mixmaster to make the dough. First, add 1 cup flour to the sponge and use the paddle attachment at low speed to combine them. Switch to the dough hook, and add more flour, mixing at medium speed until the dough forms a ball around the hook.

Whether you've mixed the dough by hand or machine, lightly flour your hands and a work surface, and turn the dough out onto the surface to knead until it's smooth and springy, about 15 minutes. (Pinch the dough and pull it back. If it springs into place, it's ready.) Shape into a firm ball.

Lightly grease a bowl and place the dough inside. Cover with plastic wrap and a towel, and set aside in a draft-free place to rise until doubled, about 1½ hours.

Press down the dough in the center, and deflate it. Turn it out onto a lightly floured surface and knead it briefly, just to squeeze out the air.

Divide the dough into 2 pieces. Cupping one piece between your hands, rotate it while tucking the dough under to form a perfect round. Repeat with the other piece. Dust the center of 2 clean dish towels with about ¼ cup flour each, and rub the flour into the towels. Place each towel, floured side up, in a soup bowl about 8 inches in diameter. Place the rounds of dough upside down in the bowls.

Cover loosely with plastic wrap and set aside in a draft-free place to rise until doubled, about 1½ hours.

Forty-five minutes before you plan to bake the bread, place the baking stone on the center rack of the oven, and heat to 450°F.

Sprinkle a baking sheet or baker's peel with cornmeal. Using a dish towel to assist you, carefully turn the dough out of the bowls onto the baking sheet or peel so their top sides are down. If it deflates a bit, try to pat the rounds gently back into shape. Using a serrated knife, quickly score the top of each loaf with 3 slashes or an X and put the loaves in the oven, either on the baking sheet or by sliding them off the peel onto the baking stone.

Close the oven door for about 15 seconds. Open the oven and squirt inside with water to make steam, using a water pistol or a spritzer bottle. If you don't have either, simply splash water from a cup onto the oven floor. (Make sure you don't splash the hot lightbulb.) Close the door for 30 seconds, then repeat.

Bake until the loaves are golden brown and each, when tapped on the bottom, sounds as if it's hollow inside, about 40 minutes. If the bread is browning but doesn't sound hollow, cover the loaves loosely with foil, lower the heat to 400°F., and continue baking until they're done, checking every 5 minutes.

Transfer the loaves to a wire rack and let them cool completely before slicing.

PER SERVING: CALORIES 175 • PROTEIN 5 G • CARBOHYDRATE 36.7 G • FAT 0 G • CHOLESTEROL 0 MG • SODIUM 401 MG • 3% CALORIES FROM FAT

STRAIGHT DOUGH METHOD: In a large mixing bowl, combine the water, sugar, and yeast. Let the mixture sit until it turns creamy, and tiny bubbles appear on the surface, about 5 to 7 minutes.

In a separate mixing bowl, whisk together 3 cups of the flour with the salt. Stir this flour mixture into the yeast mixture, and beat by hand or with the dough hook of a Mixmaster at low speed until very elastic. Proceed as directed in the main recipe, skipping the fermentation period and starting from the point of adding the remaining flour.

BREAD BASICS

Until recently I couldn't bake bread at all, a fact I've attributed variously to a threatening demeanor that scares the life out of tiny organisms such as yeast, a free spirit that can't bother to distinguish between a half cup and a whole one, and an artistic temperament that favors impulse and

ASK THE EXPERT

Q. What about bread machines?

A. Lora Brody, author of *Bread Machine Baking: Perfect Every Time, Desserts from Your Bread Machine,* and *Pizza, Focaccia, Flat and Filled Breads from Your Bread Machine,* and creator of a line of bread machine products that carry her name, emphatically endorses not only the bread machine, but any gadget that gets most of us into the kitchen. To those purists who insist that machines strip the baking process of soul and yield uninspired, uniform loaves, Brody has two sensible things to say. First, she says, how many people do you know who have the time to make bread entirely by hand? She'd rather encourage everyone to find a way—*any* way—to make their own bread than tell them, if you can't do it this way, forget it. Second, she says, you can make terrific bread with a machine, if you start with a recipe for a good dough, then use the appliance only to knead the dough and proof it (allow it to rise). Where critics of the bread machine go wrong, she says, is baking the bread in the appliance. Instead, take out the dough, shape it yourself, and bake it in your oven. In this way, Brody says, you have pizza dough in sixty minutes, clarifying, "The *machine* works for sixty minutes; you work for two."

Q. I've mixed the water, sugar, and yeast, and waited ten minutes, but the water's still flat!

A. Start again with fresh yeast. The ten minutes after you blend the yeast and warm water is called the proofing stage, as in when the yeast is meant to exhibit proof, in the form of bubbles, that it's alive. In this case, it's proven to be lifeless. It's possible that you inadvertently killed it by using water that was too hot. If the water feels hot, it's too hot.

But it may also be that the yeast had already died, possibly from old age. When buying yeast, check the "use by" date. If you're not going to bake with it immediately, store it in the refrigerator or freezer. If you freeze it, you don't have to let it thaw before proofing it.

improvisation over meticulous measuring and timing. In actual fact, the reason is that I'm impatient, disorganized, and way too undisciplined for an art that requires such precision and care.

Then came the coldest, snowiest winter in years. While it would be nice to say that I learned to bake out of a determination to impose self-discipline, I have to admit it had less to do with my will to reform than with the idea of being indoors that season, with the oven on.

So I picked up several inspiring, instructive books on the subject (see page 600), suspended my "creative" impulses, and followed a few of the recipes to the letter.

The breads were perfect. I continued to follow the recipes until I understood them well enough to improvise.

Now I rely less on recipes and more on what I've learned from them, such as how much flour to add and when, how the dough should feel at what stage, how long to let the dough rest, and how long to bake it at what temperature.

Good bread requires two things above all: patience and good flour (see page 595). It's also essential to have live, active yeast and a warm, draft-free place where the yeast, once added to the dough, can thrive. Also important:

• Use warm water (between 98°F. and 115°F.) to activate (proof) the yeast. If the water feels hot, it's too hot.

• Try not to add much flour as you knead. While it may make the dough easier to handle, it will make the bread heavy in the end.

• Let the bread cool thoroughly before you slice it. The interior of the bread continues to bake once out of the oven, and if you cut it while it's warm, you'll mash the grain, and your bread may be mushy.

• Bread keeps well in the freezer, but not the refrigerator. Wrap whole loaves or unused portions tightly in plastic and freeze up to six months. To defrost, wrap the bread in foil and place in a 350°F. oven until it's thawed all the way through. The time will vary, depending on the size and density of the loaf. Alternatively, wrap the frozen bread in damp paper towels and microwave until it's thawed, starting with two minutes, then repeating at one-minute intervals until the bread is thawed. Be careful not to microwave too long, or the bread will get tough.

Make It Your Own

Whole Wheat Flour. You can substitute up to half whole wheat flour (preferably whole wheat bread flour or kamut flour, another form of whole wheat flour) for half of the all-purpose flour in the basic recipe. If you use more than that, the bread may be too heavy in flavor and texture. Also, regardless how much whole wheat flour you add to the dough, use all-purpose flour to dust your kneading surface. Whole wheat flour is too coarse.

Other Flours. Gluten is what enables dough to trap the carbon monoxide released by live yeast, making the bread rise. Only wheat flour contains enough gluten to do this. Yeast breads made entirely of cornmeal, rye, or oats would be like bricks. However, you can combine other grains with wheat flour with success, provided you keep each in proportion. Use no more than 1 cup of another grain (cornmeal,

rye, oat flour or rolled oats, barley flour, or soy flour) to 3 cups wheat flour (either whole wheat or all-purpose or both). For example, you can use 1 cup oat flour, 1 cup whole wheat flour, and 2 cups all-purpose flour.

Sweeteners. Replace the sugar with a sweetener that complements the type of grain you're using. Molasses goes well with corn bread, for example, and dark brown sugar and/or maple syrup are delicious with oat flour or rolled oats. When you use liquid sweetener, expect to use a little more flour in the final dough.

Milk. Use nonfat milk in place of water for a more nourishing loaf with a softer crumb. The milk must be fat free; fat inhibits the action of the yeast.

Herbs. When you knead the dough for the last time, knead in about 1 cup loosely packed minced fresh herbs, or a couple of tablespoons crumbled dried herbs. Divide and shape the dough, and bake as directed in the basic recipe. Try basil, oregano, rosemary (use no more than ¼ cup minced fresh rosemary—it's very strong), chives, chervil, or parsley. For a lighter flavor, beat together 1 large egg white, 2 tablespoons cold water, and ¼ cup minced fresh herbs, or 2 tablespoons crumbled dried herbs, and brush them on the loaves with a pastry brush, just before baking.

Seeds. Beat together 1 large egg white, 2 tablespoons cold water, and between 2 tablespoons and ¼ cup sesame seeds or poppy seeds. Brush them on the loaves with a pastry brush just before baking.

Cheese. When you knead the dough for the last time, knead in between ¼ cup and 1 cup grated or shredded cheese, such as Parmesan, cheddar, Monterey Jack (including Jack cheese with peppers), Emmentaler, feta, or smoked mozzarella. Match a cheese with an herb (above), if you'd like, pairing Parmesan with basil and oregano, and cheddar with cilantro, for example.

🌿 *Roasted Garlic.* When you knead the dough for the last time, knead in two mashed roasted garlic cloves (see page 529). Shape the loaves and bake as directed in the basic recipe. Try this with ½ cup combined minced fresh basil and parsley (see "Herbs," above).

🌿 *Sun-Dried Tomatoes and/or Olives.* Blot dry six oil-cured sun-dried tomatoes. Mince them finely. Mince ⅓ cup cured black or green olives. When you knead the dough for the last time, knead in the tomatoes and/or olives. Add herbs and/or cheese, if you'd like—especially grated Parmesan and basil and oregano, or smoked mozzarella and basil. Shape and bake as directed in the basic recipe.

MY FAVORITE BREAD-BAKING AIDS

Mixmaster. The dough hook stirs the dough through the icky-sticky stage to the point where it's a pleasure to handle. I let the machine bind the water and flour into a dough, which I turn out and knead by hand. A food processor fitted with a plastic dough blade will do the same, but can be harder to clean.

Marble Slab. Dough doesn't stick easily to marble, so it's ideal for the "lightly floured surface" that kneading requires.

Large Ceramic Bowl. Similarly, dough won't stick to the sides of a ceramic bowl, making it the ideal place to leave it to rise.

Also, you can punch the dough down and do the second kneading right in the bowl.

Baker's Peel. A long-handled, flat "shovel" that allows you to slide your bread and pizzas in and out of the oven without burning your hands or deflating the dough.

Baker's Stone. Also called a pizza stone, it's a heavy ceramic slab that absorbs moisture from the dough and regulates the oven temperature, rendering breads that are crisp on the outside and moist within.

Plus I still rarely bake bread without consulting one of the following books on the subject: *King Arthur Flour 200th Anniversary Cookbook*, by Brinna Sands (Countryman Press); *Bread Alone*, by Daniel Leader and Judith Blahnik (William Morrow); *The Italian Baker*, by Carol Field (William Morrow); *Brother Juniper's Bread Book*, by Peter Reinhart (Addison Wesley); *Breads*, by Bernard Clayton (Fireside).

WHEAT BERRY BREAD

Makes 2 loaves; serves 16

TOTAL TIME: ABOUT 16 HOURS, 30 MINUTES, INCLUDING
  TIME TO SOAK THE BERRIES AND FOR THE DOUGH TO RISE
TIME TO PREPARE: ABOUT 40 MINUTES
COOKING TIME: 50 MINUTES
EQUIPMENT: BAKING STONE, BAKER'S PEEL (OPTIONAL)
REFRIGERATION/FREEZING: DO NOT REFRIGERATE. FREEZE
  UP TO 6 MONTHS.

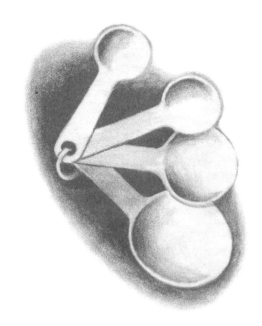

There were eight boulangeries on our street in Paris, and while all offered a similar selection of breads, each was best at only one kind. There was one for whole wheat (pain complete), another for seven grain (sept cereal), another for baguettes, another for organic wheat (ble biologique), and another whose pain au levain (sourdough) has been made every day for three hundred years in the same wood-burning oven.

If I were to open a shop, in Paris or anywhere else, I'd want to be known for this bread, studded with chewy wheat berries and lightly sweetened with barley malt.

1 cup wheat berries (for mail-order information,
  see page 596)
2 teaspoons dry active yeast
2 cups warm water (98° to 115°F.)
5 cups unbleached all-purpose flour,
  approximately
2½ cups whole wheat flour
2 tablespoons barley-malt syrup (for mail-order
  information, see page 596) or brown sugar
1 tablespoon salt
Cornmeal, for dusting

At least 8 hours before you plan to make the dough, place the wheat berries in a small bowl.

Add water to cover. Cover with plastic wrap and refrigerate.

At the same time, make the sponge for the bread, combine 1 teaspoon of the yeast and 1 cup of the warm water in a large bowl. Stir in 1 cup of the all-purpose flour and ½ cup of the wheat flour and beat until you have a stretchy batter that pulls away from the sides of the bowl in thick strands. (You'll stir about 100 strokes to reach this stage.) Cover with plastic wrap and a clean kitchen towel, and set aside in a warm place, away from drafts, to ferment.

Eight to twelve hours later, drain the wheat berries. By now the sponge should be very bubbly and smell of yeast. Stir into it the remaining yeast and warm water, the barley-malt syrup or brown sugar, salt, the remaining whole wheat flour, and wheat berries. Add additional all-purpose flour until you have a dough that is firm enough to handle.

If you're using a Mixmaster to make the

dough, after you've added the remaining ingredients up to the whole wheat flour and berries to the sponge, use the paddle at low speed to combine them. Switch to the dough hook, and add the all-purpose flour 1 cup at a time, mixing at medium speed until the dough forms a ball around the hook.

Whether you've mixed the dough by hand or machine, lightly flour your hands and a work surface, and turn the dough out onto the surface to knead until smooth and springy, about 15 minutes. (Pinch the dough and pull it back. When it springs into place, it's ready.) Shape into a firm ball.

Lightly grease a bowl and place the dough inside. Cover with plastic wrap and a towel, and set aside in a draft-free place to rise until doubled, about 1½ hours.

Press down the dough in the center, and deflate it. Turn it out onto a lightly floured surface and knead it briefly, just to squeeze out the air.

Divide the dough into 2 pieces. Cupping one piece between your hands, rotate it while tucking the dough under to form a perfect round. Repeat with the other piece. Dust the center of 2 clean dish towels with about ¼ cup flour each, and rub the flour into them. Place each towel, floured side up, in a soup bowl about 8 inches in diameter. Place the rounds of dough upside down in the bowls. Cover loosely with plastic wrap and set aside in a draft-free place to rise until doubled, about 1½ hours.

Forty-five minutes before you plan to bake the bread, place the baking stone on the center rack of the oven, and heat to 450°F.

Sprinkle a baking sheet or baker's peel with cornmeal. Using a dish towel to assist you, carefully turn the dough out of the bowls onto the baking sheet or peel so their top sides are down. If it deflates a bit, try to pat the rounds gently back into shape. Using a serrated knife, quickly score the top of each loaf with 3 slashes or an X and put the loaves in the oven, either on the baking sheet or by sliding them off the peel onto the baking stone.

Close the oven door for about 15 seconds. Open the oven and squirt inside with water to make steam, using a water pistol or a spritzer bottle. If you don't have either, simply splash a bit of water from a cup onto the oven floor. (Make sure you don't hit the hot lightbulb with the water.) Close the door for 30 seconds, then repeat.

Bake until the loaves are golden brown and, when tapped on the bottom, sound as if they're hollow inside, about 40 minutes. If the bread is browning but doesn't sound hollow, cover the loaves loosely with foil, lower the heat to 400°F., and continue baking until they're done, checking every 5 minutes.

Transfer the loaves to a wire rack and let them cool completely before slicing.

PER SERVING: CALORIES 216 • PROTEIN 6.9 G • CARBOHYDRATE 45.9 G • FAT 0 G • CHOLESTEROL 0 MG • SODIUM 402 MG • 3% CALORIES FROM FAT

BREAD MACHINE OPTION: Place all of the ingredients in your breadmaker, according to the manufacturer's instructions. Once the dough has risen, take it out of the machine, shape it as directed in the recipe, and continue to follow the recipe from that point.

•

POTATO RYE BREAD WITH CARAWAY

Makes 1 loaf; serves 8

TOTAL TIME: ABOUT 7 HOURS, INCLUDING TIME FOR THE DOUGH TO RISE
TIME TO PREPARE: ABOUT 1 HOUR
COOKING TIME: ABOUT 1 HOUR, 40 MINUTES
EQUIPMENT: BAKING STONE, BAKER'S PEEL (OPTIONAL)
REFRIGERATION/FREEZING: DO NOT REFRIGERATE. FREEZE UP TO 6 MONTHS.

Potato softens the dough, caraway seasons it, and rye flour adds hearty flavor, as well as fiber and B vitamins. Together, they make a chewy, delicious loaf. It's good toast, too!

1 teaspoon dry active yeast

2½ cups warm water (98° to 115°F.)

2¾ cups unbleached all-purpose flour

1 or 2 medium high-starch potatoes (enough for 1 cup mashed), such as russet

1 tablespoon salt

2 cups rye flour

2½ cups whole wheat flour, plus up to 1 cup if needed

1 tablespoon caraway seeds

Cornmeal, for dusting

Heat the oven to 425°F.

In a medium mixing bowl, combine ½ teaspoon of the yeast and ½ cup of the water. Let the mixture sit until the yeast dissolves, about 1 minute. Stir in ¾ cup of the all-purpose flour, cover with plastic wrap, and set aside for 2 hours in a warm, draft-free place.

Meanwhile, scrub the potatoes and carve an X at each end. Place on a baking sheet and bake until cooked through, about 50 minutes. When they're cool enough to handle, strip away the peel, and mash them.

Transfer the yeast mixture to a large bowl. Gently stir in the remaining yeast, water, and all-purpose flour, and the salt. Add the mashed potatoes, rye flour, and the whole wheat flour, incorporating it 1 cup at a time, until you have a dough that is soft and pliant, but firm enough to handle. (It helps to moisten your hands while you knead.) Or use the dough hook on your Mixmaster, kneading by machine until the dough pulls away from the bowl and forms a ball around the hook.

Turn the dough out onto a lightly floured surface and knead until it's smooth and springy, about 5 minutes. Add flour only when absolutely necessary to prevent sticking. Let the dough rest on a lightly floured surface while you wash out the mixing bowl.

Lightly grease the inside of the mixing bowl, then place the dough inside, turning it once to coat it lightly. Cover with a lightweight towel and set aside until doubled in bulk, about 1½ hours.

Punch down the dough and knead it inside the bowl for 1 minute to press out the air. Turn it out onto a lightly floured surface, sprinkle the dough with the caraway seeds, and knead for about 4 minutes, until the dough is springy and the seeds are well distributed throughout.

Shape the dough into a ball. Cupping it between your hands, rotate it while tucking the dough under to form a perfect round. Dust the center of a large dish towel with about ⅓ cup flour, and rub the flour into it. Place the towel, floured side up, in a bowl about 12 inches in diameter. Place the round of dough upside down in the bowl. Cover loosely with plastic wrap and set aside in a draft-free place to rise until doubled, about 1½ hours.

Forty-five minutes before you plan to bake the bread, place the baking stone on the center rack in the oven, and heat to 450°F.

Sprinkle a baking sheet or baker's peel with cornmeal. Using a dish towel to assist, you carefully turn the dough out of the bowl onto the baking sheet or peel so the top side is down. Using a serrated knife, quickly score the top of the loaf with 3 slashes or an **X** and put it in the oven, either on the baking sheet or by sliding it off the peel onto the baking stone.

Close the oven door for about 15 seconds. Open the oven and squirt inside with water to make steam, using a water pistol or a spritzer bottle. If you don't have either, simply splash water from a cup onto the oven floor. (Make sure you don't splash the hot lightbulb.) Close the door for 30 seconds, then repeat.

Bake until the loaf is golden brown and, when tapped on the bottom, sounds as if it's hollow inside, about 40 minutes. If the bread is browning but doesn't sound hollow, cover it loosely with foil, lower the heat to 400°F., and continue baking until it's done, checking every 5 minutes.

Transfer the loaf to a wire rack and let it cool completely before slicing.

PER SERVING: CALORIES 180 • PROTEIN 5.7 G • CARBOHYDRATE 38.6 G • FAT 0 G • CHOLESTEROL 0 MG • SODIUM 402 MG • 4% CALORIES FROM FAT

BREAD MACHINE OPTION: Place all of the ingredients in your breadmaker according to the manufacturer's instructions. Once the dough has risen, take it out of the machine, shape it as directed in the recipe, and continue to follow the recipe from that point.

WHOLE WHEAT CHICKPEA BREAD

Makes 2 loaves; serves 16

TOTAL TIME: ABOUT 4 HOURS, 45 MINUTES, INCLUDING TIME FOR THE DOUGH TO RISE
TIME TO PREPARE: ABOUT 30 MINUTES
COOKING TIME: 50 MINUTES
EQUIPMENT: BAKING STONE, BAKER'S PEEL (OPTIONAL)
DO AHEAD: YOU CAN COOK THE CHICKPEAS UP TO 5 DAYS IN ADVANCE. REFRIGERATE UNTIL READY TO USE.
FREEZING: FREEZE UP TO 6 MONTHS.

You'd think that bread made with mashed chickpeas would be heavy and pasty. In fact, this loaf is remarkably light. Moreover, it's a nearly perfect food, containing a complete protein, a range of B vitamins, and an uncommon amount of fiber. And it makes crisp toast that tastes delicate and sweet.

1 teaspoon dry active yeast
1¼ cups warm water (98° to 115°F.)
2 cups whole wheat flour
2 teaspoons salt
1 tablespoon barley-malt syrup (for mail-order information, see page 596) or sugar
1 cup cooked chickpeas, drained, rinsed, and mashed
3 cups unbleached all-purpose flour, approximately
Cornmeal, for dusting

In a medium mixing bowl, combine the yeast and ¼ cup of the water. Let the mixture sit until the yeast dissolves, about 1 minute.

In a separate mixing bowl, combine the whole wheat flour and the salt, and stir this flour mixture into the yeast mixture.

In a small bowl, stir the barley-malt syrup

or sugar into the remaining cup of warm water and add the mixture to the dough, along with the chickpeas. Add enough all-purpose flour to make a firm but pliant dough.

Turn the dough out onto a lightly floured surface, and knead until smooth (the surface will be coarse, but the consistency of the dough should be even, not lumpy), about 15 minutes. Alternatively, knead with the dough blade in a food processor or hook in a Mixmaster.

Place the dough in a deep bowl, cover with a lightweight towel, and let it rise until doubled, about 1½ hours.

With well-floured hands, knead the dough in the bowl to press out the air, about 3 minutes. Cover it again, and let it rest for 45 minutes.

Knead out the air again, and divide the dough into 2 pieces. Cupping one piece between your hands, rotate it while tucking the dough under to form a perfect round. Repeat with the other piece. Dust the center of 2 clean dish towels with about ¼ cup flour each, and rub the flour into them. Place each towel, floured side up, in a soup bowl about 8 inches in diameter. Place the rounds of dough upside down in the bowls. Cover loosely with plastic wrap and set aside in a draft-free place to rise until doubled, about 1½ hours.

Forty-five minutes before you plan to bake the bread, place the baking stone on the center rack in the oven, and heat to 450°F.

Sprinkle a baking sheet or baker's peel with cornmeal. Using a dish towel to assist you, carefully turn the dough out of the bowls onto the baking sheet or peel so their top sides are down. If the rounds deflate a bit, try to pat them gently back into shape. Using a serrated knife, quickly score the top of each loaf with 3 slashes or an **X** and put the loaves in the oven, either on the baking sheet or by sliding them off the peel onto the baking stone.

Close the oven door for about 15 seconds. Open the oven and squirt inside with water to make steam, using a water pistol or a spritzer bottle. If you don't have either, simply splash a bit of water from a cup onto the oven floor. (Make sure you don't splash the hot lightbulb.) Close the door for 30 seconds, then repeat.

Bake until the loaves are golden brown and each, when tapped on the bottom, sounds as if it's hollow inside, about 40 minutes. If the bread is browning but doesn't sound hollow, cover the loaves loosely with foil, lower the heat to 400°F., and continue baking until they're done, checking every 5 minutes.

Transfer the loaves to a wire rack and let them cool completely before slicing.

PER SERVING: CALORIES 156 • PROTEIN 5.4 G • CARBOHYDRATE 32.4 G • FAT 0 G • CHOLESTEROL 0 MG • SODIUM 268 MG • 4% CALORIES FROM FAT • GOOD SOURCE OF VITAMINS B₁, B₂, B₃; IRON

BREAD MACHINE OPTION: Place all of the ingredients in your breadmaker according to the manufacturer's instructions. Once the dough has risen, take it out of the machine, shape it as directed in the recipe, and continue to follow the recipe from that point.

•

OATMEAL BREAD

Makes 2 loaves; serves 16

TOTAL TIME: ABOUT 3 HOURS, 30 MINUTES, INCLUDING
    TIME FOR THE DOUGH TO RISE
TIME TO PREPARE: 40 MINUTES
COOKING TIME: 50 MINUTES
DO AHEAD: YOU CAN MAKE THE OATMEAL UP TO 3 DAYS IN
    ADVANCE. REFRIGERATE UNTIL READY TO USE.
REFRIGERATION/FREEZING: DO NOT REFRIGERATE. FREEZE
    UP TO 6 MONTHS.

What's good in a bowl is great in a bread as well. You're best off making this bread in a food processor, Mixmaster, or bread machine because the dough tends to be too soft and sticky to knead by hand.

1 cup rolled oats (not instant) plus 2 cups water,
    or 2 cups leftover cooked oatmeal
1 tablespoon (1 packet) dry active yeast
2 tablespoons plus 1 teaspoon brown sugar
¼ cup warm water (98° to 115°F.)
2 teaspoons salt
3 cups whole wheat flour
2 cups unbleached all-purpose or bread flour,
    plus more as needed
½ cup warm milk (98° to 115°F.)

In a medium saucepan, combine the oats and 2 cups water and bring the mixture to a boil over medium-high heat. Cook, stirring often, until you have a thick porridge, about 5 minutes. Set it aside to cool. If you already have oatmeal prepared, skip this step.

In a large mixing bowl, combine the yeast and brown sugar. Add the ¼ cup warm water, and set aside for 5 minutes, until bubbly. In a separate bowl stir together the salt, whole wheat flour, and 2 cups all-purpose or bread flour. Add the oatmeal and milk to the yeast mixture, and stir in the flour mixture 1 cup at a time, until you have a dough with enough body to knead. You may have to add more flour, but add it ½ cup at a time. The dough should be a bit sticky, so don't add enough to make it stiff.

Knead the dough on a lightly floured surface or in a food processor or Mixmaster until it's supple and elastic, about 10 minutes, or until it forms a ball around the blade or dough hook. Transfer the dough to a lightly greased bowl, cover with a light towel, and let rise in a draft-free place until doubled, about 1 hour.

Heat the oven to 375°F.

Punch down the dough, and knead it to press out the airholes, about 3 minutes. Divide the dough in two, and pat each into a fat log. Place each in a lightly greased 8 × 4 × 2-inch loaf pan. Cover loosely with a towel and let the dough rise again until doubled, about 35 to 40 minutes.

Bake until golden brown, and the bread, sounds as if it's hollow when it is tapped on the bottom, about 50 minutes.

Turn the bread out of the loaf pans and let the loaves cool on a rack for 20 minutes before slicing.

PER SERVING: CALORIES 187 • PROTEIN 6.7 G • CARBOHYDRATE 38.7 G • FAT 1 G • CHOLESTEROL 0 MG • SODIUM 273 MG • 5% CALORIES FROM FAT • GOOD SOURCE OF IRON

BREAD MACHINE OPTION: Place all of the ingredients in your breadmaker according to the manufacturer's instructions. Once the dough has risen, take it out of the machine, shape it as directed in the recipe, and continue to follow the recipe from that point.

GRAPE-NUTS BRAN BREAD

Makes 2 loaves; serves 16

TOTAL TIME: ABOUT 3 HOURS, INCLUDING TIME FOR THE DOUGH TO RISE
TIME TO PREPARE: ABOUT 30 MINUTES
COOKING TIME: ABOUT 40 MINUTES
EQUIPMENT: BAKING STONE, BAKER'S PEEL (OPTIONAL)
FREEZING: FREEZE UP TO 6 MONTHS.

There are certain commercial products I love to endorse, especially when they're uniquely suited for a specific purpose. Grape-Nuts cereal, for instance. Its malty flavor makes bread that's tastier than your average whole wheat. Moreover, it's fortified with minerals and vitamins, which make it more nourishing, too.

⅔ cup Grape-Nuts cereal

⅓ cup wheat bran (not bran cereal)

⅓ cup packed dark brown sugar

1⅓ cups boiling water

1 tablespoon (1 packet) dry active yeast

1 teaspoon granulated sugar

⅔ cup warm water (98° to 115°F.)

2 cups whole wheat flour

½ teaspoon salt

2 to 3 cups unbleached all-purpose flour

Cornmeal, for dusting

In a mixing bowl, combine the Grape-Nuts, wheat bran, and brown sugar. Stir in the boiling water and set aside until cool.

In a large mixing bowl or a Mixmaster or food processor, combine the yeast, granulated sugar, and warm water. Let the mixture stand until frothy, about 5 minutes.

Give the Grape-Nuts mixture a good stir, then add it to the yeast mixture. Stirring by hand or using the dough hook or dough blade in a Mixmaster or food processor, blend in the whole wheat flour, salt, and as much all-purpose flour as necessary to make a dough that's soft, but firm enough to handle, starting with 2 cups and adding more as needed.

Lightly flour a flat work surface. Turn out the dough and knead until it's smooth and springy, about 15 minutes if you've been working entirely by hand, 7 minutes if you've started in a machine. Roll it into a ball.

Rinse out the bowl you used to mix the dough, and dry it well. Place the dough inside, cover it with plastic wrap, and set aside to rise until doubled, about 1 hour.

Punch down the dough, turn it out again, and knead until you've pressed out all of the air, about 3 minutes.

Shape it into a ball. Cut the ball into 2 equal pieces. Shape each piece into a tight ball.

Dust the center of 2 clean kitchen towels with ¼ cup flour each, and rub the flour into the towels. Place the towels, flour side up,

the baking sheet or peel so their top sides are
down. If the rounds deflate a bit, try to pat
them gently back into shape. Using a serrated
knife, quickly score the top of each loaf with 3
slashes or an X and put the loaves in the oven,
either on the baking sheet or by sliding them
off the peel onto the baking stone.

Close the oven door for about 15 seconds.
Open the oven and squirt inside with water to
make steam, using a water pistol or a spritzer
bottle. If you don't have either, simply splash
water from a cup onto the oven floor. (Make
sure you don't splash water on the hot lightbulb.) Close the door for 30 seconds, then
repeat.

Bake until the loaves are dark brown and
you get a hollow sound when you tap on the
bottom, about 40 minutes. Cool completely on
a wire rack. Slice and serve, or slice and freeze,
taking out individual pieces to toast.

PER SERVING: CALORIES 146 • PROTEIN 4.6 G • CARBOHYDRATE 32.3 G • FAT
0.5 G • CHOLESTEROL 0 MG • SODIUM 102 MG • 3% CALORIES FROM FAT • GOOD
SOURCE OF VITAMINS B₁, B₂, B₃; FOLACIN, IRON

BREAD MACHINE OPTION: Place all of the
ingredients in your breadmaker according to
the manufacturer's instructions. Once the
dough has risen, take it out of the machine,
shape it as directed in the recipe, and continue
to follow the recipe from that point.

inside 2 soup bowls, about 8 inches in diameter. Place the round loaves upside down in the
bowls and cover loosely with plastic wrap. Set
aside until doubled, about 50 minutes.

Forty-five minutes before baking, place the
baking stone on the center rack in the oven,
and heat to 450°F.

Sprinkle a baking sheet or baker's peel with
cornmeal. Using a dish towel to assist you,
carefully turn the dough out of the bowls onto

•

SOFT AND CHEWY DINNER ROLLS

Makes 12

TOTAL TIME: ABOUT 1 HOUR, 35 MINUTES, INCLUDING
  TIME FOR THE DOUGH TO RISE
TIME TO PREPARE: 20 MINUTES
COOKING TIME: 12 TO 15 MINUTES TO BAKE
EQUIPMENT: OVENPROOF GRIDDLE (OPTIONAL)

A combination quick bread and yeast bread with the convenience of one and the flavor of the other. Cottage cheese fortifies these rolls with calcium, and makes them luscious and light.

2 teaspoons dry active yeast
¼ cup warm water (98° to 115°F.)
1 cup whole wheat flour
2 cups unbleached all-purpose flour
1 teaspoon salt
1½ teaspoons baking powder
½ teaspoon baking soda
1 cup low-fat cottage cheese
2 tablespoons fresh lemon juice
⅓ cup plain nonfat yogurt

In a small mixing bowl, dissolve the yeast in the warm water, about 1 minute.

In a large mixing bowl, stir together the whole wheat flour, all-purpose flour, salt, baking powder, and baking soda with a long-tined fork or a wire whisk.

In a food processor or blender, blend together the cottage cheese, lemon juice, and yogurt until smooth.

Add the yeast mixture and the yogurt mixture to the flour mixture, and stir until you have a stiff dough. Knead it in the bowl until it's smooth, about 3 minutes.

Turn the dough out onto a lightly floured board and roll to a thickness of about ½ inch. Cut it into rounds with a 3-inch biscuit cutter. Gather up the scraps of dough, if there are any, roll it out again, and cut more rounds.

Transfer the rolls to an ungreased baking sheet or ovenproof griddle. Cover with a cloth napkin or lightweight towel and let them rest for 1 hour.

Meanwhile, heat the oven to 450°F.

Bake the rolls for 12 to 15 minutes, until golden brown. Serve right away, or cool on a wire rack.

PER SERVING (1 ROLL): CALORIES 129 • PROTEIN 6.4 G • CARBOHYDRATE 24.6 G • FAT 0 G • CHOLESTEROL 0 MG • SODIUM 328 MG • 4% CALORIES FROM FAT

Sourdough Breads

SOURDOUGH STARTER

Makes about 4 cups

TOTAL TIME: 3 TO 5 DAYS
TIME TO PREPARE: ABOUT 5 MINUTES
COOKING TIME: NONE
REFRIGERATION/FREEZING: REFRIGERATE, REPLENISHING
  ACCORDING TO THE DIRECTIONS IN THE RECIPE. FREEZE
  IN A LARGE PLASTIC CONTAINER UP TO 6 MONTHS.

A side from gardening and maternity, I can't think of an occupation more grounded in optimism than making a sourdough starter. It signifies a faith, first, that there'll be a tomorrow and, second, that you'll be here then to enjoy your bread. It's a self-perpetuating optimism, because with each loaf you bake you'll anticipate the next, the next, and the one after that.

2 cups warm water (98° to 115°F.)

1 tablespoon (1 packet) dry active yeast

2 cups unbleached all-purpose flour

Put the water in a 2-quart glass or ceramic mixing bowl, stir in the yeast, and let it dissolve, about 1 minute. Stir in the flour until you have a smooth, sticky batter that pulls away from the sides of the bowl in strands.

Cover the bowl with plastic wrap, and let the starter rest in a moderately warm (74°F.) place for 3 to 5 days, until the surface is frothy.

Stir until it has the smooth, medium-dense consistency of pancake batter. Transfer the starter to a 2-quart glass jar with a lid or several smaller jars (it should take up no more than two-thirds of the jar[s] because it needs room to expand). Refrigerate the starter until you're ready to use it.

ALTERNATE METHOD: In the thousands of years' history of bread, making a starter with yeast is a relatively new phenomenon. You can make a starter the old-fashioned way, by mixing together the flour and water and leaving them to attract the "wild yeast" from the air in your kitchen. But dry yeast gives the basic mixture a boost, making a vital, active starter in less time, with less fuss. Also, breads made with a yeast starter tend to rise a bit more than those made without it. If you were to make the starter without yeast, you would proceed as follows: Stir together ½ cup unbleached all-purpose flour and ¼ cup warm water (98° to 115°F.) in a medium ceramic mixing bowl. Stir until you have a thick, sticky batter. Cover the bowl with plastic wrap and leave overnight at room temperature.

The next day, stir in ½ cup more of unbleached all-purpose flour and ¼ cup more of warm water. Cover the bowl with plastic wrap and leave overnight again. Repeat for the next 2 days, adding ½ cup more of unbleached all-purpose flour and ¼ cup more of warm water each day.

On the fifth day, transfer your starter to a large glass jar with a lid (it should take up no more than two-thirds of the jar because it needs room to expand).

SOURDOUGH BASICS

USING YOUR STARTER

When you take your starter out for the first time, your heart will sink. You'll see that much of it has settled, while an unwholesome-looking scum has risen to the top. You will despair that you have killed it and prepare to throw it away.

But wait! Give it a stir with a wooden spoon, and you'll find you have an active, thriving starter after all.

REPLENISHING YOUR STARTER

For each cup of starter you use, stir 1 cup of flour and 1 cup of water into the jar. Cover and let the starter sit at room temperature for about 12 hours. Return it to the refrigerator.

MAINTAINING YOUR STARTER

In the Refrigerator: Whenever you go for 2 weeks or more without using and replenishing your starter, you'll have to feed it to keep it going. Stir it well, scoop out 1 cup of the starter, and stir in 1 cup of flour and 1 cup of water. Continue stirring until you have a smooth, medium-thick pancake-batter consistency. Cover and let it sit at room temperature for about 12 hours, then refrigerate.

In the Freezer: If you want to keep a portion of your starter for a month or two without worrying about feeding it, you can freeze it. Transfer as much starter as you'd like (at least 1 cup) to a large plastic container (it should fill only half of the container; the starter will expand in the cold), and freeze.

To revive a frozen starter, transfer it to the refrigerator and let it thaw for at least a day. Stir in 2 cups of flour and 2 cups of water, cover, and let the starter rest at room temperature for 12 hours, then refrigerate.

YOUR OWN SOURDOUGH BREAD

Makes 2 loaves; serves 16

TOTAL TIME: ABOUT 16 TO 29 HOURS, INCLUDING TIME FOR THE DOUGH TO RISE, NOT INCLUDING THE 3 TO 5 DAYS TO MAKE THE SOURDOUGH STARTER
TIME TO PREPARE: ABOUT 20 MINUTES
COOKING TIME: ABOUT 50 MINUTES
EQUIPMENT: BAKING STONE, BAKER'S PEEL (OPTIONAL)
DO AHEAD: YOU CAN MAKE THE STARTER UP TO A YEAR IN ADVANCE.
FREEZING: FREEZE UP TO 6 MONTHS.

A s if you haven't waited long enough for your starter, you have to wait through yet one more day for the dough itself to ferment. *They say virtue is its own reward. However, the reward for the virtue of patience in this case is more desirable: beautiful, fragrant, delicious loaves of bread.*

1 cup Sourdough Starter (see page 408)
3 cups warm water (98° to 115°F.)
7 cups unbleached all-purpose flour, approximately, or 2 cups whole wheat flour plus 4 cups unbleached all-purpose flour
1 tablespoon salt
1 tablespoon sugar
Cornmeal, for dusting

Using a wooden spoon, stir the starter, 1 cup of the warm water, and 1 cup of all-purpose flour together in a large ceramic mixing bowl until the batter pulls away from the sides in strands. Cover with a lightweight towel or plastic wrap and set aside for 12 to 24 hours.

Stir the remaining water into your sourdough starter, breaking it up as you go. Combine the salt and sugar with 2 cups of the flour, and stir the mixture into the starter. Continue stirring and adding flour until the dough is soft and pliant, but firm enough to handle.

Lightly flour a flat surface and turn the dough out onto it. Knead, adding flour as necessary to keep the dough from sticking. Continue kneading until you have a smooth, firm, pliant dough, about 15 minutes. Alternatively, knead the dough in a food processor or Mixmaster.

Clean out the mixing bowl. Pat the dough into a tight ball, place it in the bowl, and cover it with a lightweight towel or plastic wrap. Let it rest at a warm room temperature (about 72°F.) until doubled, about 2 hours.

Lightly flour your hands, then press the dough down and knead it lightly in the bowl (about 3 minutes). Divide the dough into 2 pieces. Cupping one piece between your hands, rotate it while tucking the dough under to form a perfect round. Repeat with the other piece. Dust the center of 2 clean dish towels with about ¼ cup flour each, and rub the flour into the towels. Place each towel, floured side up, in a soup bowl about 8 inches in diameter. Place the rounds of dough upside down in the bowls. Cover loosely with plastic wrap, and set aside in a draft-free place to rise until doubled, about 1½ hours.

Forty-five minutes before you plan to bake the bread, place the baking stone on the center rack in the oven, and heat to 450°F.

Sprinkle a baking sheet or baker's peel with cornmeal. Using a dish towel to assist you, carefully turn the dough out of the bowls onto the baking sheet or peel so their top sides are down. If it deflates a bit, try to pat the loaves gently back into shape. Using a serrated knife, quickly score the top of each loaf with 3 slashes or an **X** and put the loaves in the oven, either on the baking sheet or by sliding them off the peel onto the baking stone.

Close the oven door for about 15 seconds. Open the oven and squirt inside with water to make steam, using a water pistol or a spritzer bottle. If you don't have either, simply splash a bit of water from a cup onto the oven floor. (Make sure the water doesn't splash on the hot lightbulb.) Close the door for 30 seconds, then repeat.

Bake until the loaves are golden brown and each, when tapped on the bottom, sounds as if it's hollow inside, about 40 minutes. If the bread is browning but doesn't sound hollow, cover the loaves loosely with foil, lower the heat to 400°F., and continue baking until they're done, checking every 5 minutes.

Transfer the loaves to a wire rack and let them cool completely before slicing.

Note: Don't forget to replenish your starter: Add 1 cup each flour and water, stir well, cover, and let it rest for 12 hours at room temperature.

PER SERVING: CALORIES 209 • PROTEIN 5.8 G • CARBOHYDRATE 44 G • FAT 0 G • CHOLESTEROL 0 MG • SODIUM 401 MG • 2% CALORIES FROM FAT

•

Flat Breads

SWIFT CHAPATI-STYLE FLAT BREAD

Makes 8 to 12 loaves

TOTAL TIME: ABOUT 1 HOUR, INCLUDING TIME FOR THE
   DOUGH TO REST
TIME TO PREPARE: ABOUT 40 MINUTES
COOKING TIME: INCLUDED IN TIME TO PREPARE
DO AHEAD: YOU CAN MAKE THE DOUGH UP TO 1 DAY IN
   ADVANCE. REFRIGERATE UNTIL READY TO USE.
FREEZING: FREEZE UP TO 6 MONTHS.

Semolina flour makes this flat bread sturdy and soft at the same time. Be vigilant in your rolling—it must be paper thin to have the right texture. Use it to wrap grilled vegetables or to accompany curry.

1 cup semolina flour
1 1/2 cups unbleached all-purpose flour
1 cup whole wheat flour
1/2 teaspoon salt
1 cup warm water (98° to 115°F.)

In a large mixing bowl, combine the semolina flour, all-purpose flour, whole wheat flour, and salt with a long-tined fork or wire whisk. Stir in the water to make a thick dough.

Knead the dough briefly until it becomes elastic, about 6 minutes. Roll it into a ball, return it to the mixing bowl, and cover the bowl with a lightweight towel or plastic wrap. Let it rest for 30 minutes.

Divide the dough into walnut-sized pieces. You should have between 8 and 12.

Heat a nonstick griddle or small skillet over medium-high heat. To make each bread, dust a flat surface with flour, and roll out the piece of dough until it's paper thin. Place it on the hot griddle or in the skillet and cook until it blisters, about 2 minutes. Using tongs, turn the bread over to brown the other side, about 1 minute more. Transfer to wax or parchment paper and wrap to enclose. The paper keeps the bread from drying out as it cools. Repeat the process until you have used all the dough. Serve right away, or cool completely and freeze, wrapped in plastic with layers of wax paper between each bread.

PER SERVING: CALORIES 211 • PROTEIN 7.1 G • CARBOHYDRATE 44 G • FAT 0 G •
CHOLESTEROL 0 MG • SODIUM 135 MG • 3% CALORIES FROM FAT

•

LAVOSH
Soft Flat Bread

Makes 8 loaves

TOTAL TIME: ABOUT 1 HOUR, 20 MINUTES, INCLUDING
   TIME FOR THE DOUGH TO REST
TIME TO PREPARE: ABOUT 45 MINUTES
COOKING TIME: INCLUDED IN TIME TO PREPARE
EQUIPMENT: BAKING STONE (OPTIONAL)
DO AHEAD: YOU CAN MAKE THE DOUGH 1 DAY IN
   ADVANCE. REFRIGERATE UNTIL READY TO USE.
FREEZING: FREEZE UP TO 6 MONTHS.

A devoted reader of the funny pages, I was baffled by the running joke in Blondie concerning the title character's penchant for buying expensive hats. Every so often—or so very often—the punch line hinged on how she'd break the news that she'd bought a silly bonnet, or on how her husband would take it.

First of all, I didn't understand why she needed his okay. And second, why hats? When my mother ran amok it wasn't at the milliner's, but at the Middle Eastern market. Driving home to Virginia from New

York, we had to cradle jars of grape leaves and olives, sit on sacks of bulgur and special long grain rice, and straddle huge wheels of lavosh, Armenian flat bread, which she bought in cracker form. To soften it, we'd soak it in warm water just before serving. It was good, but it's so much better when it's fresh and soft from the start.

Use this flat bread as a wrapper for grilled foods or as a scoop for Tabbouleh (see page 139) or Couscous (see page 338).

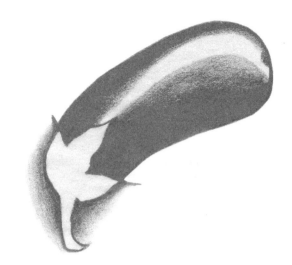

1 cup warm water (98° to 115°F.)
½ teaspoon dry active yeast
3½ to 4½ cups unbleached all-purpose flour
½ tablespoon salt

Combine the water and yeast in a large mixing bowl. When the mixture bubbles, after about 5 minutes, give it a stir, and add 2 cups of flour and the salt. Continue adding flour until you can no longer stir. Dust your hands with flour and transfer the dough to a floured work surface. Knead until the dough is smooth and springy, about 10 minutes. Alternatively, knead the dough in a food processor or Mixmaster.

Roll the dough into a ball, cover it loosely with a lightweight towel, and let it rest 30 minutes.

Place a baking sheet or stone in the lower third of the oven, and heat to 500°F.

Cut the dough into 8 equal portions. (For larger breads, make that 4 portions.) On a well-floured surface, roll the dough until it's about ¼ inch thick. Then pick it up and stretch it by hand, making it as thin as possible without tearing it.

Carefully place the dough on the hot baking sheet or stone. Shut the door and bake

until bubbles form, about 1 minute, then turn over to brown the other side, about 45 seconds more. It's easiest to bake one piece at a time.

Transfer the finished loaves to wax paper or parchment paper. Wrap each as it's done; the paper will trap the steam, keeping the breads moist as they cool. Serve right away, or cool completely and freeze, wrapped in plastic with a layer of wax paper between each loaf.

PER SERVING: CALORIES 228 • PROTEIN 6.5 G • CARBOHYDRATE 47 G • FAT 0 G • CHOLESTEROL 0 MG • SODIUM 401 MG • 3% CALORIES FROM FAT

ALTERNATE METHOD: Since this doesn't involve turning on the oven, it's the method I prefer in summer. Invert a wok over a burner and turn the heat up to medium-high. When the wok is hot, reduce the heat to medium, and coat lightly with vegetable oil. Drape the dough over the mound. Cook until bubbles form, about 30 seconds. Using wooden tongs, turn the dough over and cook the other side until it browns, about 1 minute. Turn it over to cook the other side more thoroughly, about 40 seconds, depending on the thickness of the dough. Repeat with the remaining pieces.

PITA BREAD

Makes 8 loaves

TOTAL TIME: ABOUT 1 HOUR, 45 MINUTES, INCLUDING
TIME FOR THE DOUGH TO REST
TIME TO PREPARE: ABOUT 1 HOUR, 15 MINUTES
COOKING TIME: ABOUT 6 TO 8 MINUTES
EQUIPMENT: BAKING STONE, BAKER'S PEEL (OPTIONAL)
DO AHEAD: YOU CAN MAKE THE DOUGH UP TO 1 DAY IN
ADVANCE. REFRIGERATE UNTIL READY TO USE.
FREEZING: FREEZE UP TO 6 MONTHS.

Pita was not a bread I'd ever intended to make, since a commercial brand, which was available locally, was excellent. However, the company NEW AND IMPROVED it, adding stabilizers and more potent sweeteners to appeal to a wider market out of state, losing the delightful texture and distinctive yeasty flavor I'd loved so much. I could recapture the taste only by making it myself, which I do every Sunday. It's easy—especially if you have a food processor, Mixmaster, or bread machine to handle the dough for you.

2 teaspoons dry active yeast

1 1/2 cups warm water (98° to 115°F.)

2 teaspoons sugar

4 cups unbleached all-purpose flour or 3 cups
    unbleached all-purpose flour plus 1 cup
    whole wheat

2 teaspoons salt

Combine the yeast and water in a large mixing bowl. When the mixture bubbles, give it a stir, and add the sugar, 2 cups of the flour, and the salt. Continue adding flour until you can no longer stir it with ease. Dust your hands with flour and transfer the dough to a floured work surface. Knead the dough until it is smooth and springy, about 5 minutes. Alternatively, knead the dough in a food processor or Mixmaster.

Roll the dough into a ball, cover loosely with a lightweight towel, and let it rest for 30 minutes.

Place a baking sheet or baking stone in the lower third of the oven, and heat to 500°F.

Cut the dough into 8 equal portions. On a well-floured surface, roll the dough until it's about 1/2 inch thick. Cover the rounds with a damp, not wet towel, and let them rest for 15 minutes.

Using a baker's peel or your hands, place the loaves carefully on the baking sheet or baking stone. Bake until the loaves puff up and brown, about 6 to 8 minutes.

Transfer the loaves to a wire rack, and let cool 15 minutes before serving.

PER SERVING: CALORIES 233 • PROTEIN 6.6 G • CARBOHYDRATE 49 G • FAT 0 G •
CHOLESTEROL 0 MG • SODIUM 536 MG • 3% CALORIES FROM FAT

BREAD MACHINE OPTION: Place all of the ingredients in your breadmaker according to the manufacturer's instructions. Once the dough has risen, take it out of the machine, shape it as directed in the recipe, and continue to follow the recipe from that point.

NAAN

Makes 6 loaves

TOTAL TIME: ABOUT 3 HOURS, 50 MINUTES TO 6 HOURS,
50 MINUTES, INCLUDING TIME FOR THE DOUGH TO REST
TIME TO PREPARE: ABOUT 30 MINUTES
COOKING TIME: ABOUT 9 TO 18 MINUTES
FREEZING: FREEZE UP TO 6 MONTHS.

Soft pillows of bread, naan is a traditional accompaniment to curry, but you'll enjoy it with soups and salads, too.

¼ cup nonfat milk

½ cup plain nonfat yogurt

1 teaspoon baking powder

2 teaspoons sugar

1½ teaspoons dry active yeast

2½ to 3 cups all-purpose flour

2 teaspoons salt

2 tablespoons Nigella seeds (see Note; optional)

Combine the milk and yogurt in a medium saucepan and heat gently over medium-low heat until just warmed through.

In a large mixing bowl, stir together the baking powder, sugar, and yeast, and make a well in the center. Pour the milk mixture into the well, and stir. Let it rest until the mixture starts to bubble, about 5 minutes. Stir in 2½ cups of the flour and the salt, adding more flour as needed to make a dough that's firm enough to knead.

Turn out the dough onto a floured surface and knead until it's smooth. Shape it into a ball, return it to the bowl, cover it with plastic wrap, and let it rest for at least 3 hours, until puffy and light. (Six hours are ideal.)

Punch the dough down and knead it again for about 5 minutes, folding in the nigella seeds

if you'd like. Tear the dough into 6 pieces of equal size. Roll each piece into an oblong shape, about ⅓ inch thick. Cover with a damp paper towel and let the dough rest for 10 minutes. Meanwhile, heat the broiler.

Place the pieces of dough, one or two at a time, in an ungreased ovenproof skillet, and put them under the broiler until they puff up, about 3 minutes. Using tongs, turn the bread and brown the other side, about 1 minute. Transfer the bread to wax or parchment paper while you broil the rest. (The paper keeps the loaves moist as they cool.) Serve right away.

Note: Nigella are chunky black seeds that have a mild black pepper taste. They're available at Indian-specialty stores, and by mail (see page 596).

PER SERVING: CALORIES 212 • PROTEIN 7.1 G • CARBOHYDRATE 43 G • FAT 0 G • CHOLESTEROL 0 MG • SODIUM 814 MG • 3% CALORIES FROM FAT • GOOD SOURCE OF CALCIUM

Pizzas

DOUGH FOR PIZZA

Serves 4 to 6

TOTAL TIME: ABOUT 2 HOURS
TIME TO PREPARE: ABOUT 30 MINUTES
REFRIGERATION/FREEZING: REFRIGERATE UP TO 3 DAYS.
   FREEZE UP TO 6 MONTHS.

1 tablespoon (1 packet) dry active yeast

2 teaspoons sugar

1 cup warm water (98° to 115°F.)

2 teaspoons salt

2½ to 3 cups unbleached all-purpose flour

In a large mixing bowl, combine the yeast and sugar. Stir in the water and let the mixture rest until bubbly, about 5 minutes. Stir lightly. Add the salt and enough flour to make a dough that's soft and pliable, but not sticky. Lightly flour a large, flat work surface, turn the dough out of the bowl, and knead until it's smooth. Alternatively, knead the dough in a food processor or Mixmaster.

   Clean out the mixing bowl, dry it thoroughly, and grease it lightly or squirt it with nonstick spray. Shape the dough into a ball and place in the bowl. Cover the bowl with plastic wrap and set the dough aside in a warm, draft-free place until doubled in bulk, about 1 hour, 15 minutes.

Note: The above recipe can also be used as a base for calzones, see page 419.

PER SERVING: CALORIES 298 • PROTEIN 8.7 G • CARBOHYDRATE 62.4 G • FAT 0 G • CHOLESTEROL 0 MG • SODIUM 1068 MG • 3% CALORIES FROM FAT

BREAD MACHINE OPTION: Place all of the ingredients in your breadmaker according to the manufacturer's instructions. Once the dough has risen, take it out of the machine, shape it as directed in the recipe, and continue to follow the recipe from that point.

PIZZA BASICS

It's not trendy, but it's true: I like pizza plain. I like the crust lean and crisp, the topping simple and spare. If you have a pizza with "everything," on it, chances are you won't taste any of it.

• Use fresh ingredients and apply them sparingly. If you're going to cook the toppings, prepare them simply, by sautéing (see page 507) lightly in extra virgin olive oil or steaming (see page 509). You can also use ingredients that need no cooking, such as olives and sun-dried tomatoes. See the topping suggestions in "Make It Your Own" (page 418) for specific examples.

• When adding cheese, grate it or shred it, and add no more than a handful or two. Sprinkle it evenly over the crust, underneath the rest of the toppings, to keep the crust from getting soggy.

• For whole wheat crust, substitute whole wheat *pastry* flour or kamut flour (see page 580) for half of the all-purpose flour. Regular whole wheat flour tends to make crusts that are coarse and heavy.

• If you want to make a pizza with "everything" on it, distribute the toppings evenly, alternating the ingredients in a pattern instead of piling all of them on top of one another.

• If you'll be making pizza often, it's worth springing for a baking stone, a heavy ceramic slab that makes crusts crispy by drawing moisture out of the dough. Always put the baking stone in the oven before you turn on the heat; the stone must be hot when you bake the pizza.

• To get the pizza in and out of the oven, it helps to have a "peel," a long-handled wooden paddle. Dust the peel with cornmeal, slide the pizza onto it, open the oven, and slide the pizza from the peel onto the hot baking stone.

• At least twenty minutes before baking, place the oven rack on the lowest rung, and heat the stone at the highest temperature (usually 500°F.). Bake the pizza at that temperature, until the crust is just golden, about five to eight minutes.

PIZZA PARTY TIME!

It may be considered rude to invite people over to make their own dinner, but then, maybe it's a pizza party! Since pizzas bake quickly, you can have your guests assemble their own from a variety of ingredients that you provide.

For a party for eight, double the basic pizza dough recipe (see page 416). Prepare it through the first rising, then divide it into eight pieces.

Make four to six toppings and place them in serving bowls. Fill additional bowls with trimmings, such as grated cheeses, raw onions, fresh minced herbs, and red pepper flakes. Set everything out within easy reach.

Pour extra virgin olive oil into a bowl and place a pastry brush next to it.

Thirty minutes before you plan to start baking, roll out each piece of dough into a thin disk. Heat the oven to 500° F., and sprinkle a baking sheet (if you're using one) with cornmeal. If you're using a baking stone, make sure it's in place in the oven, but don't add the cornmeal yet. Have your guests assemble their pizzas.

Sprinkle the baking stone, if using, with cornmeal. Bake as many pizzas at once as you can, and serve them right away.

Make It Your Own

There aren't any rules governing what goes on a pizza. Just take care with moist ingredients that can seep into the crust and make it soggy. You can prevent that by sprinkling any cheese you might be adding underneath the rest of the topping. Or you can let your topping drain on paper towels and blot it dry before putting it on the dough. Spread the topping sparingly, allowing some of the dough to show through. What's true for fresh pasta goes for pizza: once you've gone to the trouble to make the dough, you should allow yourself the pleasure of tasting it.

WHAT TO ADD AND WHEN TO ADD IT

⌘ Try dry-packed sun-dried tomatoes, plumped in olive oil to cover. Drain the oil and brush it on the pizza crust before you top the pizza with the reconstituted tomatoes. (Reserve any remaining oil for salad dressings.)

⌘ Make a Greek-style pizza by scattering roughly ⅓ cup chopped oil-cured Greek olives, ½ cup crumbled feta cheese, and ¼ cup minced oregano on top of the crust.

⌘ For a pizza to serve on the side with soup, top the crust with 2 cups thinly sliced roasted potato, 4 sprigs rosemary, and drizzle over 1 tablespoon extra virgin olive oil.

Here are more sensational combinations:

⌘ ½ cup shredded smoked mozzarella cheese, 1 eggplant, sliced and baked (see page 527), and 1 sliced and peeled roasted bell pepper (see page 534)

⌘ 1 cup crumbled feta cheese, 2 cups loosely packed shredded fresh spinach, and 1 tablespoon chopped fresh oregano, or 2 teaspoons crumbled dried oregano

⌘ 4 Roasted Fresh Tomatoes (see page 218), sliced, ¼ cup minced fresh mint, ½ cup grated Asiago cheese

⌘ 1 cup crumbled ricotta salata, 1 cup fresh ricotta cheese with 2 large sliced fresh tomatoes, 2 teaspoons capers, and ½ cup combined shredded fresh basil and oregano

⌘ 2 cups loosely packed chopped fresh spinach, 2 tablespoons toasted pine nuts (see Note, page 122), ¼ cup minced red onions, and ¼ cup raisins tossed with 1 tablespoon extra virgin olive oil

⌘ Spread 2 cups chili (see page 352) and ½ cup shredded Monterey Jack and/or cheddar cheese over the crust, and garnish with minced fresh cilantro.

⌘ Sprinkle with 1 cup crumbled ricotta salata and/or 2 tablespoons grated Parmesan or Asiago cheese over 2 cups Ratatouille (see page 343).

PIZZA WITH TOMATO, MOZZARELLA, AND BASIL

Serves 4 to 6

TOTAL TIME: ABOUT 20 MINUTES, NOT INCLUDING TIME TO
MAKE THE DOUGH
TIME TO PREPARE: ABOUT 10 MINUTES
COOKING TIME: ABOUT 10 MINUTES
EQUIPMENT: BAKING STONE, BAKER'S PEEL (OPTIONAL)
DO AHEAD: YOU CAN MAKE THE DOUGH AND/OR THE
SAUCE UP TO 3 DAYS IN ADVANCE. REFRIGERATE UNTIL
READY TO USE. BRING THE DOUGH TO ROOM TEMPERA-
TURE BEFORE PREPARING THE PIZZA.
REFRIGERATION/FREEZING: REFRIGERATE UP TO 2 DAYS.
FREEZE UP TO 6 MONTHS.

1 recipe Dough for Pizza (see page 416)

1 recipe Simplest Fresh Tomato Sauce
   (see page 278)

1 cup shredded part-skim mozzarella cheese

½ cup grated Parmesan cheese

½ cup minced fresh basil

1 tablespoon crushed red pepper flakes (optional)

Place a rack on the lowest rung of the oven. If
you're using a baking stone, insert it now. Heat
the oven to 500°F.

Divide the dough into four or six equal
pieces. Roll out each piece into a round about
¼ inch thick. Spread each round with as much
tomato sauce as you'd like. Top each with an
equal amount of mozzarella, Parmesan, and basil.
Sprinkle with red pepper flakes, if you'd like.

Using a baker's peel or your hands, place
the pizzas on the baking stone or on a baking
sheet. Bake until the crust turns golden and
crisp, about 8 to 10 minutes.

PER SERVING (¼ RECIPE): CALORIES 454 • PROTEIN 227 G • CARBOHYDRATE
108.4 G • FAT 9.5 G • CHOLESTEROL 25 MG • SODIUM 1465 MG • 19% CALORIES
FROM FAT • OUTSTANDING SOURCE OF CALCIUM • VERY GOOD SOURCE OF IRON
• GOOD SOURCE OF VITAMIN A; ZINC

Calzones

SPINACH-RICOTTA CALZONE

Makes 4 calzones

TOTAL TIME: ABOUT 1 HOUR, 15 MINUTES, NOT INCLUD-
ING TIME TO MAKE THE DOUGH
TIME TO PREPARE: ABOUT 20 MINUTES
COOKING TIME: 25 MINUTES
EQUIPMENT: BAKING STONE, BAKER'S PEEL (OPTIONAL)
DO AHEAD: YOU CAN MAKE THE FILLING UP TO 3 DAYS IN
ADVANCE. REFRIGERATE UNTIL READY TO USE.
REFRIGERATION/FREEZING: REFRIGERATE UP TO 2 DAYS.
FREEZE UP TO 6 MONTHS.

Try them once, and you'll make these soft,
scrumptious—and simple!—spinach-filled
pizzas again and again.

Two 10-ounce packages frozen chopped spinach,
   thawed and squeezed dry

½ cup grated Parmesan cheese

1½ cups nonfat or part-skim ricotta cheese

1½ cups shredded part-skim mozzarella cheese

2 teaspoons crumbled dried oregano

Pinch ground nutmeg

Cornmeal, for dusting

1 recipe Dough for Pizza (see page 416)

In a medium mixing bowl, combine the spinach, Parmesan, ricotta, mozzarella, oregano,
and nutmeg.

Heat the oven to 350°F. If you're using a
baking stone, put it in the center of the oven
now. Sprinkle a rimless nonstick baking sheet
or a baker's peel with cornmeal.

Punch down the dough to eliminate the airholes. Turn it out of the bowl and knead it until
it's smooth, about 5 minutes. Divide the dough

into 4 equal pieces. Working with one section at a time, roll it out to a round 7 inches in diameter. Place one-fourth of the filling in the center, and pat it down lightly, leaving a border of about 1 inch. Fold the top portion of dough over the filling, as for a turnover. Wet your fingers and pinch the border to seal the calzone. Press a fork along the edge to complete the seal. Use the fork to puncture airholes in the top. Place on the prepared baking sheet or peel. Cover with a light towel while you repeat the process with the remaining ingredients.

Let the calzone rest, covered with the towel, for 15 minutes. Slide the calzone from the baking sheet or peel onto the baking stone or place the baking sheet in the center of the oven. Bake until golden brown, about 25 minutes. Serve hot.

PER SERVING (1 CALZONE): CALORIES 696 • PROTEIN 46.5 G • CARBOHYDRATE 98.2 G • FAT 12 G • CHOLESTEROL 32.7 MG • SODIUM 1630 MG • 16% CALORIES FROM FAT • OUTSTANDING SOURCE OF VITAMINS A, C; FOLACIN, CALCIUM • VERY GOOD SOURCE OF ZINC

Make It Your Own

You can put anything you'd put on a pizza inside a calzone, provided you bind it with something such as nonfat ricotta cheese, low-fat cottage cheese, or mashed potatoes (roughly 1 cup for four calzones) if necessary to make it a substantial filling. You can also borrow fillings from the savory pies (see pages 433), and the filled pastas (see pages 299 to 304). Just make sure the filling isn't runny, or the crust will be soggy and may not fuse to encase it.

WHAT TO ADD AND WHEN TO ADD IT

Ratatouille. Try Ratatouille (see page 343), and if it seems watery, let it drain in a sieve for thirty minutes before you fill the calzones.

Early Spring Ravioli Filling. Double the recipe (see page 299) to fill four calzones.

Sautéed Mushrooms. Sauté 4 cups loosely packed sliced firm mushrooms (such as cremini, portobello, or white button) in olive oil with a minced whole scallion and the herbs of your choice—for example, basil and oregano. Mix the mushrooms with 1 cup nonfat ricotta cheese, then add other cheeses of your choice—for example, 1/2 cup part-skim mozzarella cheese and 2 tablespoons grated Parmesan, or 1/2 cup shredded sharp cheddar cheese.

Sun-Dried Tomatoes, Olives, and Cheese. Reconstitute 1 cup dry-packed sun-dried tomatoes by soaking them in warm water for 10 to 15 minutes. Drain, puree, then stir them into 1 cup Mashed Potatoes (see page 226). Stir in about 1/3 cup mixed chopped olives and the cheese of your choice, such as 1/3 cup grated Parmesan or 1/2 cup shredded provolone or 1/2 cup crumbled feta. Season with ¼ cup minced fresh, or 2 tablespoons crumbled dried, oregano and basil, combined.

•

CAYOTE CALZONE

Makes 4 calzones

TOTAL TIME: 1 HOUR, 25 MINUTES, NOT INCLUDING TIME TO MAKE THE DOUGH
TIME TO PREPARE: ABOUT 1 HOUR
COOKING TIME: 25 MINUTES
EQUIPMENT: BAKING STONE, BAKER'S PEEL (OPTIONAL)
DO AHEAD: YOU CAN MAKE THE FILLING UP TO 3 DAYS IN ADVANCE. REFRIGERATE UNTIL READY TO USE.
REFRIGERATION/FREEZING: REFRIGERATE UP TO 2 DAYS. FREEZE UP TO 6 MONTHS.

If it weren't a calzone, it would be a burrito. In fact, you can use the first filling to stuff tortillas, if you'd like. But, you could also try it like this with pizza dough or the corn dough variation on page 484.

1½ teaspoons canola or vegetable oil
1 onion, chopped
2 garlic cloves, minced
1 ancho chili, roasted, peeled, and minced (see page 534; see Note)
1 jalapeño pepper, roasted, peeled, and minced (see page 534; see Note)
1 tomatillo, husked and chopped, or 1 tablespoon green salsa
¼ cup minced fresh cilantro
2 teaspoons ground cumin
1 tablespoon chili powder
2 teaspoons crumbled dried oregano
½ cup canned or boxed tomato puree
1½ cups cooked black beans, drained and rinsed

Red pepper flakes to taste
½ cup shredded cheddar cheese
¼ cup grated Parmesan cheese
2 tablespoons nonfat or reduced-fat sour cream
Cornmeal, for dusting
1 recipe Dough for Pizza (see page 416)

Heat the oil in a large, nonstick skillet over medium-high heat, swirling the pan to coat the bottom. Add the onion, garlic, ancho chili, jalapeño, tomatillo or salsa, cilantro, cumin, chili powder, and oregano. Reduce the heat to medium and sauté, stirring often, until the vegetables have softened, about 15 minutes. Add the tomato puree, and continue cooking until you have a thick paste, about 10 minutes. Stir in the black beans and red pepper flakes and remove the mixture from the heat.

In a large bowl, combine the cheddar cheese, Parmesan, and sour cream to make a thick paste. Stir into the black bean mixture.

Heat the oven to 350° F. If you're using a baking stone, put it in the center of the oven now. Sprinkle a rimless nonstick baking sheet or a baker's peel with cornmeal.

Punch down the dough to eliminate the airholes. Turn it out of the bowl and knead it until it's smooth, about 5 minutes. Divide the dough into 4 equal pieces. Working with one section at a time, roll it out to a round 7 inches in diameter. Place a quarter of the filling in the center, and pat it down lightly, leaving a border of about 1 inch. Fold the top portion of dough over the filling, as for a turnover. Wet your fingers and pinch the border to seal. Press a fork along the edge to complete the seal. Use the fork to puncture airholes in the top. Place on the prepared baking sheet or peel. Cover with a light towel while you repeat the process with the remaining ingredients.

Let the calzone rest, covered with the towel, for 15 minutes. Slide the calzone from the baking sheet or peel onto the baking stone or place the baking sheet in the center of the oven. Bake until golden brown, about 25 minutes. Serve hot.

Note: If you can't find a fresh ancho chili and jalapeño pepper, use the same amount of dried peppers. Soak them in warm water to cover for 30 minutes, until they're soft. Drain the water, slice open the pepper, remove the seeds, mince and proceed with the recipe. (For sources of dried peppers, see mail-order information, page 596.)

PER SERVING (1 CALZONE): CALORIES 626 • PROTEIN 23.7 G • CARBOHYDRATE 107 G • FAT 11.5 G • CHOLESTEROL 19.8 MG • SODIUM 1345 MG • 12% CALORIES FROM FAT • OUTSTANDING SOURCE OF VITAMINS B₁, B₂, B₃, C; IRON • VERY GOOD SOURCE OF FOLACIN, CALCIUM • GOOD SOURCE OF VITAMIN A; ZINC

•

SWEET AND CREAMY CARROT CALZONE

Makes 4 calzones

TOTAL TIME: ABOUT 1 HOUR, 15 MINUTES, NOT INCLUDING TIME TO MAKE THE DOUGH
TIME TO PREPARE: ABOUT 20 MINUTES
COOKING TIME: 25 MINUTES
EQUIPMENT: BAKING STONE, BAKER'S PEEL (OPTIONAL)
DO AHEAD: YOU CAN MAKE THE FILLING UP TO 3 DAYS IN ADVANCE. REFRIGERATE UNTIL READY TO USE.
REFRIGERATION/FREEZING: REFRIGERATE UP TO 2 DAYS. FREEZE UP TO 3 MONTHS.

My favorite way to get vitamin A, these may seem exceedingly strange to you. But please suspend such (albeit reasonable) suspicions, and give them a try. I'm willing to bet you'll love them, too!

1 medium onion, thinly sliced
¹/₂ cup dried apricots
6 medium carrots, scrubbed and thinly sliced into rounds
1 bay leaf
1 cup fresh orange juice
1 cup nonfat ricotta cheese
¹/₂ cup shredded Gruyère cheese
Pinch ground cinnamon

Pinch ground ginger

Cornmeal, for dusting

1 recipe Dough for Pizza (see page 416)

Place the onion, apricots, carrots, and bay leaf in the bottom of a medium saucepan. Add the orange juice, plus as much water as necessary to cover by an inch. Bring to a boil over medium-high heat. Cover, lower the heat to medium, and simmer until the carrots and apricots are very soft, about 40 minutes. Check often, adding water as needed to prevent burning.

Remove from the heat, drain off and discard the liquid, and let cool, about 15 minutes. Discard the bay leaf, transfer the carrots and apricots to a food processor, and puree them together. Add the ricotta, Gruyère, cinnamon, and ginger, and process until smooth.

Heat the oven to 350°F. If you're using a baking stone, put it in the center of the oven now. Sprinkle a rimless nonstick baking sheet or a baker's peel with cornmeal.

Punch down the dough to eliminate the airholes. Turn it out of the bowl and knead it until it's smooth, about 5 minutes. Divide the pizza dough into 4 pieces of equal size. Working with one section at a time, roll it out to a round 7 inches in diameter. Place one-fourth of the filling in the center, and pat it down lightly, leaving a border of about 1 inch. Fold the top portion of the dough over the filling, as for a turnover. Wet your fingers and pinch the border to seal the calzone. Press a fork along the edge to complete the seal. Use the fork to puncture airholes in the top. Place on the prepared baking sheet or peel. Cover with a light towel while you repeat the process with the remaining ingredients.

Let the calzone rest, covered with the towel, for 15 minutes. Slide the calzone from the baking sheet or peel onto the baking stone or place the baking sheet in the center of the oven. Bake until golden brown, about 25 minutes. Serve hot.

PER SERVING (1 CALZONE): CALORIES 589 • PROTEIN 28.7 G • CARBOHYDRATE 95.7 G • FAT 5.5 G • CHOLESTEROL 31.1 MG • SODIUM 1205 MG • 16% CALORIES FROM FAT • OUTSTANDING SOURCE OF VITAMINS A, B₁, B₂, C • VERY GOOD SOURCE OF FOLACIN, CALCIUM, IRON • GOOD SOURCE OF ZINC

•

TRIPLE-CORN CALZONE

Makes 4 calzones

TOTAL TIME: ABOUT 1 HOUR, 25 MINUTES, NOT INCLUD-
ING TIME TO MAKE THE DOUGH OR THE BROTH

TIME TO PREPARE: ABOUT 1 HOUR

COOKING TIME: 25 MINUTES

EQUIPMENT: BAKING STONE, BAKER'S PEEL (OPTIONAL)

DO AHEAD: YOU CAN MAKE THE FILLING UP TO 3 DAYS IN
ADVANCE. REFRIGERATE UNTIL READY TO USE.

REFRIGERATION/FREEZING: REFRIGERATE UP TO 2 DAYS.
FREEZE UP TO 6 MONTHS.

Your teeth sink into a paradise of corn when you eat this calzone—soft cornmeal dough chock-full of fresh kernels of corn.

1 cup vegetable broth (see page 165) or water

¼ cup stone-ground cornmeal

6 ears of corn

½ cup shredded cheddar or Monterey Jack cheese

1 cup nonfat or part-skim ricotta cheese

⅓ cup nonfat or reduced-fat sour cream

1 recipe Corn Bread Dough for Calzone (see page 424)

In a medium saucepan, bring the vegetable broth or water to a boil over medium-high heat. Whisking constantly, pour in the cornmeal. Turn the heat down to medium, and continue stirring until the mixture is very thick, about 15 minutes. Remove from the heat.

Bring a large pot of water to a boil. Add the corn and let the water return to a boil. Cover the pot, turn off the heat, and leave the corn for 8 to 10 minutes. (If you're using an electric stove, take the pot off the burner.) Transfer the corn to a plate to let it cool. (Or cook the corn in the microwave according to the directions on page 526.)

Scrape the kernels into a food processor or blender. Process in short pulses until coarsely chopped. Transfer to a large mixing bowl.

Add the cornmeal mush, cheddar or Jack cheese, ricotta, and sour cream. Stir well.

Heat the oven to 350°F. If you're using a baking stone, put it in the center of the oven now. Sprinkle a rimless nonstick baking sheet or a baker's peel with cornmeal.

Punch down the dough to eliminate the airholes. Turn it out of the bowl and knead it until it's smooth, about 5 minutes. Divide the dough into 4 equal pieces. Working with one section at a time, roll it out to a round 7 inches in diameter. Place a quarter of the filling in the center, and pat it down lightly, leaving a border of about 1 inch. Fold the top portion of dough over the filling, as for a turnover. Wet your fingers and pinch the border to seal the calzone. Press a fork along the edge to complete the seal. Use the fork to puncture airholes in the top. Place on the prepared baking sheet or peel. Cover with a light towel while you repeat the process with the remaining ingredients.

Let the calzone rest, covered with the towel, for 15 minutes. Slide the calzone from the baking sheet or peel onto the baking stone or place the baking sheet in the center of the oven. Bake until golden brown, about 25 minutes. Serve hot.

PER SERVING (1 CALZONE): CALORIES 386 • PROTEIN 17.2 G • CARBOHYDRATE 70 G • FAT 4.5 G • CHOLESTEROL 9.9 MG • SODIUM 797 MG • 10% CALORIES FROM FAT • VERY GOOD SOURCE OF VITAMINS B₁, B₂, B₃; CALCIUM, IRON • GOOD SOURCE OF FOLACIN

•

CORN BREAD DOUGH FOR CALZONE

Serves 4

TOTAL TIME: ABOUT 2 HOURS
TIME TO PREPARE: ABOUT 30 MINUTES
REFRIGERATION/FREEZING: REFRIGERATE UP TO 3 DAYS.
    FREEZE UP TO 6 MONTHS.

1 tablespoon (1 packet) dry active yeast
1 teaspoon sugar
1 cup warm water (98° to 115°F.)
¼ cup molasses
2 teaspoons salt
¼ cup stone-ground cornmeal
2½ to 3 cups unbleached all-purpose flour

In a large mixing bowl, combine the yeast and sugar. Add the water and let the mixture rest until bubbly, about 5 minutes.

Stir lightly. Add the molasses, salt, cornmeal, and enough flour to make a dough that's soft and pliable, but not sticky. Lightly flour a large, flat work surface, turn the dough out of the bowl, and knead until it's smooth, about 15 minutes. Alternatively, you can knead the dough in a food processor or Mixmaster.

Clean out the mixing bowl, dry it thoroughly, and spray it lightly with nonstick spray. Shape the dough into a ball and place in the bowl. Cover the bowl with plastic wrap and set it aside in a warm, draft-free place until the dough is doubled in bulk, about 1 hour, 15 minutes.

PER SERVING: CALORIES 370 • PROTEIN 9.4 G • CARBOHYDRATE 79.7 G • FAT 1.1 G • CHOLESTEROL 0 MG • SODIUM 1082 MG • 3% CALORIES FROM FAT • VERY GOOD SOURCE OF IRON

NOW TRY THIS: Pumpkin Cornmeal Calzone: Add ⅓ cup pumpkin puree when you add the molasses and cornmeal to the yeast. (You may need up to ½ cup additional all-purpose flour to make dough that's firm enough to knead.)

BREAD MACHINE OPTION: Place all of the ingredients in your breadmaker according to the manufacturer's instructions. Once the dough has risen, take it out of the machine, shape it as directed in the recipe, and continue to follow the recipe from that point.

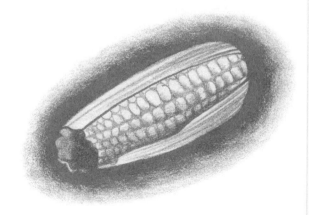

Focaccia

F O C A C C I A   D O U G H
Serves 8

TOTAL TIME: ABOUT 4 HOURS, 30 MINUTES, INCLUDING TIME TO RISE
TIME TO PREPARE: ABOUT 1 HOUR
REFRIGERATION/FREEZING: REFRIGERATE UP TO 3 DAYS. FREEZE UP TO 3 MONTHS.

It's ironic that although it came first, focaccia is always defined in terms of pizza. There are many variations of focaccia, but most are like a thick pizza, with a filling kneaded into the dough rather than placed on top. The filling can be as simple as olive oil and salt or as elaborate as anything you might find on a pizza.

In their purest forms, it's easy to distinguish focaccia from pizza: focaccia is made from dimpled dough, baked in a deep rectangular pan, slathered with olive oil, and sprinkled with rosemary and coarse salt; the crust is thick and the seasonings seep into it. Meanwhile, the definitive pizza has a thin, crisp crust and a layer of topping, most commonly tomatoes and cheese. But between the extremes, pizza and focaccia overlap. Even in Italy, you'll find that what's sold as focaccia at one place is pizza somewhere else. For instance, pizza bianca (dough topped with herbs alone or herbs and cheese) is more like focaccia than what we'd call pizza. But it's silly to get stuck on all this when we could be baking.

1½ cups warm water (98° to 115°F.)
2 teaspoons dry active yeast
1½ teaspoons extra virgin olive oil
3½ to 4 cups unbleached all-purpose flour
¼ teaspoon salt

In a large mixing bowl or a food processor or Mixmaster fitted with the plastic dough blade or the dough hook, combine ½ cup of the water with the yeast. Stir gently, and let the mixture rest until the water turns creamy, with bubbles around the edges, about 10 minutes.

Stir the olive oil with the remaining 1 cup water into the yeast mixture. In another bowl, combine 2 cups of the flour with the salt, and stir it into the yeast mixture. If using a Mixmaster, add the flour and salt to the yeast mixture with the motor running on medium-low speed. If using a food processor, add the flour mixture in pulses until incorporated. Continue adding flour until you have a dough that is firm enough to knead. Turn the dough out onto a lightly floured surface and knead by hand until the dough is smooth and elastic, about 10 minutes. Shape into a ball. Or knead by machine until the dough forms a ball around the blade or hook.

Lightly grease a large ceramic bowl with olive oil, and place the dough inside. Cover the bowl with plastic wrap and set it aside in a warm, draft-free place until it doubles in bulk, about 1½ hours.

Punch down the dough to deflate it. Turn it out onto a lightly floured surface and knead it again to eliminate airholes, about 5 minutes.

Lightly grease one 10½ × 15½-inch baking pan or two 9-inch pie plates.

Place the dough in the prepared pan or divide in 2 equal pieces if using pie plates and pat it down to fit. Cover with a damp towel and let it rest until it's puffy, about 30 minutes.

Use your fingertips or knuckles to make indentations or "dimples" on the top of the dough. Cover it again with the towel and let it rest until it's double in bulk, about 1½ hours.

PER SERVING: CALORIES 208 • PROTEIN 5.8 G • CARBOHYDRATE 42 G • FAT 1.4 G • CHOLESTEROL 0 MG • SODIUM 401 MG • 6% CALORIES FROM FAT

NOW TRY THIS: Heat the oven to 400°F. If you'll be using a baking stone, put it in the center of the oven 30 minutes before you're going to bake the focaccia. Brush the focaccia with 1 tablespoon extra virgin olive oil and sprinkle evenly with 1½ teaspoons coarse salt and the leaves of 3 sprigs fresh rosemary. Place the pan or pie plates in the oven, directly on top of the stone, if you're using one. Bake until golden, about 20 minutes. Turn the focaccia out onto a cooling rack, and let the bread cool for 5 to 10 minutes before serving. Serve the focaccia as soon as possible after baking.

BREAD MACHINE OPTION: Place all of the ingredients in your breadmaker according to the manufacturer's instructions. Once the dough has risen, take it out of the machine, shape it as directed in the recipe, and continue to follow the recipe from that point.

Make It Your Own

Remember that one of the things that distinguishes focaccia from pizza is that the flavoring is meant to go into the dough, not rest on top of it. You can press any number of things into the basic Focaccia Dough for a bread that's all your own.

WHAT TO ADD AND WHEN TO ADD IT
✐ *Flavored Olive Oils.* Instead of ordinary extra virgin olive oil, brush the focaccia with an olive oil seasoned with herbs, porcini mushrooms, or lemon. (See mail-order information, page 596.)

🖉 *Herbs.* In place of the rosemary, add about ¼ cup total minced fresh basil and/or oregano, or 2 tablespoons total dried herbs.

🖉 *Sesame Seeds.* In place of rosemary, sprinkle the dough with about 2 tablespoons sesame seeds.

🖉 *Olives and/or Sun-Dried Tomatoes.* When you dimple the dough, press into it about ½ cup total chopped cured olives and/or sun-dried tomatoes. Brush with extra virgin olive oil and sprinkle with about 2 tablespoons minced fresh basil, or 1 tablespoon dried basil.

🖉 *Caramelized Onions.* When you dimple the dough, press into it one recipe Caramelized Vidalia Onions (see page 224).

🖉 *Roasted Bell Peppers.* When you dimple the dough, press into it about ½ cup chopped peeled roasted red, yellow, and/or green bell peppers (see page 534).

🖉 *Cheese.* Just before baking, sprinkle the focaccia with about ¼ cup grated Parmesan or Asiago cheese. Brush with extra virgin olive oil.

🖉 *Raisins and Pine Nuts.* When you dimple the dough, press into it 2 tablespoons raisins and 2 tablespoons pine nuts. Brush with extra virgin olive oil.

•

SWEET ONION FOCACCIA

Serves 8

TOTAL TIME: ABOUT 1 HOUR, 35 MINUTES, NOT INCLUD-
ING TIME TO MAKE THE DOUGH
TIME TO PREPARE: ABOUT 1 HOUR, 20 MINUTES
COOKING TIME: ABOUT 15 MINUTES
DO AHEAD: YOU CAN MAKE THE DOUGH UP TO 3 DAYS IN
ADVANCE. REFRIGERATE UNTIL READY TO USE.
REFRIGERATION/FREEZING: DO NOT REFRIGERATE. FREEZE
UP TO 6 MONTHS.

The onions melt into the bread for a first course or side dish that's irresistible hot, cold, or at room temperature, with soup, salad, or stew.

3 tablespoons extra virgin olive oil
4 pounds Vidalia onions
1 recipe Focaccia Dough (see page 425)

Heat 2 tablespoons of the oil in a large nonstick skillet over medium-high heat, swirling the pan to coat the bottom. Add the onions, reduce the heat to medium, and sauté until they turn light caramel brown, about 40 minutes.

Lightly grease one 10½ × 15½-inch baking pan or two 9-inch pie plates. Place the dough in the prepared pan or divide in 2 equal pieces if using pie plates and pat it down to fit. Cover with a damp towel and let it rest until it's puffy, about 30 minutes. Use your fingertips or knuckles to make indentations or "dimples" on top of the dough. Brush the dough with the remaining tablespoon of olive oil, and spread the onions evenly on top. Cover with a lightweight towel and let the dough rest until the crust is puffy, about 40 minutes.

About 30 minutes before you're going to bake, place the oven rack in the middle of the oven and heat the oven to 400°F.

Place the focaccia in the oven. Bake until the crust is golden brown, about 15 minutes. Let it cool for about 10 minutes before slicing and serving.

PER SERVING: CALORIES 314 • PROTEIN 8.6 G • CARBOHYDRATE 62.8 G • FAT 3.4 G • CHOLESTEROL 0 MG • SODIUM 541 MG • 10% CALORIES FROM FAT • VERY GOOD SOURCE OF VITAMIN C • GOOD SOURCE OF FOLACIN

Crepes

CREPES

Makes about 12

TOTAL TIME: ABOUT 45 MINUTES
TIME TO PREPARE: ABOUT 45 MINUTES
COOKING TIME: INCLUDED IN TIME TO PREPARE
REFRIGERATION/FREEZING: REFRIGERATE UP TO 2 DAYS.
  FREEZE UP TO 6 MONTHS.

These are sturdy multipurpose crepes. The milk makes them even more substantial, for use with heavy fillings.

3 large eggs
1 cup nonfat milk
¼ teaspoon salt
1 cup unbleached all-purpose flour, sifted

In a large mixing bowl, beat together the eggs, milk, salt, and flour. Pour the mixture through a fine sieve into another mixing bowl. Let it rest for 30 minutes.

Heat an 8-inch nonstick pan over medium-high heat. Pour 3 tablespoons of batter into the center of the pan and quickly swirl the pan to coat it evenly. Cook over medium heat until the bottom has set, about 30 seconds. Loosening the crepe with a nonmetallic implement (such as a small plastic knife or spatula), turn it over with your fingers and cook until the other side has set, about 20 seconds. Transfer it to a plate, and repeat the process with the remaining batter, stacking the crepes and alternating with a sheet of wax paper as you finish them. Serve as soon as possible, or let them cool completely, wrap in plastic with a sheet of wax paper between each crepe, and refrigerate or freeze.

PER SERVING (1 CREPE): CALORIES 63.7 • PROTEIN 3.3 G • CARBOHYDRATE 9.1 G • FAT 1.3 G • CHOLESTEROL 53.6 MG • SODIUM 26.5 MG • 20% CALORIES FROM FAT

CREPE BASICS

The French have made an art of frugality (unlike those thrifty Scots, who've only made haggis of it), and crepes are a masterful example. They're so good, you'd think that some inspired chef set out deliberately to make these delicate pancakes. But given the history of French food, the first crepe probably was meant as a means to stretch a drop of batter as far as it would go. Form follows function, even in France.

• Once you've mixed the batter, pour it through a sieve to eliminate any lumps. Then let it rest for 30 minutes. (The resting period softens the gluten, which gives you lighter crepes.) Whisk the batter well before cooking. The batter should have the consistency of heavy cream at this stage. If it's too thick, add water or skim milk, 1 tablespoon at a time, until it's right. If it's too thin, whisk in another tablespoon of flour.

• Make sure the surface of your nonstick crepe pan or skillet is in good working order. You have to be able to cook the crepes quickly without worrying about peeling them off the pan. For insurance, squirt the surface lightly with nonstick spray, then wipe off the residue with a paper towel.

• Use about 3 tablespoons of batter for an 8-inch crepe. To measure and pour the correct amount, dip a ¼-cup measure into the batter and pour a quarter of it back into the bowl. Pour the rest into the crepe pan and swirl it quickly so that it sets evenly. Continue as directed in the basic recipe.

Make It Your Own

Crepe batter is too delicate to alter in any substantial way without making the crepes heavy or coarse. Rather than tinker with the crepes themselves, make them your own with the filling you choose.

WHAT TO ADD AND WHEN TO ADD IT

Ratatouille. Place about ¼ cup Ratatouille (see page 343) in the center of a crepe, and enclose it by folding all four sides over it, envelope-style. Turn seam side down to serve. Sprinkle with Parmesan cheese and brown under the broiler, if you'd like, or drizzle with tomato sauce.

Thick Stew. Try ¼ cup Potato-Fennel Stew with Mixed Beans and Tofu (see page 336) or Lentil and Mushroom Stew (see page 340).

Pasta Filling. Choose any filling offered for lasagna (see pages 302 to 303) or ravioli (see pages 299 to 301). Place about ¼ cup filling inside each crepe, enclose it by folding all four sides over it, envelope-style, and turn the crepe seam side down. Top with the pasta sauce of your choice.

Layers. Place a cooked crepe in a baking dish that's been lightly greased or squirted with nonstick spray. Sprinkle evenly with about 2 tablespoons grated or shredded cheese, or spread with any of the fillings for pasta. Cover with another crepe, and continue layering and stacking with as many crepes as you'd like. Spoon fresh tomato sauce (see page 278) over the whole thing and bake at 350° F. for about fifteen minutes, until the cheese melts, or the stack is firm. For a Southwest version, use cheddar cheese, and spread each crepe with a thin layer of Refried Bean Puree (see page 256). Spoon Spicy Fresh Tomato Sauce (see page 278) on top, and garnish after baking with nonfat or reduced-fat sour cream and diced avocado (see page 517).

MUSHROOM
CREPES

Serves 4

TOTAL TIME: ABOUT 45 MINUTES, NOT INCLUDING TIME TO
  MAKE CREPES
TIME TO PREPARE: ABOUT 20 MINUTES, INCLUDING TIME
  TO SAUTÉ
COOKING TIME: 20 MINUTES
DO AHEAD: YOU CAN MAKE THE CREPES UP TO 2 DAYS IN
  ADVANCE. KEEP EACH SEPARATE WITH A SHEET OF WAX
  PAPER. REFRIGERATE UNTIL READY TO FILL AND BAKE.
  YOU CAN MAKE THE MUSHROOM FILLING UP TO 2 DAYS
  IN ADVANCE. REFRIGERATE UNTIL READY TO USE.
REFRIGERATION/FREEZING: REFRIGERATE UP TO 2 DAYS. DO
  NOT FREEZE.

*For the mushroom mad. Serve these with Red or
Yellow Bell Pepper Soup (see page 171) or
any lentil salad (see page 142).*

1 tablespoon extra virgin olive oil
4 scallions, white part plus 1 inch of greens,
    trimmed and chopped
1 garlic clove, minced
2 teaspoons grated peeled fresh ginger
¼ cup minced fresh parsley
¼ cup minced fresh basil
¼ cup minced fresh chives
1 pound mixed fresh mushrooms, such as
    cremini, shiitake, oyster, white button, sliced
2 teaspoons red wine vinegar
1 teaspoon fresh lemon juice
¼ cup nonfat or reduced-fat sour cream
⅓ cup shredded Monterey Jack cheese
2 tablespoons grated Parmesan cheese
8 Crepes (see page 428) or store-bought crepes
    (see page 595 for brand recommendations)

Heat the oil in a medium, heavy skillet over
medium-high heat. Add the scallions, garlic,

ginger, parsley, basil, and chives and lower the
heat to medium. Sauté, stirring often until the
scallions are soft, about 8 minutes.

Add the mushrooms and stir constantly
until they begin to give up their liquid, about 3
minutes. Add the vinegar and lemon juice, and
continue stirring until the mushrooms are
cooked through and most of the liquid has
evaporated, about 10 minutes. Remove from
the heat.

Heat the oven to 375°F. Squirt a 12-inch
baking dish with nonstick spray or lightly
grease with unsalted butter.

In a mixing bowl, combine the sour cream,
Monterey Jack, and Parmesan. Stir the cheese
mixture into the mushroom mixture and blend
thoroughly.

Place an even portion in the center of each
crepe, and spread it in a strip across the diameter. Fold the bottom and sides of the crepe over
the filling, sealing it like an envelope. Transfer
the crepes to the prepared baking dish, placing

them in a single layer. Bake for 20 minutes, until bubbly. Let the crepes sit for 10 minutes before serving.

•

CORN SOUFFLÉ CREPES

Serves 6

TOTAL TIME: ABOUT 50 MINUTES, NOT INCLUDING TIME TO
    MAKE CREPES
TIME TO PREPARE: ABOUT 35 MINUTES
COOKING TIME: 15 MINUTES
DO AHEAD: YOU CAN MAKE THE CREPES UP TO 2 DAYS IN
    ADVANCE. KEEP EACH SEPARATE WITH A SHEET OF WAX
    PAPER. REFRIGERATE UNTIL READY TO FILL AND BAKE.

This is the kind of dish that gives you confidence as a cook. It looks and tastes as if it's impossibly complicated, while, in fact, it's really very simple (pssst . . . especially if you buy ready-made crepes).

3 ears of corn
1 tablespoon cornstarch
1 cup nonfat milk
2 large eggs, separated
¼ teaspoon salt
12 Crepes (see page 428) or store-bought crepes
    (see page 595 for brand recommendations)

Bring a large pot of water to a boil. Add the corn and let the water return to a boil. Cover the pot, turn off the heat, and leave the corn for 8 to 10 minutes. (If you're using an electric stove, take the pot off the burner.) Transfer the corn to a plate to let it cool. (Or cook the corn in the microwave according to the directions on page 526.)

Scrape the corn kernels off the cobs into a small bowl.

Heat the oven to 350° F. Squirt a 12-inch baking dish with nonstick cooking spray or lightly grease with unsalted butter.

In a large saucepan, whisk the cornstarch into the milk until the mixture is smooth. Heat gently over medium heat, bringing it to a simmer, taking care not to boil, and whisking constantly until thickened, about 15 minutes. Remove from the heat.

Whisk about 2 tablespoons of the hot milk into the egg yolks, then slowly pour the yolks into the milk mixture, stirring constantly. Still stirring, heat over medium-low until further thickened, about 7 minutes. Turn off the heat.

Stir in the corn and salt.

Beat the egg whites until they're stiff. Fold the whites into the corn mixture.

Lay a crepe on a flat surface. Place 3 tablespoons of the corn filling in the center, and fold all 4 sides over to enclose it. Carefully transfer the crepe to the prepared baking dish, seam side down. Repeat until you've used up all of the crepes and/or filling, placing the filled crepes in a single layer.

Bake until the filling is puffy and golden brown, about 15 minutes. Serve right away.

•

STACKED CREPES WITH SOUFFLÉED SPINACH AND CHEESE

Serves 6

TOTAL TIME: ABOUT 50 MINUTES, NOT INCLUDING TIME TO MAKE THE CREPES
TIME TO PREPARE: ABOUT 15 MINUTES
COOKING TIME: 35 MINUTES
DO AHEAD: YOU CAN MAKE THE CREPES UP TO 2 DAYS IN ADVANCE. KEEP EACH SEPARATE WITH A SHEET OF WAX PAPER. REFRIGERATE UNTIL READY TO FILL AND BAKE.

This is another deceptive dish. It looks sophisticated and tastes terrific, but it's so simple you may feel bad taking credit for it. (But go ahead: eat up the praise along with the crepes, and a crisp salad.)

1 cup nonfat milk

3 tablespoons unbleached all-purpose flour

5 large eggs, separated

½ cup grated Parmesan or cheddar cheese

Pinch ground nutmeg

4 cups fresh spinach, steamed (see page 539) and chopped, or one 10-ounce package frozen chopped spinach, thawed and squeezed dry

Salt and freshly ground black pepper to taste

8 Crepes (see page 428) or store-bought crepes (see page 595 for brand recommendations)

In a measuring cup, combine ¼ cup of the milk with the flour. Stir to make a paste, and set aside.

In a medium, heavy saucepan bring the remaining ¾ cup milk to a simmer over medium heat. When the milk is simmering, stir in the flour paste, and continue stirring until the mixture thickens, about 5 minutes.

Remove the mixture from the heat and let it sit for about 4 minutes. Stir in the egg yolks, one at a time. Stir in the cheese, nutmeg, and spinach. Season with salt and pepper and set aside.

Heat the oven to 400°F.

Beat the egg whites to stiff peaks. Fold a third of the egg whites into the spinach mixture. When these are thoroughly blended, fold in the remaining whites.

Place one crepe in the bottom of a 9-inch round gratin dish. Spread an eighth of the spinach mixture on top. Cover with another crepe, and continue to alternate crepes and spinach, ending with a layer of spinach.

Cover with foil and bake for 20 minutes, until the soufflé starts to set. Remove the foil and continue baking until the soufflé is puffy and lightly browned, about 15 minutes more. Serve immediately.

PER SERVING (1 CREPE): CALORIES 254 • PROTEIN 17.5 G • CARBOHYDRATE 25.5 G • FAT 8.8 G • CHOLESTEROL 257 MG • SODIUM 308 MG • 32% CALORIES FROM FAT • OUTSTANDING SOURCE OF VITAMIN A • VERY GOOD SOURCE OF VITAMIN C; FOLACIN, CALCIUM • GOOD SOURCE OF IRON, ZINC

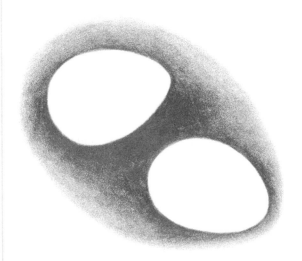

DOUGH FOR SAVORY PIES

Serves 6

TOTAL TIME: 1 HOUR, 25 MINUTES, INCLUDING TIME TO RISE

TIME TO PREPARE: ABOUT 10 MINUTES

EQUIPMENT: BAKING STONE (OPTIONAL)

REFRIGERATION/FREEZING: REFRIGERATE UP TO 2 DAYS. FREEZE UP TO 3 MONTHS.

T*his recipe makes a bready crust that's a bit crisper than calzone or pizza. It's also a lot faster because the dough is firm and easy to handle.*

1 teaspoon dry active yeast

⅓ cup warm water (98° to 115°F.)

¾ cup unbleached all-purpose flour

¾ cup whole wheat pastry flour

½ teaspoon sugar

1 teaspoon salt

1 large egg, lightly beaten

3 tablespoons nonfat or reduced-fat sour cream

In a small bowl, stir together the yeast and water. Let the mixture sit until frothy, about 10 minutes.

In a larger bowl, combine the flours, sugar, and salt. Make a well in the center, and add the egg, sour cream, and yeast mixture. Stir to make a soft dough. Turn out onto a lightly floured board and knead briefly until smooth.

Clean the larger mixing bowl, and return the dough to it. Cover with plastic wrap or a light towel and place in a warm spot until doubled, about 45 minutes.

PER SERVING: CALORIES 127 • PROTEIN 5.3 G • CARBOHYDRATE 24.2 G • FAT 1.2 G • CHOLESTEROL 35.5 MG • SODIUM 372 MG • 9% CALORIES FROM FAT

SAVORY PIE BASICS

Before they were appropriated for dessert, all pies were savory, named (or so I'm told) for the magpie, a notorious winged scavenger. The name is an oblique reference to the versatility of the dish, indicating pies can contain as many different ingredients as that bird might collect when it's out on a spree.

• For a whole wheat crust, substitute whole wheat pastry flour for half or all of the all-purpose flour. Don't use regular whole wheat flour, which will make the crust coarse and heavy.

• Make sure the filling isn't watery or the crust will get soggy. If you have doubts, let the filling drain in a colander for 15 to 30 minutes before putting it into the pie. If you're still worried about it, stir in ½ cup soft bread crumbs for each cup of filling. The bread will absorb excess moisture and add body to the dish.

Make It Your Own

You can fill a savory pie with anything you'd put into lasagna, calzone, or a thick stew or casserole. Then you can shape it like a conventional free-form pie, as directed in the basic recipe, or you can make individual turnovers, by following the instructions for shaping calzone (see page 419).

ARTICHOKE AND MUSHROOM SAVORY PIE

Serves 4 to 6

TOTAL TIME: 1 HOUR, 10 MINUTES, NOT INCLUDING TIME
   TO MAKE THE DOUGH
TIME TO PREPARE: ABOUT 45 MINUTES
COOKING TIME: 25 MINUTES
EQUIPMENT: BAKING STONE (OPTIONAL)
DO AHEAD: YOU CAN PREPARE THE ARTICHOKES UP TO 3
   DAYS IN ADVANCE. REFRIGERATE UNTIL READY TO USE.
REFRIGERATION/FREEZING: REFRIGERATE UP TO 3 DAYS.
   FREEZE UP TO 6 MONTHS.

This chunky lemon filling makes a marvelous pie, and fabulous focaccia (see page 425), calzone (see page 419), crepe (see page 428), and filled vegetables (see page 361).

2 large fresh artichokes

2 teaspoons extra virgin olive oil

1 shallot, minced

2 scallions, white part only, minced

2 garlic cloves, minced

2 tablespoons minced fresh mint

2 tablespoons minced fresh flat-leaf parsley

1 tablespoon white wine, or 2 teaspoons wine
   vinegar

¼ pound firm mushrooms, such as cremini,
   portobello, or white button, sliced

½ cup vegetable broth (see page 165),
   approximately

1 tablespoon fresh lemon juice

1 recipe Dough for Savory Pies (see page 433)

Prepare the artichokes as directed on page 288. When they are cool, strip away the tough leaves, scrape out the choke, and coarsely chop the rest.

Heat the oil in a large skillet over medium-high heat, swirling the pan to coat the bottom. Add the shallot, scallions, garlic, mint, and parsley. Reduce the heat to medium and sauté, stirring often, until the shallot has softened, about 7 minutes. Add the wine or vinegar and stir until the liquid has evaporated, about 1 minute.

Add the mushrooms and stir until they start to release liquid, about 3 minutes, adding vegetable broth as necessary to prevent sticking. Add the artichokes, lemon juice, and only as much broth as necessary to keep the filling from burning. (The mixture should not be soupy.)

Let the mixture cool slightly.

To fill and bake, heat the oven to 400°F. If you're using a baking stone, put it in the center of the oven now.

Press the air out of the dough and turn it out onto a large (12-inch square) piece of parchment paper. Roll out the dough to a round 10 inches in diameter. Place the filling in the center, leaving a 2-inch margin all around. Pull up the sides to hold the filling like a bowl, with a small "window" at the top where the filling shows through. Pinch the dough around the window tight to flute it.

Carefully transfer the pie to a baking sheet or the stone. Bake until the filling has set and the crust is golden brown, about 25 minutes. The crust may spread during baking, so that the filling is much more exposed than it was when you put the pie into the oven. Don't worry about this; the results will taste wonderful. Serve hot.

PER SERVING: CALORIES 176 • PROTEIN 7.4 G • CARBOHYDRATE 31.5 G • FAT 2.9 G • CHOLESTEROL 35.5 MG • SODIUM 413 MG • 15% CALORIES FROM FAT • GOOD SOURCE OF VITAMIN C; FOLACIN, IRON

•

SOUR CREAM AND ONION SAVORY PIE

Serves 6

TOTAL TIME: ABOUT 1 HOUR, NOT INCLUDING TIME TO
   MAKE THE DOUGH
TIME TO PREPARE: ABOUT 25 MINUTES
COOKING TIME: 35 TO 40 MINUTES
DO AHEAD: YOU CAN SAUTÉ THE ONIONS UP TO 2 DAYS IN
   ADVANCE. REFRIGERATE UNTIL READY TO USE.
REFRIGERATION/FREEZING: REFRIGERATE UP TO 2 DAYS.

Made with a breadlike crust rather than the conventional butter pastry shell, this wholesome version of classic onion tart, served with soup or salad, makes a soothing lunch or light supper.

1 tablespoon unsalted butter or canola oil

4 cups thinly sliced yellow onions

1 1/2 tablespoons unbleached all-purpose flour

2 large eggs, lightly beaten

1/2 cup reduced-fat or nonfat sour cream

1 recipe Dough for Savory Pies (see page 433)

Heat the oven to 400°F.

In a large, heavy skillet, melt the butter or heat the oil over medium heat. Add the onions and sauté until they're soft and limp, about 20 minutes. Sprinkle the flour evenly over the onions, and stir well. Turn off the heat.

In a mixing bowl, beat together the eggs and sour cream until the mixture is smooth. Add the onions and stir well. Set aside while you prepare the crust.

For a free-form pie, roll out the dough on a marble slab or lightly floured board into a thin oblong shape, about 10 inches long and 8 inches wide. Transfer to a baking sheet. Form a border by pinching up 1 1/2 inches of dough around the edge. Stir the onion mixture, then spread it evenly over the dough. Bake until the crust is golden brown and the filling is firm, 35 to 40 minutes.

Transfer the pie to a wire cooling rack and let it cool at least 10 minutes before slicing and serving. Serve warm, at room temperature, or cold.

PER SERVING: CALORIES 226 • PROTEIN 10.2 G • CARBOHYDRATE 36.5 G • FAT 5 G • CHOLESTEROL 112 MG • SODIUM 410 MG • 20% CALORIES FROM FAT • GOOD SOURCE OF VITAMINS A, C; FOLACIN, IRON

FOR A ROUND PIE: You'll need a 9-inch quiche pan with a removable bottom. Roll the dough out to a round 11 inches in diameter. Carefully lift it and place it in the quiche or tart pan. Trim the edges, place the pan on a baking sheet, fill, bake, and cool as in the main recipe.

WINTER GARDEN SAVORY PIE

Serves 6

TOTAL TIME: 1 HOUR, 10 MINUTES, NOT INCLUDING TIME
TO MAKE THE DOUGH OR THE BROTH
TIME TO PREPARE: ABOUT 45 MINUTES
COOKING TIME: 25 MINUTES TO BAKE
EQUIPMENT: BAKING STONE (OPTIONAL)
DO AHEAD: YOU CAN MAKE THE FILLING UP TO 3 DAYS IN
ADVANCE. REFRIGERATE UNTIL READY TO USE.
REFRIGERATION/FREEZING: REFRIGERATE UP TO 3 DAYS.
FREEZE UP TO 6 MONTHS.

This hearty filling makes an excellent pie, and a terrific topping for whole wheat pasta. If you've never cooked with ruta-bagas, here's a splendid chance. And, if you already enjoy cooking with them, you know how good this dish will be.

2 teaspoons extra virgin olive oil
1 onion, thinly sliced
2 cups shredded red or green cabbage
2 teaspoons cumin seeds
2 medium Yukon Gold potatoes, peeled and cut
    into 1-inch chunks
1 medium rutabaga, peeled and cut into 1-inch
    chunks
2 beets, peeled and diced
1/2 cup vegetable broth (see page 165) or water
1/3 cup shredded Havarti cheese
Salt and freshly ground black pepper to taste
1 recipe Dough for Savory Pies (see page 433)

Heat the olive oil in a large skillet over medium heat. When it's hot, add the onion, cabbage, and cumin seeds. Turn down the heat to medium-low and sauté until the vegetables are soft and limp, about 10 minutes. Add the pota-toes, rutabaga, and beets. Stir in the vegetable broth or water, cover, and simmer gently until the vegetables are soft and most of the liquid has evaporated, about 10 minutes. Stir in the cheese. Season with salt and pepper.

Transfer the mixture to a bowl and let it cool until it stops steaming.

To fill and bake, heat the oven to 400°F. If you're using a baking stone, put it in the center of the oven now.

Press the air out of the dough and turn it out onto a large (12-inch square) piece of parchment paper. Roll out the dough to a round 10 inches in diameter. Place the filling in the center, leaving a 2-inch margin all around. Pull up the sides to hold the filling like a bowl, with a small "window" at the top where the filling shows through. Pinch the dough around the window tight to flute it.

Carefully transfer the pie to a baking sheet or the stone. Bake until the filling has set and the crust is golden brown, about 25 minutes. The crust may spread during baking, so that the filling is much more exposed than it was when you put the pie into the oven. Don't worry about this; the results will taste wonder-ful. Serve hot.

PER SERVING: CALORIES 355 • PROTEIN 14 G • CARBOHYDRATE 60 G • FAT 7.8 G •
CHOLESTEROL 63.6 MG • SODIUM 672 MG • 19% CALORIES FROM FAT • OUTSTAND-
ING SOURCE OF VITAMIN C • VERY GOOD SOURCE OF FOLACIN • GOOD SOURCE
OF VITAMIN A; IRON, ZINC

Phyllo

SPINACH STRUDEL

Serves 8

TOTAL TIME: ABOUT 50 MINUTES

TIME TO PREPARE: ABOUT 30 MINUTES

COOKING TIME: 15 TO 20 MINUTES

DO AHEAD: YOU CAN MAKE THE FILLING UP TO 2 DAYS IN
ADVANCE. REFRIGERATE UNTIL READY TO USE.

REFRIGERATION/FREEZING: REFRIGERATE UP TO 3 DAYS. DO
NOT FREEZE.

Even people who don't like spinach will eat this—tons of it—prepared like this. Mixed with tangy cheese and baked in flaky phyllo, spinach is irresistible. If you've never worked with phyllo, here's a chance to discover how easy it is and how rewarding.

2 teaspoons extra virgin olive oil

2 shallots, minced

2 teaspoons crumbled dried oregano

One 10-ounce package frozen chopped spinach,
thawed and squeezed dry

1 large egg

1 large egg white

1 cup nonfat ricotta cheese

½ cup nonfat sour cream

⅔ cup crumbled feta cheese

6 sheets phyllo dough

1 tablespoon unsalted butter, approximately,
melted

Heat the oil in a medium skillet over medium heat. When it's hot, add the shallots, and sauté until they're soft, about 7 minutes. Add the oregano and spinach and continue to sauté until they're well mixed, about 2 minutes. Remove from the heat.

In a mixing bowl, combine the whole egg, egg white, ricotta cheese, sour cream, and feta cheese. Stir in the spinach, and mix until they're thoroughly combined.

Heat the oven to 350°F.

On your work surface, place a damp kitchen towel, the long edge parallel to the table's edge nearest you. Cover the towel with a piece of wax paper of equal size. Place 3 sheets of phyllo on top of the wax paper, stacking them one on top of another. Meanwhile, keep the remaining sheets covered with a sheet of wax paper, topped with a damp kitchen towel (see page 438). Brush the top layer of phyllo lightly with the melted butter. Spread half of the spinach mixture along the bottom edge of the dough, leaving an inch margin from both sides. Using the towel as a guide, fold the dough up over the spinach mixture. Keep folding the dough over, taking care not to get the towel caught in the roll, until the log is complete. Lift carefully and place on a non-stick baking sheet. Brush the top lightly with melted butter.

Repeat with the remaining ingredients to make a second roll.

Bake for 15 to 20 minutes, until golden brown. Serve hot.

PER SERVING: CALORIES 176 • PROTEIN 11.8 G • CARBOHYDRATE 13.7 G • FAT 8.4 G • CHOLESTEROL 48.6 MG • SODIUM 347 MG • 43% CALORIES FROM FAT • VERY GOOD SOURCE OF VITAMIN A • GOOD SOURCE OF VITAMIN C; FOLACIN, CALCIUM

RATATOUILLE STRUDEL: Substitute 1 recipe Ratatouille (see page 343) for the spinach filling. Let the ratatouille drain in a sieve for 20 minutes before filling the phyllo. Fill, fold, and bake as directed in the main recipe.

PHYLLO BASICS

As confessions go, mine isn't very shocking, but you might as well know that phyllo used to terrify me. The dough is so delicate, and I'm such a klutz, I was sure that to open a carton would be courting disaster. Never mind that my great-grandmother not only baked with it all the time but made the stuff from scratch. Some traits aren't heritable.

But recently I spilled all to my husband's Aunt Barrie, an innkeeper in Georgia whose food is famous down there. She suggested I go out and get some and "just throw it around the kitchen. You'll see it can take a lot more than you think."

She was right.

Nevertheless, there *are* some tricks to handling phyllo, but they're easily mastered.

• Defrost the phyllo in the refrigerator the night before you plan to use it. It may dry out if you let it thaw at room temperature.

• Use the dough as soon as it has defrosted, and don't refreeze leftover dough.

• Always use at least four layers of phyllo, (not necessarily four *sheets*, but you can put the filling on the end of a single sheet and roll it over four times to encase it in four layers). If you use fewer, the filling will seep into the dough and make a soggy mess.

• You can keep the dough from cracking and crumbling if you cover with wax paper the portion you're not working with, and top that with a damp (not wet) cloth. Be careful not to let the cloth touch the phyllo, or the dough will be soggy and impossible to shape.

• Always brush the dough lightly with melted unsalted butter or extra virgin olive oil. This step is essential for the golden, flaky results phyllo is all about.

• As with any savory pie, don't use watery fillings. If in doubt, add fine bread crumbs to absorb the moisture.

Try these fillings, too: Ratatouille (page 343), Artichoke and Mushroom (page 434), and Carrot and Apricot (page 422).

•

TORTA DI PASQUA
Easter Pie
Serves 8

TOTAL TIME: ABOUT 1 HOUR, 20 MINUTES
TIME TO PREPARE: ABOUT 45 MINUTES
COOKING TIME: 35 MINUTES
EQUIPMENT: 8-INCH SPRINGFORM PAN
DO AHEAD: YOU CAN MAKE THE SPINACH FILLING UP TO 2
DAYS IN ADVANCE. REFRIGERATE UNTIL READY TO USE.
REFRIGERATION/FREEZING: REFRIGERATE UP TO 3 DAYS. DO
NOT FREEZE.

Geography is destiny when it comes to the origin of most cuisines. Tropical foods tend to be hot because peppers precipitate perspiration, which cools you off as it evaporates on the skin. By the same token, the foods of the far north contain lots of fat, which insulates you from the cold.

There are exceptions, though—namely, Sicily. It's hot down there, but a typical meal involves several deep-fried dishes, each doused with additional olive oil. Sicilians deep-fry rice, chickpeas, cheeses, and ravioli. They also make a stupefying Easter pie, comprising layers of butter-brushed phyllo filled with spinach, ricotta, dried fruits, sausage, and hard-boiled eggs.

This version is leaner and lighter than the genuine article, and—comparisons aside—festive and good in its own right.

4 cups fresh spinach, chopped, or one 10-ounce
    package frozen chopped spinach, thawed
    and squeezed dry
1 tablespoon extra virgin olive oil
1 large onion, chopped
2 scallions, including greens, chopped
2 tablespoons pine nuts
1 teaspoon crumbled dried oregano
1 teaspoon crumbled dried basil
Pinch ground cinnamon
Pinch ground nutmeg
¼ cup raisins
2 cups nonfat or part-skim ricotta cheese
¼ cup grated Parmesan cheese
¼ cup shredded smoked mozzarella cheese
½ cup shredded whole-milk or part-skim
    mozzarella cheese
12 sheets phyllo dough
1 tablespoon unsalted butter, melted
4 hard-boiled large eggs (see page 65), sliced

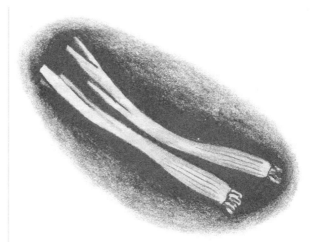

In a large saucepan, bring 1 inch of water to a boil. Add the spinach, cover the pan, and remove from the heat. Wait 3 minutes, lift out the spinach, transfer it to a colander, and let it cool and drain at room temperature.

Heat the oil in a medium skillet over medium-high heat. When it's hot, add the onion and scallions. Reduce the heat to medium and sauté, stirring often, until the vegetables are soft, about 7 minutes. Add the pine nuts, oregano, basil, cinnamon, and nutmeg, and continue sautéing until the pine nuts begin to color, about 4 minutes. Stir in the raisins and spinach and remove from the heat.

In a large mixing bowl, combine the ricotta, Parmesan, smoked mozzarella, and mozzarella. Mix well to combine. Add the spinach mixture and stir thoroughly. Cover and refrigerate while proceeding with the recipe.

Heat the oven to 350° F.

Place the bottom of an 8-inch springform pan on top of a layer of phyllo 4 sheets thick. Keep the rest of the phyllo covered with wax paper; drape a damp towel on top. Trace the outline of the pan on the phyllo with a sharp knife, cutting out a circle of dough the same diameter as the pan. Repeat twice with the remaining dough. You should have 3 circles, each 4 layers thick.

Place 2 of the dough circles side by side on a baking sheet and brush the surface of each with butter. Keep the third covered with wax paper draped with the damp towel. Bake the 2 dough circles for 6 minutes, until golden. Turn them over and brush the bottoms with butter. Return them to the oven until golden, about 6 minutes more. Leave the oven on.

Reinsert the bottom into the springform pan. Place one of the baked dough circles into the bottom of the pan. Spread half of the spinach mixture on top. Distribute half of the egg slices over that. Top with the second circle of baked dough. Spread the rest of the spinach mixture on top, and distribute the remaining egg slices over it. Lay the remaining circle of dough on top of the pie, and lightly brush it with butter. Bake in the center of the oven until golden brown, about 35 minutes.

Let the pie cool thoroughly in the pan on a rack before unmolding. Serve warm, at room temperature, or chilled.

PER SERVING: CALORIES 264 • PROTEIN 19.5 G • CARBOHYDRATE 22.4 G • FAT 10.9 G • CHOLESTEROL 119 MG • SODIUM 296 MG • 37% CALORIES FROM FAT • VERY GOOD SOURCE OF VITAMINS A, C; FOLACIN • GOOD SOURCE OF CALCIUM, IRON

Stratas and Savory Bread Puddings

STRATA
A Basic Savory Bread Pudding
Serves 4

TOTAL TIME: ABOUT 1 HOUR
TIME TO PREPARE: ABOUT 5 MINUTES
COOKING TIME: ABOUT 50 MINUTES
DO AHEAD: THIS DISH IS MADE ALMOST ENTIRELY OF LEFT-OVERS. ADDITIONALLY, YOU CAN ASSEMBLE THE STRATA UP TO 8 HOURS IN ADVANCE. REFRIGERATE UNTIL READY TO BAKE.

Strata and savory bread puddings are always better than the sum of their parts. Stale bread, eggs, and cheese wouldn't make the most lip-smacking combination if it weren't for the magic that occurs when you bake them. The unpromising mixture goes into the oven looking like mush and comes out puffed and golden, with a toasty top and a consistency like custard.

6 cups loosely packed day-old French bread chunks, crusts removed, or 8 thick slices whole wheat bread
2 large eggs
2 large egg whites
¾ cup nonfat milk
¼ cup grated hard cheese, such as Parmesan or Asiago, or ½ cup shredded soft cheese, such as cheddar, mozzarella, or Havarti
2 cups filling, approximately, such as sautéed sliced onions and cabbage; mushrooms; steamed fresh vegetables, such as broccoli, asparagus, corn; sliced peeled roasted mixed bell peppers (see page 534); thick tomato sauce (see "Make It Your Own," for more ideas)

Heat the oven to 350°F. Squirt an 8-inch baking dish with nonstick spray or lightly grease with unsalted butter.

Place half of the bread chunks or 4 bread slices in a single layer at the bottom of the prepared baking dish.

In a mixing bowl whisk together the eggs, egg whites, milk, cheese, and filling of your choice. Pour half of this mixture over the bread. Place the remaining bread on top and cover with the rest of the egg mixture.

Bake, uncovered, until brown, bubbly, and firm but springy to the touch, about 50 minutes. If the top seems to have browned before the pudding is firm, drape foil loosely over the dish and continue baking.

Transfer the strata to a rack and let it sit for about 5 minutes before slicing and serving. It may be too goopy to slice neatly, in which case use a big serving spoon to scoop it onto plates.

PER SERVING: CALORIES 260 • PROTEIN 16.4 G • CARBOHYDRATE 36.3 G • FAT 6.5 G • CHOLESTEROL 114 MG • SODIUM 567 MG • 22% CALORIES FROM FAT • VERY GOOD SOURCE OF CALCIUM • GOOD SOURCE OF FOLACIN, IRON, ZINC

STRATA AND SAVORY BREAD PUDDING BASICS

The difference between a strata and a savory bread pudding is that a strata involves layering milk-soaked bread with a filling, while for bread pudding, you chuck everything into a baking dish at once. Make strata when you have sliced bread, and pudding when you have chunks.

• Use day-old bread and, if you have time, let it sit uncovered for several hours before making the strata. Trim away the crusts before you soak the bread in the eggs and milk.

• Don't use pita bread. You need bread with volume to get the right texture, and pita is too thin. Also, you'll need yeast breads—quick breads like muffins won't do the trick.

• Distribute the ingredients as evenly as possible, beating the filling thoroughly with the eggs and milk and pouring the mixture evenly over the bread.

• Soak the bread thoroughly with the milk mixture, or portions of your bread pudding will be dry.

Make It Your Own

Once you've got the basic formula down, you may find that you never make the same strata or bread pudding twice, using whatever happens to be on hand or on the verge of languishing in the refrigerator.

WHAT TO ADD AND WHEN TO ADD IT

Breads. Try different types of bread, such as challah (egg bread), dark rye, and multigrain as well as standards like French or Italian. Slice them at least a half inch thick for strata; tear them into fat chunks—about two inches thick —for puddings.

✐ *Cheese.* Change the cheese, and you'll change the flavor. Lower-fat cheeses don't work very well because they don't melt sufficiently to blend in with the other ingredients. If you're concerned about fat, instead of using a skim cheese, use a small amount—between 2 tablespoons and ¼ cup finely grated—of strong-flavored full-fat cheese, such as Parmesan or sharp cheddar. Distribute it thoroughly. Good combinations include cheddar, broccoli, and French bread; Swiss or Gruyère cheese, chopped spinach, and whole wheat bread; Roasted Fresh Tomatoes (see page 218) and hearty white bread; and Parmesan, Havarti, sautéed mushrooms, and rye bread.

✐ *Fillings.* Use about 2 cups leftover Ratatouille (see page 343); thick pasta sauce, such as Tomato and Mushroom Ragout (see page 285); or any of the fillings for savory pies (see pages 433 to 436). If you don't have any leftovers, use prepared ingredients, such as chopped drypacked sun-dried tomatoes (about 1 cup loosely packed), pitted oil-cured olives (about ½ cup), marinated artichoke hearts (about 1 cup loosely packed). Or roast, peel, and slice a variety of bell peppers (see page 534), and add roughly 2 cups to the dish.

•

BASIC FRENCH TOAST SANDWICH

Serves 1

TOTAL TIME: ABOUT 15 MINUTES
TIME TO PREPARE: ABOUT 3 MINUTES
COOKING TIME: 10 MINUTES

Here's the same basic strata and pudding idea, adapted for individual servings in sandwich form. Use any vegetable and cheese combinations you'd like (hints: mushrooms, spinach, cheddar, eggplant, tomato, and fontina).

½ egg (beat 1 egg and pour off half of it)
¼ cup nonfat milk
2 slices day-old bread
Filling, such as about ⅔ cup loosely packed sliced tomatoes and red or Vidalia onions; four ½-inch slices baked eggplant (see page 528); ⅔ cup steamed vegetables; ⅔ cup sautéed mushrooms; four ½-inch slices firm tofu; 1 cup chopped fresh spinach
2 tablespoons grated cheese

Beat together the egg and the milk in a pie plate or wide bowl. Dip the bread slices into the mixture, turning them over to soak both sides. Handle the soaked slices carefully, so they don't tear.

Heat a small nonstick griddle or skillet over medium heat. (If you're not thoroughly confident that nothing will stick to the surface, grease it lightly with olive oil or squirt it with nonstick spray.)

Meanwhile, place the filling and cheese evenly on one slice of bread. Cover it with the other piece of bread to make a sandwich.

Cook on the griddle or in the skillet until golden brown underneath, about 6 minutes. Turn gently with a spatula and brown the other side, about 4 minutes. Serve immediately.

PER SERVING: CALORIES 300 • PROTEIN 14.6 G • CARBOHYDRATE 36.6 G • FAT 9.7 G • CHOLESTEROL 124.7 MG • SODIUM 476.7 MG • 30% CALORIES FROM FAT • GOOD SOURCE OF CALCIUM

•

BASIC BRUSCHETTA
Garlic Bread
Serves 8

TOTAL TIME: 8 MINUTES
TIME TO PREPARE: ABOUT 3 MINUTES
COOKING TIME: 5 MINUTES

W*hen you make it yourself, you can restore to garlic bread the good name that's been sullied by the greasy, over-seasoned stuff commonly sold in supermarkets. Serve it as an appetizer, along with crostini, if you'd like (see page 262), or beside a big bowl of soup.*

1 baguette
1 garlic clove, halved lengthwise
2 tablespoons extra virgin olive oil
Ripe tomatoes or cherry tomatoes, chopped, for garnish (optional)
Minced fresh basil, for garnish (optional)

Heat the oven to 300°F.

Slice the baguette into pieces about 1 inch thick. Place the slices in a single layer on a baking sheet. Put them in the oven until golden brown, about 3 minutes. Turn the slices over and brown the other side, about 2 minutes. Watch closely to make sure the bread doesn't burn.

Rub each piece of bread well with the garlic. Drizzle the slices with extra virgin olive oil, being careful not to douse them. You may find you'll have better control if you pour some oil onto a teaspoon, then drizzle it over the bread from the spoon.

Distribute the tomatoes, if using, on top, and/or sprinkle with minced basil, if you'd like. Serve right away.

PER SERVING: CALORIES 197 • PROTEIN 5.1 G • CARBOHYDRATE 37.2 G • FAT 2.7 G • CHOLESTEROL 0 MG • SODIUM 401 MG • 13% CALORIES FROM FAT

G R I L L I N G

Ever feel that the more things change, the more you wish they'd stayed the way they were before? I feel that way about grilling, which for a number of reasons—primarily too many chefs with too much mesquite—has become pointlessly complicated. It's time to "take back the barbecue!" and make grilling easy once again.

Here, in 10 simple steps, is as much as you *need* to know and do to have fun (and good food) with your grill.

GUIDE TO GRILLING • A–Z,

1, 2, 3 GUIDE TO GRILLING FRESH

VEGETABLES • GRILLING MENUS

• MARINADES • GRILLED MAIN

DISHES • GRILLED SIDE DISHES

Guide to Grilling

STEP 1: CHOOSE A GRILL

Most large hardware stores offer an adequate selection. Your first option will be gas or charcoal. Gas grills are convenient, and if you've had problems with guests nibbling on the lawn furniture while waiting for your coals to light, you might consider one. Many places that sell grilling supplies carry special wood chips to place near the heat source on gas grills, so you won't have to sacrifice the taste of charcoal for the convenience of gas.

Next, how many people will you be feeding? If you'll be cooking for only two or three, a round or rectangular portable grill may be adequate. Look into larger kettle-shaped grills if you'll be cooking for more. A cover is optional. Many cooks prefer not to use one, since covers can trap the flavor of foods, transferring the taste of last week's meal to the one you're making tonight. If a dish must be covered during grilling, you can use aluminum foil instead.

Last, don't buy a grill because it's cute. "Cute" is short for "cleaning this grill will drive you insane." Instead, make sure:
a. It's sturdy and the surfaces are wide and smooth enough to wipe easily.
b. It has vents on the sides to give you some control over the temperature of the coals.
c. It has an adjustable cooking surface that allows you to move food closer to or further from the coals as necessary.

STEP 2: CHOOSE A FUEL

Mesquite charcoal gives a rich char-cooked flavor to foods. Unfortunately, pure mesquite costs a bundle and takes wizardry to light. However, several popular brands of briquettes combine mesquite with less expensive charcoal, for an affordable, ignitable fuel.

When you buy charcoal, also pick up a package of solid fire starters. These safe, nontoxic alternatives to lighter fluid look like cork and come in cubes, bricks, or golfball-sized balls. Instructions for use vary, so be sure to read them before you begin.

STEP 3: BLANCH AND MARINATE THE VEGETABLES

Many vegetables absorb optimum flavor when they've been blanched and then marinated for several hours. Also, when they're blanched, some vegetables cook more quickly and evenly than when you grill them raw.

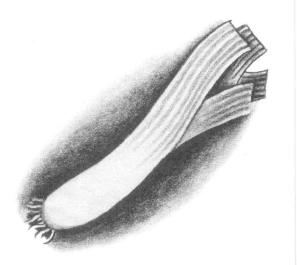

Whether you marinate (let your vegetables soak in a dressing or marinade) or baste (brush them with the marinade just before and/or during grilling) depends on the type of vegetable, how much flavor you want it to absorb, and what texture you want in the end. The more time a vegetable spends in the marinade, the more flavor it will soak in, and the more tender it will become. Basted, vegetables take on a hint of flavor and tend to stay crisp.

STEP 4: LIGHT THE FIRE
If you are cooking with charcoal, this can be the most challenging part of the process.

First, check to see that you've placed your grill away from hanging branches, sporadic drafts, and curious toddlers. And make sure that it's standing square and stable. Then:

a. Spread the charcoal in a single layer at the bottom of your grill. Pour half again as much charcoal on top and spread that out.
b. Gather all of the charcoal into a pile in the center of the grill. (Why did you spread it out in the first place instead of starting with a pile? To make sure it wouldn't be more than 1½ layers thick for cooking.) Scatter chunks of the solid fire starter among the coals, and light them following package instructions.
c. As soon as the coals are blazing, use a poker to spread them back into a layer. Now wait for the flames to subside and a white ash to form over the coals, usually about twenty minutes.

STEP 5: SOAK THE WOODEN SKEWERS
If you're going to be making vegetable kabobs, use wooden rather than metal skewers because metal heats up and cooks the vegetables from the inside. You'll have to soak the wooden skewers in water for thirty minutes in advance so they won't catch fire. Don't marinate the vegetables on the skewers; thread them on the soaked skewers just before grilling.

STEP 6: PREPARE THE BASTING MARINADES
Do this now unless your recipe calls for marinating for more than 1 hour.

STEP 7: TEST THE HEAT AFTER THE FLAMES HAVE SUBSIDED
Most vegetables will cook best on high heat. To determine whether your grill is hot enough, hold your hand over the coals at the level where you'll put the food. If you can hold it there for only three or four seconds, your fire is ready.

HOW TO BLANCH VEGETABLES FOR GRILLING

1. Fill a large pot with enough water to cover the vegetables you plan to blanch. Bring it to a rolling boil over medium-high heat. Meanwhile, put some ice cubes in a large bowl and add enough cold water to cover the vegetables.

2. When the water has reached a boil, add the vegetables and cook just long enough to soften them. (Time will vary depending on the type of vegetable and the size of the pieces. For example, it may take thirty seconds for slender asparagus and two minutes for broccoli.)

3. Remove the vegetables with tongs or a slotted spoon, and plunge them into the cold water. (The cold water keeps the vegetables from overcooking.) Lift them out of the cold water and let them drain on paper towels. Marinate or baste according to your recipe before grilling.

STEP 8: PREPARE THE GRILLING SURFACE

Use a surface with fine mesh, or you'll lose a lot of food through the cracks (see mail-order information, for suppliers). Before you place the food on the surface, squirt it with nonstick spray or brush it with olive oil or canola oil.

STEP 9: ARRANGE THE VEGETABLES ON THE GRILL ACCORDING TO TYPE

Vegetables cook at varying rates, depending on how thick or dense they are to begin with and how you've cut them. They'll cook fairly evenly if you cut each type of vegetable to a uniform size and grill all of the eggplant, for example, together on the same area of the grill, and all of the mushrooms together in another, removing each type as it's done.

What about kabobs? Although they look lovely threaded with a variety of vegetables, they don't cook all that well that way. If you want to serve skewers with mixed vegetables, fake it:

a. Thread each skewer with a single kind of vegetable (all green pepper, all shiitake mushrooms, and so on).

b. Grill until each is done, remove, and cover with foil to keep warm while waiting for the rest to cook.

c. When all of the vegetables are done, rethread the skewers, alternating the peppers, mushrooms, eggplant, tomatoes, and so on, as you'd like.

STEP 10: MAKE SURE YOUR FIRE IS COMPLETELY OUT

Before you call it a night. A single flying ember could be calamitous.

A—Z, 1, 2, 3 Guide to Grilling Fresh Vegetables

Where I'm coming from: I'm not much for baking, stir-frying, or steaming on the grill. It's never any easier than using the oven or stovetop, and I don't think the results are worth it. The grill is best at what it simply does and does simply.

Again, many vegetables must be blanched before grilling, or they'll take forever to cook. If you're going to be marinating the vegetables, light your coals toward the end of the marinating time. If you'll be basting, you can prepare the marinade while the coals are heating.

ARTICHOKES HEARTS

1. Fill a large pot with enough water to cover the artichokes. Bring to a boil over medium-high heat and add the juice of one lemon.

2. Add the artichokes, reduce the heat to medium-low, cover, and simmer until the leaves pull away easily, about fifteen to twenty minutes, depending on their size. Be careful not to overdo it, or they'll be too mushy to grill. Remove the artichokes with a slotted spoon, and drain them on paper towels.

3. When they're cool enough to handle, pull off the leaves, throwing out the tough ones and saving the tender ones for a snack. Scoop out and discard the fuzz in the center. Marinate up to eight hours, or brush with basting marinade before grilling over high heat.

Whole Baby Artichokes: Pull away the tough outer leaves, and snip off the sharp tips of the remaining leaves with kitchen shears. Plunge them into boiling water until you can just pierce them with a knife, about eight minutes, depending on their size. Marinate and grill as directed for artichoke hearts.

ASPARAGUS

1. Choose asparagus spears of equal size so they'll cook at the same rate.

2. Blanch, following the directions in "How to Blanch Vegetables for Grilling" (see page 448), until bright green, about two minutes.

3. Marinate up to three hours, or simply baste with marinade before grilling the asparagus over high heat until cooked through, about 3 minutes.

BEETS

1. Scrub the beets well, then boil them in their skin in water to cover until you can just pierce them with a paring knife, twenty to forty minutes, depending on their size.
2. Remove the beets with a slotted spoon, and drain them in a colander lined with paper towels.
3. When they're cool enough to handle, peel and slice them ¼ inch thick, and marinate them up to eight hours, or simply baste them with marinade before grilling them on high heat until tender, about eight minutes.

BELL PEPPERS

Grilled bell peppers taste so good as they are, you don't have to marinate or baste them.

1. Slice the peppers in half lengthwise and remove the core and seeds.

2. Place them skin side down on the grill over high heat. When the skin has buckled and charred, about ten to fifteen minutes, remove them from the grill.
3. Let them cool (place them in a paper bag and toss it into the freezer for five minutes to speed the process), then peel and slice them.

BROCCOLI AND CAULIFLOWER

1. Cut the vegetables into pieces of the same size, so they'll cook evenly.
2. Blanch them according to the directions in "How to Blanch Vegetables for Grilling" (see page 448), until the broccoli is bright green, about five minutes.
3. Marinate the broccoli and cauliflower up to three hours, or simply baste them with marinade before grilling them over high heat until tender, three to four minutes.

CARROTS

1. Peel, then cut the carrots into pieces of the same size so they'll cook evenly.
2. Blanch the carrots according to the directions in "How to Blanch Vegetables for Grilling" (see page 448), until just soft, about four to eight minutes, depending on their size.
3. Marinate the carrots up to eight hours, or baste them with marinade before grilling them over high heat until tender, about eight minutes.

CHERRY TOMATOES

1. Thread the tomatoes onto skewers and brush them with marinade.

2. Sprinkle the tomatoes with fresh herbs if you'd like, such as basil, oregano, rosemary, cilantro, or mint.

3. Grill the tomatoes over medium-high heat until they're soft and lightly charred, about four to six minutes, turning them often to prevent burning.

CORN ON THE COB

1. Strip the husk down without removing it altogether, leaving it attached at the base of the cob.

2. Spread the corn with unsalted butter, corn oil, and/or fresh herbs, such as oregano, basil, or cilantro. Salt it to taste. Replace the husk, then wrap the corn loosely in a single layer of foil.

3. Grill the corn over high heat for twenty to thirty minutes, turning it often to cook it evenly.

EGGPLANT

1. Cut off the root and stem ends of the eggplants. Without peeling it, slice it into ¼-inch-thick rounds.

2. Brush the eggplant with marinade and grill it over high heat, brushing it frequently, until it's lightly browned, about eight minutes.

3. Turn the eggplant and brown the other side, about eight minutes more.

Marinated Eggplant: You can also marinate the eggplant slices, and grill them in the same way, brushing on the leftover marinade as you grill.

GARLIC

1. Wrap at least six unpeeled garlic cloves in a single piece of foil. You can wrap a whole head if you'd like.

2. Place the garlic cloves over high heat, turning them often until the garlic is soft, about ten minutes.

3. Remove the garlic from the grill, and unwrap the foil to cool. When the garlic is cool enough to handle, remove the peel and serve it as a spread for grilled bread or puree it for use in salad dressings or with other grilled vegetables on sandwiches, in ratatouille, and so on.

LEEKS

1. Use only the white part and about two inches of the greens. Trim off the root and peel off the tough outer layer.

2. Blanch the leeks according to the directions in "How to Blanch Vegetables for Grilling" (see page 448), until the layers are just pliable enough to separate, but not mushy, about three minutes. When the leeks are cool enough to handle, separate the layers.

3. Marinate the leeks up to three hours, or simply baste them with marinade before

grilling them over high heat until very tender, eight to ten minutes.

MUSHROOMS

1. If you're using large firm mushrooms such as portobello or cremini, slice them according to what texture you want and how long you're willing to wait; the thinner they are the more quickly they'll cook. I like mine thick, so I'll wait the extra few minutes for them to grill.

2. Marinate the mushrooms, without blanching, for three to eight hours. Give thick, meaty mushrooms, such as portobello, more time.

3. Grill the mushrooms over high heat until they're soft, five to ten minutes, depending on their size and type.

ONIONS

1. Peel the onions and blanch them according to the directions in "How to Blanch Vegetables for Grilling" (see page 448), until the layers are just pliable enough to separate, but not mushy, about twenty minutes. When the onions are cool enough to handle, separate the layers into rings. Don't worry about tearing them.

2. Marinate the rings up to three hours, or simply baste them with marinade before grilling.

3. Grill the onions over high heat until they're lightly browned, about seven to ten minutes, turning them halfway through.

POTATOES

1. Choose small boiling potatoes or cut larger boiling potatoes into quarters. Don't peel them unless they really prefer your potatoes without the skin.

2. In a large saucepan, bring enough water to cover the potatoes to a boil. Add the potatoes and boil them until you can just pierce them with a knife, five to seven minutes, depending on their size.

3. Marinate the potatoes up to eight hours, or simply baste them with marinade before grilling them over high heat until browned, about eight minutes, turning them halfway through.

RUTABAGA

1. Peel and cut the rutabagas into 1-inch chunks.

2. In a large saucepan, bring enough water to cover the rutabagas to a boil. Add the rutabagas and boil them until you can just pierce them with a knife, seven to ten minutes.

3. Marinate the rutabagas up to eight

hours, or simply baste them with marinade before grilling them over high heat until browned, about eight minutes, turning them halfway through.

SNOW PEAS OR SUGAR SNAP PEAS

1. Choose only bright green, crisp peas. Only the freshest peas can hold up to grilling.
2. Marinate the peas, without blanching them, up to three hours.
3. If you're grilling a variety of vegetables, save these for last, grilling over medium or low heat for less than a minute.

SWEET POTATOES

1. Cut off the potatoes' tapered ends. Scrub the potatoes and cut them into 1-inch chunks or into ½-inch-thick rounds.
2. In a large saucepan, bring enough water to cover the potatoes to a boil. Add the potatoes and boil them until you can just pierce them with a knife, about five minutes, depending on their size.
3. Marinate the sweet potatoes up to eight hours, or simply baste them with marinade before grilling them over high heat until browned, about eight minutes, turning them halfway through.

SUMMER SQUASH

See "Zucchini," below.

TOFU OR TEMPEH

1. Use only extra-firm tofu. Anything softer will fall through the cracks.
2. Marinate the tofu or tempeh up to eight hours. The longer you marinate tofu, the more flavor it will absorb.
3. Grill the tofu or tempeh over high heat, turning it every five minutes and basting it with marinade, until the marinade has thoroughly permeated the tofu, about twenty minutes.

TURNIPS

1. Cut off the root and stem ends. Peel the turnips and cut them into 1-inch chunks.
2. In a large saucepan, bring enough water to cover the turnips to a boil. Add the turnips and boil them until you can just pierce them with a knife, about five minutes.
3. Marinate the turnips up to eight hours, or simply baste them with marinade before grilling them over high heat until they're browned, about eight minutes, turning them halfway through.

ZUCCHINI

1. Cut the zucchini into rounds about ½ inch thick. Try to make each round the same size, so all will cook evenly.
2. Blanch the zucchini according to the directions in "How to Blanch Vegetables for Grilling" (see page 448), until just pliant, about two minutes.
3. Marinate the zucchini up to three hours, or simply baste it with marinade before grilling it over high heat for about three minutes on each side.

•

Grilling Menus

Cold Apricot Soup (*page 206*)
Grilled Vegetable Pockets (*page 462*)

Cold Curried Peach Soup (*page 208*)
Tofu and Mushrooms
with Peanut Sauce (*page 457*)

Grilled Black Bean Patties (*page 461*)
Plum Salsa (*page 159*)
Grilled Corn and Pepper Salad
with Tomatoes (*page 465*)

Cantaloupe Soup (*page 207*)
Grilled Fresh Corn and Chickpea Patties
(*page 460*)
Rosemary New Potatoes (*page 464*)
Basic Bruschetta (*page 443*)

Fresh Tomato Soup
with Cilantro Pistou (*page 178*)
Grilled Fajitas (*page 459*)

Cool and Spicy Eggplant Salad with
Roasted Garlic, Ginger, and Mint (*page 135*)
Grilled Pepper and
Provolone Sandwich (*page 463*)

Marinades

YOGURT MARINADE FOR BASTING OR MARINATING

Serves 4; Makes about 1 cup, enough for
1 to 1½ pounds prepared vegetables

TOTAL TIME: FEWER THAN 5 MINUTES, NOT INCLUDING
  TIME TO PREPARE THE VEGETABLES
TIME TO PREPARE: FEWER THAN 5 MINUTES
COOKING TIME: NONE
REFRIGERATION/FREEZING: REFRIGERATE UP TO 3 DAYS. DO
  NOT FREEZE.

A lightly curried marinade for (especially) cherry tomatoes, eggplants, mushrooms, potatoes, sweet potatoes, and tofu or tempeh.

2 garlic cloves, grated
One 2-inch piece fresh ginger, peeled and grated
2 tablespoons fresh lemon juice
¼ cup minced fresh cilantro
1 tablespoon curry powder
2 teaspoons ground cumin
1 cup plain nonfat yogurt
1 to 1½ pounds prepared vegetables (see pages
    449 to 453)

In a medium mixing bowl, whisk together the garlic, ginger, lemon juice, cilantro, curry powder, cumin, and yogurt.

For marinating, place the mixture in a large glass bowl and add the vegetables.

For basting, brush the marinade directly onto the vegetables before and during grilling.

PER SERVING: CALORIES 55 • PROTEIN 4 G • CARBOHYDRATE 9 G • FAT 0 G •
CHOLESTEROL 1.02 MG • SODIUM 48.2 MG • 10% CALORIES FROM FAT • GOOD
SOURCE OF CALCIUM

MEDITERRANEAN MARINADE FOR BASTING OR MARINATING

Serves 8; Makes about ¾ cup, enough for
2 pounds prepared vegetables

TOTAL TIME: ABOUT 5 MINUTES, NOT INCLUDING TIME TO
PREPARE THE VEGETABLES
TIME TO PREPARE: ABOUT 5 MINUTES
COOKING TIME: NONE
REFRIGERATION/FREEZING: REFRIGERATE UP TO 5 DAYS. DO
NOT FREEZE.

A wonderful aromatic seasoning for artichoke hearts, asparagus, broccoli, cherry tomatoes, eggplant, leeks, mushrooms, onions, tofu, and zucchini.

½ cup extra virgin olive oil

¼ cup white wine vinegar or balsamic vinegar

¼ cup minced onions

1 garlic clove, crushed

1 tablespoon crumbled dried oregano

Salt and freshly ground black pepper to taste

2 pounds prepared vegetables (see pages 449
    to 453)

In a medium mixing bowl, whisk together the olive oil, vinegar, onions, garlic, oregano, and salt and pepper.

For marinating, place the mixture in a large glass bowl and add the vegetables.

For basting, brush the marinade directly onto the vegetables before and during grilling.

PER SERVING: CALORIES 123 • PROTEIN 0 G • CARBOHYDRATE 0 G • FAT 13.6 G •
CHOLESTEROL 0 MG • SODIUM 0 MG • 97% CALORIES FROM FAT

•

ASIAN-STYLE MARINADE FOR BASTING OR MARINATING

Serves 4; Makes about 1 cup, enough for
2 to 2½ pounds prepared vegetables

TOTAL TIME: ABOUT 5 MINUTES, NOT INCLUDING TIME TO
PREPARE THE VEGETABLES
TIME TO PREPARE: ABOUT 5 MINUTES
COOKING TIME: NONE
REFRIGERATION/FREEZING: REFRIGERATE UP TO 5 DAYS. DO
NOT FREEZE.

Sweet and tangy, this marinade is made for asparagus, beets, broccoli, carrots, mushrooms, onions, and tofu.

½ cup rice vinegar

1 tablespoon light sesame oil

¼ cup honey

1 garlic clove, crushed

One 2-inch piece fresh ginger, peeled and grated

¼ cup pineapple juice

2 to 2½ pounds prepared vegetables (see pages
    449 to 453)

In a medium mixing bowl, whisk together the rice vinegar, sesame oil, honey, garlic, ginger, and pineapple juice.

For marinating, place the mixture in a large glass bowl and add the vegetables.

For basting, brush the marinade directly onto the vegetables before and during grilling.

PER SERVING: CALORIES 105 • PROTEIN 0 G • CARBOHYDRATE 20 G • FAT 3.4 G •
CHOLESTEROL 0 MG • SODIUM 1.3 MG • 28% CALORIES FROM FAT

•

GINGER MARINADE
FOR BASTING

Serves 4; Makes about ⅔ cup, enough for
2 pounds prepared vegetables

TOTAL TIME: ABOUT 5 MINUTES, NOT INCLUDING TIME TO
    PREPARE THE VEGETABLES
TIME TO PREPARE: ABOUT 5 MINUTES
COOKING TIME: NONE
DO AHEAD: THIS MARINADE CAN BE MADE UP TO 4 DAYS IN
    ADVANCE. REFRIGERATE UNTIL READY TO USE.
REFRIGERATION/FREEZING: REFRIGERATE UP TO 3 DAYS. DO
    NOT FREEZE.

Try this Eastern-influenced marinade with
assorted vegetables, such as asparagus,
broccoli, carrots, and mushrooms. Serve the
works over tofu and steamed rice.

4 scallions, including greens, sliced

3 garlic cloves, minced

2 tablespoons grated peeled fresh ginger

6 tablespoons soy sauce

2 tablespoons honey

2 tablespoons balsamic vinegar

2 pounds prepared vegetables (see pages 449 to
    453)

Combine the scallions, garlic, ginger, soy
sauce, honey, and balsamic vinegar in a large
shallow bowl or baking dish. Baste the vegetables with the marinade before and during
grilling.

PER SERVING: CALORIES 58 • PROTEIN 2.9 G • CARBOHYDRATE 13 G • FAT 1 G •
CHOLESTEROL 0 MG • SODIUM 1219 MG • 1% CALORIES FROM FAT • GOOD SOURCE
OF VITAMIN C

•

Grilled Main Dishes

GRILLED TOFU IN
MIDEAST MARINADE

Serves 4

TOTAL TIME: ABOUT 3 HOURS, 15 MINUTES, TO 12 HOURS,
    15 MINUTES, INCLUDING TIME TO MARINATE
TIME TO PREPARE: ABOUT 5 MINUTES
COOKING TIME: ABOUT 10 MINUTES
EQUIPMENT: CHARCOAL, GAS, OR STOVETOP GRILL
DO AHEAD: YOU CAN MAKE THE MARINADE UP TO 3 DAYS
    IN ADVANCE. YOU CAN MARINATE THE TOFU OVERNIGHT.
    REFRIGERATE BOTH UNTIL READY TO GRILL.

Serve this tangy main course with Lavosh (see
page 412) and Cucumber Raita (see page
156). If you can't find extra-firm tofu, press
firm tofu according to the directions on page 589.

4 scallions, white part and 1 inch of greens,
    chopped

1 small white onion, chopped

1 garlic clove, minced

2 tablespoons minced fresh parsley

2 tablespoons minced fresh cilantro

1 tablespoon crumbled dried oregano

¼ cup fresh lemon juice

2 teaspoons grated lemon zest

½ teaspoon salt

Freshly ground black pepper to taste

⅔ cup plain nonfat yogurt

1 pound extra-firm tofu, sliced into ⅓-inch-thick
    strips

In a shallow baking dish, combine the scallions, onion, garlic, parsley, cilantro, oregano,
lemon juice, lemon zest, salt, pepper, and
yogurt. Mix well. Add the tofu and turn it over
to coat both sides with the marinade. Cover

the dish with plastic wrap and refrigerate for at least 3 hours, and as many as 12, turning the tofu over at least once during that time.

Heat a charcoal, gas, or stovetop grill. Drain the tofu, reserving the marinade. Cook the tofu on high heat until it's lightly browned underneath, about 5 minutes. Drizzle with the reserved marinade, turn the pieces over, and grill until the other sides are browned, too, about 5 minutes.

PER SERVING: CALORIES 223 • PROTEIN 21.3 G • CARBOHYDRATE 16.5 G • FAT 10.3 G • CHOLESTEROL 0 MG • SODIUM 319 MG • 38% CALORIES FROM FAT • OUT-STANDING SOURCE OF VITAMIN C • VERY GOOD SOURCE OF CALCIUM • GOOD SOURCE OF VITAMINS B₁, B₂, B₆; FOLACIN, ZINC

•

TOFU AND MUSHROOMS WITH PEANUT SAUCE

Serves 4

TOTAL TIME: ABOUT 1 HOUR 20 MINUTES, INCLUDING TIME TO MARINATE
TIME TO PREPARE: ABOUT 10 MINUTES
COOKING TIME: ABOUT 10 MINUTES
EQUIPMENT: CHARCOAL, GAS, OR STOVETOP GRILL AND WOODEN SKEWERS
DO AHEAD: YOU CAN MAKE THE PEANUT SAUCE UP TO 5 DAYS IN ADVANCE. YOU CAN MARINATE THE TOFU OVERNIGHT. REFRIGERATE BOTH UNTIL READY TO USE.

L*ike many dishes made with peanut sauce, this one can be habit forming. Use your favorite brand of peanut butter, since the flavor will come through in the end. For extra crunch, sprinkle some chopped peanuts onto each serving.*

Sauce
½ cup unsalted, unsweetened crunchy peanut butter

1 cup warm water
1 tablespoon low-sodium soy sauce
2 tablespoons brown sugar
1 garlic clove, grated
One 2-inch piece fresh ginger, peeled and grated
Generous pinch red pepper flakes
1 large onion, coarsely chopped

1 pound extra-firm tofu
2 cups quartered mushrooms, such as cremini, shiitake, oyster, white button
1 red bell pepper, cored, seeded, and cut into 1-inch chunks

For the Sauce
Combine the peanut butter, water, soy sauce, brown sugar, garlic, ginger, and pepper flakes.

Add the onion, and refrigerate for 1 hour, stirring occasionally. Meanwhile, soak eight wooden skewers in water to cover for at least 30 minutes.

Heat a charcoal, gas, or stovetop grill. Thread the tofu, mushrooms, and bell pepper on the skewers, alternating tofu, pepper, mushroom, so the flavors will meld as they cook.

Brush the skewered vegetables with the peanut sauce.

Grill over high heat, turning the skewers and basting often with the sauce, until the mushrooms are cooked through and the tofu is lightly charred, about 10 minutes.

PER SERVING: CALORIES 280 • PROTEIN 19.4 G • CARBOHYDRATE 17.8 G • FAT 17.6 G • CHOLESTEROL 0 MG • SODIUM 152 MG • 52% CALORIES FROM FAT • OUT-STANDING SOURCE OF IRON • VERY GOOD SOURCE OF VITAMINS B₁, B₂, B₃ • GOOD SOURCE OF VITAMIN B₆; FOLACIN, CALCIUM, ZINC

•

SESAME GRILLED TOFU AND MUSHROOMS

Serves 4

TOTAL TIME: 1 HOUR, 15 MINUTES, INCLUDING TIME TO MARINATE

TIME TO PREPARE: 5 MINUTES

COOKING TIME: 10 MINUTES

EQUIPMENT: CHARCOAL, GAS, OR STOVETOP GRILL AND WOODEN SKEWERS

DO AHEAD: YOU CAN MAKE THE MARINADE UP TO 3 DAYS IN ADVANCE. YOU CAN MARINATE THE INGREDIENTS OVERNIGHT. REFRIGERATE BOTH UNTIL READY TO USE.

L*et the vegetables marinate as long as you can —the more marinade the tofu absorbs, the more flavor it will give back to you.*

Marinade

½ cup hoisin sauce

¼ cup mirin (rice wine, available at Asian-specialty stores and in the Asian-specialty section of some supermarkets)

¼ cup soy sauce

2 tablespoons brown sugar

2 tablespoons ketchup

4 garlic cloves, finely grated

3 tablespoons finely grated peeled fresh ginger

1 teaspoon dark sesame oil

Generous pinch red pepper flakes

1 pound extra-firm tofu

2 cups quartered mushrooms, such as cremini, shiitake, oyster, white button

1 red bell pepper, cored, seeded, and cut into 1-inch chunks

1 Vidalia onion, quartered, then cut into bite-sized chunks

For the Marinade

Combine the hoisin sauce, mirin, soy sauce, brown sugar, ketchup, garlic, ginger, sesame oil, and pepper flakes.

To the marinade add the tofu, mushrooms, bell pepper, and onion, and refrigerate for at least 1 hour, stirring occasionally. Meanwhile, soak wooden skewers in water to cover for at least 30 minutes.

Heat a charcoal, gas, or stovetop grill. Thread the ingredients on the skewers, alternating tofu, pepper, mushroom, onion, so the flavors will meld as they cook.

Grill over high heat until the mushrooms are cooked through and the tofu is lightly charred, turning every few minutes, about 10 minutes in all.

PER SERVING: CALORIES 280 • PROTEIN 23.3 G • CARBOHYDRATE 25.9 G • FAT 11.4 G • CHOLESTEROL 0 MG • SODIUM 2303 MG • 34% CALORIES FROM FAT • OUTSTANDING SOURCE OF IRON • VERY GOOD SOURCE OF VITAMIN B₂; CALCIUM • GOOD SOURCE OF VITAMINS A, B₁, B₃, B₆; FOLACIN, ZINC

G R I L L E D   F A J I T A S

Serves 4

TOTAL TIME: ABOUT 3 HOURS, 30 MINUTES, TO 6 HOURS,
   30 MINUTES, INCLUDING TIME TO MARINATE
TIME TO PREPARE: ABOUT 10 MINUTES
COOKING TIME: ABOUT 20 MINUTES
EQUIPMENT: CHARCOAL, GAS, OR STOVETOP GRILL AND
   WOODEN SKEWERS.
DO AHEAD: YOU CAN MAKE THE MARINADE UP TO 3 DAYS
   IN ADVANCE. YOU CAN MARINATE THE TOFU OVERNIGHT.
   REFRIGERATE BOTH UNTIL READY TO USE.

*A*t first "fajitas" referred to the cut of beef that
went into a dish made in a manner similar
to this one. Shortly it came to apply to any
dish made in this style regardless of the main ingredi-
ent, which may be chicken, shrimp, mushrooms . . .
or tofu.

Marinate the tofu for several hours, so it will
have ample time to absorb the seasoning.

Marinade
Juice of 2 limes
1 garlic clove, minced
¼ cup minced fresh cilantro
2 teaspoons chili powder
1 teaspoon ground cumin
½ teaspoon cayenne pepper

1 pound extra-firm tofu, cut into 1-inch-thick
   strips
1 large red onion, quartered
1 large red bell pepper, cored, seeded, and cut
   into 1-inch-square chunks
1 large green bell pepper, cored, seeded, and cut
   into 1-inch-square chunks
12 cherry tomatoes
4 large flour tortillas or Lavosh (see page 412)
Red salsa, for garnish
Green salsa, for garnish

Nonfat or reduced-fat sour cream, for garnish
Minced fresh cilantro, for garnish

For the Marinade
Three to 6 hours before you plan to light the
fire, combine the lime juice, garlic, cilantro,
chili powder, cumin, and cayenne in a large
glass bowl. Stir well. Add the tofu, cover, and
refrigerate. Stir gently several times before
cooking.

Soak wooden skewers in water to cover for
at least 30 minutes.

Heat a charcoal, gas, or stovetop grill.
When the coals are glowing and very hot,
thread the onion quarters on one skewer, the
red pepper chunks on another, the green pepper chunks on another, and the cherry tomatoes on 2 or 3 more, depending on the length
of the skewers. Drain the tofu, reserving the
marinade. Brush the skewers lightly with the
marinade from the tofu, and grill, turning
often, until lightly charred, about 6 minutes.
Remove the skewers from the grill as the vegetables are done. Place the tofu on the grill,
cover it with the grill lid or with foil, and cook,
basting occasionally with the reserved marinade, until lightly browned, about 10 minutes.

Using tongs, place each tortilla or Lavosh
briefly on the grill and flip it, just to heat. For
each fajita, distribute an even amount of vegetables and tofu among the four tortillas. Pass
the salsas, sour cream, and cilantro.

PER SERVING: CALORIES 306 • PROTEIN 15 G • CARBOHYDRATE 45.2 G • FAT
10.5 G • CHOLESTEROL 0 MG • SODIUM 245 MG • 28% CALORIES FROM FAT • OUT-
STANDING SOURCE OF IRON • VERY GOOD SOURCE OF VITAMINS A, B₁ • GOOD
SOURCE OF VITAMINS B₂, B₃, B₆; FOLACIN, CALCIUM, ZINC

•

GRILLED FRESH CORN AND CHICKPEA PATTIES

Makes 4

TOTAL TIME: ABOUT 40 MINUTES, NOT INCLUDING TIME TO
   COOK CHICKPEAS OR MAKE THE DRESSING
TIME TO PREPARE: ABOUT 20 MINUTES, INCLUDING TIME
   TO SAUTÉ
COOKING TIME: 11 MINUTES
EQUIPMENT: CHARCOAL, GAS, OR STOVETOP GRILL
   (OPTIONAL)
DO AHEAD: YOU CAN MAKE THE BURGERS 1 OR 2 DAYS IN
   ADVANCE. REFRIGERATE UNTIL READY TO GRILL OR BROIL.
REFRIGERATION/FREEZING: REFRIGERATE UP TO 3 DAYS.
   FREEZE UP TO 6 MONTHS.

When my editor at a food magazine asked me for a piece about vegetarian barbecue dinners, she was firm on one point: no burgers. I couldn't blame her. "Veggie burgers" can be dry and bland, intended primarily as pacifiers for people moving away from meat.

These "burgers" aren't meant to mimic meat, but to make it possible to combine flavorful beans with complementary ingredients, cook them on the grill, and eat them neatly and with ease.

3 ears of corn
1 teaspoon canola or vegetable oil
1 small onion, chopped
2 cups cooked chickpeas, drained and rinsed
$\frac{1}{2}$ cup fresh bread crumbs
1 teaspoon Dijon mustard
$\frac{1}{2}$ teaspoon honey
$\frac{1}{2}$ teaspoon ground cumin
Salt and freshly ground black pepper
   to taste
4 pita pockets or burger buns
Avocado-Buttermilk Dressing (see page 120;
   optional)

Bring a large pot of water to a boil. Add the corn and let the water return to a boil. Cover the pot, turn off the heat, and leave the corn for 8 to 10 minutes. (If you're using an electric stove, take the pot off the burner.) Transfer the corn to a plate to let it cool. (Or cook the corn in the microwave according to the directions on page 526.)

Heat the oil in a small skillet over medium-high heat, swirling the pan to coat the bottom. Add the onion and sauté until it's soft, about 7 minutes.

Light your grill or heat the broiler. Scrape the kernels off the corncobs, and place them in a food processor or blender. Add the onion, chickpeas, bread crumbs, mustard, honey, and cumin, and process in short bursts until well combined but not pasty. Transfer to a mixing bowl, and using your hands to blend, season with salt and pepper. Shape into 4 patties.

Grill or broil until the patties are brown on one side, about 6 minutes. Turn and cook to brown the other side, about 5 minutes. Serve on pita bread or buns with Avocado-Buttermilk Dressing, if you'd like.

PER SERVING: CALORIES 390 • PROTEIN 14.8 G • CARBOHYDRATE 77 G • FAT 6.18 G • CHOLESTEROL 0 MG • SODIUM 159 MG • 13% CALORIES FROM FAT • OUTSTANDING SOURCE OF FOLACIN • VERY GOOD SOURCE OF VITAMINS B₁, B₃, C; IRON • GOOD SOURCE OF VITAMINS B₂, B₆; ZINC

•

GRILLED BLACK BEAN PATTIES

Makes 6

TOTAL TIME: ABOUT 45 MINUTES, NOT INCLUDING TIME TO COOK THE BEANS AND RICE OR MAKE THE SALSA AND ONIONS
TIME TO PREPARE: ABOUT 20 MINUTES, INCLUDING TIME TO SAUTÉ
COOKING TIME: ABOUT 20 MINUTES
EQUIPMENT: CHARCOAL, GAS, OR STOVETOP GRILL
DO AHEAD: YOU CAN MAKE THE BURGERS, UNCOOKED, UP TO 2 DAYS IN ADVANCE. REFRIGERATE UNTIL READY TO GRILL.
REFRIGERATION/FREEZING: REFRIGERATE UP TO 3 DAYS. FREEZE UP TO 6 MONTHS.

If you're short on time, skip the salsa and onions—just brush these patties with mustard and tuck them into pockets of pita bread, with tomatoes and sprouts, if you'd like.

2 teaspoons canola or vegetable oil

1 red onion, chopped

2 scallions, including greens, minced

2 garlic cloves, minced

1 tablespoon grated orange zest

2 teaspoons ground cumin

2 teaspoons ground coriander

¼ cup minced fresh cilantro

1 teaspoon crumbled dried oregano

2 teaspoons red wine vinegar

2 cups cooked black beans, drained and rinsed

1 cup cooked medium-grain or short-grain brown rice

6 pita pockets or burger buns

Plum Salsa (see page 158; optional), for garnish

Caramelized Vidalia Onions (see page 224; optional), for garnish

Heat the oil in a medium skillet over medium-high heat, swirling the pan to coat the bottom. Add the onion, scallions, garlic, orange zest, cumin, coriander, cilantro, and oregano. Turn the heat down to medium-low and sauté, stirring often, until the vegetables have softened, about 7 minutes. Stir in the vinegar and the beans, and continue cooking until the mixture is dry, and the beans mash easily, about 10 minutes. Remove from the heat.

Heat a charcoal, gas, or stovetop grill. Transfer the bean mixture to a small mixing bowl, and add the rice, using your hands to blend it in with the beans. Shape the mixture into 6 patties. Grill each patty over hot coals or on a stovetop grill until lightly browned on both sides, about 10 minutes altogether.

Serve in pita or buns with Plum Salsa and/or Caramelized Vidalia Onions, if you'd like.

PER SERVING: CALORIES 199 • PROTEIN 9.5 G • CARBOHYDRATE 34 G • FAT 3.5 G • CHOLESTEROL 0 MG • SODIUM 6.4 MG • 16% CALORIES FROM FAT • VERY GOOD SOURCE OF FOLACIN • GOOD SOURCE OF VITAMIN B₁; IRON

•

GRILLED VEGETABLE POCKETS

Serves 2

TOTAL TIME: ABOUT 1 HOUR, 30 MINUTES, TO 8 HOURS, 30 MINUTES, INCLUDING TIME TO MARINATE
TIME TO PREPARE: ABOUT 10 MINUTES
COOKING TIME: ABOUT 20 MINUTES
EQUIPMENT: CHARCOAL, GAS, OR STOVETOP GRILL AND WOODEN SKEWERS
DO AHEAD: YOU CAN MAKE THE MARINADE UP TO 5 DAYS IN ADVANCE. YOU CAN MAKE THE SPREAD UP TO 3 DAYS IN ADVANCE. REFRIGERATE BOTH UNTIL READY TO USE.

This recipe originally appeared in my book Grilling from the Garden. *I love it so much, I'm offering it here as well.*

⅓ cup extra virgin olive oil

2 tablespoons dry white wine

1 tablespoon minced fresh oregano, or 1½ teaspoons crumbled dried oregano

Salt and freshly ground black pepper to taste

2 stalks broccoli, cut into bite-sized pieces and blanched (see page 448)

1 large carrot, peeled, sliced into wafer-thin rounds and blanched (see page 448)

1 large red onion, blanched (see page 448)

1 slender miniature or Japanese eggplant, sliced into ¼-inch rounds

8 cherry tomatoes

1 cup loosely packed snow peas, stems and strings removed

1 small red bell pepper, cored, seeded, and cut into ½-inch-wide strips

12 fresh basil leaves

Two 8-inch pita pockets

1 recipe Sandwich Spread (recipe follows)

Alfalfa sprouts, for garnish

Up to 8 hours before you'll be cooking, combine the olive oil, wine, oregano, and salt and pepper in a large glass mixing bowl. Add the broccoli and carrot. Press lightly on the center of the onion to push out a series of rings. Add them to the marinade, along with the eggplant, cherry tomatoes, snow peas, and red pepper. Cover and refrigerate for at least an hour and up to 8 hours, stirring several times before grilling.

Soak wooden skewers in water to cover for at least 30 minutes.

Heat a charcoal, gas, or stovetop grill. Drain the vegetables, reserving the marinade. Thread the skewers, filling each with a single type of vegetable. Depending on the length of your skewers, you may need up to 4 skewers for each vegetable. Alternate the cherry tomatoes with the basil leaves.

Brush the skewers with the reserved marinade, and grill, turning often, until the vegetables are lightly charred, about 8 to 10 minutes per side. Remove the skewers from the grill as the vegetables are done, keeping them covered with foil.

Distribute the grilled vegetables evenly between the pita pockets. Drizzle with the Sandwich Spread and top with alfalfa sprouts.

Sandwich Spread

½ cup plain nonfat yogurt

1 tablespoon tahini

1 tablespoon fresh lemon juice

1 teaspoon ground cumin

1 teaspoon paprika

¼ teaspoon grated garlic

In a medium mixing bowl, whisk together the yogurt, tahini, lemon juice, cumin, paprika, and garlic.

PER SERVING: CALORIES 370 • PROTEIN 10.5 G • CARBOHYDRATE 37.5 G • FAT 21.3 G • CHOLESTEROL 0 MG • SODIUM 228 MG • 50% CALORIES FROM FAT • OUT-STANDING SOURCE OF VITAMIN A • VERY GOOD SOURCE OF VITAMINS B₁, B₆; FOLACIN, IRON • GOOD SOURCE OF VITAMINS B₂, B₃; CALCIUM, ZINC

•

GRILLED PEPPER AND PROVOLONE SANDWICH

Serves 2

TOTAL TIME: ABOUT 30 MINUTES
TIME TO PREPARE: ABOUT 10 MINUTES
COOKING TIME: ABOUT 20 MINUTES
EQUIPMENT: CHARCOAL, GAS, OR STOVETOP GRILL
DO AHEAD: YOU CAN MAKE THE MARINADE UP TO 5 DAYS
    IN ADVANCE. REFRIGERATE UNTIL READY TO USE.

S o simple and good, this sandwich will become a standard item on your summer lunch table. Serve it with any cold soup (see pages 200 to 203).

2 green bell peppers, halved lengthwise, cored, and seeded

2 red bell peppers, halved lengthwise, cored, and seeded

1 small red onion

1 tablespoon extra virgin olive oil

1 tablespoon balsamic vinegar

2 tablespoons minced fresh oregano, or 1 tablespoon crumbled dried oregano

1 small garlic clove, minced

2 Italian-style hard rolls, split, or 4 thick slices Italian-style bread

⅔ cup shredded provolone cheese

Heat the grill.

Place the peppers skin side down on the grate, and grill until the skin chars, about 5 minutes. Remove and set them aside to cool. When they're cool enough to handle, peel off the skin.

Meanwhile, blanch the onion according to the instructions on page 448. Cut it into 4 slices.

Stir together the olive oil, vinegar, oregano, and garlic, and brush the mixture onto the onion slices. Grill the onion until it's lightly browned, about 7 minutes. Place the bottoms of the rolls, or 4 slices of bread, on a large piece of foil. Distribute an even amount of peppers, onion, and cheese on each roll or bread slices. Top with the roll tops or remaining bread, and fold the foil over the sandwiches. Grill until heated through, 5 to 7 minutes.

PER SERVING: CALORIES 376 • PROTEIN 15 G • CARBOHYDRATE 50.8 G • FAT 13.1 G • CHOLESTEROL 20.2 MG • SODIUM 603 MG • 31% CALORIES FROM FAT • OUT-STANDING SOURCE OF VITAMINS A, C • VERY GOOD SOURCE OF VITAMINS B₁, B₆; CALCIUM, IRON • GOOD SOURCE OF VITAMINS B₂, B₃; FOLACIN, ZINC

Grilled Side Dishes

GRILLED RATATOUILLE

Serves 4

TOTAL TIME: ABOUT 1 HOUR, 30 MINUTES, TO 8 HOURS,
   30 MINUTES, INCLUDING TIME TO MARINATE
TIME TO PREPARE: ABOUT 10 MINUTES
COOKING TIME: ABOUT 20 MINUTES
EQUIPMENT: CHARCOAL, GAS, OR STOVETOP GRILL AND
   WOODEN SKEWERS
DO AHEAD: YOU CAN MAKE THE MARINADE UP TO 5 DAYS
   IN ADVANCE. YOU CAN MARINATE THE VEGETABLES
   OVERNIGHT. REFRIGERATE BOTH UNTIL READY TO USE.
REFRIGERATION: REFRIGERATE UP TO 3 DAYS.

Strictly speaking, "Grilled Ratatouille" is non-sense, meaning "grilled stew." Speaking sub-jectively, it is delicious—the ingredients of the Mediterranean stew (see page 343) prepared over coals.

1 large eggplant, quartered and sliced ¼ inch
   thick
12 cherry tomatoes
2 large zucchini, blanched (see page 448) and
   sliced 1 inch thick
2 onions, blanched (see page 448) and quartered
6 garlic cloves, unpeeled
1 large red bell pepper, cored, seeded, and sliced
1 large yellow or orange bell pepper, cored,
   seeded, and sliced
1 recipe Mediterranean Marinade (see page 455)
12 whole fresh basil leaves

Marinate the eggplant, tomatoes, zucchini, onions, garlic, and bell peppers in the marinade, covered and refrigerated, for 30 minutes up to 8 hours. Soak about 12 wooden skewers in water to cover at least 30 minutes.

Heat a charcoal, gas, or stovetop grill. Drain the vegetables, reserving the marinade. Thread the skewers, filling each with a single type of vegetable, taking care not to pack them too tightly. Alternate the cherry tomatoes with the basil leaves.

Brush the skewered vegetables with the reserved marinade, and grill, turning often, until the vegetables are lightly charred, about 8 to 10 minutes per side. Remove the skewers from the grill as the vegetables are done, keeping them covered with foil. When all of the vegetables are done, mix them well in a large bowl and serve warm.

PER SERVING: CALORIES 235 • PROTEIN 3.4 G • CARBOHYDRATE 17.2 G • FAT 18.6 G • CHOLESTEROL 0 MG • SODIUM 12 MG • 67% CALORIES FROM FAT • OUTSTANDING SOURCE OF VITAMIN C • VERY GOOD SOURCE OF VITAMIN A • GOOD SOURCE OF VITAMINS B1, B6; CALCIUM, IRON

•

ROSEMARY NEW POTATOES

Serves 4

TOTAL TIME: ABOUT 25 MINUTES, INCLUDING TIME TO
   BLANCH
TIME TO PREPARE: ABOUT 10 MINUTES
COOKING TIME: ABOUT 12 MINUTES
EQUIPMENT: CHARCOAL, GAS, OR STOVETOP GRILL AND
   WOODEN SKEWERS
DO AHEAD: YOU CAN MAKE THE MARINADE UP TO 5 DAYS
   IN ADVANCE. YOU CAN BLANCH THE POTATOES UP TO 2
   DAYS IN ADVANCE. REFRIGERATE BOTH UNTIL READY TO
   USE.

In the Middle Ages, when herbs were a kind of code, rosemary stood for both love and remembrance. Here's proof the code is still current; rosemary makes for memorable potatoes that you will love.

¼ cup extra virgin olive oil

2 tablespoons minced fresh rosemary

1 teaspoon coarse salt

1 pound tiny new potatoes, scrubbed and
   blanched (see page 448)

In a mixing bowl, combine the olive oil, rosemary, and salt.

Soak about 6 wooden skewers in water to cover for at least 30 minutes.

Heat a charcoal, gas, or stovetop grill. Thread the potatoes on the skewers and brush them with the olive oil mixture. Grill until the potatoes are crispy brown, about 12 minutes, turning them halfway through. Serve right away.

PER SERVING: CALORIES 199 • PROTEIN 4.3 G • CARBOHYDRATE 26.2 G • FAT 9.2 G • CHOLESTEROL 0 MG • SODIUM 377 MG • 40% CALORIES FROM FAT • GOOD SOURCE OF VITAMIN B₆

•

GRILLED CORN AND PEPPER SALAD WITH TOMATOES

Serves 4

TOTAL TIME: ABOUT 35 TO 45 MINUTES
TIME TO PREPARE: ABOUT 10 MINUTES
COOKING TIME: ABOUT 25 TO 35 MINUTES
EQUIPMENT: CHARCOAL, GAS, OR STOVETOP GRILL AND
   WOODEN SKEWERS
REFRIGERATION/FREEZING: REFRIGERATE UP TO 3 DAYS.

Fresh-picked corn is best straight off the grill *(see page 451). But one or two days after harvest, it's better made with some perky seasoning, like this one.*

1 tablespoon unsalted butter or corn oil

1 tablespoon minced fresh oregano

1 tablespoon minced fresh basil

1 teaspoon ground cumin

4 ears of corn, in their husks

1 large red bell pepper, halved, cored, and
   seeded

6 cherry tomatoes

2 teaspoons balsamic vinegar

Salt and freshly ground black pepper to taste

Soak about 8 wooden skewers in water to cover for at least 30 minutes.

Heat a charcoal, gas, or stovetop grill. Combine the butter or oil, oregano, basil, and cumin. Strip down the husks of the corn, but don't remove them. Spread the herb mixture on the corn. Replace the husk, then wrap the corn lightly in foil. Grill over very hot coals for 20 to 30 minutes, turning the corn often to cook evenly.

Place the red pepper skin side down on the grill. Grill until charred. Remove and let cool. When cool enough to handle, peel off the skin and chop.

Thread the cherry tomatoes on the skewers and grill until they're soft and lightly charred, about 6 minutes. When the corn is done grilling, scrape the kernels off the cob and into a mixing bowl. Add the tomatoes, peppers, and vinegar, and toss well. Season with salt and pepper.

PER SERVING: CALORIES 119 • PROTEIN 2.9 G • CARBOHYDRATE 21.7 G • FAT 3.9 G • CHOLESTEROL 7.7 MG • SODIUM 16.2 MG • 27% CALORIES FROM FAT • OUTSTANDING SOURCE OF VITAMIN C • GOOD SOURCE OF VITAMINS A, B₁; FOLACIN

•

DESSERTS

Sooner or later, in one way or another, even the most health-conscious home cooks must come to terms with dessert. It may seem you can go one way or another—offering plain fruit, to be strictly wholesome, or serving a rich, gooey sweet, as a "reward" for having eaten virtuously in preceding courses.

But your choice is not limited to that, as you'll discover when you prepare what follows: cakes, cookies, puddings, and creamy frozen desserts that give pleasure and nourishment in equal measure. These desserts are truly part of the meal, providing not only the sweet finish we crave, but an extra helping of the nutrients we need.

It's easy to make wholesome desserts, and to make desserts wholesome. Often it involves modifying favorite recipes to replace the shortening with healthful ingredients that taste good. For example, when you replace oil with buttermilk, you can make a rich-tasting chocolate cake (see page 475) that's high in calcium and free of fat. And when you substitute fruit puree for shortening in spiced bar cookies (see page 485), you enhance the fruity flavor of the treats, enriching them with vitamins and fiber at the same time.

But my emphasis on health may be misleading. True, these cakes, cookies, and treats are wholesome, but that's not why you'll want to eat them and serve them to your friends. They are delicious. They are dessert.

CUTTING THE FAT FROM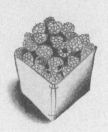

 CAKE RECIPES • DESSERTS IN

MEAL PLANNING • DESSERT

PANTRY • CAKES • COOKIES

 • GLACES • SORBETS •

PUDDINGS • SOUFFLÉS

Cutting the Fat from Cake Recipes

To make fat-free cakes, you'll be changing a few ingredients and the way you bake them. First, you have to substitute something for the butter or oil, which, rumors aside, isn't there *just* to make you shudder when you stand in front of the mirror. Shortening makes cakes light and moist, enhances their flavor, and extends their shelf life. The fat substitutes listed below do a fine job with the moisture and flavor, but not with shelf life. Fat-free baked goods don't keep well, but then, do you really expect to keep them? (These guidelines for replacing fat will make more sense to you once you've used them in the recipes that follow.)

FAT SUBSTITUTES: FRUIT PUREES

You're after the tenderizing effect of the fruit puree, not the taste, so you'll want to use a puree that won't take over the final

product. When you replace the fat in cake and cookie recipes, substitute an equal amount of fruit puree for the shortening. If a cake recipe calls for ½ cup butter, use ½ cup prune puree, apple butter, or pureed pear instead.

Here are some recipes for purees and when to use them.

PRUNE PUREE

Makes 1 cup

I t's easy to make. (It's even easier to open a jar of prune baby food, which works just as well.) Prune melds with chocolate and also with the rich spices that season gingerbread and spice cookies.

8 ounces pitted prunes
6 tablespoons boiling water

Put the ingredients into a food processor or blender and blend until smooth.

PEAR PUREE

Makes a little over 1 cup

P ear puree (or pear baby food) has the mildest flavor of the fruit purees, so it can stand in for the fat in plain sheet or layer cakes without affecting the taste very much.

One (16-ounce) can pears, packed in juice

Drain the pears and place them in a food processor or blender. Process just until smooth. Transfer the puree to a saucepan. Bring it to a gentle simmer over medium-high heat. Reduce the heat, and continue cooking, stirring often, until it's thickened and reduced by a third.

UNSWEETENED APPLE BUTTER

You may see recipes recommending applesauce, but I've found that it's too watery for the job. Apple butter is more subtle than prune puree and works much better in lightly seasoned treats such as oatmeal cookies and apple cakes. Choose a favorite from the brands recommended on page 596, or make the Apple Butter recipe on page 103, omitting the syrup and spices.

NONFAT BUTTERMILK AND YOGURT

Nonfat buttermilk can replace the fat in cakes and cookies that call for a combination of plain milk and shortening. It can be hard to find, so you can use plain nonfat yogurt instead; simply whip it with a whisk or electric beater to thin it out before measuring for recipes.

To convert a cake, muffin, or quickbread recipe, omit the plain milk and shortening. Substitute nonfat buttermilk or yogurt for the full amount of the plain milk *plus* half the amount of shortening.

For example, if the recipe calls for 1 cup of milk and 4 tablespoons butter, use 1 cup plus 2 tablespoons nonfat buttermilk instead. Or you can use 1 cup of buttermilk and 4 tablespoons of fruit puree.

SYRUP SWEETENERS

Finally, you'll get the best results if you use liquid sweeteners with the fat substitutes.

When a recipe calls for sugar, replace half of the sugar with maple syrup or barley-malt syrup. (I've found that honey is so dense that the results are too heavy, and corn syrup can be too sweet.)

Let's say a recipe calls for 1 cup of sugar, 4 tablespoons of butter, and 1 cup of plain milk. Use ½ cup of sugar, ½ cup of malt syrup, 4 tablespoons of fruit puree, and 1 cup of buttermilk. Or leave out the fruit puree and use 1½ cups buttermilk.

EGGS: NO YOLK

Since egg yolks contain fat, you may want to eliminate them along with the shortening. (Before you do, consider that a single yolk has 5.5 grams of fat, which amounts to only 0.7 grams per portion in a cake that serves eight.) Simply substitute two egg whites for each whole egg. Or use one whole egg and one egg white for every *two* whole eggs called for in a recipe.

BAKE AT A LOWER TEMPERATURE FOR LESS TIME

When you take out the fat, cakes and cookies become hypersensitive to heat, which means you should bake them at a lower temperature for less time than usual. If the cake recipe says to bake at 400° F., bake it at 375° F. instead.

Remove it the very second the tester (knife or toothpick) you insert in the center comes out clean. If you leave fat-free baked goods in the oven even a few minutes too long, they turn out tough and chewy. If you're adapting a recipe that calls for baking for forty minutes, start testing the cake after thirty. Even at the lower temperature, it may be ready.

THERE ARE LIMITS

Finally, this business of replacing shortening is an evolving art and isn't very precise. You'll learn a lot through trial and error. Take notes as you go, so you can keep track of what works for you and what you don't ever want to try again. And while you can make terrific fat-free chocolate cakes, fruit-based cakes, spice cakes, and various types of cookies, you can't adapt everything. Pound cake, sponge cake, sugar cookies, and shortbread all depend on butter and/or whole eggs. Fat-free pie crust is impossible and should not be attempted. But if you make fat-free desserts on a regular basis, you can enjoy genuine shortbread and butter crusts on occasion.

Desserts in Meal Planning

As mentioned above, desserts can help you round out your vitamins, minerals, and nutrients for the day.

APRICOT SOUFFLÉ (PAGE 497)
13% daily value for protein
37% daily value for vitamin A
15% daily value for vitamin B_2
14% daily value for iron

SWEET-POTATO-BISCUIT STRAWBERRY SHORTCAKE (PAGE 486)
17% daily value for protein
73% daily value for vitamin C
23% daily value for vitamin B_1
19% daily value for vitamin B_2
15% daily value for vitamin B_3
21% daily value for calcium
15% daily value for iron

PRUNE PUDDING CAKE (PAGE 476)
12% daily value for iron

LEMON-BERRY PUDDING (PAGE 495)
20% daily value for protein
24% daily value for vitamin B_2
18% daily value for calcium

STRAWBERRY GLACE II (PAGE 486)
20% daily value for protein
105% daily value for vitamin C
10% daily value for calcium

CARROT CAKE (PAGE 474)
58% daily value for vitamin A
13% daily value for calcium
12% daily value for iron

Dessert Pantry

You'll find my brand-name recommenda-tions for most of these items on page 595. If you can't find what you want where you shop, see the mail-order information on page 596.

All-purpose flour
Cake flour
Whole wheat pastry flour or kamut flour
Oat flour
Cornstarch
Baking powder
Baking soda
Evaporated skim milk
Brown sugar
Granulated or raw sugar
Superfine sugar

Molasses
Maple syrup
Barley-malt syrup
Prune juice
Apple butter
Canned Pears
Prunes
Currants
Raisins
Walnuts
Almonds
Vanilla extract
Vanilla beans
Ground cinnamon
Ground nutmeg
Ground cloves
Ground ginger

In the Refrigerator
Large eggs
Nonfat buttermilk
Nonfat milk
Lemons
Low-fat cottage cheese
Nonfat ricotta cheese
Nonfat or reduced-fat sour cream

Cakes

ANGEL FOOD CAKE

Serves 8

TOTAL TIME: ABOUT 1 HOUR, 25 MINUTES
TIME TO PREPARE: ABOUT 40 MINUTES
COOKING TIME: 45 MINUTES
EQUIPMENT: ANGEL FOOD CAKE PAN
DO AHEAD: 30 MINUTES BEFORE BEATING LET THE EGG
   WHITES COME TO ROOM TEMPERATURE
REFRIGERATION/FREEZING: REFRIGERATE UP TO 3 DAYS.
   FREEZE UP TO 2 MONTHS. THAW AT ROOM
   TEMPERATURE.

To whom, or what, does the "angel" in "angel food cake" refer? The heavenly baker who bothers beating all those egg whites and folding them gently into the batter? The diner who chooses it over richer desserts? Or the cake itself, which is, and has been since the first slice was served in the late 1800s, entirely fat free?

1 cup cake flour

1 cup superfine sugar

10 large egg whites at room temperature

1 teaspoon cream of tartar

1 teaspoon vanilla extract

Heat the oven to 325°F.

Sift the cake flour into a large bowl. Add ½ cup of the sugar, then sift the two together into another bowl.

In a very large bowl or in the work bowl of a Mixmaster, combine the egg whites and cream of tartar. Whip the egg whites until frothy. While whipping, sprinkle the remaining ½ cup sugar over the whites. Continue whipping until the whites are satiny and glossy. Stir in the vanilla.

Sprinkle 3 tablespoons of the flour mixture over the egg white mixture, and using a rubber spatula, gently fold them together. When the flour mixture is evenly incorporated, add 3 tablespoons more, and fold gently but thoroughly again. Repeat the process until all of the flour mixture has been incorporated.

Gently transfer the mixture to an ungreased angel food cake pan. Bake until golden and firm, about 45 minutes.

Arrange 4 custard cups or ramekins, spaced so they can serve as a stand for the cake pan. Turn the pan upside down so it rests on this improvised stand, and let it cool completely. Remove the cake from the pan, wrap tightly, and chill.

PER SERVING: CALORIES 162 • PROTEIN 5.3 G • CARBOHYDRATE 34.8 G • FAT 0 G • CHOLESTEROL 0 MG • SODIUM 69 MG • 1% CALORIES FROM FAT

Make It Your Own

The basic Angel Food Cake recipe invites adaptation. Just keep the additions light, so they won't weigh down the batter.

WHAT TO ADD AND WHEN TO ADD IT

🍃 *Lemon or Orange:* Add 2 teaspoons grated lemon or orange zest to the flour and sugar mixture. Fold it into the egg whites as directed in the basic recipe, and proceed from there.

🍃 *Ginger.* Instead of vanilla extract, add 1 tablespoon grated peeled fresh ginger, or 1 teaspoon ground ginger, to the flour and sugar mixture.

🍃 *Chocolate.* Replace 2 tablespoons of cake flour with 2 tablespoons cocoa powder. Sift the cocoa into the flour before adding the sugar. Add the sugar to the flour as directed in the basic recipe, and proceed from there.

❧ *Fruit Syrup or Fruit Puree.* When the cake has cooled completely, slice it into serving pieces. Pour fruit syrup or puree into a baking dish and arrange the cake slices in a single layer on top. Douse the cake with additional fruit syrup or fruit puree. Wrap it tightly and refrigerate overnight. The cake will be very squishy; eat it with vanilla frozen yogurt and a spoon.

•

BAKED ALASKA

Serves 8

TOTAL TIME: ABOUT 3 HOURS, 15 MINUTES, INCLUDING TIME TO FREEZE, BUT NOT INCLUDING TIME TO MAKE ANGEL FOOD CAKE
TIME TO PREPARE: ABOUT 10 MINUTES
COOKING TIME: 5 MINUTES
DO AHEAD: YOU CAN MAKE THE ANGEL FOOD CAKE UP TO 2 DAYS IN ADVANCE. REFRIGERATE UNTIL READY TO USE.

When he wasn't busy inciting revolution or establishing a university, Thomas Jefferson could be found coaxing his cook to try some neat trick he'd learned in Italy or France. A guest at Monticello in 1802 reported with some degree of wonder, eating a pudding that had been baked around a core of ice cream. This dessert was clearly a forerunner of what Fanny Farmer introduced as "baked Alaska" in her 1909 Boston Cooking School Cookbook. It's a cinch to adapt for a low-fat diet—just switch angel food for the traditional sponge cake, and nonfat frozen yogurt for ice cream.

1 Angel Food Cake, homemade or store-bought, sliced into 8 pieces (see page 472)
1 pint frozen yogurt, flavor of your choice
6 large egg whites
2 tablespoons sugar

Place the slices of cake at the bottom of a large casserole dish or inside 8 individual ramekins. Cover evenly with the frozen yogurt. Wrap tightly in plastic and freeze for at least 3 hours.

Heat the oven to 450° F. In a medium bowl, beat the egg whites until they're frothy. Continue beating, sprinkling the sugar over the whites, until stiff peaks form. Unwrap the yogurt-covered cake and spread the meringue evenly on top. Bake until golden brown, about 5 minutes. Serve immediately.

PER SERVING: CALORIES 140 • PROTEIN 8.1 G • CARBOHYDRATE 26.7 G • FAT 0 G • CHOLESTEROL 1.5 MG • SODIUM 114 MG • 1% CALORIES FROM FAT

CARROT CAKE

Serves 8

TOTAL TIME: ABOUT 1 HOUR
TIME TO PREPARE: ABOUT 15 MINUTES
COOKING TIME: 40 MINUTES
DO AHEAD: YOU CAN MAKE THE CAKE AND/OR ICING UP TO
   3 DAYS IN ADVANCE. REFRIGERATE UNTIL READY TO USE.
FREEZING: FREEZE UP TO 6 MONTHS.

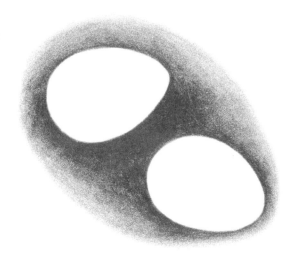

M oist, sweet, spicy, and much more wholesome than conventional versions, which may call for up to a cup of oil. Serve it for dessert, and even for breakfast the next day.

2 large egg whites

½ cup nonfat buttermilk

¼ cup unsweetened unseasoned homemade apple butter (see page 103), or store-bought (see brand recommendations, page 595)

½ cup packed dark brown sugar

2 teaspoons vanilla extract

1 cup unbleached all-purpose flour

¾ cup whole wheat pastry flour or unbleached all-purpose flour

1 teaspoon baking powder

½ teaspoon baking soda

1 teaspoon ground cinnamon

½ teaspoon ground ginger

Pinch ground nutmeg or mace

1 cup grated carrots (about 2 large carrots)

One 8-ounce can unsweetened crushed pineapple, drained

½ cup golden raisins

1 recipe Lemon Filling (see page 496)

Heat the oven to 400°F. Lightly grease an 8-inch square pan or squirt it with nonstick spray.

In a large mixing bowl, whisk together the egg whites, buttermilk, apple butter, brown sugar, and vanilla.

In a separate bowl, combine the all-purpose flour, whole wheat pastry flour, baking powder, baking soda, cinnamon, ginger, and nutmeg or mace. Sift the dry ingredients into the wet ingredients. Stir to blend.

Stir in the carrots, pineapple, and raisins.

Turn the batter into the prepared pan. Bake for 30 minutes. Turn the heat down to 350°F. and bake for 10 minutes more, or until a knife or toothpick inserted in the center comes out clean. Cool on a cake rack for 10 minutes. Turn out of the pan and cool completely.

Carefully slice the cake horizontally into 2 layers. Spread the cut side of 1 layer with half of the Lemon Filling. Sandwich with the other layer, and spread the top with the remaining filling.

PER SERVING: CALORIES 223 • PROTEIN 5.3 G • CARBOHYDRATE 52.5 G • FAT 0 G • CHOLESTEROL 0 MG • SODIUM 334 MG • 3% CALORIES FROM FAT • OUTSTANDING SOURCE OF VITAMIN A • GOOD SOURCE OF CALCIUM

•

CHOCOLATE-BUTTERMILK CAKE

Serves 8

TOTAL TIME: ABOUT 45 MINUTES
TIME TO PREPARE: ABOUT 25 MINUTES
COOKING TIME: 20 MINUTES
DO AHEAD: YOU CAN MAKE THE CAKE AND FILLING UP TO 3
    DAYS IN ADVANCE. REFRIGERATE UNTIL READY TO USE.
FREEZING: FREEZE UP TO 6 MONTHS.

It happens every time—my guests stare long-ingly at the chocolate cake until I tell them it's fat free, at which point they dive for it, again and again. The buttermilk gives it a moist, soft crumb, and the prune enhances the chocolate flavor without asserting a taste of its own.

1½ cups unbleached all-purpose flour

1 cup cocoa powder

2 teaspoons baking powder

1 teaspoon baking soda

1⅓ cups granulated sugar

1¼ cups nonfat buttermilk

¾ cup prune puree (see page 468) or prune baby
    food

4 large egg whites

1 teaspoon vanilla extract

½ cup raspberry jam plus ½ cup confectioners'
    sugar or 1 recipe Vanilla-Ricotta Icing
    (recipe follows)

Heat the oven to 350°F. Lightly grease two 9-inch layer-cake pans or squirt them with non-stick spray.

In a mixing bowl, whisk together the flour, cocoa, baking powder, baking soda, and granulated sugar.

In a separate bowl combine the buttermilk, prune puree or baby food, egg whites, and vanilla. Stir until smooth.

Pour the wet ingredients into the dry, and stir just to mix. Divide evenly between the 2 prepared pans.

Bake until the top is springy and a knife inserted in the center comes out clean, about 20 minutes. Cool in the pan on a rack for 5 to 10 minutes, then turn out the cake onto the rack and let it cool completely.

To serve, carefully slice the rounded top off one of the cakes, just to create a flat surface. Spread the flat surface with a layer of raspberry jam, cover with the other cake, and sift confectioners' sugar liberally on top. Or spread the bottom layer with half the Vanilla-Ricotta Icing, sandwich with the top layer, and spread the remaining icing on top.

PER SERVING: CALORIES 284 • PROTEIN 7.7 G • CARBOHYDRATE 64.6 G • FAT 2 G • CHOLESTEROL 1.3 MG • SODIUM 350 MG • 6% CALORIES FROM FAT • GOOD SOURCE OF CALCIUM, IRON

Vanilla-Ricotta Icing

Serves 8

1 cup nonfat or reduced-fat sour cream

1 cup nonfat ricotta cheese

½ cup confectioners' sugar

1 teaspoon vanilla extract

Place the sour cream, ricotta cheese, confectioners' sugar, and vanilla extract in a mixing bowl. Beat with an electric mixer until smooth and fluffy.

PER SERVING: CALORIES 68.5 • PROTEIN 6.5 G • CARBOHYDRATE 10.7 G • FAT 0 G • CHOLESTEROL 0 MG • SODIUM 20 MG • 0% CALORIES FROM FAT

•

CHOCOLATE SOUFFLÉ CAKE

Serves 4

TOTAL TIME: ABOUT 50 TO 55 MINUTES
TIME TO PREPARE: FEWER THAN 10 MINUTES
COOKING TIME: 40 TO 45 MINUTES
REFRIGERATION/FREEZING: REFRIGERATE OVERNIGHT. DO
    NOT FREEZE.

Part pudding, part cake, this delicious dessert bakes while you enjoy dinner. And unlike genuine soufflés, it doesn't have to be served the second it's ready.

3 large eggs, separated
1 cup nonfat buttermilk
1 teaspoon vanilla extract
¼ cup nonfat dry milk
¼ cup cocoa powder
⅓ cup sugar
3 tablespoons unbleached all-purpose flour or
    whole wheat pastry flour

Heat the oven to 350°F.

In a mixing bowl, combine the egg yolks, buttermilk, vanilla, dry milk, cocoa, sugar, and flour. Blend well.

Beat the egg whites to stiff peaks. Fold them into the yolk mixture just until incorporated. Pour the batter into four 6-inch custard cups, ramekins, or individual soufflé dishes. Place them in a large baking pan, and pour water into the outer pan until it comes halfway up the sides of the ramekins or soufflé dishes. Bake until the tops are puffy and firm and a knife inserted in the center of the soufflés comes out clean, about 40 to 45 minutes. Serve warm or at room temperature.

PER SERVING: CALORIES 138 • PROTEIN 7.4 G • CARBOHYDRATE 20.8 G • FAT 3.4 G • CHOLESTEROL 109 MG • SODIUM 102 MG • 21% CALORIES FROM FAT • GOOD SOURCE OF CALCIUM

•

PRUNE PUDDING CAKE

Serves 8

TOTAL TIME: ABOUT 45 MINUTES
TIME TO PREPARE: ABOUT 15 MINUTES
COOKING TIME: 25 MINUTES
REFRIGERATION/FREEZING: REFRIGERATE UP TO 4 DAYS. DO
    NOT FREEZE.

Serve this sweet, dense, wintertime treat topped with any vanilla- or cappuccino-flavored ice cream or yogurt. A dollop of whipped cream wouldn't hurt, either.

2 cups pitted prunes, chopped
1 cup prune juice
¼ cup unsweetened unseasoned homemade
    apple butter (see page 103), or store-bought
    (see brand recommendations, page 595)
¼ cup light brown sugar
1 teaspoon ground cinnamon
¼ teaspoon ground cloves
1 cup whole wheat pastry flour or kamut flour
1 teaspoon baking soda

Heat the oven to 350°F.

Place the prunes, prune juice, apple butter, brown sugar, cinnamon, and cloves in a large saucepan. Bring the mixture to a simmer over medium-high heat. Lower the heat to medium, and continue simmering, stirring often, until the prunes soften and the mixture thickens slightly, about 5 minutes.

Meanwhile, place the flour and baking soda in a large mixing bowl, and combine with a whisk. Pour the prune mixture into the bowl, and stir quickly and thoroughly. (The mixture will foam as the baking soda reacts with the fruit juice.) Pour the batter into a nonstick or lightly greased 7- to 8-inch round baking dish. Bake until the cake is firm, and a knife inserted in the center comes out clean, about 25 minutes.

PER SERVING:: CALORIES 209 • PROTEIN 3.3 G • CARBOHYDRATE 51.8 G • FAT 0 G • CHOLESTEROL 0 MG • SODIUM 163 MG • 2% CALORIES FROM FAT • GOOD SOURCE OF IRON

APPLE PUDDING CAKE: Substitute dried apples and freshly pressed apple juice for the prunes and prune juice. Proceed as directed in the main recipe.

•

FRESH APPLE-SPICE CAKE

Serves 8

TOTAL TIME: ABOUT 1 HOUR
TIME TO PREPARE: ABOUT 20 MINUTES
COOKING TIME: 30 TO 35 MINUTES
FREEZING: FREEZE UP TO 6 MONTHS.

This fat-free cake is so moist and so rich with flavor, it would have nothing to gain from shortening of any kind. It travels well, so pack it with lunches, or send it off to college or camp.

½ cup whole wheat pastry flour or unbleached all-purpose flour
1 cup unbleached all-purpose flour
1 teaspoon baking soda
¼ teaspoon ground cloves
½ teaspoon ground ginger
1 teaspoon ground cinnamon
½ cup packed light brown sugar
⅓ cup unsweetened unseasoned homemade apple butter (see page 103), or store-bought (see brand recommendations, page 595)
⅔ cup nonfat buttermilk
1 large egg white
1½ cups chopped peeled apples, preferably Granny Smith or Rome
3 tablespoons granulated maple sugar (see mail-order information, page 596) or brown sugar

Heat the oven to 350° F.

In a large mixing bowl, combine the whole wheat pastry flour, all-purpose flour, baking soda, cloves, ginger, and cinnamon with a wire whisk.

In a separate medium bowl, combine the brown sugar, apple butter, buttermilk, and egg white. Stir thoroughly until well blended.

Add the wet ingredients to the dry and stir well. Fold in the apples to distribute throughout the batter.

Pour the batter (it will be very thick) into an 8-inch round nonstick cake pan. Sprinkle evenly with the maple sugar. Bake 30 to 35 minutes, until a paring knife inserted in the center comes out clean. Transfer the cake to a cooling rack. Let it cool for 30 minutes before turning out onto a plate and serving.

PER SERVING: CALORIES 170 • PROTEIN 3.7 G • CARBOHYDRATE 38.3 G • FAT 0 G • CHOLESTEROL 0 MG • SODIUM 190 MG • 3% CALORIES FROM FAT

•

CITRUS PUDDING CAKE

Serves 4

TOTAL TIME: ABOUT 50 TO 55 MINUTES
TIME TO PREPARE: FEWER THAN 10 MINUTES
COOKING TIME: 40 TO 45 MINUTES
REFRIGERATION/FREEZING: REFRIGERATE UP TO 2 DAYS. DO NOT FREEZE.

A marvel: as it bakes, this mixture separates into a tangy, not-too-sweet custard with a soft cakelike top.

1 lemon or orange, or 2 limes
3 large eggs, separated
1 cup nonfat milk
¼ cup nonfat dry milk
⅓ cup sugar
3 tablespoons unbleached all-purpose flour or whole wheat pastry flour

Heat the oven to 325°F. Lightly grease four 6-ounce custard cups or one 4-cup soufflé dish with unsalted butter or coat with nonstick spray.

Into a mixing bowl, grate the zest from the lemon, orange, or limes, and extract all of the juice. Add the egg yolks, milk, dry milk, sugar, and flour. Blend well.

Beat the egg whites to stiff peaks. Fold them into the yolk mixture. Distribute the batter evenly among the custard cups, or pour it into the prepared soufflé dish. Place in a large baking pan and pour water into the outer pan until it comes halfway up the sides of the custard cups or soufflé dish. Bake until golden brown and a knife inserted in the center comes out clean, about 40 to 45 minutes. Serve warm or chilled.

PER SERVING: CALORIES 187 • PROTEIN 5.1 G • CARBOHYDRATE 40.8 G • FAT 0 G • CHOLESTEROL 2.8 MG • SODIUM 124 MG • 4% CALORIES FROM FAT • GOOD SOURCE OF VITAMIN C; CALCIUM

•

LEMON TEA CAKES

Makes 12 tea cakes

TOTAL TIME: ABOUT 30 MINUTES
TIME TO PREPARE: ABOUT 10 MINUTES
COOKING TIME: 18 MINUTES
REFRIGERATION/FREEZING: REFRIGERATE UP TO 4 DAYS. FREEZE UP TO 4 MONTHS.

Light and lovely, these cakes aren't particularly sweet. If they're too tart for your taste, increase the amount of sugar to ½ cup.

1 cup whole wheat pastry flour
½ cup oat flour
⅓ cup sugar
1 teaspoon baking soda
¾ cup nonfat buttermilk or plain nonfat yogurt
2 large egg whites, lightly beaten
1 tablespoon fresh lemon juice
2 tablespoons grated lemon zest

Heat the oven to 350°F.

In a large mixing bowl, whisk together the whole wheat flour, oat flour, sugar, and baking soda.

In a separate bowl beat together the buttermilk or yogurt, egg whites, lemon juice, and lemon zest. Add them to the flour mixture and stir just to moisten.

Spoon the mixture into 12 cups in a non-stick muffin tin, filling each cup only one-fourth full. If you have a miniature-muffin tin, fill each cup two-thirds full. Bake until golden and a toothpick inserted in the center comes out clean, about 18 minutes.

Remove the tin from the oven and let it cool completely on a rack before turning the cakes out.

•

MAPLE-APPLE-CRANBERRY CRUMBLE

Serves 8

TOTAL TIME: ABOUT 30 MINUTES
TIME TO PREPARE: ABOUT 10 MINUTES
COOKING TIME: 20 MINUTES
REFRIGERATION/FREEZING: REFRIGERATE UP TO 2 DAYS.
  REHEAT AT 325° F., COVERED IN FOIL, OR SERVE COLD.

*M*ost crisps start out wholesome, with a base of fresh fruit lightly sweetened with sugar. But then the butter crumble topping goes on, and your wholesome dessert, while sure enough delicious, is no longer consistent with any promises you may have made to yourself regarding your heart or your weight. Here's one that tastes terrific, and won't set you swearing to starve yourself the next day.

1 cup rolled oats, preferably organic
1 cup fresh cranberries, rinsed
¼ cup maple syrup
¼ cup fruit juice concentrate, barley-malt syrup
  (for mail-order information see page 596), or
  honey
1 teaspoon vanilla extract

4 large apples, such as Rome or Stayman, peeled,
  cored, and quartered
⅓ cup light brown sugar
1 teaspoon ground cinnamon
Vanilla nonfat frozen yogurt or soy-based
  equivalent (optional)

Heat the oven to 375° F.

Place the oats and cranberries in a food processor and process in short spurts to pulverize. Transfer to a large mixing bowl.

In a small saucepan, combine the maple syrup, fruit juice concentrate, barley-malt syrup, or honey, and vanilla. Bring the mixture to a simmer over medium-high heat and pour over the oat-and-cranberry mixture. Stir well, working the syrup into the oats with your hands.

Place the apples in a deep baking dish. In a mixing bowl, combine the brown sugar and cinnamon. Sprinkle the mixture over the fruit. Cover with the oat-and-cranberry mixture.

Bake until the oats turn light brown and the fruit softens, about 20 minutes. If the oats brown too quickly, cover the dish with foil, lower the heat to 325° F., and continue baking until the apples are tender.

Serve topped with vanilla frozen yogurt or a soy equivalent, if you'd like.

•

JELLY ROLL

Serves 8

TOTAL TIME: ABOUT 1 HOUR, 30 MINUTES
TIME TO PREPARE: ABOUT 15 MINUTES
COOKING TIME: 15 MINUTES
EQUIPMENT: JELLY-ROLL PAN
REFRIGERATION/FREEZING: Refrigerate overnight. Do
   NOT FREEZE.

J elly rolls are a bit richer than angel cake, because the batter contains egg yolks. But no fat's added in the form of shortening, so it's legit to call it light. More important, it's also legit to call it luscious.

4 large eggs, separated
½ cup plus 2 tablespoons granulated sugar
1 teaspoon vanilla extract
1 cup whole wheat pastry flour, sifted
Confectioners' sugar, for dusting
1¼ cups fresh fruit preserves, or 1½ cups filling
   (see suggestions below)

Heat the oven to 350°F. Line a jelly-roll pan with a single sheet of parchment paper.

In a large mixing bowl, beat the egg yolks lightly just to break them up. Add the ½ cup granulated sugar, and beat with an electric mixer until the mixture is light and sunny yellow in color. Beat in the vanilla. Gently stir in the flour in 3 additions.

In another bowl, beat the egg whites until they're stiff, sprinkling in the remaining 2 tablespoons granulated sugar halfway through. Fold the whites into the flour mixture in 6 additions, until the batter is light and smooth.

Spread the batter evenly over the paper in the prepared pan. Bake in the center of the oven until set and springy, about 15 minutes.

Remove the cake from the oven and let it cool in the pan on a rack for 5 minutes. Spread a kitchen towel on a flat surface, and place a piece of parchment paper, the same size as that lining the pan, on top. Dust it with confectioners' sugar. Turn the cake out of the pan. Carefully peel the cake off the paper, and lay it upside down on the parchment. Using the towel as a guide, roll the cake into a tight log, rolling the parchment inside. Let it cool for an hour.

Unroll the cake on the towel and spread with the preserves or filling of your choice. Roll it up again, this time taking care not to include the parchment.

PER SERVING: CALORIES 261 • PROTEIN 4.7 G • CARBOHYDRATE 59 G • FAT 2.2 G • CHOLESTEROL 79.9 MG • SODIUM 44.5 MG • 7% CALORIES FROM FAT

NOW TRY THIS: Fill the Jelly Roll with 1½ cups of vanilla, lemon, strawberry, or cappuccino yogurt cheese (see page 102); dried prunes, dried Bing cherries, or dried apricots soaked in warm water to cover until soft (about 40 minutes), drained, and pureed; Lemon Filling (see page 496); or Vanilla-Ricotta Icing (see page 475).

SWEET-POTATO-BISCUIT STRAWBERRY SHORTCAKE

Serves 8

TOTAL TIME: 30 MINUTES
TIME TO PREPARE: 10 MINUTES
COOKING TIME: 20 MINUTES
REFRIGERATION/FREEZING: REFRIGERATE UP TO 2 DAYS.
    FREEZE UP TO 6 MONTHS.

The name is a mouthful, and the dish itself offers a lot to chew on: a biscuitlike shortcake, enriched, seasoned, and tenderized with sweet potatoes, topped with fresh strawberries and sweet ricotta cream.

2 cups unbleached all-purpose flour

1 cup oat flour

2½ tablespoons sugar

1 tablespoon baking powder

1 teaspoon baking soda

1 cup nonfat buttermilk or plain nonfat yogurt

⅓ cup Mashed Sweet Potatoes (see page 228) or
    canned pumpkin

1 recipe Strained Yogurt (see page 102), or
    nonfat vanilla frozen yogurt

2 cups Fruit Sauce, made with strawberries (see
    page 104)

Heat the oven to 375° F.

In a mixing bowl, whisk together the all-purpose flour, oat flour, sugar, baking powder, and baking soda.

In a separate bowl, beat together the buttermilk or yogurt and sweet potatoes or pumpkin until the mixture is smooth. Add it to the flour mixture and stir just to moisten. Be careful not to beat rigorously, or the shortcakes will be tough.

Drop heaping spoonfuls of the batter into a nonstick baking pan, making 16 mounds of equal size. Press down lightly in the center of each. Bake until lightly browned, about 20 minutes.

Remove the cakes from the oven and let them cool completely on a rack before turning them out.

To serve, place one shortcake on each of 8 serving plates. Place 2 tablespoons of Ricotta Cream or a small scoop of frozen yogurt on top. Top with a second shortcake and spoon strawberry sauce over it.

PER SERVING: CALORIES 265 • PROTEIN 7.5 G • CARBOHYDRATE 57 G • FAT 0 G • CHOLESTEROL 0 MG • SODIUM 320 MG • 3% CALORIES FROM FAT • OUTSTANDING SOURCE OF VITAMIN C • VERY GOOD SOURCE OF CALCIUM

TORTA DI BUDINO DI RISO INTEGRALE
Rice Pudding Cake
Serves 8

TOTAL TIME: ABOUT 1 HOUR, 25 MINUTES, INCLUDING
  TIME TO MAKE THE RICE
TIME TO PREPARE: ABOUT 5 MINUTES
COOKING TIME: 30 MINUTES
EQUIPMENT: 8-INCH SPRINGFORM PAN
DO AHEAD: YOU CAN COOK THE RICE SEVERAL HOURS IN
  ADVANCE, AND LET COOL TO ROOM TEMPERATURE.
REFRIGERATION/FREEZING: REFRIGERATE UP TO 3 DAYS. DO
  NOT FREEZE.

Here's how to have your cake and eat your pudding, too. This cake is made from sweet and chewy rice pudding.

½ cup sweet or short-grain brown rice

3 cups milk

One 1-inch vanilla bean, minced

⅓ cup plus ¼ cup sugar

2 large eggs, lightly beaten

1 tablespoon grated lemon zest

1 tablespoon fresh lemon juice

2 tablespoons all-purpose flour

Combine the rice, milk, vanilla bean, and ⅓ cup of sugar in a medium, heavy saucepan. Heat gently over medium-low heat, and simmer, with the cover slightly ajar so the pan isn't completely covered, until the rice is plump and soft, about 30 minutes.

Remove the pan from the heat and let the rice cool to room temperature. Or to speed up the cooling process, you can place the pan in a larger pan filled with ice cubes, then transfer the works to the refrigerator for 15 to 20 minutes.

Meanwhile, heat the oven to 350°F.

In a food processor, blend together the rice mixture, the additional ¼ cup sugar, eggs, lemon zest, lemon juice, and flour. Pour into an 8-inch springform pan. Bake until firm and golden brown on top, about 30 minutes.

Serve warm, at room temperature, or chilled.

PER SERVING: CALORIES 157 • PROTEIN 5.8 G • CARBOHYDRATE 29.7 G • FAT 1.7 G • CHOLESTEROL 54.9 MG • SODIUM 64 MG • 10% CALORIES FROM FAT • GOOD SOURCE OF CALCIUM

●

RICOTTA CHEESECAKE
Serves 8

TOTAL TIME: ABOUT 55 MINUTES
TIME TO PREPARE: ABOUT 5 MINUTES
COOKING TIME: 50 MINUTES TO BAKE
EQUIPMENT: 9-INCH SPRINGFORM PAN
REFRIGERATION/FREEZING: REFRIGERATE UP TO 3 DAYS. DO
  NOT FREEZE.

I'm not big on parlor games, but from time to time I enjoy a round of "Desert Island Dish." It's my version of an old BBC radio program, Desert Island Disks, in which a celebrity would be asked to name the ten records and two books he'd want to have with him if stranded on an island. I, of course, ask my guests what foods they'd request. I've modified my own list over the years, substituting one dish for another, but Ricotta Cheesecake has always been on it. In fact, if confinement on the island meant eating it indefinitely, I just might choose to stay.

4 large egg whites

2 large egg yolks

1 cup sugar

3 cups nonfat or part-skim ricotta cheese

½ cup nonfat sour cream

½ cup all-purpose flour

1 teaspoon vanilla extract

2 teaspoons grated lemon zest

Heat the oven to 425°F.

Using a food processor or powerful hand mixer, blend together the egg whites, yolks, sugar, ricotta, sour cream, flour, vanilla, and lemon zest. Pour the mixture into a 9-inch springform pan and cover loosely with foil.

Bake for 40 minutes. Remove the foil and bake 10 minutes more, until firm and golden brown. Cool in the pan for 5 minutes, then remove and cool completely on a wire rack.

PER SERVING: CALORIES 183 • PROTEIN 23.7 G • CARBOHYDRATE 16.4 G • FAT 1.81 G • CHOLESTEROL 11 MG • SODIUM 52.5 MG • 9% CALORIES FROM FAT

PUMPKIN CHEESECAKE: Omit the lemon zest. Substitute ½ cup pumpkin puree for ½ cup of the ricotta cheese. Add 2 tablespoons molasses, 1 teaspoon ground cinnamon, 1 teaspoon ground ginger, ½ teaspoon ground cloves, and a pinch of nutmeg.

CHOCOLATE CHEESECAKE: Omit the lemon zest. Add 2 tablespoons cocoa powder.

Cookies

CARROT BAR COOKIES

Makes 8 cookies

TOTAL TIME: 1 HOUR
TIME TO PREPARE: 20 MINUTES
COOKING TIME: 40 MINUTES
DO AHEAD: YOU CAN PUREE THE FIGS AND/OR GRATE THE
 CARROTS UP TO 2 DAYS IN ADVANCE. REFRIGERATE BOTH
 UNTIL READY TO USE.
REFRIGERATION/FREEZING: REFRIGERATE UP TO 4 DAYS.
 FREEZE UP TO 6 MONTHS.

The problem with most commercial fat-free cookies and cakes is the amount of sweeteners added to them, as if all that sugar will compensate for the missing fat. I'm sure lots of people would appreciate products made without cloying compounds comprising fruit juice concentrates, granulated fructose, date sugar, honey, and the like. These cookies get no more sweetening than they need from figs, pineapple, and a bit of brown sugar.

2 cups dried figs

⅓ cup warm water

1⅔ cups whole wheat pastry flour

1½ teaspoons baking powder

1½ teaspoons baking soda

1 teaspoon ground cinnamon

1 cup canned unsweetened crushed pineapple, drained

2 large egg whites, lightly beaten

⅔ cup brown sugar

1 teaspoon vanilla extract

1½ cups grated peeled carrots (about 2 medium carrots)

Heat the oven to 350°F.

Combine the figs and water in a food processor or blender, and puree in short pulses. Set aside.

Stir together the flour, baking powder, baking soda, and cinnamon in a large mixing bowl using a wire whisk. In a separate bowl, combine the pineapple, egg whites, brown sugar, vanilla, carrots, and fig puree. Stir well to combine.

Stir the dry ingredients into the fig mixture, and blend thoroughly. Pour into a 8-inch square pan and bake until golden brown, about 40 minutes. Let the cookies cool on a wire rack.

PER SERVING (I COOKIE): CALORIES 188 • PROTEIN 4.3 G • CARBOHYDRATE 44.3 G • FAT 0 G • CHOLESTEROL 0 MG • SODIUM 286 MG • 3% CALORIES FROM FAT • OUTSTANDING SOURCE OF VITAMIN A • GOOD SOURCE OF CALCIUM

OATMEAL COOKIES

Makes 20 cookies

TOTAL TIME: ABOUT 30 MINUTES
TIME TO PREPARE: 15 MINUTES
COOKING TIME: 10 TO 12 MINUTES TO BAKE
REFRIGERATION/FREEZING: STORE AT ROOM TEMPERATURE
  UP TO 5 DAYS. FREEZE UP TO 6 MONTHS.

These are everything you want oatmeal cookies to be: chewy, delicious, and utterly wholesome. Be careful not to bake them too long, or they will be hard to chew (but then, of course, you can always dunk them in milk to soften them up).

⅔ cup unsweetened unseasoned homemade
  apple butter (see page 103), or store-bought
  (see brand recommendations, page 595)
1 cup granulated brown sugar
⅓ cup dark corn syrup or barley-malt syrup (for
  mail-order information, see page 596)
¼ cup nonfat buttermilk or plain nonfat yogurt
1 large egg white
1 teaspoon vanilla extract
2 cups whole wheat pastry flour or unbleached
  all-purpose flour
1 cup oat flour or unbleached all-purpose flour
1 cup rolled oats
1 teaspoon baking soda
1 teaspoon baking powder
1 cup raisins, soaked in hot water for 15 minutes
  (optional)

Heat the oven to 350°F.

Place the apple butter in a large mixing bowl, and beat in the brown sugar, corn or barley-malt syrup, buttermilk or yogurt, egg white, and vanilla.

In a separate large mixing bowl, combine

the pastry flour, oat or all-purpose flour, oats, baking soda, and baking powder. Stir with a fine whisk or long-tined fork to blend.

Stir the dry ingredients into the wet ingredients until you have a firm dough. Add the raisins, if desired, at this point. Drop the dough by spoonfuls onto a nonstick baking sheet. Lightly flour the bottom of a drinking glass. Press the glass down lightly to flatten each cookie. Bake until browned on the edges, 10 to 12 minutes. Let the cookies cool on a rack.

PER SERVING (I COOKIE): CALORIES 134 • PROTEIN 3.2 G • CARBOHYDRATE 30 G • FAT 0 G • CHOLESTEROL 0 MG • SODIUM 105 MG • 5% CALORIES FROM FAT

•

HERMITS
Spicy Bar Cookies
Makes 12 squares

TOTAL TIME: 40 MINUTES
TIME TO PREPARE: 15 MINUTES
COOKING TIME: 25 MINUTES
FREEZING: FREEZE UP TO 6 MONTHS.

The hermits I ate as a child contained a quarter pound of butter, and I set out to convert my mother's recipe warily, prepared for disappointment. Instead, I was delighted. The butter's gone, but the rich, spicy taste that I remember is all there.

½ cup prune puree (see page 468) or prune baby food
½ cup granulated sugar
½ cup packed brown sugar
2 large eggs, lightly beaten
1 cup nonfat buttermilk
1 cup molasses

2 cups unbleached all-purpose flour
2 cups whole wheat flour
1 teaspoon baking soda
1 teaspoon baking powder
1 teaspoon ground cinnamon
½ teaspoon ground nutmeg or mace
½ teaspoon ground allspice
½ teaspoon ground cloves
1 cup currants
½ cup chopped walnuts (optional)

Heat the oven to 350°F. Lightly grease a 13 × 18-inch shallow baking pan or squirt it with nonstick spray.

In a large mixing bowl, combine the prune puree or baby food, granulated sugar, brown sugar, eggs, buttermilk, and molasses. Blend until smooth.

In a separate large bowl, use a whisk to combine the all-purpose flour, whole wheat flour, baking soda, baking powder, cinnamon, nutmeg or mace, allspice, and cloves.

Pour the liquid ingredients into the dry, and stir to blend. Fold the currants and nuts, if using, into the batter.

Spread the dough in the prepared baking pan. Bake until the top is firm and dry, about 25 minutes. Let cool on a rack before turning out. Cut into squares.

PER SERVING (I COOKIE): CALORIES 246 • PROTEIN 5.4 G • CARBOHYDRATE 55.5 G • FAT 1.2 G • CHOLESTEROL 27.2 MG • SODIUM 148 MG • 4% CALORIES FROM FAT • VERY GOOD SOURCE OF CALCIUM, IRON

•

Glaces

GLACE BASE I

Makes 4 cups frozen glace

TOTAL TIME: 10 MINUTES, NOT INCLUDING TIME TO
FREEZE, WHICH VARIES AMONG ICE-CREAM MAKERS
TIME TO PREPARE: ABOUT 10 MINUTES
COOKING TIME: NONE
EQUIPMENT: ICE-CREAM MAKER

This makes a smooth, light glace that's great with delicate fruits, such as cantaloupe, peaches, or lemons.

1 cup nonfat buttermilk

½ cup plain or vanilla nonfat yogurt

¼ cup nonfat dry milk

⅔ cup superfine sugar, or ½ cup maple syrup or
light honey

1 teaspoon vanilla extract

2 cups pureed fruit (see page 468)

Blend together the buttermilk, yogurt, and dry milk until the mixture is smooth. Add the sugar or syrup or honey, vanilla, and fruit. Blend until perfectly smooth.

Freeze the mixture in an ice-cream maker according to the manufacturer's instructions.

PER SERVING (WITH STRAWBERRIES): CALORIES 212 • PROTEIN 3.2 G • CARBOHYDRATE 50 G • FAT 0 G • CHOLESTEROL 1.8 MG • SODIUM 59.9 MG • 3% CALORIES FROM FAT • OUTSTANDING SOURCE OF VITAMIN C • GOOD SOURCE OF CALCIUM

GLACE BASE II

Makes 4 cups frozen glace

TOTAL TIME: 10 MINUTES, NOT INCLUDING TIME TO
FREEZE, WHICH VARIES AMONG ICE-CREAM MAKERS
TIME TO PREPARE: ABOUT 10 MINUTES
COOKING TIME: NONE
EQUIPMENT: ICE-CREAM MAKER

Ricotta cheese makes this glace denser and creamier than Glace Base I. I use this with richer-tasting fruits, such as fresh figs, mangoes, or cherries.

1 cup nonfat or part-skim ricotta cheese

½ cup plain or vanilla nonfat yogurt

3 tablespoons nonfat dry milk

⅔ cup superfine sugar, or ½ cup maple syrup or
light honey

1 teaspoon vanilla extract

2 cups pureed fruit (see page 468)

Blend the ricotta and yogurt together in a food processor or blender. Add the dry milk, sugar or syrup or honey, vanilla, and fresh fruit. Blend.

Freeze the mixture in an ice-cream maker according to the manufacturer's instructions.

PER SERVING (WITH STRAWBERRIES): CALORIES 243 • PROTEIN 9.2 G • CARBOHYDRATE 52 G • FAT 0 G • CHOLESTEROL 1.1 MG • SODIUM 37.2 MG • 2% CALORIES FROM FAT • OUTSTANDING SOURCE OF VITAMIN C • GOOD SOURCE OF CALCIUM

GLACE BASICS

Glace refers to "ice cream" in French, but I've appropriated the word for chewy frozen desserts made with yogurt, buttermilk, or ricotta cheese. Like genuine glace, they're creamy, and like sorbet, they're full of fresh fruit flavor and free of fat.

• Make sure the base is perfectly smooth before adding the fruit or other ingredients. If you start with a smooth base, the texture will be even and the flavor well distributed.

• Nonfat dry milk gives the glace body and helps to make it smooth. If possible, use organic nonfat dry milk. It has a milder flavor than ordinary commercial dry milk, which can taste chalky.

• Use the proportions given in the recipes for adding ingredients, no more than 2 cups fruit puree for each batch of base. Stir additional ingredients into the base just before processing it in your ice-cream maker.

• You can't store these glaces—they freeze rock solid and are impossible to scoop—so make only as much as you can eat and share at one time.

Make It Your Own

The base recipes are just that—bases. You can build on them in any of the following ways.

WHAT TO ADD AND WHEN TO ADD IT

✍ *Fresh Fruit.* Add any prepared chopped fresh fruit to the base. Puree or process in spurts for a chunkier glace. Freeze in an ice-cream maker according to the manufacturer's directions.

✍ *Nuts.* Add chopped nuts, about ½ cup per cup of base, near the end of the freezing time, before the glace is completely set.

✍ *Chocolate Pieces.* Add chocolate pieces, about ¼ cup per cup of base, near the end of the freezing time, before the glace is completely set.

✍ *Dried Fruit.* Soak dried fruit in warm fruit juice or water until it's soft and plump. Dice it and add it near the end of the freezing time.

✍ *Fruit Syrups or Flavored Syrups.* Blend ½ cup fruit syrup or ¼ cup vanilla, chocolate, or liqueur-flavored syrup into the base before freezing.

BERRY GLACE

Makes about 4 cups frozen glace

TOTAL TIME: 10 MINUTES, NOT INCLUDING TIME TO
   FREEZE, WHICH VARIES AMONG ICE-CREAM MAKERS
TIME TO PREPARE: ABOUT 10 MINUTES
COOKING TIME: NONE
EQUIPMENT: ICE-CREAM MAKER
DO AHEAD: YOU CAN MAKE THE FRUIT MIXTURE UP TO A
   DAY AHEAD. REFRIGERATE UNTIL READY TO USE. STIR
   WELL BEFORE FREEZING.

U se the sweetest, fruitiest berries of the season for this light mid-summer treat. Try it
on Waffles (see page 89).

2 pints fresh blueberries, raspberries, or hulled
   and chopped strawberries
¼ cup maple syrup
¼ cup sugar
2 cups nonfat buttermilk
⅓ cup nonfat dry milk
1 tablespoon fresh lemon juice
1 large egg white

Puree the berries in a blender or food processor. Strain through a fine sieve into a large mix-

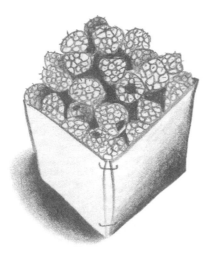

ing bowl. (This should yield about 1 cup of
strained puree.)

Blend the puree with the maple syrup,
sugar, buttermilk, nonfat dry milk, and lemon
juice. In a small bowl, beat the egg white until
it's stiff, and fold it into the berry mixture.

Freeze in an ice-cream maker according to
the manufacturer's directions.

PER SERVING (WITH BLUEBERRIES): CALORIES 182 • PROTEIN 9 G • CARBOHY-
DRATE 34.7 G • FAT 1.4 G • CHOLESTEROL 6.2 MG • SODIUM 201 MG • 7% CALORIES
FROM FAT • VERY GOOD SOURCE OF VITAMIN B₂; CALCIUM • GOOD SOURCE OF
VITAMINS B₁₂, C; ZINC

•

FIG GLACE

Makes about 4 cups frozen glace

TOTAL TIME: 25 MINUTES, NOT INCLUDING TIME TO
   FREEZE, WHICH VARIES AMONG ICE-CREAM MAKERS
TIME TO PREPARE: 25 MINUTES
COOKING TIME: NONE
EQUIPMENT: ICE-CREAM MAKER

H early, dense, and sweet, fresh figs make
great glace. Try this over Fresh Apple-
Spice Cake (see page 477).

1 pound fresh figs, tough stems removed
⅓ cup plus 1 tablespoon sugar
1 cup nonfat buttermilk
⅓ cup nonfat dry milk
1 teaspoon vanilla extract, or more to taste
1 large egg white

Bring about 2 cups of water to a boil. Plunge
the figs into the water and allow it to return to
a boil. After 20 seconds, turn off the heat and
drain the water. Set the figs aside to cool (if

you're in a rush, toss them into the freezer for 5 minutes).

Peel away as much of the skin as possible. Place the figs in a large mixing bowl. Add the ⅓ cup of sugar, and mash thoroughly with a fork. Beat the buttermilk and dry milk together with an electric mixer or wire whisk (it won't get perfectly smooth, but that's okay), and add this to the fig mixture. Stir in the vanilla.

Beat the egg white in another bowl until frothy, and sprinkle it with the remaining sugar. Resume beating until white is stiff but not dry. Fold the egg white into the fig mixture.

Freeze in an ice-cream maker according to the manufacturer's directions.

PER SERVING: CALORIES 227 • PROTEIN 73 G • CARBOHYDRATE 49.6 G • FAT 0 G • CHOLESTEROL 4 MG • SODIUM 132 MG • 4% CALORIES FROM FAT • VERY GOOD SOURCE OF CALCIUM • GOOD SOURCE OF VITAMIN B₂

Sorbets

SORBET

Makes about 4 cups frozen sorbet

TOTAL TIME: ABOUT 5 MINUTES, NOT INCLUDING TIME TO FREEZE, WHICH VARIES AMONG ICE-CREAM MAKERS
TIME TO PREPARE: ABOUT 5 MINUTES
COOKING TIME: NONE
EQUIPMENT: ICE-CREAM MAKER

G*iven the number of good commercial sorbets in the shops, you might wonder whether it's worth the effort to make your own. In fact, it isn't always. If you can't find great fruit, sorbet from a carton is bound to be better than what you'd churn out at home. But when your favorite fruits are at their best, the sorbet you make from them will beat even the best brands.*

4 cups chopped or mashed fresh fruit (to prepare fruit for pureeing, see page 468)
1 to 2 cups superfine sugar (see Note)
2 tablespoons fresh lemon or orange juice

Puree the prepared fruit with an immersion blender or in a food processor.

Beat together the fruit puree, sugar, and juice. Pour the mixture into an ice-cream maker and process according to the manufacturer's directions.

Note: You can try other sweeteners, such as honey, maple syrup, and fruit juice concentrate, but sugar promotes a smoother texture and creamier consistency.

PER SERVING (WITH STRAWBERRIES): CALORIES 163 • PROTEIN 0 G • CARBO-HYDRATE 41.6 G • FAT 0 G • CHOLESTEROL 0 MG • SODIUM 1.4 MG • 2% CALORIES FROM FAT • OUTSTANDING SOURCE OF VITAMIN C

SORBET BASICS

• Taste the fruit you plan to use. If you're not tempted to keep right on eating it, it's probably not good enough for sorbet. The fruit has to be the best of its kind. Cold blunts the taste, so if the flavor of the fruit

TO PREPARE FRUITS FOR PUREEING

Apples and Pears: Soften fruits.

1. Peel, core, and slice the fruit.

2. Place an inch of apple juice or water in a saucepan and bring it to a simmer over medium-high heat. Add the fruit.

3. Reduce the heat to medium-low and simmer until the fruit is soft enough to puree. Let it cool completely before using it for sorbet or glace. (You can speed up the cooling by filling a large bowl with ice cubes, putting the puree in a smaller bowl, and nesting it in the ice. Stir well to cool the whole mixture evenly.)

Blueberries: Just pick them off the stems and puree them as they are.

Cherries: Pit them. If you love cherries, it's worth buying a pitter. Although you'll only use it for a few weeks each year, it will make life easier when the time comes to cook with them.

Peaches, Apricots, and Plums: These fruits must be peeled.

1. In a saucepan, bring enough water to cover the fruit to a boil. Make four evenly spaced 1/2-inch vertical slits through the skin at the top of each fruit.

2. Plunge the fruit into the water. Bring it to a second boil and boil the fruit for 40 seconds.

3. Remove the fruit with a slotted spoon. When it's cool enough to handle, slip off the skin, and proceed with the recipe.

Strawberries: Pull off the stems and slice off the hull.

---

isn't strong at the start, the sorbet will be bland.

• If your fruit was good, but your sorbet is bland nonetheless, add more sugar next time. Sugar doesn't just sweeten; it amplifies the taste.

• Make sure to puree the fruit thoroughly before freezing, or the texture of the sorbet will be uneven, and perhaps icy. (See page 468 for pureeing instructions.)

• Homemade sorbet doesn't keep well; it becomes impossibly hard. Serve it—*all* of it—straight from the ice-cream maker.

Make It Your Own

Every batch of sorbet is going to taste different, determined entirely by the flavor of the fruit and the amount and proportions of other ingredients.

WHAT TO ADD AND WHEN TO ADD IT

✒ *Dried Fruit.* You can intensify the flavor of any sorbet by using pureed softened dried fruit. Soak 1/4 cup of the dried fruit (apricots, Bing cherries, or peaches, for example) in any flavor fruit juice to cover. When the fruit is thoroughly soft, puree the dried fruit together with

the fresh fruit. Proceed with the basic recipe.
✐ *Liqueur and Other Alcohol.* Give a kick to
your sorbet with a tablespoon of rum, vodka,
or Grand Marnier. Add it to the basic mixture
before freezing.

•

CHERRY SORBET

Makes about 4 cups frozen sorbet

TOTAL TIME: ABOUT 15 MINUTES, NOT INCLUDING TIME TO
FREEZE, WHICH VARIES AMONG ICE-CREAM MAKERS
TIME TO PREPARE: ABOUT 15 MINUTES
COOKING TIME: NONE
EQUIPMENT: ICE-CREAM MAKER, CHERRY PITTER (OPTIONAL)

Here's a great way to enjoy the gobs of
cherries you're likely to grab toward the
end of the fruit's short season.

4 cups pitted cherries

1 cup sugar

2 tablespoons fresh lemon juice

Puree the cherries in a food processor. Blend in
the sugar and lemon juice. Freeze in an ice-
cream maker according to the manufacturers'
instructions.

PER SERVING: CALORIES 200 • PROTEIN 1.1 G • CARBOHYDRATE 49.8 G • FAT 0 G •
CHOLESTEROL 0 MG • SODIUM 0 MG • 4% CALORIES FROM FAT • GOOD SOURCE OF
VITAMIN C

•

CHOCOLATE-CHERRY SORBET

Makes about 4 cups frozen sorbet

TOTAL TIME: 5 MINUTES, NOT INCLUDING TIME TO FREEZE,
WHICH VARIES AMONG ICE-CREAM MAKERS
TIME TO PREPARE: ABOUT 5 MINUTES
COOKING TIME: NONE
EQUIPMENT: ICE-CREAM MAKER

2 cups water

1 cup sugar

1 cup cocoa powder

1 teaspoon vanilla extract

2 cups pitted cherries

In a large mixing bowl, combine the water,
sugar, cocoa, and vanilla. Puree the cherries
with an immersion blender or food processor
and blend into the sugar mixture. Freeze in an
ice-cream maker according to the manufacturer's instructions.

PER SERVING: CALORIES 198 • PROTEIN 3.4 G • CARBOHYDRATE 49.2 G • FAT
2.4 G • CHOLESTEROL 0 MG • SODIUM 3.3 MG • 9% CALORIES FROM FAT • GOOD
SOURCE OF IRON

BASIC CLAFOUTIS

Serves 6

TOTAL TIME: 1 HOUR, 15 MINUTES
TIME TO PREPARE: FEWER THAN 5 MINUTES
COOKING TIME: 40 MINUTES
DO AHEAD: YOU CAN MAKE THE BATTER UP TO 1 DAY IN
    ADVANCE. REFRIGERATE UNTIL READY TO USE. WHISK
    WELL BEFORE BAKING.
REFRIGERATION/FREEZING: REFRIGERATE OVERNIGHT. DO
    NOT FREEZE.

From the files of "Real Estate: Brooklyn" . . . Some bright spark in the Limousin region of France came up with this dessert to make the most of the annual cherry harvest. As French confections go, it's easy, calling for nothing more than a custard-based batter and a whole lot of cherries—or a lot of whole cherries. According to the classic recipe, you're not supposed to pit the cherries. It was the creator's contention that the pits actually season the dish. And if you believe that, I've got this bridge to sell you.

Anyone who's cooked with stone fruits knows the pits are bitter. Clearly, leaving in the pits was meant only as a shortcut, and the bit about seasoning was a feeble rationalization. For goodness' sake, pit the cherries.

Or use another fruit.

⅓ cup unbleached all-purpose flour

1 cup nonfat milk

⅓ cup evaporated skim milk

¼ cup nonfat dry milk

2 large eggs

1 large egg white

¾ cup sugar

1 teaspoon vanilla extract

1½ cups fruit filling (see suggestions below)

In a large mixing bowl, beat together the flour, nonfat milk, evaporated skim milk, nonfat dry milk, eggs, egg white, sugar, and vanilla. Set the mixture aside for 30 minutes. Meanwhile, heat the oven to 400° F.

Spread the fruit evenly over the bottom of a shallow round ovenproof dish, 6 to 8 inches in diameter. Pour the batter through a sieve over the fruit, using a wooden spoon to help force it through. Bake until puffy and firm, about 40 minutes. Let cool briefly on a rack. Serve warm, at room temperature, or chilled.

Fruit Fillings
• Dried cherries soaked in warm water for 30 minutes, then drained
• Blueberries, stems removed
• Chopped, peeled fresh peaches or apricots. (To peel, bring a large pot of water to a boil. Drop in the fruit and bring to a second boil. Let the fruit boil for 40 seconds, and remove it with a slotted spoon. When it's cool enough to handle, slip off

the skin. Chop the pulp and proceed with the recipe.)
• Prunes, plumped in warm water to cover for 40 minutes, and drained
• Apple or pear slices, peeled and sprinkled with ½ teaspoon cinnamon and 1 tablespoon brown sugar
• Fresh figs, stems removed, mashed

PER SERVING: CALORIES 196 • PROTEIN 7.5 G • CARBOHYDRATE 35.8 G • FAT 2.7 G • CHOLESTEROL 108 MG • SODIUM 86.6 MG • 12% CALORIES FROM FAT • GOOD SOURCE OF CALCIUM

Puddings

COTTAGE CHEESE PUDDING

Serves 4

TOTAL TIME: ABOUT 1 HOUR, 10 MINUTES, NOT INCLUDING TIME TO CHILL
TIME TO PREPARE: FEWER THAN 10 MINUTES
COOKING TIME: 1 HOUR TO BAKE
DO AHEAD: YOU CAN MAKE THE PUDDING, UNCOOKED, UP TO 2 DAYS IN ADVANCE. REFRIGERATE UNTIL READY TO BAKE.
REFRIGERATION/FREEZING: REFRIGERATE OVERNIGHT.

Support groups exist for all kinds of conditions, from divorce to drug addiction, but I may be unique in having formed one to cope with erratic and unreliable access to cottage cheese.

There were just two of us—my friend Cynthia and myself—harboring a secret that was shameful because we, Americans both, were living in Italy. We knew we should have been thanking our lucky stars that our corner market carried fresh mozzarella of any kind that did, truly, melt in your mouth, ricotta so light and sweet it was practically dessert, and Parmesan so nutty you'd swear it was dusted with just-toasted almonds. Provolone, Asiago, mascarpone of inimitable quality were ours for the asking (and a few thousand lire). Yet we would have killed for cottage cheese.

Each of us would have suffered in lonely silence if it hadn't been for Cynthia's (Milanese) husband, Ricchi, who made a wisecrack one evening about her crazy American fixation. I leapt to her defense, while my (Florentine) husband joined Ricchi in wondering aloud how, among the World's Greatest Cheeses, we could pine for a Lousy Mess of Curds.

While most support groups are meant to help members overcome their obsessions, we helped each other indulge ours, calling when the Standa or Galli supermarket had just received a shipment, or when we found a merchant who had some in stock. It was bad enough that we had to have the stuff, but to compound our humiliation, the name for it in Italian is distinctly—I suspect deliberately—unappetizing: fiocchi di latte (milk flakes).

We wanted the cottage cheese mostly for topping baked potatoes. But now that I'm home, and can have it anytime, I also love it like this.

2 cups low-fat cottage cheese
½ cup nonfat sour cream
¼ cup plus 1 tablespoon sugar
1 tablespoon grated lemon or orange zest
2 large egg whites
1 large egg
1 teaspoon vanilla extract

Heat the oven to 350°F.

In a food processor or blender, combine the cottage cheese, sour cream, sugar, lemon or orange zest, egg whites, egg, and vanilla extract. Process until smooth.

Spoon the mixture into four 6-ounce ramekins or custard cups. Place the cups in a large baking dish. Pour water into the outer dish until it comes halfway up the sides of the ramekins or custard cups. Bake until a knife inserted in the center comes out clean, about 1 hour. Let them cool on a rack, then chill thoroughly. Serve cold.

PER SERVING: CALORIES 91 • PROTEIN 2.3 G • CARBOHYDRATE 21 G • FAT 0 G • CHOLESTEROL 1.1 MG • SODIUM 32 MG • 2% CALORIES FROM FAT • VERY GOOD SOURCE OF VITAMINS A, C

•

FRUITY RICE PUDDING WITH MERINGUE

Serves 6

TOTAL TIME: ABOUT 40 MINUTES
TIME TO PREPARE: ABOUT 25 MINUTES
COOKING TIME: ABOUT 7 MINUTES

I love rice pudding and am reconciled to the fact that I will never find a recipe so perfect I won't ever try another or return to one I liked before. But here's a version with a twist—or, rather, a top —a layer of fruit puree capped with sweet meringue. Use short-grain brown rice, Wehani-brand rice, medium-grain white rice, or arborio rice.

½ cup nonfat milk

½ cup nonfat or part-skim ricotta cheese

⅓ cup plus 2 tablespoons sugar

1 cup cooked rice

1 teaspoon grated lemon zest

2 large eggs, separated

1 teaspoon vanilla extract

⅓ cup pure fruit preserves

In a medium mixing bowl, blend together the milk and ricotta until smooth. Pour the mixture into a medium, heavy saucepan, and stir in the ⅓ cup sugar, rice, and lemon zest. Beat the egg yolks together lightly to break them up, then stir them in, too. Bring to a gentle simmer over medium heat and stir often until thickened, about 20 minutes.

Turn off the heat, stir in the vanilla, and transfer the mixture to a 4-cup-capacity baking dish.

Heat the oven to 350° F.

Beat the egg whites until frothy and then sprinkle with the remaining sugar. Resume beating the egg whites until stiff but not dry. Using a spatula, spread the fruit preserves on top of the pudding. Then spread the egg whites on top of that.

Bake until the meringue is firm and golden brown, about 7 minutes. If part of the meringue seems to be browning too quickly, move the pudding to a lower rack in the oven. Serve immediately.

PER SERVING: CALORIES 196 • PROTEIN 6.7 G • CARBOHYDRATE 38.6 G • FAT 1.8 G • CHOLESTEROL 71.4 MG • SODIUM 38.7 MG • 8% CALORIES FROM FAT

•

LEMON-BERRY PUDDING

Serves 2

TOTAL TIME: ABOUT 3 HOURS, 40 MINUTES, INCLUDING TIME TO CHILL
TIME TO PREPARE: FEWER THAN 10 MINUTES
COOKING TIME: 30 MINUTES
DO AHEAD: YOU CAN MAKE THE PUDDING, UNCOOKED, UP TO 3 DAYS IN ADVANCE. REFRIGERATE UNTIL READY TO BAKE.
REFRIGERATION/FREEZING: KEEP REFRIGERATED UP TO 2 DAYS. DO NOT FREEZE.

Scratch a good cook, and you'll find her lemon stash. The aptly named zest gives life to savory dishes and makes for awfully good desserts.

1 lemon, preferably organic or unwaxed
1 large egg, lightly beaten
¼ cup plus 1 tablespoon sugar
⅓ cup nonfat milk
2 tablespoons nonfat dry milk
2 tablespoons unbleached all-purpose flour
1 teaspoon cornstarch
1 cup fresh berries, such as blueberries, sliced and hulled strawberries, or raspberries

Heat the oven to 350°F. Lightly butter two 6-ounce custard cups or squirt them with nonstick spray.

Grate 2 teaspoons of zest from the lemon, and set it aside. Squeeze out all of the juice, and set that aside, too.

Using an electric mixer, beat the egg until it's frothy, about 1 minute. Add the ¼ cup sugar and beat again until the mixture is lemon colored, about 1 minute. Add the nonfat milk, dry milk, lemon juice, and flour and beat again until smooth.

Pour half of the mixture into each prepared custard cup. Place the cups in a baking pan, and add water to the outer pan until it comes halfway up the custard cups. Bake until the custard is set, about 30 minutes. Let them cool on a rack.

For the sauce, combine the remaining 1 tablespoon sugar, cornstarch, lemon zest, and berries in a small saucepan. Stir well. Heat over medium-high heat until thickened and bubbly, about 3 to 5 minutes, stirring often.

Alternatively, place the ingredients in the microwave and cook, uncovered, on full power for 3 minutes.

Spoon the sauce over the custards, let them cool until the sauce stops steaming, cover them with plastic wrap, and chill them thoroughly, for at least 3 hours. Serve cold.

PER SERVING: CALORIES 266 • PROTEIN 8.8 G • CARBOHYDRATE 53 G • FAT 3.1 G • CHOLESTEROL 109 MG • SODIUM 94.4 MG • 10% CALORIES FROM FAT • OUTSTANDING SOURCE OF VITAMIN C • VERY GOOD SOURCE OF VITAMIN B₂ • GOOD SOURCE OF VITAMIN B₁₂

•

LEMON FILLING

Makes about 3 cups

TOTAL TIME: ABOUT 4 HOURS, 15 MINUTES, INCLUDING
   TIME TO CHILL
TIME TO PREPARE: ABOUT 15 MINUTES
COOKING TIME: INCLUDED IN TIME TO PREPARE
REFRIGERATION/FREEZING: REFRIGERATE UP TO 3 DAYS. DO
   NOT FREEZE.

Not quite as creamy as butter-based lemon curd, this sweet-tart spread makes ideal icing nevertheless. *Try it on Carrot Cake (see page 474) and gingerbread and inside a Jelly Roll (see page 480). Or spoon it into a custard cup and eat it as it is.*

¾ cup raw sugar (see mail-order information,
   page 596)
½ cup cornstarch
2 cups nonfat buttermilk
1 tablespoon grated lemon zest
4 large egg whites
Juice of 2 lemons (about ½ cup)

Combine the sugar and cornstarch in a medium, heavy saucepan. Whisk in the buttermilk, and set over medium-high heat. Continue whisking until the mixture is thick and begins to bubble, about 8 minutes. Whisk in the lemon zest. Remove from the heat.

Place the egg whites in a nonreactive mixing bowl. Pour half of the buttermilk mixture into the bowl and whisk well. Return the saucepan and its contents to the stove, turn the heat to medium-low, and whisk in the buttermilk–egg white mixture. Continue whisking until it's thickened, about 2 minutes. Take care not to boil it. Remove from the heat and stir in the lemon juice.

Spoon the mixture into 4 to 6 individual custard cups, cover with plastic wrap, and chill until set, about 4 hours. If using as a cake filling, let it cool to room temperature before spreading it on a baked, cooled cake.

PER SERVING: CALORIES 187 • PROTEIN 5.1 G • CARBOHYDRATE 40 G • FAT 0 G • CHOLESTEROL 2.8 MG • SODIUM 124 MG • 4% CALORIES FROM FAT • GOOD SOURCE OF VITAMINS B₂, C; CALCIUM

ORANGE VARIATION: Substitute 1 tablespoon orange zest for the lemon zest, and ½ cup freshly squeezed orange juice for the lemon juice.

•

MANGO CREAM

Makes about 3 cups

TOTAL TIME: 3 HOURS, 25 MINUTES, INCLUDING TIME TO
   CHILL
TIME TO PREPARE: 25 MINUTES
COOKING TIME: INCLUDED IN TIME TO PREPARE
REFRIGERATION/FREEZING: REFRIGERATE UP TO 3 DAYS. DO
   NOT FREEZE.

A ripe mango can be dessert enough, but when ripe mangoes are going cheap, it's fun to get fancy, as follows. *Serve this after a curry or a meal made on the grill.*

1 ripe fresh mango
2 teaspoons fresh lime juice
1 cup nonfat milk
2 tablespoons sugar
1½ tablespoons cornstarch
2 tablespoons water

Peel the mango (see Note) and cut all of the fruit away from the pit. Place the fruit in a food processor or blender along with the lime juice. Puree. Set aside.

In a medium saucepan, stir together the milk and sugar and bring to a simmer over medium heat. Combine the cornstarch with the water to make a paste, and add it to the milk. Lower the heat to medium-low, and continue stirring until the milk thickens, about 7 minutes. Remove from the heat.

Distribute half of the milk mixture evenly among 4 small (4-ounce) custard cups. Top with half of the mango mixture. Add an even amount of the remaining milk mixture to the cups and finish with a layer of mango. Refrigerate until chilled through, about 3 hours.

Note: To peel the mango, make 4 equally spaced slices lengthwise from the stem. Pull off the skin as if peeling a banana.

PER SERVING: CALORIES 91.4 • PROTEIN 2.3 G • CARBOHYDRATE 21 G • FAT 0 G • CHOLESTEROL 1.1 MG • SODIUM 32.9 MG • 2% CALORIES FROM FAT • VERY GOOD SOURCE OF VITAMINS A, C

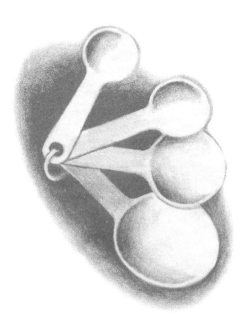

Soufflés

FRUIT SOUFFLÉ
Serves 4

TOTAL TIME: ABOUT 45 MINUTES
TIME TO PREPARE: ABOUT 20 MINUTES, DEPENDING ON THE FRUIT
COOKING TIME: 25 MINUTES
DO AHEAD: YOU CAN MAKE THE FRUIT PUREE (EXCEPT BANANA, WHICH WON'T KEEP) UP TO 5 DAYS IN ADVANCE. REFRIGERATE UNTIL READY TO USE.
REFRIGERATION/FREEZING: DO NOT REFRIGERATE OR FREEZE.

*I*f you like the mystique that surrounds soufflés, and want to remain awed by them, skip this recipe: I'm about to disclose how easily you can make them.

A soufflé provides a unique sensation; it's so light and flavorful, it's like eating nothing that tastes like something. But this seeming miracle is a simple matter of folding air, via stiffly beaten egg whites, into a dense puree.

With the exception of banana, I use dried fruit rather than fresh for these soufflés because the flavor of dried fruit tends to be highly concentrated, and consequently stronger. Also, dried fruit isn't watery, so the soufflés turn out firm, rather than runny.

1 recipe fruit puree (recipes follow)
2 teaspoons fresh lemon juice
1/3 cup plus 1 tablespoon sugar
4 large egg whites
1/2 teaspoon baking powder

Heat the oven to 375° F. Coat four 8-ounce custard cups or individual soufflé dishes with nonstick spray or grease them lightly with unsalted butter.

In a mixing bowl, beat together the fruit puree, lemon juice, and ⅓ cup sugar until smooth.

In a separate bowl, beat the egg whites until they're foamy. Sprinkle the baking powder and the remaining tablespoon of sugar on top. Resume beating until the whites are stiff but not dry (like shaving foam).

Fold about a third of the egg whites into the fruit mixture until the mixture becomes lighter and you can't see any whites. Fold in another third, and then the last third, just until incorporated.

Using a rubber spatula, carefully distribute the soufflé mixture evenly among the prepared dishes. Place the dishes inside a large, deep baking dish. Add enough water to the larger dish to come halfway up the sides of the custard cups or soufflé dishes.

Bake until the soufflés are puffed and golden brown, about 25 minutes. Serve right away.

Puree for Prune Soufflé

Makes about 2 cups; serves 4

1 ½ cups pitted prunes

1 cup prune juice

1 teaspoon vanilla extract

Place the prunes and prune juice in a medium, heavy saucepan. Bring to a simmer over medium-high heat. Cover, and turn down the heat to medium-low. Simmer until the prunes are very soft, about 15 minutes. Transfer to a food processor and puree. Add the vanilla and process to blend. Let it cool completely before folding the egg whites into the puree.

PER SERVING: CALORIES 202 • PROTEIN 4.5 G • CARBOHYDRATE 47 G • FAT 0 G • CHOLESTEROL 0 MG • SODIUM 120 MG • 1% CALORIES FROM FAT

Puree for Apricot Soufflé

Makes about 2 cups; serves 4

1 ½ cups dried apricots

1 cup fresh orange juice

Place the apricots and orange juice in a medium, heavy saucepan. Bring to a simmer over medium-high heat. Cover and turn down the heat to medium-low. Simmer until the apricots are very soft, about 30 minutes. Transfer to a food processor and puree. Let it cool completely before folding the egg whites into the puree.

PER SERVING: CALORIES 237 • PROTEIN 5.7 G • CARBOHYDRATE 56.9 G • FAT 0 G • CHOLESTEROL 0 MG • SODIUM 122 MG • 1% CALORIES FROM FAT • OUTSTANDING SOURCE OF VITAMIN C • VERY GOOD SOURCE OF VITAMIN A • GOOD SOURCE OF IRON

Puree for Cherry Soufflé

Makes about 2 cups; serves 4

1 ½ cups dried cherries
1 cup fresh cherry juice (see Note) or apple juice
1 teaspoon vanilla extract

Place the cherries and cherry juice in a medium, heavy saucepan. Bring to a simmer over medium-high heat. Cover and turn down the heat to medium-low. Simmer until the cherries are plump and very soft, about 15 minutes. Transfer to a food processor and puree. Add the vanilla and process to blend. Let it cool completely before folding the egg whites into the puree.

Note: Cherry juice is available in the bottled-juice section of most health-food supermarkets. See page 595 for brand recommendations.

PER SERVING: CALORIES 229 • PROTEIN 5.4 G • CARBOHYDRATE 51.8 G • FAT 1.4 G • CHOLESTEROL 0 MG • SODIUM 118 MG • 5% CALORIES FROM FAT • VERY GOOD SOURCE OF VITAMIN C • GOOD SOURCE OF VITAMIN B₂

Puree for Apple Soufflé

Makes about 2 cups; serves 4

1 ½ cups dried apples
1 cup fresh apple juice
1 teaspoon ground cinnamon

Place the apples and apple juice in a medium, heavy saucepan. Bring to a simmer over medium-high heat. Cover and turn down the heat to medium-low. Simmer until the apricots are very soft, about 15 minutes. Transfer to a food processor and puree. Add the cinnamon

and process to blend. Let it cool completely before folding the egg whites into the puree.

PER SERVING: CALORIES 162 • PROTEIN 3.7 G • CARBOHYDRATE 38.2 G • FAT 0 G • CHOLESTEROL 0 MG • SODIUM 132 MG • 1% CALORIES FROM FAT

Puree for Banana Soufflé

Makes about 2 cups; serves 4

3 large bananas
1 teaspoon vanilla extract

Mash the bananas well with a potato masher. Add the vanilla and stir well to blend.

PER SERVING: CALORIES 175 • PROTEIN 4.4 G • CARBOHYDRATE 40.4 G • FAT 0 G • CHOLESTEROL 0 MG • SODIUM 117 MG • 2% CALORIES FROM FAT • VERY GOOD SOURCE OF VITAMIN B₆ • GOOD SOURCE OF VITAMINS B₂, C

Puree for Pumpkin or Sweet Potato Soufflé

Makes about 2 cups; serves 4

1 ½ cups canned or fresh pumpkin or sweet potato puree
¼ cup molasses
1 teaspoon ground cinnamon
1 teaspoon ground ginger
½ teaspoon ground cloves
Pinch ground nutmeg

In a mixing bowl, beat together the pumpkin or sweet potato puree, molasses, cinnamon, ginger, cloves, and nutmeg.

PER SERVING: CALORIES 173 • PROTEIN 4.5 G • CARBOHYDRATE 40.3 G • FAT 0 G • CHOLESTEROL 0 MG • SODIUM 132 MG • 1% CALORIES FROM FAT • OUTSTANDING SOURCE OF VITAMIN A • VERY GOOD SOURCE OF CALCIUM • GOOD SOURCE OF VITAMIN B₂

A P P E N D I X

How to Cook to Maximize Flavor and Nourishment and Modify Fat and Calories

It's hardly ever true that the easiest, fastest way of doing something is also the best way to do it. But it *is* true when it comes to preparing food. When you cook fresh produce quickly and simply, you not only save time and effort, you preserve the flavor, vitamins, and nutrients in whatever you're making.

THE BASIC METHODS

Baking
You bake by cooking food in an oven, surrounded by dry, hot air. Although you can bake any vegetable, baking is best for root vegetables such as potatoes, sweet potatoes, turnips, and beets.

TO PREPARE THE FOOD FOR BAKING
Recipes that call for baking usually give specific directions for preparing the food. You may be instructed to stuff the vegetables and stand them upright or on their sides, puree the ingredients, layer the ingredients with pasta and sauce, and so on. If you're simply baking root vegetables, bake at 375°F.

Beets and Turnips: Scrub them, then wrap each in foil, unpeeled, before baking beets for fifty minutes, turnips for forty.

Rutabagas: Wrap unwaxed, unpeeled rutabagas in foil, but peel waxed rutabagas before you wrap them. Bake for one hour.

Potatoes and Sweet Potatoes: Scrub but don't wrap them in foil, or they'll taste as if they've been steamed. A medium russet takes about one hour to bake. A red sweet potato takes about forty minutes to bake.

You'll find additional basic instructions for specific vegetables in the "1-2-3 Guide," starting on page 514. You'll find instructions for specific grains starting on page 572.

TO PREPARE THE PAN
When you're baking vegetables, make sure your pan is ovenproof, the right size for the amount of food you're baking (check your recipe for the dimensions), and in good condi-

FOR GOOD TASTE AND GOOD HEALTH THE BEST WAYS TO COOK CALL FOR . . .

1. Brief and minimal exposure to water or other liquid. Whenever you boil vegetables, vitamins seep into the liquid. This is fine if you're making a stew, soup, or sauce, because you'll be eating all of it. But if you're just boiling the vegetables and dumping the water, the vitamins will go down the drain. Rather than boil them, steam or microwave fresh vegetables until they're just cooked through.

2. Brief exposure to air and heat, both of which destroy vitamins. To limit exposure to heat, choose quick-cooking methods.

To limit exposure to air, wait until you're ready to cook before you chop, peel, or slice fresh vegetables.

3. Little or no added fat. Most vegetables and grains will absorb any available oil or butter, going from virtually fat free to phenomenally fatty in no time. Eggplant is a good example. An entire eggplant baked plain has about 40 calories and no fat at all. But it can absorb just about as much fat as you add to it when cooking, up to 400 calories if you fry it in 1/4 cup of oil.

---

tion—not buckled or cracked—so the heat is conducted evenly.

If your pan doesn't have a nonstick surface, grease it lightly with canola oil or squirt it—lightly—with nonstick spray. If you use nonstick spray, wipe off the residue with a paper towel. There'll be plenty left on the surface to do the job, but not enough to affect the flavor of the food.

TO COOK

Follow your recipe. More often than not, baking temperatures and times are precise and meant to be taken literally.

TO BAKE VEGETABLES "EN PAPILLOTE"

Purchase a roll of parchment paper (available at specialty food shops, cookware stores, some supermarkets, and by mail [see page 596]). Tear off a large sheet and place raw vegetables in the center. The vegetables should be of similar size, shape, and density so they'll cook in the same amount of time. For extra flavor, toss in a crushed garlic clove and some minced fresh herbs. Sprinkle the vegetables and paper with vegetable broth or brush the paper lightly with extra virgin olive oil. Fold in the sides of the paper to cover the vegetables. Then roll up the packet from the bottom to seal them inside. Bake at 425° F. until the packet puffs up, for tender vegetables such as asparagus, or until you can pierce the thickest part with a fork for others, such as leeks or sweet potatoes.

To Bake Flans, Terrines, and Custards in a Water Bath

This method involves putting water between the ingredients and the heat to keep the dish cooking slowly and evenly. Custard-type dishes that aren't cooked in a water bath may cook unevenly and/or curdle.

Place the pan containing the dish you're cooking inside a deeper baking pan. Pour water into the outer pan until it comes halfway up the dish inside. Bake until your food is firm, checking the water level and adding more as necessary to maintain it.

Blanching

When you blanch vegetables you boil them until they're partly cooked. Many grilling and stir-frying recipes call for starting with blanched vegetables such as asparagus, broccoli, beets, and potatoes, because they'll cook more quickly and evenly on the grill or in the wok if they're partially done beforehand.

To Prepare the Vegetables for Blanching

Cut vegetables such as broccoli and cauliflower into uniform pieces. If using whole vegetables such as small beets or new potatoes, scrub them well. To preserve the vitamins, peel them after they've been blanched.

To Cook

Fill a saucepan with enough water to cover the vegetables and bring it to a rolling boil. Meanwhile, fill a large bowl with enough cold water and ice cubes to cover the vegetables. Line a colander with paper towels.

When the water has reached a boil, plunge the vegetable into it, and boil just until

you can pierce it with a paring knife. Time will vary according to the vegetable you're blanching. Allow between thirty and forty-five seconds for slender asparagus, about two minutes for broccoli florets, and four to six minutes for new potatoes and beets.

BRAISING

IT HAPPENS TO THE BEST OF US

Problem: The pan dries out and the food sticks and burns!
Solution: Check the food often, adding vegetable broth or water ¼ cup at a time when it looks dangerously dry, and cover loosely with foil. Turn down the heat by about 25 degrees.

Remove the vegetable with a slotted spoon and transfer it to the ice water for fifteen seconds to stop the cooking, then transfer to the colander to drain.

Braising

To braise vegetables, you sauté them briefly, then let them cook slowly in a tightly sealed pan on top of the stove or in the oven. You use a small amount of fat and a flavorful liquid, such as very strong broth, wine, or balsamic vinegar, and give them plenty of time to cook through. To preserve as many vitamins as possible, serve the braising liquid along with the vegetables.

TO PREPARE THE FOOD FOR BRAISING

Slice or chop the vegetables into uniform sizes, or select vegetables of roughly the same size so they'll cook at the same rate.

TO COOK

In a heavy skillet over medium-high heat, heat 1 tablespoon extra virgin olive oil. Add up to 4 cups loosely packed vegetables such as peeled pearl onions, chopped carrots, quartered potatoes, turnips, and/or rutabagas. Sauté the vegetables (see page 507), just until they're coated with oil. Stir in a splash (about 2 tablespoons) of wine or balsamic vinegar. Turn the heat down to medium-low and cover the skillet. Cook, stirring occasionally, until the vegetables are very tender, about forty minutes. Or after sautéing using an ovenproof skillet with a lid or transferring the vegetables to a covered baking dish, heat the oven to 375°F., and cook, stirring occasionally, for about fifty minutes, until tender.

Broiling

Like grilling, broiling is a straightforward matter of food meeting heat, except that the source of heat is above the food

BROILING

IT HAPPENS TO THE BEST OF US

Problem: The food touches the heat source and catches fire!
Solution: Don't heat the broiler until you've made a trial run. Place the dish on the broiler tray and put it in the broiler, noting the distance between the food and the heat source. If the fit is tight, lower the broiler rack. If it won't go down farther, transfer the food to a shallower pan, even if this means broiling in two batches.

rather than below it. If your barbecue dinner gets rained out, you can use your broiler to cook the food you've prepared.

You'll also use the broiler to crisp and brown the tops of dishes that have been baked, steamed, or sautéed already.

And you'll use your broiler to prepare vegetables for further cooking. For example, you have to broil bell peppers before you can peel them. And to make anything with eggplant puree, you have to broil an eggplant first. See the "1-2-3 Guide" (page 514) for broiling instructions for specific vegetables.

To Prepare the Food for Broiling

Slice or chop the vegetables into uniform sizes, if necessary, so they'll broil at the same rate. Brush them lightly with oil or melted butter and place them on a broiler pan. Or marinate the vegetables first, as you would if you were going to grill them (see page 446).

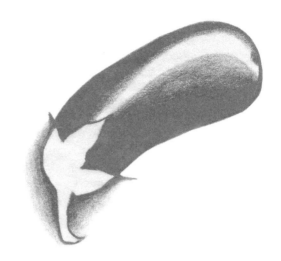

To Prepare the Broiler

Heat the broiler fifteen minutes before you plan to use it. Adjust the rack so the food is at least an inch away from the heat—or far enough from the source so it won't ignite. Depending on the thickness of the food, the rack may have to be even farther from the heat source, so that vegetables cook through before they brown too much.

To Cook

Place the food under the broiler and *don't go away!* Foods broil quickly, and burn a second later. Make sure you're wearing mitts or grasping hefty pot holders when you remove the pan.

Grilling
See the grilling chapter, starting on page 444.

Microwaving
When microwave ovens first came on the market, we heard that they were going to revolutionize the way we cook, making it possible to produce a five-

---

BROILING

BLAZING BROILERS

For a fast gratin, steam 2 cups of any vegetable over vegetable broth. Puree, then stir in 1 cup dried bread crumbs and ¼ cup grated cheese. Pour the puree into a gratin dish and dot the top with 1 teaspoon unsalted butter, thinly shaved. Broil 1½ inches from the heat until the top is golden brown.

course meal in as many minutes. If you use your microwave to thaw complete frozen dinners on a regular basis, you've come close to realizing that dream. But if you've been using a microwave at all, it's probably been for small tasks, such as boiling water, defrosting vegetables, and baking potatoes. My microwave's always assisted me with conventional cooking, but rarely replaced it, mostly because I enjoy cooking too much to resort to this antiseptic way of preparing food.

I make an exception for steamed vegetables, which I prepare in the microwave all the time. Microwaving preserves more nutrients than any other method. And when you know your microwave oven well enough to get the timing right, the vegetables always turn out just the way you want them.

To Prepare the Food for Microwaving

While you'll find microwave instructions for specific vegetables in the "1-2-3 Guide" (see page 514), here are the basic preparation guidelines:

• Pierce hard-shelled or thick-skinned vegetables such as squash, potatoes, and beets in several places, or steam will build up inside them as they cook, and they will explode.

• Cut or trim other large vegetables into uniform-sized pieces so that they'll cook evenly.

To Prepare the Pan for Microwaving

Make sure that any plate, pan, or container you plan to use in the microwave will survive the experience. Plastic melts down, paper can burn, and some types of glass can crack or shatter. Metals block or deflect the microwaves, so nix to aluminum, copper, and enamel ware. You're safe with Pyrex or ovenproof porcelain. I use Pyrex pie plates for steaming vegetables and

large (one- and two-quart-capacity) Pyrex bowls or measuring cups for boiling.

If you have frozen broths or leftovers in a plastic container, such as a yogurt carton, put the container in the microwave just enough to loosen the contents so you can transfer them to a sturdier bowl to finish the job. In most cases, one to two minutes on full power will be enough to free the food but not to melt the container. Once you've transferred the contents, break up the ice as much as possible with a fork, then return the food to the microwave to thaw, stopping every few minutes to break up the chunks.

TO COOK

First remember that every oven is different, and cooking times vary from one to another. It may take a few trials and as many errors before you know how long yours takes to make various vegetables the way you want them.

Space the vegetables evenly on the plate, tray, or paper towel. If the type or volume of food is going to take longer than four minutes to cook, turn the food over 180 degrees halfway through the cooking time, unless you have a rotating tray. For example, it takes six

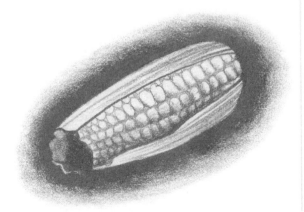

minutes to cook two ears of corn. Place the ears side by side in the center of the microwave. Microwave on full power for three minutes. Switch sides, placing the ear that's on the left on the right and vice versa. Microwave for two minutes longer.

To steam a sliced or chopped vegetable, place it in a microwavable pan with ¼ to ½ inch of water. Cover it completely with a damp paper towel and cook on full power for one to five minutes, depending on the vegetable and volume. Let it rest with the towel in place for one minute. If it's not done, return it to the oven for one minute at a time, allowing one minute of rest in between. (The food continues to cook during the rest period.)

Pressure-Cooking
I treasure my Kuhn Tikow pressure cooker for two reasons: beans and broth. Because it cooks beans quickly without soaking, I can decide to serve them an hour before the meal instead of a day ahead. And because it seals in flavor instead of letting it slip out in steam, my pressure cooker makes marvelous vegetable broth. Consequently, everything I make with the broth—soups, risottos, stews of all kinds—is that much better.

But the pressure cooker can be maddening for other purposes. I've never been able to regulate the heat well enough to make anything that requires precise timing, such as grains. Although lots of people report better results, my grains either burn or turn to mush. And despite its reputation for efficiency, the pressure cooker doesn't always save time. Once you've brought the appliance up to adequate pressure, cooked for the specified time, then allowed the pressure to come down again, you might as well have made the rice or whatever on the stove or in the oven.

But test it out; it may be that, unlike me, you're one of those people with the pressure-cooker touch, able to enjoy its celebrated versatility.

Like my microwave, my pressure cooker is an essential tool for specific purposes rather than a substitute for skillets, saucepans, and conventional ovens.

Sautéing
"Sauté" means "jump" in French, describing what food should do when you stir it into a hot skillet or saucepan with a bit of butter or oil. It's fast and it's healthy, and it's essential to most good recipes: sautéing releases flavor from aromatic vegetables such as onions, garlic, leeks, and shallots, preparing them to season the rest of the dish.

Whenever you sauté you have to add some fat, but not much, in the scheme of things. For most recipes serving 4 to 6 people, you'll need no more than 1 tablespoon of oil or butter.

Finally, you usually add the entire sauté preparation to the dish, so many of those vitamins that leach out of the vegetables while they're cooking get into the meal in the end.

SAUTÉING
QUICK CALCULATION

1 tablespoon of oil or butter = 100 calories

Divide by 4 servings and you have *25 calories per serving*. With a good nonstick pan, you can get by with 2 teaspoons of oil in a recipe that serves 4, for fewer than *17 calories of fat per serving*. Not bad!

To Prepare the Food for Sautéing

Chop the vegetables well, but don't mince them (chop very, very fine) unless the recipe calls for it. When vegetables have been minced, they tend to release a lot of moisture, stewing slowly in their own juice, rather than cooking quickly as they should.

To Prepare the Pan for Sautéing

If you're going to be cooking a lot, you'll be sautéing a lot. So it's worth buying a good non-stick skillet and saucepan. As long as the surface holds up, you won't need much oil, and you won't have to depend on nonstick sprays, which can taste peculiar.

Drop the oil or butter into the center of the pan. Heat the pan over medium-high heat, swirling it so the oil runs over the surface. Test the heat by dropping some chopped onion, or whatever you're going to sauté, into the pan. If it sizzles, the pan is ready. If it smokes, it's already too hot. Take it off the heat, let it cool, and start over. If the oil has turned brown, let it

SAUTÉING

IT HAPPENS TO THE BEST OF US

Problem: The food sticks to the pan!
Solution: Have some vinegar, wine, or vegetable broth next to you at the stove and add about 1 tablespoon at a time, stirring to loosen the food that sticks. Also make sure the heat is no longer on high.
Problem: The food starts cooking in its own juice!
Solution: Turn up the heat and stir constantly until the liquid evaporates.

cool until it's no longer smoking, wash out the pan, and begin again with fresh oil.

To Cook

Add the rest of the ingredients to the pan and turn down the heat to medium or medium-low. (If you're using an electric stove, set another burner to medium-low at the same time you set the first burner to high. Instead of turning down the heat at this stage—which won't register as quickly as you need it—transfer the skillet to the medium-low burner.)

Stir often until the vegetables have softened, usually between seven and twelve minutes, depending on the type of vegetable and the size of the pieces.

Steaming Steaming is the least you can do to a food and still call it cooked. Aside from preserving the true flavors of vegetables and keeping them crisp, steaming doesn't leach vitamins as boiling does or involve even the small amount of fat needed for sautéing or stir-frying. And steamed vegetables are versatile: you can top them any way you'd like and serve them hot or chilled.

To Prepare the Food for Steaming
Cut or trim the vegetables to uniform sizes, if necessary, so they'll cook at the same rate.

To Prepare the Pan for Steaming
To steam, vegetables have to be suspended above simmering liquid. You can buy a pan or utensil designed for that purpose or rig up your own. Bamboo steamers are inexpensive and easy to use, but nearly impossible to maintain. I've had to throw out a few because I've been unable to clean them. Consequently, I recommend using a large steamer pot—a big perforated basket that fits into a stockpot several inches from the bottom, or a small collapsible metal steamer basket that expands or folds to fit pans of all sizes.

If you don't have a steamer of any kind, you can improvise with more common utensils:
• Fit a wire cooling rack inside a saucepan. Add water just to touch the base of the rack.
• Fit a metal colander or sieve into the rim of a saucepan.

To Cook
You'll find instructions for steaming specific vegetables in the "1-2-3 Guide" (see page 514), but here is the basic technique.

Bring the water to a simmer over medium-high heat. Place the food in the steamer and cover the pot. If you're using a colander or sieve and the lid won't fit, cover the post with foil.

Reduce the heat to medium-low and keep the water simmering until the food is just cooked through. How long this will take depends on the food, from fifteen seconds for snow peas to forty minutes for whole new potatoes.

If the food will be steaming for more than

five minutes, check the water level often, replenishing as necessary, taking care not to add enough to touch the food.

To enhance the flavor, steam the vegetables over vegetable broth. Or place aromatic vegetables in the water, and generate a broth as it simmers.

Stewing When you stew vegetables you simmer them at length in seasoned sauce or broth of some kind, infusing them with flavor in the process. Although you cook them for a long time, you'll retain vitamins as long as you serve the entire stew, broth and all.

To Prepare the Food for Stewing
Chop the aromatic vegetables called for in the recipe. Cut the remaining ingredients into bite-sized pieces.

To Prepare the Pan for Stewing
Proceed as directed for sautéing (see page 507) or sweating (see page 512).

To Cook
Once you've added all of the ingredients according to your recipe, bring the stew to a simmer, cover the pot, and continue to cook it at a low simmer over medium-low heat, or transfer it to a 350° to 425° F. oven for the length of time given in the recipe.

Stir-Frying Like sautéing, stir-frying involves cooking vegetables quickly at high heat with little fat. And like sautéing, it's fast and healthy, releasing flavor while preserving nutrients. But rather than a way to prepare the vegetables for further cooking, a stir-fry is an

STIR-FRYING
IT HAPPENS TO THE BEST OF US

Problem: The vegetables cook unevenly. The snow peas are soggy by the time I've cooked the broccoli!

Solution: Blanch long-cooking vegetables as directed (see page 502) until they're all at the same stage, that is, nearly cooked through. This way you can add them at the same time without overcooking any one of them. Or add the vegetables to your wok in the order of how long it takes each one to cook. Mushrooms (which you wouldn't blanch) first, then thick asparagus, broccoli stems, carrots, cauliflower, and bell peppers, then thinner asparagus, broccoli florets, and sugar snap peas, and finally snow peas. Before you add the snow peas, bite into one of the tougher vegetables, such as a broccoli stem, to make sure it's done.

end in itself. You may toss some seasoning sauce or broth into the wok, but there's nothing to do beyond that, besides break out the noodles or rice and dig in.

TO PREPARE THE FOOD FOR STIR-FRYING

Use a cheese grater to grate the ginger and garlic called for in the recipe. Mince any scallions, shallots, or onions you'll be adding (unless the recipe tells you otherwise). Cut the rest of the vegetables into uniform bite-sized pieces so they'll cook evenly.

To make sure the vegetables cook evenly, you can blanch them before you put them in the wok. If you blanch each type of vegetable until it's almost cooked through, you can finish cooking them all at once. (See blanching instructions, page 502.)

Or you can add them to the wok in order of size, starting with the thickest, so that the denser vegetables such as carrots and fresh mushrooms will have more time to cook than delicate vegetables such as slender asparagus and snow peas. I prefer blanching because I don't have to think about when to add which vegetable.

Put the prepared vegetables in bowls or on a large plate and place them right beside the stove in the order in which you'll be adding them to the pan. Also make sure that everything else you need, such as broth and seasoning sauces, is right there. The vegetables will cook so quickly, you don't want to let them get overdone while you rummage around for the hoisin sauce.

TO PREPARE THE PAN FOR STIR-FRYING

Heat a wok over medium-high heat until water dropped on the surface sizzles. Add the amount of oil called for in the recipe, swirl the wok quickly to coat the surface, and start to cook immediately.

TO COOK

Add the aromatic vegetables first and stir them quickly to season the oil, about thirty seconds. If you've blanched the remaining vegetables, add them all at once and cook, stirring constantly, until they're cooked through. If you haven't blanched, add the vegetables as directed above, starting with the most dense and finishing with the most delicate.

Sweating
I wish it were called something else, but this is the term for sautéing without fat, a cross between steaming and sautéing. Instead of tossing aromatic vegetables into hot butter or oil, you cook them in vegetable broth and vinegar or wine. If you're after every conceivable way to cut fat from your diet, substitute sweating for sautéing, following the directions below instead of taking the steps to sauté. Then proceed as directed in your recipe from that point on.

TO PREPARE THE FOOD FOR SWEATING

Do as you would to sauté (see page 507). Also, you'll need vegetable broth and good balsamic vinegar.

SWEATING
IT HAPPENS TO THE BEST OF US

Problem: The water disappears and the pan—and everything in it—burns!

Solution: There's nothing you can do about it now, other than resolve that next time you'll stand by and peek into the saucepan periodically, adding water a couple of tablespoons at a time when necessary.

TO PREPARE THE PAN FOR SWEATING

Pour about ¼ to ½ cup broth into a nonstick skillet or saucepan. Add 2 tablespoons balsamic vinegar.

TO COOK

Bring the broth mixture to a simmer over medium-high heat. Add the aromatic vegetables and continue simmering, stirring often, until the liquid has reduced almost to nothing and the vegetables are soft, as if you'd sautéed. Proceed with the rest of your recipe.

SWEAT OR NO SWEAT?

A representative—but not all-inclusive—list of dishes you can sweat instead of sauté, and suggestions for liquid in which to sweat them.

Soups

Chili Bean Soup (page 193) Sweat the aromatics in a combination of vegetable broth and red wine vinegar, or in broth alone. If using broth, use 1 tablespoon vinegar to 3 tablespoons broth.

Winter Tomato–Wheat Berry Soup (page 197) Sweat the aromatics in vegetable broth.

Winter Garden Soup (page 198) Sweat the aromatics in vegetable broth.

Simple Soothing Mushroom Soup (page 177) Sweat the aromatics in vegetable broth or a combination of vegetable broth or white wine (about 1 tablespoon wine to 3 tablespoons broth).

Pastas

Lasagna with Stewed Vegetables (page 302) Sweat the aromatics in a combination of vegetable broth and red wine, or in broth alone. If using both, use half wine and half broth.

Sweet Black Beans on Whole Wheat Penne (page 289) Sweat the aromatics in vegetable broth.

Three-Mushroom Sauce (page 286) Sweat the aromatics in vegetable broth or a combination of vegetable broth and white wine. If using both, use about 1 tablespoon wine to 3 tablespoons broth.

Rich Savory Lentil Ragout (page 284) Sweat the aromatics in a combination of vegetable broth and balsamic vinegar or red wine, or in broth alone. If using broth and vinegar, use about 1 tablespoon vinegar to 3 tablespoons broth. If using broth and wine, use half broth and half wine.

One-Dish Dinners

Couscous (page 338) Sweat the aromatics in vegetable broth.

Tangy Tofu Sauce (page 351) Sweat the aromatics in a combination of vegetable broth and rice vinegar or in broth alone. If using both, use 1 tablespoon vinegar to 3 tablespoons broth.

Chunky Bean Burritos (page 354) Sweat the aromatics in a combination of vegetable broth and red wine vinegar, or in broth alone. If using broth, use 1 tablespoon vinegar to 3 tablespoons broth.

Cabbage-Filled Cabbage Stir-Fry (page 376) Sweat the aromatics in a combination of vegetable broth and rice vinegar or in broth alone. If using both, use 1 tablespoon vinegar to 3 tablespoons broth.

Potato Curry (page 356) Sweat the aromatics in vegetable broth, ideally Broth for Far Eastern–Flavored Dishes (page 168).

1,2,3 GUIDE TO FRESH PRODUCE

HOW TO CHOOSE THEM, USE THEM, AND STORE THEM

Some clichés that are perfectly true when applied to people must be modified when evaluating produce. Take, for instance, "Beauty is only skin deep." With vegetables it can go deeper than that. Produce that's blotchy, withered, or badly bruised may in fact be rotten. As for judging a book by its cover, sprouts and mold that appear on the outside may signal real trouble within. But some imperfections are innocuous and inconsequential, with no effect on the flavor or nutritional content of the vegetable or fruit. The more produce you buy, the better you'll get at telling the difference between a harmless blemish and serious blight.

Just to complicate things, not all produce that looks good *is* good. Imported vegetables and fruits may have traveled too far to taste of much when they arrive. And a lot of domestic produce, bred to look perfect or to grow out of season, is flavorless, too.

So even in this Wonder Age of Amazing Agricultural Advancement and high-speed transport, the best produce is pretty much what it's always been: vegetables and fruits in season, grown close to home.

Artichokes
Thorny and tough, resembling a cudgel more than a delicacy, an artichoke isn't, on the face of it, the most enticing plant in the garden. So, you have to wonder, was it desperation, daring, or ingenuity that drove some ancestors of ours to try one? Whatever the motive, they did posterity a favor when they found that artichokes can be eaten, then figured out how that could be done. Sweet and nutty, artichokes would be habit forming if it weren't for the work involved in preparing them. Even so, they're hard to resist steamed, baked, and in risottos, pastas, and salads.

I SERVING: I MEDIUM ARTICHOKE • CALORIES: 50 • FIBER: HIGH • GOOD SOURCE OF VITAMIN C; FOLACIN

To Choose
1. A good artichoke has a firm, compact head

2. It feels heavy for its size (indicating that it's full of moisture and hasn't dried out or rotted inside).

3. The color is a nice, even shade of green —not blotchy or yellow.

To Use Whole for Steaming or Baking

1. Trim the stem so the artichoke stands upright on its own.
2. Pull off the tough, dark outer leaves, then cut off the sharp tips of the remaining leaves with kitchen shears.
3. Sprinkle with fresh lemon juice to keep the leaves from turning black.

To Use Sliced or Chopped for Casseroles, Risottos, or Pastas

1. Cut away the stem and snap off all of the tough outer leaves. Don't panic when you find that this amounts to more than half of the artichoke. As you strip away the leaves, you may think you're going too far. But you can't use more than a small part of the whole artichoke for dishes like these.
2. Once you're down to the light green, tender leaves, cut the artichoke in half lengthwise. With a melon scoop, paring knife, or teaspoon, scoop out the fuzz at the center.
3. Cut the artichoke into quarters lengthwise, then cut each quarter in half across the middle.

To Store Raw Artichokes

1. Sprinkle with cold water.
2. Wrap in an airtight plastic bag.
3. Refrigerate for up to five days.

To Use Baby Artichokes

1. Pull off the tough outer leaves.
2. Trim the stem entirely.
3. Steam in a basket steamer or on a rack, as directed above, until tender, about 10 minutes.

To Steam

1. Put a cooling rack or a collapsible metal steaming basket on the bottom of a large saucepan.
2. Add water until it almost touches the rack or basket. Bring the water to a boil.
3. Add the artichokes, cover the pot, and steam over medium heat until you can pluck a petal from the center easily, about forty minutes. Serve hot or cool.

To Steam in the Microwave

1. Place the prepared artichokes in a microwavable bowl or dish.
2. Add ¼ inch of water. Cover the bowl with a microwavable plate or damp paper towel.
3. Microwave on full power for five to seven minutes. The cooking time will vary with the size of the artichokes and the number you're cooking. Let the artichokes rest for three minutes before lifting the plate or paper towel and testing for doneness. If they're not done, return them to the oven at full power for one minute more.

To Blanch (to prepare quartered artichoke hearts for grilling or stir-frying)

1. Fill a large saucepan with water and bring to a boil.
2. Meanwhile, fill a large bowl with cold water and ice cubes. Line a colander with paper towels.
3. Plunge the quartered artichoke hearts into the boiling water. The moment you can pierce them with a paring knife, about one minute—remove them with a slotted spoon and transfer to the ice water for fifteen sec-

onds, to stop the cooking, then transfer to the colander to drain.

Asparagus

When you consider the current craze for cultivating *everything* all year 'round, you might assume that no one served asparagus at Christmastime before us. Not so. Louis XIV insisted on asparagus in December, and his gardener, mindful that it was curtains if he failed, forced the plants from September until March. Evidently the king was pleased because the gardener lived on, turning next to growing exotic greens, which Louis enjoyed to excess. But that's another story.

The Sun King may have liked it, but asparagus grown out of season doesn't compare with what arrives when it should, in the spring. It's not as tender or as sweet, and the flavor, while distinct enough, is merely reminiscent of the "real" thing.

Regardless of *when* you eat it, there's the problem of how it should be eaten. Unless it's dripping with dressing, asparagus is fine finger food. And as long as you refrain from eating it sword-swallower style, no one should object. If they do? Remind them it's accepted practice in France, flourish a spear, and wish them *Bon apetit!*

I SERVING: 5 SPEARS • CALORIES: 22 • FIBER: LOW • GOOD SOURCE OF VITAMINS C, E; FOLACIN

To Choose

1. Good asparagus stalks are firm and straight.
2. The tips are compact and closed tight like a bud.
3. The color is vibrant, the stalks deep green, and the tips green or splashed with purple.

To Use

1. Rinse the tips with cold water to get out any grit that may be lodged in them.
2. Trim away the tough ends of the stalks.
3. If the remaining lower third or so of the stalks is rough or woody, use a vegetable peeler to pare away the outer layer. The asparagus will be stringy or tough if you leave that layer in place.

To Store Raw Asparagus

1. Place the asparagus in a tall drinking glass or tumbler.
2. Add an inch or two of cold water.
3. Refrigerate for up to three days, changing the water daily.

To Steam Whole Spears

1. Choose asparagus of similar length and thickness, so all of the spears will be done at the same time.
2. Place ¼ inch of water in a skillet or wide saucepan. Bring it to a simmer.
3. Add the prepared asparagus, placing the spears in a single layer if possible. Cover and

steam until the asparagus turns bright green and bends easily when you pick it up at the base and pull the tip back toward you, between one and a half and seven minutes, depending on the thickness.

TO STEAM WHOLE SPEARS IN THE MICROWAVE

I. Stand the spears upright in a two-cup measure, or any microwavable glass tall enough to hold them. Add ¼ inch of water.

2. Drape a damp paper towel over them.

3. Microwave on full power for one and a half to two minutes, depending on how many spears you have and how thick they are. If they're not done after the first cooking cycle, return them to the microwave for one minute at a time until they are, keeping in mind that the spears will continue to cook for a short time once they're out of the oven. The asparagus is done when it's bright green and bends easily when you pull it back toward you. (If it droops, it's overdone.)

TO STEAM CHOPPED ASPARAGUS

I. Put a rack or a steamer basket on the bottom of a large saucepan.

2. Add water until it almost touches the rack or basket. Bring the water to a boil.

3. Add the asparagus, cover the pot, and steam until the asparagus is bright green and crisp but cooked in the center, about one and a half to seven minutes.

TO STEAM CHOPPED ASPARAGUS IN THE MICROWAVE

I. Place the prepared asparagus in a microwavable bowl.

2. Add ¼ inch of water. Cover the bowl with a plate or damp paper towel.

3. Microwave on full power for two minutes. Let the asparagus rest one minute before lifting the plate or paper towel and testing for doneness. If it's not done, return it to the oven at full power for one minute more.

TO BLANCH (TO PREPARE QUARTERED ASPARAGUS SPEARS FOR GRILLING OR STIR-FRYING)

I. Fill a large saucepan with water and bring to a boil.

2. Meanwhile, fill a large bowl with cold water and ice cubes. Line a colander with paper towels.

3. Plunge the spears into the boiling water. The moment they turn bright green—about thirty to forty-five seconds for slender spears, up to one and a half minutes for thicker spears—remove it with a slotted spoon and transfer it to the ice water for fifteen seconds, to stop the cooking, then transfer to the colander to drain.

Avocados
Botanically speaking, avocados are fruit. Mercifully, they're seldom served as such. The last time I had an avocado for dessert was literally the last time. It was avocado ice cream, and the opportunity to appreciate the culinary potential of the avocado's true identity was lost on me as I lamented the waste of good guacamole.

There are two types of avocado: Hass, the dark green, pocked, thick-skinned kind from California, and the smoother, light green fruit from Florida. Whole, each contains more fat than you should eat at one sitting, but Florida's are leaner by half—nine grams of fat to the Hass's seventeen grams of fat. Naturally, the Hass tastes better.

I SERVING: ⅓ MEDIUM AVOCADO (ROUGHLY 3½ OUNCES) • CALORIES: HASS 180; FLORIDA 110 • FIBER: HIGH • GOOD SOURCE OF FOLACIN

To Choose

1. A good avocado's skin is unblemished, and there's no mold growing around the stem.
2. Its color is vibrant and even in tone.
3. It gives slightly when you squeeze it.

To Use

1. Strip off the peel.
2. Cut the avocado in half and remove the pit.
3. Chop or puree according to your recipe.

To Store Unripe Avocados

1. Place them in a paper bag in a dark cupboard for twenty-four to forty-eight hours.
2. To speed ripening, put a ripe pear or banana in the bag with them.

To Store Uncut Ripe Avocados

1. Keep them at room temperature for up to three days.
2. Refrigerate them when they're ripe, and use them within three days.

To Store Cut Ripe Avocados

1. Sprinkle the exposed fruit with lemon juice.
2. Wrap the avocados loosely in plastic and refrigerate them for up to four days.
3. When they get gray-black and mushy, throw them out.

Beets
If natural selection truly works to sustain plants that can endure abuse, then beets should be with us forever. Few vegetables have been treated as badly. Pickled in vinegar, stewed in cinnamon syrup, and shredded on iceberg lettuce, beets have managed somehow to survive. If you've only had beets served in those ways, you may well think they *should* be extinct. But try them fresh, and prepared simply as follows, and you'll surely change your mind.

I SERVING: I CUP SLICED (ABOUT 1½ MEDIUM BEETS) • CALORIES: 50 • FIBER: MEDIUM • GOOD SOURCE OF VITAMIN C; FOLACIN

To Choose

1. A good beet is deep, vibrant crimson-maroon.
2. The leaves are perky and rich green with deep crimson veins.
3. The skin is smooth, and the beet is firm.

To Use

1. Cut off the leaves—leaving two inches of stem—and save them to cook separately if you want. (If you don't want, I'll understand. I *know* that the leaves are the most nourishing part of the beet, but I don't like them as much as spinach, collards, and kale.)
2. Wash the beets gently but thoroughly; don't scrub, or you'll scrape away the nutrients that lie just under the skin.
3. Leave the peel intact until you've cooked them.

To Store Raw Beets

1. Cut off the leaves, leaving two inches of stem. (The remaining stem will help the beets keep their color and nutrients.)

2. Place the beets, unwashed, in a paper bag.
3. Refrigerate for up to one week. If they start to sprout, cut off the affected area and carry on with your recipe as if nothing's happened.

To Boil

1. Bring water to a boil in a large saucepan.
2. Add the prepared whole beets. Bring to a second boil. Cover and reduce the heat to low.
3. Boil until you can pierce the beets with a paring knife, about forty minutes, depending on their size. Cool and peel.

To Boil in the Microwave

1. Cut the prepared beets into quarters.
2. Place them in a microwavable bowl. Add one inch of water. Cover the bowl with a plate or drape it with a damp paper towel.
3. Microwave one beet on full power about seven minutes, depending on the beet's size. Add two minutes for each additional beet. Leave the plate or paper towel in place for four minutes. Cool and peel.

To Bake

1. Heat the oven to 425°F.
2. Carve an X at both ends of each beet and wrap them in foil.
3. Place the beets directly on the oven rack, and bake until they're soft, about fifty minutes, depending on their size.

To Bake in the Microwave

1. Prick the beets in several places with a sharp knife. (If you forget, the beets will explode inside your oven. Guaranteed you'll remember next time!)
2. Place a paper towel on the bottom of the microwave and put the beets on top.

3. Microwave one beet on high for five to ten minutes, depending on its size. (Add two to three minutes of cooking for each additional beet.) To ensure even cooking, remove from the oven and wrap in foil (the beets will continue cooking inside the foil). Let them rest for three to five minutes before unwrapping and peeling. Or you can skip the foil, and simply rotate the beets in the oven at 180 degrees and cook for one to two minutes longer before removing and peeling.

To Blanch (to prepare beets for grilling)

1. Fill a large saucepan with water and bring to a boil.
2. Meanwhile, fill a large bowl with cold water and ice cubes. Line a colander with paper towels.
3. Plunge the beets into the boiling water. When you can pierce them with a paring knife (about four minutes for small beets), remove them with a slotted spoon and transfer to the ice water for fifteen seconds, to stop the cooking, then transfer to the colander to drain.

Broccoli
Broccoli is a great polarizer. How people feel about it tends to reflect their attitude toward vegetables overall; you'll find that lots of people who love broccoli feel virtuous about it, while those who hate it make their disdain a point of pride.

Neither stance makes much sense, especially since most people who hate broccoli feel as they do because they've never had it cooked correctly. While the rest of us know it as crisp and sweet, broccoli as *they* know it is mushy and stringy and stinks to high heaven. To convert them you may have to pull a fast one, concealing it in a creamy cold soup (see page 200). If they go for it, great. If they don't, that's fine; you get to eat the leftovers.

I SERVING: ½ CUP, CHOPPED • CALORIES: 22 • FIBER: HIGH • GOOD SOURCE OF VITAMINS A, C; FOLACIN

TO CHOOSE

1. Good broccoli is a deep green.
2. The buds on the florets are tight and compact.
3. The stalks are firm and straight.

TO USE

1. To get grit out of the heads, dunk them in cold water and swish them around for a minute or so. Rinse well.
2. Cut off the woody ends.
3. If the lower part of the stems are tough and dry, use a vegetable peeler to pare away the outer layer, or the broccoli will be stringy and tough. If you want only the florets, cut high up on the stem, so the head separates into distinct pieces.

TO STORE RAW BROCCOLI

Refrigerate in a loose plastic bag or a perforated vegetable bag for up to five days.

TO STEAM

1. Put a rack or a steamer basket on the bottom of a large saucepan.
2. Add water until it almost touches the rack or steamer. Bring the water to a boil.
3. Add the broccoli, cover the pot, and steam until the broccoli is bright green and cooked, but still crisp in the center, about four minutes for florets, eight minutes for stems, ten to twelve minutes for a full head.

TO STEAM IN THE MICROWAVE

1. Place the prepared broccoli in a microwavable bowl.
2. Add ¼ inch of water and cover the bowl with a plate or damp paper towel.
3. Microwave on full power for three minutes for florets, six minutes for stems; eight to ten minutes for a full head. Let the broccoli rest one minute before lifting the plate or paper towel and testing for doneness. If the broccoli is not done, return it to the oven at full power for one minute more.

TO BLANCH

1. Fill a large saucepan with water and bring it to a boil.
2. Meanwhile, fill a large bowl with cold water and ice cubes. Line a colander with paper towels.

3. Plunge the broccoli into the boiling water. The moment it turns bright green, about forty-five seconds to one minute, remove it with a slotted spoon and transfer it to the ice water for fifteen seconds to stop the cooking, then transfer the broccoli to the colander to drain.

Brussels Sprouts
They look like cabbage and smell like cabbage, but brussels sprouts taste more like broccoli and are even less popular. If you're wise you won't serve them to guests without knowing where they stand on the subject or offering a simple salad as an alternative.

I SERVING: I CUP • CALORIES: 45 • FIBER: MEDIUM • GOOD SOURCE OF VITAMINS A, C; FOLACIN

To Choose

1. Good brussels sprouts are small, firm, compact, with leaves bound in a tight ball.
2. They're deep green, without yellow leaves. (If the outer leaf has yellowed, it may be okay if the leaves underneath have not.)
3. The leaves are smooth, without insect holes.

To Use

1. If the stem is still attached, cut it off.
2. If the outer leaf is yellow, droopy, or torn, remove it.
3. Soak the sprouts in water to cover for fifteen minutes to loosen grit. Rinse well.

To Store Raw Brussels Sprouts

1. If the sprouts come in a container with cellophane wrap, store them as is in the refrigerator for up to three days.
2. If you bought brussels sprouts loose, place them, unwashed, in a perforated plastic bag and refrigerate for up to three days.
3. If you bought the sprouts on the stem, cut them off, transfer them to a perforated plastic bag, and refrigerate for up to three days.

To Steam

1. Put a rack or a steamer basket on the bottom of a large saucepan.
2. Add water until it almost touches the rack or basket. Bring the water to a boil.
3. Add the brussels sprouts, cover the pot, and steam until tender, about six to ten minutes.

To Steam in the Microwave

1. Place the prepared brussels sprouts in a microwavable bowl.
2. Add ¼ inch of water. Cover the bowl with a plate or damp paper towel.
3. Microwave on full power for three minutes. Let the brussels sprouts rest one minute before lifting the plate or paper towel and testing them for doneness. If they're not done, return the brussels sprouts to the oven at full power in one-minute increments until tender.

Cabbage
The *Dictionary of American Slang* says that "cabbage" was once a colloquialism for "money," which is odd, since cabbage is what people eat when they don't have any. The association with poverty has cost cabbage some prestige, but none of its value as a rich source of vitamins, fiber, and—if lightly steamed, not boiled to death—sweet, subtle flavor.

I SERVING: I ½ CUPS, SHREDDED • CALORIES: 25 • FIBER: HIGH • GOOD SOURCE OF VITAMIN C; FOLACIN

To Choose

1. A good head of cabbage has tightly packed leaves. (Buy heads; don't buy halved, shredded, or sliced cabbage. Cabbage loses nutrients as soon as it's cut.)

2. The color, whether green or red, is vibrant and even, not dull or spotty.

3. It's clean, with few, if any, signs that bugs have been at it.

To Use

1. Trim off the stem.

2. Cut off the droopy outer leaves.

3. Don't bother washing the cabbage, unless you find that it's gritty. If it has to be washed, rinse it *just* before cooking or shredding.

To Use for Stuffing

1. If the cabbage is very tender, and the leaves are not too tightly packed, cut the leaf at the stem end, and peel it off the head, taking care not to tear it.

2. Blanch the leaves to soften them for stuffing. If the leaves are too firm and too tightly packed to peel off without tearing, steam the head to loosen them.

To Store Raw Cabbage

1. Place unwashed whole cabbage heads in a perforated plastic bag.

2. Refrigerate in the crisper compartment for up to two weeks.

3. Wrap cut cabbage tightly in plastic, refrigerate, and use within two days.

To Blanch the Leaves

1. Fill a large saucepan with water and bring it to a boil.

2. Meanwhile, fill a large bowl with cold water and ice cubes. Line a colander with paper towels.

3. Plunge the cabbage leaves into the boiling water. Let them boil for one minute, then remove them with tongs or a slotted spoon and transfer them to the ice water for fifteen seconds. Transfer to the colander to drain.

To Steam the Head

1. Put a rack or a steamer basket on the bottom of a large saucepan.

2. Add water until it almost touches the rack or basket. Bring the water to a boil.

3. Add the cabbage head, cover the pot, and steam until the leaves peel away easily, about eight to ten minutes.

To Steam the Head in the Microwave

1. Place the prepared cabbage head in a microwavable bowl.

2. Add one inch of water. Cover the bowl with a plate or damp paper towel.

3. Microwave on full power for four minutes. Let the cabbage rest one minute before lifting the plate or paper towel and testing to see whether the leaves peel easily. If they do not, return the cabbage to the oven at full power at one-minute intervals until they do.

Carrots
When "health food" became fashionable in the 1960s, dessert was a problem for everyone involved. What sort of treat would be consistent with their principles? Carrot cake! The vegetable's reputation as a healthy food was so unassailable, no one questioned the relative value of a shredded carrot or two in a batter that also included a cup of oil

and enough honey to afford a hiveful of bees early retirement.

Inadvertently, the cake made a great contribution, demonstrating that carrots can be versatile. Until then they'd been pretty much confined to those awful canned-vegetable combos and to the lunch bags of weight-obsessed schoolgirls, not to mention photo shoots for onion-dip mix. Now we enjoy them in soups (see page 162), gnocchi (see page 316), and unusual salads (see page 108).

I SERVING: ½ CUP • CALORIES: 35 • FIBER: MEDIUM • GOOD SOURCE OF VITAMIN A

To Choose

1. A good carrot is deep orange.

2. The carrot is firm and uncracked.

3. Packaged carrots shouldn't have the leafy top. (The package keeps them fresh; the tops sap the moisture and nutrients from carrots.)

To Use

1. Cut off the tip and the root end.

2. Pare with a vegetable peeler or scrub with a vegetable brush.

To Store Raw Carrots

1. If the leafy tops are still on, twist them off and discard them as soon as you get home.

2. Place the carrots in a plastic bag or leave them in their original package and store them in the crisper compartment of the refrigerator for up to two weeks.

3. Don't store them close to apples or pears, which give off a gas that will spoil them.

To Blanch

1. Cut the carrots into thin (¼ inch) slices lengthwise, or into rounds. Fill a large saucepan with water and bring to a boil.

2. Meanwhile, fill a large bowl with cold water and ice cubes. Line a colander with paper towels.

3. Plunge the carrots into the boiling water. The moment they begin to soften, about forty-five seconds to one minute, remove them with a slotted spoon and transfer to the ice water for fifteen seconds, to stop the cooking, then transfer to the colander to drain.

To Steam

1. Slice the carrots as thin as you'd like, lengthwise or into rounds. Put a rack or a steamer basket on the bottom of a large saucepan.

2. Add water until it almost touches the rack. Bring the water to a boil.

3. Add the carrots, cover the pot, and steam until tender, about eight to ten minutes.

To Steam in the Microwave

1. Place the prepared carrots in a microwavable bowl.

2. Add one inch of water. Cover the bowl with a plate or damp paper towel.

3. Microwave on full power for 4 minutes. Let rest one minute before lifting the plate or paper towel and testing to see whether the carrots are tender. If not, return to the oven at full power at one-minute intervals until they are.

Cauliflower Food writers love to quote Mark Twain on cauliflower, as if his observation (he called it "cabbage with a college education") is so profound it doesn't have to be explained. To be honest, I didn't know

what he meant until I consulted the source (his novel *Puddin' Head Wilson*) and found the lines that precede this quotation. "Training is everything," he wrote. "A peach was once a bitter almond; a cauliflower is nothing but a cabbage with a college education." I *think* he's saying that cauliflower is essentially a cabbage that resembles a brain.

What's most interesting about the passage is that no one ever cites the part referring to peaches. I suspect this is because we have enough to say about peaches without resorting to Twain. But cauliflower, which does in fact look like a brain (and tastes like a turnip), isn't as inspiring, so we'll borrow what words we can on the subject. I'd rather cite recipes that make the most of cauliflower than spend more time trying to describe it. See Cream of Cauliflower Soup on page 176.

I SERVING: I CUP, FLORETS • CALORIES: 25 • FIBER: MEDIUM • GOOD SOURCE OF VITAMIN C; FOLACIN

TO CHOOSE

1. A good cauliflower is pure white or pale ivory.
2. The buds on the florets are firm, not crumbly.
3. It's not bruised or marked with brown or yellow blotches.

TO USE

1. Cut off the stem and leaves at the base. Cut the stem higher up if you want to separate the florets.
2. Soak the whole head or the florets in cold water for fifteen minutes to get rid of any bugs that may be lodged there.
3. Rinse with fresh water.

TO STORE RAW CAULIFLOWER

1. Place the unwashed head in a perforated plastic bag.
2. Store in the refrigerator for up to five days.
3. If you're storing florets, they'll keep, refrigerated, in a perforated plastic bag for up to two days.

TO BLANCH

1. Fill a large saucepan with water and bring it to a boil.
2. Meanwhile, fill a large bowl with cold water and ice cubes. Line a colander with paper towels.
3. Plunge the cauliflower into the boiling water. After two minutes remove it with tongs or a slotted spoon, transfer it to the ice water for fifteen seconds to stop the cooking, then transfer it to the colander to drain.

TO STEAM

1. Put a rack or a steamer basket on the bottom of a large saucepan.
2. Add water until it almost touches the rack or basket. Bring the water to a boil.
3. Add the florets or whole cauliflower, cover the pot, and steam until tender but still firm, about three to five minutes for florets; twelve to fifteen for a whole head.

TO STEAM IN THE MICROWAVE

1. Place the prepared cauliflower in a microwavable bowl.
2. Add water, and cover the bowl with a plate or damp paper towel.
3. Microwave on full power for four to six minutes for florets, ten to fifteen minutes for a full head. Let the cauliflower rest two min-

utes before lifting the plate or paper towel and testing it for doneness. If the cauliflower is not done, return it to the oven at full power at one-minute intervals.

Celery
You have to admire the imagination and daring of the good folks at the Michigan Celery Promotion Board. Or applaud their sense of humor. The recipes in their informational packet include several that are way-out wacky, notably one for celery Parmesan. Call me conservative, but I can't see it. I'll stick with more conventional uses for the sharp-flavored stalks, chopping them raw for salads, steeping them to season broths, and pureeing them with potatoes and milk for soothing soup (see page 176).

I SERVING: 2 STALKS • CALORIES: 20 • FIBER: LOW • GOOD SOURCE OF NO SINGLE NUTRIENT

TO CHOOSE
1. Good celery stalks are firm and smooth.
2. The surface is glossy and ice green.
3. The leaves are bright green and aren't wilted.

TO USE
1. Separate and rinse the ribs, making sure to get at any dirt that may be lodged inside the crevice.
2. Trim off the wide root end.
3. Check the recipe to see whether you need the leaves. If not, cut them off and save them—for up to three days refrigerated, wrapped loosely in plastic—for vegetable broth.

TO STORE RAW CELERY
1. Place in a perforated plastic bag.
2. Keep in the crisper in the refrigerator for up to ten days.
3. When the surface gets slimy, it's time to toss the celery.

Corn
Jonathan Swift said, and I agree, "Whoever could make two ears of corn grow upon a spot of ground where only one grew before would deserve better of mankind, and do more essential service to his country than the whole race of politicians put together."

For eleven months of the year, my community is a model of civility. Neighbors are neighborly but not intrusive, everyone drives cautiously, mindful of each other's kids, and except for the occasional yelping pup or squealing child, peace prevails night and day. But then July comes around, and it's dog eat dog, or, to be precise, *we* eat corn. When the native ears arrive at the local market, elbows go out, teeth are bared, and hands shovel into the bin until there's nothing left for those whose poor timing or good manners kept them from the fray.

1 SERVING: ½ CUP, KERNELS • CALORIES: 70 • FIBER: MEDIUM • GOOD SOURCE OF FOLACIN, THIAMIN

TO CHOOSE

1. On a good ear of corn, the husk fits snugly, and the silk is light and moist.
2. The kernels are plump, even, and perfectly aligned, not protruding or crooked.
3. The color—whether white, pale yellow, or deep yellow—is vibrant and glossy, not dull.

TO USE

1. Peel off the husk and silks unless you're going to microwave the corn, in which case you should strip away only the tough outer layer of husk and leave the bright green inner leaves intact.
2. If you need raw kernels, hold the ear over a large bowl and scrape closely with a very sharp serrated knife, letting the kernels and the milk fall into the bowl.

TO STORE RAW CORN

1. Reconsider. Corn doesn't keep no matter what you do.
2. Invite extra guests to help eat it all at once. Failing that . . .
3. Place the ears in a plastic bag and refrigerate until tomorrow.

TO BOIL

1. In a large pot, bring enough water to cover the corn to a boil.
2. Add the corn and bring the water to a second boil.

3. Cover the pot, turn off the heat, and let the corn sit for eight to ten minutes. (If you're using an electric stove, transfer the pot to an inactive burner as soon as you turn off the heat.) Remove with tongs or a large slotted spoon.

TO MICROWAVE

1. Remove the tough outer husk, leaving the tender light green layer in place.
2. Place a paper towel on the bottom of the microwave and put the ears of corn on top.
3. Microwave one ear at full power for three to four minutes. Add two minutes for each additional ear. Let the corn sit for two minutes before stripping the husk.

TO GRILL

See page 451.

Cucumbers If we took Dr. Johnson's advice regarding cucumbers, "discard them as good for nothing," how would we make refreshing Gazpacho (see page 202) or Cucumber and Bulgur Wheat with Fresh Herbs (see page 138) —which explains why Johnson made his mark as a wag, not a cook.

1 SERVING: ⅓ MEDIUM CUCUMBER • CALORIES: 18 • FIBER: LOW • GOOD SOURCE OF NO SINGLE NUTRIENT

To Choose

1. A good cucumber is firm and well formed, not gnarly or bruised.

2. It's deep green and evenly colored.

3. It has thin skin and few seeds.

4. You can also buy hothouse or English cucumbers, commonly sold tightly wrapped in cellophane. They are available in most markets that have a wide variety of produce. They're seedless and therefore easier to use and more attractive to serve than ordinary cukes. They're also exceptionally crisp, great for salads and sandwiches. Their skin is thick, so peel hothouse cukes before you use them.

To Use

1. Rinse with cold water.

2. If you're slicing the cucumber very thin, and the skin is unwaxed, you won't have to peel it. Just cut off the tapered ends and slice with a razor-sharp knife.

3. If you want larger chunks, pare away the skin with a vegetable peeler. Cut the cucumber lengthwise into quarters, skim off the seeds by running a knife along the top, and chop.

To Store Raw Cucumbers

1. Place whole cucumbers in a plastic bag. Refrigerate for up to ten days.

2. Wrap cut cucumbers in plastic and refrigerate for five days.

Eggplants
The English call them aubergines, and it's just as well we don't, largely because "eggplant" is easier to pronounce. Which begs the question, "Why egg?" Because the first European eggplants were white. Purple has since become the norm, although you can find white in specialty stores. It has a milder flavor than the purple kind, but tends to be mealy, too.

Versatile and hearty, eggplants have been a mainstay of vegetarian cultures for centuries. Consequently, you'll find it highly spiced (see page 135), baked with lentils (see page 346), grilled (see page 462), and pureed (see page 133).

I SERVING: I CUP, SLICED • CALORIES: 25 • FIBER: LOW • GOOD SOURCE OF NO SINGLE VITAMIN OR MINERAL, BUT A SMATTERING OF SEVERAL

To Choose

1. A good eggplant is firm and smooth.

2. Its skin is a glossy deep purple.

3. It's slender and nicely tapered, not bulbous and squat. Small and medium eggplants tend to have fewer seeds; fewer seeds mean sweeter pulp.

To Use Chopped or Pureed Cooked Eggplant

1. Heat the broiler. Trim off the root end and place the eggplant, lying down, on the broiler tray.

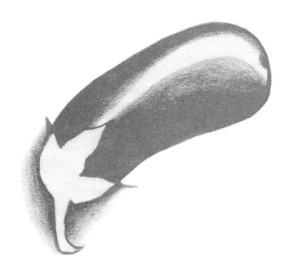

2. Broil until the skin buckles, then turn the eggplant and broil the other side, about seven minutes on each side.

3. Remove the eggplant from the heat. When it's cool enough to handle, peel off the skin and use the pulp as directed in your recipe.

To Store Raw Eggplant

1. Place the raw eggplant in a perforated plastic bag. Refrigerate in the crisper compartment for up to five days.

2. You can keep cooked eggplant pulp or baked eggplant slices, wrapped in plastic and refrigerated, for up to two days.

To Use Eggplant Slices or Pieces

1. Cut off the root end and slice the eggplant ½ inch thick.

2. If it's full of seeds, sprinkle it with coarse salt, and place it in a colander lined with paper towels for thirty minutes.

3. Rinse off the salt and immediately blot the pieces dry with paper towels.

To Bake

1. Heat the oven to 425°F.

2. Slice the eggplant, and place the slices on a nonstick baking sheet.

3. Bake until the eggplant is tender, about twenty minutes. Loosen the slices with a spatula, turn, and bake until the other side is tender, too, about seven minutes.

Fennel (Anise)
In the medieval language of plants, fennel stood for flattery. Maybe some monk found, as I have, that he got more compliments when he seasoned his stews with the stuff. More likely, it's because vintners discovered that eating fennel while drinking made their wine taste better (a notorious sales scheme involved feeding potential clients fennel-studded sausages when they arrived at a winery for a sampling).

Light green with feathery, leafy tops, crispy, and a bit sharp, fennel has a licorice flavor that makes it distinct from celery, which it resembles in some ways. Cooking tames that taste, and broths, stews, and sauces made with fennel in place of celery are sweeter for the switch.

I SERVING: I CUP, CHOPPED (ABOUT ½ BULB) • CALORIES: 25 • FIBER: MEDIUM • GOOD SOURCE OF VITAMINS A, C; IRON

To Choose

1. A good fennel bulb's surface is smooth and firm.

2. The color is a vibrant ice green.

3. The leaves look perky.

To Use

1. Rinse well with cold water, scrubbing very lightly with a vegetable brush if necessary.

2. Cut off the tough stem at the base before slicing or chopping.

3. If the recipe calls for the fronds, trim just the tips of the branches. If the recipe doesn't call for them, cut off the branches with the fronds attached, and save them for broth.

To Store Raw Fennel

1. Place unwashed fennel bulbs in a perforated plastic bag.

2. Refrigerate for up to eight days.

3. When you feel slime on the surface, it's time to toss them.

Garlic
Some say it's variety, but in fact it's *garlic* that's the spice of life. The proof is in the global repertoire of dishes that depend on it:

curries, chilies, stir-fries, sautés, salad dressings. . . . Plainly, for most people in most places, garlic is a staple.

There's more lore concerning garlic than any other food, some of it hokum, and some of it not. For instance, there's good research behind the notion that garlic protects against some cancers and cardiovascular conditions. Meanwhile, claims that it wards off vampires remain unproven. And while dietitians debate the optimum dose for a healthy heart, the rest of us may limit our consumption only in proportion to the amount that's eaten by our companions; one of garlic's peculiar properties is that you can't smell it on anyone else's breath if you've had enough yourself.

1 SERVING: 1 CLOVE • CALORIES: 5 • FIBER: NONE • GOOD SOURCE OF NO SINGLE NUTRIENT

TO CHOOSE

1. A good head of garlic has plump and tightly packed cloves.

2. The head is heavy for its size (indicating

that it's full of moisture, not dry or rotten inside).

3. The cloves are smooth, not bruised.

TO USE

1. Lay a garlic clove flat on a hard surface.

2. Hold the flat edge of a heavy knife over the clove, and press down with your palm to crack the skin.

3. Peel off the skin, then slice or crush the clove with the same heavy knife and mince or grate with a cheese grater according to your recipe.

TO STORE RAW GARLIC

1. Keep garlic unwrapped in a cool, dark place, such as a cupboard or the refrigerator.

2. Don't keep garlic that's been peeled.

3. Once garlic sprouts, throw it out.

TO ROAST

1. Heat an oven or toaster oven to 425°F.

2. Wrap unpeeled cloves (up to a whole head) in a piece of foil. Bake until the cloves are soft, about fifteen to twenty minutes.

3. Unwrap and let it cool. Using your fingers, squeeze out the garlic from the skins.

Jerusalem Artichokes (See Sunchokes, page 542.)

Leeks
It's hard to know whether to pity the Welsh or envy their having leeks as a national symbol. On the one hand, Welsh warriors look pretty silly depicted in films and commemorative statues brandishing leeks as they head into battle. Saber rattling's one thing. Waving a bunch of leeks around doesn't quite have the same effect.

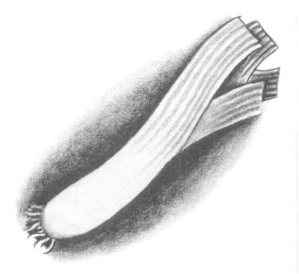

On the other hand, leeks are the most lus-cious member of the lily family, whose mem-bers include onions, scallions, garlic, and shallots. Leeks became the symbol of Wales because Saint David, the nation's patron saint, is said to have survived on them for quite some time. There are worse ways to martyrdom.

I SERVING: I CUP, CHOPPED • CALORIES: 60 • FIBER: NONE • GOOD SOURCE OF VITAMIN C; FOLACIN

To Choose

1. A good leek is firm and rigid, not droopy or shriveled.

2. The surface is smooth and glossy.

3. The tops are deep green, and the color tapers off nicely to ice green, then to white.

To Use

1. Cut off the green part, unless the recipe calls for it. Save it for broth.

2. Slit the leek lengthwise, without slicing it in half.

3. Peel back the layers and rinse under run-ning water to wash away grit.

To Store Raw Leeks

1. Place unwashed leeks in perforated plas-tic bags.

2. Store them in the refrigerator's crisper compartment for up to five days.

3. When the color fades and the surface feels slimy, it's time to toss them.

Lettuce (See page 112.)

Mushrooms Everyone knows the risk involved in foraging for wild mushrooms: you have to be able to tell the ones that will work well in a salad or sauce from those that will kill you.

But what about the hazards of shopping for mushrooms at your supermarket? You may not have to worry about poisons, but the staggering selection may be just as intimidating. Not long ago stores carried "mushrooms." Now those mushrooms are called white button mushrooms to distinguish them from cremini, morel, oyster, portobello, shiitake, and a perpetually prolifer-ating assortment of exotic varieties that, like heirloom lettuces and legumes, have become widely available. Generally, mushrooms of simi-lar size, shape, and density are interchangeable. You'll find that mushrooms that look notably different from the rest, such as enoki and shi-itake, taste much different, too.

I SERVING: 5 MEDIUM MUSHROOMS • CALORIES: 25 • FIBER: NONE • GOOD SOURCE OF RIBOFLAVIN, NIACIN

To Choose

1. A good mushroom is smooth and firm.

2. The surface is dry, not slimy.

3. The veil (the dark membrane between the stem and cap) is firmly attached.

POPULAR MUSHROOMS: SELECTION AND USE

White Button

LOOKS: White with short, stubby stems; wide umbrella heads

TEXTURE: Firm

FLAVOR: Sweet and faintly nutty when raw; rich and "meaty" when cooked

USE IN: Simple Soothing Mushroom Soup (page 177); Mushroom Pâté (page 240)

Cremini

LOOKS: Beige with short, stubby stems; wide umbrella heads

TEXTURE: Firm

FLAVOR: Nutty when raw; rich, meaty, and mushroomy when cooked

USE IN: Tomato and Mushroom Ragout (page 285); Mushroom Flan (page 242); Mushroom Risotto (page 311)

Portobello

LOOKS: Brown with short, narrow stems; wide, enormous heads

TEXTURE: Medium firm

FLAVOR: Bitter-bland when raw; rich and mushroomy when cooked

USE IN: Grilled Mushrooms and Sour Cream (page 226); Radicchio with Grilled Portobello Mushrooms on Mesclun (page 127)

Shiitake

LOOKS: Tawny with thin stems; wide, flat top

TEXTURE: Medium soft

FLAVOR: Don't eat raw; pleasantly pungent when cooked

USE IN: Moo-Shu Mushrooms (page 374)

Oyster

LOOKS: Ivory with thick, short stems with floppy fanlike heads

TEXTURE: Soft

FLAVOR: Don't eat raw; mild and faintly sweet when cooked

USE IN: Tomato and Mushroom Ragout (page 285); Artichokes and Mushrooms (page 225)

Morels

LOOKS: Small, brown, honeycomb cones

TEXTURE: Spongy

FLAVOR: Don't eat raw; rich and earthy when cooked

USE IN: Morels with Spinach and Cream (page 215); Tomato and Mushroom Ragout (page 285)

Porcini

LOOKS: Most sold in the United States are imported, sliced and dried

TEXTURE: Chewy when reconstituted

FLAVOR: Ultraintense, winey

USE IN: Mushroom Risotto (page 311); Mushroom Flan (page 242)

To Use

1. Wipe the caps with a damp paper towel just before using.
2. Cut off the stubby end of the stem.
3. If the mushrooms are large, or you'll be chopping rather than slicing them, separate the stem from the cap.

To Store Raw Mushrooms

1. Leave them, unwashed, in their original container or put in a paper—not plastic—bag.
2. Drape a damp paper towel loosely over them.
3. Refrigerate them for up to four days on a middle shelf, not in a bin or on the refrigerator's bottom; they need circulating air.

Onions
If there were primary colors in cooking, onions would be one of them, and in a just world, they'd be praised as much as the exotic produce that's got everyone so excited these days. Onions have two seasons: spring and autumn. Springtime onions include Vidalia, Maui, and Texas Sweet. They have a lighter, more delicate taste than the yellow, white, and red onions we get throughout the year. When their season comes around, Vidalias et al. get a degree of glory denied the autumn varieties known as storage onions. They're the workhorses of the kitchen, and, as such, they're taken for granted.

If it were possible, I'd suggest storage onions stage a strike. After a day or two, I'm sure food fanatics worldwide would lavish less praise on radicchio and rare root vegetables and express some appreciation for the inimitable, indispensable onion.

1 SERVING: 1 MEDIUM ONION • CALORIES: 60 • FIBER: HIGH • GOOD SOURCE OF VITAMIN C

To Choose

1. A good onion has tight, smooth skin.
2. It feels heavy for its size (indicating that it's full of moisture and hasn't dried out or rotted inside).
3. It's firm, unbruised, and has a faint savory-sweet aroma.

To Use

1. (Optional) Chill in freezer for ten minutes before slicing; very cold, onions are less prone to make your eyes water.

2. Slice off the top and bottom, then slice from top to bottom through the outer layer.

3. Peel off the outer layer.

To Store Raw Onions

1. Keep storage onions in a cool, dark place for four to five weeks.

2. Keep spring and summer onions in the refrigerator for one to two weeks.

3. If the onions sprout, throw them out.

Parsnips

They look like bleached carrots and taste like turnips, celery, and raw almonds combined. The French roast them or put them in stews. The Italians won't touch them. You decide.

I SERVING: ¾ CUP • CALORIES: 75 • FIBER: HIGH • GOOD SOURCE OF VITAMIN C; FOLACIN

To Choose

1. A good parsnip is no more than eight inches long.

2. It is firm and rigid, not shriveled or limp.

3. The parsnip is relatively smooth—without hairy roots, moist spots, or nicks.

To Use

1. Cut off the tip and root end.

2. Peel as you would a carrot or simply scrub well to remove surface grit.

To Store Raw Parsnips

1. If the green tops are attached when you buy them, cut them off.

2. Place the parsnips in a perforated plastic bag.

3. Refrigerate in the crisper compartment for up to three weeks.

Peas

There's no better example of the pernicious influence of English cooking in America than canned peas. Slimy, mushy, and the shade of green associated with seasickness, they could only be tolerated by people who've lost all taste for what's fresh.

So perhaps there's no better tribute to the redeeming influence of immigrants from Asia than the tender snow peas and crisp sugar snap peas that we can buy instead.

I SERVING: ½ CUP • CALORIES: 67 • FIBER: HIGH • GOOD SOURCE OF VITAMIN C; FOLACIN

To Choose

1. Good peas have shells that are vibrant green, smooth, and firm.

2. The pea bumps on snow peas are small, the pod almost translucent, and the stem crisp, not droopy.

3. The pod of sugar snap peas is firm, fat, and free of blotches.

To Use

1. Shell green peas by peeling back the pod along the inner seam.

2. String snow peas and sugar snap peas by snapping the stem end back and stripping off the string along the seam of the pod.

To Store Raw Peas

1. Place unwashed peas in a perforated plastic bag.

2. Refrigerate for up to three days.

3. When the peas look dull and limp, it's time to toss them.

Peppers

If Peter Piper picked a peck of them, I wonder not how *many* peppers he had (one peck = 2 gallons), but what *kind* they were and *what* he was going to do with all of them. His plans would depend on whether those peppers were treacherous or tame, searing or sweet. If Mr. Piper were clever, he'd have chosen an assortment so he could sample the broad range of flavors and sensations peppers provide.

1 SERVING: 1 MEDIUM BELL PEPPER • CALORIES: 25 • FIBER: MEDIUM • GOOD SOURCE OF VITAMINS A, C

To Choose

1. A good pepper is firm and smooth, not soft in spots or shriveled.
2. It's well formed, stands up straight, and is heavier than it looks.
3. You can't smell it.

To Use Unpeeled Chopped or Sliced Peppers

1. Slice the peppers in half vertically.
2. Pull out the core, seeds, and stem.
3. Slice or chop according to your recipe.

To Store Raw Peppers

1. Place, unwashed, in a perforated plastic bag.
2. Refrigerate for up to one week.
3. If moist spots develop, cut around them.

To Roast

1. Heat the broiler.
2. Slice the peppers in half lengthwise and pull out the core, seeds, and stem. Place the pepper halves skin side up on a broiler pan.
3. Broil until the skin buckles and chars, about five to eight minutes. Cool by transferring to a paper bag and refrigerating for about

twenty-five minutes or freezing for seven to ten. Peel and proceed with your recipe.

Potatoes

Yes, we have no potatoes. We have Katahdins and Kennebecs and Alleghanies and Caribes and Red Dales and Ruby Crescents and Yukon Golds. We have yellow fins and Blushing and Blossoms and a tasty little number called Desiree. We even have some called bananas—*Russian* bananas.

But we haven't had the plain old potatoes that come in plastic sacks at my house ever since I got the *Maine Potato Catalogue* from a place called WoodPrairie Farm. The catalog listed a dozen potatoes I'd never tasted, and reading it was like discovering that Mozart had written more than one piece, or finding that apples are not all McIntosh.

Everyone likes potatoes, but this hasn't always been true. Cultivated in Peru since Neolithic times, they weren't welcome when they arrived in Europe with Pisarro in 1534. The Spaniards called them "edible stones," the

When you're handling hot peppers, wear either rubber gloves or plastic bags on your hands. The seeds—which contain the hot stuff—will burn your skin if it's not covered. Remove as many of the seeds from hot peppers as possible, or the heat will overwhelm any seasoning you add to the dish and singe a few throats on the way down. To use dried chilies, reconstitute them by placing them in hot water to cover until soft—usually about thirty minutes. Drain, slice down the center, and remove the seeds before using.

Anaheim
Long, curved, and slender, green or red, it's the mildest of the "hot" chilies.

Ancho
Anchos are poblanos (see below).

Cherry
Named for its appearance, this small chili is moderately hot.

Habanero (Scotch Bonnets)
Small and orange-red, this chili is a firebomb.

Jalapeño
Small, oblong, orange or green peppers, jalapeños are medium-hot. They give a kick without a burn.

Poblano
Small, bell pepper–shaped chilies, poblanos can be mild or hot. You'll know only by tasting, so sample the pepper before you add it to your dish.

Serrano
A small, firm torpedo-shaped red or green chili, it tends to be very hot.

Germans fed them to farm animals, and the pious Scots denounced them on the basis that they aren't mentioned in the Bible. The French thought they caused leprosy and wouldn't touch them until the Revolution, when wheat shortages forced them into it.

Potatoes have distinct flavors and textures because they contain varying amounts of starch. You'll get the best results if you use starch content as your guide. When cooked, high-starch potatoes are very dry. They're best baked or used in potato-based doughs.

Medium-starch potatoes are dense, rich, and smooth, and they're wonderful baked, mashed, steamed, or used in stews or soups. Low-starch potatoes are moist and light, which makes them great for salads and gratins. True new potatoes are potatoes that are picked before they're mature—in other words, before their starch has fully developed. They're the lightest potatoes of all and available only briefly, before the mature-potato season's in full swing.

I SERVING: I MEDIUM POTATO • CALORIES: 110 • FIBER: WITH SKIN HIGH; PEELED, MEDIUM • GOOD SOURCE OF VITAMIN C

To Choose

1. A good potato is well formed for its kind (for example, long and oval if it's a russet, round or egg shaped if it's a new potato).
2. The surface is smooth and free of sprouts.
3. The color is even, with no trace of green (indicating bitter toxins).

High-Starch Potatoes: Use them for baking and in doughs such as that for gnocchi that call for potatoes; include russet, Idaho, and all-purpose potatoes.

Medium-Starch Potatoes: Use them for roasting, mashing, and cooking in stews; include Yukon Gold, Purple Peruvian, long red, and long white potatoes.

Low-Starch Potatoes: Use them for steaming or boiling and potato salads; include round red, small round white, new, and tiny purple potatoes.

To Use

1. Scrub the potato's surface with a vegetable brush to get rid of dirt and grit.
2. If the recipe calls for peeling, use a vegetable peeler, and skim away just the skin. The nutrients lie just under the skin, and you'll want to preserve as many as possible.
3. If you'll be microwaving the potatoes, poke several holes in the surface. These will allow steam to escape and keep the spuds from exploding in the oven.

To Store Raw Potatoes

1. Keep potatoes in a cool, dry place, where air can circulate around them (a good case for a hanging wire basket).
2. Don't refrigerate potatoes—the cold speeds the conversion of sugars to starches, making the spuds tough and bland.

3. If your potatoes start to sprout or turn green in places, cut away the affected area, and carry on with your recipe as if nothing has happened.

To Steam

1. Put about an inch of water in a saucepan, insert a steamer basket, and bring the water to a boil.

LAST WORD ON SPUDS

Now that we know they don't cause leprosy, let's eliminate the myth that they make you fat.

A 7-ounce potato has 210 calories, 4 grams of protein, 50 grams of carbohydrate, and no fat at all. With this you get 39 percent of the RDA for vitamin B6, 44 percent of vitamin C, and as much potassium as you need all day. There's fiber and iron in the skin, but you don't have to eat the skin to get vitamins and protein from a potato; much of the nourishment is *just under* the skin. So when you're preparing a dish that calls for peeled potatoes, cook the potato with the skin on to seal the vitamins and nutrients inside, then strip away the skin without cutting the flesh.

2. Cut large potatoes into two-inch chunks or thick slices. Leave tiny new potatoes (up to 1½ inches in diameter) whole. Place them in the steamer.

3. Cover the pan, turn the heat down to medium-low, and let the potatoes steam until tender, twenty to forty minutes, depending on the size of the pieces. Check the water level often, adding more as it evaporates.

TO BOIL

1. Fill a large saucepan with enough to cover the potatoes with water, and bring it to a boil.

2. Meanwhile, cut large potatoes into quarters. Leave tiny new potatoes (up to 1½ inches in diameter) whole.

3. Place the potatoes in the boiling water, turn the heat down to medium, and simmer gently until they're cooked through, about fifteen minutes.

TO BOIL IN THE MICROWAVE

1. Cut the potatoes into quarters or sixths, depending on their size.

2. Place the potatoes in a microwavable bowl. Add 1½ inches of water. Cover the bowl with a plate or drape it with a damp paper towel.

3. Microwave on full power five to seven minutes for one potato, depending on its size. Add two minutes for each additional potato. Leave the plate or paper towel in place for four minutes.

TO BAKE

1. Heat the oven to 425°F.

2. Carve an X at both ends of each potato.

3. Place the potatoes directly on the oven rack and bake until they're soft, about forty-five to fifty minutes.

TO BAKE A MEDIUM RUSSET IN THE MICROWAVE

1. Prick the potato in several places with a sharp knife. The holes let steam escape, keeping the potato from exploding in your oven.

2. Place a paper towel on the bottom of the oven and put the potato on it.

3. Microwave the potato on high for five to eight minutes, depending on its size. (Add two to three minutes of cooking time for each additional potato.) Remove the potato and wrap it in foil (it will continue cooking). Let it rest for three to five minutes before unwrapping.

4. For crispy skin, put the microwaved potato in a toaster oven at 500°F. for five minutes.

TO BLANCH (TO PREPARE POTATOES FOR GRILLING)

1. Fill a large saucepan with water and bring to a boil.

2. Meanwhile, fill a large bowl with cold water and ice cubes. Line a colander with paper towels.

3. Plunge the potatoes into the boiling water. When you can pierce them with a paring knife (about four minutes for new potatoes), remove them with a slotted spoon and transfer to the ice water for fifteen seconds to stop the cooking, then transfer to the colander to drain.

Rutabagas If you want to know what's
in a name, consider that *every* time I reach the checkout with this vegetable, the following exchange occurs. "What is this?" "It's a rutabaga." "A *rutabaga*?" (As in: "You gotta be kiddin' me.") It's like saying you're from Hoboken. No one takes you seriously after that.

The cashiers where I shop have been trained to tell a habanero from a pasilla and a cremini from a morel. They know cherimoyas and tomatillos. But someone decided to draw the line at rutabagas. What do you bet things would be different if, like the English, we called them Swedes or Yellow turnips? Given their deep, sweet flavor (like turnips, but richer), I'm sure they'd command more respect and more customers, too.

1 SERVING: 1 CUP, CUBED • CALORIES: 30 • FIBER: LOW • GOOD SOURCE OF VITAMIN C

To Choose
1. A good rutabaga is relatively smooth, without gouges and cracks.
2. It's unwaxed and/or no bigger than four inches in diameter.
3. It isn't covered with hairlike roots.

To Use
1. Cut off both ends.
2. Peel off the skin with a vegetable peeler. Make sure to cut deeply enough if it's been waxed.
3. Slice or chop according to your recipe.

To Store Raw Rutabagas
1. Keep them in a cool, dark place where the air circulates well.
2. If they sprout, cut away the affected area, and carry on with your recipe as if nothing's happened.
3. When the surface gets slimy, it's time to toss them.

To Steam
1. Slice the rutabagas.
2. Put a rack or a steamer basket on the bottom of a large saucepan.
3. Add water until it almost touches the rack or basket. Bring the water to a boil.

4. Add the sliced rutabagas, cover the pot, and steam until you can pierce them easily with a knife, about twenty-five minutes, depending on the thickness of the slices.

To Steam in the Microwave

1. Place the prepared rutabaga in a microwavable bowl.

2. Add one inch of water. Cover the bowl with a plate or damp paper towel.

3. Microwave on full power for ten minutes. Let the rutabaga rest for three minutes before lifting the plate or paper towel and testing it for doneness. If you can't pierce the rutabaga easily with a knife, return it to the oven at full power for one-minute intervals until cooked.

Salad Greens (See page 112.)

Scallions Green Onions, Spring
Onions Scallions put the zip and zing in stir-fries (see page 374), Nori Rolls (page 370), and salad dressings. It's virtually two ingredients in one; the greens work like an herb (I often use them in place of chives), while the white acts like an onion.

I SERVING: I CUP, CHOPPED • CALORIES: 30 • FIBER: LOW • GOOD SOURCE OF VITAMIN C; FOLACIN

To Choose

1. Good scallions have greens that are dark at the tips and taper off to white.

2. They're firm and rigid with tassel-like roots.

3. They're dry, not slimy.

To Use

1. Trim off the tip and root end.

2. Slice, chop, or mince, according to your

recipe, using as much of the scallions as called for.

3. If the recipe calls for the white only, save the greens—refrigerated in a perforated plastic bag for up to two days—for broth.

To Store Raw Scallions

1. Place in a perforated plastic bag.

2. Refrigerate for up to five days.

3. When the surface is slimy, it's time to toss them.

Spinach "What a world of gammon and
spinach it is!" David Copperfield observes at one point on his journey, using an expression that was common at the time. He means "nonsense," and why "spinach" was used in that context, I don't know. It's even more puzzling when you consider that spinach was one of the few popular vegetables in Copperfield's England, which held most greens in contempt.

The English chose a good green to enjoy; raw or lightly cooked, it's nearly as nourishing as they come.

I SERVING: 2 CUPS, CHOPPED • CALORIES: 30 • FIBER: LOW • GOOD SOURCE OF VITAMINS A, B6, C; FOLACIN, RIBO-FLAVIN, CALCIUM, IRON

To Choose

1. Good spinach leaves are jade green, without yellow on the edges or near the ribs.

2. The leaves aren't withered, and they don't curl at the edges.

3. It's been washed by the packager (highly recommended).

To Use

1. If the spinach hasn't been washed, fill a large bowl with water just before using. Dunk the spinach and swish it around.

2. Lift out the leaves after five minutes and place them in a colander. Dump the water.

3. Rinse the leaves with fresh water.

4. If you're using the spinach for salad, blot the leaves dry, then run them through a salad spinner. If you're cooking them, leave them wet.

To Store Raw Spinach

1. Wrap loose spinach leaves in paper towels. Place them in a plastic bag (not perforated). Refrigerate for up to three days.

2. Leave packaged spinach sealed in the refrigerator for up to three days.

To Steam

1. Place the damp leaves in a saucepan or skillet.

2. Cover and heat over low heat for two minutes.

To Cook in the Microwave

1. Place the damp leaves in a microwavable bowl. Cover loosely with a damp paper towel.

2. Microwave on full power for 1½ minutes.

Sprouts

It's ironic that sprouts have become a symbol of health food because there's not a lot to them but water and fiber. When you put them in sandwiches and stir-fries, you get virtually no vitamins, but you'll enjoy their crisp crinkly texture and delicate flavor.

I SERVING: I CUP ALFALFA SPROUTS • CALORIES: 10 • FIBER: LOW • GOOD SOURCE OF NO SINGLE NUTRIENT

To Choose

1. Good sprouts are crisp looking, with vibrant color.

2. They're dry on the surface, not slimy.

3. You can't smell them.

To Use

1. Take the sprouts out of their container.

To Store Sprouts

1. Keep sprouts refrigerated in their original container for up to three days.

2. Place loose sprouts in a perforated plastic bag, and refrigerate for up to three days.

Squash

The name "squash" comes from a verb, but unless you're up on your Narraganset, it's probably not the one you have in mind. The root word is *asquatasquash,* meaning "to eat raw or green," a fine suggestion for very young zucchini, but not the best recipe for acorn squash, which is far better baked with maple syrup and cinnamon.

Rich with beta-carotene, winter squash is more nourishing than summer varieties. It all evens out, though, because winter squash compensate for a shortage of fresh produce, while zucchini, yellow summer squash, and crooknecks appear when there are plenty of vitamins available from other vegetables.

Summer Squash: zucchini, yellow summer squash, and crooknecks

I SERVING: ½ CUP, CHOPPED • CALORIES: 18 • FIBER: LOW • GOOD SOURCE OF NO SINGLE NUTRIENT

To Choose

1. Good squash is no longer than eight inches and no more than two inches in diameter.

2. It's firm and rigid.

3. The surface is smooth and dry, with vibrant color.

To Use

1. Scrub the outside gently with a vegetable brush.

2. Cut off both ends.

3. Peel with a vegetable peeler only if the skin seems tough.

To Store Raw Summer Squash

1. Place in a perforated plastic bag.

2. Refrigerate for up to five days.

3. When it gets soft and slimy, it's time to toss it.

To Blanch

1. Fill a large saucepan with water and bring it to a boil.

2. Meanwhile, fill a large bowl with cold water and ice cubes. Line a colander with paper towels.

3. Plunge sliced or chopped squash into the boiling water. The moment the skin turns a brighter shade—thirty seconds to one minute—remove it with tongs or a slotted spoon, and transfer it to the ice water for fifteen seconds to stop the cooking, then transfer the squash to the colander to drain.

To Steam

1. Put a rack or a steamer basket on the bottom of a large saucepan.

2. Add water until it almost touches the rack or basket. Bring the water to a boil.

3. Add the sliced or chopped squash, cover the pot, and steam until tender but still crisp, about two to six minutes.

To Steam in the Microwave

1. Place the prepared squash in a microwavable bowl.

2. Add ¼ inch of water. Cover the bowl with a plate or damp paper towels.

3. Microwave on full power for one to four minutes, until tender, but still crisp. Let the squash rest for three minutes before lifting the plate or paper towel and testing it for doneness. If the squash is not done, return it to the oven at full power for one minute more.

Winter Squash: acorn and butternut

I SERVING: I CUP, CUBED • CALORIES: 45 • FIBER: LOW • GOOD SOURCE OF VITAMINS A, C

To Choose

1. Good winter squash is so pretty and well formed you can't decide whether to cook it or bronze it.

2. The color is deep and vibrant, and the surface is smooth, not gouged, cracked, or soft in spots.

3. It's heavier than it looks.

TO STORE RAW WINTER SQUASH

1. Keep it unwrapped at a cool room temperature for up to a month.
2. When the color fades and the shell feels soft, it's time to toss it.

TO STEAM IN THE OVEN

1. Heat the oven to 375°F. Place a rack in a baking dish. Add water or vegetable broth until it almost touches the rack.
2. Put the whole squash on the rack and cover the pan with foil.
3. Bake until the squash is soft enough for use in your recipe, from thirty to sixty minutes. It will have to be completely soft for pureeing for use in soups and terrines. It should stay partly firm if you're going to stuff it.

TO STEAM IN THE MICROWAVE

1. Place the prepared squash in a microwavable bowl.
2. Add two inches of water, and cover the bowl with a plate or damp paper towel.
3. Microwave on full power for five to ten minutes. Let the squash rest for three minutes before lifting the plate or paper towel and testing it for doneness. If it's not done, return it to the oven at full power at one-minute intervals.

Sunchokes Jerusalem Artichokes

These gnarly roots have little to do with the sun (they grow underground) or Jerusalem (they're native to North America). And while they taste a lot like artichokes, there's no botanical link between them. The name "Jerusalem artichoke" owes more to savvy marketing than anything else. Importers from England, catering to a craze for exotic produce, hoped that "Jerusalem" would lend an alluring mystique to a food that had little frankly to recommend it. Meanwhile, American marketers, afraid the exotic name would put off more people than it drew, chose the simpler "sunchoke."

1 SERVING: ¾ CUP, SLICED • CALORIES: 75 • FIBER: HIGH • GOOD SOURCE OF IRON

TO CHOOSE

1. A good sunchoke is firm and rigid.
2. It's evenly colored, not faded or tinged with green.
3. It's relatively smooth, without soft spots.

TO USE

1. Cut off all of the ends.
2. Scrub thoroughly with a vegetable brush.
3. Don't peel—too much of the vegetable will come off with the skin.

TO STORE RAW SUNCHOKES

1. Keep them, unwashed and unwrapped, in a cool, dark place for up to one week.
2. When the sunchokes sprout, toss them out.

Sweet Potatoes

The sweet potato suffered a demotion of sorts in the late 1700s when after several centuries as "the potato," it had to yield the title to the tuber we now know by that name. Until then, the sweet potato was a staple in France and Spain, partly because it tastes good, and partly (largely?) because it was supposed to be an aphrodisiac.

To the extent that nutrition affects virility, it may be. According to the Center for Science in the Public Interest, an authoritative nutrition advocacy group, sweet potatoes are the most nourishing vegetable by a long shot. On a point system scoring for vitamins, minerals, complex carbohydrates, protein, and fiber, sweet potatoes rank higher than their closest competitor (the potato) by 100 points. They lead spinach by slightly more than that, and broccoli by 131. They're way ahead of carrots (154 points higher), corn, and tomatoes.

I SERVING: I MEDIUM SWEET POTATO • CALORIES: 140 • FIBER: MEDIUM • GOOD SOURCE OF VITAMINS A, C

TO CHOOSE
1. A good sweet potato is well shaped— tapered nicely at each end and rounded in the middle.
2. It's deep orange and evenly colored, not faded in spots.
3. It's heavy for its size, indicating that it's full of moisture, not dry or rotten inside.

TO USE
1. Scrub with a vegetable brush.
2. To preserve nutrients, don't peel before boiling, steaming, or baking.
3. Peel the sweet potato after cooking if you'd like or if the recipe calls for pureeing.

TO STORE RAW SWEET POTATOES
1. Keep in a cool place away from direct light, where the air can circulate around them.
2. Don't refrigerate sweet potatoes. The cold speeds the conversion of sugar to starches, making the potatoes tough and bland.
3. If they start to sprout, cut out the affected area, and use the rest as if nothing has happened.

TO BOIL IN THE MICROWAVE
1. Cut the unpeeled potatoes into quarters or sixths, depending on their size.
2. Place them in a microwavable bowl. Add 1½ inches of water. Cover the bowl with a plate or drape it with a damp paper towel.
3. Microwave on full power five to seven minutes for one potato, depending on its size. (Add two minutes for each additional potato.) Leave the plate or paper towel in place for two minutes.

TO BAKE
1. Heat the oven to 425°F.
2. Carve an X at both ends of each sweet potato.
3. Place them directly on the oven rack and bake until they're soft, about forty-five minutes.

TO BAKE MEDIUM SWEET POTATOES IN THE MICROWAVE
1. Prick the potato in several places with a sharp knife. The holes will let steam escape and keep the potato from exploding in your oven.
2. Place a paper towel on the bottom of the microwave and put the potato on top.
3. Microwave on high for five to eight minutes. (Add two to three minutes of cooking for each additional potato.) To ensure even cooking, remove the sweet potato and wrap it in foil. (The potato will continue cooking in the foil.) Let it rest for three to five minutes before unwrapping it. You can skip this step by simply turning the potato 180 degrees in the microwave and cooking for one to two minutes longer.

To Blanch (to prepare sweet potatoes for grilling)

1. Fill a large saucepan with water and bring to a boil.
2. Meanwhile, fill a large bowl with cold water and ice cubes. Line a colander with paper towels.
3. Plunge the sweet potatoes into the boiling water. When you can pierce them with a paring knife (about five minutes, depending on size), remove them with a slotted spoon and transfer to the ice water for fifteen seconds to stop the cooking, then transfer to the colander to drain.

Tomatoes

The great present-day misconception concerning tomatoes is that fresh is best. For a short while each year, and in the nation's Sunbelt, this is true enough. But the rest of the time in the rest of this land, you'll do better with a box of Pomi or a can of Redpack than with whatever may be in the produce bin. I am secretly glad to know this because it's easier to crack open a can of prepared tomatoes than to peel, seed, and chop a few pounds of fresh tomatoes.

But today's misconception is nothing compared with the myth that moved sixteenth-century botanists to name the tomato *mala insana,* or "unhealthy apple." This myth—that tomatoes are poisonous—persisted over here long after the Italians had disproved it in their own country. Tomatoes aren't even mentioned in an American cookbook until 1848, and then the point of the passage is how to temper the taste. Several years later, the United States Supreme Court defied botanical science and decreed the tomato, which is a fruit, a veg-etable. The ruling had to do with whether tomatoes should be taxed as fruits or vegetables; since tomatoes are served as vegetables, the Court decided they should be subject to the same commerce laws pertaining to broccoli, onions, et al.

I SERVING: I MEDIUM TOMATO • CALORIES: 35 • FIBER: LOW • GOOD SOURCE OF VITAMINS A, C

To Choose

1. A good tomato's color is vibrant, deep orange.
2. It gives slightly when you squeeze it.
3. It has a faint, sweet aroma.

To Use Peeled Tomatoes in Sauces, Stews, and Other Cooked Dishes

1. With a sharp paring knife, make two slits in the skin at the top of the tomato.
2. Bring enough water to cover the tomatoes to a boil in a saucepan. Add three or four tomatoes at a time, and boil for thirty seconds.

3. Remove the tomatoes with a slotted spoon. When they're cool enough to handle, slip off the skin. Slice and scoop out and discard as many seeds as possible.

TO STORE RAW TOMATOES

1. Place unripe tomatoes in a brown paper bag until they're deep red. Don't refrigerate them; the cold keeps them from ripening and makes them mealy.

2. Keep ripe tomatoes at room temperature for up to two days.

3. Refrigerate very ripe tomatoes (those that seem about to turn into sauce all by themselves) in a perforated plastic bag for up to two days.

Turnips
What do brown rice, corn, parsnips, and turnips have in common? In some places where they've been fed to livestock, people have refused to eat them, thinking it beneath their dignity to dine like swine. For a short time, the French, for instance, tried to pretend they didn't have a taste for turnips, commonly fed to pigs. But never ones to substitute symbolism for a good meal, they gave up and resumed eating the tender, top-shaped vegetable.

I SERVING: I CUP, CUBED • CALORIES: 30 • FIBER: LOW • GOOD SOURCE OF VITAMIN C

TO CHOOSE

1. A good turnip is small—no more than 2½ inches in diameter—and well formed, shaped like a top.

2. It's smooth, without gouges, pits, sprouts, or hairlike roots on the surface.

3. The color bands are bright and distinct, not faded and run together.

TO USE

1. Slice off the ends.

2. Pare away the outer layer of skin with a vegetable peeler, taking care to get only the thinnest outer layer so you won't remove the vitamins.

3. Slice, chop, or leave whole, according to your recipe.

TO STORE RAW TURNIPS

1. Keep them in a cool, dark place or place in a perforated plastic bag and refrigerate for up to two weeks.

2. If they sprout, toss them out.

TO STEAM

1. Put a rack or a steamer basket on the bottom of a large saucepan.

2. Add water until it almost touches the rack or basket. Bring the water to a boil.

3. Add the turnips, cover the pot, and steam until they're tender, about eight to forty minutes, depending on the size and thickness of the pieces.

TO STEAM IN THE MICROWAVE

1. Place the prepared cut-up turnip in a microwavable bowl.

2. Add ¼ inch water. Cover the bowl with a plate or damp paper towel.

3. Microwave on full power for five minutes or more, depending on the size and thickness of the pieces. Let the turnip rest for one minute before lifting the plate or paper towel and testing it for doneness. If it's not done, return it to the oven at full power at one-minute intervals until tender.

To Boil a Medium Turnip in the Microwave

1. Cut the unpeeled turnips into quarters.

2. Place the quarters in a microwavable bowl. Add ½ inch of water. Cover the bowl with a plate or drape it with a damp paper towel.

3. Microwave on full power about six minutes for one turnip, depending on its size. Add two minutes for each additional turnip. Leave the plate or paper towel in place for two minutes before removing.

To Bake

1. Heat the oven to 425°F.

2. Carve an **X** at the end of each whole turnip.

3. Wrap in foil, place directly on the oven rack, and bake until soft, about fifty minutes, depending on its size.

To Bake a Medium Turnip in the Microwave

1. Prick the turnip in several places with a sharp knife. The holes will let steam escape and keep the turnip from exploding in your oven.

2. Place a paper towel on the bottom of the oven and put the turnip on top of it.

3. Microwave on high for five to eight minutes, depending on size. (Add two to three minutes of cooking for each additional turnip.) Remove and wrap in foil (it will continue cooking). Let the turnip rest for three to five minutes before unwrapping.

GUIDE TO EVERYDAY FRUITS

Refrigerate ripe fruit. Discard the fruit when it discolors and/or turns mushy.

Apples Actually, blueberries are more authentically American, so it's hard to say why *apple* pie is a national emblem. Maybe it's be-cause the Pilgrims planted apples with the first crops at Plymouth. But then, pie wasn't on their minds. Wary of the water, they drank hard cider instead, a fact that may account for the other-wise implausible image of the jolly Pilgrims we see each Thanksgiving; life in the colony was relentlessly grim, and it's hard to imagine how they'd look so happy without some help, per-haps in the form of fermented fruit juice.

While you may *think* there's a good selec-tion where you shop, consider that more than seven thousand varieties of apples are classified in America, and tens of thousands more grow in other countries.

1 SERVING: 1 MEDIUM APPLE • CALORIES: 80 • FIBER: HIGH

THE CHILD IN ALL OF US WANTS TO KNOW

Q. Was there a Johnny Appleseed?
A. Yes! John Chapman, 1774–1845, a vegetarian given to wearing a saucepan on his head (no causal relation between those facts, we hope), walked barefoot from Penn-sylvania to Indiana, planting orchards and setting up nurseries in every state along the way. In legend he strew the seeds at random. In fact his approach to agriculture was disciplined and methodical. He'd hoped to plant orchards right up to the Pacific, but he died in Fort Wayne, short of his goal, but having inspired many others to pursue it.

Apricots If you've read an ad for reduced airfares, long-distance phone rates, or anything else for that matter, you know it's rare when fine print carries something besides dis-claimers and disheartening clarifications. But in lettering tiny relative to the significance of the words, the latest brochure from the Washing-ton State Fruit Commission informs us that apricot production "continues to increase" and that the fragile, tangy, peachlike fruit, which used to hit its peak for one week only, in early summer, is now available clear into August.

Buy ripened apricots, which are deep orange-yellow with a peachy blush and feel soft, but not mushy. They don't ripen well at

POPULAR APPLES: SELECTION AND USE

Red Delicious
LOOKS: Red, bell shaped

FLAVOR AND TEXTURE: Sweet, juicy, firm, and crisp (can get soft and mealy; keep very cold)

BEST FOR: Eating raw

Golden Delicious
LOOKS: Yellow-green with speckles

FLAVOR AND TEXTURE: Very sweet, crisp, and smooth

BEST FOR: Eating raw

Winesap
LOOKS: Deep purple-red, small, round, with flat top

FLAVOR AND TEXTURE: Spicy, mild-tart, firm, and juicy

BEST FOR: Apple butter

Jonagold
LOOKS: Red blushed with gold, bell shaped

FLAVOR AND TEXTURE: Sweet, tart, very crisp

BEST FOR: Eating raw

Jonathan
LOOKS: Red, small to medium

FLAVOR AND TEXTURE: Tart, mildly spicy with sweet finish, crisp

BEST FOR: Eating raw, pies, applesauce

Granny Smith
LOOKS: Bright green, medium

FLAVOR AND TEXTURE: Tart, crisp, and (tooth alert!) very firm

BEST FOR: Baked apples, apple butter, apple crisp, and pies

Rome
LOOKS: Deep red, large, round

FLAVOR AND TEXTURE: Rich sweet-tart, firm, dense, and smooth (can get soft and mealy; keep very cold)

BEST FOR: Eating raw, baked apples, apple butter, apple crisp, and pies

Gala
LOOKS: Slashes of red, green, and gold, small

FLAVOR AND TEXTURE: Sweet, slightly spicy, crisp, and light

BEST FOR: Eating raw, applesauce

McIntosh
LOOKS: Red with spots of green, squat, round

FLAVOR AND TEXTURE: Mild sweet, smooth, soft (bruises and becomes mealy easily; keep very cold and eat as soon as possible)

BEST FOR: Eating raw

home—you may find that they mold on one side before they've even softened on the other.

I SERVING: 3 APRICOTS • CALORIES: 60 • FIBER: MEDIUM • GOOD SOURCE OF VITAMINS A, C; POTASSIUM

Bananas
If the numbers are correct (twenty-five pounds per person each year), they're America's favorite fruit, figuring in cream puddings and quick breads and in brochures advising you to get adequate potassium, a mineral abundant in this fruit.

Buy firm bananas and keep them at room temperature. When they start to get blotchy, refrigerate them. The skin will turn black, but the fruit will stay fresh.

I SERVING: I MEDIUM BANANA • CALORIES: 120 • FIBER: HIGH • GOOD SOURCE OF VITAMINS B6, C; POTASSIUM

Blackberries
There's no in-between with blackberries. They're either juicy, winey, and sweet, or they're bland as paper pellets or painfully sour. Aroma is a clue: if there's a faint,

sweet smell, they may be good. If there's nothing at all, you'll find the same true for flavor.

I SERVING: ⅔ CUP • CALORIES: 50 • FIBER: HIGH • GOOD SOURCE OF VITAMIN C

Blueberries
If Ben Franklin had had his way, the turkey, a strictly native bird, would festoon our nation's seal rather than the eagle, which inhabits other countries, too. By the same logic, we should say "As American as *blueberry* pie." Apples grow all over the world, while no other continent can boast of its blueberries.

Thanks to prolific cultivation, the season begins well before August. But the best berries still grow in the wild and appear in late summer.

I SERVING: I CUP • CALORIES: 100 • FIBER: HIGH • GOOD SOURCE OF VITAMIN C

Cantaloupes
If it's a flaw to be finicky, your choices are clear: compromise your character, or forget about cantaloupe. A good melon can be hard to find, and you'll

RED BANANAS? THREE-INCH BANANAS?

Make way for strange bananas, showing up in supermarkets, perhaps near you. Both red-skinned bananas and miniature yellow bananas tend to be sweeter and creamier than the usual kind.

probably have to pick through a pile of them for one that's neither impossibly underripe nor partially fermented. Look for melon that's firm like a well-inflated basketball, not hard like a boulder; that's heavy for its size (indicating it's full of moisture), and smells faintly sweet. Some say you should also insist on even netting and no bald spots. But this is asking too much and has no bearing on the taste.

I SERVING: ½ MEDIUM MELON • CALORIES: 50 • FIBER: LOW • GOOD SOURCE OF VITAMINS A, C; FOLACIN

Cherries
Some may idolize particular presidents, generals, or Supreme Court justices, but my Great American Heroes are Henderson and Seth Lewelling. In 1847, the Lewelling brothers put several hundred saplings into oxcarts and traveled west from Iowa to plant cherries in Oregon. Once they'd arrived, they played around with hybrids and harvested a perfect cherry, which they named for their farm's Chinese foreman. They called that cherry Bing, but I call it the Truffle of Fruits.

YOU WANTED TO KNOW

Q. What about those red-splattered yellow cherries?
A. Ranier and Queen Anne cherries are firm, crisp cherries with a mild flavor, edging toward plum. They're not for cooking, but for eating, obsessively.

Cherries should be firm and glossy, not muddy and dull. Check for mold, then eat them promptly, before it can accumulate. Washed and drained, cherries keep well frozen for up to a year.

I SERVING: 20 CHERRIES • CALORIES: 100 • FIBER: MEDIUM • GOOD SOURCE OF VITAMIN C

Cranberries
Like blueberries, cranberries are exclusively North American and make good muffins. For most practical purposes, though, they have more in common with rhubarb, which isn't sweet until you make it so by adding sugar (or honey) and simmering just long enough to soften. (If you cook cranberries too long, they turn bitter.) If it all seems like too much trouble, you can reconstitute dried cranberries by soaking them in hot water to cover, then use them instead of fresh.

I SERVING: I CUP • CALORIES: 50 • FIBER: MEDIUM • GOOD SOURCE OF NO SINGLE NUTRIENT

Dates
There's a county just north of Los Angeles where the word "date" is invariably followed by "shake," referring not to a strange social ritual, but to a drink comprising milk, vanilla ice cream, and the finger-shaped fruit. Middle Eastern immigrants brought dates to California at the turn of the century, but—except as an ingredient in dense nut bread—they haven't caught on in the country at large. Their gooey consistency may have something to do with it, and the fact that, even as fruits go, they're awfully sweet. But fresh organic Medjools are delicious, and as they make their way east, these dates may win over the nation.

I SERVING: I2 DATES • CALORIES: 275 • FIBER: HIGH • GOOD SOURCE OF NO SINGLE NUTRIENT

Figs Fresh figs make a fleeting appearance in most parts of the country, where the fruit is best known for filling a famous cookie named for the Boston suburb of Newton. In Italy, the arrival of figs in early fall is an occasion for frenzy, but we tend to let them rot in the store. This would have shocked the ancient Greeks, who so cherished figs that they made the annual harvest a sacred rite.

Maybe we ignore fresh figs because the season is so short that no one has time to learn what to do with them. Choose plump figs with a mild sweet aroma and firm, unruptured skin. Calimyrna figs are greenish yellow when ripe; mission figs turn blue-black, while Kadota become yellow-brown. When fresh figs aren't in season, dried mission figs are delicious stuffed with ricotta cheese and chopped nuts.

1 SERVING: 2 MEDIUM FIGS • CALORIES: 75 • FIBER: HIGH • GOOD SOURCE OF CALCIUM, MAGNESIUM

Grapefruit Why *grape*fruit? The horticulturalist who first took note of them (1814) thought they tasted like grapes. I guess there *is* no accounting for taste, unless the grapes he had in mind were spectacularly sour.

In one respect, grapefruit epitomizes a merciful side of nature; the sweeter grapefruit are better for you than the sour kind. Red grapefruit contains more of the anticancer agent beta-carotene than white.

1 SERVING: ½ GRAPEFRUIT • CALORIES: 50 • FIBER: LOW • GOOD SOURCE OF VITAMIN C

Grapes Leery of the weird new plants they found in the New World, the early colonists were relieved to recognize grapes. Being good Europeans, they set about making wine, only to have to settle for jam in the end. The grapes just weren't good enough for vinifying. This brought relief and opportunity to prohibitionist preacher Thomas Welch, who squeezed the grapes for "unfermented wine," aka grape juice. Eventually his company went on to manufacture the definitive jelly for peanut butter sandwiches. Welch did us all a favor by using Concord grapes in his products, so we can enjoy the taste without the pesky seeds.

Buy firm grapes that look as if they're ready to burst out of their skins. Green grapes should be translucent, with a touch of yellow, not opaque frosty green.

1 SERVING: 1½ CUPS • CALORIES: ABOUT 100 • FIBER: LOW • GOOD SOURCE OF VITAMIN C

Honeydew If you think you're peculiarly inept at choosing melon, you'll be heartened by a French proverb quoted by Maguelonne Toussaint-Samat in her magnificent *A History of Food* (Blackwell, 1992). Translated, it goes, "Friends of the present day are like melons. You must try fifty of them to find a good one." Honeydew is more inscrutable than cantaloupe, largely because the skin is thicker, so you can't gauge ripeness by touch. I'm not qualified to offer advice, since I usually wing it myself, finding that a faint sweet smell may be all there is to signal that the melon is good.

1 SERVING: ¹⁄₁₀ LARGE MELON • CALORIES: 50 • FIBER: LOW • GOOD SOURCE OF VITAMIN C

Kiwifruit Some say it tastes like strawberries and oranges sprinkled with lime, a description that inflates expectations for what I say tastes more like citrus-infused sugar water.

Sliced and peeled they're very pretty, but all but the best tend to be bland. Use them for garnish or in salads with other fruit.

1 SERVING: 2 MEDIUM KIWIFRUITS • CALORIES: 100 • FIBER: MEDIUM • GOOD SOURCE OF VITAMINS C, E; POTASSIUM

Lemons

There are three aspects of lemon in the kitchen: chemical, flavorful, and magical.

Chemically, lemon juice preserves the color of sliced vegetables by inhibiting oxidation.

The flavor is refreshing in desserts of all kinds, and surprisingly mellow in savory sauces.

And lemon juice and zest are magical in the way they act as culinary caffeine; a drop of juice or a pinch of zest animates other flavors, so foods taste livelier and more vivid.

Buy firm, well-formed fruit with a light, lemony scent. If you're going to be using the zest, try to find unwaxed, organic lemons, so the zest will be pure.

1 SERVING: 1 MEDIUM LEMON • CALORIES: 18 • FIBER: NONE • GOOD SOURCE OF VITAMIN C

LEMON, LIME, OR ORANGE ZEST

Lightly rub a whole lemon or lime against the fine teeth of a cheese grater. You want to remove only the colored part of the peel; the white underneath is bitter. Rotate the lemon or lime until you've grated as much zest as you need.

Limes

It's ironic that "to be in the limelight" means to be the center of attention, because no one pays much attention to limes. You'll find that like lemon, lime accents the taste of other foods, adding a faint, sweet flavor of its own. Reverse the trend and enjoy a revelation while you're at it: the next time a recipe calls for lemon juice or zest, use lime instead. Buy firm, well-formed fruit with a light scent of lime. If you're going to be using the zest, try to find unwaxed, organic limes, so the zest will be pure.

1 SERVING: 1 MEDIUM LIME • CALORIES: 20 • FIBER: NONE • GOOD SOURCE OF VITAMIN C

Mangoes

If the flood comes again, and a voice on high tells me to get an ark and fill it with fruits, I'd stuff the hold with mangoes. And in the space that remains, I'll squeeze in some more. Mangoes are a perfect fruit, sweet, substantial, and big enough for breakfast. There's something citrusy about them, but they have much more body than oranges or grapefruit.

Choosing a mango can be tricky because different types ripen in different ways. I learned this when I chewed out a local greengrocer for selling rotten fruit. Her mangoes were yellow, I said. "Some nerve charging a buck fifty for compost," I think is how I put it.

She assured me the fruit was fine. "Impossible," I replied. In my experience a mango that had gone from orange to yellow had *gone*. At this point she brandished a knife and, while I'm sure I made the more tempting target, sliced a mango instead. The flesh was blazing orange, pulpy, but still firm. There were no bruises and no sign of the soggy, rusty ring that forms around the seed of rotting fruit. I bought half a dozen off her "compost" pile, and left enlightened and contrite.

Some mangoes (for example, Tommy Atkins, the type most commonly sold in this country) are red-orange when they're ripe, and yellow when they're rotten. Others (the S-shaped mangoes from Haiti) stay green. Consequently, touch and smell are much better guides than color. You want one that gives slightly when you press it and smells faintly sweet. If it gives easily and has a cloying stench, you can call it compost without offending anyone.

I SERVING: ½ AVERAGE MANGO • CALORIES: 70 • FIBER: LOW • GOOD SOURCE OF VITAMINS A, C

Nectarines

If you consider the difference between a nectarine and a peach, you might first think of fuzz. But it's also the "nectar" part that makes them distinct. Nectarines, generally, are juicier and sweeter than peaches. They're also slightly hardier, giving you up to two additional days to eat them once they're ripe.

I SERVING: I NECTARINE • CALORIES: 70 • FIBER: LOW • GOOD SOURCE OF VITAMINS A, C

Oranges

Two assumptions about oranges represent the triumph of marketing over truth. One is that they're native to Florida. The other is that they're uniquely high in vitamin C. The Spanish brought oranges to the Sunshine State in the sixteenth century, and they've flourished in Florida ever since. And while it's true that oranges are a rich source of vitamin C, they're not unique—or even superior—in that respect. Red bell peppers have

more than twice as much. But then again, which would you welcome at breakfast?

I SERVING: I ORANGE • CALORIES: 80 • FIBER: LOW • GOOD SOURCE OF VITAMIN C; FOLACIN

Peaches

Peaches have cult status in several parts of the world: Asia, where they represent fertility and life; Georgia, where they provide the livelihood and a justified source of pride for tens of thousands; and my house, where we eat them compulsively from June till September.

I SERVING: 2 MEDIUM PEACHES OR I LARGE PEACH • CALORIES: 70 • FIBER: LOW • GOOD SOURCE OF NO SINGLE NUTRIENT

PUZZLED PEACH LOVERS WANT TO KNOW

Q. Why are white peaches so much more expensive than the rest?
A. The same qualities that make them desirable make them difficult to transport and preserve. The thin skin and tender pulp unique to this variety make them vulnerable to damage from slight temperature change and minimal impact. Few make it to the market, at which point the law of supply and demand applies, and prices are set accordingly.

POPULAR PEARS: SELECTION AND USE

Bartletts

LOOKS: Deep green or red, medium, nicely tapered

FLAVOR AND TEXTURE: Spicy, juicy when fully ripe, dense, and smooth

BEST FOR: Eating raw, poaching, and baking

Anjou

LOOKS: Pale green, squat

FLAVOR AND TEXTURE: Very sweet, juicy when fully ripe, dense

BEST FOR: Eating raw, poaching, and baking

Bosc

LOOKS: Reddish brown, long, narrow

FLAVOR AND TEXTURE: Spicy, crunchy, dense, slightly mealy

BEST FOR: Eating raw and poaching

Comice

LOOKS: Dull yellow-green, squat

FLAVOR AND TEXTURE: Very sweet, very juicy, thin and mealy

BEST FOR: Eating raw (too watery to cook)

Seckels

LOOKS: Green with deep red splotches, tiny, bite sized

FLAVOR AND TEXTURE: Spicy-sweet, crunchy

BEST FOR: Eating raw and poaching

Pears

Pears present an intractable problem to the impulsive eater. They don't get ripe. *Ever.* Or at least that's how it seems when you crave one. Pear eating takes planning, which is frustrating to those of us accustomed to thinking of fruit as a spur-of-the-moment snack.

To speed the process, put the pears in a paper bag along with a ripe banana. The bag will trap the gases that convert the starches that sweeten and soften the fruit.

I SERVING: I PEAR • CALORIES: 100 • FIBER: LOW • GOOD SOURCE OF NO SINGLE NUTRIENT

Pineapples

History is full of profound injustice, including the fate of Captain James Cook, explorer and navigator, who introduced the pineapple to Hawaii from the West Indies in 1778. Two years later, he was slaughtered by island natives. The pineapple, needless to say, survived him, becoming a major cash crop and a critical source of sustenance for the archipelago, which was short on native foods.

Hawaiian pineapple is ripe when it's blazing yellow-orange under the eyes and smells like something you want to eat *right now.* Costa Rican pineapple (which is more plentiful, less expensive, and not as sweet) turns pale yellow under the eyes and may not smell of anything until it's too late. Don't buy either kind if the fruit is leaking or if the bottom feels squishy.

I SERVING: 2 SLICES • CALORIES: 90 • FIBER: LOW • GOOD SOURCE OF VITAMIN C

Plums

Why is a desirable job called a plum?

It has to do with Little Jack Horner, who, you may recall, sat in the corner playing with his food. He stuck in his thumb and pulled out a plum. Ergo.

Yet "plum" hasn't always referred to a treat. In the nineteenth century "to give a taste of plum" meant to shoot someone. Presumably this was a play on "plumb," the piece of lead fixed to a line to gauge the depth of a river, the lead in this case being a bullet.

I'm drifting a long way from plums, which in actuality I find hard to do, as long as they're ripe (soft to the touch) and, preferably, purple. You may prefer green (mellow) or red (sharp and succulent) but I'll take Black Friars, the sweetest of them all.

1 SERVING: 2 PLUMS • CALORIES: 70 • FIBER: LOW • GOOD SOURCE OF VITAMIN C

Raspberries

The fruit is fragile, and the season is short. But the raspberry's lease on life has been greatly lengthened now that raspberry vinegar is widely available.

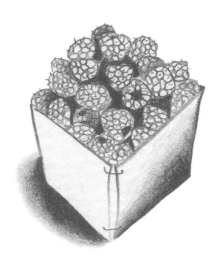

Look for berries that aren't mashed or moldy, and don't expect to keep them very long. Lay them in a single layer on a paper towel, without rinsing, and refrigerate for up to two days.

1 SERVING: 1 CUP • CALORIES: 50 • FIBER: HIGH • GOOD SOURCE OF VITAMIN C

Rhubarb

The most alarming item I've ever seen in a corrections column concerned a recipe for rhubarb pie. The recipe had run in the weekly feature pitched at children and called for rhubarb, leaves and all. Rhubarb leaves, the correction advised, are highly toxic.

The fruit itself looks like red celery and tastes of nothing much until you stew it with sugar. Then it has a citrusy flavor that blends well with other stewed fruits, especially apples, strawberries, and peaches, for dessert sauces, cobblers, and crisps.

1 SERVING: ¾ CUP • CALORIES: 20 • FIBER: MEDIUM • GOOD SOURCE OF NO SINGLE NUTRIENT

Strawberries

Politicians attack each other's record, conduct, and credibility, but rarely make an issue of their opponent's favorite foods. So the presidential campaign of 1840 stands out for the unique role that strawberries had in the race between William Henry Harrison and Martin Van Buren. Harrison's supporters depicted him as a he-man, who, according to an account in Waverly Root's *Eating in America*, lived on "raw beef without salt," while that sybarite Van Buren indulged in such fey luxuries as *strawberries*. Worse, Van Buren's chef was French and said to be serving foreign things like pâté de foie gras *in the White House!*

Harrison won, proving that an eclectic appetite is no asset in the American political system.

California exports them almost year-round, but everybody knows the best strawberries are the ones harvested locally for two or three short weeks in late spring to early summer.

1 SERVING: 8 STRAWBERRIES • CALORIES: 50 • FIBER: HIGH • GOOD SOURCE OF VITAMIN C

Watermelon
Botanically speaking, a watermelon is a big sweet cucumber. But you're less likely to care about classifying it than storing it; it's too big for the refrigerator, but too perishable to be left out. I *would* suggest that you slice it and carve out the fruit first, but the last time I tried this, I succumbed to the obvious temptation and felt the full force of the fact that the melon is 92 percent water. Now I buy it by the half or quarter.

Good whole watermelon is symmetrical and pale yellow underneath.

Cut watermelon should reveal deep pink fruit, not frosted with white or rusted near the rind—unless it happens to be a yellow-fleshed watermelon, in which case the fruit should be a deep yellow-orange.

1 SERVING: 2 CUPS, CHOPPED • CALORIES: 90 • FIBER: LOW • GOOD SOURCE OF VITAMINS A, C

GUIDE TO HERBS
AND SELECT DISHES THAT USE THEM TO THEIR BEST EFFECT

Glad You Asked

FRESH OR DRIED?

In an ideal world, every home, however small, would include a flourishing herb garden. In the world as it is, I, for one, can coax no form of plant life higher than mold to grow. Consequently, whenever I want to cook with fresh herbs, I have to buy them. I spend a lot on herbs. But when the herbs I want are out of season, out of stock, or out of my price range, I use dried herbs instead. Few herbs taste the same dried as they do fresh (dill is one of the few that does), but provided they come from good plants and haven't been sitting around for more than a few months, dried herbs aren't necessarily inferior, especially in dishes that call for lots of seasoning. And if the choice is between making a recipe with dried herbs or not cooking at all, by all means, head for the spice rack and heat up the stove!

ORGANIC OR CONVENTIONAL?

Like other organic crops, organic herbs are cultivated in smaller quantities and moved to the market—or, in the case of dried herbs, to the dehydrator—much faster than ordinary herbs. Consequently, organic herbs—fresh or dried —are often more flavorful than the rest. How-ever, no herb, organic or otherwise, will taste good if it's wilted, moldy, or just plain old. Simply, freshness determines flavor more than any particular farming practice.

Basil
Warm, sweet, with a touch of pepper, stupefyingly fragrant. It's the principal seasoning in Mediterranean, Middle Eastern, and Far Eastern foods.

You Can Taste It In: Pesto (see page 280), Roasted Fresh Tomatoes (see page 218), Simplest Fresh Tomato Sauce (see page 278), Chilled Pasta Salad (see page 295), Lasagna with Stewed Vegetables (see page 302), Cold Curried Peach Soup (see page 208).

Substitutes: There is none. Most dishes that call for basil shouldn't be made without it. Dishes that specify fresh basil won't taste the same made with dried, but may well be as good.

Bay Leaves
Spicy, aromatic, somewhere between savory and sweet.

You Can Taste Them In: Savory Carrot Flan (see page 245), Cream of Fresh Tomato Soup (see page 182), Early Spring Minestrone (see page 196), Chilled Cream of Carrot Soup with Ginger and Lime (see page 201).

Substitutes: No herb can replicate the flavor of bay, but you can try using rosemary or mint in its place. Or since it's usually one of many seasonings in a dish, you can—in most cases—omit it altogether.

Bouquet Garni
A mix of fresh or dried herbs tied in cheesecloth or tea bags and steeped in stews and soups for seasoning. You can fill a bouquet garni of any size with any herbs you'd like—it's a way of infusing a dish with flavor without the risk of overdoing it.

You Can Try It In: Lemon-Spiked Lentil Salad (see page 142), Ratatouille (see page 343), Chunky Chickpea Soup (see page 191).

CONVENTIONAL METHOD
1. Cut a square out of cheesecloth, large enough to hold the amount of herbs you're using. The size of the square depends on how much seasoning you'll need for the size dish you're making. Roughly, for a large stew (six servings or more), cut a seven-inch square. For a soup to serve four or fewer, make it five inches.
2. Fill the cheesecloth with herbs. The conventional combination is three sprigs of parsley, one sprig of thyme, and one bay leaf. But you can fill it with anything that will complement the dish—rosemary, cloves, celery leaves. . . .

3. Tie the cheesecloth closed with twine.

MY METHOD
1. Take the staple out of a tea bag, reserving the string. (Make sure it contains mild tea, or the residue will mingle with the herbs.)
2. Remove the tea. Replace it with herbs.
3. Shape the bag into a bundle and tie it with the string.

Chili Powder
Each brand makes its own blend, but typically the components are ground dried chili peppers, garlic, onions, cumin, and oregano.

Chives
Lively, biting; the Italians call them *erba cippollina*, or "onion herbs," a description that is comprehensive.

You Can Taste Them In: Creamy Chive Dressing (see page 120), Raspberry Dressing I (see page 122), Spicy Spinach Nuggets with Cooling Chive Sauce (see page 216), Bulgur and Red Lentil Soup (see page 199), Beet and Vidalia Onion Salad (see page 136), Quick Fresh Corn Salad (see page 128).

Substitutes: Minced scallion greens taste much like chives. Or you can use parsley, a multipurpose herb, which doesn't taste like chives, but can cover for them.

Cilantro
Musty lemon.

You Can Taste It In: Fresh Tomato Soup with Cilantro Pistou (see page 178), Hummus (see page 254), Chili (see page 352), Orange-and-Cilantro Bean Salad (see page 136), Moo-Shu Mushrooms (see page 136).

Substitutes: No herb tastes enough like cilantro to substitute for it, but often you can use a combination of fresh mint and basil in its place. Or you can use parsley, if you don't mind that the resulting dish won't be as zesty.

Curry Powder Each brand makes its own blend, but it typically contains cumin, turmeric, coriander, chili peppers, ground mustard, cardamom, ginger, cloves, nutmeg, and cinnamon.

You can amplify the flavor of commercial curry powder by putting it in an ungreased skillet over low heat and stirring until it is lightly toasted. Once it's toasted, use it right away.

Dill Sweet, sharp, lively.
You Can Taste It In: Chilled Spinach and Herb Soup (see page 203), Three-Mushroom Sauce (see page 286), Beet Raita (see page 154), Tomato Raita (see page 155), Cucumber and Bulgur Wheat (see page 138).

Substitutes: You can use the fronds from fresh fennel, which taste like dill. Or you can use parsley, with milder results.

Herbes de Provence Aromatic blend of thyme, oregano, savory, rosemary, and marjoram.
You Can Taste Them In: Chunky Chickpea Soup (see page 191), Tomato and Mushroom Ragout (see page 285).
Substitutes: If you don't have the entire blend, you can use any combination of the herbs involved.

Mint Sharp, refreshing, and sweet; call it basil with bite.
You Can Taste It In: Chilled Spinach and Herb Soup (see page 203), Angel Hair Pasta with Asparagus and Cherry Tomatoes (see page 294), Asparagus Risotto with Lemon and Mint (see page 314), Spinach Raita (see page 156), Beet and Vidalia Onion Salad (see page 136), Chilled Filled Spinach Rolls (see page 369).
Substitutes: Nothing tastes quite like mint, but if you have none, you can use oregano or a combination of cilantro and basil. Or you can use parsley in its place.

Oregano Rich, peppery, savory, and complex.
You Can Taste It In: Greek-Style Panzanella (see page 154), Tomato and Herb Topping for Pasta (see page 273), Spinach Risotto (see page 309), Lasagna with Stewed Vegetables (see page 302), Highly Spiced Black Bean Soup (see page 190), Chili (see page 352).
Substitutes: Marjoram is an herb that tastes

very much like oregano. But because its flavor is so pronounced, oregano is essential to dishes that call for it. If you have neither oregano nor marjoram, get some before you proceed with dishes that call for them.

Parsley
Mild, grassy . . . too good as a seasoning to waste as a garnish. Flat-leaf parsley is milder and more aromatic than curly leaf, which can be bitter.

You Can Taste It In: Red or Yellow Bell Pepper Soup (see page 171), Tender Soup Dumplings (see page 169), Creamy Herb Soup (see page 180), Lentils with Spinach (see page 282), Rolled Roasted Red Peppers (see page 249).

Substitutes: Fortunately fresh parsley is easy to find, because there's no substitute for it—including dried parsley, which is no good at all.

Rosemary
Piney, perfumey, wonderful in proportion, but potentially overpowering.

You Can Taste It In: Chickpea and Rosemary Passata (see page 192), Pasta e Fagioli (see page 194), Winter Tomato–Wheat Berry Soup (see page 197).

Substitutes: Nothing tastes like rosemary, but because they tend to complement the same foods, you can often use bay leaf in its place.

Sage
Astringent start, savory finish.

You Can Taste It In: Lentil Salad with Minced Vegetables (see page 142).

Substitutes: Nothing tastes like sage, but you can use a number of aromatic herbs in its place, such as tarragon, thyme, or savory.

Thyme
Supremely aromatic and savory.

You Can Taste It In: Light Lemony Lentil Sauce (see page 283).

Substitutes: Thyme's delightful, delicate, complex flavor is unique. But dishes that call for it taste good if you use other savory herbs such as marjoram, tarragon, or sage.

GUIDE TO SPICES

Allspice One spice tasting of several, including cinnamon, nutmeg, and—especially —cloves.

You Can Taste It In: Bulgur Wheat with Spinach, Raisins, and Pine Nuts (see page 262).

Substitutes: Since it tastes like a blend of sweet spices, you can use equal parts cinnamon, nutmeg, and cloves in its place.

Cinnamon If brown sugar weren't sweet, it would taste like cinnamon.

You Can Taste It In: Sweet Potato Drop Gnocchi (see page 320), Grain-Filled Onions (see page 365), Butternut Squash Soup (see page 181), Fresh Apple-Spice Cake (see page 477), Couscous (see page 338).

Substitutes: Cinnamon is distinctive, but often optional. If you're not intent on that cinnamon taste, you can often leave it out or use ginger, allspice, or a touch of nutmeg or cloves in its place.

Cloves Rich, deep, pungent—a darker shade of cinnamon.

You Can Taste Them In: Cold Curried Peach Soup (see page 208), Butternut Squash Soup (see page 181), Rich, Savory Lentil Ragout (see page 284), Lovely Lentil Sauce (see page 283).

Substitutes: It won't taste exactly the same, but you can use a pinch of allspice in place of a pinch of cloves for good results.

Coriander Musty lemon.

You Can Taste It In: Highly Spiced Black Bean Soup (see page 190), My Favorite Chickpeas (see page 360), Grain-Filled Onions (see page 365), Potato Curry (see page 356).

Substitutes: Coriander is the seed of the cilantro plant, and you can substitute minced fresh cilantro for it, about two measures minced fresh cilantro to one ground coriander. However, coriander is usually one of many spices in a dish, so often you can leave it out without missing it.

Cumin Smoky caraway with a citrus finish.

You Can Taste It In: Chili (see page 352), Highly Spiced Black Bean Soup (see page 190), Hummus (see page 254), My Favorite Chickpeas (see page 360), Refried Bean Puree (see page 256), Peanut Curry with Sweet Potato and Collard Greens (see page 359).

Substitutes: Cumin is essential to dishes that call for it. There's no substitute and no joy in eating something that's meant to have it but doesn't.

Fennel Seeds Sweet licorice (love it or leave it out).

You Can Taste Them In: Potato-Fennel Stew with Mixed Beans and Tofu (see page 336), Chunky Saffron-Bean Sauce (see page 287).

Substitutes: Anise seeds taste a lot like fennel. If you have neither, you can use rosemary instead. It doesn't taste like fennel, but it tends to complement the same foods.

Ginger Sweet, zesty.

You Can Taste It In: Cold Apricot Soup (see page 206), Breakfast Gingerbread (see page 78), Carrot Cake (see page 474), Pumpkin Soufflé (see page 499), Carrot Gnocchi (see page 318), My Favorite Chickpeas (see page 360), Butternut Squash Soup (see page 181).

Substitutes: There is no substitute for fresh or ground ginger, and you'll probably be disappointed if you try to make something that calls for it without it. And when a dish specifies fresh ginger, don't substitute ground. However, when a muffin or cake calls for a number of sweet spices, you might be able to get away with adding a little more cinnamon to compensate. But wherever ginger is the only spice or the one used in the largest quantity, replenish your supply before you proceed.

Mace Concentrated nutmeg (see below) made from the netting around the nutmeg.

Substitutes: Nutmeg.

Mustard Seeds Mellow start, sharp finish.

You Can Taste Them In: Peanut Curry with Sweet Potato and Collard Greens (see page 359), Coconut Curry with Potato, Cauliflower, and Eggs (see page 358).

Substitutes: There is no substitute for mustard seeds (don't use ground mustard in their place). Since they're usually one of many spices called for in a dish, they're rarely essen-

tial; you can omit mustard seeds with little consequence.

Nutmeg Sweet used sparingly, bitter in larger amounts.

You Can Taste It In: Sweet Potato Soufflé (see page 232), Sweet Potato Drop Gnocchi (see page 320), Hermits (see page 485), Carrot Cake (see page 474).

Substitutes: You can use half as much mace in place of nutmeg. Although they taste quite different, you can use cinnamon or allspice in some cases, too.

Paprika "Light" pepper—mild heat with a distinctly sweet finish. Available in hot and mild.

You Can Taste It In: Tangy Tofu Sauce (see page 351), Simple Soothing Mushroom Soup (see page 177).

Substitutes: Nothing taste like paprika, but you can try a little cayenne instead, if you don't mind the heat.

Pepper Sharp and hot. White is finely ground and blends more evenly with food than black, which is coarser and consequently more distinct. Red pepper raises the heat without affecting the flavor.

You Can Taste It In: My Favorite Chickpeas (see page 360).

Substitutes: You can't substitute anything for pepper, but you can switch a hotter pepper with a milder one or vice versa.

Saffron Perfume, bitterness, but buffered by a mild sweet finish.

You Can Taste It In: Chunky Saffron-Bean

SALT

No other food has fallen as far from grace. Salt was so precious in the ancient world, that "salary" meant—literally—"money to buy salt." And until recently, "salt of the earth" was considered a compliment.

Today it has different connotations, thanks to fairly conclusive evidence linking excessive sodium with high blood pressure and the risk of heart disease and stroke. No one knows just how much sodium we can eat risk free, but authorities agree it shouldn't exceed 2,400 milligrams, or the amount in roughly 1 teaspoon, each day. When you consider that many foods contain sodium to begin with, there's not a lot of leeway.

This wouldn't be such a big deal if the subject were allspice or turmeric, which we could eliminate more easily. But we crave salt to the point where most foods taste bland without it. You don't have to be obsessed with counting milligrams, but try to control the amount of sodium you eat by using fresh ingredients or salt-free canned goods when you cook. Adjust the salt to taste at the stove, and don't put any on the table. And remember that dishes that call for ingredients such as soy sauce, capers, and most cheeses may get enough salt from these foods, and not need any extra from you.

For more on sodium, see page 15.

Sauce (see page 287), Potato-Fennel Stew with Mixed Beans and Tofu (see page 336), Black Beans with Orange and Saffron (see page 341), Couscous (see page 338).

Substitutes: None. Saffron is so expensive (the process to procure it is uniquely labor-intensive) recipes rarely include it unless they *mean* it. If a recipe calls for saffron and you have none, don't make the dish until you do. Some people use turmeric instead, but the only thing the spices have in common is their yellow coloring. The results will be bitter and chalky, and very disappointing.

Sesame Seeds
Mild, smooth nutty taste. For sharper, more assertive flavor, place them in an ungreased skillet over low heat and stir just until they're lightly toasted. Or spread the seeds in a single layer on a piece of foil and place them in a toaster oven at 300° F. until golden brown, about three minutes.

You Can Taste Them In: Quick Cold Sesame Noodles (see page 298), Orange-Sesame Tabbouleh (see page 140), Savory Fresh Peach Salad (see page 132), Quick Crunchy Collards (see page 218).

Substitutes: You can use lightly toasted pine nuts, although the flavor will be milder, and you'll be adding more fat to the dish.

Turmeric Bitter, chalky—strictly a supporting player, to balance sweet and pungent spices in curries and similar dishes.
You Can Taste It In: Lightly Curried Split Pea Soup (see page 195), My Favorite Chickpeas (see page 360).
Substitutes: In most cases, you can use curry powder in its place.

Vanilla Whoever coined the phrase "plain vanilla," probably didn't think truffles were any big deal, either. This heady, fragrant spice deserves its standing as the world's favorite seasoning. You can buy it by the bean, in powder, or in liquid extract. The flavor varies with place of origin. Try Mexican, Bourbon (from the Indian Ocean), and Tahitian.
You Can Taste It In: Clafoutis (see page 492), Ricotta Cheesecake (see page 482), Fruity Rice Pudding with Meringue (see page 494), Angel Food Cake (see page 472).
Substitutes: None.

GUIDE TO LEGUMES
HOW TO CHOOSE THEM AND USE THEM

"Fresh dried beans" may appear to be a contradiction in terms, but it's not, as you'll discover if you compare ordinary supermarket beans with the legumes available from specialty firms. Because they produce fewer of them, specialty companies (including most organic brands) get their products to the store more swiftly than mass-producers, who keep their goods in warehouses for ages. You can see the difference right away; the fresher beans are glossy, vibrant, and plump, while the others look sallow, withered, and dull. More important, the difference in appearance corresponds to a difference in flavor, texture, and cooking time: the fresher the beans, the quicker they'll cook, the more tender they'll become, and the better—and more distinct—they'll taste.

Ask the Expert

Elizabeth Berry, who grows more than 650 types of beans (and counting . . .) on her ranch in New Mexico, offers these cooking tips:
• Soak the beans overnight in water to cover to shorten the cooking time.
• While cooking the beans, don't let them boil, or the skins may burst. Keep them at a simmer instead.
• Make sure the water covers the beans throughout cooking.

• Don't add salt to the beans until they're done. Salting the water toughens the beans.

ADDITIONAL TIPS
• If the beans you're using look old and dull, you can restore the texture by putting a strip of kombu (seaweed, available at most health-food and Japanese-specialty stores) into the water when you boil them. Kombu tenderizes the beans.
• If you haven't soaked the beans overnight, you can still serve them for dinner, in one of two ways: "boil and rest" method or the pressure cooker method.
  1. Bring the beans to a boil in water to cover by two inches.
  2. Cover the pot and turn off the heat. Let the beans sit for one hour.
  3. Drain the soaking water and proceed as if the beans had soaked overnight.

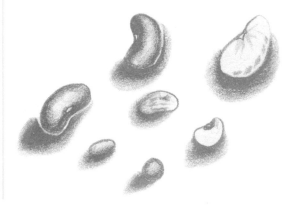

Q. Is it ever okay to use canned beans?

A. Yes! Canned beans are fine in recipes that call for lots of seasoning, such as chili, curry, vegetable stew, and filled vegetables. They won't work as well as fresh beans in salads, soups, or pastas, where the flavor really counts. And your selection is very limited.

Q. Are some canned beans better than others?

A. Yes! Chickpeas and white beans tend to hold up pretty well to the canning process, while kidney beans, pintos, and black beans generally—but not always—emerge as muddy-flavored mush. (Goya and Eden brands are two exceptions.)

Q. How can I get good results with canned beans?

A. Put them in a colander and rinse them thoroughly with cold water. Let them drain before adding them to your dish. Since the beans are probably very tender, take care not to let them boil once you've put them on to cook, or they'll fall apart.

Or use a pressure cooker, as I do. You don't have to soak the beans before you cook them under pressure. For precise instructions, consult the manual that came with your model.

BEFORE YOU BEGIN . . .

1 serving beans = ½ to ¾ cup cooked

1 pound dry beans = 2½ cups dry = 5 to 6 cups cooked = 10 to 12 servings

1 cup dry beans = 2½ cups cooked = 4 to 5 servings

1 can (15½ ounces) beans = 2 cups = 3 to 4 servings

Reference bean(s) in italics

Note: *"Try Them In"* means try these beans in place of the beans called for in the recipe indicated.

Appaloosa

How They Look: Spotted black and white, narrow.

How They Taste: Mild *kidney bean* flavor.

Soak Them For: 6 hours or overnight (or use the hour-long "boil and rest" method on page 565).

Cook Them For: 45 minutes on the stovetop; 15 minutes in a pressure cooker.

Try Them In: Raspberry-Cannellini Succotash (see page 137), Hummus (see page 254), Spring Garden Tortillas (see page 355).

Barlotti

How They Look: Medium size, beige with red-black streaks.

How They Taste: Mild, beany *chickpea* flavor.

Soak Them For: 6 hours or overnight (or use the hour-long "boil and rest" method on page 565).
Cook Them For: 1 hour on the stovetop; 15 minutes in a pressure cooker.
Try Them In: Early Spring Minestrone (see page 196), Chunky Saffron-Bean Sauce (see page 287), Pasta e Fagioli (see page 194).

Black-Eyed Peas
How They Look: Ivory with a single black spot (the eye).
How They Taste: More like a green garden pea than like any of the reference beans
Soak Them For: 6 hours or overnight (or use the hour-long "boil and rest" method on page 565).
Cook Them For: 1 hour on the stovetop; 15 minutes in a pressure cooker.
Try Them In: Orange-and-Cilantro Bean Salad (see page 136).

Black Turtle
How They Look: Small black pellets.
How They Taste: Mild, sweet *black bean* flavor.
Soak Them For: 8 hours or overnight (or use the hour-long "boil and rest" method on page 565).
Cook Them For: 50 minutes on the stovetop; 8 minutes in a pressure cooker.
Try Them In: Chili (see page 352), Highly Spiced Black Bean Soup (see page 190), Your Basic Heartwarming Black Bean Soup (see page 188), Orange-and-Cilantro Bean Salad (see page 136), Sweet Black Beans on Whole Wheat Penne (see page 289).

Calypso
How They Look: Ivory with black paisley print.
How They Taste: Sharp, creamy *kidney bean* flavor.
Soak Them For: 6 hours or overnight (or use the hour-long "boil and rest" method on page 565).
Cook Them For: 45 minutes on the stovetop; 6 minutes in a pressure cooker.
Try Them In: Raspberry-Cannellini Succotash (see page 137), Early Spring Minestrone (see page 196), Chunky Bean Burritos (see page 354).

Cannellini
How They Look: Ivory color, plump kidney shape.
How They Taste: Mild creamy *chickpea* flavor.
Soak Them For: 8 hours or overnight (or use the hour-long "boil and rest" method on page 565).
Cook Them For: 1 hour on the stovetop; 10 minutes in a pressure cooker.
Try Them In: Early Spring Minestrone (see page 196), Swift, Delicious Bean Salad (see page 148).

Great Northern
How They Look: Torpedo shaped, white.
How They Taste: Beany-pea flavor.
Soak Them For: 6 hours or overnight (or use the hour-long "boil and rest" method on page 565).
Cook Them For: 1 hour on the stovetop; 6 minutes in a pressure cooker.
Try Them In: Cannellini Bean and Spinach Salad (see page 138), Raspberry-Cannellini Succotash (see page 137).

REFERENCE BEANS

The most telling way to describe how one bean tastes is to compare it to another. These four legumes cover the range of flavors for all of the beans below. If you're not familiar with the flavor of each of these, try them first, so you can make sense of the descriptions that follow.

VERSATILITY: Once you've found the bean you want to use and the reference bean for comparison, check the versatility index to see whether the bean you've chosen lends itself to the dish you have in mind.

Note: *There are advantages to both the more versatile beans and those that have more limited uses. Flavorful beans (such as runner beans, lentils) are less versatile than blander legumes (such as chickpeas), because they're compatible with a narrower range of seasonings. However, they won't need much seasoning, making life (or at least fixing supper) simpler for you.*

Black Runner Beans

Sweet flavor with a winey undertone.

VERSATILITY: Moderate. Best with chili spices, citrus, and subtle seasonings, such as onions and bay leaf.

Chickpeas

(Garbanzo Beans) Mild peanut flavor.

VERSATILITY: High. Superb for most purposes, including chili, curry, and Mediterranean dishes.

Kidney Beans

Mild sweet-smoky flavor.

VERSATILITY: Moderate. Excellent for chili and baked beans.

Lentils

Earthy, peppery.

VERSATILITY: Poor. Lentils are interchangeable only with split peas. You can substitute lentils for other beans, but they will change the dish altogether.

I can't say enough for lentilles du Puy, tiny deep green lentils grown in the volcanic soil of the Auvergne region of France. People who don't like lentils usually cite a muddy, chalky taste. These lentils have none of that. They're spicy and rich, with a subtle sweetness that you can play up or subdue as you wish. They hold their shape through cooking, so they're ideal for salads. And they blend beautifully into a dense puree, which makes them perfect for sauces and soups.

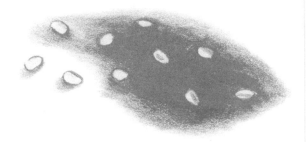

Jacob's Cattle

How They Look: Ivory with rust-colored spots.

How They Taste: Sweet *kidney bean* flavor.

Soak Them For: 6 hours or overnight (or use the hour-long "boil and rest" method on page 565).

Cook Them For: 1 hour on the stovetop; 6 minutes in a pressure cooker.

Try Them In: Chunky Saffron-Bean Sauce (see page 287), Chili Bean Soup (see page 193), Swift, Delicious Bean Salad (see page 148), Stewed Beans with Potatoes and Olives (see page 322).

Navy

How They Look: Kidney shape, white.

How They Taste: Beany-pea flavor (kidney shape, but they don't taste like kidney beans).

Soak Them For: 6 hours or overnight (or use the hour-long "boil and rest" method on page 565).

Cook Them For: 1 hour on the stovetop; 6 minutes in a pressure cooker.

Try Them In: bean spread (see page 255), Orange-and-Cilantro Bean Salad (see page 136), Chickpea-Rosemary Passata (see page 192).

Pinto

How They Look: Light brown, speckled with rust.

How They Taste: Mild *kidney bean* flavor.

Soak Them For: 8 hours or overnight (or use the hour-long "boil and rest" method on page 565).

Cook Them For: 1 hour, 10 minutes, on the stovetop; 6 minutes in a pressure cooker.

Try Them In: Baked Beans (see page 214), Chili (see page 352), bean spread (see page 255), Spring Garden Tortillas (see page 355).

Rattlesnake

How They Look: Medium size, mottled beige and rust.

How They Taste: Milk *kidney bean* flavor.

Soak Them For: 6 hours or overnight (or use the hour-long "boil and rest" method on page 565).

Cook Them For: 1 hour on the stovetop; 8 minutes in a pressure cooker.

Try Them In: Baked Beans (see page 214), Chili (see page 352), Refried Bean Puree (see page 256), Chunky Bean Burritos (see page 354).

Rice Beans

How They Look: Fat grains of ivory-colored rice.

How They Taste: Faint beany flavor.

Soak Them For: 6 hours or overnight (or use the hour-long "boil and rest" method on page 565).

Cook Them For: 45 minutes on the stovetop; 4 minutes in a pressure cooker.

Try Them In: Early Spring Minestrone (see page 196), Pasta e Fagioli (see page 194).

Scarlet Runner

How They Look: Huge, plump, and deep maroon.

How They Taste: Piquant, sweet *black bean* flavor.

Soak Them For: 8 hours or overnight (or use the hour-long "boil and rest" method on page 565).

Cook Them For: 1 hour, 15 minutes, on the stovetop; 15 minutes in a pressure cooker.

Try Them In: Chili (see page 352), Black Beans with Orange and Saffron (see page 341), Sweet Black Beans on Whole Wheat Penne (see page 289), Black Beans in Bell Peppers (see page 368).

Split Peas

How They Look: Like lentils: flat green or gold disks.

How They Taste: Chalky *lentil* flavor.

Soak Them For: Do not soak them.

Cook Them For: 35 minutes on the stovetop; not recommended in a pressure cooker.

Try Them In: (Lightly) Curried Split Pea Soup (see page 195), Bulgur and Red Lentil Soup (see page 199).

Swedish Buckskin

How They Look: Small beige peas.

How They Taste: Beany *chickpea* flavor.

Soak Them For: 6 hours or overnight (or use the hour-long "boil and rest" method on page 565).

Cook Them For: 45 minutes on the stovetop; 10 minutes in a pressure cooker.

Try Them In: Baked Beans (see page 214), Pasta e Fagioli (see page 194), Winter Tomato–Wheat Berry Soup (see page 197).

Tongues of Fire

How They Look: Deep tan with brown splatters.

How They Taste: Musty *kidney bean* flavor.

Soak Them For: 8 hours or overnight (or use the hour-long "boil and rest" method on page 565).

Cook Them For: 1 hour, 10 minutes, on the stovetop; 8 minutes in a pressure cooker.

Try Them In: Chili (see page 352), Baked Beans (see page 214), Baked Bean Soup (see page 191), Chunky Bean Burritos (see page 354).

The Best Bean(s) for the Dish

The list of beans recommended for the dishes below isn't all-inclusive. It's meant to indicate the type of bean that's best for each dish. So wherever you see kidney beans, for example, suggested in a recipe, any bean that's described above as similar to kidney beans—such as pintos—will work well, too.

BAKED BEANS: Kidney, Swedish buckskin

BEAN DIPS AND SPREADS: Kidney, pinto, black runner, black turtle, cannellini

BEANS AND RICE: Kidney, black runner, black turtle, scarlet runner, tongues of fire

CHILI: Kidney, pinto, black runner, scarlet runner, tongues of fire, chickpeas, Appaloosas

CURRY: Chickpeas, pinto, lentils

HUMMUS: Chickpeas

MINESTRONE: Cannellini, barlotti, kidney

PASTA E FAGIOLI: Cannellini, barlotti, kidney, chickpeas

SALADS: Cannellini, chickpeas, lentils, black runner, scarlet runner

GUIDE TO RICE AND OTHER GRAINS
HOW TO CHOOSE THEM AND USE THEM

Whether you buy them in bulk from a bin or in packs off the shelf, make sure the grains you get are fresh. If you're buying in bulk, take a quick sniff at the scoop. Basmati, jasmine, and Texmati rices have a smoky aroma, but other grains should give off a light, sweet scent, if any at all. If there's a musty or sour odor, tell the manager it's time to fill the bin with fresh stock.

Whenever you buy packaged grains, check the "sell by" date on the box or bag before you bring them home. If you buy your rice, oats, and so on in clear cellophane packs, shake the package gently, then look closely to see whether there's stringy filament between the grains, a sure sign of spoilage. Finally, unless you tend to go through gobs of a particular grain, buy in small batches. Store the grain in a cool place away from direct sunlight.

Be sure to also look for these rices: Black Japonica, Kashmati, and Organic Sushi Rice.

NO-FAIL BASIC METHOD FOR COOKING THE MOST POPULAR GRAINS

Although you're more often told to cook grain on top of the stove, you may get better results if you use the oven. Surrounded by heat that's at a steady temperature, the grain cooks evenly. If you own an electric stove, this is much easier than trying to regulate the heat on the burners.

1. Heat the oven to 350°F. On the stovetop, in a saucepan with a tight lid, bring to a boil the amount of water or other liquid (see Note) you need for the grain you're cooking.

2. Add the grain, and bring the water to a boil again.

3. Cover the saucepan, transfer it to the oven, and bake for the amount of time given below.

Note: *You can use vegetable broth, milk, or tomato or fruit juice instead of water. If you're using milk or juice, increase the amount of liquid by ½ cup. If the grains are too dry and still hard at the core, add water ¼ cup at a time and continue cooking until they're tender.*

See the listings for specific instructions and cooking times for each type of grain.

NO-FAIL PILAF METHOD FOR COOKING RICE, COUSCOUS, BULGUR WHEAT, AND BARLEY (AN EFFECTIVE WAY TO COOK FLAVOR INTO THE GRAIN)

1. Heat the oven to 350°F. In a saucepan over medium-high heat, heat 2 teaspoons extra virgin olive oil. When it's hot, add minced onions, shallots, or scallions, as well as any minced fresh or crumbled dried herbs you'd like. Reduce the heat to medium and sauté, stirring often, until they're soft.

2. Add the grain and stir well to coat it with the oil and seasonings, about one minute. Add vegetable broth in place of the

amount of water noted in the specific legumes, beginning on page 574, and bring to a boil.

3. Cover the saucepan, transfer it to the oven, and bake for the time given, until the grain is tender and the broth has been absorbed.

What About Cooking Grains in the Microwave?

Grains take as long to cook in the microwave as they do in a conventional oven. What's more, you have to watch them (they tend to erupt volcanically), and you have to take them out and stir every so often to make sure they cook evenly.

What About a Pressure Cooker?

For grains, pressure-cooking can be much faster than conventional methods. I have come to count on this appliance for long-cooking grains such as brown rice, barley, and wheat berry. It will take some tinkering to find the right ratio of liquid to grain when you use this method, so follow the guidelines in the owner's manual that comes with your cooker.

What About a Rice Cooker?

A rice cooker is supposed to regulate the heat and render the fabled "perfect rice every time." Unfortunately, the thermostats on those things aren't always accurate, and you can get gummy guck instead. If you find a model you can trust, it can be very convenient, especially in the summer when you'd rather not use the oven.

Rices

Once upon a time, when pasta was "spaghetti" and you couldn't get an espresso if your life depended it, there were two types of rice: white, the kind that normal people ate, and brown, which was for hippies.

Now it's not possible to talk about rice without getting far more specific. You can get rice in flavors and colors that are as different from each other as they are from other grains. Although they're all called rice, they're not necessarily interchangeable. Once you get to know the taste and texture of various rices, you'll also know which you can substitute for another.

Arborio

In the eighteenth century, Italy's Po Valley was so dependent on producing this rice it was a capital crime to take the seeds to cultivate else-

where. In a now legendary (and we'd hope uncharacteristic) act of lawlessness, Thomas Jefferson smuggled a few grains back to Monticello, where justly enough they did not take. The reason the rice was precious to the Po, and so tempting to the future president, is that it's uniquely chewy when tender, it holds together without getting gummy, and it fully absorbs the flavor of anything that's cooked with it. Consequently, it's the rice to use for risotto (see Note).

1 SERVING: ¼ CUP DRY; ⅔ CUP COOKED • CALORIES: 170 • FAT: 1 G • FIBER: 1 G • COOK ACCORDING TO RECIPES FOR RISOTTO (SEE PAGE 304).

Note: *If you can get carnaroli rice, do. The nutritional profile and cooking instructions are identical to arborio, but carnaroli is slightly sweeter, and the grains a bit chewier when fully cooked. It's not as widely available as arborio, which is grown domestically by Lundberg and Rice Tea.*

Short-Grain Brown

Sweet and a little bit sticky, it's ideal for sushi and rice pudding.

1 SERVING: ¼ CUP DRY; ⅔ CUP COOKED • CALORIES: 170 • FAT: 1.5 G • FIBER: 1.5 G • COOK 1 CUP DRY IN 2 CUPS WATER FOR 40 MINUTES.

Try It In: Fruity Rice Pudding with Meringue (see page 494), Torta di Budino di Riso Integrale (see page 482), Nori Rolls (see page 370).

Wehani-Brand

Mahogany colored, with a caramel flavor, this grain, cultivated uniquely by the Lundberg family, is the sweetest, richest of the "new" rices. Wonderful for rice puddings and for any main course or salad that contains dried or fresh fruits and/or nuts.

1 SERVING: ¼ CUP DRY; ¾ CUP COOKED • CALORIES: 170 • FAT: 1.5 G • FIBER: 3 G • COOK 1 CUP DRY IN 2 CUPS WATER FOR 45 MINUTES. REMOVE FROM THE HEAT AND LEAVE COVERED FOR 10 MINUTES BEFORE SERVING.

Try It With: Black Beans with Orange and Saffron (see page 34), Tangy Tofu Sauce (see page 351).

Long-Grain Brown

A mild, neutral-tasting rice, an unassertive accompaniment for any main course.

1 SERVING: ¼ CUP DRY; ¾ CUP COOKED • CALORIES: 110 • FAT: 1 G • FIBER: 1 G • COOK 1 CUP DRY IN 2 CUPS WATER FOR 40 MINUTES. REMOVE FROM THE HEAT AND LEAVE COVERED FOR 10 MINUTES BEFORE SERVING.

Try It With: Stir-fries (see pages 374 to 376).

Brown Basmati

The distinct smoky flavor complements curry and chili, but won't go well with Mediterranean dishes or anything with cheese.

1 SERVING: ¼ CUP DRY; ¾ CUP COOKED • CALORIES: 110 • FAT: 1 G • FIBER: 1 G • COOK 1 CUP DRY IN 2 CUPS WATER FOR 40 MINUTES. REMOVE FROM THE HEAT AND LEAVE COVERED FOR 10 MINUTES BEFORE SERVING.

Try It With: My Favorite Chickpeas (see page 360), Peanut Curry (see page 359).

Long-Grain White

The basic all-purpose rice.

1 SERVING: ¼ CUP DRY; ¾ CUP COOKED • CALORIES: 150 • FAT: 0 G • FIBER: 0 G • COOK 1 CUP DRY IN 1½ CUPS WATER FOR 15 TO 20 MINUTES. REMOVE FROM THE HEAT AND LEAVE COVERED FOR 10 MINUTES BEFORE SERVING.

Try It With: Stir-fries (see pages 374 to 376).

White Basmati

With a distinct smoky flavor, white basmati is lighter and cleaner tasting than brown basmati, which is the same rice with the bran layer in place. It comes coated with a starchy powder,

so place it in a sieve and rinse until the water runs clear.

1 SERVING: ¼ CUP DRY; ¾ CUP COOKED • CALORIES: 180 • FAT: 0.5 G • FIBER: 0 G • RINSE IT IN A SIEVE, THEN COOK 1 CUP DRY IN 1½ CUPS WATER FOR 20 MINUTES. REMOVE FROM THE HEAT AND LEAVE COVERED FOR 10 MINUTES BEFORE SERVING.

Try It With: Curries (see pages 356 to 360).

Jasmine

Sweeter than basmati, and more tender, but otherwise quite similar, it comes coated with a starchy powder, so place it in a sieve and rinse until the water runs clear.

1 SERVING: ¼ CUP DRY; ¾ CUP COOKED • CALORIES: 180 • FAT: 0.5 G • FIBER: 0 G • RINSE IT IN A SIEVE, THEN COOK 1 CUP DRY IN 1½ CUPS WATER FOR 20 MINUTES. REMOVE FROM THE HEAT AND LEAVE COVERED FOR 10 MINUTES BEFORE SERVING.

Try It With: My Favorite Chickpeas (see page 360), curries (see pages 356 to 360) Ratatouille (see page 343).

Texmati

A domestic basmati-style rice, firmer than genuine basmati, with a milder smoky flavor, it's less expensive than imported basmati and easier to prepare; you don't have to rinse it before cooking.

1 SERVING: ¼ CUP DRY; ¾ CUP COOKED • CALORIES: 180 • FAT: 0.5 G • FIBER: 0 G • COOK 1 CUP DRY IN 1⅔ CUPS WATER FOR 20 MINUTES. REMOVE FROM THE HEAT AND LEAVE COVERED FOR 10 MINUTES BEFORE SERVING.

Try It With: Chili (see page 352), Black Beans in Bell Peppers (see page 368), Chunky Bean Burritos (see page 354).

Jasmati

A domestic version of jasmine rice, much firmer than genuine jasmine and not as sweet or smoky, it tastes more like conventional long-grain white rice than like the rice it's meant to resemble and works well when you want not more than a hint of flavor. It's less expensive than imported jasmine and easier to prepare; you don't have to rinse it before cooking.

1 SERVING: ¼ CUP DRY; ¾ CUP COOKED • CALORIES: 180 • FAT: 0.5 G • FIBER: 0 G • COOK 1 CUP DRY IN 1⅔ CUPS WATER FOR 20 MINUTES. REMOVE FROM THE HEAT AND LEAVE COVERED FOR 10 MINUTES BEFORE SERVING.

Try It With: Curries (see pages 356 to 360), Ratatouille (see page 343).

Short-Grain White

The regulation sushi rice.

1 SERVING: ¼ CUP DRY; ¾ CUP COOKED • CALORIES: 180 • FAT: 0.5 G • FIBER: 0 G • COOK 1 CUP DRY IN 1¼ CUPS WATER FOR 15 MINUTES.

Try It With: Nori Rolls (see page 370).

Short-Grain Sweet Brown

Aka Mochi Rice Too sticky and sweet to use in place of regular short-grain brown rice, it makes good gooey desserts.

I SERVING: ¼ CUP DRY; ¾ CUP COOKED • CALORIES: 180 • FAT: I G • FIBER: I G • COOK I CUP DRY IN I¼ CUPS WATER FOR I5 MINUTES.

Try It With: Torta di Riso (see page 482).

Medium-Grain White

Plumper than long-grain rice, not as gummy or sweet as short grain, it's perfect for stuffings and rice puddings.

I SERVING: ¼ CUP DRY; ¾ CUP COOKED • CALORIES: 150 • FAT: 0 G • FIBER: 0 G • COOK I CUP DRY IN I½ CUPS WATER FOR I5 MINUTES. REMOVE FROM THE HEAT AND LEAVE COVERED FOR I0 MINUTES BEFORE SERVING.

Try It With: Chili (see page 352), Fruity Rice Pudding with Meringue (see page 494), Rice Salad with Snow Peas (see page 146), Tomato and Rice Soup (see page 172).

Wild

Its strong, heavy flavor is best diluted by cooking in aromatic broth and blending with lighter-tasting rices and dried fruits and nuts.

I SERVING: ¼ CUP DRY; ¾ CUP COOKED • CALORIES: 180 • FAT: 0.5 G • FIBER: 2 G • COOK I CUP DRY IN 4 CUPS WATER FOR 55 MINUTES. REMOVE FROM THE HEAT AND LEAVE COVERED FOR I0 MINUTES BEFORE SERVING.

Try It With: Potato-Fennel Stew with Mixed Beans and Tofu (see page 336), Lentil and Mushroom Stew (see page 340).

Switching Grains

Grains are interchangeable up to a point. You can switch some rices around, substituting brown basmati for white to serve with curries, for example, or using jasmine rice instead of either type of basmati. But none of those, which have a distinct smoky flavor, is a good match for sushi. Further, you can use couscous or barley instead of bulgur for a richer, more substantial version of tabbouleh (see page 139), but buckwheat "risotto" gives innovation a bad name. When you're thinking of replacing one grain with another, consider whether:

1. The flavor will complement the other ingredients. As mentioned above, smoky rice will overpower the more subtle ingredients in sushi. Similarly, sushi rice is too sticky and sweet to complement curries.

2. The texture will work with whatever you're making. If, for example, you want the grain to absorb juice from the food without getting soggy, use a substantial grain such as barley, bulgur, wheat berries, or medium-grain brown rice. If you want the grain to sop up the liquid and get slightly mushy, use couscous or jasmine or medium-grain white rice.

Barley

For all its virtues as a high-fiber, iron-rich, vitamin-packed source of protein and complex carbohydrates, barley is not your basic, everyday grain. It's heavy, and the flavor, neither as distinct as that of bulgur nor as delicate as that of rice, always needs enhancement. Whether you steam

GRITS

Definition: Finely ground dried corn, virtually unknown—or deliberately ignored—in the North.

There was a competition every morning at my summer camp to get the seat at breakfast closest to the buttered grits. It was the only way to guarantee that there'd be butter on your portion, because whoever got to the bowl first scooped most of the butter for herself, passing the grits devoid of their single source of flavor. It was a custom so well established that even the cherubs among us, inclined to be charitable in all other circumstances, made no more effort to distribute the butter than the born gluttons.

Grits are bland and, without something to season them, pretty much pointless. I've tried every alternative I can think of, but butter does it best. If you use it sparingly—½ teaspoon is enough for one ¾-cup serving—the calories (roughly thirty-five) won't hurt you.

I SERVING: ¼ DRY; ¾ CUP COOKED • CALORIES: 140 • FAT: 0 G • FIBER: 0 G • COOK I CUP DRY IN 3 CUPS WATER FOR 6 MINUTES.

it in vegetable broth or prepare it as pilaf with garlic, onions, and herbs, it's worth the trouble for a hearty winter dinner. But when you're too busy, or when hefty foods are out of season, you can enjoy the benefits of barley more easily by having Grape-Nuts cereal for breakfast.

I SERVING: ¼ CUP DRY; ¾ CUP COOKED • CALORIES: 350 • FAT: 2 G • FIBER: 3 G • COOK I CUP DRY IN 3 CUPS WATER FOR 55 MINUTES.

Try It In: Grain-Filled Onions (see page 364), breakfast pudding with prunes (see page 99).

Bulgur Wheat

I've been told that bulgur is an acquired taste. I wouldn't know, since I've been biased from birth; my great-grandfather was one of the first American grocers to import it, and I grew up eating what I describe as the "wheatiest" of wheats. The flavor is strong and not easy to characterize in terms of anything *but* wheat, although there's a touch of nut to the taste, which you can enhance by adding chopped walnuts, toasted almonds, or sesame seeds.

You might expect a grain with such a strong flavor to have a heavy texture, too. But bulgur, while coarse, is surprisingly light. That's why it's perfect for tabbouleh, the definitive grain salad.

Bulgur comes coarsely ground, for pilaf and tabbouleh, and finer, for mixing with bread flour and using for stuffings.

In a medium saucepan, bring the water to a boil. Stir in the bulgur wheat. Let the water come to a second boil, then immediately remove from the heat and cover the pan. Let it sit for twenty minutes without lifting the lid. Pour the bulgur into a sieve and press it with the back of a wooden spoon to squeeze out the excess water.

I SERVING: ¼ CUP DRY; ¾ CUP COOKED • CALORIES: 110 • FAT: 0.5 G • FIBER: 6 G • SOAK 1 CUP DRY IN 1½ CUPS BOILING WATER FOR 30 MINUTES.

Try It In: Tabbouleh (see page 139), Bulgur and Red Lentil Soup (see page 198).

Cornmeal

The colonists hated it and wrote bitter letters home about having to make do with it. They desperately set about planting other grains, especially wheat. But it took more than a century for the wheat to take, and by then Americans didn't mind cornmeal so much. Driven by that fundamental determination to have something good to eat, they'd developed a repertoire of cornmeal quick breads, puddings, and stews that have come to represent New England and southern cooking.

Ironically, during a period when Americans would have traded every last stalk for a shaft of wheat, the Italians were going crazy for cornmeal, planting their imported seeds to make a savory porridge. They called it polenta, which may explain why the dish caught on in Italy, while cornmeal mush, which is the American name for the very same thing, gave way to rice and mashed potatoes. (For more on polenta, see page 324.)

Stone-ground cornmeal tastes more like corn than any other you can buy, which makes it the best for baking and for making polenta and tamales. Cornmeal doesn't contain gluten, so you'll need wheat flour when you make muffins and yeast breads with it. Quick-cooking cornmeal loses much of its flavor during processing, so only use it to sprinkle on

your baking surface when you're making bread.

I SERVING: ¼ CUP DRY; ¾ CUP COOKED • CALORIES: 120 • FAT: 1 G • FIBER: 3 G • COOK 1 CUP DRY IN 4 CUPS WATER FOR 25 MINUTES.

Try It In: Polenta (see page 324), Triple-Corn Calzone (see page 423), Tamale-Style Fresh Corn Nuggets (see page 246).

Couscous

Which came first, the couscous or the couscous? The name applies to a spicy Algerian stew (see page 338) and to the form of semolina that's served underneath it. Couscous has a light, neutral/sweet taste, a flavor more similar to that of fine pasta than to that of wheat in other forms.

Ordinarily critical of "quick cooking" grains of any kind, I make an exception for couscous, which requires heroic efforts to prepare from scratch. It's a tedious process that involves soaking, rinsing, and drying the wheat and then rolling it between your fingers to make uniform granules. Even if it were to taste better than what comes precooked in a box, it's going to be buried in a highly seasoned stew in the end. So who'll know the difference?

I SERVING: ¼ CUP DRY; ½ CUP COOKED • CALORIES: 100 • FAT: 0.5 G • FIBER: 1 G • SOAK 1 CUP DRY IN 1¼ CUPS WATER FOR 10 MINUTES.

Try It In: Couscous (see page 338).

Oats

When Samuel Johnson derisively defined oats as "a grain which in England is generally given to horses but in Scotland supports the people," he meant to vex the Scots. But he only betrayed his own ignorance and poor taste. Naturally sweet, chewy, soothing, and revitalizing, oats are also phenomenally nourishing, containing 50 percent more protein than bulgur wheat and twice as much as brown rice, plus more iron, folacin, vitamin E, and zinc than any other grain. And recent authoritative studies indicate that oat bran can lower blood cholesterol substantially, perhaps as effectively as some prescription drugs. (If you're being treated for high cholesterol, don't switch to oat bran without consulting your doctor.)

Oat flour has an astonishing quality: a buttery flavor that makes fat-free baked goods taste rich. It doesn't contain gluten, so you have to combine it with wheat flour in breads and most quick breads.

1 SERVING (ROLLED OATS): ⅓ CUP DRY; ⅓ CUP COOKED • CALORIES: 140 • FAT: 2.5 G • FIBER: 4 G • COOK 1 CUP DRY IN 2 CUPS WATER FOR 10 MINUTES.

Try It In: Oatmeal Pudding (see page 98), Muesli (see page 56), Granola (see page 50), Oatmeal Cookies (see page 484).

1 SERVING (STEEL-CUT OATS): ¼ CUP DRY; ¾ CUP COOKED • CALORIES: 170 • FAT: 3 G • FIBER: 4 G • COOK 1 CUP DRY IN 2 CUPS WATER FOR 15 MINUTES.

Try It In: Oatmeal Pudding (see page 98).

Quinoa

I'm all for the movement to bring back "lost crops," grateful for the broader selection of legumes, fresh produce, and grains we have as a result. Inevitably, though, we'll "rediscover" a number of things that are just as well forgotten. I personally include quinoa in that category. Quinoa's being promoted as the "ancient food of the Incas," as if its role in the diet of a tragi-

cally annihilated civilization exempts it from the first rules governing what we choose to eat —that it must taste good and have a decent texture. Quinoa is mushy and its muddy flavor defies pleasant seasoning. As for the fact that the Incas ate it—they also ate dogs, but no one's suggesting we follow suit.

It's true that quinoa has more protein than most grains. But protein deficiency is rare even among strict vegetarians. Given that it's also uncommonly high in fat, there's no reason to eat it, unless you truly like the way it tastes.

1 SERVING: ½ CUP DRY; ¾ CUP COOKED • CALORIES: 375 • FAT: 6 G • FIBER: 0 G • COOK 1 CUP DRY IN 2 CUPS WATER FOR 15 MINUTES. YOU CAN IMPROVE THE FLAVOR BY POURING THE GRAIN INTO AN UNGREASED SKILLET OVER MEDIUM HEAT, STIRRING CONSTANTLY, AND TOASTING IT, ABOUT 5 MINUTES, BEFORE COOKING.

Wheat Berries

The kernel of the wheat grain, including the germ and the bran, are sweet and nutty and fun to chew. They take forever to cook (well, more than an hour anyway) unless you soak them overnight. Wheat berries can be too spongy to enjoy on their own, so mix them with other grains (having cooked each separately), especially barley or Wehani-brand rice. They also make nice nuggets for yeast breads and a tasty and substantial hot breakfast cereal (see pages 52 to 56).

1 SERVING: ¼ CUP DRY; ¾ CUP COOKED • CALORIES: 160 • FAT: 1 G • FIBER: 7 G • COOK 1 CUP DRY IN 3 CUPS WATER FOR 55 MINUTES.

Try It In: Supper Fruit Salad (see page 144).

GUIDE TO FLOURS

First, it can be hard or soft. The difference between the two is the amount of gluten, or protein, they contain; hard wheat has more gluten than soft wheat. This matters to you because gluten makes dough sturdy and elastic, and allows it to trap the gas given off by yeast, and so to rise. Consequently, hard wheat flour is best for yeast breads, while soft wheat, which yields a lighter, less manageable dough, is better for quick breads and pastries.

Second, wheat flours differ according to how they're ground. A grain of wheat has a core (the endosperm) that nourishes the wheat seedling. The endosperm is encased in the germ, which is the embryo of a new seedling. The germ is in turn encased in the bran, a hard shell that protects the germ and the endosperm.

To make white flour, most large commercial flour companies crush the wheat with steel rollers, stripping away the germ and the bran. The flour consists of the endosperm alone.

Pause to Point Out an Important Fact

There is a malicious rumor making the rounds that white flour isn't nourishing. While whole wheat flour, which contains the bran and germ as well as the endosperm, has more fiber than white flour, keep in mind that in nature, the endosperm feeds the wheat; it is *the* source of nourishment in the plant. What's more, all white flours that don't contain the germ, which contains critical vitamins and irons, have to be enriched with niacin, riboflavin, and iron (it's the law!). So if you're not crazy about whole wheat bread, or you enjoy a plain bagel or pita from time to time, don't worry that you *must* eat whole wheat exclusively to be healthy. However, if you don't get enough fiber from the other sources, such as whole-grain cereal and fresh fruits and vegetables, you'll be better off if you choose whole wheat bread as often as possible (see page 15 for the benefits of fiber). Smaller mills preserve some of the germ and bran in their white flours by milling wheat with slow-moving stones. This is sold as stone-ground flour.

All-Purpose

What It Is: A combination of hard (high-gluten) and soft (low-gluten) wheat.

How You Use It: True to its name, you can use all-purpose flour in anything calling for flour. Some brands have a higher proportion of hard to soft wheat, making them better for yeast breads, while other brands reverse the ratio, so they're best for muffins and pastries. You may have to test a number of brands to find which is which. Most all-purpose flour is white, although some whole wheat flours call themselves all-purpose. You take a risk when you substitute whole wheat "all-purpose" flour in recipes that call for all-purpose flour; the whole wheat may be too heavy and coarse for the dish.

Bread

What It Is: Depends on the manufacturer, but most often a blend of high-gluten (hard-wheat) flours, malted-barley flour (a high-sugar flour that makes yeast act more rigorously), and vitamin C, which acts with the gluten to make a dough that's more elastic and retains more gas so the bread will rise higher.

How You Use It: For yeast breads only. Quick breads and pastries made with high-gluten flour are heavy and tough.

Cornmeal

What It Is: Ground corn. Look for stone-ground cornmeal, which contains the nourishing germ and tastes more like corn than steel-ground meal.

How You Use It: Because cornmeal has no gluten, you have to combine it with a wheat flour to make breads. See the corn muffin recipe on page 76 for an example of a good proportion of cornmeal to flour. If cornmeal is stone-ground, it says so on the label.

Kamut

What It Is: A nourishing strain of wheat cultivated by the Egyptians and recently revived. It's unusual because although it's high in gluten, it makes delicate baked goods. It has a faint, sweet flavor, similar to whole wheat, but lighter and less coarse.

How You Use It: In place of whole wheat pastry flour or pastry flour in baked goods. Also, you can use it to replace up to half of the white flour called for in any bread recipe.

Oat

What It Is: Ground oats. (You can make your own by pulverizing oatmeal in a food processor or blender.) It has a wonderful sweet, buttery flavor.

How You Use It: Oat flour has no gluten, so you must blend it with wheat flour to use it in yeast breads (I suggest ⅓ oat flour to ⅔ white).

Q. Aren't all flours basically alike? Why would one brand be better than another?

A. Because flours look pretty much the same, few people other than professional bakers and dedicated hobbyists tend to give much thought to the qualities that make one brand better than another. But as with any other ingredient, the better the flour, the better your results. Brands differ a lot, in ways you can taste. They use different types of wheat and different milling processes, both affecting the flavor, texture, and nutritional value of the foods you make with their flour. What's more, some companies process wheat in such great volume, they end up storing tons of flour before shipping it to market. What you get from those guys is far from fresh. Others mill smaller amounts and sell it right away.

You'll find my brand-name recommendations on page 595.

Pastry

What It Is: Finely ground soft wheat.

How You Use It: Soft wheat has little gluten, so the flour made from it makes soft doughs and tender baked goods. If you use it for yeast dough, it won't rise as much as dough made with bread flour or all-purpose flour. The results you get with white pastry flour are more delicate than what you get with pastry flour made with whole wheat.

Rice

What It Is: Ground white or brown rice. It contains no gluten.

How You Use It: You can use it as a thickener for sauces or soups or in pancakes, waffles, or quick breads if you're allergic to the gluten in wheat flour.

Rye

What It Is: Ground rye berries.

How You Use It: With all-purpose or bread flour to make bread (see page 402). Rye contains very little gluten, so you have to blend it with all-purpose or bread flour to make breads that rise.

Semolina

What It Is: Flour milled from durham wheat, the hardest of hard wheats.

How You Use It: For pasta dough or, blended with all-purpose flour, for chewy bread. Use up to half semolina flour in place of ordinary white flour in yeast bread recipes.

Soy

What It Is: Ground defatted soybeans.

How You Use It: When you combine it with wheat flour, soy flour boosts the protein content of breads and other baked goods. To use it in recipes, replace up to (but no more than) a quarter of the wheat flour with soy flour. It won't affect the flavor, but will make the bread lighter and more nourishing.

Whole Wheat

What It Is: Wheat flour that retains the germ and bran. It is coarse, and it inhibits the action of the gluten, which explains why whole wheat breads tend to be heavier than breads made with white flour.

How You Use It: You can use it in place of white flour, as long as you're prepared for the possibility that what you get in the end will be heavier and coarser than you might have imagined. Instead of replacing white flour with whole wheat in baked goods, I recommend

using half and half at most, or up to two-thirds white flour. Either way, you'll get good flavor and fiber from the whole wheat and optimum texture from the white.

Terms

Enriched: All white flours must—by law—be fortified with several B vitamins and iron.

Organic: Flour milled from wheat that has been grown without chemical pesticides or fertilizers, according to state laws regulating organic farming. Organic flours may taste better than conventional flours, not necessarily because they are organic, but because they're produced in smaller quantities and sold fresher than flours that are made in abundance and end up spending more time on the shelf.

Self-rising: Flour that contains baking powder and salt. Strictly for quick breads. Read the directions on the package before you use it to avoid duplicating ingredients.

Unbleached: Freshly milled flour is yellowish. To whiten it quickly, some manufacturers add chemical bleaches. Unbleached flours have been left to whiten naturally, a process that takes time, but no chemicals.

TO KEEP IT FRESH

Store whole-grain and stone-ground flours in the refrigerator for up to six months, or freeze for up to one year. (You won't have to defrost them; just be sure to sift thoroughly when you take the flour out of the freezer.) Keep other flours tightly covered, in a cool place away from direct sunlight, for up to three months.

GUIDE TO MILK, YOGURT, AND CHEESE

In these all-too-acrimonious times, there are some things that should not be controversial. One is the value of dairy products. Certainly if you're truly allergic to milk, avoid them. But somehow dairy products have come to be widely condemned as unwholesome and worse when they've proven throughout time to be among the most nourishing of natural foods.

Here are some reasons people reject dairy products and why those reasons don't stand up to serious consideration:

Dairy Products Are Fattening Full-fat milk products are high in saturated fat. But there are so many good nonfat dairy goods that you can eat a satisfying variety of yogurt, milk, and soft cheeses without having more than a gram or so of fat (see page 595 for my brand-name recommendations). Moreover a one-inch cube or wedge of real cheese, a two-tablespoon sprinkling of Parmesan, or a pat of pure creamery butter—for anyone who doesn't suffer a serious heart condition or obesity—can only complement a diet that is otherwise low in fat and high in complex carbohydrates.

Dairy Farming Is Bad for Cows If inhumane modern farming practices have put you off dairy products, you should know that it's possible to buy milk and cheese produced by people who care as much about the environment and the well-being of their animals as you do. Throughout the country, small regional dairies have their cows graze on organic fields and keep the animals free of antibiotics and hormones, including rBST, which increases milk yield but shortens the life of the cows. Look for organic milk where you shop, or ask your store to stock it. It ordinarily costs more, but if it buys you peace of mind—and keeps these good farmers in business—it's worth it.

Dairy Products Are Harmful Milk bashers may have told you that dairy products increase the amount of mucus in the system. It's a lie, disproved by one authoritative study after another. Another myth is that lactose intolerance (the inability to digest milk) is a common condition. One recent university study found that most participants who thought they were lactose intolerant actually had plenty of lactase, the enzyme that's missing in people who can't handle milk. This doesn't mean no one has this condition, just that it isn't as rampant as you may have heard. And many people who are truly lactose intolerant *can* eat dairy foods after popping the lactase tablets you can purchase at the pharmacy or supermarket.

In fact, nonfat milk and yogurt are near-miraculous sources of nourishment. Rich in complete protein, the essential vitamins A and D, and the critical mineral calcium, milk products provide more nourishment per unit than most other single foods: two cups of nonfat milk or yogurt provide one-third of the protein and nearly half of the calcium you need each day. And if you look at it demographically, people who live in countries where dairy products are consumed tend to be taller and to have lower rates of osteoporosis (degenerative bone disease associated with inadequate calcium) than people in places where milk comes from soy or other plant sources. And whenever the news reports on the oldest person in the world, it's always someone from the Caucuses who goes through a gallon of yogurt a week.

So if you've sworn off milk or other dairy products for "health reasons," reconsider. You're missing not only substantial health benefits, but some of the most delicious foods in the world.

Types of Milk

Buttermilk
A tangy, low-fat milk (see page 45).

Evaporated Skim
This is concentrated nonfat milk, with 60 percent less water than ordinary skim milk. Because it's concentrated, it has more protein and calcium per measure than fresh milk and a thicker consistency. In small amounts, it's great for thickening cream-style soups and sauces, acting like cream without adding fat. Use it sparingly, though, because it tastes peculiar. A little bit goes a long way toward making dishes seem richer, but a lot goes too far, making them taste strange.

Lactose-Reduced
If you have trouble digesting dairy products, it may be that you don't have enough lactase, the enzyme that breaks down milk sugar. Lactose-reduced milk has had lactase added to it and is otherwise identical to ordinary milk.

Low-Fat
Two-percent-fat milk is labeled "low fat," although it is far too close to whole milk in fat content to be *truly* low fat. Two percent milk gets 35 percent of its calories from fat and contains about 120 calories per cup. If you don't like nonfat milk, pass up the 2 percent and choose 1 percent milk instead. One percent low-fat milk gets 23 percent of its calories from fat and contains about 110 calories per cup.

Nonfat or Skim
Fewer than 5 percent of the calories in nonfat milk come from fat. Moreover, it has nearly half as many calories as whole milk, about eighty per cup. And because it has less fat per volume, it contains more calcium than whole milk: 123 milligrams in skim milk versus 119 in whole.

HOW NOW ORGANIC COW?

I have never been without a carton of nonfat milk in my refrigerator. I wouldn't know how to start the day without one. I pour milk liberally on my cereal and froth it for my coffee. Later, it goes into my tea and often into soups and puddings. Until last summer, I had always bought a carton for its milk, not vice versa. But a surprise on a routine trip to the market changed that. In the refrigerator section was a row of the most beautiful milk cartons I'd ever seen. They were pastel shades of blue, pink, and yellow, with a sweet sketch of a cow in a garland of flowers. The milk came from the Organic Cow of Vermont and cost considerably more than the brand I normally bought. But I couldn't resist the carton. Now I can't resist the milk, which tastes so much richer than ordinary skim milk, I had to call the company to find out why. According to Bunny Flint, who runs the Organic Cow with her husband, Peter, their milk comes exclusively from colored-breed cows: Jerseys, Ayrshires, Brown Swiss, and Guernseys. These cows produce milk that is more robust than Holstein milk, which dominates the market. The Flints, and the select family farmers who sell milk to them, graze their cows on pasture that hasn't been treated with pesticides or chemical fertilizers, and all use homeopathic remedies rather than antibiotics when their cows fall ill.

Gary and Linda Shaneberger, whose Ayrshire cows provide milk for the Organic Cow, have assuring words for those of us who worry about the nature of farming today: "We take great pride in producing a food of the highest quality, free of chemicals, and we feel that organic farming is humane and healthy for the cows, our number-one concern."

The Flints and Shanebergers are not alone. Wherever you live, it's likely you can buy milk from conscientious dairy farmers who think and work like them.

For information about organic dairies near you, contact the Northeast Organic Farming Association (NOFA), at (508) 355-2853. For information about the Organic Cow, call (802) 685-3123 or write P.O. Box 55, Tunbridge, VT 05077.

Whole

Typically, whole milk contains 3.25 percent milk fat; 50 percent of its calories come from fat, most of it saturated, and it contains about 150 calories per cup. It's the best milk for children under age two, but not for everyday use for anyone older than that.

Glad You Asked

WHAT IS YOGURT?

Chances are you can't remember a time when you didn't have a choice of plain, nonfat, lemon-chiffon, mixed-berry, or chocolate-cappuccino yogurt, much less soft-serve or solid frozen yogurt in various flavors and percentages of fat. So you may well know what it is without knowing what it *is*.

In its purest form, yogurt is milk that's been infused with a culture of two types of bacteria,

heated, then left in an incubator to curdle. When the milk is nonfat milk, the manufacturer may add nonfat milk solids to thicken the final product, which also increase the calcium and protein content of the yogurt. (The label will indicate whether the solids have been added.)

Aside from producing a creamy, versatile, nourishing food, the bacteria have other beneficial effects. For instance, if you're lactose intolerant, you should be able to eat yogurt because the bacteria that curdle the milk also create lactase, the enzyme that helps you digest milk sugars. Also, the bacteria in yogurts labeled "With active cultures" help maintain a healthful balance of good bacteria in your intestines, which is good for your digestion overall.

But most of the yogurt we eat is not in its purest form; much of it has been sweetened with sugar fruit juice concentrate or aspartame; thickened with milk solids, pectin, guar gum, or gelatin; freeze-dried, then reconstituted as soft-serve frozen yogurt; or sweetened, stabilized, and frozen solid. Check the carton and choose the brand, refrigerated or frozen, with the most wholesome ingredients and the least fat. (See page 595 for my brand-name recommendations.)

Cheese

If you can tell how desirable a food is by the number of low-fat versions on the market (and I think you can), then a quick survey of the supermarket will show that we want cheese more than we want chocolate. However, most fat-free chocolate cakes taste a lot better than

any nonfat cheddar I've tried. This is not a tragedy. It's just an incentive to keep your daily diet low in fat, so you can enjoy genuine cheese as a regular treat.

Some cheeses are low in fat by nature: 3½ ounces of 1 percent cottage cheese, for instance, contains only 1 gram of fat, versus 33 grams in the same amount of cheddar. The cottage cheese has seventy-two calories, while the cheddar contains four hundred. (For optimum taste at minimum fat, choose 1 percent cottage cheese. Fat-free cottage cheese is awful, and the difference in fat content isn't worth the sacrifice in flavor and texture. See page 595 for my brand-name recommendations.)

But if you love cheese, adapt your eating habits to allow for it. Make room for the fat and calories in a chunk of glorious genuine cheddar (or Jarlsberg or Gouda or Muenster or . . .) by routinely eating skim dairy products, whole grains, legumes, and fresh produce and limiting oils and other fats. When you're cooking with cheese, use one with a strong flavor so you can get away with less. A few tablespoons of grated good imported Parmesan goes a long way. Ditto shredded aged cheddar and finely shaved Gruyère.

Reduced-fat cheeses are fine when you want only a hint of cheese—for instance, as a garnish for burritos or to flavor a frittata, sandwich, or scrambled eggs. (See page 595 for my brand-name recommendations.) Otherwise, it's ironic—but true!—you may end up getting *more* fat and calories from reduced-fat cheeses in the long run; they tend to be blander than the originals, so you'll want to eat more or add more to recipes to get as much flavor as you'd like. So you'll be better off altogether if you enjoy genuine cheese from time to time.

Conscientious Vegetarians Want to Know

WHAT ABOUT RENNET?

Rennet is a coagulating agent made from the lining of the stomach of calves, and most commercial dairies here and abroad use it to make their cheese. However, rennetless cheese is widely available and labeled clearly. Dairies simply substitute a vegetable stabilizer for the rennet. (You'll find that most of the organic cheese on the market is rennetless.)

SOME FACTS ABOUT SOY

Miso This seasoning paste is made from fermented grains—usually rice or barley—and soybeans. It comes in various flavors, determined by the type of grain involved, and how long it's been fermented. Miso is pungent and very salty, so use it sparingly to season soups and salad dressing, and to serve as a condiment with grilled tofu (see pages 456 to 458).

Soy Milk Is made by grinding soybeans with water, boiling, then straining. If you've chosen to or must eliminate dairy foods from your diet, you can use soy milk measure for measure to substitute for real milk in recipes. Several companies produce soy milks in flavors, including vanilla, chocolate, strawberry, and coffee.

Tempeh Comes in thin, chewy slabs that have a mild smoky-nutty flavor. It's made from cooked soybeans—sometimes combined with rice or barley—that have been infused with a bacterial culture that makes them bind and ferment. Check the refrigerator section of the health-foods supermarket, and you may find barbecue, teriyaki, and Southwest-flavored tempehs that you can heat and eat or use in other recipes.

I SERVING: 3½ OUNCES • CALORIES: 200 • FAT: 8 G

Tofu As impetuous and rash as I may be in other realms of life, I am judicious and prudent where tofu is concerned. I'm just as unwilling to embrace it as an all-purpose ingredient as to dismiss it altogether. Some say it's always as good as whatever it's cooked in, but that's not entirely true. The tofu itself may be runny and taste of soap, in which case you don't have a chance. But if it's fresh and firm, and soaks up enough sauce or marinade, you just might have something really superb.

To make tofu, soy milk is infused with a coagulant that separates the "curds" from the "whey" much as dairy milk is treated to become cheese. Once separated, the curds are compressed into blocks, then sold moist and creamy as soft tofu or with excess moisture extracted as firm tofu.

To Press Tofu: Put several layers of absorbent paper towel inside a baking pan or wide bowl. Put a one-pound block of firm or extra-firm tofu on top and put another few layers of paper towel over it. Weigh it down with something very heavy, such as a cast-iron pot or a pile of ceramic plates, and refrigerate overnight.

I SERVING: 3½ OUNCES FIRM TOFU • CALORIES: 145 • FAT: 9 G

STRATEGIES

Care Package Strategies

You want your care package to be received with utter and absolute delight, not "Well, it's the thought that counts." So send foods that will hold up for roughly five days, using the swiftest service you can afford. Unless you're shipping the package for overnight delivery, don't mail a care package on Thursday or Friday, when it's likely to sit in the post office over the weekend.

FOODS THAT TRAVEL WELL

Granola (see page 50)
Granola Bars (see page 51)
Carrot Bar Cookies (see page 483)
Hermits (see page 485)
Chocolate-Buttermilk Cake (see page 475)
Zucchini Bread (see page 77)
Fresh Apple-Spice Cake (see page 477)
Jam, in sterilized, sealed jars (see pages 105 to 107)
Fruit Vinegars (see page 116)

CARE PACKAGE LABEL

Nutrition Facts
Serving size: 1 Granola Bar
Servings per container: 4

	% Daily Value
Love	100%
Hugs	100%
Kisses	100%
Smiles	100%

—

Vitamin C* 100%   Vitamin D** 100%   Vitamin A***
* Caring
**Devotion
***Adoration

• Prepare and wrap the food in small portions. Instead of sending a whole chocolate cake, for example, bake the batter in muffin tins or miniature Bundt pans, and wrap each cake individually. Wrap cookies in short stacks of three or four. Instead of baking one large zucchini bread, use mini–loaf pans and make two or, if you can find pans small enough, four or six.

• If you have instructions and serving suggestions, include them, such as "Heat in a 350° F. oven for five minutes. Serve warm with ice cream, frozen yogurt, or milk."

• Don't send anything that's likely to spoil and poison the recipient, unless of course that's your intention, in which case you should review your state's penal code, just so you know what's coming.

• Don't feel compelled to make everything you send. Combine your own products with complementary store-bought goods. For instance, homemade granola and assorted dried fruits, or homemade preserves and imported crackers.

• If you want to send a care package, but don't have the time for it, you can order one from a food-by-mail company and have it sent wherever you'd like (see Shop from Home, page 596).

Bag Lunch Strategies

Soon after we moved to Paris, my husband and I discovered that "light lunch" is a contradiction in terms over there. We found that to go out for a meal at midday was to acknowledge that we would not be working in the afternoon. "Lunch" in local parlance was three quite-considerable courses plus wine, which, roughly translated, meant "so much for the momentum we had this morning."

If we'd been less keen to keep our jobs, we would have been happy to assimilate, spending the hours between one and two eating our way into a stupor. But as it happened, we began packing our own lunch. At first I just wrapped up leftovers from the night before. But after finding that (*a*) we didn't always have leftovers and (*b*) some things didn't taste so great the next day, I began to make dishes expressly for lunch.

The dishes fell into four categories:

• Stewlike soups, such as Winter Tomato–Wheat Berry Soup (see page 197) and curries such as My Favorite Chickpeas (see page 360) are good because their flavors deepen over time. You can make them on Saturday or Sunday and enjoy them later in the week. Pastas absorb flavors, too, and as long as they're not overcooked, they'll hold up well for a few days.

• Packet-style foods, such as Nori Rolls (see page 370), are easy to eat.

• Bread-based dishes such as pizza (see page 416) or calzone (see page 419) are hearty and handy. You can make the dough in advance, keeping it frozen until you're ready for it.

• Salads made with grains, such as Tabbouleh (see page 139), contain ingredients that are soft to begin with, so there's nothing to wilt or go soggy. (Whenever you pack a salad of this kind, bring pita bread along; if you forget your utensils, you can make a sandwich by stuffing the salad inside with your fingers.)

HOW TO SEND THEM PACKING

• Use good, sturdy containers, which make the difference between lunch and a trip to the dry cleaner. Recycling yogurt or cottage cheese cartons may seem a neat idea, but they can be a colossal mess in reality. The tops may lose their grip, and the sides may puncture or give way. You're better off with Tupperware or thermoses.

• Get a lunch box! "Brown-bag " may be a nice catch phrase, but it's not ideal for carrying your food. Sauces seep through it, people sit on it, and hungry dogs paw at it. Look for a solid, insulated case, with containers and utensils to use instead.

• Don't forget napkins and utensils. One of the handiest items I've ever owned is a cloth place mat made from heavy cotton with pockets for utensils and a cloth napkin and ties on both ends. When you're through, just put the utensils back in the pockets, roll up the mat, and tie it until next time. Look for it in gift shops and wherever offbeat housewares are sold.

• Freeze individual juice boxes. They'll keep other items chilled, and they'll be cold but no longer frozen when it's time for lunch.

• Pack the bread and filling separately, and sandwiches won't go soggy.

SAFETY FIRST

On those days when you don't get around to eating your lunch (or you get an offer for something better) don't save it for the next day unless you've kept it cold.

Last-Minute Guest Strategies

The best strategy concerning last-minute guests is to avoid ever having them in the first place.

But many of us are prone to inexplicable bouts of enthusiasm from time to time, and the invitation is out of our mouth before we've had time to think, "What on earth am I going to feed these people?" No fair defrosting macaroni and cheese. You offered the invitation; it's not right to punish your guests for accepting it.

• Get to work. The minute you know they're coming, plan your menu *in writing*. Find the recipes for the dish(es) you'd like to serve and take inventory of your kitchen, making a list of

things you'll need to buy. If the list is too long, or involves stopping at more than one store, revise the menu.

• Compile a to-do list, then rewrite it in order of attack.

• Make judicious use of prepared foods, such as packaged salad greens and bottled low-fat dressings. For hors d'oeuvres, pick up cured olives, hummus, and mini-pitas; low-fat cream cheese spreads and whole wheat crackers; salsas and fat-free tortilla chips. Buy prepared foods from shops or companies you know and trust; don't serve anything you haven't tried.

• Best last-minute dish: risotto takes forty minutes to prepare and tastes best served the moment it's made. Also, you can start to prepare it once your guests have arrived, so you'll have until then to do everything else that has to be done. And risotto calls for only a few ingredients, usually of a kind that are easy to find. One drawback is the main ingredient, arborio rice; not every store carries it, and if you have none on hand, risotto isn't an option.

• Other last-minute dishes are panzanellas (see pages 150 to 154), frittatas (see pages 68 to 70), and some pastas (see pages 273 to 275).

Last-Minute Guest Menus

Orange-and-Cilantro Bean Salad (page 136)
    Mushroom Risotto (page 311)
    Maple-Apple-Cranberry Crumble (page 479)

Coconut Curry (page 358)
    Spinach Raita (page 156)
    Lemon-Berry Pudding (page 495)

Spring Garden Tortillas (page 355)
Rice
Pumpkin Soufflé (page 499)

Caesar-Style Summertime Panzanella
(page 152)
Cream of Cauliflower Soup (page 176)
Mango Sorbet with Fruit Sauce
(page 104)

Chili Rice (page 260)
Creamy Spinach Soup (page 183)
Apricot Soufflé (page 498)

Ask the Expert: Express Meal Strategies

Sarah Fritschner, "Express Lane" columnist for the *Louisville Courier Journal*, author of the *Express Lane Cookbook* and the *Express Lane Vegetarian Cookbook*, and self-anointed Queen of Convenience, offers these tips for speedy supper preparation:

• Use flavorful ingredients. You can use fewer total ingredients—which means you'll spend less time putting a dish together—when you cook with bold foods such as cured olives, capers, feta cheese, toasted almonds or sesame seeds, grated fresh ginger, and garlic.

• Make one-dish dinners, calling for rice, beans, and vegetables or some other combination of grain, legume, and/or cheese and vegetables. (For example, see pages 336, 346, and 351.) By preparing everything in one pan, you'll save preparation and clean-up time. Supplement with all-natural applesauce from a jar (see page 595 for brand recommendations).

• To cook quickly, get some sharp knives and use a wide skillet. No preparation is fast or easy if you're fighting with the food—so effective knives are essential. As for the skillet, foods cook more rapidly in wide skillets than in those that are narrow.

• Simple seasonings can do as much for a dish as more exotic spices. A pinch of salt and a grinding of black pepper give flavors a substantial boost.

Strategies for Improving the Flavor of Packaged Foods

Too tired to cook? Too finicky to take whatever you can get? Here's how to tailor prepared foods to taste:

CANNED OR FROZEN SOUPS

Check the ingredients listed on the can package, then before heating, add fresh herbs or vegetables of the same kind or that blend with them. For instance, add fresh minced basil or pesto to minestrone. To curried soup, add grated peeled fresh ginger, minced fresh cilantro, unsweetened coconut, and lightly toasted ground cumin and curry powder (see Note). Lentil soups get a lift from fresh lemon juice and minced fresh chives.

PREPARED PASTA SAUCES

To a basic fresh frozen or jarred tomato sauce, add pesto; defrosted frozen artichoke hearts and fresh minced garlic sautéed in extra virgin olive oil; sliced fresh mushrooms and minced parsley sautéed in extra virgin olive oil; ricotta and Parmesan cheeses blended in a food processor; capers and minced cured olives.

CANNED OR FROZEN CHILI

Before heating add minced fresh cilantro, grated fresh garlic, lightly toasted ground cumin, and chili powder (see Note).

POWDERED DRIED MIXES

Before reconstituting mixes for curry, couscous, rice pilaf, and similar dishes, sauté minced garlic and proceed according to package directions.

Note: Toasting amplifies the flavor of spices. To toast spices: Heat a toaster oven or oven to 350° F. Sprinkle a very thin layer onto a piece of foil, place on a baking tray, and put in the oven until light golden brown, about 3 minutes. Watch carefully to avoid burning. If it burns, it will taste acrid; throw it out and start again.

Small Kitchen Strategies

I speak from experience; I've rarely had a kitchen larger than six by five feet. Once I had a kitchen that could be measured in yards, but the stove had only two burners, and the refrigerator was just big enough for a carton of milk. So, be assured, these tips are practical, not theoretical.

• Clean as you go. Don't let your work surface get cluttered. I can't cite you any studies, but years of personal experience indicate that clutter can make you crazy. Keep a trash bag next to you at all times, and as you skin, slice, and seed, toss the refuse straight into it. Otherwise you'll mix the garbage into the main course; rinds and peels will fall on the floor, you'll slip, break your back, and have to cancel dinner.

• Cover your work surface with paper. When you've got tons of chopping to do, or when you're working with flour or something as likely to fly all over the place, lay down a few sheets of newspaper or a large paper shopping bag (tear it open and spread it flat). Place the chopping board on top. When you're done, just fold up the paper, enclosing the spillover, and throw the whole mess away. It's much easier than wiping down the counter after each spill.

• Put away everything you don't immediately need. Rinse and store mixing bowls, appliances, cutting boards, and utensils as soon as you're through with them. It only takes a minute or two, and beats facing a sink full of them in the end. Even if you're going to be using a particular utensil later in the process, rinse it and put it back in its place—off the work surface—until you're ready for it.

• Hang it up. Small kitchens tend to be short on storage space as well as work space. Get wall racks for everything from knives and spices to measuring spoons and a cordless mixer. Place the racks within easy reach of your work space. Don't fall for racks that fit inside your cabinets. Whatever you hang on them is bound to jut into the cabinet, cutting into your shelf and storage space.

BRAND NAMES

Playing Favorites

While a certain amount of skill sure helps, the success of a dish often hinges on good ingredients. All other things being equal, a better product will yield better results. And when things aren't *quite* equal, a good product can compensate to some degree. Here are my favorite brand names for a number of common ingredients, many of which (marked with an *) are available by mail. The rest are sold in stores nationwide.

Baking Powder: Maine Bakewell Cream*

Balsamic Vinegar: Fini

Beans, canned: Eden, Goya

Beans, dried: Gallina Canyon Ranch*, Frieda's Finest, Arrowhead Mills

Cheese, Cheddar: Organic Cow of Vermont, Tillamook, Cabot
  Low-fat Cottage: Friendship
  Monterey Jack: Cabot
  Domestic Asiago: Stella
  Domestic Ricotta Salata: Stella
  Domestic Mozzarella: Mozzarella Company*
  Ricotta: Calabro, Sargento

Cocoa (defatted): Wonderslim*

Cornmeal: Butte Creek Mill, Arrowhead Mills

Crepes: Frieda's Finest

Dijon Mustard: Grey Poupon

Dried Fruit: Timber Crest*, Chukar Cherries*

Flour, All-purpose: King Arthur*, Arrowhead Mills

Oat: King Arthur*, Arrowhead Mills

Whole Wheat Bread Flour: Arrowhead Mills

Semolina: Zarenga, King Arthur*

Grains (such as bulgur, barley, wheat berries): Arrowhead Mills

Lettuce, packaged mixes: TKO Organics

Nonfat Dry Milk: Organic Valley*

Oatmeal: Vermont Cereal Company, Arrowhead Mills

Olive Oils: Domestic, Corsica*

Orange Juice: Tropicana Pure Premium Grovestand

Pasta: Rustichella

Rice: Lundberg's rices*, including Wehani-Brand, specialty blends, short-grain brown rice, sushi rice, domestic basmati. Rice Select—domestic arborio, Kasmati

Sour Cream, nonfat: Land O' Lakes

Spices and herbs: The Spice Hunter, Williams Sonoma*

Sugar: Billington's; Sucanat*

Sun-dried tomatoes: Timber Crest*

Tofu: White Wave (including reduced fat)

Tomatoes: Pomi chopped tomatoes, Redpack chopped or whole

Vanilla Extract: Nielson-Massey*

Vegetable Broth: Williams Sonoma Concentrate*

Walnut Oil: Loriva

Yeast: Saf-Instant* or Red Star*

Yogurt, nonfat plain: Stonyfield Farms

SHOP FROM HOME

Depending where you live, ordering by mail may be the easiest—or only—way to get high quality and/or specialty ingredients. Here are some of my favorite mail-order sources for ingredients mentioned throughout the book.

KING ARTHUR FLOUR

Everything about this company is wonderful: its catalog, its staff (phoning in an order is a delight), its service (orders arrive swiftly), and above all, its flour. I have yet to try flours that give better results than King Arthur's, particularly the organic unbleached featured in their catalog. King Arthur is also a source for my favorite baking powder, defatted cocoa, maple sugar crystals, maple syrup, nonfat dry milk, vanilla extract, and yeast.
1-800-827-6836
http://www.kingarthurflour.com

VERMONT CEREAL COMPANY

Eric Allen and Andy Leinoff provide—as they say—"the very best organically grown oatmeal." Even if you love oatmeal, I am willing to bet you have never had any this good. You can order a small amount, but if you buy the ten pound package, you get a thirty-two page booklet of recipes for oaty goodies, from muesli to scones.
R.D. #2 Box 2599
Cabot, Vermont 05647
1-802-563-2229

ARROWHEAD MILLS

Superior organic flours and grains, such as bulgur wheat, barley, stone-ground cornmeal, Kamut flour, oatmeal—and oat flour—and a variety of rices. If you can't find their products where you shop, call for a list of stores in your area that carry their goods.
1-800-749-0730

TIMBER CREST

Organic dried fruits and sun-dried tomatoes. First rate.
1-707-433-8251

WILLIAMS SONOMA

Justly famous for cookware, Williams Sonoma sells some wonderful kitchen staples, such as spices, pastas, and a superb vegetable broth concentrate.
1-800-541-2233

FRIEDA'S FINEST

Excellent dried beans in extraordinary variety, and the best prepared crepes on the market. Exotic vegetables (check out the squashes!) and fantastic dried fruits, too.
1-800-421-9477

CORSICA EXTRA VIRGIN OLIVE OIL

Corsica is the best domestic olive oil available today, better even than most expensive imported oils. Light and fruity, it's ideal for cooking and salad dressing. If your specialty retailer doesn't carry it, call 1-203-531-0267.

GALLINA CANYON RANCH

Elizabeth Berry grows big, beautiful heirloom beans on her farm in New Mexico. Write for a descriptive "menu" and price list.

P.O. Box 706
Abiquiu, New Mexico 87510

PENZEY'S SPICE HOUSE, LTD.

Every spice and every conceivable blend, all fresh. Call for a current catalog.

1-414-579-0277

CHUKAR CHERRIES

The first commercial dried cherry company, and still the best. Their dried Bings taste better than fresh. Call for a current price list.

1-800-624-9544

GUIDE TO KITCHENWARE

Kitchen Gear

"Basic" is a relative concept, depending entirely on what you make most often. If you bake a lot, you'll need equipment that someone who doesn't bake would never use. I know someone who puts her pasta machine through its paces three times a week, and someone else who hasn't taken hers out of the box it came in eight months ago. And things I was living contentedly without for years—a pressure cooker, for example—are indispensable to me now, while others I thought would be immensely useful have turned out to be good only for cluttering my cabinets.

• Items in bold type are *basic basics*—everyone needs them.

• Items in demi-bold type are *specialty basics*—everyone who bakes or makes pasta, for example, needs them.

• Items in plain type may not be needed, but you might have fun with them.

Aluminum foil
Angel food cake pan
Apple corer and peeler

Baking pans: one 2-quart deep rectangular casserole, one 2-quart shallow rectangular casserole

Baking peel
Baking sheet, nonstick
Baking stone
Biscuit cutter
Bowls, stainless steel: small, medium, and large
Bowls, earthenware

Cheesecloth
Cheese grater, board or box
Cherry pitter
Coffee filters, paper
Colander
Cooling rack
Crepe pan, nonstick
Custard cups: six ½-cup capacity
Cutting board

Dishwashing detergent

English-muffin rings

Food processor or blender

Griddle, nonstick

Ice-cream maker
Immersion blender

Kitchen shears
Knives: 4-inch paring knife, 6- to 8-inch slicing knife, 6- to 8-inch utility knife, 9- to 12-inch carving knife

Loaf pan, nonstick, one 9 × 5 × 3 inches

Mandoline
Measuring cup, plastic dry level, complete set
Microwave oven
Mini–Bundt pans
Mixer, cordless electric
Mixmaster
Muffin tins, nonstick

Oven thermometer

Paper towels
Parchment paper
Pasta maker
Plastic wrap
Popover pans
Pressure cooker
Pyrex bowls: small, medium, and large (you'll need them if you use your microwave often)
Pyrex measuring cups: 2-cup capacity, optional 1-cup and 1-quart capacity

Rice cooker
Rolling pin
Rubber gloves

Salad bowl
Saucepans: one 1½-quart (preferably enamel) with cover, one 2½-quart (preferably enamel) with cover
Sieve
Skillets, nonstick two 1- to 6-inch; one 12-inch skillet with cover
Slotted spoon
Soufflé dish or round deep baking dish: 1½- to 2-quart capacity
Spatulas, plastic, in 2 sizes (plastic won't scrape your nonstick cookware)
Sponges in various sizes
Spoon and fork for tossing salad
Springform pan, nonstick
Spritzer bottle
Steamer basket
Steel wool
Stockpot, 4- to 6-quart
Stovetop grill

Toaster oven
Towels

Vegetable peeler

Waffle iron
Wire whisks
Wooden skewers
Wooden spoons
Wooden tongs

SOURCE BOOKS
AND RECOMMENDED READING HISTORY

Audacious, irreverent, and highly subjective, *Eating in America* by Waverly Root and Richard de Rouchemont is both commentary on our dismal eating habits and chronicle of how we got them. You'll find a more sober and comprehensive treatment of the *History of Food* in the magnificent book by that title by Maguelonne Toussaint-Samat. Translated from French, it deals mostly with European staples, while *Food in History*, by Reay Tannahill, although not as detailed, has a more global scope. The anecdotal *Much Depends on Dinner*, by Margaret Visser focuses on nine familiar menu items, exploring the history of lettuce, salt, corn, olive oil, and more. Visser's *The Rituals of Dinner*, an account of mealtime etiquette and convention, is also good fun.

Odds and Ends

For useless facts to know and tell, nothing beats *The Diner's Dictionary*, by John Ayto, and *The Dictionary of American Food and Drink*, by John F. Mariani. Don't open either volume unless you have nothing planned for the rest of the day—the entries are so enticing, you won't stop at one or two and may be tempted to plow straight through.

As a food writer, I consider *On Food and Cooking*, by Harold McGee, more than

admirable; it's *enviable*, comprising chemistry, botany, folklore, and historical facts, arcane information, and practical tips. McGee's fascination with his subject is infectious, and reading the results of his inquiries, analyses, and experiments, you'll find that you're much more interested in the minutiae than you knew.

Why is a good job called a plum? Why does "waffle" mean "to equivocate"? Why is a silly joke "corny"? I found the answers in *The Penguin Dictionary of Historical Slang* and *American Slang*, by Robert L. Chapman.

The *Larousse Gastronomique*, 1988 edition, has the strengths and shortcomings of any encyclopedia: some entries are too terse, some too long, and some outdated. But if you're looking for the definition of any Western dish, and the story behind it, you'll find it here.

Cookbooks

The New Vegetarian, by Colin Spencer, has long been my favorite vegetarian cookbook. Spencer's light hand and simple flair set his inspiring collection apart from all others. His recipes are short, ingredients are spare, and the results wholesome and delicious. Years after it first appeared, I still consult *World-of-the-East Vegetarian Cooking*, by Madhur Jaffrey, for luscious, easily prepared dishes from India, China,

Korea, Japan, and the Philippines. While not strictly vegetarian, the marvelous *Flatbreads and Flavors*, by Jeffrey Alford and Naomi Duguid, is meant to showcase flat breads enjoyed around the world and the simple dishes (enough of them meatless to justify a mention here) commonly served with them. The authors roamed the earth to compile this collection, which includes everything from tortillas and salsa to lavosh and hummus.

I owe my confidence as a bread baker to *Bread Alone*, by Daniel Leader and Judith Blahnik, and *Brother Juniper's Bread Book*, by Brother Peter Reinhart. *Techniques of Healthy Cooking*, by the Culinary Institute of America, is still the best book I know of on the title subject. Thorough and thoroughly reliable, it presents simple basic recipes and gives you the know-how to adapt them. In *Vegetarian Cooking Under Pressure*, Lorna Sass's enthusiasm for her subject, as well as her trustworthy recipes, makes you wonder how you ever lived without a pressure cooker, and Elisabeth Lambert Ortiz offers more in *The Encyclopedia of Herbs, Spices and Seasonings* than detailed definitions and exquisite illustrations. Her recipes are simple and superb.

Stumped by a cooking term? Have a recipe that calls for a utensil you've never heard of? Want to know what you can substitute for arrowroot? Consult *The Essential Cook*, by Charles Delmar, a straightforward, authoritative, comprehensive how-to-cook book.

Nutrition

I used the Food Processor software program, by ESHA, to calculate the nutritional content of each recipe.

For additional nutrition information, I relied on *The Wellness Encyclopedia of Food and Nutrition*, by Shelden Margen, M.D., and the staff of the *Wellness Letter*, published by the University of California at Berkeley, as well as the monthly *Wellness Letter* itself, *Prevention's Book of Food and Nutrition*, the newsletter *Environmental Nutrition*, and the monthly *Nutrition Action*, published by the Center for Science in the Public Interest.

I gathered miscellaneous facts, figures, and practical tips from material sent to me by the following: American Celery Council; American Egg Board; American Spice Trade Association; California Avocado Commission; California Artichoke Advisory Board; California Dry Bean Advisory Board; California Tomato Board; Maine Potato Board; Idaho Bean Commission; Idaho Potato Commission; International Dairy Foods Association; Mushroom Council; National Onion Association, Oregon, Washington; California Pear Bureau; Soy Protein Council; Sun World International; Sweet Potato Council; Washington State Apple Commission; Wheat Council; and United States Department of Agriculture.

I N D E X

CONVERSION CHART
EQUIVALENT IMPERIAL AND METRIC MEASUREMENTS

American cooks use standard containers, the 8-ounce cup and a tablespoon that takes exactly 16 level fillings to fill that cup level. Measuring by cup makes it very difficult to give weight equivalents, as a cup of densely packed butter will weigh considerably more than a cup of flour. The easiest way therefore to deal with cup measurements in recipes is to take the amount by volume rather than by weight. Thus the equation reads: 1 cup = 240 ml = 8 fl. oz.; ½ cup = 120 ml = 4 fl. oz. It is possible to buy a set of American cup measures in major stores around the world.

In the States, butter is often measured in sticks. One stick is the equivalent of 8 tablespoons. One tablespoon of butter is therefore the equivalent to ½ ounce/15 grams.

Liquid Measures

Fluid ounces	U.S.	Imperial	Milliliters
	1 teaspoon	1 teaspoon	5
¼	2 teaspoons	1 dessertspoon	7
½	1 tablespoon	1 tablespoon	15
1	2 tablespoons	2 tablespoons	28
2	¼ cup	4 tablespoons	56
4	½ cup or ¼ pint		110
5		¼ pint or 1 gill	140
6	¾ cup		170
8	1 cup or ½ pint		225
9			250, ¼ liter
10	1¼ cups	½ pint	280
12	1½ cups	¾ pint	340
15	¾ pint		420
16	2 cups or 1 pint		450
18	2¼ cups		500, ½ liter
20	2½ cups	1 pint	560
24	3 cups		675
	or 1½ pints		
25		1¼ pints	700
27	3½ cups		750, ¾ liter
30	3¾ cups	1½ pints	840
32	4 cups or 2 pints		900
	or 1 quart		

Solid Measures

U.S. and Imperial Measures		Metric Measures	
ounces	pounds	grams	kilos
1		28	
2		56	
3½		100	
4	¼	112	
5		140	
6		168	
8	½	225	
9		250	¼
12	¾	340	
16	1	450	
18		500	½
20	1¼	560	
24	1½	675	
27		750	¾
28	1¾	780	
32	2	900	
36	2¼	1000	1
40	2½	1100	
48	3	1350	
54		1500	1½
64	4	1800	
72	4½	2000	2

Equivalents for Ingredients

all-purpose flour—plain flour
arugula—rocket
buttermilk—ordinary milk
confectioners' sugar—icing sugar
cornstarch—cornflour
eggplant—aubergine
granulated sugar—caster sugar
half-and-half—12% fat milk
heavy cream—double cream
light cream—single cream
lima beans—broad beans
scallion—spring onion
squash—courgettes or marrow
unbleached flour—strong, white flour
zest—rind
zucchini—courgettes

Oven Temperature Equivalents

Fahrenheit	Celsius	Gas Mark	Description
225	110	¼	Cool
250	130	½	
275	140	1	Very Slow
300	150	2	
325	170	3	Slow
350	180	4	Moderate
375	190	5	
400	200	6	Moderately Hot
425	220	7	Fairly Hot
450	230	8	Hot
475	240	9	Very Hot
500	250	10	Extremely Hot

Linear and Area Measures

1 inch	2.54 centimeters